Third Edition

D1584808

Quentin Charatan and
Aaron Kans

**McGraw-Hill
Higher Education**

London Boston Burr Ridge, IL Dubuque, IA Madison, WI New York San Francisco
St. Louis Bangkok Bogotá Caracas Kuala Lumpur Lisbon Madrid Mexico City
Milan Montreal New Delhi Santiago Seoul Singapore Sydney Taipei Toronto

Java in Two Semesters, 3e
Quentin Charatan and Aaron Kans
ISBN-13 978-0-07-712267-6
ISBN-10 0-07-712267-4

McGraw-Hill
Higher Education

Published by McGraw-Hill Education
Shoppenhangers Road
Maidenhead
Berkshire
SL6 2QL
Telephone: 44 (0) 1628 502 500
Fax: 44 (0) 1628 770 224
Website: www.mcgraw-hill.co.uk

British Library Cataloguing in Publication Data
A catalogue record for this book is available from the British Library

Library of Congress Cataloguing in Publication Data
The Library of Congress data for this book has been applied for from the Library of Congress

Acquisitions Editor: Catriona Hoyle
Marketing Manager: Alice Duijser
Senior Production Editor: James Bishop

Text Design by Hardlines
Cover design by Ego Creative Ltd
Printed and bound in Great Britain by Ashford Colour Press Ltd

ISBN-13 978-0-07-712267-6
ISBN-10 0-07-712267-4

The McGraw·Hill Companies

Dedication

In memory of our friend and mentor David Hatter (1939–2009)

Brief Table of Contents

Preface to third edition   *ix*
Guided tour   *xi*
Technology to enhance learning and teaching   *xiii*

SEMESTER ONE   *1*

1 The first step   *3*
2 Building blocks   *20*
3 Selection   *38*
4 Iteration   *63*
5 Methods   *95*
6 Arrays   *121*
7 Classes and objects   *163*
8 Implementing classes   *191*
9 Inheritance   *237*
10 Graphics   *270*
11 Case study – part 1   *307*
12 Case study – part 2   *336*

SEMESTER TWO   *357*

13 Interfaces and adapters   *359*
14 Exceptions   *384*
15 The Java Collections Framework   *416*
16 Advanced graphics programming   *445*
17 Enhancing the user interface   *487*
18 Working with files   *516*
19 Multi-threaded programs   *545*
20 Packages   *571*
21 Advanced Case Study   *588*
22 Java in a network environment   *631*
23 Mobile Java   *673*
24 Java in context   *716*

Detailed Table of Contents

Preface to third edition	ix
Guided tour	xi
Technology to enhance learning and teaching	xiii

SEMESTER ONE — 1

1 The first step — 3
Introduction — 3
Software — 3
Compiling programs — 4
Programming in Java — 5
Your first program — 11
Output in Java — 14
Self-test questions — 17
Programming exercises — 18

2 Building blocks — 20
Introduction — 20
Simple data types in Java — 20
Declaring variables in Java — 21
Assignments in Java — 23
Creating constants — 25
Arithmetic operators — 25
Expressions in Java — 27
More about output — 30
Input in Java: the Scanner class — 31
Program design — 34
Self-test questions — 35
Programming exercises — 37

3 Selection — 38
Introduction — 38
Making choices — 38
The 'if' statement — 40
The 'if...else' statement — 46
Logical operators — 48
Nested 'if...else' statements — 50
The 'switch' statement — 52
Self-test questions — 58
Programming exercises — 61

4 Iteration — 63
Introduction — 63
The 'for' loop — 65

The 'while' loop — 76
The 'do...while' loop — 78
Picking the right loop — 83
The 'break' statement — 83
The 'continue' statement — 86
Self-test questions — 88
Programming exercises — 92

5 Methods — 95
Introduction — 95
Declaring and defining methods — 96
Calling a method — 98
Method input and output — 99
More examples of methods — 103
Variable scope — 107
Method overloading — 109
Using methods in menu-driven programs — 114
Self-test questions — 118
Programming exercises — 120

6 Arrays — 121
Introduction — 121
Creating an array — 122
Accessing array elements — 125
Passing arrays as parameters — 129
Returning an array from a method — 132
The enhanced 'for' loop — 135
Some useful array methods — 136
Multi-dimensional arrays — 147
Creating a two-dimensional array — 148
Initializing two-dimensional arrays — 148
Processing two-dimensional arrays — 149
The *MonthlyTemperatures* program — 150
Ragged arrays — 156
Self-test questions — 159
Programming exercises — 161

7 Classes and objects — 163
Introduction — 163
Classes as data types — 163
Objects — 165
The *Rectangle* class — 166
Strings — 172
Our own *Scanner* class for keyboard input — 179
The *Console* class — 180

The *BankAccount* class   181
Arrays of objects   184
Self-test questions   188
Programming exercises   189

8 Implementing classes   191
Introduction   191
Designing classes in UML notation   191
Implementing classes in Java   194
The *static* keyword   201
Initializing attributes   205
The *EasyScanner* class   206
Passing objects as parameters   207
Collection classes   208
The benefits of object-oriented
programming   227
Self-test questions   228
Programming exercises   231

9 Inheritance   237
Introduction   237
Defining inheritance   238
Implementing inheritance in Java   238
Method overriding   249
Abstract classes   253
Abstract methods   256
The *final* modifier   261
The *Object* class   261
Wrapper classes and autoboxing   263
Self-test questions   265
Programming exercises   269

10 Graphics   270
Introduction   270
The Swing package   270
The *SmileyFace* class   271
Event-handling in Java: The
ChangingFace class   277
An interactive graphics class   284
A graphical user interface (GUI) for the
Rectangle class   287
A metric converter   292
Number formatting   297
Layout policies   299
Compound containers   300
GUIs for collections of objects   302
Self-test questions   303
Programming exercises   305

11 Case study – part 1   307
Introduction   307
The requirements specification   308
The design   308
Implementing the *Payment* class   310
The *ObjectList* class   313
The *PaymentList* class   325
Implementing the *Tenant* class   328
Implementing the *TenantList* class   330
Self-test questions   335
Programming exercises   335

12 Case study – part 2   336
Introduction   336
Keeping permanent records   336
Design of the GUI   337
Designing the event-handlers   339
Implementing the *Hostel* class   343
Testing the system   351
What next?   355
Self-test questions   356
Programming exercises   356

SEMESTER TWO   357

13 Interfaces and adapters   359
Introduction   359
An example   360
Interfaces   361
Some more interfaces   366
Adapters and inner classes   373
Polymorphism and polymorphic
types   377
Self-test questions   379
Programming exercises   381

14 Exceptions   384
Introduction   384
Pre-defined exception classes in Java   384
Handling exceptions   386
The 'finally' clause   394
Exceptions in GUI applications   398
Using exceptions in your own classes   400
Throwing exceptions   405
Creating your own exception classes   408
Re-throwing exceptions   410
Documenting exceptions   411
Self-test questions   413
Programming exercises   414

15 The Java Collections Framework   *416*
Introduction   *416*
The *List* interface and the *ArrayList*
class   *417*
Using the enhanced classes   *423*
The *Set* interface and the *HashSet* class   *424*
The *Map* interface and the *HashMap*
class   *429*
Using your own classes with Java's
collection classes   *433*
Developing a collection class for
Book objects   *437*
Self-test questions   *441*
Programming exercises   *442*

16 Advanced graphics programming   *445*
Introduction   *445*
More layout policies   *445*
Making choices   *456*
The *JFileChooser* class   *472*
The *JSlider* class   *478*
Self-test questions   *481*
Programming exercises   *483*

17 Enhancing the user interface   *487*
Introduction   *487*
The *Border* interface   *487*
Combining text and graphics with
the *Icon* interface   *489*
The *ImageIcon* class   *492*
Creating message boxes and input
boxes   *495*
Creating new colours   *502*
Creating new fonts   *504*
The *Graphics2D* class   *506*
Guidelines for creating good user
interfaces   *512*
Self-test questions   *514*
Programming exercises   *515*

18 Working with files   *516*
Introduction   *516*
Input and output   *517*
Input and output devices   *517*
File-handling   *518*
Reading and writing to text files   *520*
Reading and writing to binary files   *529*
Reading a text file character by
character   *531*
Object serialization   *533*
Random access files   *536*

Self-test questions   *543*
Programming exercises   *544*

19 Multi-threaded programs   *545*
Introduction   *545*
Concurrent processes   *545*
Threads   *546*
The *Thread* class   *549*
Thread execution and scheduling   *552*
An alternative implementation   *553*
Synchronizing threads   *556*
Thread states   *557*
Animations   *558*
The *Timer* class   *564*
Self-test questions   *569*
Programming exercises   *570*

20 Packages   *571*
Introduction   *571*
Understanding packages   *571*
Accessing classes in packages   *572*
Developing your own packages   *575*
Package scope   *577*
Setting the *classpath* environment
variable   *578*
Running applications from the
command line   *578*
Deploying your packages   *581*
Self-test questions   *586*
Programming exercises   *587*

21 Advanced Case Study   *588*
Introduction   *588*
System overview   *588*
Requirements analysis and
specification   *589*
Design   *590*
Implementation   *593*
Testing   *616*
Design of the GUI   *617*
The *JTabbedPane* class   *618*
The *AirportFrame* class   *620*
Airport dialogue boxes   *623*
Self-test questions   *630*
Programming exercises   *630*

22 Java in a network environment   *631*
Introduction   *631*
Applets   *632*
Accessing remote databases   *636*
Sockets   *642*

A simple server application   643
A simple client application   650
A client–server chat application   655
Self-test questions   669
Programming exercises   671

23 **Mobile Java**   673
Introduction   673
Java Micro Edition   674
Java ME configurations and profiles 675
Developing MIDP applications   676
Your first mobile program   676
The Canvas class   684
Adding more commands   689
Sprites   694

Using a timer   702
Selecting items from a list   707
Self-test questions   714
Programming exercises   714

24 **Java in context**   716
Introduction   716
Language size   716
Language reliability   719
The role of Java   730
What next?   730
Self-test questions   732
Programming exercises   733

Index   735

Preface

As with previous editions, this book is designed for university students taking a first module in software development or programming, followed by a second, more advanced module. The book uses Java as the vehicle for the teaching of programming concepts – design concepts are explained using the UML notation. The topic is taught from first principles and assumes no prior knowledge of the subject.

The book is organized so as to support two twelve-week, one-semester modules, which might typically comprise a two-hour lecture, a one-hour tutorial and a one- or two-hour laboratory session. The self-test questions at the end of each chapter ensure that the learning objectives for that chapter have been met, while the programming exercises that follow allow these learning objectives to be applied to complete programs. In addition to these exercises and questions, a case study is developed in each semester to illustrate the use of the techniques covered in the text to develop a non-trivial application. Lecturers who teach on modules that run for fewer than twelve weeks in a semester could treat these case studies as a self-directed student learning experience, rather than as taught topics.

The approach taken in this book is ideal for students entering university with no background in the subject matter, often coming from pre-degree courses in other disciplines, or perhaps returning to study after long periods away from formal education. It is the authors' experience that such students have enormous difficulties in grasping the fundamental programming concepts the first time round, and therefore require a simpler and gentler introduction to the subject than is presented in most standard texts.

The book takes an integrated approach to software development by covering such topics as basic design principles and standards, testing methodologies and the user interface, as well as looking at detailed implementation topics.

In the first semester, considerable time is spent concentrating on the fundamental programming concepts such as declarations of variables and basic control structures, methods and arrays, prior to introducing students to the concepts of classes and objects, inheritance, graphics and event-driven programming.

The second semester covers more advanced topics such as interfaces, exceptions, collection classes from the Java Collections Framework, advanced graphics, file-handling techniques, the implementation of multi-threaded programs, network programming, packages and programming for mobile devices.

The third edition achieves three main goals. Firstly, it incorporates all the very useful feedback on the second edition that we have received from students and lecturers over the past three years. Secondly, it includes many new questions and programming exercises at the end of the chapters. Finally, it includes new material to bring it completely up to date with the current developments in the field.

Those familiar with the previous edition will notice that some of the material has been re-ordered and updated. In particular, in the first semester, the material on software quality has now been incorporated into the case study rather than being a chapter on its own. This enables students to learn about the principles and techniques of software development in a practical setting, rather than dealing with the theory and practice separately. This has also enabled the material which was previously in the first chapter to be spread across the two chapters, providing a somewhat gentler introduction. Another change is the moving of two-dimensional arrays from the second to the first semester, so that this topic is covered along with one-dimensional arrays. Also, in the second semester, the chapter on packages has been moved towards the end of the book, as it was felt that it is better to cover this topic once students were in a position to create and deploy large-scale applications. The second semester is now introduced by the chapter on interfaces, which has been completely renewed and updated in response to many useful suggestions.

The new edition is fully compliant with the latest release of Java, namely Java 6. It includes an entirely new chapter, Mobile Java, that introduces readers to Java Micro Edition and takes them through a step-by-step guide to producing applications for small devices such as mobile phones and PDAs, and includes a number of full applications that students can create. Other new material includes the `Graphics2D` class in the chapter on enhancing the user interface, and additional examples in the chapter on network programming.

As before, the accompanying CD contains a Java IDE, with instructions for installation and use, and the source code for many of the classes from the book. If your CD does not run automatically, open my computer, expand the CD-Rom folder and double-click on the file called "CD-start.exe".

We would like to thank our publisher, McGraw-Hill, for the encouragement and guidance that we have received throughout the production of this book.

Additionally, we would like to thank especially the computing students of the University of East London for their thoughtful comments and feedback. For support and inspiration, special thanks are due once again to our families and friends.

Acknowledgements

Our thanks go to the following reviewers for their comments at various stages in the text's development:

Frank Neven, University of Hasselt, Belgium
Marina De Vos, University of Bath, UK
Amanda Peart, University of Portsmouth, UK
Dave Elliman, University of Nottingham, UK

Every effort has been made to trace and acknowledge ownership of copyright and to clear permission for material reproduced in this book. The publishers will be pleased to make suitable arrangements to clear permission with any copyright holders whom it has not been possible to contact.

Guided Tour

Objectives

Each chapter opens with a set of learning objectives introducing the reader to the topics they should have come to understand after having worked through the chapter.

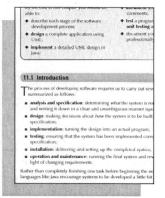

Introduction

Each chapter opens with an introduction to the key themes of the chapter.

Self-test Questions

Each chapter includes self-test questions to ensure that the learning objectives for that chapter have been met.

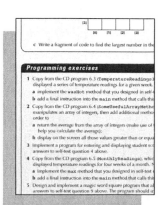

Programming Exercises

Each chapter concludes with a set of programming exercises that allow the learning objectives to be applied to complete programs.

xi

Technology to Enhance Learning and Teaching

Visit www.mcgraw-hill.co.uk/textbooks/charatan

Online Learning Centre (OLC)

After completing each chapter, log on to the supporting Online Learning Centre website. Take advantage of the study tools offered to reinforce the material you have read in the text, and to develop your knowledge of Java in a fun and effective way.

Resources for lecturers include:

■ Power Point Slides
■ Solutions to Tutorial
■ Artwork from the Book

Resources for students include:

■ Multiple Choice Questions for Semester One and Semester Two

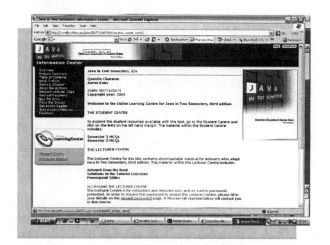

Custom Publishing Solutions: Let us help make our **content** your **solution**

At McGraw-Hill Education our aim is to help lecturers to find the most suitable content for their needs delivered to their students in the most appropriate way. Our **custom publishing solutions** offer the ideal combination of content delivered in the way which best suits lecturer and students.

Our custom publishing programme offers lecturers the opportunity to select just the chapters or sections of material they wish to deliver to their students from a database called Primis at www. primisonline.com

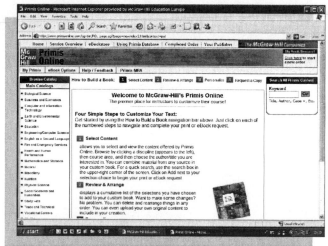

xiv   Java in Two Semesters

Primis contains over two million pages of content from:

- textbooks
- professional books
- case books – Harvard Articles, Insead, Ivey, Darden, Thunderbird and BusinessWeek
- Taking Sides – debate materials

across the following imprints:

- McGraw-Hill Education
- Open University Press
- Harvard Business School Press
- US and European material

There is also the option to include additional material authored by lecturers in the custom product – this does not necessarily have to be in English.

We will take care of everything from start to finish in the process of developing and delivering a custom product to ensure that lecturers and students receive exactly the material needed in the most suitable way.

With a Custom Publishing Solution, students enjoy the best selection of material deemed to be the most suitable for learning everything they need for their courses – something of real value to support their learning. Teachers are able to use exactly the material they want, in the way they want, to support their teaching on the course.

Please contact your local McGraw-Hill representative with any questions or alternatively contact Warren Eels **e:** warren_eels@mcgraw-hill.com.

Semester One

The first step

❖ **OBJECTIVES**

By the end of this chapter you should be able to:

❖ explain the meaning of the word **software**;

❖ explain how Java programs are compiled and run;

❖ provide examples of different types of Java applications;

❖ write Java programs that display text on the screen;

❖ join messages in output commands by using the **concatenation** (+) operator;

❖ add comments to your programs.

1.1 Introduction

Like any student starting out on a first programming module, you will be itching to do just one thing – get started on your first program. We can well understand that, and you won't be disappointed, because you will be writing programs in this very first chapter. Designing and writing computer programs can be one of the most enjoyable and satisfying things you can do, although it can seem a little daunting at first because it is like nothing else you have ever done. But, with a bit of perseverance, you will not only start to get a real taste for it but you may well find yourself sitting up till two o'clock in the morning trying to solve a problem. And just when you have given up and you are dropping off to sleep, the answer pops into your head and you are at the computer again until you notice it is getting light outside! So if this is happening to you, then don't worry – it's normal!

However, before you start writing programs we need to make sure that you understand what we mean by important terms such as *program, software* and *programming languages*.

1.2 Software

A computer is not very useful unless we give it some instructions that tell it what to do. This set of instructions is called a **program**. Programs that the computer can use can be stored on electronic chips that form part of the computer, or can be stored on devices like hard disks, CDs, DVDs, and USB drives (sometimes called memory sticks).

The word **software** is the name given to a single program or a set of programs. There are two main kinds of software:

- **Application software.** This is name given to useful programs that a user might need; for example, word-processors, spreadsheets, accounts programs, games and so on. Such programs are often referred to simply as **applications**.

- **System software.** This is the name given to special programs that help the computer to do its job; for example, operating systems (such as UNIX or Windows, which help us to use the computer) and network software (which helps computers to communicate with each other).

Of course software is not restricted simply to computers themselves. Many of today's devices – from mobile phones to microwave ovens to games consoles – rely on computer programs that are built into the device. Such software is referred to as **embedded software**.

Both application and system software are built by writing a set of instructions for the computer to obey. **Programming** is the task of writing these instructions. These instructions have to be written in a language specially designed for this purpose. These **programming languages** include C++, Visual Basic, Pascal and many more. The language we are going to use in this book is Java. Java is an example of one of the more recent advances in the development of programming languages – it is an **object-oriented** language. Right now, that phrase might not mean anything to you, but you will find out all about its meaning as we progress through this book.

1.3 Compiling programs

Like most modern programming languages, the Java language consists of instructions that look a bit like English. For example, words such as `while` and `if` are part of the Java language. The set of instructions written in a programming language is called the **program code** or **source code**.

Ultimately these instructions have to be translated into a language that can be understood by the computer. The computer understands only **binary** instructions – that means instructions written as a series of 0's and 1's. So, for example, the machine might understand 01100111 to mean add. The language of the computer is often referred to as **machine code**. A special piece of system software called a **compiler** translates the instructions written in a programming language into machine instructions consisting of 0's and 1's. This process is known as **compiling**. Figure 1.1 illustrates how this process works for many programming languages.

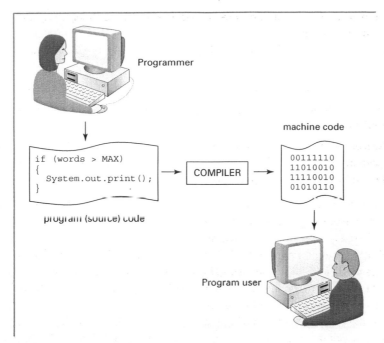

FIGURE 1.1 The compilation process

Programming languages have a very strict set of rules that you must follow. Just as with natural languages, this set of rules is called the **syntax** of the language. A program containing syntax errors will not compile. You will see when you start writing programs that the sorts of things that can cause compiler errors are the incorrect use of special Java keywords, missing brackets or semi-colons, and many others. If, however, the source code is free of such errors the compiler will successfully produce a machine code program that can be run on a computer, as illustrated.

Once a program has been compiled and the machine code program saved, it can be run on the target machine as many times as necessary. When you buy a piece of software such as a game or a word processor, it is this machine code program that you are buying.

1.4 Programming in Java

Before the advent of Java, most programs were compiled as illustrated in figure 1.1. The only problem with this approach is that the final compiled program is suitable only for a particular type of computer. For example, a program that is compiled for a PC will not run on a Mac or a UNIX machine.

But this is not the case with Java! Java is **platform-independent**. A Java program will run on any type of computer.

How is this achieved? The answer lies in the fact that any Java program requires the computer it is running on to also be running a special program called a **Java Virtual Machine**, or **JVM** for short. This JVM is able to run a Java program for the particular computer on which it is running.

For example, you can get a JVM for a PC running windows; there is a JVM for a MAC, and one for a Unix or Linux box. There is a special kind of JVM for mobile phones; and there are JVMs built into machines where the embedded software is written in Java.

We saw earlier that conventional compilers translate our program code into machine code. This machine code would contain the particular instructions appropriate to the type of computer it was meant for. Java compilers do not translate the program into machine code – they translate it into special instructions called **Java byte code**. Java byte code, which, like machine code, consists of 0's and 1's, contains instructions that are exactly the same irrespective of the type of computer – it is *universal*, whereas machine code is specific to a particular type of computer. The job of the JVM is to translate each byte code instruction for the computer it is running on, before the instruction is performed. See figure 1.2.

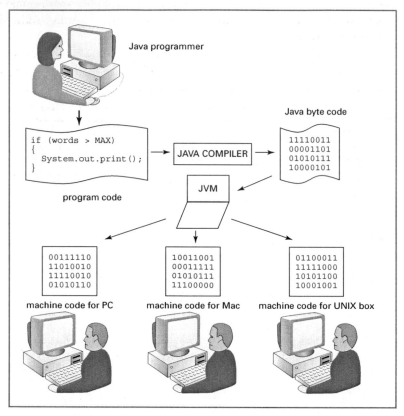

FIGURE 1.2 Compiling Java programs

There are various ways in which a JVM can be installed on a computer. In the case of some operating systems – for example Mac OS X and Linux – a JVM comes packaged with the system, along with the Java libraries (pre-compiled Java modules that can be integrated with the programs you create) and a compiler. Together the JVM and the libraries are known as the **Java Runtime Environment (JRE)**. If you do not have a JRE on your computer (as will be the case with any Windows operating system), then the entire **Java Development Kit (JDK)**, comprising the JRE, compiler and other tools, can be downloaded from Sun Microsystems (the original developers of the Java platform). This is obtained from the following website:

java.sun.com

We strongly recommend that you visit this site from time to time, because not only does it provide downloads such as the above; it also contains a wealth of information about the Java language. The JDK is updated by Sun at regular intervals. The latest release at time of writing this book is version 6.

To save you the trouble, we have provided the JDK for Windows for you on the accompanying CD – we have also provided a simple-to-use *Integrated Development Environment (IDE)*, the meaning of which we will explain to you now.

1.4.1 Integrated Development Environments (IDEs)

It is very common to compile and run your programs by using a special program called an **Integrated Development Environment** or **IDE**. An IDE provides you with an easy-to-use window into which you can type your code; other windows will provide information about the files you are using; and a separate window will be provided to tell you of your errors.

Not only does an IDE do all these things, it also lets you run your programs as soon as you have compiled them. Depending on the IDE you are using, your screen will look something like that in figure 1.3.

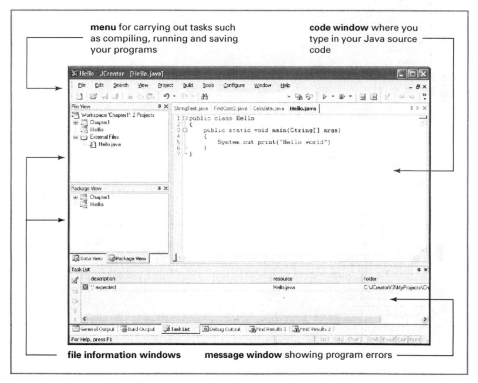

FIGURE 1.3 A typical Java IDE screen

Common IDEs include *Borland JBuilder, JCreator, NetBeans* and *Eclipse*. Instructions for installing and using the IDE provided with this book are contained on the disk.

It is perfectly possible to compile and run Java programs without the use of an IDE – but not nearly so convenient. You would do this from a command line in a console window. The source code that you write is saved in the form of a simple text file which has a .java extension. The compiler that comes as part of the JDK is called javac.exe, and to compile a file called, for example, MyProgram.java, you would write at the command prompt:

```
javac MyProgram.java
```

This would create a file called `MyProgram.class`, which is the compiled file in Java byte code. The name of the JVM is `java.exe` and to run the program you would type:

> **java MyProgram**

To start off with, however, we strongly recommend that you use an IDE such as the one we have provided for you on the CD.

1.4.2 Java applications

As we explained in section 1.2, Java applications can run on a computer, on such devices as mobile phones and games consoles, or sometimes can be embedded into an electronic device. In the last case you would probably be unaware of the fact that the software is running at all, whereas in the former cases you would be seeing output from your program on a screen and providing information to your program via a keyboard and mouse or via a joystick or game controller.

The screen that provides output from your program, and prompts you to enter information, is known as the **user interface**. There are two principal types of user interface:

- **text** based;
- **graphics** based.

With text-based user interfaces, information is displayed simply as text – with no pictures. Text-based programs make use of the keyboard for user input. Often text-based programs run in a black and white window and are known as **console applications**. You can see an example of this in figure 1.4.

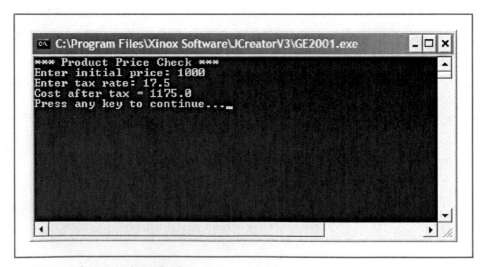

FIGURE 1.4 A Java console application

You are probably more accustomed to running programs that have a **graphical user interface (GUI)**. Such interfaces allow for pictures and shapes to be drawn on the screen (such as text boxes and buttons) and make use of the mouse as well as the keyboard to collect user input. An example of a GUI is given in figure 1.5.

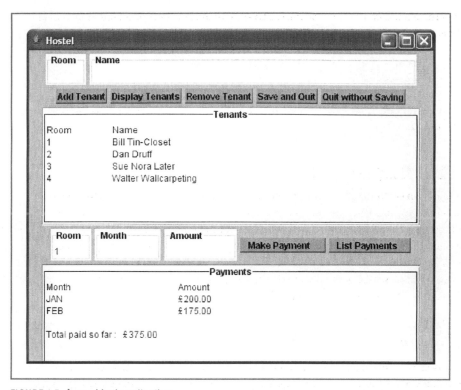

FIGURE 1.5 A graphical application

Eventually we want all your programs to have graphical interfaces, but these obviously require a lot more programming effort to create than simple console applications. So, for most of the first semester, while we are teaching you the fundamentals of programming in Java, we are going to concentrate on getting the program logic right and we will be sticking to console-style applications. Once you have mastered these fundamentals, however, you will be ready to create attractive graphical interfaces before the end of this very first semester!

Programs can run in many different environments. For example, in the second semester you will learn how to create a special kind of Java program called an **applet**. An applet is a program that is designed to be available over the Internet and to run in a browser such as Internet Explorer or Firefox. Figure 1.6 shows an example.

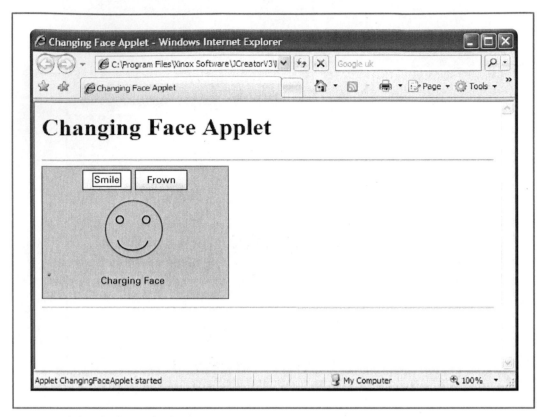

FIGURE 1.6 A Java Applet running in a browser

You will also find that in the second semester you will be able to create applications that communicate with each other over a network, and link into remote databases. You will also be introduced to Java applications that can run on mobile devices as shown in figure 1.7.

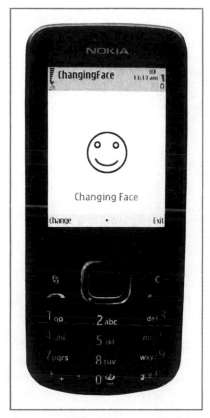

FIGURE 1.7 A Java application running on
a mobile phone

1.5 Your first program

Now it is time to write your first program. Anyone who knows anything about programming will tell you that the first program that you write in a new language has always got to be a program that displays the words "Hello world" on the screen; so we will stick with tradition, and your first program will do exactly that!

When your program runs you will see the words "Hello world" displayed.[1] The type of window in which this is displayed will vary according to the particular operating system you are running, and the particular IDE you are using.

The code for the "Hello world" program is written out for you below as program 1.1.

---

[1] In some systems you might find that the words "Press any key to continue …" are displayed immediately after the output – for example as in figure 1.4.

PROGRAM 1.1

```java
public class Hello
{
  public static void main(String[] args)
  {
    System.out.println ("Hello world");
  }
}
```

1.5.1 Analysis of the "Hello world" program

Let's start with the really important bit – the line of code that represents the instruction *display "Hello world" on the screen*. The line that does this looks like this:

```java
System.out.println("Hello world");
```

This is the way we are always going to get stuff printed on a simple text screen; we use `System.out.println` (or sometimes `System.out.print`, as explained below) and put whatever we want to be displayed in the brackets. The `println` is short for "print line" by the way. You won't understand at this stage why it has to be in this precise form (with each word separated by a full stop, and the actual phrase in double quotes), but do make sure that you type it exactly as you see it here, with an upper case *S* at the beginning. Also, you should notice the semi-colon at the end of the statement. This is important; every Java instruction has to end with a semi-colon.

Now we can consider the meaning of the rest of the program. The first line, which we call the header, looks like this:

```java
public class Hello
```

The first, and most important, thing to pay attention to is the word **class**. We noted earlier that Java is referred to as an *object-oriented* programming language. Now, the true meaning of this will start to become clear in chapter 7 – but for the time being you just need to know that object-oriented languages require the program to be written in separate units called **classes**. The simple programs that we are starting off with will contain only one class (although they will interact with other classes from the "built-in" Java libraries). We always have to give a name to a class and in this case we have simply called our class `Hello`.

When choosing a name for a class, you can choose any name as long as:

- the name is not already a keyword in the Java language (such as **static**, **void**);
- the name has no spaces in it;
- the name does not include operators or mathematical symbols such as + and –;
- the name starts either with a letter, an underscore (_), or a dollar sign ($).

So, the first line tells the Java compiler that we are writing a class with the name `Hello`. However, you will also have noticed the word **public** in front of the word **class**; placing this word here makes our class accessible to the outside world and to other classes – so, until we learn about specific ways of restricting access (in the second semester), we will always include this word in the header. A **public** class should always be saved in a file with the same name as the class itself – so in this case it should be saved as a file with the name `Hello.java`.

Notice that everything in the class has to be contained between two curly brackets (known as **braces**) that look like this { }; these tell the compiler where the class begins and ends.

There is one important thing that we must emphasize here. Java is *case-sensitive* – in other words it interprets upper case and lower case characters as two completely different things – it is very important therefore to type the statements exactly as you see them here, paying attention to the case of the letters.

The next line that we come across (after the opening curly bracket) is this:

```
public static void main(String[] args)
```

This looks rather strange if you are not used to programming – but you will see that every application we write is going to contain one class with this line in it. In chapter 7 you will find out that this basic unit called a class is made up of, among other things, a number of **methods**. You will find out a lot more about methods in chapter 5, but for now it is good enough for you to know that a method contains a particular set of instructions that the computer must carry out. Our `Hello` class contains just one method and this line introduces that method. In fact it is a very special method called a `main` method. Applications in Java must always contain a class with a method called `main`: this is where the program begins. A program starts with the first instruction of `main`, then obeys each instruction in sequence (unless the instruction itself tells it to jump to some other place in the program). The program terminates when it has finished obeying the final instruction of `main`.

So this line that we see above introduces the `main` method; the program instructions are now written in a second set of curly brackets that show us where this `main` method begins and ends. At the moment we will not worry about the words **public static void** in front of `main`, and the bit in the brackets afterwards (`String[] args`)[2] – we will just accept that they always have to be there; you will begin to understand their significance as you learn more about programming concepts. The top line of a method is referred to as the method **header** and words such as **public** and **static**, that are part of the Java language, are referred to as **keywords**.[3]

As we have said, we place instructions inside a method by surrounding them with opening and closing curly brackets. In Java, curly brackets mark the beginning and end of a group of instructions. In this case we have only one instruction inside the curly brackets but, as you will soon see, we can have many instructions inside these braces.

By the way, you should be aware that the compiler is not concerned about the layout of your code, just that your code meets the rules of the language. So we could have typed the method header, the curly brackets and the `println` command all on one line if we wished! Obviously this would look very messy, and it is always important to lay out your code in a way that makes it easy to read and to follow.

---

[2] In fact, if you left out the words in brackets your program would still compile – but it wouldn't do what you wanted it to do!

[3] You will notice that we are using bold Courier font for Java keywords.

So throughout this book we will lay out our code in a neat easy-to-read format, lining up opening and closing braces.

1.5.2 Adding comments to a program

When we write program code, we will often want to include some comments to help remind us what we were doing when we look at our code a few weeks later, or to help other people to understand what we have done.

Of course, we want the compiler to ignore these comments when the code is being compiled. There are two ways of doing this. For short comments we place two slashes (//) at the beginning of the line – everything after these slashes, up to the end of the line, is then ignored by the compiler.

For longer comments (that is, ones that run over more than a single line) we usually use another approach. The comment is enclosed between two special symbols; the opening symbol is a slash followed by a star (/*) and the closing symbol is a star followed by a slash (*/). Everything between these two symbols is ignored by the compiler. The program below shows examples of both types of comment; when you compile and run this program you will see that the comments have no effect on the code, and the output is exactly the same as that of the original program.

PROGRAM 1.1 – with added comments

```java
// this is a short comment, so we use the first method

public class Hello
{
    public static void main(String[] args)
    {
      System.out.println("Hello world");
    }

  /* this is the second method of including comments - it is more convenient to use this
      method here, because the comment is longer and goes over more than one line */
}
```

In chapter 11 you will learn about a special tool called Javadoc for documenting your programs. In that chapter you will see that in order to use this tool you must comment your classes in the Javadoc style – as you will see, Javadoc comments must begin with /** and end with */.

1.6 Output in Java

As you have already seen when writing your first program, to output a message on to the screen in Java we use the following command:

```java
System.out.println (message to be printed on screen);
```

For example, we have already seen:

```
System.out.println("Hello world");
```

This prints the message "Hello world" onto the screen. There is in fact an alternative form of the `System.out.println` statement, which uses `System.out.print`. As we said before, `println` is short for *print line* and the effect of this statement is to start a new line after displaying whatever is in the brackets. You can see the effect of this below – we have adapted program 1.1 by adding an additional line.

PROGRAM 1.1 – with an additional line

```
public class Hello
{
  public static void main(String[] args)
  {
    System.out.println("Hello world"); // notice the use of println
    System.out.println("Hello world again!");
  }
}
```

When we run this program, the output looks like this:

```
Hello world

Hello world again!
```

Now let's change the first `System.out.println` to `System.out.print`:

PROGRAM 1.1 – adapted to show the effect of using *print* instead of *println*

```
public class Hello
{
  public static void main(String[] args)
  {
    System.out.print("Hello world"); // notice the use of print
    System.out.println("Hello world again!");
  }
}
```

Now our output looks like this:

    Hello worldHello world again!

You can see that the output following the `System.out.print` statement doesn't start on a new line, but follows straight on from the previous line.

By the way, if you want a blank line in the program, then you can simply use `println` with empty brackets:

```
System.out.println();
```

Messages such as `"Hello world"` are in fact what we call **strings** (collections of characters). In Java, literal strings like this are always enclosed in speech marks. We shall explore strings in depth in chapter 7. However, it is useful to know now how several strings can be printed on the screen using a single output command.

In Java, two strings can be joined together with the plus symbol (+). When using this symbol for this purpose it is known as the **concatenation operator**. For example, instead of printing the single string "Hello world", we could have joined two strings, "Hello" and "world", for output using the following command:

```
System.out.println("Hello " + "world");
```

Note that spaces are printed by including them within the speech marks (`"Hello "`), not by adding spaces around the concatenation operator (which has no effect at all).

Self-test questions

1 Explain the meaning of the following terms:
   - program;
   - software;
   - application software;
   - system software;
   - machine code;
   - source code;
   - embedded software;
   - compilation;
   - Java byte code;
   - Java virtual machine;
   - integrated development environment.

2 Explain how Java programs are compiled and run, and how this differs from the way many other programs are compiled and run.

3 Describe the various types of Java program that can be created – such as console applications, graphical applications, applets and mobile applications.

4 Describe two different ways of adding comments to a Java program.

5 What is the difference between using `System.out.println` and `System.out.print` to produce output in Java?

6 What, precisely, would be the output of the following programs?

   a

```
public class FirstStepQ1
{
  public static void main(String[] args)
  {
    System.out.print("Hello, how are you? ");
    System.out.println("Fine thanks.");
  }
}
```

b

```
public class FirstStepQ2
{
  public static void main(String[] args)
  {
    System.out.println("Hello, how are you? ");
    System.out.println("Fine thanks.");
  }
}
```

c

```
public class FirstStepQ3
{
  public static void main(String[] args)
  {
    System.out.println("1 + 2 " + "+ 3" + " = 6");
  }
}
```

7 Identify the syntax errors in the following program:

```
public class
{
  public Static void main(String[] args)
  {
    system.out.println( I want this program to compile)
  }
```

Programming exercises

1 If you do not already have access to a Java IDE, install the software that is supplied on the accompanying CD. There are instructions on this CD that tell you exactly how to do this. They also tell you how to use the software in order to compile and run your programs.

2 Type and compile program 1.1. If you make any syntax errors, the compiler will indicate where to find them. Correct them and re-compile your program. Keep doing this until you no longer have any errors. You can then run your program.

3 Make the changes to the *Hello world* program that are made in this chapter, then each time re-compile and run the program again.

4 Type and compile the program given in self-test question 7 above. This program contained compiler errors that you should have identified in your answer to that question. Take a look at how the compiler reports these errors, then fix them so that the program can compile and run successfully.

5 Write a program that displays your name, address and telephone number, each on a separate line.

6 Adapt the above program to include a blank line between your address and telephone number.

7 Write a program that displays your initials in big letters made of asterisks. For example:

Do this by using a series of `println` commands, each printing one row of asterisks.

CHAPTER

Building blocks

02

❖ **OBJECTIVES**

By the end of this chapter you should be able to:

❖ distinguish between the eight built-in **primitive types** of Java;

❖ **declare** and **assign** values to **variables**;

❖ create **constant** values with the keyword `final`;

❖ use the input methods of the `Scanner` class to get data from the keyboard;

❖ design the functionality of a method using **pseudocode**.

2.1 Introduction

The "Hello world" program that we developed in chapter 1 is of course very simple indeed. One way in which this program is very limited is that it has no *data* to work on. All interesting programs will have to store data in order to give interesting results; what use would a calculator be without the numbers the user types in to add and multiply? For this reason, one of the first questions you should ask when learning any programming language is "what types of data does this language allow me to store in my programs?"

2.2 Simple data types in Java

We begin this topic by taking a look at the basic types available in the Java language. The types of value used within a program are referred to as **data types**. If you wish to record the *price* of a cinema ticket in a program, for example, this value would probably need to be kept in the form of a **real number** (a number with a decimal point in it). However, if you wished to record *how many* tickets have been sold you would probably need to keep this in the form of an **integer** (whole number). It is necessary to know whether suitable types exist in the programming language to keep these bits of data.

In Java there are a few simple data types that programmers can use. These simple types are often referred to as the **primitive types** of Java; they are also referred to as the **scalar types**, as they relate to a single piece of information (a single real number, a single character etc.)

Table 2.1 lists the names of these types in the Java language, the kinds of value they represent, and the exact range of these values.

Java type	Allows for	Range of values
byte	very small integers	−128 to 127
short	small integers	−32 768 to 32 767
int	big integers	−2 147 483 648 to 2 147 483 647
long	very big integers	−9 223 372 036 854 775 808 to 9 223 372 036 854 775 807
float	real numbers	+/− $1.4 * 10^{-45}$ to $3.4 * 10^{38}$
double	very big real numbers	+/− $4.9 * 10^{-324}$ to $1.8 * 10^{308}$
char	characters	Unicode character set
boolean	true or false	not applicable

TABLE 2.1 The primitive types of Java

As you can see, some kinds of data, namely integers and real numbers, can be kept as more than one Java type. For example, you can use the **byte** type, the **short** type or the **int** type to hold integers in Java. However, while each numeric Java type allows for both positive and negative numbers, *the maximum size of numbers that can be stored varies from type to type*.

For example, the type **byte** can represent integers ranging only from −128 to 127, whereas the type **short** can represent integers ranging from −32 768 to 32 767. Unlike some programming languages, these ranges are *fixed* no matter which Java compiler or operating system you are using.

The character type, **char**, is used to represent characters from a standard set of characters known as the **Unicode** character set. This contains nearly all the characters from most known languages. For the sake of simplicity, you can think of this type as representing any character that can be input from your keyboard.

Finally, the **boolean** type is used to keep only one of two possible values: **true** or **false**. This type can be useful when creating tests in programs. For example, the answer to the question "have I passed my exam?" will either be either *yes* or *no*. In Java a **boolean** type could be used to keep the answer to this question, with the value **true** being used to represent *yes* and the value **false** to represent *no*.

2.3 Declaring variables in Java

The data types listed in table 2.1 are used in programs to create named locations in the computer's memory that will contain values while a program is running. This process is known as **declaring**. These named locations are called **variables** because their values are allowed to *vary* over the life of the program.

For example, a program written to develop a computer game might need a piece of data to record the player's score as secret keys are found in a haunted house. The value held in this piece of data will vary as more keys are found. This piece of data would be referred to as a variable. To create a variable in your program you must:

- give that variable a name (of your choice);
- decide which data type in the language best reflects the kind of values you wish to store in the variable.

What name might you choose to record the score of the player in our computer game?

The rules for naming *variables* are the same as those we met when discussing the rules for naming *classes* in the previous chapter. However, the convention in Java programs is to begin the name of a variable with a *lower case* letter (whereas the convention is to start class names with an upper case letter). We could just pick a name like x, but it is best to pick a name that describes the purpose of the item of data; an ideal name would be score.

Which data type in table 2.1 should you use if you wish to record a player's score? Well, since the score would always be a whole number, an integer type would be appropriate. There are four Java data types that can be used to hold integers (**byte**, **short**, **int** and **long**). As we said before, the only difference among these types is the range of values that they can keep. Unless there is specific reason to do otherwise, however, the **int** type is normally chosen to store integer values in Java programs. Similarly, when it comes to storing real numbers we will choose the **double** type rather than the **float** type.

Once the name and the type have been decided upon, the variable is **declared** as follows:

```
dataType variableName;
```

where dataType is the chosen primitive type and variableName is the chosen name of the variable. So, in the case of a player's score, the variable would be declared as follows:

```
int score;
```

Figure 2.1 illustrates the effect of this instruction on the computer's memory. As you can see, a small part of the computer's memory is set aside to store this item. You can think of this reserved space in memory as being a small box, big enough to hold an integer. The name of the box will be score.

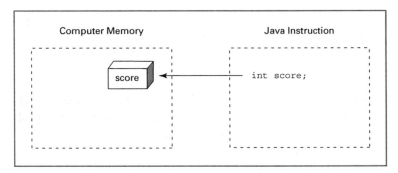

FIGURE 2.1 The effect of declaring a variable in Java

In this way, many variables can be declared in your programs. Let's assume that the player of a game can choose a difficulty level (A, B, or C); another variable could be declared in a similar way.

What name might you give this variable? An obvious choice would be *difficulty level* but remember names cannot have spaces in them. You could use an underscore to remove the space (*difficulty_level*) or start the second word with a capital letter to distinguish the two words (*difficultyLevel*). Both are well-established naming conventions in Java. Alternatively you could just shorten the name to, say, *level*; that is what we will do here.

Now, what data type in table 2.1 best represents the difficulty level? Since the levels are given as characters (A, B and C) the **char** type would be the obvious choice. At this point we have two variables declared: one to record the score and one to record the difficulty level:

```
int score;
char level;
```

Finally, several variables can be declared on a *single line* if they are *all of the same type*. For example, let's assume that there are ghosts in the house that hit out at the player; the number of times a player gets hit by a ghost can also be recorded. We can call this variable *hits*. Since the type of this variable is also an integer, it can be declared along with score in a single line as follows:

```
int score, hits; // two variables declared at once
char level ; // this has to be declared separately
```

Figure 2.2 illustrates the effect of these three declarations on the computer's memory.

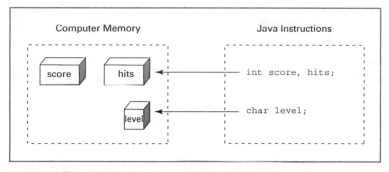

FIGURE 2.2 The effect of declaring many variables in Java

Notice that the character box, level, is half the size of the integer boxes score and hits. That is because, in Java, the **char** type requires half the space of the **int** type. You should also be aware that the **double** type in Java requires twice the space of the **int** type.

You're probably wondering: if declaring a variable is like creating a box in memory, how do I put values into this box? The answer is with assignments.

2.4 Assignments in Java

Assignments allow values to be put into variables. They are written in Java with the use of the equality symbol (=). In Java this symbol is known as the **assignment operator**. Simple assignments take the following form:

```
variableName = value;
```

For example, to put the value zero into the variable score, the following assignment statement could be used:

```
score = 0;
```

This is to be read as "*set* the value of score *to* zero" or alternatively as "score *becomes equal to* zero". Effectively, this puts the number zero into the box in memory we called score. If you wish, you may combine the assignment statement with a variable declaration to put an initial value into a variable as follows:

```
int score = 0;
```

This is equivalent to the two statements below:

```
int score;
score = 0;
```

Although in some circumstances Java will automatically put initial values into variables when they are declared, this is not always the case and it is better explicitly to initialize variables that require an initial value.

Notice that the following declaration will not compile in Java:

```
int score = 2.5 ;
```

Can you think why?

The reason is that the right-hand side of the assignment (2.5) is a *real* number. This value could not be placed into a variable such as score, which is declared to hold only integers, without some information loss. In Java, such information loss is not permitted, and this statement would therefore cause a compiler error.

You may be wondering if it is possible to place a whole number into a variable declared to hold real numbers. The answer is yes. The following is perfectly legal:

```
double someNumber = 1000;
```

Although the value on the right-hand side (1000) appears to be an integer, it can be placed into a variable of type **double** because this would result in no information loss. Once this number is put into the variable of type **double**, it will be treated as the real number 1000.0.

Clearly, you need to think carefully about the best data type to choose for a particular variable. For instance, if a variable is going to be used to hold whole numbers *or* real numbers, use the **double** type as it can cope with both. If the variable is only ever going to be used to hold whole numbers, however, then although the **double** type might be adequate, use the **int** type as it is specifically designed to hold whole numbers.

When assigning a value to a character variable, you must enclose the value in single quotes. For example, to set the initial difficulty level to A, the following assignment statement could be used:

```
char level = 'A';
```

Remember: you need to declare a variable only once. You can then assign values to it as many times as you like. For example, later on in the program the difficulty level might be changed to a different value as follows:

```
char level = 'A'; // initial difficulty level
// other Java instructions
level = 'B'; // difficulty level changed
```

2.5 Creating constants

There will be occasions where data items in a program have values *that do not change*. The following are examples of such items:

- the maximum score in an exam (100);
- the number of hours in a day (24);
- the mathematical value of π (approximately 3.1416).

In these cases the values of the items do not vary. Values that remain constant throughout a program (as opposed to variable) should be named and declared as **constants**.

Constants are declared much like variables in Java except that they are preceded by the keyword **final**. Once they are given a value, then that value is fixed and cannot later be changed. Normally we fix a value when we initialize the constant. For example:

```
final int HOURS = 24;
```

Notice that the standard Java convention has been used here of naming constants in upper case. Any attempt to change this value later in the program will result in a compiler error. For example:

```
final int HOURS = 24; // create constant
HOURS = 12; // will not compile!
```

2.6 Arithmetic operators

Rather than just assign simple values (such as 24 and 2.5) to variables, it is often useful to carry out some kind of arithmetic in assignment statements. Java has the four familiar arithmetic operators, plus a remainder operator, for this purpose. These operators are listed in table 2.2.

Operation	Java operator
addition	+
subtraction	−
multiplication	*
division	/
remainder	%

TABLE 2.2 The arithmetic operators of Java

You can use these operators in assignment statements, much as you might use a calculator. For example, consider the following instructions:

```
int x;
x = 10 + 25;
```

After these instructions the variable x would contain the value 35: the result of adding 10 to 25. Terms on the right-hand side of assignment operators (like 10 + 25) that have to be *worked out* before they are assigned are referred to as **expressions**. These expressions can involve more than one operator.

Let's consider a calculation to work out the price of a product after a sales tax has been added. If the initial price of the product is 500 and the rate of sales tax is 17.5%, the following calculation could be used to calculate the total cost of the product:

```
double cost;
cost = 500 * (1 + 17.5/100);
```

After this calculation the final cost of the product would be 587.5.

By the way, in case you are wondering, the order in which expressions such as these are evaluated is the same as in arithmetic: terms in brackets are calculated first, followed by division, then multiplication, then addition and finally subtraction. This means that the term in the bracket

```
(1 + 17.5/100)
```

evaluates to 1.175, not 0.185, as the division is calculated before the addition. The final operator (%) in table 2.2 returns the remainder after *integer division* (this is often referred to as the **modulus**). Table 2.3 illustrates some examples of the use of this operator together with the values returned.

Expression	Value
29 % 9	2
6 % 8	6
40 % 40	0
10 % 2	0

TABLE 2.3 Examples of the modulus operator in Java

As an illustration of the use of both the division operator and the modulus operator, consider the following example:

A large party of 30 people is going to attend a school reunion. The function room will be furnished with a number of tables, each of which seats four people.

To calculate how many tables of four are required, and how many people will be left over, the division and modulus operators could be used as follows:

```
int tablesOfFour, peopleLeftOver;
tablesOfFour = 30/4; // number of tables
peopleLeftOver = 30%4; // number of people left over
```

After these instructions the value of `tablesOfFour` will be 7 (the result of dividing 30 by 4) and the value of `peopleLeftOver` will be 2 (the remainder after dividing 30 by 4). You may be wondering why the calculation for `tablesOfFour`

```
30/4
```

did not yield 7.5 but 7. The reason for this is that there are, in fact, two different in-built division routines in Java, one to calculate an integer answer and another to calculate the answer as a real number.

Rather than having two division operators, however, Java has a single division symbol (/) to represent *both* types of division. The division operator is said to be **overloaded**. This means that the same operator (in this case the division symbol) can behave in different ways. This makes life much easier for programmers as the decision about which routine to call is left to the Java language.

How does the Java compiler know which division routine we mean? Well, it looks at the values that are being divided. If *at least one value* is a real number (as in the product cost example), it assumes we mean the division routine that calculates an answer as a real number, otherwise it assumes we mean the division routine that calculates an answer as a whole number (as in the reunion example).[1]

2.7 Expressions in Java

So far, variable names have appeared only on the left-hand side of assignment statements. However, the expression on the right-hand side of an assignment statement can itself contain variable names. If this is the case then the name does not refer to *the location*, but to *the contents of the location*. For example, the assignment to calculate the cost of the product could have been rewritten as follows:

```
double price, tax, cost; // declare three variables
price = 500; // set price
tax = 17.5; // set tax rate
cost = price * (1 + tax/100); // calculate cost
```

[1] To force the use of one division routine over another, a technique known as **type casting** can be used. We will return to this technique in later chapters.

Here, the variables `price` and `tax` that appear in the expression

```
price * (1 + tax/100)
```

are taken to mean *the values contained in* `price` and `tax` respectively. This expression evaluates to 587.5 as before. Notice that although this price happens to be a whole number, it has been declared to be a **double** as generally prices are expressed as real numbers.

There is actually nothing to stop you using the name of the variable you are assigning to in the expression itself. This would just mean that the old value of the variable is being used to calculate its new value. Rather than creating a new variable, `cost`, to store the final cost of the product, the calculation could, for example, have updated *the original price* as follows:

```
price = price * (1 + tax/100);
```

Now, only two variables are required, `price` and `tax`. Let's look at this assignment a bit more closely.

When reading this instruction, the `price` in the right-hand expression is to be read as the *old value* of `price`, whereas the `price` on the left-hand side is to be read as *the new value* of `price`.

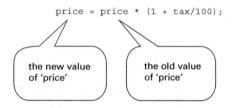

You might be wondering what would happen if we used a variable in the right-hand side of an expression before it had been given a value. For example, look at this fragment of code:

```
double price = 500;
double tax;
cost = price * (1 + tax/100);
```

The answer is that you would get a compiler error telling you that you were trying to use a variable before it has been initialized.

You will find that one very common thing that we have to do in our programs is to increase (or increment) an integer by 1. For example, if a variable x has been declared as an **int**, then the instruction for incrementing x would be:

```
x = x + 1;
```

In fact, this is so common that there is a special shorthand for this instruction, namely:

```
x++;
```

The '++' is therefore known as the increment operator. Similarly there exists a decrement operator, '--'. Thus:

```
x--;
```

is shorthand for:

```
x = x - 1;
```

It is possible to use the increment and decrement operators in expressions. We will show you a couple of examples of this here, as you might easily come across them in other texts. However, we will not be using this technique in the remainder of this book, because we think it can sometimes be confusing for new programmers. If x and y are **int**s, the expression:

```
y = x++;
```

means assign the value of x to y, then increment x by 1.

However, the expression:

```
y = ++x;
```

means increment x by 1, then assign this new value to y. The decrement operator can be used in the same way.

While we are on the subject of shortcuts, there is one more that you might come across in other places, but which, once again, we won't be using in this text:

```
y += x;
```

is shorthand for:

```
y = y + x;
```

The code fragments we have been writing so far in this chapter are, of course, not complete programs. As you already know, to create a program in Java you must write one or more classes. In program 2.1, we write a class, `FindCost`, where the `main` method calculates the price of the product.

PROGRAM 2.1

```
/* a program to calculate the cost of a product after a sales tax has been added */

public class FindCost
{
  public static void main(String[] args)
  {
    double price, tax;
    price = 500;
    tax = 17.5;
    price = price * (1 + tax/100);
  }
}
```

What would you see when you run this program? The answer is nothing! There is no instruction to display the result on to the screen. You have already seen how to display messages onto the screen. It is now time to take a closer look at the output command to see how you can also display results onto the screen.

2.8 More about output

As well as displaying messages, Java also allows any values or expressions of the primitive types that we showed you in table 2.1 to be printed on the screen using the same output commands. It does this by implicitly converting each value/expression to a string before displaying it on the screen. In this way numbers, the value of variables, or the value of expressions can be displayed on the screen. For example, the square of 10 can be displayed on the screen as follows:

```
System.out.print(10*10);
```

This instruction prints the number 100 on the screen. Since these values are converted into strings by Java they can be joined on to literal strings for output.

For example, let's return back to the party of 30 people attending their school reunion that we discussed in section 2.6. If each person is charged a fee of 7.50 for the evening, the total cost to the whole party could be displayed as follows:

```
System.out.print("cost = " + (30*7.5) );
```

Here the concatenation operator (+), is being used to join the string, `"cost = "`, on to the value of the expression, `(30*7.5)`. Notice that when expressions like `30*7.5` are used in output statements it is best to enclose them in brackets. This would result in the following output:

```
cost = 225.0
```

Bear these ideas in mind and look at program 2.2, where we have rewritten program 2.1 so that the output is visible.

PROGRAM 2.2

```
// a program to calculate and display the cost of a product after sales tax has been added

public class FindCost2
{
  public static void main(String[] args)
  {
    double price, tax;
    price = 500;
    tax = 17.5;
    price = price * (1 + tax/100); // calculate cost
    // display results
    System.out.println("*** Product Price Check ***");
    System.out.println("Cost after tax = " + price);
  }
}
```

This program produces the following output:

```
*** Product Price Check ***
Cost after tax = 587.5
```

Although being able to see the result of the calculation is a definite improvement, this program is still very limited. The formatting of the output can certainly be improved, but we shall not deal with such issues until later on in the book. What does concern us now is that this program can only calculate the cost of products when the sales tax rate is 17.5% and the initial price is 500!

What is required is not to fix the rate of sales tax or the price of the product but, instead, to get the *user of your program* to *input* these values as the program runs.

2.9 Input in Java: the Scanner class

Java provides a special class called `Scanner`, which makes it easy for us to write a program that obtains information that is typed in at the keyboard. `Scanner` is provided as part of what is known, in Java, as a **package**. A package is a collection of pre-compiled classes – lots more about that in the second semester! The `Scanner` class is part of a package called `util`. In order to access a package we use a command called **import**. So, to make the `Scanner` class accessible to the compiler we have to tell it to look in the `util` package, and we do this by placing the following line at the top of our program:

```
import java.util.*;
```

This asterisk means that all the classes in the particular package are made available to the compiler.

As long as the `Scanner` class is accessible, you can use all the input methods that have been defined in this class. We are going to show you how to do this now. Some of the code might look a bit mysterious to you at the moment, but don't worry about this right now. Just follow our instructions for the time being – after a few chapters, it will become clear to you exactly why we use the particular format and syntax that we are showing you.

Having imported the `util` package, you will need to write the following instruction in your program:

```
Scanner keyboard = new Scanner(System.in)
```

What we are doing here is creating an object, `keyboard`, of the `Scanner` class. Once again, the true meaning of the phrase *creating an object* will become clear in the next few chapters, so don't worry too much about it now. However, you should know that, in Java, `System.in` represents the keyboard, and by associating our `Scanner` object with `System.in`, we are telling it to get the input from the keyboard as opposed to a file on disk or a modem, for example.

The `Scanner` class has several input methods, each one associated with a different input type, and once we have declared a `Scanner` object we can use these methods. Let's take some examples. Say we wanted a user to type in an integer at the keyboard, and we wanted this value to be assigned to an integer variable called x. We would use the `Scanner` method called `nextInt`; the instruction would look like this:

```
x = keyboard.nextInt();
```

In the case of a **double**, y, we would use this:

```
y = keyboard.nextDouble();
```

Notice that to access a method of a class you need to join the name of the method (getInt or getDouble) to the name of the object (keyboard) by using the full-stop. Also you must remember the brackets after the name of the method.

What about a character? Unfortunately this is a little bit more complicated, as there is no nextChar method provided. Assuming c had been declared as a character, we would have to put this:

```
c = keyboard.next().charAt(0);
```

You won't understand exactly why we use this format until chapter 7 – for now just accept it and use it when you need to.

Let us return to the haunted house game to illustrate this. Rather than *assigning* a difficulty level as follows:

```
char level;
level = 'A';
```

you could take a more flexible approach by asking the user of your program to *input* a difficulty level while the program runs. Since level is declared to be a character variable, then, after declaring a Scanner object, keyboard, you could write this line of code:

```
level = keyboard.next().charAt(0);
```

Some of you might be wondering how we would get the user to type in strings such as a name or an address. This is a bit more difficult, because a string is not a simple data type like an **int** or a **char**, but contains many characters. In Java a String is not a simple data type but a class – so to do this you will have to wait until chapter 7 where we will study classes and objects in depth.

Let us re-write program 2.2 so that the price of the product and the rate of sales tax are not fixed in the program, but are input from the keyboard. Since the type used to store the price and the tax is a **double**, the appropriate input method is nextDouble, as can be seen in program 2.3.

PROGRAM 2.3

```
import java.util.*; // in order to access the Scanner class

/* a program to input the initial price of a product and then calculate and
   display its cost after tax has been added */

public class FindCost3
```

```
{
  public static void main(String[] args )
  {
    Scanner keyboard = new Scanner(System.in);
    // create Scanner object
    double price, tax;
    System.out.println("*** Product Price Check ***");
    System.out.print("Enter initial price: "); // prompt for input
    price = keyboard.nextDouble(); // input method called
    System.out.print("Enter tax rate: "); // prompt for input
    tax = keyboard.nextDouble(); // input method called
    price = price * (1 + tax/100); // perform the calculation
    System.out.println("Cost after tax = " + price);
  }
}
```

Note that, by looking at this program code alone, there is no way to determine what the final price of the product will be, as the initial price and the tax rate will be determined *only when the program is run*.

Let's assume that we run the program and the user interacts with it as follows:[2]

```
*** Product Price Check ***
Enter initial price: 1000
Enter tax rate: 12.5
Cost after tax = 1125.0
```

You should notice the following points from this test run:

- whatever the price of the computer product and the rate of tax, this program could have evaluated the final price;
- entering numeric values with additional formatting information, such as currency symbols or the percentage symbol, is not permitted;
- after an input method is called, the cursor always moves to the next line.

The programs we are looking at now involve input commands, output commands and assignments. Clearly, the order in which you write these instructions affects the results of your programs. For example, if the instructions to calculate the final price and then display the results were reversed as follows:

```
System.out.println("Cost after tax = " + price);
price = price * (1 + tax/100);
```

---

[2] We have used **_bold italic_** font to represent user input.

The price that would be displayed would not be the price *after* tax but the price *before* tax! In order to avoid such mistakes it makes sense *to design your code* by sketching out your instructions before you type them in.

2.10 Program design

*D*esigning a program is the task of considering exactly *how to build* the software, whereas writing the code (the task of *actually building* the software) is referred to as *implementation*. As programs get more complex, it is important to spend time on program design, before launching into program implementation.

As we have already said, Java programs consist of one or more classes, each with one or more methods. In later chapters we will introduce you to the use of diagrams to help design such classes. The programs we have considered so far, however, have only a single class and a single method (`main`), so a class diagram would not be very useful here! We will therefore return to this design technique as we develop larger programs involving many classes.

At a lower level, it is the instructions *within* a method that determine the *behaviour* of that method. If the behaviour of a method is complex, then it will also be worthwhile spending time on designing the instructions that make up the method. When you sketch out the code for your methods, you don't want to have to worry about the finer details of the Java compiler such as declaring variables, adding semi-colons and using the right brackets. Very often a general purpose "coding language" can be used for this purpose to convey the meaning of each instruction without worrying too much about a specific language syntax.

Code expressed in this way is often referred to as **pseudocode**. The following is an example of pseudocode that could have been developed for the `main` method of program 2.3:

```
BEGIN
  DISPLAY program title
  DISPLAY prompt for price
  ENTER price
  DISPLAY prompt for tax
  ENTER tax
  SET price TO price * (1 + tax/100)
  DISPLAY new price
END
```

Note that these pseudocode instructions are not intended to be typed in and compiled as they do not meet the syntax rules of any particular programming language. So, exactly how you write these instructions is up to you: there is no fixed syntax for them. However, each instruction conveys a well-understood programming concept and can easily be translated into a given programming language. Reading these instructions you should be able to see how each line would be coded in Java.

Wouldn't it be much easier to write your `main` method if you have pseudocode like this to follow? In future, when we present complex methods to you we will do so by presenting their logic using pseudocode.

Self-test questions

1 What would be the most appropriate Java data type to use for the following items of data?

   - the maximum number of people allowed on a bus;
   - the weight of a food item purchased in a supermarket;
   - the grade awarded to a student (for example 'A', 'B' or 'C').

2 Explain which, if any, of the following lines would result in a compiler error:

```
int x = 75.5;
double y = 75;
```

3 Identify and correct the errors in the program below, which prompts for the user's age and then attempts to work out the year in which the user was born.

```
import java.util.*;

public class SomeProg
{
  public static void main (String[] args)
  {
    Scanner keyboard = new Scanner(System.in);
    final int YEAR;
    int age, bornIn;
    System.out.print(How old are you this year? );
    age = keyboard.nextDouble();
    bornIn = YEAR - age;
    System.out.println("I think you were born in " + BornIn);
  }
}
```

4 What would be the final output from the program below if the user entered the number 10?

```
import java.util.*;

public class Calculate
{
  public static void main(String[] args )
  {
    Scanner keyboard = new Scanner(System.in);
    int num1, num2;
```

```
    num2 = 6;
    System.out.print("Enter value ");
    num1 = keyboard.nextInt();
    num1 = num1 + 2;
    num2 = num1 / num2;
    System.out.println("result = " + num2);
  }
}
```

5 Use pseudocode to design a program that asks the user to enter values for the length and height of a rectangle and then displays the area and perimeter of that rectangle.

6 The program below was written in an attempt to swap the value of two variables. However, it does not give the desired result:

```
/* This program attempts to swap the value of two variables - it doesn't give
   the desired result however! */

import java.util.*;

public class SwapAttempt
{
  public static void main(String[] args)
  {
    // declare variables
    int x, y;
    // enter values
    System.out.print("Enter value for x ");
    x = keyboard.nextInt();
    System.out.print("Enter value for y ");
    y = keyboard.nextInt();
    // code attempting to swap two variables
    x = y;
    y = x;

    //display results
    System.out.println("x = " + x);
    System.out.println("y = " + y);
  }
}
```

> **a** Can you see why the program doesn't do what we hoped?
>
> **b** What would be the actual output of the program if the user enters 10 and 20 when prompted?
>
> **c** How could you modify the program above so that the values of the two variables are swapped successfully?

Programming exercises

1 Implement the programs from self-test questions 3, 4 and 6 above in order to verify your answers to those questions.

2 Implement the rectangle program that you designed in self-test question 5.

3 Some while ago, the European Union decreed that all traders in the UK sell their goods by the kilo and not by the pound (1 kilo = 2.2 pounds). The following pseudocode has been arrived for a program that carries this conversion:

```
BEGIN
  PROMPT for value in pounds
  ENTER value in pounds
  SET value to old value ÷ 2.2
  DISPLAY value in kilos
END
```

Implement this program, remembering to declare any variables that are necessary.

4 A group of students has been told to get into teams of a specific size for their coursework. Design and implement a program that prompts for the number of students in the group and the size of the teams to be formed, and displays how many teams can be formed and how many students are left without a team.

5 Design and implement a program that asks the user to enter a value for the radius of a circle; then displays the area and circumference of the circle.

Note that the area is calculated by evaluating πr^2 and the circumference by evaluating $2\pi r$. You can take the value of π to be 3.1416 – and ideally you should declare this as a constant at the start of the program.[3]

---

[3] Of course, you will not be able to use the Greek letter π as a name for a variable or constant. You will need to give it a name like PI.

CHAPTER 03

Selection

❖ OBJECTIVES

By the end of this chapter you should be able to:

❖ explain the difference between **sequence** and **selection**;

❖ use an **if** statement to make a single choice in a program;

❖ use an **if...else** statement to make a choice between two options in a program;

❖ use nested **if...else** statements to make multiple choices in a program;

❖ use a **switch** statement to make multiple choices in a program.

3.1 Introduction

One of the most rewarding aspects of writing and running a program is knowing that *you* are the one who has control over the computer. But looking back at the programs you have already written, just how much control do you actually have? Certainly, it was you who decided upon which instructions to include in your programs but *the order in which these instructions were executed was not* under your control. These instructions were always executed in **sequence**, that is one after the other, from beginning to the end of the main method. You will soon find that there are numerous instances when this order of execution is too restrictive and you will want to have much more control over the order in which instructions are executed.

3.2 Making choices

Very often you will want your programs to make *choices* among different courses of action. For example, a program processing requests for airline tickets could have the following choices to make:

- display the price of the seats requested;
- display a list of alternative flights;
- display a message saying that no flights are available to that destination.

A program that can make choices can behave *differently* each time it is run, whereas programs in which instructions are just executed in sequence behave the *same way* each time they are run.

As we have already mentioned, unless you indicate otherwise, program instructions are always executed in sequence. **Selection**, however, is a method of program control in which a choice can be made about which instructions to execute.

For example, consider the following program, which welcomes customers queuing up for a roller-coaster ride:

PROGRAM 3.1

```java
import java.util.*;


public class RollerCoaster
{
  public static void main(String[] args)
  {
    // declare variables
    int age;
    Scanner keyboard = new Scanner (System.in);

    // four instructions to process information
    System.out.println("How old are you?");
    age = keyboard.nextInt();
    System.out.println("Hello Junior!");
    System.out.println("Enjoy your ride");
  }
}
```

As you can see, following the variable declarations, there are *four* remaining instructions in this program. Remember that at the moment these instructions will be executed in sequence, from top to bottom. Consider the following interaction with this program:

```
How old are you?
10
Hello Junior!
Enjoy your ride
```

This looks fine but the message "Hello Junior!" is only meant for children. Now let's assume that someone older comes along and interacts with this program as follows:

```
How old are you?
45
Hello Junior!
Enjoy your ride
```

The message "Hello Junior!", while flattering, might not be appropriate in this case! In other words, it is not always appropriate to execute the following instruction:

```
System.out.println("Hello Junior!");
```

What is required is a way of deciding (while the program is running) whether or not to execute this instruction. In effect, this instruction needs to be *guarded* so that it is only executed *when appropriate*. Assuming we define a child as someone under 13 years of age, we can represent this in pseudocode as follows:

```
DISPLAY "How old are you?"
ENTER age
IF age is under 13
BEGIN
    DISPLAY "Hello Junior!"
END
DISPLAY "Enjoy your ride"
```

In the above, we have emboldened the lines that have been added to guard the "Hello Junior!" instruction. The emboldened lines that have been added are not to be read as *additional* instructions; they are simply a means to *control the flow* of the *existing* instructions. The emboldened lines say, in effect, that the instruction to display the message "Hello Junior!" should only be executed if the age entered is under 13.

This, then, is an example of the form of control known as selection. Let's now look at how to code this selection in Java.

3.3 The 'if' statement

The particular form of selection discussed above is implemented by making use of Java's **if** statement. The general form of an **if** statement is given as follows:

```
if ( /* a test goes here */)
{
  // instruction(s) to be guarded go here
}
```

As you can see, the instructions to be guarded are placed inside the braces of the **if** statement. A **test** is associated with the **if** statement. A test is any expression that produces a result of **true** or **false**. For example, x>100 is a test as it is an expression that gives an answer of either **true** or **false** (depending upon the value of x). We call an expression that returns a value of **true** or **false** a **boolean expression**, as **true** and **false** are **boolean** values. Examples of tests in everyday language are:

- this password is valid;
- there is an empty seat on the plane;
- the temperature in the laboratory is too high.

The test must follow the **if** keyword and be placed in round brackets. When the test gives a result of **true** the instructions inside the braces of the **if** statement are executed. The program then continues by executing the instructions after the braces of the **if** statement as normal. If, however, the **if** test gives a result of **false** the instructions inside the **if** braces are *skipped* and not executed.

We can rewrite program 3.1 by including an appropriate **if** statement around the "Hello Junior!" message with the test (age < 13) as follows:

PROGRAM 3.2

```java
import java.util.*;

// This program is an example of the use of selection in a Java program

public class RollerCoaster2
{
  public static void main(String[] args)
  {
    int age;
    Scanner keyboard = new Scanner (System.in);
    System.out.println("How old are you?");
    age = keyboard.nextInt();
    if (age < 13) // test controls if the next instruction is executed
    {
      System.out.println("Hello Junior!");
    }
    System.out.println("Enjoy your ride");
  }
}
```

Now the message "Hello Junior!" will only be executed if the test (age<13) is **true**, otherwise it will be skipped (see figure 3.1).

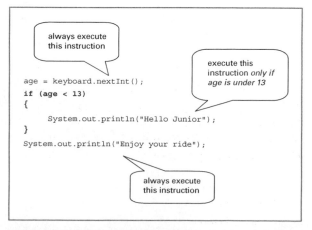

FIGURE 3.1 The *if* statement allows a choice to be made in programs

Let's assume we run program 3.2 with the same values entered as when running program 3.1 before. First, the child approaches the ride:

```
How old are you?
10
Hello Junior!
Enjoy your ride
```

In this case, the **if** statement has allowed the "Hello Junior!" message to be displayed as the age entered is less than 13. Now the adult approaches the ride:

```
How old are you?
45
Enjoy your ride
```

In this case the **if** statement has not allowed the given instruction to be executed as the associated test was not true. The message is skipped and the program continues with the following instruction to display "Enjoy your ride".

In this program there was only a *single* instruction inside the **if** statement.

```
age = keyboard.nextInt();

if (age < 13)

{

  System.out.println("Hello Junior!"); // single instruction inside 'if'

}

System.out.println("Enjoy your ride");
```

When there is only a single instruction associated with an **if** statement, the braces can be omitted around this instruction, if so desired, as follows:

```
age = keyboard.nextInt();

if (age < 13)

System.out.println("Hello Junior!"); // braces can be omitted around this line

System.out.println("Enjoy your ride");
```

The compiler will always assume that the first line following the **if** test is the instruction being guarded. For clarity, however, we will always use braces around instructions.

3.3.1 Comparison operators

In the example above, the "less than" operator (<) was used to check the value of the age variable. This operator is often referred to as a **comparison operator** as it is used to compare two values. Table 3.1 shows all the Java comparison operator symbols.

Operator	Meaning
= =	equal to
! =	not equal to
<	less than
>	greater than
> =	greater than or equal to
< =	less than or equal to

TABLE 3.1 The comparison operators of Java

Since comparison operators give a **boolean** result of **true** or **false** they are often used in tests such as those we have been discussing. For example, consider a temperature variable being used to record the temperature for a particular day of the week. Assume that a temperature of 18 degrees or above is considered to be a hot day. We could use the "greater than or equal to" operator (>=) to check for this as follows:

```
if (temperature >= 18) // test to check for hot temperature
{
  // this line executed only when the test is true
  System.out.println("Today is a hot day!");
}
```

You can see from table 3.1 that a double equals (= =) is used to check for equality in Java and not the single equals (=), which, as you know, is used for assignment. To use the single equals is a very common error! For example, to check whether an angle is a right angle the following test should be used:

```
if (angle == 90) // note the use of the double equals
{
  System.out.println("This IS a right angle");
}
```

To check if something is *not equal* to a particular value we use the exclamation mark followed by an equals sign (! =). So to test if an angle is *not* a right angle we can have the following:

```
if (angle != 90)
{
  System.out.println("This is NOT a right angle");
}
```

3.3.2 Multiple instructions within an 'if' statement

You have seen how an `if` statement guarding a single instruction may or may not be implemented with braces around the instruction. When *more than one* instruction is to be guarded by an `if` statement, however, the instructions *must* be placed in braces. As an example, consider once again program 2.3 that calculates the cost of a product.

REMINDER OF PROGRAM 2.3

```java
import java.util.*;
public class FindCost3
{
  public static void main(String [] args)
  {
    Scanner keyboard = new Scanner(System.in);
    double price, tax;
    System.out.println("*** Product Price Check ***");
    System.out.print("Enter initial price: ");
    price = keyboard.nextDouble();
    System.out.print("Enter tax rate: ");
    tax = keyboard.nextDouble();
    price = price * (1 + tax/100);
    System.out.println("Cost after tax = " + price);
  }
}
```

Now assume that a special promotion is in place for those products with an initial price over 100. For such products the company pays half the tax. Program 3.3 makes use of an `if` statement to apply this promotion, as well as informing the user that a tax discount has been applied. Take a look at it and then we will discuss it.

PROGRAM 3.3

```java
import java.util.*;
public class FindCostWithDiscount
{
  public static void main(String[] args )
  {
    double price, tax;
    Scanner keyboard = new Scanner(System.in);
    System.out.println("*** Product Price Check ***");
    System.out.print("Enter initial price: ");
    price = keyboard.nextDouble();
    System.out.print("Enter tax rate: ");
    tax = keyboard.nextDouble();
```

```
    // the following 'if' statement allows a selection to take place
    if (price > 100) // test the price to see if a discount applies
    {
      // these two instructions executed only when test is true
      System.out.println("Special Promotion: We pay half your tax!");
      tax = tax * 0.5;
    }
    // the remaining instructions are always executed
    price = price * (1 + tax/100);
    System.out.println("Cost after tax = " + price);
  }
}
```

Now, the user is still always prompted to enter the initial price and tax as before:

```
System.out.print("Enter initial price: ");
price = keyboard.nextDouble();
System.out.print("Enter tax rate: ");
tax = keyboard.nextDouble();
```

The next two instructions are then placed inside an **if** statement. This means they may not always be executed:

```
if (price > 100)
{
  System.out.println("Special Promotion: We pay half your tax!");
  tax = tax * 0.5;
}
```

Notice that if the braces were omitted in this case, only the *first* instruction would be taken to be inside the **if** statement – the second statement would not be guarded and so would *always* be executed!

With braces around both instructions, they will be executed only when the test (price > 100) returns a **boolean** result of **true**. So, for example, if the user had entered a price of 150 the tax discount would be applied; but if the user entered a price of 50 these instructions would not be executed and a tax discount would not be applied.

Regardless of whether or not the test was **true** and the instructions in the **if** statement executed, the program always continues with the remaining instructions:

```
price = price * (1 + tax/100);
System.out.println("Cost after tax = " + price);
```

Here is a sample program run when the test returns a result of **false** and the discount is not applied:

```
*** Product Price Check ***
Enter initial price: 20
Enter tax rate: 10
Cost after tax = 22.0
```

In this case the program appears to behave in exactly the same way as the original program (program 2.3). Here, however, is a program run when the test returns a result of **true** and a discount does apply:

```
*** Product Price Check ***
Enter initial price: 1000
Enter tax rate: 10
Special Promotion: We pay half your tax!
Cost after tax = 1050.0
```

3.4 The 'if...else' statement

Using the **if** statement in the way that we have done so far has allowed us to build the idea of a choice into our programs. In fact, the **if** statement made one of two choices before continuing with the remaining instructions in the program:

- execute the conditional instructions, or
- do not execute the conditional instructions.

The second option amounts to "do nothing". Rather than do nothing if the test is **false**, an extended version of an **if** statement exists in Java to state an *alternative* course of action. This extended form of selection is the **if...else** statement. As the name implies, the instructions to be executed if the test evaluates to **false** are preceded by the Java keyword **else** as follows:

```
if ( /* test goes here */ )
{
  // instruction(s) if test is true go here
}
else
{
  // instruction(s) if test is false go here
}
```

This is often referred to as a **double-branched** selection as there are two alternative groups of instructions, whereas a single **if** statement is often referred to as a **single-branched** selection. Program 3.4 illustrates the use of a double-branched selection.

PROGRAM 3.4

```java
import java.util.*;
public class DisplayResult
{
  public static void main(String[] args)
  {
    int mark;
    Scanner keyboard = new Scanner(System.in);
    System.out.println("What exam mark did you get? ");
    mark = keyboard.nextInt();
    if (mark >= 10)
    {
      // executed when test is true
      System.out.println("Congratulations, you passed");
    }
    else
    {
      // executed when test is false
      System.out.println("I'm sorry, but you failed");
    }
    System.out.println("Good luck with your other exams");
  }
}
```

Program 3.4 checks a student's exam mark and tells the student whether or not he or she has passed (gained a mark greater than or equal to 40), before displaying a good luck message on the screen. Let's examine this program a bit more closely.

Prior to the **if...else** statement the following lines are executed in sequence:

```java
int mark;
Scanner keyboard = new Scanner(System.in);
System.out.println("What exam mark did you get? ");
mark = keyboard.nextInt();
```

Then the following condition is tested as part of the **if...else** statement:

```java
(mark >= 40)
```

When this test is **true** the following line is executed:

```java
System.out.print("Congratulations, you passed");
```

When the test is **false**, however, the following line is executed *instead*:

```
System.out.println("I'm sorry, but you failed");
```

Finally, whichever path was chosen the program continues by executing the last line:

```
System.out.println("Good luck with your other exams");
```

The **if...else** form of control has allowed us to choose from *two* alternative courses of action. Here is a sample program run:

> *What exam mark did you get?*
> *52*
> *Congratulations, you passed*
> *Good luck with your other exams*

Here is another sample run where a different course of action is chosen.

> *What exam mark did you get?*
> *35*
> *I'm sorry, but you failed*
> *Good luck with your other exams*

3.5 Logical operators

As we've already pointed out, the test in an **if** statement is an expression that produces a **boolean** result of **true** or **false**. Often it is necessary to join two or more tests together to create a single more complicated test.

As an example, consider a program that checks the temperature in a laboratory. Assume that, for the experiments in the laboratory to be successful, the temperature must remain between 5 and 12 degrees Celsius. An **if** statement might be required as follows:

```
if (/* test to check if temperature is safe */)
{
  System.out.println ("TEMPERATURE IS SAFE!");
}
else
{
  System.out.println("UNSAFE: RAISE ALARM!!");
}
```

The test should check if the temperature is safe. This involves combining two tests together:

1 check that the temperature is greater than or equal to 5 (`temperature >= 5`)

2 check that the temperature is less than or equal to 12 (`temperature <= 12`)

Both of these tests need to evaluate to **true** in order for the temperature to be safe. When we require two tests to be **true** we use the following symbol to join the two tests:

`&&`

This symbol is read as "AND". So the correct test is:

```
if (temperature >= 5 && temperature <= 12)
```

Now, if the temperature were below 5 the first test (`temperature >= 5`) would evaluate to **false** giving a final result of **false**; the **if** statement would be skipped and the **else** statement would be executed:

`UNSAFE: RAISE ALARM!!`

If the temperature were greater than 12 the second part of the test (`temperature <= 12`) would evaluate to **false** also giving an overall result of **false** and again the **if** statement would be skipped and the **else** statement would be executed.

However, when the temperature is between 5 and 12 *both* tests would evaluate to **true** and the final result would be **true** as required; the **if** statement would then be executed instead:

`TEMPERATURE IS SAFE!`

Notice that the two tests must be *completely* specified as each needs to return a **boolean** value of **true** or **false**. It would be wrong to try something like the following:

```
// wrong! second test does not mention 'temperature'!
if (temperature >= 5 && <= 12)
```

This is wrong as the second test (`<= 12`) is not a legal **boolean** expression. Symbols that join tests together to form longer tests are known as **logical operators**. Table 3.2 lists the Java counterparts to the three common logical operators.

Logical operator	Java counterpart
AND	&&
OR	||
NOT	!

TABLE 3.2 The logical operators of Java

Both the AND and OR operators join two tests together to give a final result. While the AND operator requires both tests to be **true** to give a result of **true**, the OR operator requires only that *at least one* of the tests be **true** to give a result of **true**. The NOT operator flips a value of **true** to **false** and a value of **false** to **true**. Table 3.3 gives some examples of the use of these logical operators.

Expression	Result	Explanation
10>5 && 10>7	true	Both tests are true
10>5 && 10>20	false	The second test is false
10>15 && 10>20	false	Both tests are false
10>5 || 10>7	true	At least one test is true (in this case both tests are true)
10>5 || 10>20	true	At least one test is true (in this case just one test is true)
10>15 || 10>20	false	Both tests are false
! (10 > 5)	false	Original test is true
! (10 > 15)	true	Original test is false

TABLE 3.3 Logical operators: some examples

As an example of the use of the NOT operator (!), let us return to the temperature example. We said that we were going to assume that a temperature of greater than 18 degrees was going to be considered a hot day. To check that the day is not a hot day we could use the NOT operator as follows:

```java
if (!(temperature > 18) ) // test to check if temperature is not hot
{
  System.out.println("Today is not a hot day!");
}
```

Of course, if a temperature is not greater than 18 degrees then it must be less than or equal to 18 degrees. So, another way to check the test above would be as follows:

```java
if (temperature <= 18) // this test also checks if temperature is not hot
{
  System.out.println("Today is not a hot day!");
}
```

3.6 Nested 'if...else' statements

Instructions within **if** and **if...else** statements can themselves be *any* legal Java commands. In particular they could contain other **if** or **if...else** statements. This form of control is referred to as **nesting**. Nesting allows multiple choices to be processed.

As an example, consider program 3.5 below, which asks a student to enter his or her tutorial group (A, B, or C) and then displays on the screen the time of the software lab.

PROGRAM 3.5

```java
import java.util.*;
public class Timetable
{
  public static void main(String[] args)
  {
    char group; // to store the tutorial group
    Scanner keyboard = new Scanner(System.in);
    System.out.println("***Lab Times***"); // display header
    System.out.println("Enter your group (A,B,C)");
    group = keyboard.next().charAt(0);
    // check tutorial group and display appropriate time
    if (group == 'A')
    {
      System.out.print("10.00 a.m"); // lab time for group A
    }
    else
    {
      if (group == 'B')
      {
        System.out.print("1.00 p.m"); // lab time for group B
      }
      else
      {
        if (group == 'C')
        {
          System.out.print("11.00 a.m"); // lab time for group C
        }
        else
        {
          System.out.print("No such group"); // invalid group
        }
      }
    }
  }
}
```

As you can see, nesting can result in code with many braces that can become difficult to read, even with our careful use of tabs. Such code can be made easier to read by not including the braces associated with all the **else** branches.

```
if (group == 'A')
{
  System.out.print("10.00 a.m");
}
else if (group == 'B')
{
  System.out.print("1.00 p.m");
}
else if(group == 'C')
{
  System.out.print("11.00 a.m");
}
else
{
  System.out.print("No such group");
}
```

This program is a little bit different from the ones before because it includes some basic **error checking**. That is, it does not *assume* that the user of this program will always type the *expected* values. If the wrong group (not A, B or C) is entered, an error message is displayed saying "*No such group*".

```
// valid groups checked above
else // if this 'else' is reached, group entered must be invalid
{
  System.out.print("No such group"); // error message
}
```

Error checking like this is a good habit to get into.

This use of nested selections is okay up to a point, but when the number of options becomes large the program can again look very untidy. Fortunately, this type of selection can also be implemented in Java with another form of control: a **switch** statement.

3.7 The 'switch' statement

Program 3.6 behaves in exactly the same way as program 3.5 but using a **switch** instead of a series of nested **if...else** statements allows a neater implementation. Take a look at it and then we'll discuss it.

PROGRAM 3.6

```java
import java.util.*;
public class TimetableWithSwitch
{
  public static void main(String[] args)
  {
    char group;
    Scanner keyboard = new Scanner(System.in);
    System.out.println("***Lab Times***");
    System.out.println("Enter your group (A,B,C)");
    group = keyboard.next().charAt(0);
    switch(group) // beginning of switch
    {
      case 'A': System.out.print("10.00 a.m ");
                break;
      case 'B': System.out.print("1.00 p.m ");
                break;
      case 'C': System.out.print("11.00 a.m ");
                break;
      default: System.out.print("No such group");
    } // end of switch
  }
}
```

As you can see, this looks a lot neater. The **switch** statement works in exactly the same way as a set of nested **if** statements, but is more compact and readable. A **switch** statement may be used when

- only one variable is being checked in each condition (in this case every condition involves checking the variable group);
- the check involves specific values of that variable (e.g. 'A', 'B') and not ranges (for example >=40).

As can be seen from the example above, the keyword **case** is used to precede a possible value of the variable that is being checked. There may be many **case** statements in a single **switch** statement. The general form of a **switch** statement in Java is given as follows:

```java
switch(someVariable)
{
  case value1: // instructions(s) to be executed
               break;
  case value2: // instructions(s) to be executed
               break;
  // more values to be tested can be added
  default: // instruction(s) for default case
}
```

where

- someVariable is the name of the variable being tested. This variable is usually of type **int** or **char** but may also be of type **long**, **byte**, or **short**.
- value1, value2, etc. are the possible values of that variable.
- **break** is a command that forces the program to skip the rest of the **switch** statement.
- **default** is an optional (last) case that can be thought of as an "otherwise" statement. It allows you to code instructions that deal with the possibility of none of the cases above being **true**.

The **break** statement is important because it means that once a matching case is found, the program can skip the rest of the cases below. If it is not added, not only will the instructions associated with the matching case be executed, but also all the instructions associated with all the cases below it. Notice that the last set of instructions does not need a **break** statement as there are no other cases to skip.

3.7.1 Grouping case statements

There will be instances when a particular group of instructions is associated with more than one **case** option. As an example, consider program 3.7 again. Let's assume that both groups A and C have a lab at 10.00 a.m. The following **switch** statement would process this without grouping case 'A' and 'C' together:

```
// groups A and C have labs at the same time
switch(group)
{
  case 'A': System.out.print("10.00 a.m ");
            break;
  case 'B': System.out.print("1.00 p.m ");
            break;
  case 'C': System.out.print("10.00 a.m ");
            break;
  default: System.out.print("No such group");
}
```

While this will work, both **case** 'A' and **case** 'C' have the same instruction associated with them:

```
System.out.print("10.00 a.m ");
```

Rather than repeating this instruction, the two **case** statements can be combined into one as follows:

```
// groups A and C have been processed together
switch(group)
{
  case 'A': case 'C': System.out.print("10.00 a.m ");
                      break;
  case 'B': System.out.print("1.00 p.m ");
            break;
  default: System.out.print("No such group");
}
```

In the example above a time of 10.00 a.m will be displayed when the group is either 'A' or 'C'. The example above combined two **case** statements, but there is no limit to how many such statements can be combined.

3.7.2 Removing `break` statements

In the examples above we have always used a **break** statement to avoid executing the code associated with more than one **case** statement. There may be situations where it is *not* appropriate to use a **break** statement and we *do* wish to execute the code associated with more than one case statement.

For example, let us assume that spies working for a secret agency are allocated different levels of security clearance, the lowest being 1 and the highest being 3. A spy with the highest clearance level of 3 can access all the secrets, whereas a spy with a clearance of level of 1 can see only secrets that have the lowest level of security. An administrator needs to be able to view the collection of secrets that a spy with a particular clearance level can see. We can implement this scenario by way of a **switch** statement in program 3.7 below. Take a look at it and then we will discuss it.

PROGRAM 3.7

```
import java.util.*;
public class SecretAgents
{
  public static void main(String[] args)
  {
    int security;
    Scanner keyboard = new Scanner(System.in);
    System.out.println("***Secret Agents***");
    System.out.println("Enter security level (1,2,3)");
    security = keyboard.nextInt();
    switch(security) // check level of security
    {
      case 3: System.out.println("The code to access the safe is 007."); // level 3 security
```

```
      case 2: System.out.println("Jim Kitt is really a double agent."); // level 2 security
      case 1: System.out.println("Martinis in the hotel bar may be poisoned."); // level 1 security
             break; // necessary to avoid error message below
      default: System.out.println("No such security level.");
   }
  }
}
```

You can see that there is just a single **break** statement at the end of **case** 1.

```
case 3: System.out.println("The code to access the safe is 007.");
case 2: System.out.println("Jim Kitt is really a double agent.");
case 1: System.out.println("Martinis in the hotel bar may be poisoned.");
       break; // the only break statement
```

If the user entered a security level of 3, for example, the println instruction associated with this case would be executed:

```
case 3: System.out.println("The code to access the safe is 007.");
```

However, as there is no **break** statement at the end of this instruction, the instruction associated with the **case** below is then also executed:

```
System.out.println("Jim Kitt is really a double agent.");
```

We have still not reached a **break** statement so the instruction associated with the next **case** statement is then executed:

```
System.out.println("Martinis in the hotel bar may be poisoned.");
break; // the only break statement
```

Here we do reach a **break** statement so the **switch** terminates. Here is a sample test run:

```
***Secret Agents***
Enter security level (1,2,3)
3
The code to access the safe is 007.
Jim Kitt is really a double agent.
Martinis in the hotel bar may be poisoned.
```

Because the security level entered is 3 *all* secrets can be revealed. Here is another sample test run when security level 2 is entered:

```
***Secret Agents***
Enter security level (1,2,3)
2
Jim Kitt is really a double agent.
Martinis in the hotel bar may be poisoned.
```

Because the security level is 2 the first secret is not revealed.

The last **break** statement is necessary in program 3.7 as we wish to avoid the final error message if a valid security level (1, 2 or 3) is entered. The error message is only displayed if an invalid security level is entered:

```
***Secret Agents***
Enter security level (1,2,3)
8
No such security level.
```

Self-test questions

1 Explain the difference between *sequence* and *selection*.

2 When would it be appropriate to use

- an **if** statement?
- an **if...else** statement?
- a **switch** statement?

3 Consider the following Java program, which is intended to display the cost of a cinema ticket. Part of the code has been replaced by a comment:

```
import java.util.*;
public class SelectionQ3
{
  public static void main(String[] args)
  {
    double price = 10.00;
    int age;
    Scanner keyboard = new Scanner(System.in);
    System.out.print("Enter your age: ");
    age = keyboard.nextInt();
      // code to reduce ticket price for children goes here
    System.out.println("Ticket price = " + price);
  }
}
```

Replace the comment so that children under the age of 14 get half price tickets.

4 Consider the following program:

```
import java.util.*;
public class SelectionQ4
{
  public static void main(String[] args)
  {
    int x;
    Scanner keyboard = new Scanner(System.in);
    System.out.print("Enter a number: ");
    x = keyboard.nextInt();
    if (x > 10)
```

```
        {
          System.out.println("Green");
          System.out.println("Blue");
        }
        System.out.println("Red");
      }
  }
```

What would be the output from this program if

a the user entered 10 when prompted?

b the user entered 20 when prompted?

c the braces used in the **if** statement are removed, and the user enters 10 when prompted?

d the braces used in the **if** statement are removed, and the user enters 20 when prompted?

5 Consider the following program:

```
import java.util.*;
public class SelectionQ5
{
  public static void main(String[] args)
  {
    int x;
    Scanner keyboard = new Scanner(System.in);
    System.out.print("Enter a number: ");
    x = keyboard.nextInt();
    if (x > 10)
    {
      System.out.println("Green");
    }
    else
    {
      System.out.println("Blue");
    }
    System.out.println("Red");
  }
}
```

What would be the output from this program if

a the user entered 10 when prompted?

b the user entered 20 when prompted?

6 Consider the following program:

```
import java.util.*;
public class SelectionQ6
{
  public static void main(String[] args)
  {
    int x;
    Scanner keyboard = new Scanner(System.in);
    System.out.print("Enter a number: ");
    x = keyboard.nextInt();
    switch (x)
    {
      case 1: case 2: System.out.println("Green"); break;
      case 3: case 4: case 5: System.out.println("Blue"); break;
      default: System.out.println("numbers 1-5 only");
    }
    System.out.println("Red");
  }
}
```

What would be the output from this program if

a the user entered 1 when prompted?

b the user entered 2 when prompted?

c the user entered 3 when prompted?

d the user entered 10 when prompted?

e the **break** statements were removed from the **switch** statement and the user entered 3 when prompted?

f the default were removed from the **switch** statement and the user entered 10 when prompted?

▶ ## Programming exercises

1 Design and implement a program that asks the user to enter two numbers and then displays the message "NUMBERS ARE EQUAL", if the two numbers are equal and "NUMBERS ARE NOT EQUAL", if they are not equal.

   Hint: Don't forget to use the double equals (==) to test for equality.

2 Adapt the program developed in the question above so that as well as checking if the two numbers are equal, the program will also display "FIRST NUMBER BIGGER" if the first number is bigger than the second number and display "SECOND NUMBER BIGGER" if the second number is bigger than the first.

3 Design and implement a program that asks the user to enter two numbers and then guess at the sum of those two numbers. If the user guesses correctly a congratulatory message is displayed, otherwise a commiseration message is displayed along with the correct answer.

4 Implement program 3.4 which processed an exam mark and then adapt the program so that marks of 70 or above are awarded a distinction rather than a pass.

5 Write a program to take an order for a computer system. The basic system costs 375.99. The user then has to choose from a 38 cm screen (costing 75.99) or a 43 cm screen (costing 99.99). The following extras are optional.

Item	Price
DVD/CD Writer	65.99
Printer	125.00

The program should allow the user to select from these extras and then display the final cost of the order.

6 Consider a bank that offers four different types of account ('A', 'B', 'C' and 'X'). The following table illustrates the annual rate of interest offered for each type of account.

Account	Annual rate of interest
A	1.5%
B	2%
C	1.5%
X	5%

Design and implement a program that allows the user to enter an amount of money and a type of bank account, before displaying the amount of money that can be earned in one year as interest on that money for the given type of bank account. You should use the **switch** statement when implementing this program.

Hint: be careful to consider the case of the letters representing the bank accounts. You might want to restrict this to, say, just upper case. Or you could enhance your program by allowing the user to enter either lower case or upper case letters.

▶

7 Consider the bank accounts discussed in exercise 6 again. Now assume that each type of bank account is associated with a minimum balance as given in the table below:

Account	Minimum balance
A	250
B	1000
C	250
X	5000

Adapt the **switch** statement of the program in exercise 6 above so that the interest is applied only if the amount of money entered satisfies the minimum balance requirement for the given account. If the amount of money is below the minimum balance for the given account an error message should be displayed.

CHAPTER

Iteration

04

❖ OBJECTIVES

By the end of this chapter you should be able to:

❖ explain the term **iteration**;

❖ repeat a section of code with a **for** loop;

❖ repeat a section of code with a **while** loop;

❖ repeat a section of code with a **do...while** loop;

❖ select the most appropriate loop for a particular task;

❖ use a **break** statement to terminate a loop;

❖ use a **continue** statement to skip an iteration of a loop;

❖ explain the term **input validation** and write simple validation routines.

4.1 Introduction

So far we have considered sequence and selection as forms of program control. One of the advantages of using computers rather than humans to carry out tasks is that they can repeat those tasks over and over again without ever getting tired. With a computer we do not have to worry about mistakes creeping in because of fatigue, whereas humans would need a break to stop them becoming sloppy or careless when carrying out repetitive tasks over a long period of time. Neither sequence nor selection allows us to carry out this kind of control in our programs. As an example, consider a program that needs to display a square of stars (five by five) on the screen as follows:

```
*  *  *  *  *

*  *  *  *  *

*  *  *  *  *

*  *  *  *  *

*  *  *  *  *
```

This could be achieved with five output statements executed in sequence, as shown in program 4.1:

PROGRAM 4.1

```
public class DisplayStars
{
  public static void main (String[] args)
  {
    System.out.println("*****"); // instruction to display one row
    System.out.println("*****"); // instruction to display one row
    System.out.println("*****"); // instruction to display one row
    System.out.println("*****"); // instruction to display one row
    System.out.println("*****"); // instruction to display one row
  }
}
```

While this produces the desired result, the program actually consists just of the following instruction to print out one row, but repeated 5 times:

```
System.out.println("*****"); // this instruction is written 5 times
```

Writing out the same line many times is somewhat wasteful of our precious time as programmers. Imagine what would happen if we wanted a square 40 by 40!

Rather than write out this instruction five times we would prefer to write it out once and get the program to *repeat that same line* five times. Something like:

```
public class DisplayStars
{
  public static void main (String[] args)
  {
    // REPEAT THE FOLLOWING 5 TIMES
    System.out.println("*****");
  }
}
```

Iteration is the form of program control that allows us to instruct the computer to carry out a task several times by repeating a section of code. For this reason this form of control is often also referred to as **repetition**. The programming structure that is used to control this repetition is often called a **loop**. There are three types of loop in Java:

- **for** loop;
- **while** loop;
- **do...while** loop.

We will consider each of these in turn.

4.2 The 'for' loop

I f we wish to repeat a section of code a *fixed* number of times (five in the example above) we would use
Java's **for** loop. For example, program 4.2 rewrites program 4.1 by making use of a **for** loop. Take a look
at it and then we will discuss it:

PROGRAM 4.2

```
public class DisplayStars2
{
  public static void main (String[] args)
  {
    for(int i = 1; i <= 5; i++) // loop to repeat 5 times
    {
      System.out.println("*****"); // instruction to display one row
    }
  }
}
```

As you can see, there are three bits of information in the header of the **for** loop, each bit separated by a
semi-colon:

```
for(int i = 1; i <= 5; i++) // three bits of information in the brackets
{
  System.out.println("*****");
}
```

All three bits of information relate to a **counter**. A counter is just another variable (usually integer) that has
to be created. We use it to keep track of how many times we have been through the loop so far. In this case
we have called our counter 'i' but we could give it any variable name – often though, simple names like 'i'
and 'j' are chosen.

Let's look carefully at how this **for** loop works. First the counter is initialized to some value. We have
decided to initialize it to 1:

```
for(int i = 1; i <= 5; i++) // counter initialized to 1
{
  System.out.println("*****");
}
```

Notice that the loop counter 'i' is *declared* as well as initialized in the header of the loop. Although it is possible to declare the counter variable *prior* to the loop, declaring it within the header restricts the use of this variable to the loop itself. This is often preferable.

The second bit of information in the header is a test, much like a test when carrying out selection. When the test returns a **boolean** value of **true** the loop repeats; when it returns a **boolean** value of **false** the loop ends. In this case the counter is tested to see if it is less than or equal to 5 (as we wish to repeat this loop 5 times):

```
for(int i = 1; i <= 5; i++) // counter tested
{
   System.out.println("*****");
}
```

Since the counter was set to 1, this test is **true** and the loop is entered. We sometimes refer to the instructions inside the loop as the **body** of the loop. As with **if** statements, the braces of the **for** loop can be omitted when only a single instruction is required in the body of the loop – but for clarity we will always use braces with our loops. When the body of the loop is entered, all the instructions within the braces of the loop are executed. In this case there is only one instruction to execute:

```
for(int i = 1; i <= 5; i++)
{
   System.out.println("******"); // this line is executed
}
```

This line prints a row of stars on the screen. Once the instructions inside the braces are complete, the loop *returns to the beginning* where the third bit of information in the header of the **for** loop is executed. The third bit of information *changes* the value of the counter so that eventually the loop test will be **false**. If we want the loop to repeat 5 times and we have started the counter off at 1, we should *add 1* to the counter each time we go around the loop:

```
for(int i = 1; i <= 5; i++) // counter is changed
{
   System.out.println("*****");
}
```

After the first increment, the counter now has the value of 2. Once the counter has been changed the test is examined again to see if the loop should repeat:

```
for(int i = 1; i <= 5; i++) // counter tested again
{
   System.out.println("*****");
}
```

This test is still **true** as the counter is still not greater than 5. Since the **test** is **true** the body of the loop is entered again and another row of stars printed. This process of checking the test, entering the loop and changing the counter repeats until five rows of stars have been printed. At this point the counter is incremented as usual:

```
for(int i = 1; i <= 5; i++) // counter eventually equals 6
{
  System.out.println("*****");
}
```

Now when the test is checked it is **false** as the counter is greater than five:

```
for(int i = 1; i <= 5; i++) // now test is false
{
  System.out.println("*****");
}
```

When the test of the **for** loop is **false** the loop stops. The instructions inside the loop are skipped and the program continues with any instructions after the loop.

Now that you have seen one example of the use of a **for** loop, the general form of a **for** loop can be given as follows:

```
for( /* start counter */ ; /* test counter */ ; /* change counter */)
{
  // instruction(s) to be repeated go here
}
```

Be very careful that the loop counter and the test achieve the desired result. For example, consider the following test:

```
for(int i = 1; i >= 10; i++) // something wrong with this test!
{
  // instruction(s) to be repeated go here
}
```

Can you see what is wrong here?

The test to continue with the loop is that the counter be *greater* than or equal to 10 (i >= 10). However, the counter starts at 1 so this test is immediately **false**! Because this test would be **false** immediately, the loop does not repeat at all and it is skipped all together!

Now consider this test:

```
for(int i = 1; i >= 1; i++) // something wrong with this test again!
{
  // instruction(s) to be repeated go here
}
```

Can you see what is wrong here?

The test to continue with the loop is that the counter be greater than or equal to 1 (i >= 1). However, the counter starts at 1 and increases by 1 each time, so this test will always be **true**! Because this test would be **true** always, the loop will never stop repeating when it is executed!

As long as you are careful with your counter and your test, however, it is a very easy matter to set your **for** loop to repeat a certain number of times. If, for example, we start the counter at 1 and increment it by 1 each time, and we need to repeat some instructions 70 times, we could have the following test in the **for** loop:

```
for(int i = 1; i <= 70; i++) // this loop repeats 70 times
{
  // instruction(s) to be repeated goes here
}
```

4.2.1 Varying the loop counter

Program 4.2 illustrated a common way of using a **for** loop; start the counter at 1 and add 1 to the counter each time the loop repeats. However, you may start your counter at *any* value and change the counter in any way you choose when constructing your **for** loops.

For example, we could have rewritten the **for** loop of program 4.2 so that the counter starts at 0 instead of 1. In that case, if we wish the **for** loop to still repeat 5 times the counter should reach 4 and not 5:

```
// this counter starts at 0 and goes up to 4 so the loop still repeats 5 times
for(int i = 0; i <= 4; i++)
{
  System.out.println("*****");
}
```

Another way to ensure that the counter does not reach a value greater than 4 is to insist that the counter stays below 5. In this case we need to use the "less than" operator (<) instead of the "less than or equal to" operator(<=):

```
// this loop still repeats 5 times
for(int i = 0; i < 5; i++)
{
  System.out.println("*****");
}
```

We can also change the way we modify the counter after each iteration. Returning to the original **for** loop, we would increment the counter by 2 each time instead of 1. If we still wish the loop to repeat 5 times we now need the counter to go up to 10:

```
// this loop still repeats 5 times
for(int i = 1; i <= 10; i = i+2) // the counter moves up in steps of 2
{
  System.out.println("*****");
}
```

Finally, counters can move down as well as up. As an example, look at program 4.3, which prints out a countdown of the numbers from 10 down to 1.

PROGRAM 4.3

```
public class Countdown
{
  public static void main(String[] args)
  {
    System.out.println("*** Numbers from 10 to 1 ***");
    System.out.println();
    for (int i=10; i >= 1; i--) // counter moving down from 10 to 1
    {
      System.out.println(i);
    }
  }
}
```

Here the counter starts at 10 and is reduced by 1 each time. The loop stops when the counter falls below the value of 1. Note the use of the loop counter *inside* the loop:

```
System.out.println(i); // value of counter 'i' used here
```

This is perfectly acceptable as the loop counter is just another variable. However, when you do this, be careful not to inadvertently *change* the loop counter within the loop body as this can throw the test of your **for** loop off track! Running program 4.3 gives us the following result:

```
*** Numbers from 10 to 1 ***
10
9
8
7
6
5
4
3
2
1
```

4.2.2 The body of the loop

The body of the loop can contain any number and type of instructions, including variable declarations, **if** statements, **switch** statements, or even another loop! For example program 4.4 modifies the countdown of program 4.3 by including an **if** statement inside the **for** loop so that only the *even* numbers from 10 to 1 are displayed:

PROGRAM 4.4

```java
public class DisplayEven
{
  public static void main(String[] args)
  {
    System.out.println("*** Even numbers from 10 to 1 ***");
    System.out.println();
    for(int i=10; i >= 1; i--) // loop through the numbers 10 down to 1
    {
      // body of the loop contains in 'if' statement
      if (i%2 == 0) // check if number is even
      {
        System.out.println(i); // number displayed only when it is checked to be even
      }
    }
  }
}
```

You can see that the body of the **for** loop contains within it an **if** statement. The test of the **if** statement checks the current value of the loop counter i to see if it is an even number:

```
for(int i=10; i >= 1; i--)
{
  if (i%2 == 0) // use the modulus operator to check the value of the loop counter
  {
    System.out.println(i);
  }
}
```

An even number is a number that leaves no remainder when divided by 2, so we use the modulus operator (%) to check this. Now the loop counter is displayed only if it is an even number. Running program 4.4 gives us the obvious results:

```
*** Even numbers from 10 to 1 ***
10
8
6
4
2
```

In this example we included an **if** statement inside the **for** loop. It is also possible to have one **for** loop inside another. When we have one loop inside another we refer to these loops as **nested** loops. As an example of this consider program 4.5, which displays a square of stars as before, but this time uses a pair of nested loops to achieve this:

PROGRAM 4.5

```
public class DisplayStars3
{
  public static void main (String[] args)
  {
    for(int i = 1; i <= 5; i++) // outer loop as before
    {
      for (int j = 1; j <= 5; j++) // inner loop to display one row of stars
      {
        System.out.print("*");
      } // inner loop ends here
      System.out.println(); // necessary to start next row on a new line
    } // outer loop ends here
  }
}
```

You can see that the outer **for** loop is the same as the one used in program 4.2. Whereas in the original program we had a single instruction to display a single row of stars inside our loop:

```
System.out.println("*****"); // original instruction inside the 'for' loop
```

In program 4.6 we have replaced this instruction with *another* **for** loop, followed by a blank `println` instruction:

```
// new instructions inside the original 'for' loop to print a single row of stars
for (int j = 1; j <= 5; j++) // new name for this loop counter
{
    System.out.print("*");
}
System.out.println();
```

Notice that when we place one loop inside another, we need a fresh name for the loop counter in the nested loop. In this case we have called the counter j. These instructions together allow us to display a single row of five stars and move to a new line, ready to print the next row.

Let's look at how the control in this program flows. First the outer loop counter is set to 1:

```
for(int i = 1; i <= 5; i++) // outer loop counter initialized
{
  for (int j = 1; j <= 5; j++)
  {
    System.out.print("*");
  }
  System.out.println();
}
```

The test of the outer loop is then checked:

```
for(int i = 1; i <= 5; i++) // outer loop counter tested
{
  for (int j = 1; j <= 5; j++)
  {
    System.out.print("*");
  }
  System.out.println();
}
```

This test is found to be **true** so the body of the outer loop is executed. First the inner loop repeats five times:

```
for(int i = 1; i <= 5; i++)
{
  for (int j = 1; j <= 5; j++) // this loop repeats 5 times
  {
    System.out.print("*");
  }
  System.out.println();
}
```

The inner loop prints five stars on the screen as follows:

```
*****
```

After the inner loop stops, there is one more instruction to complete: the command to move the cursor to a new line:

```
for(int i = 1; i <= 5; i++)
{
  for (int j = 1; j <= 5; j++)
  {
    System.out.print("*");
  }
  System.out.println(); // last instruction of outer loop
}
```

This completes one cycle of the outer loop, so the program returns to the beginning of this loop and increments its counter:

```
for(int i = 1; i <= 5; i++) // counter moves to 2
{
  for (int j = 1; j <= 5; j++)
  {
    System.out.print("*");
  }
  System.out.println();
}
```

The test of the outer loop is then checked and found to be **true** and the whole process repeats, printing out a square of five stars as before.

Program 4.5 displayed a five by five square of stars. Now take a look at program 4.6 and see if you can work out what it does. Look particularly at the header of the inner loop:

PROGRAM 4.6

```
public class DisplayShape
{
  public static void main (String[] args)
  {
    for(int i = 1; i <= 5; i++) // outer loop controlling the number of rows
    {
      for (int j = 1; j <= i; j++) // inner loop controlling the number of stars in one row
```

```
  {
    System.out.print("*");
  }
    System.out.println();
  }
 }
}
```

You can see this is very similar to program 4.5 except that in program 4.5 the inner loop displayed 5 stars each time. In this case the number of stars is not fixed to a number, but to the value of the outer loop counter i:

```
for(int i = 1; i <= 5; i++) // outer loops controls the number of rows
{
  // inner loop determines how many stars in each row
  for (int j = 1; j <= i; j++) // inner loop displays 'i' number of stars
  {
    System.out.print("*");
  }
  System.out.println();
}
```

The first time around this loop the inner loop will display only one star in the row as the i counter starts at 1. The second time around this loop it will display two stars as the i counter is incremented, then three stars. Eventually it will display five stars the last time around the loop when the outer i counter reaches 5. Effectively this means that program 4.6 will display a *triangle* of stars as follows:

```
*
*  *
*  *  *
*  *  *  *
*  *  *  *  *
```

4.2.3 Revisiting the loop counter

Before we move on to look at other kinds of loops in Java it is important to understand that, although a **for** loop is used to repeat something a fixed number of times, you don't necessarily need to know this fixed number when you are writing the program. This fixed number could be a value given to you by the user of your program, for example. This number could then be used to test against your loop counter. Program 4.7 modifies program 4.5 by asking the user to determine the size of the square of stars.

PROGRAM 4.7

```
import java.util.*;
public class DisplayStars4
{
  public static void main(String[] args)
  {
    int num; // to hold user response
    Scanner keyboard = new Scanner(System.in);
    // prompt and get user response
    System.out.println("Size of square?");
    num = keyboard.nextInt();
    // display square
    for(int i = 1; i <= num; i++) // number of rows fixed to 'num'
    {
      for (int j = 1; j <= num; j++) // number of stars in a row fixed to 'num'
      {
        System.out.print("*");
      }
      System.out.println();
    }
  }
}
```

In this program you cannot tell from the code exactly how many times the loops will iterate, but you can say that they will iterate *num* number of times – whatever the user may have entered for *num*. So in this sense the loop is still fixed. Here is a sample run of program 4.7:

```
Size of square?
7
* * * * * * *
* * * * * * *
* * * * * * *
* * * * * * *
* * * * * * *
* * * * * * *
* * * * * * *
```

Here is another sample run of program 4.7:

```
Size of square?
3
* * *
* * *
* * *
```

4.3 The 'while' loop

Much of the power of computers comes from the ability to ask them to carry out repetitive tasks, so iteration is a very important form of program control. The **for** loop is an often-used construct to implement fixed repetitions.

Sometimes, however, a repetition is required that is *not fixed* and a **for** loop is not the best one to use in such a case. Consider the following scenarios, for example:

- a racing game that repeatedly moves a car around a track until the car crashes;
- a ticket issuing program that repeatedly offers tickets for sale until the user chooses to quit the program;
- a password checking program that does not let a user into an application until he or she enters the right password.

Each of the above cases involves repetition; however, the number of repetitions is not fixed but depends upon some condition. The **while** loop offers one type of non-fixed iteration. The syntax for constructing this loop in Java is as follows:

```
while ( /* test goes here */ )
{
  // instruction(s) to be repeated go here
}
```

As you can see, this loop is much simpler to construct than a **for** loop. As this loop is not repeating a fixed number of times, there is no need to create a counter to keep track of the number of repetitions.

When might this kind of loop be useful? The first example we will explore is the use of the **while** loop to check data that is input by the user. Checking input data for errors is referred to as **input validation**.

For example, look back at program 3.4 in the last chapter, which asked the user to enter an exam mark:

```
System.out.println("What exam mark did you get?");
mark = keyboard.nextInt();
if (mark >= 40)
// rest of code goes here
```

The mark that is entered should never be greater than 100 or less than 0. At the time we assumed that the user would enter the mark correctly. However, good programmers never make this assumption!

Before accepting the mark that is entered and moving on to the next stage of the program, it is good practice to check that the mark entered is indeed a valid one. If it is not, then the user will be allowed to enter the mark again. This will go on until the user enters a valid mark.

We can express this using pseudocode as follows:

```
PROMPT for mark
ENTER mark
KEEP REPEATING WHILE mark < 0 OR mark > 100
BEGIN
  DISPLAY error message to user
  ENTER mark
END
// REST OF PROGRAM HERE
```

The design makes clear that an error message is to be displayed every time the user enters an invalid mark. The user may enter an invalid mark many times so an iteration is required here.

However, the number of iterations is not fixed as it is impossible to say how many, if any, mistakes the user will make.

This sounds like a job for the **while** loop:

```
System.out.println("What exam mark did you get?");
mark = keyboard.nextInt();
while (mark < 0 || mark > 100) // check for invalid input
{
  // display error message and allow for re-input
  System.out.println("Invalid mark: Re-enter!");
  mark = keyboard.nextInt();
}
if (mark >= 40)
// rest of code goes here
```

Program 4.8 below shows the whole of the program 3.4 rewritten to include the input validation. Notice how this works – we ask the user for the mark; if it is within the acceptable range, the **while** loop is not entered and we move past it to the other instructions. But if the mark entered is less than zero or greater than 100 we enter the loop, display an error message and ask the user to input the mark again. This continues until the mark is within the required range.

PROGRAM 4.8

```
import java.util.*;
public class DisplayResult2
{
  public static void main(String[] args)
  {
    int mark;
    Scanner keyboard = new Scanner (System.in);
    System.out.println("What exam mark did you get?");
    mark = keyboard.nextInt();
```

```
    // input validation
    while (mark < 0 || mark > 100) // check if mark is invalid
    {
        // display error message
        System.out.println("Invalid mark: please re-enter");
        // mark must be re-entered
        mark = keyboard.nextInt();
    }
    // by this point loop is finished and mark will be valid
    if (mark >= 40)
    {
        System.out.println("Congratulations, you passed");
    }
    else
    {
        System.out.println("I'm sorry, but you failed");
    }
    System.out.println("Good luck with your other exams");
  }
}
```

Here is a sample program run:

```
What exam mark did you get?
101
Invalid mark: please re-enter
-10
Invalid mark: please re-enter
10
I'm sorry, but you failed
Good luck with your other exams
```

4.4 The 'do…while' loop

There is one more loop construct in Java that we need to tell you about: the **do…while** loop.

The **do…while** loop is another variable loop construct, but, unlike the **while** loop, the **do…while** loop has its test at the *end* of the loop rather than at the *beginning*.

The syntax of a **do…while** loop is given below:

```
do
{
    // instruction(s) to be repeated go here
} while ( /* test goes here */ ); // note the semi-colon at the end
```

You are probably wondering what difference it makes if the test is at the end or the beginning of the loop. Well, there is one subtle difference. If the test is at the end of the loop, the loop will iterate *at least once*. If the test is at the beginning of the loop, however, there is a possibility that the condition will be **false** to begin with, and the loop is never executed. A **while** loop therefore executes *zero or more times* whereas a **do...while** loop executes *one or more times*.

To make this a little clearer, look back at the **while** loop we just showed you for validating exam marks. If the user entered a valid mark initially (such as 66), the test to trap an invalid mark (mark < 0 || mark > 100) would be **false** and the loop would be skipped altogether. A **do...while** loop would not be appropriate here as the possibility of never getting into the loop should be left open.

When would a **do...while** loop be suitable? Well, any time you wish to code a non-fixed loop that must execute at least once. Usually, this would be the case when the test can take place only *after* the loop has been entered.

To illustrate this, think about all the programs you have written so far. Once the program has done its job it terminates – if you want it to perform the same task again you have to go through the whole procedure of running the program again.

In many cases a better solution would be to put your whole program in a loop that keeps repeating until the user chooses to quit your program. This would involve asking the user each time if he or she would like to continue repeating the program, or to stop.

A **for** loop would not be the best loop to choose here as this is more useful when the number of repetitions can be predicted. A **while** loop would be difficult to use, as the test that checks the user's response to the question cannot be carried out at the beginning of the loop. The answer is to move the test to the end of the loop and use a **do...while** loop as follows:

```
char response; // variable to hold user response
do // place code in loop
{
  // program instructions go here
  System.out.println("another go (y/n)?");
  response = keyboard.next().charAt(0); // get user reply
} while (response == 'y' || response == 'Y'); // test must be at the end of the loop
```

Notice the test of the **do...while** loop allows the user to enter either a lower case or an upper case 'Y' to continue running the program:

```
while (response == 'y' || response == 'Y');
```

As an example of this application of the **do...while** loop, program 4.9 below amends program 2.3, which calculated the cost of a product, by allowing the user to repeat the program as often as he or she chooses.

PROGRAM 4.9

```java
import java.util.*;
public class FindCost4
{
  public static void main(String[] args )
  {
    double price, tax;
    char reply;
    Scanner keyboard = new Scanner(System.in);
    do
    {
      // these instructions as before
      System.out.println("*** Product Price Check ***");
      System.out.print("Enter initial price: ");
      price = keyboard.nextDouble();
      System.out.print("Enter tax rate: ");
      tax = keyboard.nextDouble();
      price = price * (1 + tax/100);
      System.out.println("Cost after tax = " + price);
      // now see if user wants another go
      System.out.println();
      System.out.print("Would you like to enter another product(y/n)?: ");
      reply = keyboard.next().charAt(0);
      System.out.println();
    } while (reply == 'y' || reply == 'Y');
  }
}
```

Here is sample program run:

```
*** Product Price Check ***
Enter initial price: 50
Enter tax rate: 10
Cost after tax = 55.0

Would you like to enter another product (y/n)?: y

*** Product Price Check ***
Enter initial price: 70
Enter tax rate: 5
Cost after tax = 73.5

Would you like to enter another product (y/n)?: y

*** Product Price Check ***
Enter initial price: 200
```

```
Enter tax rate: 15
Cost after tax = 230.0

Would you like to enter another product (y/n)?: n
```

Another way to allow a program to be run repeatedly using a **do...while** loop is to include a *menu* of options within the loop (this was very common in the days before windows and mice). The options themselves are processed by a **switch** statement. One of the options in the menu list would be the option to quit and this option is checked in the **while** condition of the loop. Program 4.10 is a reworking of program 3.5 of the previous chapter using this technique.

PROGRAM 4.10

```java
import java.util.*;
public class TimetableWithLoop
{
  public static void main(String[] args)
  {
    char group, response;
    Scanner keyboard = new Scanner(System.in);
    System.out.println("***Lab Times***");
    do // put code in loop
    {
      // offer menu of options
      System.out.println(); // create a blank line
      System.out.println("[1] TIME FOR GROUP A");
      System.out.println("[2] TIME FOR GROUP B");
      System.out.println("[3] TIME FOR GROUP C");
      System.out.println("[4] QUIT PROGRAM");
      System.out.print("enter choice [1,2,3,4]: ");
      response = keyboard.next().charAt(0); // get response
      System.out.println(); // create a blank line
      switch(response) // process response
      {
        case '1': System.out.println("10.00 a.m ");
                  break;
        case '2': System.out.println("1.00 p.m ");
                  break;
        case '3': System.out.println("11.00 a.m ");
                  break;
        case '4': System.out.println("Goodbye ");
                  break;
```

```
        default: System.out.println("Options 1-4 only!");
    }
  } while (response != '4'); // test for Quit option
  }
}
```

Notice that the menu option is treated as a character here, rather than an integer. So option 1 would be interpreted as the character '1' rather than the number 1, for example. The advantage of treating the menu option as a character rather than a number is that an incorrect menu entry would not result in a program crash if the value entered was non-numeric. Here is a sample run of this program:

```
***Lab Times***

[1] TIME FOR GROUP A
[2] TIME FOR GROUP B
[3] TIME FOR GROUP C
[4] QUIT PROGRAM
enter choice [1,2,3,4]: 2

1.00 p.m

[1] TIME FOR GROUP A
[2] TIME FOR GROUP B
[3] TIME FOR GROUP C
[4] QUIT PROGRAM
enter choice [1,2,3,4]: 5

Options 1-4 only!

[1] TIME FOR GROUP A
[2] TIME FOR GROUP B
[3] TIME FOR GROUP C
[4] QUIT PROGRAM
enter choice [1,2,3,4]: 1

10.00 a.m

[1] TIME FOR GROUP A
[2] TIME FOR GROUP B
[3] TIME FOR GROUP C
[4] QUIT PROGRAM
enter choice [1,2,3,4]: 3

11.00 a.m
```

```
[1]  TIME FOR GROUP A
[2]  TIME FOR GROUP B
[3]  TIME FOR GROUP C
[4]  QUIT PROGRAM enter choice [1,2,3,4]: 4

Goodbye
```

4.5 Picking the right loop

With three types of loop to choose from in Java, it can sometimes be difficult to decide upon the best one to use in each case, especially as it is technically possible to pick *any type of loop* to implement *any type of repetition*! For example, **while** and **do...while** loops *can* be used for fixed repetitions by introducing your own counter and checking this counter in the test of the loop. However, it is always best to pick the most appropriate loop construct to use in each case, as this will simplify the logic of your code. Here are some general guidelines that should help you:

- if the number of repetitions required can be determined prior to entering the loop – use a **for** loop;
- if the number of repetitions required cannot be determined prior to entering the loop, and you wish to allow for the possibility of zero repetitions – use a **while** loop;
- if the number of repetitions required cannot be determined before the loop, and you require at least one repetition of the loop – use a **do...while** loop.

4.6 The 'break' statement

In the previous chapter we met the **break** statement when looking at **switch** statements. Here for example is a **switch** statement from the previous chapter that processed a student's timetable:

```
switch(group)
{
  case 'A': System.out.print("10.00 a.m ");
            break; // terminates switch
  case 'B': System.out.print("1.00 p.m ");
            break; // terminates switch
  case 'C': System.out.print("11.00 a.m ");
            break; // terminates switch
  default: System.out.print("No such group");
}
```

Here the **break** statement allowed the **switch** to terminate without processing the remaining **cases**. The **break** statement can also be used with Java's loops to terminate a loop before it reaches its natural end. For example, consider a program that allows the user a maximum of three attempts to guess a secret number. This is an example of a non-fixed iteration but the iteration does have a fixed upper limit of three.

We could use any of the loop types to implement this. If we wished to use a **for** loop, however, we would need to make use of the **break statement**. Take a look at program 4.11, which does this for a secret number of 27:

PROGRAM 4.11

```java
import java.util.*;

// This program demonstrates the use of the 'break' statement inside a 'for' loop

public class SecretNumber
{
  public static void main(String[] args)
  {
    Scanner keyboard = new Scanner (System.in);
    final int SECRET = 27; // secret number
    int num; // to hold user's guess
    boolean guessed = false; // so far number not guessed

    System.out.println("You have 3 goes to guess the secret number");
    System.out.println("HINT: It is a number less than 50!");
    System.out.println();

    // look carefully at this loop
    for (int i= 1; i <= 3; i++) // loop repeats 3 times
    {
      System.out.print("Enter guess: ");
      num = keyboard.nextInt();
      // check guess
      if (num == SECRET) // check if number guessed correctly
      {
          guessed = true; // record number has been guessed correctly
          break; // exit loop
      }
    }
    // now check to see if the number was guessed correctly or not
    if (guessed)
    {
      System.out.println("Number guessed correctly");
    }
    else
```

```
  {
    System.out.println("Number NOT guessed");
  }
 }
}
```

The important part of this program is the **for** loop. You can see that it has been written to repeat three times:

```
for (int i= 1; i <= 3; i++) // loop repeats 3 times
{
  System.out.print("Enter guess: ");
  num = keyboard.nextInt();
  // code here to check the guess
}
```

Each time around the loop the user gets to have a guess at the secret number. We need to do two things if we determine that the guess is correct. Firstly, set a **boolean** variable to **true** to indicate a correct guess. Then, secondly, we need to terminate the loop, even if this is before we reach the third iteration. We do so by using a **break** statement if the guess is correct:

```
for (int i= 1; i <= 3; i++)
{
  System.out.print("Enter guess: ");
  num = keyboard.nextInt();
  if (num == SECRET) // check if number guessed correctly
  {
    guessed = true; // record number has been guessed correctly
    break; // exit loop even if it has not yet finished three repetitions
  }
}
```

Here is a sample program run of program 4.11:

```
You have 3 goes to guess the secret number
HINT: It is a number less than 50!
Enter guess: 49
Enter guess: 27
Number guessed correctly
```

Here the user guessed the number after two attempts and the loop terminated early due to the **break** statement. Here is another program run where the user fails to guess the secret number:

```
You have 3 goes to guess the secret number
HINT: It is a number less than 50!

Enter guess: 33
Enter guess: 22
Enter guess: 11
Number NOT guessed
```

Here the **break** statement is never reached so the loop iterates three times without terminating early.

4.7 The 'continue' statement

Whereas the **break** statement forces a loop to terminate, a **continue** statement forces a loop to skip the remaining instructions in the body of the loop and to *continue* to the next iteration. As an example of this here is a reminder of a program that displayed the even numbers from 10 down to 1:

PROGRAM 4.4 – a reminder

```
public class DisplayEven
{
  public static void main(String[] args)
  {
    System.out.println("*** Even numbers from 10 to 1 ***");
    System.out.println();
    for(int i=10; i>=1; i--)
    {
      if (i%2 == 0) // check if number is even
      {
        System.out.println(i); // number displayed only when it is checked to be even
      }
    }
  }
}
```

Here the body of the loop displayed the loop counter if it was an even number. An alternative approach would have been to skip a number if it was odd and move on to the next iteration of the loop. If the number is not skipped then it must be even, so can be displayed. This is what we have done in program 4.12 below:

PROGRAM 4.12

```
public class DisplayEven2
{
  public static void main(String[] args)
  {
    System.out.println("*** Even numbers from 10 to 1 ***");
    System.out.println();
    for(int i=10; i>=1; i--)
    {
      if (i%2 != 0) // check if number is NOT even
      {
        continue; // skips the rest of this iteration and moves to the next iteration
      }
      // even number only displayed if we have not skipped this iteration
      System.out.println(i);
    }
  }
}
```

The **if** statement checks to see if the number is odd (not even). If this is the case the rest of the instructions in the loop can be skipped with a **continue** statement, so the loop moves to the next iteration:

```
if (i%2 != 0) // check if number is NOT even
{
  continue; // skips the rest of the loop body and moves to the next iteration
}
System.out.println(i); // this line only executed if this iteration is not skipped
```

The last `println` instruction is only executed if the number is even and the iteration has not been skipped. Of course, the result of running this program will be the same as the result of running the original program 4.4.

Self-test questions

1 Consider the following program:

```
public class IterationQ1
{
  public static void main(String[] args)
  {
    for(int i= 1; i<= 4; i++)
    {
      System.out.println("YES");
    }
    System.out.println("OK");
  }
}
```

   a How many times does this **for** loop repeat?

   b What would be the output of this program?

2 Consider the following program:

```
public class IterationQ2
{
  public static void main(String[] args)
  {
    for(int i= 1; i< 4; i++)
    {
      System.out.println("YES");
      System.out.println("NO");
    }
    System.out.println("OK");
  }
}
```

   a How many times does this **for** loop repeat?

   b What would be the output of this program?

3 Consider the following program:

```
import java.util.*;
public class IterationQ3
{
  public static void main(String[] args)
```

```
  {
    int num;
    Scanner keyboard = new Scanner(System.in);

    System.out.print("Enter a number: ");
    num = keyboard.nextInt();

    for(int i= 1; i< num; i++)
    {
      System.out.println("YES");
      System.out.println("NO");
    }
    System.out.println("OK");
  }
}
```

a What would be the output of this program if the user entered 5 when prompted?

b What would be the output of this program if the user entered 0 when prompted?

4 Consider the following program

```
public class IterationQ4
{
  public static void main(String[] args)
  {
    for(int i=1; i<=15; i= i +2)
    {
      System.out.println(i);
    }
  }
}
```

a How many times does this **for** loop repeat?

b What would be the output of this program?

c What would be the consequence of changing the test of the loop to (i >= 15)?

5 Consider the following program:

```
public class IterationQ5
{
  public static void main(String[] args)
  {
    for(int i=5; i>=2; i--)
```

```
      {
        switch (i)
        {
          case 1: case 3: System.out.println("YES"); break;
          case 2: case 4: case 5: System.out.println("NO");
        }
      }
      System.out.println("OK");
    }
}
```

a How many times does this **for** loop repeat?

b What would be the output of this program?

c What would be the consequence of changing the loop counter to (i++) instead of (i--)?

6 What would be the output from the following program?

```
public class IterationQ6
{
  public static void main(String[] args)
  {
    for(int i=1; i <= 3; i++)
    {
      for(int j=1; j <= 7; j++)
      {
        System.out.print("*");
      }
      System.out.println();
    }
  }
}
```

7 Examine the program below, which aims to allow a user to guess the square of a number that is entered. Part of the code has been replaced by a comment:

```
import java.util.*;

public class IterationQ7
{
  public static void main(String[] args)
```

```
{
    int num, square;
    Scanner keyboard = new Scanner(System.in);
    System.out.print("Enter a number ");
    num = keyboard.nextInt();
    System.out.print("Enter the square of this number ");
    square = keyboard.nextInt();
    // loop to check answer
    while (/* test to be completed */)
    {
        System.out.println("Wrong answer, try again");
        square = keyboard.nextInt();
    }
    System.out.println("Well done, right answer");
}
}
```

a Why is a **while** loop preferable to a **for** loop or a **do...while** loop here?

b Replace the comment with an appropriate test for this loop.

8 What would be the output of the following program?

```
public class IterationQ8
{
  public static void main(String[] args)
  {
    for(int i=1; i<=10; i++)
    {
      if (i > 5)
      {
        break;
      }
      System.out.println(i);
    }
  }
}
```

9 What would be the output of the following program?

```
public class IterationQ9
{
 public static void main(String[] args)
 {
   for(int i=1; i<=10; i++)
   {
     if (i <= 5)
     {
       continue;
     }
     System.out.println(i);
   }
 }
}
```

Programming exercises

1 Implement the programs from the self-test questions above in order to verify your answers to those questions.

2 a Modify program 4.4 so that the program displays the even numbers from 1 to 20 instead of from 10 down to 1.

  b Modify the program further so that the user enters a number and the program displays all the even numbers from 1 up to the number entered by the user.

  c Modify the program again so that it identifies which of these numbers are odd and which are even. For example, if the user entered 5 the program should display something like the following:

```
1 is odd
2 is even
3 is odd
4 is even
5 is odd
```

3 Write a program that makes use of nested **for** loops to display the following shapes:

```
a * * * * * *
  * * * * * *
  * * * * * *
```

b
```
*  *  *
*  *  *
*  *  *  *  *  *  *  *  *
*  *  *  *  *  *  *  *  *
*  *  *
*  *  *
```
Hint: make use of an **if...else** *statement inside your* **for** *loops.*

c
```
*  *  *  *
*  *  *
*  *
*
```

4 a Using a **for** loop, write a program that displays a "6 times" multiplication table; the output should look like this:
```
 1 × 6 = 6
 2 × 6 = 12
 3 × 6 = 18
 4 × 6 = 24
 5 × 6 = 30
 6 × 6 = 36
 7 × 6 = 42
 8 × 6 = 48
 9 × 6 = 54
10 × 6 = 60
11 × 6 = 66
12 × 6 = 72
```

b Adapt the program so that instead of a "6 times" table, the user chooses which table is displayed.

5 Implement program 4.7 which allows the user to determine the size of a square of stars and then

a adapt it so that the user is allowed to enter a size only between 2 and 20;

b adapt the program further so that the user can choose whether or not to have another go.

6 Consider a vending machine that offers the following options:

```
[1] Get gum
[2] Get chocolate
[3] Get popcorn
[4] Get juice
[5] Display total sold so far
[6] Quit
```

Design and implement a program that continuously allows users to select from these options. When options 1–4 are selected an appropriate message is to be displayed acknowledging their choice. For example, when option 3 is selected the following message could be displayed:

```
Here is your popcorn
```

When option 5 is selected, the number of each type of item sold is displayed. For example:

```
3 items of gum sold
2 items of chocolate sold
6 items of popcorn sold
9 items of juice sold
```

When option 6 is chosen the program terminates. If an option other than 1–6 is entered an appropriate error message should be displayed, such as:

```
Error, options 1-6 only!
```

CHAPTER 05

Methods

❖ OBJECTIVES

By the end of this chapter you should be able to:

- ❖ explain the meaning of the term **method**;
- ❖ declare and define methods;
- ❖ **call** a method;
- ❖ explain the meaning of the terms **actual parameters** and **formal parameters**;
- ❖ devise simple **algorithms** with the help of pseudocode;
- ❖ identify the **scope** of a particular variable;
- ❖ explain the meaning of the term **polymorphism;**
- ❖ declare and use **overloaded** methods.

5.1 Introduction

As early as chapter 1 we were using the term **method**. There you found out that a method is a part of a class, and contains a particular set of instructions. So far, all the classes you have written have contained just one method, the `main` method. In this chapter you will see how a class can contain not just a `main` method, but many other methods as well.

Normally a method will perform a single well-defined task. Examples of the many sorts of task that a method could perform are calculating the area of a circle, displaying a particular message on the screen, converting a temperature from Fahrenheit to Celsius, and many, many more. In this chapter you will see how we can collect the instructions for performing these sorts of tasks together in a method.

You will also see how, once we have written a method, we can get it to perform its task within a program. When we do this we say that we are **calling** the method. When we call a method, what we are actually doing is telling the program to jump to a new place (where the method instructions are stored), carry out the set of instructions that it finds there, and, when it has finished (that is, when the method has terminated), return and carry on where it left off.

So in this chapter you will learn how to write a method within a program, how to call a method from another part of the program and how to send information into a method and get information back.

5.2 Declaring and defining methods

Let's illustrate the idea of a method by thinking about a simple little program. The program prompts the user to enter his or her year of birth, month of birth and day of birth; each time the prompt is displayed, it is followed by a message, consisting of a couple of lines, explaining that the information entered is confidential. This is shown below in program 5.1 – the program would obviously then go on to do other things with the information that has been entered, but we are not interested in that, so we have just replaced all the rest of the program with a comment.

PROGRAM 5.1

```java
import java.util.*;

public class DataEntry
{
  public static void main(String[] args)
  {
    Scanner keyboard = new Scanner(System.in);

    int year, month, day;

    // prompt for year of birth
    System.out.println("Please enter the year of your birth");

    // display confidentiality message
    System.out.println("Please note that all information supplied is confidential");
    System.out.println("No personal details will be shared with any third party");

    // get year from user
    year = keyboard.nextInt();

    // prompt for month of birth
    System.out.println("Please enter the month of your birth as a number from 1 to 12");

    // display confidentiality message
    System.out.println("Please note that all information supplied is confidential");
    System.out.println("No personal details will be shared with any third party");

    // get month from user
    month = keyboard.nextInt();

    // prompt for day of birth
    System.out.println("Please enter the day of your birth as a number from 1 to 31");
```

```
    // display confidentiality message
    System.out.println("Please note that all information supplied is confidential");
    System.out.println("No personal details will be shared with any third party");

    // get day from user
    day = keyboard.nextInt();

    // more code here
  }
}
```

You can see from the above program that we have had to type out the two lines that display the confidentiality message three times. It would be far less time-consuming if we could do this just once, then send the program off to wherever these instructions are stored, and then come back and carry on with what it was doing. You will probably have realized by now that we can indeed do this – by writing a *method*. The job of this particular method will be simply to display the confidentiality message on the screen – we need to give our method a name so that we can refer to it when required, so let's call it displayMessage. Here is how it is going to look:

```
static void displayMessage()
{
  System.out.println("Please note that all information supplied is confidential");
  System.out.println("No personal details will be shared with any third party");
}
```

The body of this method, which is contained between the two curly brackets, contains the instructions that we want this method to perform, namely to display two lines of text on the screen. The first line, which declares the method, is called the method header, and consists of three words – let's look into each of these a bit more closely:

static

You have seen this word in front of the main method many times now. However, we won't be explaining its meaning to you properly until chapter 8. For now, all you need to know is that methods that have been declared as **static** (such as main) can only call other methods in the class if they too are **static**. So, if we did not declare displayMessage as **static** and tried to call it from the main method then our program would not compile.

void

In the next section you will see that it is possible for a method to *send back* or *return* some information once it terminates. This particular method simply displays a message on the screen, so we don't require it to send back any information when it terminates. The word **void** indicates that the method does not return any information.

`displayMessage()`
This is the name that we have chosen to give our method. You can see that the name is followed by a pair of empty brackets. Very soon you will learn that it is possible to send some information *into* a method – for example, some values that the method needs in order to perform a calculation. When we need to do that we list, in these brackets, the types of data that we are going to send in; here, however, as the method is doing nothing more that displaying a message on the screen we do not have to send in any data, and the brackets are left empty.

5.3 Calling a method

Now that we have declared and defined our method, we can make use of it. The idea is that we get the method to perform its instructions as and when we need it to do so – you have seen that this process is referred to as *calling* the method. To call a method in Java, we simply use its name, along with the following brackets, which in this case are empty. So in this case our method call, which will be placed at the point in the program where we need it, looks like this:

```
displayMessage();
```

Now we can rewrite program 5.1, replacing the appropriate lines of code with the simple method call. The whole program is shown below in program 5.2:

PROGRAM 5.2

```
import java.util.*;

public class DataEntry2
{
    public static void main(String[] args)
    {
      Scanner keyboard = new Scanner(System.in);

      int year, month, day;

      System.out.println("Please enter the year of your birth");
      displayMessage(); // call displayMessage method
      year = keyboard.nextInt();

      System.out.println("Please enter the month of your birth as a number from 1 to 12");
      displayMessage(); // call displayMessage method
      month = keyboard.nextInt();

      System.out.println("Please enter the day of your birth as a number from 1 to 31");
```

```
    displayMessage(); // call displayMessage method
    day = keyboard.nextInt();

    // more code here
}


// the code for displayMessage method
static void displayMessage()
{
  System.out.println("Please note that all information supplied is confidential");
  System.out.println("No personal details will be shared with any third party");
}
}
```

You can see that the method itself is defined separately after the `main` method – although it could have come before it, since the order in which methods are presented doesn't matter to the compiler. When the program is run, however, it always starts with `main`. The overall result is of course that program 5.2 runs exactly the same as program 5.1.

We should emphasize again here that when one method calls another method, the first method effectively pauses at that point, and the program then carries out the instructions in the called method; when it has finished doing this, it returns to the original method, which then resumes. In most of the programs in this chapter it will be the `main` method that calls the other method. This doesn't have to be the case, however, and it is perfectly possible for any method to call another method – indeed, the called method could in turn call yet another method. This would result in a number of methods being "chained". When each method terminates, the control of the program would return to the method that called it.

You can see an example of a method being called by a method other than `main` in section 5.6.

5.4 Method input and output

We have already told you that it is possible to send some data into a method, and that a method can send data back to the method that called it. Now we will look into this in more detail.

In order to do this we will use as an example a program that we wrote in chapter 2 – program 2.3. Here is a reminder of that program:

A REMINDER OF PROGRAM 2.3

```
import java.util.*;

/* a program to input the initial price of a product and then calculate and display its cost
   after tax has been added */

public class FindCost3
```

```
{
  public static void main(String[] args)
  {
    Scanner keyboard = new Scanner(System.in);
    double price, tax;
    System.out.println("*** Product Price Check ***");
    System.out.print("Enter initial price: ");
    price = keyboard.nextDouble();
    System.out.print("Enter tax rate: ");
    tax = keyboard.nextDouble();
    price = price * (1 + tax/100);
    System.out.println("Cost after tax = " + price);
  }
}
```

The line that calculates the new price, with the sales tax added, is this one:

```
price = price * (1 + tax/100);
```

Let's create a method that performs this calculation – in a real application this would be very useful, because we might need to call this method at various points within the program, and, as you will see, each time we do so we could get it to carry out the calculation for different values of the price and the tax. We will need a way to send in these values to the method. But on top of that, we need to arrange for the method to tell us the result of adding the new tax – if it didn't do that, it wouldn't be much use!

The method is going to look like this:

```
static double addTax(double priceIn, double taxIn)
{
  return priceIn * (1 + taxIn/100);
}
```

First, take a careful look at the header. You are familiar with the first word, **static**, but look at the next one; this time, where we previously saw the word **void**, we now have the word **double**. As we have said, this method must send back – or **return** – a result, the new price of the item. So the type of data that the method is to return in this case is a **double**. In fact what we are doing here is declaring a method of *type* **double**. Thus, the *type* of a method refers to its *return* type. It is possible to declare methods of any type – **int**, **boolean**, **char** and so on.

After the type declaration, we have the name of the method, in this case addTax – and this time the brackets aren't empty. You can see that within these brackets we are declaring two variables, both of type **double**. The variables declared in this way are known as the **formal parameters** of the method. Formal parameters are variables that are created exclusively to hold values sent in from the calling method. They are going to hold, respectively, the values of the price and the tax that are going to be sent in from the calling method (you will see how this is done in a moment). Of course, these variables could be given any name we choose, but we have called them `priceIn` and `taxIn` respectively. We will use this convention of adding the suffix `In` to variable names in the formal parameter list throughout this book.

Now we can turn our attention to the body of the method, which as you can see, in this case, consists of a single line:

```
return priceIn * (1 + taxIn/100);
```

The word **return** in a method serves two very important functions. First it ends the method – as soon as the program encounters this word, the method terminates, and control of the program jumps back to the calling method. The second function is that it sends back a value. In this case it sends back the result of the calculation:

```
priceIn * (1 + taxIn/100)
```

You should note that, if the method is of type **void**, then there is no need to include a **return** instruction – the method simply terminates once the last instruction is executed.

Now we can discuss how we actually call this method and use its return value. The whole program appears below as program 5.3:

PROGRAM 5.3

```
import java.util.*;

/* we have adapted program 2.3 so that the new price is determined by calling a method that
   adds the sales tax */

public class FindCost4
{
  public static void main(String[] args )
  {
    Scanner keyboard = new Scanner(System.in);

    double price, tax;

    System.out.println("*** Product Price Check ***");

    System.out.print("Enter initial price: ");
    price = keyboard.nextDouble();

    System.out.print("Enter tax rate: ");
    tax = keyboard.nextDouble();

    price = addTax(price, tax); // call the addTax method
```

```
    System.out.println("Cost after tax = " + price);
  }


  static double addTax(double priceIn, double taxIn)
  {
    return priceIn * (1 + taxIn/100);
  }
}
```

The line in `main` that calls the method is this one:

```
price = addTax(price, tax);
```

First, we will consider the items in brackets after the method name. As you might have expected, there are two items in the brackets – these are the *actual* values that we are sending into our method. They are therefore referred to as the **actual parameters** of the method. Their values are copied onto the formal parameters in the called method. This process, which is referred to as **passing** parameters, is illustrated in figure 5.1.

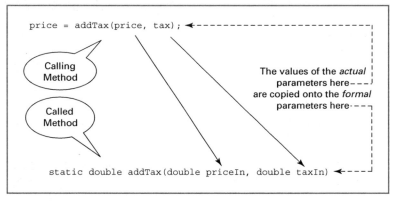

FIGURE 5.1 Passing parameters from one method to another method

You might have been wondering how the program knows which values in the actual parameter list are copied onto which variables in the formal parameter list. The answer to this is that it is the *order* that is important – you can see this from figure 5.1 – the value of `price` is copied onto `priceIn`; the value of `tax` is copied onto `taxIn`. Although the variable names have been conveniently chosen, the names themselves have nothing to do with which value is copied to which variable.

You might also be wondering what would happen if you tried to call the method with the wrong number of variables. For example:

```
price = addTax(price);
```

The answer is that you would get a compiler error, because there is no method called `addTax` that requires just one single variable to be passed into it.

You can see then that the actual parameter list must match the formal parameter list exactly. Now this is important not just in terms of the number of variables, but also in terms of the *types*. For example, using actual values this time instead of variable names, this method call would be perfectly acceptable:

```
price = addTax(187.65, 17.5);
```

However, this would cause a compiler error:

```
price = addTax(187.65, 'c');
```

The reason, of course, is that `addTax` requires two **doubles**, not a **double** and a **char**.

We can now move on to looking at how we make use of the return value of a method.

The `addTax` method returns the result that we are interested in, namely the new price of the item. What we need to do is to assign this value to the variable `price`. As you have already seen, we have done this in the same line in which we called the method:

```
price = addTax(price, tax);
```

A method that returns a value can in fact be used just as if it were a variable of the same type as the return value! Here we have used it in an assignment statement – but in fact we could have simply dropped it into the `println` statement, just as we would have done with a simple variable of type **double**:

```
System.out.println("Cost after tax = " + addTax(price, tax));
```

5.5 More examples of methods

Just to make sure you have got the idea, let's define a few more methods. To start with, we will create a very simple method, one that calculates the square of a number. When we are going to write a method, there are four things to consider:

- the name that we will give to the method;
- the inputs to the method (the formal parameters);
- the output of the method (the return value);
- the body of the method (the instructions that do the job required).

In the case of the method in question, the name `square` would seem like a sensible choice. We will define the method so that it will calculate the square of any number, so it should accept a single value of type **double**. Similarly, it will return a **double**.

The instructions will be very simple – just return the result of multiplying the number by itself. So here is our method:

```
static double square(double numberIn)
{
  return numberIn * numberIn;
}
```

Remember that we can choose any names we want for the input parameters; here we have stuck with our convention of using the suffix In for formal parameters.

To use this method in another part of the program, such as the main method, is now very easy. Say, for example, we had declared and initialized two variables as follows:

```
double a = 2.5;
double b = 9.0;
```

Let's say we wanted to assign the square of a to a **double** variable x and the square of b to a **double** variable y. We could do this as follows:

```
x = square(a);
y = square(b);
```

After these instructions, x would hold the value 6.25 and y would hold the value 81.0.

For our next illustration we will choose a slightly more complicated example. We will define a function that we will call max; it will accept two integer values, and will return the bigger value of the two (of course, if they are equal, it can return the value of either one). It should be pretty clear that we will require two integer parameters, and that the method will return an integer. As far as the instructions are concerned, it should be clear that an **if...else** statement should do the job – if the first number is greater than the second, return the first number, if not return the second. Here is our method:

```
static int max(int firstIn, int secondIn)
{
  if(firstIn > secondIn)
  {
    return firstIn;
  }
  else
  {
    return secondIn;
  }
}
```

You should note that in this example we have two **return** statements, each potentially returning a different value – the value that is actually returned is decided at run-time by the values of the variables `firstIn` and `secondIn`. Remember, as soon as a **return** statement is reached the method terminates.

Working out how to write the instructions for this method was not too hard a job. In fact it was so simple, we didn't bother to design it with pseudocode. However, there will be many occasions in the future when the method has to carry out a much more complex task, and you will need to think through how to perform this task. A set of instructions for performing a job is known as an **algorithm** – common examples of algorithms in everyday life are recipes and DIY (Do-It-Yourself) instructions. Much of a programmer's time is spent devising algorithms for particular tasks, and, as you saw in chapter 2, we can use pseudocode to help us design our algorithms. We will look at further examples as we progress through this chapter.

Let's develop one more method. There are many instances in our programming lives where we might need to test whether a number is even or odd. Let's provide a method that does this job for us. We will call our method `isEven`, and it will report on whether or not a particular number is an even number. The test will be performed on integers, so we will need a single parameter of type **int**. The return value is interesting – the method will tell us whether or not a number is even, so it will need to return a value of **true** if the number is even or **false** if it is not. So our return type is going to be **boolean**. The instructions are quite simple to devise – again, an **if...else** statement should certainly do the job. But how can we test whether a number is even or not? Well, an even number will give a remainder of zero when divided by 2. An odd number will not. So we can use the modulus operator here. Here is our method:

```
static boolean isEven(int numberIn)
{
  if(numberIn % 2 == 0)
  {
    return true;
  }
  else
  {
    return false;
  }
}
```

Actually there is a slightly neater way we could have written this method. The expression:

```
numberIn % 2 == 0
```

will evaluate to either **true** or **false** – and we could therefore simply have returned the value of this expression and written our method like this:

```
static boolean isEven(int numberIn)
{
  return (numberIn % 2 == 0);
}
```

It is interesting to note that the calling method couldn't care less how the called method is coded – all it needs is for it to do the calculation correctly, and return the desired value. This is something that will become very significant when we look at methods that call methods of other classes later in this semester.

A method that returns a **boolean** value can be referred to as a **boolean** method. In chapter 3 you came across **boolean** *expressions* (expressions that evaluate to **true** or **false**) such as:

```
temperature > 10
```

or

```
y == 180
```

Because **boolean** methods also evaluate to **true** or **false** (that is, they return a value of **true** or **false**) they can – as with boolean expressions – be used as the test in a selection or loop.

For example, assuming that the variable number had been declared as an **int**, we could write something like:

```
if(isEven(number))
{
  // code here
}
```

or

```
while(isEven(number))
{
  // code here
}
```

To test for a **false** value we simply negate the expression with the *not* operator (!):

```
if(!isEven(number))
{
  // code here
}
```

Before we leave this section, there is one thing we should make absolutely clear – a method cannot change the *original* value of a variable that was passed to it as a parameter. The reason for this is that all that is being passed to the method is a *copy* of whatever this variable contains. In other words, just a *value*. The method does not have access to the original variable. Whatever value is passed is copied to the parameter in the called method. We will illustrate this with a very simple program indeed – program 5.4 below:

PROGRAM 5.4

```java
public class ParameterDemo
{
  public static void main(String[] args)
  {
    int x = 10;
    demoMethod(x);
    System.out.println(x);
  }

  static void demoMethod(int xIn)
  {
    xIn = 25;
    System.out.println(xIn);
  }
}
```

You can see that in the `main` method we declare an integer, `x`, which is initialized to 10. We then call a method called `demoMethod`, with `x` as a parameter. The formal parameter of this method – `xIn` – will now of course hold the value 10. But the method then assigns the value of 25 to the parameter – it then displays the value on the screen.

The method ends there, and control returns to the `main` method. The final line of this method displays the value of `x`.

The output from this method is as follows:

```
25

10
```

This shows that the original value of `x` has not in any way been affected by what happened to `xIn` in `demoMethod`.

5.6 Variable scope

Looking back at program 5.3, it is possible that some of you asked yourselves the following questions: Why do we need to bother with all this stuff in the brackets? We've already declared a couple of variables called `price` and `tax` – why can't we just use them in the body of the method? Well, go ahead and try it – you will see that you get a compiler error telling you that these variables are not recognized!

How can this be? They have certainly been declared. The answer lies in the matter of *where* exactly these variables have been declared. In actual fact variables are only "visible" within the pair of curly brackets in which they have been declared – this means that if they are referred to in a part of the program outside these brackets, then you will get a compiler error. Variables that have been declared inside the brackets of a particular method are called **local** variables – so the variables `price` and `tax` are said to be *local* to the `main` method. We say that variables have a **scope** – this means that their visibility is limited to a particular part of the program. If `price` or `tax` were referred to in the `addtax` method, they would be out of scope.

Let's take another, rather simple, example. Look at program 5.5:

PROGRAM 5.5

```java
public class ScopeTest
{
  public static void main(String[] args)
  {
    int x = 1;      // x is local to main
    int y = 2;      // y is local to main
    method1(x, y); // call method1
  }


  static void method1(int xIn, int yIn)
  {
    int z; // z is local to method1
    z = xIn + yIn;
    System.out.println(z);
  }
}
```

In this program the variables `x` and `y` are local to `main`. The variable `z` is local to `method1`. The variables `xIn` and `yIn` are the formal parameters of `method1`. This program will compile and run without a problem, because none of the variables is referred to in the wrong place.

Imagine, however, that we were to rewrite program 5.5 as program 5.6, below:

PROGRAM 5.6

```java
// this program will give rise to two compiler errors

public class ScopeTest2
{
  public static void main(String[] args)
  {
    int x = 1; // x is local to main
    int y = 2; // y is local to main
    method1(x, y); // call method1
```

```
      System.out.println(z); // this line will cause a compiler error as z is local to method1
   }


   static void method1(int xIn, int yIn)
   {
      int z;      // z is local to method1
      z = x + y; // this line will cause a compiler error as x and y are local to main
      System.out.println(z);
   }
}
```

As the comments indicate, the lines in bold will give rise to compiler errors, as the variables referred to are out of scope.

It is interesting to note that, since a method is completely unaware of what has been declared inside any other method, you could declare variables with the same name inside different methods. The compiler would regard each variable as being completely different from any other variable in another method which simply had the same name. So, for example, if we had declared a *local* variable called x in method1, this would be perfectly ok – it would exist completely independently from the variable named x in main.

To understand why this is so, it helps to know a little about what goes on when the program is running. A part of the computer's memory called the **stack** is reserved for use by running programs. When a method is called, some space on the stack is used to store the values for that method's formal parameters and its local variables. That is why, whatever names we give them, they are local to their particular method. Once the method terminates, this part of the stack is no longer accessible, and the variables effectively no longer exist. And this might help you to understand even more clearly why the value of a variable passed as a parameter to a method cannot be changed by that method.

Before we move on, it will be helpful if we list the kinds of variables that a method can access:

- a method can access variables that have been declared as formal parameters;
- a method can access variables that have been declared locally – in other words that have been declared within the curly brackets of the method;
- as you will learn in chapter 8, a method has access to variables declared as *attributes of the class* (don't worry – you will understand what this means in good time!).

A method cannot access any other variables.

5.7 Method overloading

You have already encountered the term *overloading* in previous chapters, in connection with operators. You found out, for example, that the division operator (/) can be used for two distinct purposes – for division of integers, and for division of real numbers. The + operator is not only used for addition, but also for concatenating two strings. So the same operator can behave differently depending on what it is operating on – operators can be overloaded.

Methods too can be overloaded. To illustrate, let's return to the max method of section 5.5. Here it is again:

```
static int max(int firstIn, int secondIn)
{
  if(firstIn > secondIn)
  {
    return firstIn;
  }
  else
  {
    return secondIn;
  }
}
```

As you will recall, this method accepts two integers and returns the greater of the two. But what if we wanted to find the greatest of three integers? We would have to write a new method, which we have shown below. We are just showing you the header here – we will think about the actual instructions in a moment:

```
static int max(int firstIn, int secondIn, int thirdIn)
{
  // code goes here
}
```

You can see that we have given this method the same name as before – but this time it has *three* parameters instead of two. And the really clever thing is that we can declare and call both methods within the same class. Both methods have the same name but the parameter list is different – and each one will *behave* differently. In our example, the original method compares two integers and returns the greater of the two; the second one, once we have worked out the algorithm for doing this, will examine three integers and return the value of the one that is the greatest of the three. When two or more methods, distinguished by their parameter lists, have the same name but perform different functions we say that they are **overloaded**. Method overloading is actually one example of what is known as **polymorphism**. Polymorphism literally means *having many forms*, and it is an important feature of object-oriented programming languages. It refers, in general, to the phenomenon of having methods and operators with the same name performing different functions. You will come across other examples of polymorphism in later chapters.

Now, you might be asking yourself how, when we call an overloaded method, the program knows which one we mean. The answer of course depends on the actual parameters that accompany the method call – they are matched with the formal parameter list, and the appropriate method will be called. So, if we made this call somewhere in a program:

```
int x = max(3, 5);
```

then the first version of max would be called – the version that returns the bigger of two integers. This, of course, is because the method is being called with two integer parameters, matching this header:

```
static int max(int firstIn, int secondIn)
```

However, if this call, with three integer parameters, were made:

```
int x = max(3, 5, 10);
```

then it would be the second version that was called:

```
static int max(int firstIn, int secondIn, int thirdIn)
```

One very important thing we have still to do is to devise the *algorithm* for this second version. Can you think of a way to do it? Have go at it before reading on.

One way to do it is to declare an integer variable, which we could call result, and start off by assigning to it the value of the first number. Then we can consider the next number. Is it greater than the current value of result? If it is, then we should assign this value to result instead of the original value. Now we can consider the third number – if this is larger than the current value of result, we assign its value to result. You should be able to see that result will end up having the value of the greatest of the three integers. It is helpful to express this as pseudocode:

```
SET result TO first number
IF second number > result
BEGIN
  SET result TO second number
END
IF third number > result
BEGIN
  SET result TO third number
END
RETURN result
```

Here is the code:

```
static int max(int firstIn, int secondIn, int thirdIn)
{
  int result;
  result = firstIn;
  if(secondIn > result)
```

```
  {
    result = secondIn;
  }
  if(thirdIn > result)
  {
    result = thirdIn;
  }
  return result;
}
```

Program 5.7 illustrates how both versions of our max method can be used in the same program:

PROGRAM 5.7

```
public class OverloadingDemo
{
  public static void main(String[] args)
  {
    int maxOfTwo, maxOfThree;
    maxOfTwo = max(2, 10);      // call the first version of max
    maxOfThree = max(-5, 5, 3); // call the second version of max

    System.out.println(maxOfTwo);
    System.out.println(maxOfThree);
  }

  // this version of max accepts two integers and returns the greater of the two
  static int max(int firstIn, int secondIn)
  {
    if(firstIn > secondIn)
    {
      return firstIn;
    }
    else
    {
      return secondIn;
    }
  }

  // this version of max accepts three integers and returns the greatest of the three
  static int max(int firstIn, int secondIn, int thirdIn)
```

```
{
  int result;
  result = firstIn;
  if(secondIn > result)
  {
    result = secondIn;
  }
  if(thirdIn > result)
  {
    result = thirdIn;
  }
  return result;
  }
}
```

As the first call to max in the main method has two parameters, it will call the first version of max; the second call, with its three parameters, will call the second version. Not surprisingly then, the output from this program looks like this:

10

5

It might have occurred to you that we could have implemented the second version of max (that is the one that takes three parameters) in a different way. We could have started off by finding the maximum of the first two integers (using the first version of max), and then doing the same thing again, comparing the result of this with the third number.

This version is presented below – this is an example of how we can call a method not from the main method, but from another method.

```
static int max(int firstIn, int secondIn, int thirdIn)
{
  int step1, result;
  step1 = max(firstIn, secondIn); // call the first version of max
  result = max(step1, thirdIn); // call the first version of max again
  return result;
}
```

Some of you might be thinking that if we wanted similar methods to deal with lists of four, five, six, or even more numbers, it would be an awful lot of work to write a separate method for each one – and indeed it would! But don't worry – in the next chapter you will find that there is a much easier way to deal with situations like this.

5.8 Using methods in menu-driven programs

In chapter 4 we developed a program that presented the user with a menu of choices; we pointed out that this was a very common interface for programs before the days of graphics. Until we start working with graphics later in the semester, we will use this approach with some of our more complex programs.

Here is a reminder of program 4.10.

PROGRAM 4.10 – a reminder

```java
import java.util.*;

public class TimetableWithLoop
{
  public static void main(String[] args)
  {
    char group, response;
    Scanner sc = new Scanner (System.in);
    System.out.println("***Lab Times***");
    do // put code in loop


    {
      // offer menu of options
      System.out.println(); // create a blank line
      System.out.println("[1] TIME FOR GROUP A");
      System.out.println("[2] TIME FOR GROUP B");
      System.out.println("[3] TIME FOR GROUP C");
      System.out.println("[4] QUIT PROGRAM");
      System.out.print("enter choice [1,2,3,4]: ");
      response = sc.next().charAt(0); // get response
      System.out.println(); // create a blank line
      switch(response) // process response
      {
        case '1': System.out.println("10.00 a.m ");
                  break;
        case '2': System.out.println("1.00 p.m ");
                  break;
        case '3': System.out.println("11.00 a.m ");
                  break;
        case '4': System.out.println("Goodbye ");
                  break;
```

```
         default:  System.out.println("Options 1-4 only!");
      }
   } while (response != '4'); // test for Quit option
  }
}
```

In this program, each **case** statement consisted of a single instruction (apart from the **break**), which simply displayed one line of text. Imagine, though, that we were to develop a more complex program in which each menu choice involved a lot of processing. The **switch** statement would start to get very messy, and the program could easily become very unwieldy. In this situation, confining each menu option to a particular method will make our program far more manageable.

Program 5.8 is an example of such a program. The program allows a user to enter the radius of a circle and then enables the area and circumference of the circle to be calculated and displayed. Four menu options are offered. The first allows the user to enter the radius. The second displays the area of the circle, and the third the circumference. The final option allows the user to quit the program.

Study it carefully, and then we will point out some of the interesting features.

PROGRAM 5.8

```java
import java.util.*;

/* This program demonstrates how methods can be used in a menu-driven program */

public class CircleCalculation
{
  public static void main(String[] args)
  {

    Scanner keyboard = new Scanner(System.in);
    /* The variable below is local to the main method; if the value is needed by another method,
       it must be passed in as a parameter */

    double radius = -999; // initialize with a dummy value to show that nothing has been entered
    char choice;
    do
    {

      System.out.println();
      System.out.println("*** CIRCLE CALCULATIONS ***");
      System.out.println();
      System.out.println("1. Enter the radius of the circle");
```

```java
      System.out.println("2. Display the area of the circle");
      System.out.println("3. Display the circumference of the circle");
      System.out.println("4. Quit");
      System.out.println();
      System.out.println("Enter a number from 1 - 4");
      System.out.println();
      choice = keyboard.next().charAt(0);
      switch(choice)
    {
       case '1' : radius = option1(); // call method option1
                break;
       case '2' : option2(radius); // call method option2
                break;
       case '3' : option3(radius); // call method option3
                break;
       case '4' : break;
       default :  System.out.println("Enter only numbers from 1 - 4");
       System.out.println();
     }
  } while(choice != '4');
}


// option1 gets the user to enter the radius of the circle
static double option1()
{
  double myRadius; // local variable
  Scanner keyboard = new Scanner(System.in);
  System.out.print("Enter the radius of the circle: ");
  myRadius = keyboard.nextDouble();
  return myRadius;
}


// option2 calculates and displays the area of the circle
static void option2(double radiusIn)
{
  if(radiusIn == -999)
  {
    System.out.println("Radius has not been entered");
  }
  else
```

```
    {
      double area; // local variable
      area = 3.1416 * radiusIn * radiusIn; // calculate the area of the circle
      System.out.println("The area of the circle is: " + area);
    }
  }


  // option3 calculates and displays the circumference of the circle
  static void option3(double radiusIn)
  {
    if(radiusIn == -999)
    {
      System.out.println("Radius has not been entered");
    }
    else
    {
      double circumference;; // local variable
      circumference = 2 * 3.1416 * radiusIn; // calculate the circumference of the circle
      System.out.println("The circumference of the circle is: " + circumference);
    }
  }
}
```

There are no new programming techniques in this program; it is the *design* that is interesting. The comments are self-explanatory; so we draw your attention only to a few important points:

- The radius is initialized with a "dummy" value of –999. This allows us to check if the radius has been entered before attempting to perform a calculation.

- Choosing menu option 1 causes the method `option1` to be called – the value of the radius entered by the user is returned.

- Choosing menu option 2 causes the method `option2` to be called. The radius of the circle is sent in as a parameter. After using the dummy value to check that a value for the radius has been entered, the area is then calculated and displayed.

- Choosing menu option 3 causes the method `option3` to be called. This is similar to `option2`, but for the circumference instead of the area.

- Choosing option 4 causes the program to terminate – this happens because the body of the **while** loop executes only while `choice` is not equal to 4. If it is equal to 4, the loop is not executed and the program ends. The associated **case** statement consists simply of the instruction **break**, thus causing the program to jump out of the **switch** statement.

- You can see that we have had to declare a new `Scanner` object in each method where it is needed – now that you understand the notion of variable *scope*, you should understand why we have had to do this.

Self-test questions

1 Explain the meaning of the term *method*.

2 Consider the following program:

```java
public class MethodsQ2
{
  public static void main(String[] args)
  {
    System.out.println(myMethod(3, 5));
    System.out.println(myMethod(3, 5, 10));
  }

  static int myMethod(int firstIn, int secondIn, int thirdIn)
  {
    return firstIn + secondIn + thirdIn;
  }

  static int myMethod(int firstIn, int secondIn)
  {
    return firstIn - secondIn;
  }
}
```

  a By referring to this program:

   i Distinguish between the terms *actual parameters* and *formal parameters*.

   ii Explain the meaning of the terms *polymorphism* and *method overloading*.

  b What would be displayed on the screen when this program was run?

  c Explain, giving reasons, the effect of adding either of the following lines into the `main` method:

   i `System.out.println(myMethod(3));`

   ii `System.out.println(myMethod(3, 5.7, 10));`

3 What would be displayed on the screen as a result of running the following program?

```java
public class MethodsQ3
{
  public static void main(String[] args)
  {
    int x = 3;
```

```
    int y = 4;
    System.out.println(myMethod(x, y));
    System.out.println(y);
  }


  static int myMethod(int firstIn, int secondIn)
  {
   int x = 10;
   int y;
   y = x + firstIn + secondIn;
   return y;
  }
}
```

4   What would be displayed on the screen as a result of running the following program?

```
public class MethodsQ4
{
  public static void main(String[] args)
  {
    int x = 2;
    int y = 7;
    System.out.println(myMethod(x, y));
    System.out.println(y);
  }


  static int myMethod(int a, int x)
  {
   int y = 20;
   return y - a - x;
  }
}
```

Programming exercises

1 Implement the programs from the self-test questions in order to verify your answers.

2 In chapter 2, programming exercise 3, you wrote a program that converted pounds to kilograms. Rewrite this program, so that the conversion takes place in a separate method, which is called by the `main` method.

3 In the exercises at the end of chapter 2 you were asked to write a program that calculated the area and perimeter of a rectangle. Rewrite this program so that now the instructions for calculating the area and perimeter of the rectangle are contained in two separate methods.

4 a Design and implement a program that converts a sum of money to a different currency. The amount of money to be converted, and the exchange rate, are entered by the user. The program should have separate methods for:

- obtaining the sum of money from the user;
- obtaining the exchange rate from the user;
- making the conversion;
- displaying the result.

b Adapt the above program so that after the result is displayed the user is asked if he or she wishes to convert another sum of money. The program continues in this way until the user chooses to quit.

5 a Write a menu-driven program that provides three options:

- the first option allows the user to enter a temperature in Celsius and displays the corresponding Fahrenheit temperature;
- the second option allows the user to enter a temperature in Fahrenheit and displays the corresponding Celsius temperature;
- the third option allows the user to quit.

The formulae that you need are as follows, where C represents a Celsius temperature and F a Fahrenheit temperature:

$$F = \frac{9C}{5} + 32$$

$$C = \frac{5(F - 32)}{9}$$

b Adapt the above program so that the user is not allowed to enter a temperature below absolute zero; this is $-273.15C$, or $-459.67°F$.

Arrays

❖ OBJECTIVES

By the end of this chapter you should be able to:

❖ create **arrays**;

❖ use **for** loops to process arrays;

❖ use an enhanced **for** loop to process an array;

❖ use arrays as method inputs and outputs;

❖ develop routines for accessing and manipulating arrays;

❖ distinguish between **one-dimensional** arrays and **multi-dimensional** arrays;

❖ create and process **two-dimensional** arrays;

❖ create **ragged arrays**.

6.1 Introduction

In previous chapters we have shown you how to create variables and store data in them. In each case the variables created could be used to hold a *single* item of data. How, though, would you deal with a situation in which you had to create and handle a very large number of data items?

An obvious approach would be just to declare as many variables as you need. Declaring a large number of variables is a nuisance but simple enough. For example, let's consider a very simple application that records seven temperature readings (one for each day of the week):

```
public class TemperatureReadings
{
  public static void main(String[] args)
  {
    // declare 7 variables to hold readings
    double temperature1, temperature2, temperature3, temperature4, temperature5, temperature6, temperature7;
    // more code will go here
  }
}
```

Here we have declared seven variables each of type **double** (as temperatures will be recorded as real numbers). So far so good. Now to write some code that allows the user to enter values for these temperatures. Getting one temperature is easy (assuming we have created a Scanner object keyboard), as shown below:

```
System.out.println("max temperature for day 1 ?");
temperature1 = keyboard.nextDouble();
```

But how would you write the code to get the second temperature, the third temperature and all the remaining temperatures? Well, you could repeat the above pair of lines for each temperature entered, but surely you've got better things to do with your time!

Essentially you want to repeat the same pair of lines seven times. You already know that a **for** loop is useful when repeating lines of code a fixed number of times. Maybe you could try using a **for** loop here?

```
for (int i=1; i<=7; i++)
{
  // what goes here?
}
```

This looks like a neat solution, but the problem is that there is no obvious instruction we could write in the **for** loop that will allow a value to be entered into a *different* variable each time the loop repeats. As things stand there is no way around this, as each variable has a *distinct* name.

Ideally we would like each variable to be given the *same* name (temperature, say) so that we could use a loop here, but we would like some way of being able to distinguish between each successive variable. In fact, this is exactly what an **array** allows us to do.

6.2 Creating an array

An array is a special data type in Java that can be thought of as a *container* to store a *collection of items*. These items are sometimes referred to as the **elements** of the array. All the elements stored in a particular array must be of the *same type* but there is no restriction on which type this is. So, for example, an array can be used to hold a collection of **int** values or a collection of **char** values, but it cannot be used to hold a mixture of **int** and **char** values.

Let's look at how to use arrays in your programs. First you need to know how to create an array. Array creation is a two-stage process:

1 declare an array variable;
2 allocate memory to store the array elements.

An array variable is declared in much the same way as a simple variable except that a pair of square brackets is added after the type. For example, if an array was to hold a collection of integer variables it could be declared as follows:

```
int[] someArray;
```

Here a name has been given to the array in the same way you would name any variable. The name we have chosen is `someArray`. If the square brackets were missing in the above declaration this would just be a simple variable capable of holding a *single* integer value only. But the square brackets indicate this variable is an array allowing *many* integer values to be stored.

So, to declare an array `temperature` containing **double** values, you would write the following:

```
double[] temperature;
```

At the moment this simply defines `temperature` to be a variable that can be *linked* to a collection of **double** values. The `temperature` variable itself is said to hold a **reference** to the array elements. A reference is a variable that holds a *location* in the computer's memory (known as a memory *address*) where data is stored, rather than the data itself. This illustrated in figure 6.1.

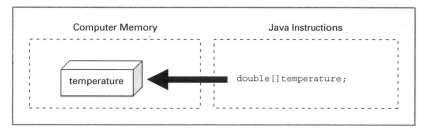

FIGURE 6.1 The effect on computer memory of declaring an array reference

At the moment the memory address stored in the `temperature` reference is not meaningful as the memory that will eventually hold the array elements has not been allocated yet. This is stage two.

What information do you think would be required in order to reserve enough space in the computer's memory for all the array elements?

Well, it would be necessary to state the size of the array, that is the *maximum* number of elements required by the array. Also, since each data type requires a different amount of memory space, it is also necessary to state the type of each individual array element (this will be the same type used in stage one of the array declaration). The array type and size are then put together with a special **new** operator. For example, if we required an array of 10 integers the following would be appropriate:

```
someArray = new int[10];
```

The **new** operator creates the space in memory for an array of the given size and element type.[1]

We will come back to look at this **new** operator when looking at classes and objects in the next chapter. Once the size of the array is set it cannot be changed, so always make sure you create an array that is big enough for your purpose. Returning to the temperature example above, if you wanted the array to hold seven temperatures you would allocate memory as follows:

```
temperature = new double[7];
```

---

[1] Of course, this size should not be a negative value. A negative value will cause an error in your program.

Let's see what effect the **new** operator has on computer memory by looking at figure 6.2.

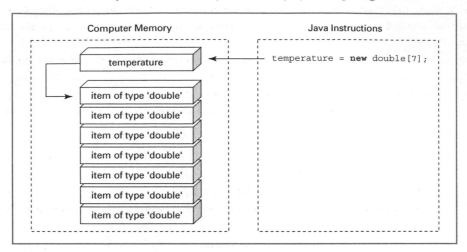

FIGURE 6.2 The effect on computer memory of declaring an array of seven 'double' values

As can be seen from figure 6.2, the array creation has created seven continuous locations in memory. Each location is big enough to store a value of type **double**. The temperature variable is linked to these seven elements by containing the address of the very first element. In effect, the array reference, tempera-ture, is linked to seven new variables. Each of these variables will automatically have some initial value placed in them. If the variables are of some number type (such as **int** or **double**), the value of each will be initially set to zero; if the variables are of type **char**, their values will be set initially to a special Unicode value that represents an empty character; if the variables are of **boolean** type, they will each be set initially to **false**.

The two stages of array creation (declaring and allocating memory space for the elements) can also be combined into one step as follows:

```
double[] temperature = new double[7];
```

You may be wondering: what names have each of these variables been given? The answer is that each element in an array shares the same name as the array, so in this case each element is called temperature. The individual elements are then *uniquely identified* by an additional **index value**. An index value acts rather like a street number to identify houses on the same street (see figure 6.3). In much the same way as a house on a street is identified by the street name and a house number, an array element is identified by the array name and the index value.

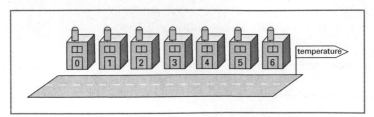

FIGURE 6.3 Elements in an array are identified in much the same way as houses on a street

Like a street number, these index values are always contiguous integers. Note carefully that, in Java, *array indices start from 0 and not from 1*. This index value is always enclosed in square brackets, so the first temperature in the list is identified as `temperature[0]`, the second temperature by `temperature[1]` and so on.

This means that the size of the array and the last index value are *not* the same value. In this case the size is 7 and the last index is 6. There is no such value as `temperature[7]`, for example. Remember this, as it is a common cause of errors in programs! If you try to access an invalid element such as `temperature[7]`, the following program error will be generated by the system:

```
java.lang.ArrayIndexOutOfBoundsException
```

This type of error is called an *exception*. You will find out more about exceptions in the second semester but you should be aware that, very often, exceptions will result in program termination.

Usually, when an array is created, values will be added into it as the program runs. If, however, all the values of the array elements are known beforehand, then an array can be created without the use of the **new** operator by initializing the array as follows:

```
double[] temperature = {9, 11.5, 11, 8.5, 7, 9, 8.5} ;
```

The initial values are placed in braces and separated by commas. The compiler determines the length of the array by the number of initial values (in this case 7). Each value is placed into the array in order, so `temperature[0]` is set to 9, `temperature[1]` to 11.5 and so on. This is the only instance in which *all the elements* of an array can be assigned explicitly by listing out the elements in a single assignment statement.

Once an array has been created, elements must be accessed *individually*.

6.3 Accessing array elements

Once an array has been created, its elements can be used like any other variable of the given type in Java. If you look back at the temperature example, initializing the values of each temperature when the array is created is actually quite unrealistic. It is much more likely that temperatures would be entered into the program as it runs. Let's look at how to achieve this.

Whether an array is initialized or not, values can be placed into the individual array elements. We know that each element in this array is a variable of type **double**. As with any variable of a primitive type, the assignment operator can be used to enter a value.

The only thing you have to remember when using the assignment operator with an array element is to specify *which* element to place the value in. For example, to allow the user of the program to enter the value of the first temperature, the following assignment could be used (again, assuming the existence of a `Scanner` object, `keyboard`):

```
temperature[0] = keyboard.nextDouble();
```

Note again that, since array indices begin at 0, the first temperature is not at index 1 but index 0.

Array elements could also be printed on the screen. For example, the following command prints out the value of the *sixth* array element:

```
System.out.println(temperature[5]); // index 5 is the sixth element!
```

Note that an array index (such as 5) is just used to *locate* a position in the array; it is *not* the item at that position.

For example, assume that the user enters a value of 25.5 for the first temperature in the array; the following statement:

```
System.out.println("temperature for day 1 is "+ temperature[0]);
```

would then print out the message:

```
temperature for day 1 is 25.5
```

Statements like the `println` command above might seem a bit confusing at first. The message refers to "temperature for day **1**" but the temperature that is displayed is `temperature[0]`. Remember though that the temperature at index position 0 *is* the first temperature! After a while you will get used to this indexing system of Java.

As you can see from the examples above, you can use array elements in exactly the same way you can use any other kind of variable of the given type. Here are a few more examples:

```
temperature[4] = temperature[4] * 2;
```

This assignment doubles the value of the *fifth* temperature. The following **if** statement checks if the temperature for the *third* day was a hot temperature:

```
if (temperature[2] >= 18)
{
  System.out.println("it was hot today");
}
```

So far so good, but if you are just going to use array elements in the way you used regular variables, why bother with arrays at all?

The reason is that the indexing system of arrays is in fact a very powerful programming tool. The index value does not need to be a literal number such as 5 or 2 as in the examples we have just shown you; it can be *any expression that evaluates to an integer*.

More often than not an integer *variable* is used, in place of a fixed index value, to access an array element. For example, if we assume that `i` is some integer variable, then the following is a perfectly legal way of accessing an array element:

```
System.out.println(temperature[i]); // index is a variable
```

Here the array index is not a literal number (like 2 or 5) but the variable i. The value of i will determine the array index. If the value of i is 4 then this will display temperature[4], if the value of i is 6 then this will display temperature[6], and so on. One useful application of this is to place the array instructions within a loop (usually a **for** loop), with the loop counter being used as the array index. For example, returning to the original problem of entering all seven temperature readings, the following loop could now be used:

```
for(int i = 0; i<7; i++) // note, loop counter runs from 0 to 6
{
  System.out.println("enter max temperature for day "+(i+1));
  temperature[i] = keyboard.nextDouble(); // use loop counter
}
```

Note carefully the following points from this loop:

- Unlike many of the previous examples of **for** loop counters that started at 1, this counter starts at 0. Since the counter is meant to track the array indices, 0 is the appropriate number to start from.
- The counter goes up to, but does not include, the number of items in the array. In this case this means the counter goes up to 6 and not 7. Again this is because the array index for an array of size 7 stops at 6.
- The println command uses the loop counter to display the number of the given day being entered. The loop counter starts from 0, however. We would not think of the first day of the week as being day 0! In order for the message to be more meaningful for the user, therefore, we have displayed (i+1) rather than i.

Effectively the following statements are executed by this loop:

```
System.out.println("enter max temperature for day 1 ");
temperature[0] = keyboard.nextDouble();                    ── 1st time round loop

System.out.println("enter max temperature for day 2 ");
temperature[1] = keyboard.nextDouble();                    ── 2nd time round loop

//as above but with indices 2-5                            ── 3rd–6th time round loop

System.out.println("enter max temperature for day 7 ");
temperature[6] = keyboard.nextDouble();                    ── 7th time round loop
```

You should now be able to see the benefit of an array. This loop can be made more readable if we make use of a built-in feature of all arrays that returns the length of an array. It is accessed by using the word length after the name of the array. The two are joined by a full stop. Here is an example:

```
System.out.print("number of temperatures = ");
System.out.println(temperature.length); // returns the size of the array
```

which displays the following on to the screen:

```
number of temperatures = 7
```

Note that `length` feature returns the size of the array, not necessarily the number of items currently stored in the array (which may be fewer). This attribute can be used in place of a fixed number in the **for** loop as follows:

```
for (int i = 0; i < temperature.length, i++)
{
  // code for loop goes here
}
```

To see this technique being exploited, look at program 6.1 to see the completed `TemperatureReadings` program, which stores and displays the maximum daily temperatures in a week.

PROGRAM 6.1

```
import java.util.*;
public class TemperatureReadings
{
  public static void main(String[] args)
  {
    Scanner keyboard = new Scanner(System.in);
    // create array
    double[] temperature;
    temperature = new double[7];
    // enter temperatures
    for (int i = 0; i < temperature.length; i++)
    {
      System.out.println("enter max temperature for day " + (i+1));
      temperature[i] = keyboard.nextDouble();
    }

    // display temperatures
    System.out.println(); // blank line
    System.out.println("***TEMPERATURES ENTERED***");
    System.out.println(); // blank line
    for (int i = 0; i < temperature.length; i++)
    {
      System.out.println("day "+(i+1)+" "+ temperature[i]);
    }
  }
}
```

Note how `length` was used to control the two **for** loops. Here is a sample test run.

```
enter max temperature for day 1 12.2
enter max temperature for day 2 10.5
enter max temperature for day 3 13
enter max temperature for day 4 15
enter max temperature for day 5 13
enter max temperature for day 6 12.5
enter max temperature for day 7 12

***TEMPERATURES ENTERED***

day 1 12.2
day 2 10.5
day 3 13.0
day 4 15.0
day 5 13.0
day 6 12.5
day 7 12.0
```

6.4 Passing arrays as parameters

In chapter 5 we looked at how methods can be used to break up a programming task into manageable chunks. Methods can receive data in the form of parameters and can send back data in the form of a return value. Arrays can be used both as parameters to methods and as return values. In the next section we will see an example of an array as a return value from a method. In this section we will look at passing arrays as parameters to a method. As an example of passing an array to a method, consider once again program 6.1, which processes temperature readings. That program contains all the processing within the `main` method. As a result, the code for this method is a little difficult to read. Let's do something about that. We will create two methods, `enterTemps` and `displayTemps`, to enter and display temperatures respectively. To give these methods access to the array they must receive it as a parameter. Here, for example, is the header for the `enterTemps` method. Notice that when a parameter is declared as an array type, the size of the array is not required but the empty square brackets are:

```
static void enterTemps( double[] temperatureIn )
{
  // rest of method goes here
}
```

Now, although in the previous chapter we told you that a parameter just receives a copy of the original variable, this works a little differently with arrays. We will explain this a little later, but for now just be aware that this method will actually fill the original array. The code for the method itself is straightforward:

```
Scanner keyboard = new Scanner(System.in); // create local Scanner object
for (int i = 0; i < temperatureIn.length; i++)
{
  System.out.println("enter max temperature for day " + (i+1));
  temperatureIn[i] = keyboard.nextDouble();
}
```

Similarly the `displayTemps` method will require the array to be sent as a parameter. Program 6.2 rewrites program 6.1 by adding the two methods mentioned above. Take a look at it and then we will discuss it.

PROGRAM 6.2

```
import java.util.*;
public class TemperatureReadings2
{
  public static void main(String[] args)
  {
    double[] temperature;
    temperature = new double[7];
    enterTemps(temperature); // call method
    displayTemps(temperature); // call method
  }
  // method to enter temperatures
  static void enterTemps(double[] temperatureIn)
  {
    Scanner keyboard = new Scanner(System.in);
    for (int i = 0; i < temperatureIn.length; i++)
    {
      System.out.println("enter max temperature for day " + (i+1));
      for temperatureIn[i] = keyboard.nextDouble();
    }
  }
  // method to display temperatures
  static void displayTemps(double[] temperatureIn)
```

```
    {
       System.out.println();
       System.out.println("***TEMPERATURES ENTERED***");
       System.out.println();
       for (int i = 0; i < temperatureIn.length; i++)
       {
          System.out.println("day "+(i+1)+" "+ temperatureIn[i]);
       }
    }
}
```

Notice that when sending an array as a parameter, the array name alone is required:

```
public static void main(String[] args)
{
   double[] temperature;
   temperature = new double[7];
   enterTemps(temperature); // array name plugged in
   displayTemps(temperature); // array name plugged in
}
```

Now let us return to the point we made earlier. You are aware that, in the case of a simple variable type such as an **int**, it is the *value* of the variable that is copied when it is passed as a parameter. This means that if the value of a parameter is altered within a method, the original variable is unaffected outside that method. This works differently with arrays.

As we said earlier, the enterTemps method actually fills the *original* array. How can this be? The answer is that in the case of arrays, the value sent as a parameter is not a copy of each array element but, instead, a copy of the array *reference*. In other words, the *location* of the array is sent to the receiving method, not the value of the contents of the array. Now, even though the receiving parameter (temperatureIn) has a different name to the original variable in main (temperature), they are both pointing to the same place in memory so both are modifying the same array! This is illustrated in figure 6.4: Sending the array reference to a method rather than a copy of the whole array is a very efficient use of the computer's resources, especially when arrays become very large.

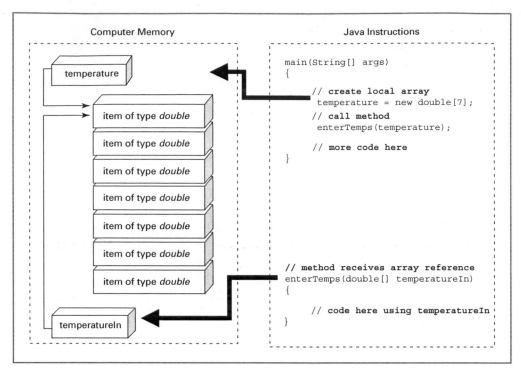

FIGURE 6.4 The effect on computer memory of passing on array as a parameter

6.5 Returning an array from a method

A method can return an array as well as receive arrays as parameters. As an example, let us reconsider the enterTemps method from program 6.2. At the moment, this method accepts an array as a parameter and fills this array with temperature values. Since this method fills the *original* array sent in as a parameter, it does not need to return a value – its return type is therefore **void**:

```
static void enterTemps (double[] temperatureIn)
{

  // code to fill the parameter, 'temperatureIn', goes here

}
```

An alternative approach would be *not* to send an array to this method but, instead, to create an array *within* this method and fill *this* array with values. This array can then be returned from the method:

```
// this method receives no parameter but returns an array of doubles
static double[] enterTemps()
{

  Scanner keyboard = new Scanner(System.in);
```

```
    // create an array within this method
    double[] temperatureOut = new double[7];
    // fill up the array created in this method
    for (int i = 0; i < temperatureOut.length; i++)
    {
      System.out.println("enter max temperature for day " + (i+1));
      temperatureOut[i] = keyboard.nextDouble();
    }
    // send back the array created in this method
    return temperatureOut;
}
```

As you can see, we use square brackets to indicate that an array is to be returned from a method:

```
static double[] enterTemps()
```

The array itself is created within the method. We have decided to call this array temperatureOut:

```
double[] temperatureOut = new double[7];
```

After the array has been filled it is sent back with a **return** statement. Notice that, to return an array, the name alone is required:

```
return temperatureOut;
```

Now that we have changed the enterTemps method, we need to revisit the original main method also. It will no longer compile now that the enterTemps method has changed:

```
// the original 'main' method will no loger compile!
public static void main(String[] args)
{
  double[] temperature = new double[7];
  enterTemps(temperature); // this line will now cause a compiler error!!
  displayTemps(temperature);
}
```

The call to enterTemps will no longer compile as the new enterTemps does not expect to be given an array as a parameter. The correct way to call the method is as follows:

```
enterTemps(); // this method requires no parameter
```

However, this method now *returns* an array. We really should do something with the array value that is returned from this method. We should use the returned array value to set the value of the original temperature array:

```
// just declare the 'temperature' array but do not allocate it memory yet
double[] temperature;
// 'temperature' array is now set to the return value of 'enterTemps'
temperature = enterTemps();
```

As you can see, we have not sized the temperature array once it has been declared. Instead the temperature array will be set to the size of the array returned by enterTemps, and it will contain all the values of the array returned by enterTemps. Program 6.3 presents the complete program:

PROGRAM 6.3

```
import java.util.*;
public class TemperatureReadings3
{
  public static void main(String[] args)
  {
    double[] temperature ;
    temperature = enterTemps(); // call new version of this method
    displayTemps(temperature);
  }
  // method to enter temperatures returns an array
  static double[] enterTemps()
  {
    Scanner keyboard = new Scanner(System.in);
    double[] temperatureOut = new double[7];
    for (int i = 0; i < temperatureOut.length; i++)
    {
      System.out.println("enter max temperature for day " + (i+1));
      temperatureOut[i] = keyboard.nextDouble();
    }
    return temperatureOut;
  }
  // this method is unchanged
  static void displayTemps(double[] temperatureIn)
  {
    System.out.println();
    System.out.println("***TEMPERATURES ENTERED***");
```

```
      System.out.println();
      for (int i = 0; i < temperatureIn.length; i++)
      {
        System.out.println("day "+(i+1)+" "+ temperatureIn[i]);
      }
   }
}
```

Program 6.3 behaves in exactly the same way as program 6.2, so whether you implement `enterTemps` as in program 6.2 or as in program 6.3 is really just a matter of preference.

6.6 The enhanced 'for' loop

As you can see from the examples above, when processing an entire array a loop is required. Very often, this will be a **for** loop. With a **for** loop, the loop counter is used as the array index within the body of the loop. In the examples above, the loop counter was used not only as an array index but also to display meaningful messages to the user. For example:

```
for (int i = 0; i < temperature.length; i++)
{
  System.out.println("day "+(i+1)+" "+ temperature[i]);
}
```

Here the loop counter was used to determine the day number to display on the screen, as well as the index of an array element. Very often, when a **for** loop is required, the *only* use made of the loop counter is as an array index to access all the elements of the array consecutively. Java provides an enhanced version of the **for** loop especially for this purpose.

Rather than use a counter, the enhanced **for** loop consists of a variable that, upon each iteration, stores consecutive elements from the array.[2] For example, if we wished to display on the screen each value from the `temperature` array, the enhanced **for** loop could be used as follows:

```
/* the enhanced for loop iterates through elements of an
   array without the need for an array index */

for (double item : temperature) // see discussion below
{
  System.out.println(item);
}
```

---

[2] The enhanced **for** loop also works with other classes in Java, which act as alternatives to arrays. We will explore some of these classes in chapter 15.

In this case we have named each successive array element as item. The loop header is to be read as "for each item in the temperature array". For this reason the enhanced **for** loop is often referred to as the *for each* loop. Notice that the type of the array item also has to be specified. The type of this variable is **double** as we are processing an array of **double** values. Remember that this is the type of each *individual* element within the array.

You should note that the variable item can be used only within the loop, we cannot make reference to it outside the loop. Within the body of the loop we can now print out an array element by referring directly to the item variable rather than accessing it via an index value:

```
System.out.println(item); // 'item' is an array element
```

This is a much neater solution than using a standard **for** loop, which would require control of a loop counter in the loop header, and array look up within the body of the loop.

Be aware that the enhanced **for** loop should *not* be used if you wish to modify the array items. Modifying array items with such a loop will not cause a compiler error, but it is unsafe as it may cause your program to behave unreliably. So you should use an enhanced **for** loop only when

- you wish to access the *entire* array (and not just part of the array);
- you wish to *read* the elements in the array, not *modify* them;
- you do not require the array index for additional processing.

Very often, when processing an array, it is the case that these three conditions apply. In the following sections we will make use of this enhanced **for** loop where appropriate.

6.7 Some useful array methods

Apart from the length feature, an array does not come with any useful built-in routines. So we will develop some of our own methods for processing an array. We will use a simple integer array for this example. Here is the outline of the program we are going to write in order to do this:

```
import java.util.*;
public class SomeUsefulArrayMethods
{
  public static void main (String[] args)
  {
    Scanner keyboard = new Scanner(System.in);
    int[] someArray; // declare an integer array
    // ask user to determine size of array
    System.out.println("How many elements to store?");
    int size = keyboard.nextInt();
```

```
    // size array now
    someArray = new int[size];


    // call methods here
  }
  // methods to process an array here
}
```

As you can see, we have delayed the second stage of array creation here until the user tells us how many elements to store in the array. Now to some methods.

6.7.1 Array maximum

The first method we will develop will allow us to find the maximum value in an array. For example, we may have a list of scores and wish to know the highest score in this list. Finding the maximum value in an array is a much better approach than the one we took in chapter 5, where we looked at a method to find the maximum of two values and another method to find the maximum of three values. This array method can instead be used with lists of two, three, four or any other number of values. The approach we will use will be similar to the max method we developed in chapter 5 for finding the maximum of three values. Here is the pseudocode again.

```
SET result TO first number
IF second number > result
BEGIN
  SET result TO second number
END
IF third number > result
BEGIN
  SET result TO third number
END
RETURN result
```

Here, the final result is initialized to the first value. All other values are then compared with this value to determine the largest value. Now that we have an array, we can use a loop to process this comparison, rather than have a series of many **if** statements. Here is a suitable algorithm:

```
SET result TO first value in array
LOOP FROM second element in array TO last element in array
BEGIN
  IF current element > result
  BEGIN
    SET result TO current element
  END
END
RETURN result
```

This method will need the array that it has to search to be sent in as a parameter. Also, this method will return the maximum item so it must have an integer return type.

```java
static int max (int[] arrayIn)
{
  int result = arrayIn[0]; // set result to the first value in the array
  // this loops runs from the 2nd item to the last item in the array
  for (int i=1; i < arrayIn.length; i++)
  {
    if (arrayIn[i] > result)
    {
      result = arrayIn[i]; // reset result to new maximum
    }
  }
  return result;
}
```

Notice we did not use the enhanced **for** loop here, as we needed to iterate from the *second* item in the array rather than through *all* items, and the standard **for** loop gives us this additional control.

6.7.2 Array summation

The next method we will develop will be a method that calculates the total of all the values in the array. Such a method might be useful, for example, if we had a list of deposits made into a bank account and wished to know the total value of these deposits. A simple way to calculate the sum is to keep a running total and add the value of each array element to that running total. Whenever you have a running total it is important to initialize this value to zero. We can express this algorithm using pseudocode as follows:

```
SET total TO zero
LOOP FROM first element in array TO last element in array
BEGIN
  SET total TO total + value of current element
END
RETURN total
```

This method will again need the array to be sent in as a parameter, and will return an integer (the value of the sum), giving us the following:

```
static int sum (int[] arrayIn)
{
  int total = 0;
  for (int currentElement : arrayIn)
  {
    total = total + currentElement;
  }
  return total;
}
```

Notice the use of the enhanced **for** loop here – as we need to iterate through *all* elements within the array.

6.7.3 Array membership

It is often useful to determine whether or not an array contains a particular value. For example, if the list were meant to store a collection of unique student ID numbers, this method could be used to check if a new ID number already exists before adding it to the list. A simple technique is to check each item in the list one by one, using a loop, to see if the given value is present. If the value is found the loop is exited. If the loop reaches the end without exiting then we know the item is not present. Here is the pseudocode:

```
LOOP FROM first element in array TO last element in array
BEGIN
  IF current element = item to find
  BEGIN
    EXIT loop and RETURN true
  END
END
RETURN false
```

Notice in the algorithm above that a value of **false** would be returned only if the given item is not found. If the value is found, the loop would terminate without reaching its end and a value of **true** would be returned.

Here is the Java code for this method. We need to ensure that this method receives the array to search and the item being searched for. Also the method must return a **boolean** value:

```
static boolean contains (int[] arrayIn, int valueIn)
{
  // enhanced 'for' loop used here
  for (int currentElement : arrayIn)
  {
    if (currentElement == valueIn)
```

```
   {
     return true; // exit loop early if value found
   }
 }
 return false; // value not present
}
```

6.7.4 Array search

One of the most common tasks relating to a list of values is to determine the position of an item within the list. For example, we may wish to know the position of a job waiting in a printer queue.

How will we go about doing this?

Just as we did when devising the contains algorithm, we will need to use a loop to examine every item in the array. Inside the loop we check each item one at a time and compare it to the item we are searching for.

What do we do if we find the item we are searching for? Well, we are interested in its position in the array so we just return the index of that item.

Now we need to decide what we do if we reach the end of the loop, having checked all the elements in the array, without finding the item we are searching for. This method needs to return an integer regardless of whether or not we find an item. What number shall we send back if the item is not found? We need to send back a value that could never be interpreted as an array index. Since array indexes will always be positive numbers we could send back a negative number, such as −999, to indicate a valid position has not been found.

Here is the pseudocode:

```
LOOP FROM first element in array TO last element in array
BEGIN
  IF current element = item to find
  BEGIN
    EXIT loop and RETURN current index
  END
END
RETURN -999
```

This approach is often referred to as a *linear search*. Here is the Java code for this method. Once again we need to ensure that this method receives the array to search and the item being searched for. This method must return an integer value:

```
static int search (int[] arrayIn, int valueIn)
{
  // enhanced 'for' loop should not be used here!
  for (int i=0; i < arrayIn.length; i++)
```

```
  {
    if (arrayIn[i] == valueIn)
    {
      return i; // exit loop with array index
    }
  }
  return -999; // indicates value not in list
}
```

Notice, in this case, we could not use the enhanced **for** loop. The reason for this is that we required the method to return the array index of the item we are searching for. This index is best arrived at by making use of a loop counter in a standard **for** loop.

6.7.5 The final program

The complete program for manipulating an array is now presented below. The array methods are accessed via a menu. We have included some additional methods here for entering and displaying an array:

PROGRAM 6.4

```
import java.util.*;

// a menu driven program to test a selection of useful array methods

public class SomeUsefulArrayMethods
{
  public static void main (String[] args)
  {
    char choice;
    Scanner keyboard = new Scanner(System.in);
    int[] someArray; // declare an integer array
    System.out.print("How many elements to store?: ");
    int size = keyboard.nextInt();
    // size the array
    someArray = new int [size];
    // menu
    do
    {
      System.out.println();
      System.out.println("[1] Enter values");
      System.out.println("[2] Find maximum");
      System.out.println("[3] Calculate sum");
```

```java
        System.out.println("[4] Check membership");
        System.out.println("[5] Search array");
        System.out.println("[6] Display values");
        System.out.println("[7] Exit");
        System.out.print("Enter choice [1-7]: ");
        choice = keyboard.next().charAt(0);
        System.out.println();
        // process choice by calling additional methods
        switch(choice)
        {
          case '1': fillArray(someArray);
                    break;
          case '2': int max = max(someArray);
                    System.out.println("Maximum array value = " + max); break;
          case '3': int total = sum(someArray);
                    System.out.println("Sum of array values = " + total); break;
          case '4': System.out.print ("Enter value to find: ");
                    int value = keyboard.nextInt();
                    boolean found = contains(someArray, value);
                    if (found)
                    {
                      System.out.println(value + " is in the array");
                    }
                    else
                    {
                      System.out.println(value + " is not in the array");
                    }
                    break;
          case '5': System.out.print ("Enter value to find: ");
                    int item = keyboard.nextInt();
                    int index = search(someArray, item);
                    if (index == -999) // indicates value not found
                    {
                      System.out.println ("This value is not in the array");
                    }
                    else
                    {
                      System.out.println ("This value is at array index " + index);
                    }
                    break;
          case '6': System.out.println("Array values");
                    displayArray(someArray);
                    break;
        }
```

```
    } while (choice != '7');

  System.out.println("Goodbye");
}


// additional methods

// fills an array with values
static void fillArray(int[] arrayIn)
{
  Scanner keyboard = new Scanner (System.in);
  for (int i = 0; i < arrayIn.length; i++)
  {
    System.out.print("enter value ");
    arrayIn[i] = keyboard.nextInt();
  }
}


// returns the total of all the values held within an array
static int sum (int[] arrayIn)
{
  int total = 0;
  for (int currentElement : arrayIn)
  {
    total = total + currentElement;
  }
  return total;
}


// returns the maximum value in an array
static int max (int[] arrayIn)
{
  int result = arrayIn[0]; // set result to the first value in the array
  // this loops runs from the 2nd item to the last item in the array
  for (int i=1; i < arrayIn.length; i++)
  {
    if (arrayIn[i] > result)
    {
      result = arrayIn[i]; // reset result to new maximum
    }
  }
```

```
  return result;
}


// checks if a given item is contained within the array
static boolean contains (int[] arrayIn, int valueIn)
{
  // enhanced 'for' loop used here
  for (int currentElement : arrayIn)
  {
    if (currentElement == valueIn)
    {
      return true; // exit loop early if value found
    }
  }
  return false; // value not present
}


/* returns the position of an item within an array or -999 if the value is not present
   within the array */
static int search (int[] arrayIn, int valueIn)
{
  for (int i = 0; i < arrayIn.length; i++)
  {
    if (arrayIn[i] == valueIn)
    {
      return i;
    }
  }
  return -999;
}


// displays the array values on the screen
static void displayArray(int[] arrayIn)
{
  System.out.println();
  // standard 'for' loop used here as the array index is required
  for (int i = 0; i < arrayIn.length; i++)
  {
    System.out.println("array[" + i + "] = " + arrayIn[i]);
  }
}
}
```

Here is a sample program run:

```
How many elements to store?: 5

[1] Enter values
[2] Find maximum
[3] Calculate sum
[4] Check membership
[5] Search array
[6] Display values
[7] Exit
Enter choice [1-7]: 1

enter value 12
enter value 3
enter value 7
enter value 6
enter value 2

[1] Enter values
[2] Find maximum
[3] Calculate sum
[4] Check membership
[5] Search array
[6] Display values
[7] Exit
Enter choice [1-7]: 2

Maximum array value = 12

[1] Enter values
[2] Find maximum
[3] Calculate sum
[4] Check membership
[5] Search array
[6] Display values
[7] Exit
Enter choice [1-7]: 3

Sum of array values = 30

[1] Enter values
[2] Find maximum
[3] Calculate sum
[4] Check membership
```

```
[5] Search array
[6] Display values
[7] Exit Enter choice [1-7]: 4

Enter value to find: 10

10 is not in the array

[1] Enter values
[2] Find maximum
[3] Calculate sum
[4] Check membership
[5] Search array
[6] Display values
[7] Exit
Enter choice [1-7]: 4

Enter value to find: 7

7 is in the array

[1] Enter values
[2] Find maximum
[3] Calculate sum
[4] Check membership
[5] Search array
[6] Display values
[7] Exit
Enter choice [1-7]: 5

Enter value to find: 7
This value is at array index 2

[1] Enter values
[2] Find maximum
[3] Calculate sum
[4] Check membership
[5] Search array
[6] Display values
[7] Exit
Enter choice [1-7]: 6

Array values

array[0] = 12
array[1] = 3
```

```
array[2] = 7
array[3] = 6
array[4] = 2

[1]  Enter values
[2]  Find maximum
[3]  Calculate sum
[4]  Check membership
[5]  Search array
[6]  Display values
[7]  Exit
Enter choice [1-7]: 7


Goodbye
```

6.8 Multi-dimensional arrays

In the temperature reading example we used at the beginning of this chapter we used an array to hold seven temperature readings (one for each day of the week). Creating an array allowed us to use loops when processing these values, rather than having to repeat the same bit of code seven times – once for each different temperature variable.

Now consider the situation where temperatures were required for the four weeks of a month. We could create four arrays as follows:

```
double[] temperature1 = new double [7]; // to hold week 1 temperatures
double[] temperature2 = new double [7]; // to hold week 2 temperatures
double[] temperature3 = new double [7]; // to hold week 3 temperatures
double[] temperature4 = new double [7]; // to hold week 4 temperatures
```

How would the temperatures for these four months be entered? The obvious solution would be to write four loops, one to process each array. Luckily there is a simpler approach – create a **multi-dimensional** array.

A multi-dimensional array is an array that has *more than one* index. So far, the arrays that we have shown you have had only one index – for this reason they are very often referred to as **one-dimensional** arrays. However, an array may have as many indexes as is necessary (up to the limit of the memory on your machine). In this particular example we need *two* indexes to access a temperature reading (one for the week number, the other for the day number). If we required temperatures for each month of the year we may require *three* indexes (one for the month number, one for the week number and one for the day number) and so on. The number of dimensions an array has corresponds to the number of indexes required. Usually, no more than two indexes will ever need to be used. An array with two indexes is called a **two-dimensional** array.

6.9 Creating a two-dimensional array

To create a two-dimensional (2D) array, simply provide the size of both indexes. In this example we have four lots of seven temperatures:

```
double [][] temperature ; // declares a 2D array
temperature = new double [4][7]; // creates memory for a 4 by 7 array
```

As you can see, this is very similar to creating a one-dimensional array except that we have *two* pairs of brackets for a two-dimensional array. For larger dimensions we can have more pairs of brackets, 3 pairs for 3 dimensions, 4 for 4 dimensions and so on. In this example we have chosen to treat the first index as representing the number of weeks (4) and the second representing the number of days (7), but we could have chosen to treat the first index as the number of days and the second as the number of weeks.

While you would think of a one-dimensional array as a list, you would probably visualize a two-dimensional array as a table with rows and columns (although actually it is implemented in Java as an array of arrays). The name of each item in a two-dimensional array is the array name, plus the row and column index (see figure 6.5).

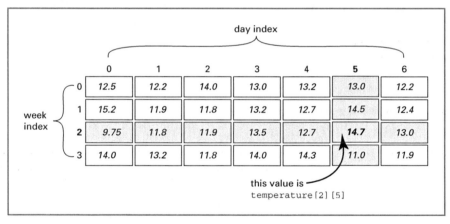

FIGURE 6.5 To access an element in a 2D array requires both a row and a column index

Note again that both indexes begin at zero, so that the temperature for the *third* week of the month and the *sixth* day of the week is actually given as `temperature[2][5]`.

6.10 Initializing two-dimensional arrays

As with one-dimensional arrays, it is possible to declare and initialize a multi-dimensional array with a collection of values all in one instruction. With a one-dimensional array we separated these values by commas and enclosed these values in braces. For example:

```
// this array of integers is initialized with four values
int[] a1DArray = { 11, -25, 4, 77};
```

This creates an array of size 4 with the given elements stored in the given order. A similar technique can be used for multi-dimensional arrays. With a two-dimensional array the sets of values in each row are surrounded with braces as above, then these row values are themselves enclosed in another pair of braces. A two-dimensional array of integers might be initialized as follows, for example:

```
// this creates a 2 dimensional array with two rows and four columns
int[][] a2DArray =    {
                         { 11, -25, 4, 77},
                         {-21, 55, 43, 11}
                      };
```

This instruction creates the same array as the following group of instructions:

```
int[][] a2DArray = new int[2][4]; // size array
// initialize first row of values
a2DArray[0][0] = 11;
a2DArray[0][1] = -25;
a2DArray[0][2] = 4;
a2DArray[0][3] = 77;
// initialize second row of values
a2DArray[1][0] = -21;
a2DArray[1][1] = 55;
a2DArray[1][2] = 43;
a2DArray[1][3] = 11;
```

As with one-dimensional arrays, however, it is not common to initialize two-dimensional arrays in this way. Instead, once an array has been created, values are added individually to the array once the program is running.

6.11 Processing two-dimensional arrays

With the one-dimensional arrays that we have met we have used a single **for** loop to control the value of the single array index. How would you process a two-dimensional array that requires two indexes?

With a two-dimensional array, a *pair* of nested loops are commonly used to process each element – one loop for each array index. Let's return to the two-dimensional array of temperature values. We can use a pair of nested loops, one to control the week number and the other the day number. As with the example of the one-dimensional array of programs 6.1–6.3, in the following code fragment we've started our day and week counters at 1, and then taken 1 off these counters to get back to the appropriate array index:

```
// create Scanner object for user input
Scanner keyboard = new Scanner (System.in);
// the outer loop controls the week row
for (int week = 1; week <= temperature.length; week++)
{
  // the inner loop controls the day column
  for (int day = 1; day <= temperature[0].length; day++)
  {
    System.out.println("enter temperature for week " + week + " and day " + day);
    /* as array indices start at zero not 1, we must take one off the loop counters */
    temperature[week-1][day-1] = keyboard.nextDouble();
  }
}
```

Notice that in a two-dimensional array, the `length` attribute returns the length of the *first* index (this is, what we have visualized as the number of rows):

```
// here, the length attribute returns 4 (the number of rows)
for (int week = 1; week <= temperature.length; week++)
```

The number of columns is determined by obtaining the length of a particular row. In the example below we have chosen the first row but we could have chosen any row here:

```
// the length of a row returns the number of columns (7 in this case)
for (int day = 1; day <= temperature[0].length; day++)
```

Here we have used a pair of nested loops as we wish to process the entire two-dimensional array. If, however, you just wished to process part of the array (such as one row or one column) then a single loop may still suffice. In the next section we present a program that demonstrates this.

6.12 The *MonthlyTemperatures* program

Program 6.5 provides the user with a menu of options. The first option allows the user to enter the temperature readings for the 4 weeks of the month. The second option allows the user to display *all* these readings. The third option allows the user to display the reading for a particular week (for example, all the temperatures for week 3). The final option allows the user to display the temperatures for a particular day of the week (for example, all the readings for the first day of each week). Take a look at it and then we will discuss it.

PROGRAM 6.5

```java
import java.util.*;

public class MonthlyTemperatures
{
  public static void main(String[] args)
  {
    Scanner keyboard = new Scanner (System.in);
    char choice;
    double[][] temperature = new double[4][7]; // create 2D array
    // offer menu
    do
    {
      System.out.println();
      System.out.println("[1] Enter temperatures");
      System.out.println("[2] Display all");
      System.out.println("[3] Display one week");
      System.out.println("[4] Display day of the week");
      System.out.println("[5] Exit");
      System.out.print("Enter choice [1-5]: ");
      choice = keyboard.next().charAt(0);
      System.out.println();
      // process choice by calling additional methods
      switch(choice)
      {
        case '1': enterTemps(temperature);
                break;
        case '2': displayAllTemps(temperature);
                break;
        case '3': displayWeek(temperature);
                break;
        case '4': displayDays(temperature);
                break;
        case '5': System.out.println ("Goodbye");
                break;
        default: System.out.println("ERROR: options 1-5 only!");
      }
    } while (choice != '5');
  }

  // method to enter temperatures into the 2D array requires a nested loop
```

```
static void enterTemps(double[][] temperatureIn)
{
  Scanner keyboard = new Scanner (System.in);
  // the outer loop controls the week number
  for (int week = 1; week <= temperatureIn.length; week++)
  {
    // the inner loop controls the day number
    for (int day = 1; day <= temperatureIn[0].length; day++)
    {
      System.out.println("enter temperature for week " + week + " and day " + day);
      temperatureIn[week-1][day-1] = keyboard.nextDouble();
    }
  }
}


// method to display all temperatures in the 2D array requires a nested loop
static void displayAllTemps(double[][] temperatureIn)
{
  System.out.println();

  System.out.println("***TEMPERATURES ENTERED***");
  // the outer loop controls the week number
  for (int week = 1; week <= temperatureIn.length; week++)
  {
    // the inner loop controls the day number
    for (int day = 1; day <= temperatureIn[0].length; day++)
    {
      System.out.println("week " +week+" day "+day+": "+ temperatureIn[week-1][day-1]);
    }
  }
}


// method to display temperatures for a single week requires a single loop
static void displayWeek(double[][] temperatureIn)
{
  Scanner keyboard = new Scanner (System.in);
  int week;
  // enter week number
  System.out.print("Enter week number (1-4): ");
  week = keyboard.nextInt();
  // input validation: week number should be between 1 and 4
  while (week<1 || week > 4)
  {
```

```
     System.out.println("Invalid week number!!");
     System.out.print("Enter again (1-4 only): ");
     week = keyboard.nextInt();
   }
   // display temperatures for given week
   System.out.println();
   System.out.println("***TEMPERATURES ENTERED FOR WEEK "+week+"***");
   System.out.println();
   // week number is fixed so loop required to process day numbers only
   for (int day = 1; day <= temperatureIn[0].length; day++)
   {
     System.out.println("week "+week+" day "+day+": "+ temperatureIn[week-1][day-1]);
   }
 }


// method to display temperatures for a single day of each week requires a single loop
static void displayDays(double[][] temperatureIn)
{
  Scanner keyboard = new Scanner (System.in);
  int day;
  // enter day number
  System.out.print("Enter day number (1-7): ");
  day = keyboard.nextInt();
  // input validation: day number should be between 1 and 7
  while (day<1 || day > 7)
  {
    System.out.println("Invalid day number!!");
    System.out.print("Enter again (1-7 only): ");
    day = keyboard.nextInt();
  }
  // display temperatures for given day of the week
  System.out.println();
  System.out.println("***TEMPERATURES ENTERED FOR DAY "+day+"***");
  System.out.println();
  // day number is fixed so loop required to process week numbers only
  for (int week = 1; week <= temperatureIn.length; week++)
  {
    System.out.println("week "+week+" day "+day+": " + temperatureIn[week-1][day-1]);
  }
 }
}
```

Here you can see that the first menu option contains the code we have just discussed for entering values into a two-dimensional array. Notice how you pass a two-dimensional array to a method. As with a one-dimensional array you do not refer to the size of the array, just its dimensions:

```java
/* As with a standard 1D array, to pass a 2D array to a method the number of dimensions
   needs to be indicated but not the size of these dimensions */
static void enterTemps(double[][] temperatureIn)
{
  // code for entering temperatures goes here
}
```

This method uses a pair of nested loops as we wish to process the entire two-dimensional array. Similarly, when we wish to display the entire array we use a pair of nested loops to control the week and day number:

```java
// method to display all temperatures in the 2D array requires a nested loop
static void displayAllTemps(double[][] temperatureIn)
{
  System.out.println();
  System.out.println("***TEMPERATURES ENTERED***");
  // the outer loop controls the week number
  for (int week = 1; week <= temperatureIn.length; week++)
  {
    // the inner loop controls the day number
    for (int day = 1; day <= temperatureIn[0].length; day++)
    {
      System.out.println("week " +week+" day "+day+": "+ temperatureIn[week-1][day-1]);
    }
  }
}
```

However, when we need to display just one of the dimensions of an array we do not need to use a pair of loops. For example, the `displayWeek` method, which allows the user to pick a particular week number so that just the temperatures for that week alone are displayed, just requires a *single* loop to move through the day numbers, as the week number is fixed by the user:

```java
// method to display temperatures for a single week requires a single loop
static void displayWeek(double[][] temperatureIn)
{
  Scanner keyboard = new Scanner(System.in);
  int week;
  // enter week number
```

```
       System.out.print("Enter week number (1-4): ");
       week = keyboard.nextInt();
       // input validation: week number should be between 1 and 4
       while (week<1 || week > 4)
       {
         System.out.println("Invalid week number!!");
         System.out.print("Enter again (1-4 only): ");
         week = keyboard.nextInt();
       }
       // display temperatures for given week
       System.out.println();
       System.out.println("***TEMPERATURES ENTERED FOR WEEK "+week+"***");
       System.out.println();
       // week number is fixed so loop required to process day numbers only
       for (int day = 1; day <= temperatureIn[0].length; day++)
       {
         System.out.println("week "+week+" day "+day+": "+ temperatureIn[week-1][day-1]);
       }
   }
```

First the user enters the week number:

```
System.out.print("Enter week number (1-4): ");
week = keyboard.nextInt();
```

We will use this week number to determine the value of the first index when looking up temperatures in the array, so we need to be careful that the user inputs a valid week number (1 to 4) as invalid numbers would lead to an illegal array index being generated. We have used a **while** loop here to implement this input validation:

```
// input validation: week number should be between 1 and 4
while (week<1 || week > 4)
{
  System.out.println("Invalid week number!!");
  System.out.print("Enter again (1-4 only): ");
  week = keyboard.nextInt();
}
```

Once we get past this loop we can be sure that the user has entered a valid week number. For example, assume that we have filled the 2D array with the temperatures given in figure 6.5. Now assume that the user calls the option to display one week's temperature, and chooses week 2. This is illustrated in figure 6.6.

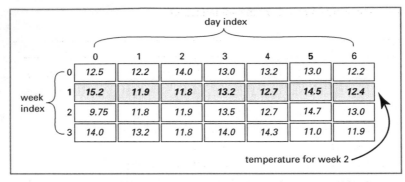

FIGURE 6.6 To access temperatures for a single week, the week index remains fixed and the day index changes

Since array indexes in Java begin at zero, the week index (1) is determined by taking one off the week number entered by the user (2). All we need to do now is to iterate through all the day numbers for that week by using a single **for** loop:

```
/* week number is fixed by the user so a single loop is required to process
    day numbers only */
for (int day = 1; day <= temperatureIn[0].length; day++)
{
  System.out.println("week "+ week +" day " + day + ": " + temperatureIn[week-1][day-1]);
}
```

The `displayDays` method works in a similar way but with the day number fixed and the week number being determined by the **for** loop.

6.13 Ragged arrays

In the examples of two-dimensional arrays discussed so far, each row of the array had the same number of columns. Each row of the two-dimensional `temperature` array, for example, had 7 columns and each row of `a2DArray` had 4 columns. Very often this will be the case. However, very occasionally, it may be necessary for rows to have a variable number of columns. A two-dimensional array with a variable number of columns is called a **ragged array**. For example, here is how we might declare and initialize a two-dimensional array of characters with a variable number of columns for each row:

```
// this creates a 2 dimensional array with a variable number of columns
char[][] animals = new char[][]
  {
    {'M', 'O', 'N', 'K', 'E', 'Y'}, // 6 columns
    {'C', 'A', 'T' }, // 3 columns
    {'B', 'I', 'R', 'D'} // 4 columns
  };
```

Figure 6.7 illustrates the array created after this initialization.

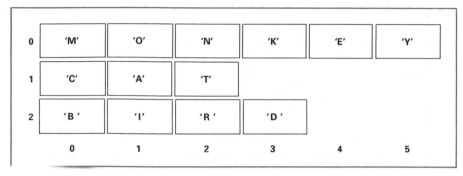

FIGURE 6.7 The array 'animals' is a *ragged array*

To declare such an array without initialization, we need to specify the number of rows first and leave the number of columns unspecified. In the example above we have 3 rows:

```
// columns left unspecified
char[][] animals = new char[3][];
```

Now, for each row we can fix the appropriate size of the associated column. In the example above the first row has 6 columns, the second row 3 columns and the last row 4 columns:

```
animals[0] = new char[6]; // number of columns in first row
animals[1] = new char[3]; // number of columns in second row
animals[2] = new char[4]; // number of columns in third row
```

You can see clearly from these instructions that Java implements a two-dimensional array as an array of arrays. When processing ragged arrays you must be careful not to use a fixed number to control the number of columns. The actual number of columns can always be retrieved by calling the `length` attribute of each row. For example, the following instructions would display the number of columns for each row:

```
System.out.println(animals[0].length); // displays 6
System.out.println(animals[1].length); // displays 3
System.out.println(animals[2].length); // displays 4
```

Program 6.6 uses a pair of nested loops to display the `animals` array:

PROGRAM 6.6

```java
public class RaggedArrays
{
  public static void main(String[] args)
  {
    // initialize ragged array
    char[][] animals = new char[][]
      {
        {'M', 'O', 'N', 'K', 'E', 'Y'}, // 6 columns
        {'C', 'A', 'T' }, // 3 columns
        {'B', 'I', 'R', 'D'} // 4 columns
      };

    for (int row = 0; row < animals.length; row++) //row number is fixed
    {
      for (int col = 0; col < animals[row].length; col++) // column number is variable
      {
        System.out.print(animals[row][col]); // display one character
      }
      System.out.println(); // new line after one row displayed
    }
  }
}
```

Notice how the inner loop, controlling the column number, instead of being fixed the length of one particular row, will vary each item depending upon the *current* row number:

```java
for (int row = 0; row < animals.length; row++)
{
  // column number is variable and is determined by current row number
  for (int col = 0; col < animals[row].length; col++)
  {
    System.out.print(animals[row][col]);
  }
  System.out.println();
}
```

As expected, program 6.6 produces the following output when run:

```
MONKEY
CAT
BIRD
```

Self-test questions

1 When is it appropriate to use an *array* in a program?

2 Consider the following explicit creation of an array:

```
int[] someArray = {2,5,1,9,11};
```

   a What would be the value of `someArray.length`?

   b What is the value of `someArray[2]`?

   c What would happen if you tried to access `someArray[6]`?

   d Create the equivalent array by using the **new** operator and then assigning the value of each element individually.

   e Write a standard **for** loop that will double the value of every item in `someArray`.

   f Explain why, in this example, it would not be appropriate to use an enhanced **for** loop.

   g Use an enhanced **for** loop to display the values inside the array.

   h Modify the enhanced **for** loop above so that only numbers greater than 2 are displayed.

3 Look back at program 6.3, which read in and displayed a series of temperature readings. Design and write the code for an additional method, `wasHot`, which displays all days that recorded temperatures of 18 degrees or over.

4 Assume that an array has been declared in `main` as follows:

```
int[] javaStudents;
```

This array is to be used to store a list of student exam marks. Now, for each of the following methods, write the code for the given method and the instruction in `main` to call this method:

   a A method, `enterExamMarks`, that prompts the user to enter some exam marks (as integers), stores the marks in an array and then returns this array.

   b A method, `increaseMarks`, that accepts an array of exam marks and increases each mark by 5.

   c A method, `allHavePassed`, that accepts an array of exam marks and returns **true** if all marks are greater than or equal to 40, and **false** otherwise.

5 Consider the following array declaration, to store a collection of student grades.

```
char [][] grades = new char[4][20];
```

Grades are recorded for 4 tutorial groups, and each tutorial group consists of 20 students.

   a How many dimensions does this array have?

   b What is the value of `grades.length`?

c What is the value of `grades[0].length`?

d Write the instruction to record the grade 'B' for the first student in the first tutorial group.

6 Consider the following scenarios and, for each, declare the appropriate array:

a `goals`: an array to hold the number of goals each team in a league scores in each game of a season. The league consist of 20 teams and a season consists of 38 games.

b `seats`: an array to record whether or not a seat in a theatre is booked or not. There are 70 rows of seats in the theatre and each row has 20 seats.

7 Consider the `MonthlyTemperatures` program of section 6.12. Write an additional method, `max`, that returns the maximum temperature recorded in the given two-dimensional array.

Hint: look back at the algorithm for finding the maximum temperature in a one-dimensional array in section 6.7.1

8 Consider an application that records the punctuality of trains on a certain route.

a Declare a 2D array, `late`, to hold the number of times a train on this route was late for each day of the week, and for each week of the year.

b Write a fragment of code that adds up the total number of days in the year when a train was late more than twice in a given day.

9 A **magic word square** is a square where a word can be formed from reading each row and each column. For example, the following is a 4 by 4 magic word square:

'P'	'R'	'E'	'Y'
'L'	'A'	'V'	'A'
'O'	'V'	'E'	'R'
'T'	'E'	'N'	'D'

a Declare and initialize a 2D array, `magicSquare`, to hold the words illustrated above.

b Write a method, `displayRow`, that accepts the `magicSquare` array and a row number and displays the word in that row.

c Write a method, `displayColumn`, that accepts the `magicSquare` array and a column number and displays the word in that column.

10 a Distinguish between a regular 2D array and a ragged array.

b Write instructions to create a ragged 2D array of integers, called `triangle`, that has the following form:

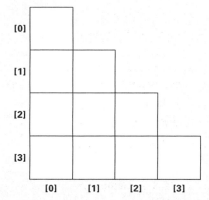

c Write a fragment of code to find the largest number in the `triangle` array.

Programming exercises

1 Copy from the CD program 6.3 (`TemperatureReadings3`), which read in and displayed a series of temperature readings for a given week. Now

a implement the `wasHot` method that you designed in self-test question 3 above;

b add a final instruction into the `main` method that calls this `wasHot` method.

2 Copy from the CD program 6.4 (`SomeUsefulArrayMethods`), which manipulates an array of integers, then add additional methods to the program in order to

a return the average from the array of integers (make use of the `sum` method to help you calculate the average);

b display on the screen all those values greater than or equal to the average.

3 Implement a program for entering and displaying student scores that tests your answers to self-test question 4 above.

4 Copy from the CD program 6.5 (`MonthlyReadings`), which read in and displayed temperature readings for four weeks of a month. Now

a implement the `max` method that you designed in self-test question 7 above;

b add a final instruction into the `main` method that calls this `max` method.

5 Design and implement a magic word square program that allows you to test your answers to self-test question 9 above. The program should initialize the word square given in the question and then use the methods `displayRow` and `displayColumn` to display all the words in the magic word square.

6   Design and implement a program that allows the user to enter into an array the price of 5 products in pounds sterling. The program should then copy this array into another array but convert the price of each product from pounds sterling to US dollars. The program should allow the user to enter the exchange rate of pounds to dollars, and should, when it terminates, display the contents of both arrays. Once again, make use of methods in your program to carry out these tasks.

7   Amend the program in exercise 6 above so that

   a   the user is asked how many items they wish to purchase and the arrays are then sized accordingly;

   b   the total cost of the order is displayed in both currencies.

8   Design and implement a program that allows you to test your answers to self-test question 10 above. The program should allow the user to enter numbers into the ragged `triangle` array and then find the largest number in the array as discussed in the question.

CHAPTER 07

Classes and objects

❖ **OBJECTIVES**

By the end of this chapter you should be able to:

- ❖ explain the meaning of the term **object-oriented**;
- ❖ explain and distinguish between the terms **class** and **object**;
- ❖ create objects in Java;
- ❖ call the methods of an object;
- ❖ use a number of methods of the `String` class;
- ❖ create and use arrays of objects.

7.1 Introduction

In the 1990s it became the norm for the programming languages to use special constructs called **classes** and **objects**. Such languages are referred to as **object-oriented programming languages**. In this chapter and the next one we will explain what is meant by these terms, and show you how we can exploit the full power of object-oriented languages like Java.

7.2 Classes as data types

So far you have been using data types such as **char**, **int** and **double**. These are simple data types that hold a *single* piece of information. But what if we want a variable to hold more than one related piece of information? Think for example of a book – a book might have a title, an author, an ISBN number and a price – or a student might have a name, an enrolment number and marks for various subjects. Types such as **char** and **int** can hold a single piece of information only, and would therefore be completely inadequate for holding all the necessary information about a book or a student. An array would also not do because the different bits of data will not necessarily be all of the same type. Earlier languages such as C and Pascal got around this problem by allowing us to create a type that allowed more than one piece of information to be held – such types were known by various names in different languages, the most common being *structure* and *record*.

Object-oriented languages such as Java and C++ went one stage further, however. They enabled us not only to create types that stored many pieces of data, but also to define within these types the methods by which we could process that data. For example a book type might have a method that adds tax to the sale price; a student type might have a method to calculate an average mark.

Do you remember that in the exercises at the end of chapter 2 you wrote a little program that asked the user to provide the length and height of a rectangle, and then displayed the area and perimeter of that rectangle? In chapter 5 you were asked to adapt this program so that it made use of separate methods to perform the calculations. Such a program might look like this:

PROGRAM 7.1

```java
import java.util.*;

public class RectangleCalculations
{
  public static void main(String[] args)
  {
    double length, height, area, perimeter;
    Scanner keyboard = new Scanner(System.in);
    System.out.print("What is the length of the rectangle? "); // prompt for length
    length = keyboard.nextDouble(); // get length from user
    System.out.print("What is the height of the rectangle? "); // prompt for height
    height = keyboard.nextDouble(); // get height from user
    area = calculateArea(length, height); // call calculateArea method
    perimeter = calculatePerimeter(length, height); // call calculatePerimeter method
    System.out.println("The area of the rectangle is " + area); // display area
    System.out.println("The perimeter of the rectangle is " + perimeter); // display perimeter
  }

  // method to calculate area
  static double calculateArea(double lengthIn, double heightIn)
  {
    return lengthIn * heightIn;
  }

  // method to calculate perimeter
  static double calculatePerimeter(double lengthIn, double heightIn)
  {
    return 2 * (lengthIn + heightIn);
  }
}
```

Can you see how useful it might be if, each time we wrote a program dealing with rectangles, instead of having to declare several variables and write methods to calculate the area and perimeter of a rectangle, we could just use a rectangle type to create a single variable, and then use its pre-written methods? In fact you wouldn't even have to know how these calculations were performed.

This is exactly what an object-oriented language like Java allows us to do. You have probably guessed by now that this special construct that holds both data and methods is called a **class**. You have already seen a class as the basic unit which contains our `main` method and any other additional methods. Now we can also use classes to define new types such as `Rectangle`.

You can see that there are two aspects to a class:

- the data that it holds;
- the tasks it can perform.

In the next chapter you will see that the different items of data that a class holds are referred to as the **attributes** of the class; the tasks it can perform, as we have seen, are referred to as the **methods** of the class – you have seen in chapter 5 how we define methods. However, in chapter 5, the methods were called only from *within* the class itself. Now we are going to see how to call the methods of *another* class. In fact you have already been doing this without quite realizing it – because you have, since the second chapter, been calling the methods of the `Scanner` class!

7.3 Objects

In order to use the methods of a class you need to create an **object** of that class. To understand the difference between classes and objects, you can think of a class as a blueprint, or template, from which objects are generated, whereas an object refers to an individual *instance* of that class. For example, imagine a system that is used by a bookshop. The shop will contain many hundreds of books – but we do not need to define a book hundreds of times. We would define a book once (in a class) and then generate as many objects as we want from this blueprint, each one representing an individual book.

This is illustrated in figure 7.1.

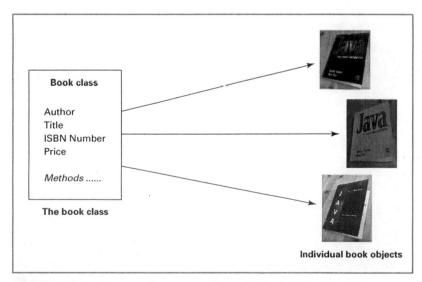

FIGURE 7.1 Many objects can be generated from a single class template

In one program we may have many classes, as we would probably wish to generate many kinds of objects. A bookshop system might have books, customers, suppliers and so on. A university administration system might have students, courses, lecturers etc.

Object-oriented programming therefore consists of defining one or more classes that may interact with each other.

We will now illustrate all of this by creating and using objects of pre-defined classes – defined either by ourselves or defined by the Java developers and provided as a standard part of the Java Development Kit. We are going to start with one of the examples we have just been discussing – the `Rectangle` class.

7.4 The *Rectangle* class

We have written a `Rectangle` class for you.[1] The class we have created is saved in a file called `Rectangle.java`. and you will need to copy this from the CD in order to use it. You must make sure that it is in the right place for your compiler to find it. You will need to place it in your project according to the rules of the particular IDE you are using.[2]

In the next chapter we will look inside this class and see how it was written. For now, however, you can completely ignore the program code, because you can use a class without knowing anything about the details.

Once you have been provided with this `Rectangle` class, instead of being restricted to making simple declarations like this:

```
int x;
```

you will now be able to make declarations like:

```
Rectangle myRectangle;
```

You can see that this line is similar to a declaration of a variable; however, what we are doing here is not declaring a variable of a primitive type such as **int**, but declaring the name of an *object* (`myRectangle`) of the *class* (`Rectangle`) – effectively we have created a new type, `Rectangle`.

You need to be sure that you understand what this line actually does; all it does in fact is to create a variable that holds a **reference** to an object, rather than the object itself. As explained in the previous chapter, a reference is simply a *name* for a location in memory. At this stage we have *not* reserved space for our new `Rectangle` object; all we have done is named a memory location `myRectangle`, as shown in figure 7.2.

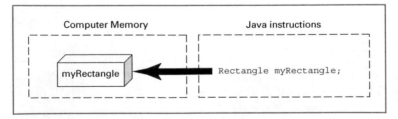

FIGURE 7.2 Declaring an object reference

---

[1] You should note that there is in fact already a class called `Rectangle` in the "built-in" Java libraries. However, as we explain in chapter 20, this is not a problem, as there are ways to avoid naming conflicts and to distinguish between different classes with the same name.

[2] If you are using the IDE supplied on the CD there are clear instructions about how to add files to your project.

Now, of course, you will be asking the question "How is memory for the `Rectangle` object going to be created, and how is it going to be linked to the reference `myRectangle`?".

As we have indicated, an object is often referred to as an *instance* of a class; the process of creating an object is referred to as **instantiation**. In order to create an object we use a very special method of the class called a **constructor**.

The constructor is a method that *always has the same name as the class*. When you create a new object this special method is always called; its function is to reserve some space in the computer's memory just big enough to hold the required object (in our case an object of the `Rectangle` class).

As we shall see in the next chapter, a constructor can be defined to do other things, as well as reserve memory. In the case of our `Rectangle` class, the constructor has been defined so that every time a new `Rectangle` object is created, the length and the height are set – and they are set to the values that the user of the class sends in. So every time you create a `Rectangle` object you have to specify its length and its height at the same time. Here, for example, is how you would call the constructor and create a rectangle with length 7.5 and height 12.5:

```
myRectangle = new Rectangle(7.5, 12.5);
```

This is the statement that reserves space in memory for a new `Rectangle`. Using the constructor with the keyword **new** reserves memory for a new `Rectangle` object. Now, in the case of the `Rectangle` class, the people who developed it (in this case, it was us!) defined the constructor so that it requires that two items of data, both of type **double**, get sent in as parameters. Here we have sent in the numbers 7.5 and 12.5. The location of the new object is stored in the named location `myRectangle`. This is illustrated in figure 7.3.

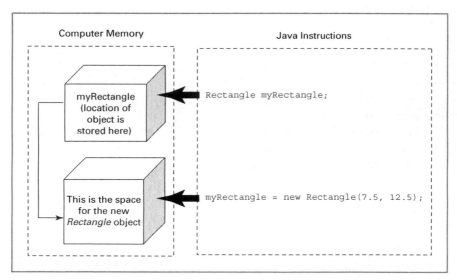

FIGURE 7.3 Creating a new object

Now every time we want to refer to our new `Rectangle` object we can use the variable name `myRectangle`.

As is the case with the declaration and initialization of simple types, Java allows us to declare a reference and create a new object all in one line:

```
Rectangle myRectangle = new Rectangle(7.5, 12.5);
```

There are all sorts of ways that we can define constructors (for example, in a BankAccount class we might want to set the overdraft limit to a particular value when the account is created) and we shall see examples of these as we go along. You have, of course, already seen another example of this, namely with the Scanner class:

```
Scanner keyboard = new Scanner(System.in);
```

You can understand now how this line creates a new Scanner object, keyboard, by calling the constructor. The parameter that we are sending in, System.in, represents a keyboard object and by using this parameter we are associating the new Scanner object with the keyboard.

You will see in the next chapter that when a class is written we make sure that no program can assign values to the attributes directly. In this way the data in the class is protected. Protecting data in this way is known as **encapsulation**. The *only way* to interact with the data is via the methods of the class.

This means that in order to use a class all we need to know are details about its methods: their names, what the methods are expected to do, and also their **inputs** and **outputs**.[3] In other words, you need to know what parameters the method requires, and its return type. Once we know this we can interact with the class by using its methods – and it is important to understand that the *only* way we can interact with a class is via its methods.

Table 7.1 lists all the methods of our Rectangle class with their inputs and outputs – including the constructor.

Method	Description	Inputs	Output
Rectangle	The constructor.	Two items of data, both of type **double**, representing the length and height of the rectangle respectively	Not applicable
setLength	Sets the value of the length of the rectangle.	An item of type **double**	None
setHeight	Sets the value of the height of the rectangle.	An item of type **double**	None
getLength	Returns the length of the rectangle.	None	An item of type **double**
getHeight	Returns the height of the rectangle.	None	An item of type **double**
calculateArea	Calculates and returns the area of the rectangle.	None	An item of type **double**
calculatePerimeter	Calculates and returns the perimeter of the rectangle.	None	An item of type **double**

TABLE 7.1 The methods of the *Rectangle* class

As far as our Rectangle class is concerned we have, as expected, provided two methods which will return values for the area and perimeter of the rectangle respectively. However, the class wouldn't be very useful if we did not have some means of giving values to the length and height of the rectangle. As you have seen, we

[3] A list of a method's inputs and outputs is often referred to as the method's **interface** – though this should not be confused with the *user interface*, the meaning of which we described in the first chapter.

do this initially via the constructor, but we might also want to be able to change these values during the course of a program. We have therefore provided methods called `setLength` and `setHeight` so that we can *write* values to the attributes. It is very likely that we will want to display these values – we have therefore provided methods to return, or *read*, the values of the attributes. These we have called `getLength` and `getHeight`.

You have used methods of the `Scanner` class on many occasions, for example:

```
x = keyboard.nextInt();
```

You can see that in order to call a method of one class from another class we use the name of the object (in this case `keyboard`) together with the name of the method (`nextInt`) separated by a full stop (often referred to as the **dot operator**).

In the case of the `Rectangle` class, we might, for example, call the `setLength` method with a statement such as:

```
myRectangle.setLength(5.0);
```

In chapter 5, when we called the methods from *within* a class, we used the name of the method on its own. In actual fact, what we were doing is form of shorthand. When we write a line such as

```
demoMethod(x);
```

we are actually saying call `demoMethod`, which is a method of *this* class. In Java there exists a special keyword **this**. The keyword **this** is used within a class when we wish to refer to an object of the class itself, rather than an object of some other class. The line of code above is actually shorthand for:

```
this.demoMethod(x);
```

You will see in chapter 10 that there are occasions when we actually have to use the **this** keyword, rather than simply allow it to be assumed.

You should be aware of the fact that, just as you cannot use a variable that has not been initialized, you cannot call a method of an object if no storage is allocated for the object; so watch out for this happening in your programs – it would cause a problem at run-time. In Java, when a reference is first created without assigning it to a new object in the same line, it is given a special value of **null**; a **null** value indicates that no storage is allocated. We can also *assign* a **null** value to a reference at any point in the program, and test for it as in the following example:

```
Rectangle myRectangle; // at this point myRectangle has a null value
myRectangle = new Rectangle(5.0, 7.5); // create a new Rectangle object with length 5.0 and height 7.5

// more code goes here
```

```
myRectangle = null; // re-assign a null value
if(myRectangle == null) // test for null value
{
  System.out.println("No storage is allocated to this object");
}
```

In the next section we will write a program that creates a `Rectangle` object and then uses the methods described in table 7.1 to interact with this object.

7.4.1 The *RectangleTester* program

Program 7.2 shows how the `Rectangle` class can be used by another class, in this case a class called `RectangleTester`. Study the program code and then we will discuss it.

PROGRAM 7.2

```
import java.util.*;

public class RectangleTester
{
  public static void main(String[] args)
  {
    Scanner keyboard = new Scanner(System.in);

    /* declare two variables to hold the length and height of the Rectangle as input
       by the user */
    double rectangleLength, rectangleHeight;

    // declare a reference to an Rectangle object
    Rectangle myRectangle;
    // now get the values from the user
    System.out.print("Please enter the length of your Rectangle: ");
    rectangleLength = keyboard.nextDouble();
    System.out.print("Please enter the height of your Rectangle: ");
    rectangleHeight = keyboard.nextDouble();

    // create a new Rectangle object
    myRectangle = new Rectangle(rectangleLength, rectangleHeight);

    /* use the various methods of the Rectangle class to display the length, height,
       area and perimeter of the Rectangle */
    System.out.println("Rectangle length is " + myRectangle.getLength());
```

```
    System.out.println("Rectangle height is " + myRectangle.getHeight());
    System.out.println("Rectangle area is " + myRectangle.calculateArea());
    System.out.println("Rectangle perimeter is " + myRectangle.calculatePerimeter());
  }
}
```

Let's analyse the `main` method line by line. After creating the new `Scanner` object, the method goes on to declare two variables:

```
double rectangleLength, rectangleHeight;
```

As you can see, these are of type **double** and they are going to be used to hold the values that the user chooses for the length and height of the rectangle.

The next line declares the `Rectangle` object:

```
Rectangle myRectangle;
```

After getting the user to enter values for the length and height of the rectangle we have this line of code:

```
myRectangle = new Rectangle(rectangleLength, rectangleHeight);
```

Here we have called the constructor and sent through the length and height as entered by the user.

Now the next line:

```
System.out.println("Rectangle Length is " + myRectangle.getLength());
```

This line displays the length of the rectangle. It uses the method of `Rectangle` called `getLength`, and, as we said in the previous section, to do this we use the dot operator to separate the name of the object and the name of the method.

The next three lines are similar:

```
System.out.println("Rectangle height is " + myRectangle.getHeight());
System.out.println("Rectangle area is " + myRectangle.calculateArea());
System.out.println("Rectangle Perimeter is "+ myRectangle.calculatePerimeter());
```

We have called the `getHeight` method, the `calculateArea` method and the `calculatePerimeter` method to display the height, area and perimeter of the rectangle on the screen.

You might have noticed that we haven't used the `setLength` and `setHeight` methods – that is because in this program we didn't wish to change the length and height once the rectangle had been created – but this is not the last you will see of our `Rectangle` class, and in future programs these methods will come in useful.

Now we can move on to look at using some other classes. The first is not one of our own, but the built-in `String` class provided with all versions of Java.

7.5 Strings

You know from chapter 1 that a string is a sequence of characters – like a name, a line of an address, a car registration number, or indeed any meaningless sequence of characters such as "h83hdu2&e£8". Java provides a `String` class that allows us to use and manipulate strings.

As we shall see in a moment, the `String` class has a number of constructors – but in fact Java actually allows us to declare a string object in the same way as we declare variables of simple type such as **int** or **char**. You should remember of course that `String` is a class, and starts with a capital letter. For example we could make the following declaration:

```
String name;
```

and we could then give this string a value:

```
name = "Quentin";
```

We could also do this in one line:

```
String name = "Quentin";
```

We should bear in mind, however, that this is actually just a convenient way of declaring a `String` object by calling its constructor, which we would do like this with exactly the same effect:

```
String name = new String("Quentin");
```

You should be aware that the `String` class is the only class that allows us to create new objects by using the assignment operator in this way.

7.5.1 Obtaining strings from the keyboard

In order to get a string from the keyboard, you should use the `next` method of `Scanner`. However, a word of warning here – when you do this you should not enter strings that include spaces, as this will give you unexpected results. We will show you in the next section a way to get round this restriction.

Program 7.3 is a little program that uses the Java `String` class. Some of you might find it amusing (although others might not!).

PROGRAM 7.3

```java
import java.util.*;

public class StringTest
{
  public static void main(String[] args)
  {
    Scanner keyboard = new Scanner(System.in);
    String name; // declaration of a String
    int age;
    System.out.print("What is your name? ");
    name = keyboard.next(); // the 'next' method is for String input
    System.out.print("What is your age? ");
    age = keyboard.nextInt();
    System.out.println();
    System.out.println("Hello " + name);
    // now comes the joke!!
    System.out.println("When I was your age I was " + age + 1));
  }
}
```

One thing to notice in this program is the way in which the + operator is used for two very different purposes. It is used with strings for concatenation – for example:

```java
"Hello" + name
```

It is also used with numbers for addition – for example:

```java
age + 1
```

Notice that we have had to enclose this expression in brackets to avoid any confusion:

```java
System.out.println("When I was your age I was "  + (age + 1));
```

Here is a sample run from program 7.3:

```
What is your name? Aaron
What is your age? 15

Hello Aaron
When I was your age I was 16
```

7.5.2 The methods of the *String* class

The String class has a number of interesting and useful methods, and we have listed some of them in table 7.2.

Method	Description	Inputs	Output
length	Returns the length of the string.	None	An item of type `int`
charAt	Accepts an integer and returns the character at that position in the string. Note that indexing starts from zero, not 1. You have been using this method in conjunction with the `next` method of the `Scanner` class to obtain single characters from the keyboard.	An item of type `int`	An item of type `char`
substring	Accepts two integers (for example `m` and `n`) and returns a copy of a chunk of the string. The chunk starts at position `m` and finishes at position `n-1`. Remember that indexing starts from zero. (Study the example below.)	Two items of type `int`	A `String` object
concat	Accepts a string and returns a new string which consists of the string that was sent in joined on to the end of the original string.	A `String` object	A `String` object
toUpperCase	Returns a copy of the original string, all upper case.	None	A `String` object
toLowerCase	Returns a copy of the original string, all lower case.	None	A `String` object
compareTo	Accepts a string (say `myString`) and compares it to the object's string. It returns zero if the strings are identical, a negative number if the object's string comes before `myString` in the alphabet, and a positive number if it comes later.	A `String` object	An item of type `int`
equals	Accepts an object (such as a `String`) and compares this to another object (such as another `String`). It returns **true** if these are identical, otherwise returns **false**.	An object of any class	A **boolean** value
equalsIgnoreCase	Accepts a string and compares this to the original string. It returns **true** if the strings are identical (ignoring case), otherwise returns **false**.	A `String` object	A **boolean** value
startsWith	Accepts a string (say `str`) and returns **true** if the original string starts with `str` and **false** if it does not (e.g. "hello world" starts with "h" or "he" or "hel" and so on).	A `String` object	A **boolean** value
endsWith	Accepts a string (say `str`) and returns **true** if the original string ends with `str` and **false** if it does not (e.g. "hello world" ends with "d" or "ld" or "rld" and so on).	A `String` object	A **boolean** value
trim	Returns a `String` object, having removed any spaces at the beginning or end.	None	A `String` object

TABLE 7.2 Some *String* methods

There are many other useful methods of the String class which you can look up. Program 7.4 provides examples of how you can use some of the methods listed above; others are left for you to experiment with in your practical sessions.

PROGRAM 7.4

```java
import java.util.*;

public class StringMethods
{
  public static void main(String[] args)
  {
    Scanner keyboard = new Scanner(System.in);
    // create a new string
    String str;
    // get the user to enter a string
    System.out.print("Enter a string: ");
    str = keyboard.next();
    // display the length of the user's string
    System.out.println("The length of the string is " + str.length());
    // display the third character of the user's string
    System.out.println("The character at position 3 is " + str.charAt(2));
    // display a selected part of the user's string
    System.out.println("Characters 2 to 4 are " + str.substring(1,4));
    // display the user's string joined with another string
    System.out.println(str.concat(" was the string entered"));
    // display the user's string in upper case
    System.out.println("This is upper case: " + str.toUpperCase());
    // display the user's string in lower case
    System.out.println("This is lower case: " + str.toLowerCase());
  }
}
```

A sample run from program 7.4:

```
Enter a string: Europe
The length of the string is 6
The character at position 3 is r
Characters 2 to 4 are uro
Europe was the string entered
This is upper case: EUROPE
This is lower case: europe
```

7.5.3 Comparing strings

When comparing two objects, such as `Strings`, we should do so by using a method called `equals`. We should *not* use the equality operator (==); this should be used for comparing primitive types only. If, for example, we had declared two strings, `firstString` and `secondString`, we would compare these in, say, an `if` statement as follows;

```
if(firstString.equals(secondString))
{

  // more code here

}
```

Using the equality operator (==) to compare strings is a very common mistake that is made by programmers. Doing this will not result in a compilation error, but it won't give you the result you expect! The reason for this is that all you are doing is finding out whether the objects occupy the same address space in memory – what you actually want to be doing is comparing the actual value of the string attributes of the objects.

The `String` class also has a very useful method called `compareTo`. As you can see from table 7.2, this method accepts a string (called `myString`, for example) and compares it to the string value of the object itself. It returns zero if the strings are identical, a negative number if the original string comes before `myString` in the alphabet, and a positive number if it comes later.

Program 7.5 provides an example of how the `compareTo` method is used.

PROGRAM 7.5

```
import java.util.*;

public class StringComparison
{
  public static void main(String[] args)
  {
    Scanner keyboard = new Scanner(System.in);
    String string1, string2;
    int comparison;
    // get two strings from the user
    System.out.print("Enter a String: ");
    string1 = keyboard.next();
    System.out.print("Enter another String: ");
    string2 = keyboard.next();

    // compare the strings
    comparison = string1.compareTo(string2);
    if(comparison < 0) // compareTo returned a negative number
```

```
      {
        System.out.println(string1 + " comes before "
                                + string2
                                + " in the alphabet");
      }
      else if(comparison > 0) // compareTo returned a positive number
      {
        System.out.println(string2 + " comes before "
                                + string1
                                + " in the alphabet");
      }
      else // compareTo returned zero
      {
        System.out.println("The strings are identical");
      }
    }
  }
}
```

Here is a sample run from the program:

```
Enter a String: hello
Enter another String: goodbye
goodbye comes before hello in the alphabet
```

You should note that `compareTo` is case-sensitive – upper-case letters will be considered as coming before lower-case letters (their Unicode value is lower). If you are not interested in the case of the letters, you should convert both strings to upper (or lower) case before comparing them.

If all you are interested in is whether the strings are identical, it is easier to use the `equals` method. If the case of the letters is not significant you can use `equalsIgnoreCase`.

7.5.4 Entering strings containing spaces

As we mentioned above, there is a problem with using the `next` method of `Scanner` when we enter strings that contain spaces. If you try this you will see that the resulting string stops at the first space, so if you enter the string "Hello world" for example, the resulting string would actually be "Hello".

To enter a string that contains spaces you need to use the method `nextLine`. Unfortunately, however, there is also an issue with this. If the `nextLine` method is used after a `nextInt` or `nextDouble` method, then it is necessary to create a separate `Scanner` object (because using the same `Scanner` object will make your program behave erratically). So, if your intention is that the user should be able to enter strings that contain spaces, the best thing to do is to declare a separate `Scanner` object for string input. This is illustrated in program 7.6.

PROGRAM 7.6

```java
import java.util.*;

public class StringExample2
{
  public static void main(String[] args)
  {
    double d;
    int i;
    String s;
    Scanner keyboardString = new Scanner(System.in); // Scanner object for string input
    Scanner keyboard = new Scanner(System.in); // Scanner object for all other types of input
    System.out.print("Enter a double: ");
    d = keyboard.nextDouble();
    System.out.print("Enter an integer: ");
    i = keyboard.nextInt();
    System.out.print("Enter a string: ");
    s = keyboardString.nextLine(); // use the Scanner object reserved for string input
    System.out.println();
    System.out.println("You entered: ");
    System.out.println("Double: " + d);
    System.out.println("Integer: " + i);
    System.out.println("String: " + s);
  }
}
```

Here is a sample run from this program:

```
Enter a double: 3.4
Enter an integer: 10
Enter a string: Hello world

You entered:
Double: 3.4
Integer: 10
String: Hello world
```

7.6 Our own *Scanner* class for keyboard input

It might have occurred to you that using the `Scanner` class to obtain keyboard input can be a bit of a bother:

- it is necessary to create a new `Scanner` object in every method that uses the `Scanner` class;
- there is no simple method such as `nextChar` for getting a single character like there is for the **int** and **double** types;
- as we have just seen, there is an issue when it comes to entering strings containing spaces.

To make life easier, we have created a new class which we have called `EasyScanner`. In the next chapter we will "look inside" it to see how it is written – in this chapter we will just show you how to use it. The methods of `EasyScanner` are described in table 7.3.

Java type	EasyScanner method
`int`	`nextInt()`
`double`	`nextDouble()`
`char`	`nextChar()`
`String`	`nextString()`

TABLE 7.3 The input methods of the *EasyScanner* class

To make life really easy we have written the class so that we don't have to create new `Scanner` objects in order to use it (that is taken care of in the class itself) – and we have written it so that you can simply use the name of the class itself when you call a method (you will see how to do this in the next chapter). Program 7.7 demonstrates how to use these methods.

PROGRAM 7.7

```java
public class EasyScannerTester
{

  public static void main(String[] args)
  {
    System.out.print("Enter a double: ");
    double d = EasyScanner.nextDouble(); // to read a double
    System.out.println("You entered: " + d);
    System.out.println();

    System.out.print("Enter an integer: ");
    int i = EasyScanner.nextInt(); // to read an int
```

```
      System.out.println("You entered: " + i);
      System.out.println();

      System.out.print("Enter a string: ");
      String s = EasyScanner.nextString(); // to read a string
      System.out.println("You entered: " + s);
      System.out.println();


      System.out.print("Enter a character: ");
      char c = EasyScanner.nextChar(); // to read a character
      System.out.println("You entered: " + c);
      System.out.println();


   }
}
```

You can see from this program how easy it is to call the methods, just by using the name of the class itself – for example:

```
double d = EasyScanner.nextDouble();
```

In the next chapter you will see how it is possible to do this. Here is a sample run:

Enter a double: **23.6**
You entered: 23.6

Enter an integer: **50**
You entered: 50

Enter a string: **Hello world**
You entered: Hello world

Enter a character: **B**
You entered: B

You are now free to use the EasyScanner class if you wish. You can copy it from the CD – as usual, make sure it is in the right place for your compiler to find it.

7.7 The *Console* class

The latest release of Java (Java 6) provides a special class called Console, which provides an alternative way to obtain strings from the keyboard. Console is provided as part of the io package, so we need to import this in order to use it.

Program 7.8 shows how the Console class can be used to obtain a string from the keyboard.

PROGRAM 7.8

```
// demonstration of the console class for keyboard input

import java.io.*; // import the io package that contains the Console class

public class FirstInput
{
  public static void main(String[] args)
  {
    Console con = System.console();
    String name; // declaration of a String
    name = con.readLine("Please enter your name: "); // allow user to enter name
    System.out.println("Hello " + name); // display a message to the user


  }
}
```

Here is a sample output from the program:

Please enter your name: **Aaron Kans**

Hello Aaron Kans

You can see from the above example that there is no problem entering a string containing spaces, so you now have another alternative for string input. If, however, you wanted to use the `Console` class for entering **doubles** or **ints**, you would have to enter a string and then convert this to the desired type. You will find out how to do this in chapter 10.

7.8 The *BankAccount* class

We have created a class called `BankAccount`, which you can copy from the CD. This could be a very useful class in the real world, for example as part of a financial control system. Once again you do not need to look at the details of how this class is coded in order to use it. You do need to know, however, that the class holds three pieces of information – the account number, the account name and the account balance. The first two of these will be `String` objects and the final one will be a variable of type **double**.

The methods are listed in table 7.4.

Method	Description	Inputs	Output
BankAccount	A constructor. It accepts two strings and assigns them to the account number and account name respectively. It also sets the account balance to zero.	Two `String` objects	Not applicable
getAccountNumber	Returns the account number.	None	An item of type `String`
getAccountName	Returns the account name.	None	An item of type `String`
getBalance	Returns the balance.	None	An item of type `double`
deposit	Accepts an item of type `double` and adds it to the balance.	An item of type `double`	None
withdraw	Accepts an item of type `double` and checks if there are sufficient funds to make a withdrawal. If there are not, then the method terminates and returns a value of `false`. If there are sufficient funds, however, the method subtracts the amount from the balance and returns a value of `true`.	An item of type `double`	An item of type `boolean`

TABLE 7.4 The methods of the *BankAccount* class

The methods are straightforward, although you should pay particular attention to the `withdraw` method. Our simple `BankAccount` class does not allow for an overdraft facility, so, unlike the `deposit` method, which simply adds the specified amount to the balance, the `withdraw` method needs to check that the amount to be withdrawn is not greater than the balance of the account; if this were to be the case then the balance would be left unchanged. The method returns a **boolean** value to indicate if the withdrawal was successful or not. A **boolean** value of **true** would indicate success and **boolean** value of **false** would indicate failure. This enables a program that uses the `BankAccount` class to check whether the withdrawal has been made successfully. You can see how this is done in program 7.9, which makes use of the `BankAccount` class.

PROGRAM 7.9

```
import java.util.*;

public class BankAccountTester
{
  public static void main(String[] args)
  {
    Scanner keyboard = new Scanner(System.in);
    double amount;
    boolean ok;

    BankAccount account1 = new BankAccount("99786754","Susan Richards");
```

```
    System.out.print("Enter amount to deposit: ");
    amount = keyboard.nextDouble();
    account1.deposit(amount);
    System.out.println("Deposit was made");
    System.out.println("Balance  = " + account1.getBalance());
    System.out.println();

    System.out.print("Enter amount to withdraw: ");
    amount = keyboard.nextDouble();
    ok = account1.withdraw(amount); // get the return value of the withdraw method
    if(ok)
    {
      System.out.println("Withdrawal made");
    }
    else
    {
      System.out.println("Insufficient funds");
    }
    System.out.println("Balance  = " + account1.getBalance());
    System.out.println();
  }
}
```

The program creates a `BankAccount` object and then asks the user to enter an amount to deposit. It then confirms that the deposit was made and shows the new balance.

It then does the same thing for a withdrawal. The `withdraw` method returns a **boolean** value indicating if the withdrawal has been successful or not, so we have assigned this return value to a **boolean** variable, ok:

```
ok = account1.withdraw(amount);
```

Depending on the value of this variable, the appropriate message is then displayed:

```
if(ok)
{
  System.out.println("Withdrawal made");
}
else
{
  System.out.println("Insufficient funds");
}
```

Two sample runs from this program are shown below. In the first the withdrawal was successful:

```
Enter amount to deposit: 1000
Deposit was made
Balance  = 1000.0

Enter amount to withdraw: 400
Withdrawal made
Balance  = 600.0
```

In the second there were not sufficient funds to make the withdrawal:

```
Enter amount to deposit: 1000
Deposit was made
Balance  = 1000.0

Enter amount to withdraw: 1500
Insufficient funds
Balance  = 1000.0
```

7.9 Arrays of objects

In chapter 6 you learnt how to create arrays of simple types such as **int** and **char**. It is perfectly possible, and often very desirable, to create arrays of objects. There, are, however, some important issues that we need to be aware of. We will illustrate this with a new version of program 7.9, the BankAccountTester. In program 7.10, instead of creating a single bank account, we have created several bank accounts by using an array. Take a look at the program, and then we will explain the important issues to you.

PROGRAM 7.10

```java
public class BankAccountTester2
{
  public static void main(String[] args)
  {
    // create an array of references
    BankAccount[] accountList = new BankAccount[3];
    // create three new accounts, referenced by each element in the array
    accountList[0] = new BankAccount("99786754","Susan Richards");
    accountList[1] = new BankAccount("44567109","Delroy Jacobs");
    accountList[2] = new BankAccount("46376205","Sumana Khan");
    // make various deposits and withdrawals
    accountList[0].deposit(1000);
    accountList[2].deposit(150);
    accountList[0].withdraw(500);
    // print details of all three accounts
    for(BankAccount item : accountList)
```

```
   {
     System.out.println("Account number: " + item.getAccountNumber());
     System.out.println("Account name: " + item.getAccountName());
     System.out.println("Current balance: " + item.getBalance());
     System.out.println();
   }
  }
}
```

The first line of the main method looks no different from the statements that you saw in the last chapter that created arrays of primitive types:

```
BankAccount[] accountList = new BankAccount[3];
```

However, what is actually going on behind the scenes is slightly different. The above statement does *not* set up an array of BankAccount objects in memory; instead it sets up an array of *references* to such objects (see figure 7.4).

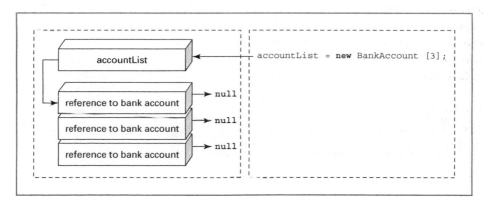

FIGURE 7.4 The effect on computer memory of creating an array of objects

At the moment, space has been reserved for the three BankAccount *references* only, *not* the three BankAccount objects. As we told you earlier, when a reference is initially created it points to the constant **null**, so at this point each reference in the array points to **null**.

This means that memory would still need to be reserved for individual BankAccount objects each time we wish to link a BankAccount object to the array. We can now create new BankAccount objects and associate them with elements in the array as we have done with these lines:

```
accountList[0] = new BankAccount("99786754","Susan Richards");
accountList[1] = new BankAccount("44567109","Delroy Jacobs");
accountList[2] = new BankAccount("46376205","Sumana Khan");
```

Three `BankAccount` objects have been created; the first one, for example, has account number of "99786754" and name "Susan Richards", and the reference at `accountList[0]` is set to point to it. This is illustrated in figure 7.5.

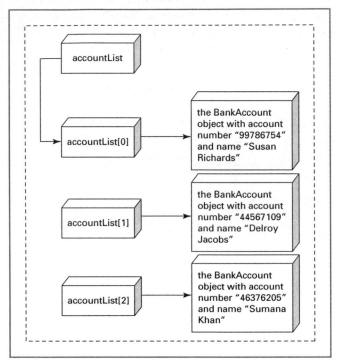

FIGURE 7.5 Objects are linked to arrays by reference

Once we have created these accounts, we make some deposits and withdrawals.

```
accountList[0].deposit(1000);
accountList[2].deposit(150);
accountList[0].withdraw(500);
```

Look carefully at how we do this. To call a method of a particular array element, we place the dot operator after the final bracket of the array index. This is made clear below:

accountList[0].deposit(1000);

returns a   calls a
BankAccount   BankAccount
   object   method

Notice that when we call the `withdraw` method we have decided not to check the **boolean** value returned.

```
accountList[0].withdraw(500); // return value not checked
```

It is not always necessary to check the return value of a method and you may ignore it if you choose.

Having done this, we display the details of all three accounts. As we are accessing the entire array, we are able to use an enhanced **for** loop for this purpose; and since we are dealing with an array of BankAccount objects here, the type of the items is specified as BankAccount.

```
for(BankAccount item : accountList) // type of items is BankAccount
{
  System.out.println("Account number: " + item.getAccountNumber());
  System.out.println("Account name: " + item.getAccountName());
  System.out.println("Current balance: " + item.getBalance());
  System.out.println();
}
```

As you might expect, the output from this program is as follows:

```
Account number: 99786754
Account name: Susan Richards
Current balance: 500.0

Account number: 44567109
Account name: Delroy Jacobs
Current balance: 0.0

Account number: 46376205
Account name: Sumana Khan
Current balance: 150.0
```

Self-test questions

1 Examine the program below and then answer the questions that follow:

```
public class SampleProgram
{
  public static void main(String[] args)
  {
    Rectangle rectangle1 = new Rectangle(3.0, 4.0);
    Rectangle rectangle2 = new Rectangle(5.0, 6.0);
    System.out.println("The area of rectangle1 is " + rectangle1.calculateArea());
    System.out.println("The area of rectangle2 is " + rectangle2.calculateArea());
  }
}
```

a By referring to the program above, distinguish between a *class* and an *object*.

b By referring to the program above, explain the purpose of the *constructor*.

c By referring to the program above, explain how you call the method of one class from another class.

d What output would you expect to see from the program above?

2 a Write the code that will create two `BankAccount` objects, `acc1` and `acc2`. The account number and account name of each should be set at the time the object is created.

b Write the lines of code that will deposit an amount of 200 into `acc1` and 100 into `acc2`.

c Write the lines of code that attempt to withdraw an amount of 150 from `acc1` and displays the message "WITHDRAWAL SUCCESSFUL" if the amount was withdrawn successfully and "INSUFFICIENT FUNDS" if it was not.

d Write a line of code that will display the balance of `acc1`.

e Write a line of code that will display the balance of `acc2`.

3 In what way does calling methods from the `EasyScanner` class differ from calling methods from the other classes you have met (`BankAccount`, `Rectangle`, `String` and `Scanner`)?

4 Consider the following fragment of code that initializes one string constant with a password ("java") and creates a second string to hold the user's guess for the password. The user is then asked to enter their guess:

```
final String PASSWORD = "java"; // set password
String guess; // to hold user's guess
System.out.print("Enter guess: ");
```

▶

a Write a line of code that uses the `EasyScanner` class to read the guess from the keyboard.

b Write the code that displays the message "CORRECT PASSWORD" if the user entered the correct password and "INCORRECT PASSWORD" if not.

5 How do arrays of objects differ from arrays of primitive types?

6 a Declare an array called `rooms`, to hold 3 `Rectangle` objects. Each `Rectangle` object will represent the dimensions of a room in an apartment.

b The 3 rooms in the apartment have the following dimensions:

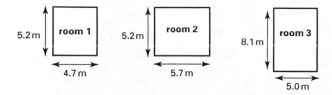

Add 3 appropriate `Rectangle` objects to the `rooms` array to represent these 3 rooms.

c Write the line of code that would make use of the `rooms` array to display the area of room 3 to the screen.

Programming exercises

In order to tackle these exercises, make sure that the classes `Rectangle`, `BankAccount` and `EasyScanner` have been copied from the CD and placed in the correct directory for your compiler to access them.

1 a Implement the program given in self-test question 1 and run it to confirm your answer to part (d) of that question.

b Adapt the program above so that the user is able to set the length and height of the two rectangles. Make use of the `EasyScanner` class to read in the user input.

2 a Write a program that asks the user to input a string, followed by a single character, and then tests whether the string starts with that character.

b Make your program work so that the case of the character is irrelevant.

3 Adapt program 7.5, which compares two strings, in the following ways:

a rewrite the program so that it ignores case;

b rewrite the program, using the `equals` method, so that all it does is to test whether the two strings are the same;

c repeat b) using the `equalsIgnoreCase` method;

d use the `trim` method so that the program ignores leading or trailing spaces.

4 Design and implement a program that performs in the following way:

- when the program starts two bank accounts are created, using names and numbers which are written into the code;
- the user is then asked to enter an account number, followed by an amount to deposit in that account;
- the balance of the appropriate account is then updated accordingly – or if an incorrect account number was entered a message to this effect is displayed;
- the user is then asked if he or she wishes to make more deposits;
- if the user answers that he or she does wish to make more deposits, the process continues;
- if the user does not wish to make more deposits, then details of both accounts (account number, account name and balance) are displayed.

5 Write a program that creates an array of `Rectangle` objects to represent the dimensions of rooms in an apartment as described in self-test question 6. The program should allow the user to:

- determine the number of rooms;
- enter the dimensions of the rooms;
- retrieve the area and dimensions of any of the rooms.

CHAPTER 08

Implementing classes

OBJECTIVES

By the end of this chapter you should be able to:

- design classes using the notation of the **Unified Modeling Language (UML)**;
- write the Java code for a specified class;
- explain the difference between **public** and **private** access to attributes and methods;
- explain the meaning of the term **encapsulation**;

- explain the use of the **static** keyword;
- pass objects as parameters;
- implement **collection classes** based on arrays;
- identify the advantages of object-oriented programming.

8.1 Introduction

This chapter is arguably the most important so far, because it is here that you are going to learn how to develop the classes that you need for your programs. You are already familiar with the concept of a class, and the idea that we can create objects that belong to a class; in the last chapter you saw how to create and use objects, and you saw how we could use the methods of a class without knowing anything about how they work.

In this chapter you will look inside the classes you have studied to see how they are constructed, and how you can write classes of your own. We start with the `Rectangle` class.

8.2 Designing classes in UML notation

In the last chapter you saw that a class consists of:

- a set of **attributes** (the data);
- a set of **methods** that can access or change those attributes.

When we design a class we must, of course, consider what data the class needs to hold, and what methods are needed to access that data. The `Rectangle` class that we develop here will need to hold two items of data – the length and the height of the rectangle; these will have to be real numbers, so **double** would be the appropriate type for each of these two attributes. You have already seen the methods that we provided for this class in table 7.1 in the previous chapter.

When we design classes, it is very useful to start off by using a diagrammatic notation. The usual way this is done is by making use of the notation of the **Unified Modeling Language (UML)**.[1] In this notation, a class is represented by a box divided into three sections. The first section provides the name of the class, the second section lists the attributes, and the third section lists the methods. The UML class diagram for the `Rectangle` class is shown in figure 8.1.

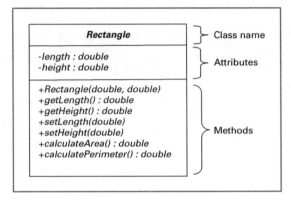

FIGURE 8.1 The design of the *Rectangle* class

You can see that the UML notation requires us to indicate the names of the attributes along with their types, separated by a colon.

In the last chapter we introduced you to the concept of *encapsulation* or information-hiding. This is the technique of making attributes accessible only to the methods of the same class, and it is this feature of object-oriented languages that has contributed to object-orientation becoming the standard way of programming in today's world. By restricting access in this way, programmers can keep the data in their classes "sealed off" from other classes, because they are the ones in control of how it is actually accessed.

The way our `Rectangle` class has been set up means that you cannot directly use the `length` and `height` attributes in another program. If you want to find out the area of the rectangle in, say, the **main** method of another program then you can't do this by a accessing the `length` and `height` data directly, because access to these attributes is denied.

Instead we would, as you know, call the `calculateArea` method of the `Rectangle` object. We design our classes like this because doing so means that no-one can inadvertently *change* the values of `length` and `height` – our data is kept secure. If access to these attributes were not restricted in this way, then the `length` and `height` data could inadvertently be changed. Instead we limit access of the `Rectangle` class to its methods. This is illustrated in figure 8.2.

---

[1] Simon Bennett et al., *Schaum's Outline UML (3rd edn)*, McGraw-Hill 2006.

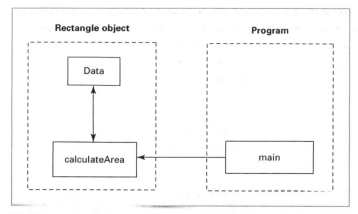

FIGURE 8.2 Encapsulation requires data be kept hidden inside an object

The plus and minus signs that you can see in the UML diagram in figure 8.1 are all to do with this idea of encapsulation; a minus sign means that the attribute or method is **private** – that is, it is accessible *only to methods of the same class*. A plus sign means that it is **public** – it is accessible to methods of other classes. Normally we make the attributes private, and the methods public, in this way achieving encapsulation. You will see how it is done in a Java class in the next section.

Now let's consider the notation for the methods. You can see from the diagram that the parameter types are given in brackets – for example:

+setLength(double)

The return types are placed after the brackets, preceded by a colon – for example:

+getLength() : double

Where there is no return type, nothing appears after the brackets, as in the `setlength` and `setHeight` methods.

The first method, `Rectangle`, is the constructor. As we know, the constructor always has the same name as the class, and in this case it requires two parameters of type **double**:

+Rectangle(double, double)

You should note that a constructor *never has a return type*. In fact you will see later that in Java we don't even put the word **void** in front of a constructor; if we did, the compiler would think it was a regular method.

As you saw in the previous chapter, we have provided our `Rectangle` class with methods for reading and writing to the attributes – and it is conventional to begin the name of such methods with `get-` and `set-` respectively. However, it is not always the case that we choose to supply methods such as `setLength` and `setHeight`, which allow us to *change* the attributes. Sometimes we set up our class so that the only way that we can assign values to the attributes is via the constructor. This would mean that the values of the `length` and `height` could be set only at the time a new `Rectangle` object was created, and could not be changed after that. Whether or not you want to provide a means of writing to individual attributes depends on the nature of the system you are developing and should be discussed with potential users. However, we believe that it is a good policy to provide write access to only those attributes that clearly require to be changed during the object's lifetime, and we have taken this approach throughout this book. In this case we have included "set" methods for `length` and `height` because we are going to need them in chapter 10.

8.3 Implementing classes in Java

8.3.1 The *Rectangle* class

Now that we have the basic design of the `Rectangle` class we can go ahead and write the Java code for it. We present the code here – when you have had a look at it we will discuss it.

THE *RECTANGLE* CLASS

```java
public class Rectangle
{
  // the attributes
  private double length;
  private double height;

  // the methods

  // the constructor
  public Rectangle(double lengthIn, double heightIn)
  {
    length = lengthIn;
    height = heightIn;
  }
  // this method allows us to read the length attribute
  public double getLength()
  {
    return length;
  }

  // this method allows us to read the height attribute
  public double getHeight()
  {
    return height;
  }

  // this method allows us to write to the length attribute
  public void setLength(double lengthIn)
```

```
   {
     length = lengthIn;
   }


   // this method allows us to write to the height attribute
   public void setHeight(double heightIn)
   {
     height = heightIn;
   }


   // this method returns the area of the rectangle
   public double calculateArea()
   {
     return length * height;
   }


   // this method returns the perimeter of the rectangle
   public double calculatePerimeter()
   {
     return 2 * (length + height);
   }
}
```

Let's take a closer look at this. The first line declares the `Rectangle` class:

```
public class Rectangle
```

Next come the attributes. A `Rectangle` object will need attributes to hold values for the length and the height of the rectangle, and these will be of type **double**. The declaration of the attributes in the `Rectangle` class took the following form in our UML diagram:

–length : double
–height : double

In Java this is implemented as:

```
private double length;
private double height;
```

As you can see, attributes are declared like any other variables, except that they are declared *outside* of any method, and they also have an additional word in front of them – the word **private**, corresponding to the minus sign in the UML notation. In Java, this keyword is used to restrict the scope of the attributes to methods of this class only, as we described above.

You should note that the attributes of a class are accessible to *all* the methods of the class – unlike *local* variables, which are accessible only to the methods in which they are declared.

Figure 8.1 makes it clear which methods we need to define within our Rectangle class. First comes the constructor. You should recall that it has the same name as the class, and, unlike any other method, it has no return type – not even **void**! It looks like this:

```
public Rectangle(double lengthIn, double heightIn)
{
  length = lengthIn;
  height = heightIn;
}
```

The first thing to notice is that this method is declared as **public**. Unlike the attributes, we want our methods to be accessible from outside so that they can be called by methods of other classes.

In our class we are defining the constructor so that when a new Rectangle object is created (with the keyword **new**) then not only do we get some space reserved in memory, but we also get some other stuff occurring; in this case two assignment statements are executed. The first assigns the value of the parameter lengthIn to the length attribute, and the second assigns the value of the parameter heightIn to the height attribute. Remember, the attributes are visible to all the methods of the class.

When we define a constructor like this in a class it is termed a *user-defined*[2] constructor. If we don't define our own constructor, then one is automatically provided for us – this is referred to as the **default** constructor. The default constructor takes no parameters and when it is used to create an object – for example in a line like this:

```
Rectangle myRectangle = new Rectangle();
```

then all that happens is that memory is reserved for the new object – no other processing takes place. Any attributes will be given initial values according to the rules that we give you later in section 8.5.

One more thing about constructors: once we have defined our own constructors, this default constructor is no longer automatically available. If we want it to be available then we have to re-define it explicitly. In the Rectangle case we would define it as:

```
public Rectangle()
{
}
```

You can see that just like regular methods, constructers can be overloaded, and we can define several constructors in one class. When we create an object it will be clear from the parameter list which constructor we are referring to.

---

[2] Here the word *user* is referring to the person *writing* the program, not the person using it!

Now let's take a look at the definition of the next method, `getLength`. The purpose of this method is simply to send back the value of the `length` attribute. In the UML diagram it was declared as:

+getLength() : double

In Java this becomes:

```
public double getLength()
{
  return length;
}
```

Once again you can see that the method has been declared as **public** (indicated by the plus sign in UML), enabling it to be accessed by methods of other classes.

The next method, `getHeight`, behaves in the same way in respect of the `height` attribute.

Next comes the `setLength` method:

+setLength(double)

We implement this as:

```
public void setLength(double lengthIn)
{
  length = lengthIn;
}
```

This method does not return a value, so its return type is **void**. However, it does require a parameter of type **double** that it will assign to the `length` attribute. The body of the method consists of a single line which assigns the value of `lengthIn` to the `length` attribute.

The next method, `setHeight`, behaves in the same way in respect of the `height` attribute.

After this comes the `calculateArea` method:

+calculateArea() : double

We implement this as:

```
public double calculateArea()
{
  return length * height;
}
```

Once again there are no formal parameters, as this method does not need any data in order to do its job; it returns a **double**. The actual code is just one line, namely the statement that returns the area of the rectangle, calculated by multiplying the value of the length attribute by the value of the height attribute.

The calculatePerimeter method is similar and thus the definition of the Rectangle class is now complete.

One important thing to note here. Unlike some of the methods we developed in chapter 5, the methods that we have defined here deal only with the basic *functionality* of the class – they do not include any routines that deal with input or output. That is because the methods of chapter 5 were only being used by the class in which they were written – but now our methods will be used by other classes that we cannot as yet predict. So when developing a class we should always strive to restrict our methods to the essential functions that define the class (in this case, for example, calculating the area and perimeter of the rectangle), and to exclude anything that is concerned with the input or output functions of a program. If we do this, then our class can be used in any sort of application, regardless of whether is it a simple console application like the ones we have developed so far, or a complex graphical application like the ones you will come across later in this book.

8.3.2 The *BankAccount* class

The UML class diagram for the BankAccount class, which we used in the previous chapter, is shown in figure 8.3.

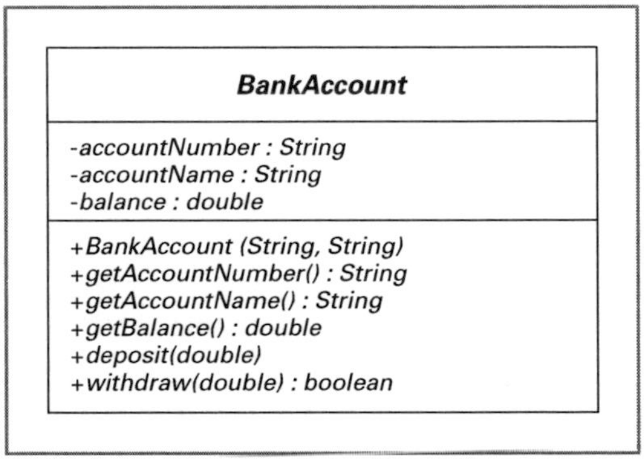

FIGURE 8.3 The design of *BankAccount* class

You will notice here that *accountNumber* and *accountName* are declared as *Strings*; it is perfectly possible for the attributes of one class to be objects of another class.

We can now inspect the code for this class:

THE *BANKACCOUNT* CLASS

```
public class BankAccount
{
  // the attributes
  private String accountNumber;
  private String accountName;
  private double balance;
```

```
// the methods


// the constructor
public BankAccount(String numberIn, String nameIn)
{
  accountNumber = numberIn;
  accountName = nameIn;
  balance = 0;
}


// methods to read the attributes
public String getAccountName()
{
  return accountName;
}


public String getAccountNumber()
{
  return accountNumber;
}


public double getBalance()
{
  return balance;
}


// methods to deposit and withdraw money
public void deposit(double amountIn)
{
  balance = balance + amountIn;
}
public boolean withdraw(double amountIn)
{
  if(amountIn > balance)
  {
    return false; // no withdrawal was made
  }
  else
  {
    balance = balance - amountIn;
    return true; // money was withdrawn successfully
  }
}
}
```

Now that we are getting the idea of how to define a class in Java, we do not need to go into so much detail in our analysis and explanation.

The first three lines declare the attributes of the class, and are as we would expect:

```
private String accountNumber;
private String accountName;
private double balance;
```

Now the constructor:

```
public BankAccount(String numberIn, String nameIn)
{
  accountNumber = numberIn;
  accountName = nameIn;
  balance = 0;
}
```

You can see that when a new object of the BankAccount class is created, the accountName and account-Number will be assigned the values of the parameters passed to the method. In this case, the balance will be assigned the value zero; this makes sense because when someone opens a new account there is a zero balance until a deposit is made.[3]

The next three methods, getAccountNumber, getAccountName and getBalance, are all set up so that the values of the corresponding attributes (which of course have been declared as **private**) can be read.

After these we have the deposit method:

```
public void deposit(double amountIn)
{
  balance = balance + amountIn;
}
```

This method does not return a value; it is therefore declared to be of type **void**. It does, however, require that a value is sent in (the amount to be deposited), and therefore has one parameter – of type **double** – in the brackets. As you would expect with this method, the action consists of adding the deposit to the balance attribute of the BankAccount object.

---

[3] You would be right in thinking that the balance attribute would automatically be assigned a value of zero if we did not specifically do that here. However it is good practice always to ensure that variables are initialized with the values that we require – particularly because in many other programming languages attributes are not initialized as they are in Java.

Now the `withdraw` method:

```
public boolean withdraw(double amountIn)
{
  if(amountIn > balance)
  {
    return false; // no withdrawal was made
  }
  else
  {
    balance = balance - amountIn;
    return true; // money was withdrawn successfully
  }
}
```

The amount is subtracted only if there are sufficient funds – in other words, if the amount to be withdrawn is no bigger than the balance. If this is not the case then a value of **false** is returned and the method terminates. Otherwise the amount is subtracted from the balance and a value of **true** is returned. The return type of the method therefore is **boolean**.

8.4 The *static* keyword

You have already seen the keyword **static** in front of the names of methods in some Java classes. A word such as this (as well as the words **public** and **private**) is called a **modifier**. A modifier determines the particular way a class, attribute or method is accessed.

Let's explore what this **static** modifier does. Consider the BankAccount class that we discussed in the previous section. Say we wanted to have an additional method which added interest, at the current rate, to the customer's balance. It would be useful to have an attribute called interestRate to hold the value of the current rate of interest. But of course the interest rate is the same for any customer – and if it changes, we want it to change for every customer in the bank; in other words, for every object of the class. We can achieve this by declaring the variable as **static**. An attribute declared as **static** is a *class* attribute; any changes that are made to it are made to all the objects in the class.

It would make sense if there were a way to access this attribute without reference to a specific object; and so there is! All we have to do is to declare methods such as setInterestRate and getInterestRate as **static**. This makes a method into a *class* method; it does not refer to any specific object. As you will see in program 8.1, we can call a class method by using the class name instead of the object name.

We have rewritten our BankAccount class, and called it BankAccount2. We have included three new methods as well as the new **static** attribute interestRate. The first two of these – setInterestRate and getInterestRate – are the methods that allow us to read and write to our new attribute. These have been declared as **static**. The third – addInterest – is the method that adds the interest to the customer's balance. As can be seen in figure 8.4, the UML notation is to underline static attributes and methods.

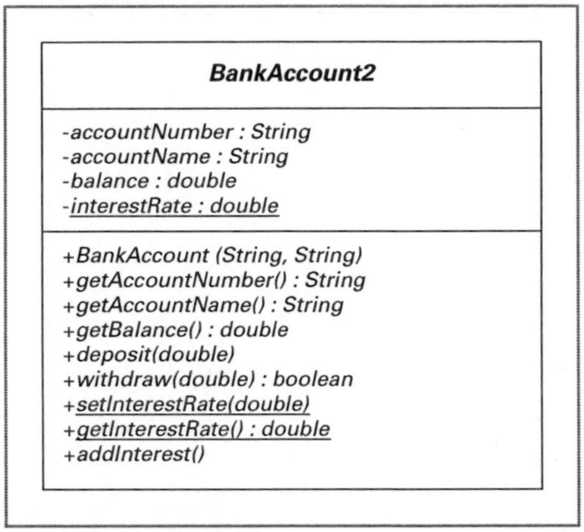

FIGURE 8.4 The design of the *BankAccount2* class

Here is the code for the class. The new items have been emboldened.

THE MODIFIED *BANKACCOUNT* CLASS

```java
public class BankAccount2
{
  private String accountNumber;
  private String accountName;
  private double balance;
  private static double interestRate;

  public BankAccount2(String numberIn, String nameIn)
  {
    accountNumber = numberIn;
    accountName = nameIn;
    balance = 0;
  }

  public String getAccountName()
  {
    return accountName;
  }
  public String getAccountNumber()
  {
    return accountNumber;
  }
```

```java
   public double getBalance()
   {
     return balance;
   }

   public void deposit(double amountIn)
   {
     balance = balance + amountIn;
   }

   public boolean withdraw(double amountIn)
   {
     if(amountIn > balance)
     {
       return false;
     }
     else
     {
       balance = balance - amountIn;
       return true;
     }
   }

   public static void setInterestRate(double rateIn)
   {
     interestRate = rateIn;
   }

   public static double getInterestRate()
   {
     return interestRate;
   }

   public void addInterest()
   {
     balance = balance + (balance * interestRate)/100;
   }
}
```

Program 8.1 uses this modified version of the `BankAccount` class.

PROGRAM 8.1

```java
public class BankAccountTester2
{
  public static void main(String[] args)
  {
    // create a bank account
    BankAccount2 account1 = new BankAccount2("99786754","Gayle Forcewind");
    // create another bank account
    BankAccount2 account2 = new BankAccount2("99887776","Stan Dandy-Liver");
    // make a deposit into the first account
    account1.deposit(1000);
    // make a deposit into the second account
    account2.deposit(2000);
    // set the interest rate
    BankAccount2.setInterestRate(10);
    // add interest to accounts
    account1.addInterest();
    account2.addInterest();
    // display the account details
    System.out.println("Account number: " + account1.getAccountNumber());
    System.out.println("Account name: " + account1.getAccountName());
    System.out.println("Interest Rate " + BankAccount2.getInterestRate());
    System.out.println("Current balance: " + account1.getBalance());
    System.out.println(); // blank line
    System.out.println("Account number: " + account2.getAccountNumber());
    System.out.println("Account name: " + account2.getAccountName());
    System.out.println("Interest Rate " + BankAccount2.getInterestRate());
    System.out.println("Current balance: " + account2.getBalance());
  }
}
```

Take a closer look at the first four lines of the `main` method of program 8.1. We have created two new bank accounts which we have called `account1` and `account2`, and have assigned account numbers and names to them at the time they were created (via the constructor). We have then deposited amounts of 1000 and 2000 respectively into each of these accounts.

Now look at the next line:

```java
BankAccount2.setInterestRate(10);
```

This line sets the interest rate to 10. Because `setInterestRate` has been declared as a **static** method, we have been able to call it by using the class name `BankAccount2`. Because `interestRate` has been declared as a **static** attribute this change is effective for any object of the class.

Therefore, when we add interest to each account as we do with the next two lines:

```
account1.addInterest();
account2.addInterest();
```

we should expect it to be calculated with an interest rate of 10, giving us new balances of 1100 and 2200 respectively.

This is exactly what we get, as can be seen from the output below:

```
Account number: 99786754
Account name: Gayle Forcewind
Interest Rate 10.0
Current balance: 1100.0

Account number: 99887776
Account name: Stan Dandy-Liver
Interest Rate 10.0
Current balance: 2200.0
```

Class methods can be very useful indeed and we shall see further examples of them in this chapter. Of course, we have always declared our `main` method, and other methods within the same class as the `main` method, as **static** – because these methods belong to the class and not to a specific object.

8.5 Initializing attributes

Looking back at the `BankAccount2` class in the previous section, some of you might have been asking yourselves what would happen if we called the `getInterestRate` method before the interest rate had been set using the `setInterestRate` method. In fact, the answer is that a value of zero would be returned. This is because, while Java does not give an initial value to *local* variables (which is why you get a compiler error if you try to use an uninitialized variable), Java always initializes attributes. Numerical attributes such as **int** and **double** are initialized to zero; **boolean** attributes are initialized to **false** and objects are initialized to **null**. Character attributes are given an initial Unicode value of zero.

Despite the above, it is nonetheless good programming practice always to give an initial value to your attributes, rather than leave it to the compiler. One very good reason for this is that you cannot assume that every programming language initializes variables in the same way – if you were using C++, for example, the initial value of any variable is completely a matter of chance – and you won't get a compiler error to warn you! In the `BankAccount2` class, it would have done no harm at all to have initialized the `interestRate` variable when it was declared:

```
private static double interestRate = 0;
```

In fact, one technique you could use is to give the `interestRate` attribute some special initial value (such as a negative value) to indicate to the user of this class that the interest rate had not been set. You will see another example where this technique can be used in question 2 of the programming exercises.

8.6 The *EasyScanner* class

In the previous chapter we used a class called `EasyScanner` that could make keyboard input a lot easier. We have now covered all the concepts you need in order to understand how this class works. Here it is:

THE *EASYSCANNER* CLASS

```java
import java.util.*;

public class EasyScanner
{
  public static int nextInt()
  {
    Scanner keyboard = new Scanner(System.in);
    int i = keyboard.nextInt();
    return i;
  }

  public static double nextDouble()
  {
    Scanner keyboard = new Scanner(System.in);
    double d = keyboard.nextDouble();
    return d;
  }
  public static String nextString()
  {
    Scanner keyboard = new Scanner(System.in);
    String s = keyboard.nextLine();
    return s;
  }

  public static char nextChar()
  {
    Scanner keyboard = new Scanner(System.in);
    char c = keyboard.next().charAt(0);
    return c;
  }
}
```

You can see that we have made every method a **static** method, so that we can simply use the class name when we call a method. For example:

```
int number = EasyScanner.nextInt();
```

You can see that the nextString method uses the nextLine method of the Scanner class – but as a new Scanner object is created each time the method is called there is no problem about using it after a nextInt or a nextDouble method as there is with nextLine itself.

We will use the EasyScanner class later, in program 8.3.

8.7 Passing objects as parameters

In chapter 5 it was made clear that when a variable is passed to a method it is simply the *value* of that variable that is passed – and that therefore a method cannot change the value of the original variable. In chapter 6 you found out that in the case of an array it is the value of the memory location (a *reference*) that is passed and consequently the value of the original array elements can be changed by the called method.

What about objects? Let's write a little program (program 8.2) to test this out.

PROGRAM 8.2

```
public class ParameterTest
{
  public static void main(String[] args)
  {
    // create new bank account
    BankAccount testAccount - new BankAccount("1", "Ann T Dote");
    test(testAccount); // send the account to the test method
    System.out.println("Account Number: " + testAccount.getAccountNumber());
    System.out.println("Account Name: " + testAccount.getAccountName());
    System.out.println("Balance: " + testAccount.getBalance());
  }

  // a method that makes a deposit in the bank account
  static void test(BankAccount accountIn)
  {
    accountIn.deposit(2500);
  }
}
```

The output from this program is as follows:

```
Account Number: 1
Account Name: Ann T Dote
Balance: 2500.0
```

You can see that the deposit has successfully been made – in other words, the attribute of the object has actually been changed. This is because what was sent to the method was, of course, a *reference* to the original `BankAccount` object, `testAccount`. Thus `accountIn` is a copy of the `testAccount` reference and so points to the original object and invokes that object's methods. So the following line of code:

```
accountIn.deposit(2500);
```

calls the `deposit` method of the original `BankAccount` object.

You might think this is a very good thing, and will make life easier for you as a programmer. However, you need a word of caution here. It is very easy inadvertently to allow a method to change an object's attributes, so you need to take care – more about this in the second semester.

8.8 Collection classes

When we studied arrays in chapter 6, we used an array only as a variable within a method. However, an array can also be used as an *attribute* of a class. In declaring an array as an attribute, we can hide some of the inconveniences of the array type (such as remembering to start array indices at zero) by providing our own methods to control array access. A class that contains many items of the same type is said to be a **collection** class. In our everyday lives we can see many examples of collections:

- a train contains a collection of passengers;
- a post bag contains a collection of letters;
- a letter contains a collection of words.

8.8.1 The *Bank* class

In chapter 7 we presented a program (program 7.10) in which three `BankAccount` objects were created and were held in an array. Now that we are able to create our own classes we can vastly improve on this approach by providing a special collection class to hold bank accounts. We will call our collection class `Bank`.

When one object itself consists of other objects, this relationship is called **aggregation**. This association, represented in UML by a diamond, is often referred to as a *part-of* relationship. For example, the association between a car object and the passengers in the car is aggregation. **Composition** (represented by a filled diamond) is a special, stronger, form of aggregation whereby the "whole" is actually dependent on the "part". For example, the association between a car and its engine is one of *composition*, as a car cannot exist without an engine. A collection class is an implementation of the aggregation relationship.

The association between the container object, `Bank`, and the contained object, `BankAccount`, is shown in the UML diagram of figure 8.5.

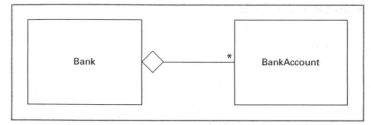

FIGURE 8.5 The *Bank* object can contain many *BankAccount* objects

The asterisk at the other end of the joining line indicates that the `Bank` object contains *zero or more* `BankAccount` objects. The design for the `Bank` class is now given in figure 8.6.

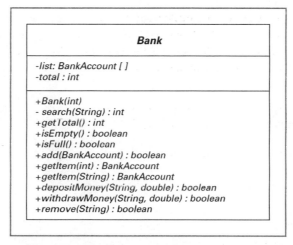

FIGURE 8.6 The design of the *Bank* class

As you can see, the class will have two attributes – a collection of `BankAccounts` and an integer to keep track of the number of accounts present.

There are 10 methods, which are described below:

+Bank(int)

This is the constructor. It receives an integer which will represent the maximum number of accounts allowed, and will create an array of bank accounts accordingly. You can see how, by this means, the size of the array is determined at run-time by the user of this class.

–search(String) : int

This is what we can term a **helper** method; it will be declared as **private** (note the minus sign in the UML notation), because it is not intended for it to be called by other classes. It accepts a `String` representing the account number. It then returns the array index of the account with that account number. If the account number does not exist, then a "phoney" index (–999) will be returned to indicate failure.

+getTotal() : int

This method simply returns the total number of accounts currently in the system.

+isEmpty() : boolean

Returns a value of **true** if the list of accounts is empty, otherwise returns **false**.

+*isFull(): boolean*

Returns a value of **true** if the list of accounts is full, otherwise returns **false**.

+*add(BankAccount): boolean*

This method receives a BankAccount object (strictly speaking, a reference to a BankAccount object) and adds this to the list of accounts. It will return a value of **true** if the operation has been completed successfully, or **false** if not.

In our first simple version of this class, the only reason that an account would not be added successfully is if the list of accounts is full. Later this could be refined to ensure that an account could not be added if there is already another account with the same account number.

+*getItem(int): BankAccount*

Receives an **int** representing the position in the list (using "natural" numbering, starting at 1), and returns the BankAccount (strictly speaking a reference to the BankAccount) with that account number.

If the position is not valid (that is, if it is a number less than 1 or greater than the total) a **null** value will be returned.

+*getItem(String): BankAccount*

An overloaded version of the above that, instead of receiving an **int**, receives a String representing an account number, and returns the BankAccount with that account number.

If the account number is not valid a **null** value will be returned.

+*depositMoney(String, double): boolean*

Accepts a String, representing the account number of a particular account, and an amount of money which is to be deposited in that account. Returns **true** if the deposit was made successfully, or **false** otherwise (no such account number).

+*withdrawMoney(String, double): boolean*

Accepts a String, representing the account number of a particular account, and an amount of money which is to be withdrawn from that account. Returns **true** if the withdrawal was made successfully, or **false** otherwise (no such account number or insufficient funds).

+*remove(String): boolean*

Accepts a String, representing an account number, and removes that account from the list. Returns **true** if the account was removed successfully, or **false** otherwise (no such account number).

The code for the Bank class is presented below. Take a careful look at it, then we will discuss it.

THE *BANK* CLASS

```
public class Bank
{
  // attributes
  private BankAccount[] list; // to hold the accounts
  private int total; // to keep track of the number of accounts in the list

  // methods
  // the constructor
  public Bank(int sizeIn)
```

```
{
  // size array with parameter
  list = new BankAccount[sizeIn];
  total = 0;
}


// helper method to find the index of a specified account
private int search(String accountNumberIn)
{
  for(int i = 0; i < total; i++)
  {
    BankAccount tempAccount = list[i]; // find the account at index i
    String tempNumber = tempAccount.getAccountNumber(); // get account number
    if(tempNumber.equals(accountNumberIn)) // if this is the account we are looking for
    {
      return i; // return the index
    }
  }
  return -999;
}


// return the total number of accounts in the list
public int getTotal()
{
  return total;
}


// check if the list is empty
public boolean isEmpty()
{
  if (total == 0)
  {
    return true; // list is empty
  }
  else
  {
    return false; // list is not empty
  }
}
// check if the list is full
public boolean isFull()
```

```
{
  if (total == list.length)
  {
    return true; // list is full
  }
  else
  {
    return false; // list is empty
  }
}


// add an item to the array
public boolean add(BankAccount accountIn)
{
  if (!isFull()) // check if list is full
  {
    list[total] = accountIn; // add item
    total++; // increment total
    return true; // indicate success
  }
  else
  {
    return false; // indicate failure
  }
}


// return an account at a particular place in the list
public BankAccount getItem(int positionIn)
{
  if(positionIn < 1 || positionIn > total)
  {
    return null; // indicate invalid index
  }
  else
  {
    return list[positionIn - 1];
  }
}
// return an account with a particular account number
public BankAccount getItem(String accountNumberIn)
{
  int index;
  index = search(accountNumberIn);
  if(index == -999)
```

```
  {
    return null; // indicate invalid index
  }
  else
  {
    return list[index];
  }
}



// deposit money in a specified account
public boolean depositMoney(String accountNumberIn, double amountIn)
{
  int index = search(accountNumberIn);
  if(index == -999) // there was no such account number
  {
    return false; // indicate failure
  }
  else
  {
    list[index].deposit(amountIn);
    return true; // indicate success
  }
}


// withdraw money from a specified account
public boolean withdrawMoney(String accountNumberIn, double amountIn)
{
  boolean okToWithdraw;
  int index = search(accountNumberIn);
  if(index == -999) // there was no such account number
  {
    return false; // indicate failure due to incorrect account number
  }
  else
  {
    okToWithdraw = list[index].withdraw(amountIn); // store boolean return value
    return okToWithdraw; // false if insufficient funds and true if withdraw successful
  }
}
```

```
// remove an account
public boolean remove(String numberIn)
{
  int index = search(numberIn); // find index of account
  if(index == -999) // if no such account
  {
    return false; // remove was unsuccessful
  }
  else
  { // overwrite items by shifting other items along
    for(int i = index; i<= total-2; i++)
    {
      list[i] = list[i+1];
    }

    total--; // decrement total number of accounts
    return true; // remove was successful
  }
}
```

As you can see, we have declared two attributes – the first an array of `BankAccounts`, the second an **int** to keep track of the total. Notice that when we declared the array we did not yet give it a size:

```
private BankAccount[] list;
```

The job of sizing the array is left to the constructor:

```
public Bank(int sizeIn)
{
  list = new BankAccount[sizeIn];
  total = 0;
}
```

As you can see, the constructor accepts an integer value representing the maximum number of accounts allowed, and creates a new array of this size. In this way the user of the class is able to decide on this number.

The second line sets the total amount of accounts to zero – the number of accounts that will be present when the application first starts.

Some of the other methods also require further discussion.

The `getTotal` method simply returns the total. This is followed by two methods, `isEmpty` and `isFull`, which are straightforward, and simply report, respectively, on whether the list is empty or full. Notice how the `isFull` method makes use of the `length` property of the array in the condition:

```
if (total == list.length)
```

Now we can turn our attention to the `search` method:

```
private int search(String accountNumberIn)
{
  for(int i = 0; i < total; i++)
  {
    BankAccount tempAccount = list[i]; // find the account at index i
    String tempNumber = tempAccount.getAccountNumber(); // get account number
    if(tempNumber.equals(accountNumberIn)) // if this is the account we are looking for
    {
      return i; // return the index
    }
  }
  return -999;
}
```

You have seen something like this before in chapter 6 when we searched an integer array – you can see we are using the same technique of sending back a "dummy" value if the account number is not valid. Notice that here, however, we are not searching the whole array, but are going only as far as the total number of elements that have been filled with accounts. You can also see that, because it is the account number we are searching for, each time we go round the loop, we have to first find the account, and then get its account number before making the comparison.

```
BankAccount tempAccount = list[i]; // find the account at index i
String tempNumber = tempAccount.getAccountNumber(); // get account number
if(tempNumber.equals(accountNumberIn)) // if this is the account we are looking for
{
  return i; // return the index
}
```

As we said before, we have made this method **private** as it is a helper method only, and does not need to be accessed by other classes.

Now we come to the add method:

```
public boolean add(BankAccount accountIn)
{
  if (!isFull())
  {
    list[total] = accountIn;
    total++;
    return true;
  }
  else
  {
    return false;
  }
}
```

We check that the list is not full, and if this is the case we assign the account which it has received to the next slot in the array, with this instruction:

```
list[total] = accountIn;
```

At first sight, you might wonder why the next available index is represented by the value `total`. This is best illustrated by an example. Imagine that there are currently 20 accounts in the list. This means that array positions 0 to 19 will be filled. Thus, the next position to be filled will be position 20 – the same as the current total of the accounts so far.

Once we have done this, we increase the total by 1, and then return a value of **true** to indicate that the account has been added successfully. If the list had been full, a value of **false** would have been returned, as you can see from the **else** clause.

Next come the overloaded `getItem` methods. The first is straightforward and simply returns the item at a particular position. The second is more complex.

```
public BankAccount getItem(String accountNumberIn)
{
  int index;
  index = search(accountNumberIn);
  if(index == -999)
  {
    return null; // indicate invalid index
  }
  else
  {
    return list[index];
  }
}
```

The method begins by calling the search method to find the index of the account in the array. As you can see, if the search method returns −999, indicating that there in no such account number in the list, then the getItem method returns a value of **null**. The user of this method will know that a **null** value indicates that the requested account does not exist.

If the account number was valid, however, the method returns the reference to the account at that position:

```
return list[index];
```

Now comes the depositMoney method:

```
public boolean depositMoney(String accountNumberIn, double amountIn)
{
  int index = search(accountNumberIn);
  if(index == -999) // there was no such account number
  {
    return false; // indicate failure
  }
  else
  {
    list[index].deposit(amountIn);
    return true; // indicate success
  }
}
```

Here we make use of the deposit method of BankAccount – but we have first to find the correct account in which to make the deposit. For this purpose we use our search method. Once we have obtained the position in the account, we check that it is valid by using the fact that the method will return a value of −999 if it is not. Having checked this, we return **false** if it was not valid; otherwise we use the deposit method of the relevant account to make the transaction. Once the deposit is made, we return a value of **true** to indicate success.

The withdrawMoney method is similar except that we need to have an additional check to see whether or not there were sufficient funds for the withdrawal to go ahead:

```
public boolean withdrawMoney(String accountNumberIn, double amountIn)
{
  boolean okToWithdraw;
  int index = search(accountNumberIn);
  if(index == -999) // same check as depositMoney method
  {
    return false; // indicate failure due to incorrect account number
  }
```

218   Java in Two Semesters

```
   else
   {
     okToWithdraw = list[index].withdraw(amountIn); // additional check
     return okToWithdraw; // false if insufficient funds, true if withdraw successful
   }
}
```

Now we come to the `remove` method, which really does need a bit of explanation. Here it is again:

```
public boolean remove(String numberIn)
{
  int index = search(numberIn); // find index of account
  if(index == -999) // if no such account
  {
    return false; // remove was unsuccessful
  }
  else
  { // overwrite items by shifting other items along
    for(int i = index; i<= total-2; i++)
    {
      list[i] = list[i+1];
    }
    total--; // decrement total number of accounts
    return true; // remove was successful
  }
}
```

The first thing we do is to use the `search` method to obtain the position of the account that has to be removed.

```
int index = search(numberIn); // find index of account
```

We then use the return value of this method to ensure that the account number actually exists, and terminate the method if it does not, returning a value of **false**.

```
if(index == -999) // if no such account
{
  return false; // remove was unsuccessful
}
```

Now let's look at a strategy to remove the given item from a list. The usual approach is to shuffle the previous items in the list along so that the given item is *overwritten*. This is shown in figure 8.7, where the accounts have been identified by the name of the account holder.

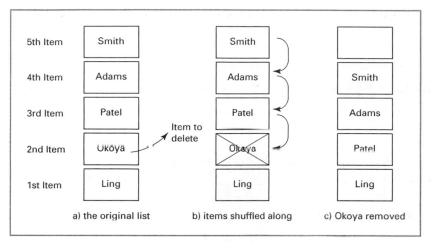

FIGURE 8.7 An item can be deleted from a list by shuffling adjacent items along

In this case the item to be removed (*Okoya*) was the second item in the list. The items to be shuffled (*Patel, Adams* and *Smith*) were the third, fourth and fifth items in the list, respectively. Remembering that this list is implemented as an array, and that array indices begin at zero, the following assignments could be used to achieve this shuffling:

```
list[1] = list[2]; // overwrite Okoya with Patel
list[2] = list[3]; // overwrite Patel with Adams
list[3] = list[4]; // overwrite Adams with Smith
```

As you can see, we are repeating the same line each time, but with a different index. In other words, we keep repeating the following line:

```
list[i] = list[i + 1];
```

with a different value of i each time. We can achieve this with a **for** loop. The only tricky bit is to work out the start and end values of the variable i – and since we are using arrays (which start at 0), this makes it a little more difficult to get it right.

Clearly we don't have to bother about any items that come before the one we are deleting. In the above example we don't have to worry about *Ling*. So we start with the item we are going to delete. In our method, this was represented by the variable index. You should be able to see from figure 8.7 that the place to stop is one before the end – *Adams* in this example. Again since we are using arrays, which start at 0, this will not be total −1, but total −2. Thus we get the following **for** loop:

```
for(int i = index; i<= total-2; i++)
{
  list[i] = list[i+1];
}
```

This isn't quite the whole story. If we used this loop on the initial list to delete *Okoya*, we would be left with the array depicted in figure 8.8.

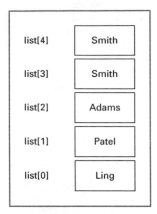

FIGURE 8.8 The 'list' array after *Okoya* has been deleted

As you can see, *Smith* is in two positions in the array. There is still a *Smith* in the last position of the list, as it hasn't been overwritten with anything. Although we don't really want that *Smith* in the last position, we can in fact simply ignore it – immediately after the **for** loop is finished, we reduce the total number of elements in the list by 1. Now the extra *Smith* is effectively hidden from the list.[4]

8.8.2 Testing the *Bank* class

Program 8.3 is a program that uses the Bank class – notice that we are using our new EasyScanner class here.

PROGRAM 8.3

```
public class BankProgram
{
  public static void main(String[] args)
  {
    char choice;
    int size;
    System.out.print("Maximum number of accounts? ");
    size = EasyScanner.nextInt();
    // create Bank object
    Bank myBank = new Bank(size);
    // offer menu
    do
```

---

[4] When a new item is added into the list it will overwrite this extra *Smith* item.

```
         {
         System.out.println();
         System.out.println("1. Create new account");
         System.out.println("2. Remove an account");
         System.out.println("3. Deposit money");
         System.out.println("4. Withdraw money");
         System.out.println("5. Check account details");
         System.out.println("6. Quit");
         System.out.println();
         System.out.print ("Enter choice [1-6]: ");

         // get choice
         choice = EasyScanner.nextChar();
         System.out.println();

         // process menu options
         switch (choice)
         {
            case '1': option1(myBank);
                      break;
            case '2': option2(myBank);
                      break;
            case '3': option3(myBank);
                      break;
            case '4': option4(myBank);
                      break;
            case '5': option5(myBank);
                      break;
            case '6': break;
            default: System.out.println("Invalid entry");
         }
      }
   while (choice != '6');
}


// add account
static void option1(Bank bankIn)
{
   // get details from user
   System.out.print("Enter account number: ");
   String number = EasyScanner.nextString();
   System.out.print("Enter account name: ");
   String name = EasyScanner.nextString();
   // create new account
```

```java
BankAccount account = new BankAccount(number, name);
// add account to list
boolean ok = bankIn.add(account); if (!ok)
{
  System.out.println("The list is full");
}
else
{
  System.out.println("Account created");
}
}


// remove account
static void option2(Bank bankIn)
{
  // get account number of account to remove
  System.out.print("Enter account number: ");
  String number = EasyScanner.nextString();
  // delete item if it exists
  boolean ok = bankIn.remove(number); if (!ok)
  {
    System.out.println("No such account number");
  }
  else
  {
    System.out.println("Account removed");
  }
}


// deposit money in an account
static void option3(Bank bankIn)
{
  // get details from user
  System.out.print("Enter account number: ");
  String number = EasyScanner.nextString();
  System.out.print("Enter amount to deposit: ");
  double amount = EasyScanner.nextDouble();
  boolean ok = bankIn.depositMoney(number, amount); // attempt to deposit
  if (!ok)
  {
    System.out.println("No such account number");
  }
  else
```

```
      {
        System.out.println("Money deposited");
      }
  }


  // withdraw money from an account
  static void option4(Bank bankIn)
  {
    // get details from user
    System.out.print("Enter account number: ");
    String number = EasyScanner.nextString();
    System.out.print("Enter amount to withdraw: ");
    double amount = EasyScanner.nextDouble();
    boolean ok = bankIn.withdrawMoney(number, amount); // attempt to withdraw
    if (!ok)
    {
      System.out.println("No such account number or insufficient funds");
    }
    else
    {
      System.out.println("Money withdrawn");
    }
  }


  // check account details
  static void option5(Bank bankIn)
  {
    // get details from user
    System.out.print("Enter account number ");
    String number = EasyScanner.nextString();
    BankAccount account = bankIn.getItem(number);
    if (account == null)
    {
      System.out.println("No such account number");
    }
    else
    {
      System.out.println("Account number: " + account.getAccountNumber());
      System.out.println("Account name: " + account.getAccountName());
      System.out.println("Balance: " + account.getBalance());
      System.out.println();
    }
  }
}
```

You are familiar with this sort of menu-driven program, so there is not too much to say about it, except to observe that this is probably the first example of an application which, although not all that complex, could actually be thought of as the kind of application that could be used in a real business environment. Of course, in the outside world such applications are much more sophisticated than this, but they are, in principle, not too different from the sort of thing we have just done. Notice that our application involves a number of classes that we have written ourselves, and have pulled together to form a single application.

It is worth drawing attention to the way that the program makes use of some of the features of the `Bank` class that we incorporated into the `BankProgram`. In `option1` (and similarly in other methods) we make use of the fact that the `add` method of `Bank` returns **true** if the new account was successfully added, and **false** otherwise:

```
boolean ok = bankIn.add(account);
if (!ok)
{
  System.out.println("The list is full");
}
else
{
  System.out.println("Account created");
}
```

In a similar way, in `option5`, we use the fact that the `getItem` method returns **null** if the account was not found:

```
BankAccount account = bankIn.getItem(number);
if (account == null)
{
  System.out.println("No such account number");
}
```

We end this chapter with an example program run from program 8.3, followed by a few ideas on how our application could be improved.

```
Maximum number of accounts? 100

1. Create new account
2. Remove an account
3. Deposit money
4. Withdraw money
5. Check account details
6. Quit

Enter choice [1-6]: 1
```

```
Enter account number: 63488965
Enter account name: Mary Land-Cookies
Account created

1. Create new account
2. Remove an account
3. Deposit money
4. Withdraw money
5. Check account details
6. Quit

Enter choice [1-6]: 1

Enter account number: 14322508
Enter account name: Laura Norder
Account created

1. Create new account
2. Remove an account
3. Deposit money
4. Withdraw money
5. Check account details
6. Quit

Enter choice [1-6]: 1

Enter account number: 90871435
Enter account name: Gary Baldi-Biscuits
Account created

1. Create new account
2. Remove an account
3. Deposit money
4. Withdraw money
5. Check account details
6. Quit

Enter choice [1-6]: 3

Enter account number: 90871435
Enter amount to deposit: 1500
Money deposited

1. Create new account
2. Remove an account
3. Deposit money
4. Withdraw money
5. Check account details
6. Quit
```

```
Enter choice [1-6]: 2

Enter account number: 14322508
Account removed

1. Create new account
2. Remove an account
3. Deposit money
4. Withdraw money
5. Check account details
6. Quit

Enter choice [1-6]: 5

Enter account number: 14322508
No such account number

1. Create new account
2. Remove an account
3. Deposit money
4. Withdraw money
5. Check account details
6. Quit

Enter choice [1-6]: 5

Enter account number: 90871435
Account number: 90871435
Account name: Gary Baldi-Biscuits
Balance: 1500.0

1. Create new account
2. Remove an account
3. Deposit money
4. Withdraw money
5. Check account details
6. Quit

Enter choice [1-6]: 6
```

As we pointed out, there are a few improvements that could be made to our application. Two of these are identified below:

1 The final program could provide an option that allows all accounts to be displayed.

2 The add method of the Bank class could be adapted so that duplicate account numbers are not allowed.

These changes are left as practical exercises.

Finally, we should point out that for our application to be useful to any organization, it would need to be able to store the account information even after the application terminates. However, before you are able to achieve this you will have to wait until the second semester, where you will find out how to create files to hold permanent records.

8.9 The benefits of object-oriented programming

In this chapter and the previous one you have seen how to create classes and use them as data types in your programs. You have seen how the process of building classes enables us to hide data within a class. Programming languages based on classes and objects – in other words, object-oriented languages – have brought a number of benefits, and are now the standard. Below we have summarized some of the benefits that this has brought us.

- As we have demonstrated, the ability to encapsulate data within a class has enabled us to build far more secure systems.

- The object-oriented approach makes it far easier for us to *reuse* classes again and again. Having defined a `BankAccount` class or a `Student` class for example, we can use them in many different programs without having to write a new class each time. In the next chapter you will also see how it is possible to refine existing classes to meet additional needs by the technique known as **inheritance**. If systems can be assembled from reusable objects, this leads to far higher productivity.

- With the object-oriented approach it is possible to define and use classes which are not yet complete. They can then be extended without upsetting the operation of other classes. This greatly improves the testing process. We can easily build prototypes without having to build a whole system before testing it and letting the user of the system see it.

- The object-oriented approach makes it far easier to make changes to systems once they have been completed. Whole classes can be replaced, or new classes can easily be added.

- The object-oriented way of doing things is a far more "natural" approach. We base our programs on objects that exist in the real world – students, bank accounts, customers and so on.

- The modular nature of object-oriented programming improves the whole development process. The modular approach means that the old methodologies whereby systems were first analysed, then designed, and then implemented and tested were able give way to new methods whereby these processes were far more integrated and systems were developed far more rapidly.

Self-test questions

1 In question 5 of the programming exercises at the end of chapter 2 you wrote a program that calculated the area and circumference of a circle. Now consider a `Circle` class that we could develop for this purpose. Here is the UML design:

Circle
-radius : double
+Circle(double) *+setRadius(double)* *+getRadius( ) : double* *+calculateArea() : double* *+calculateCircumference() : double*

a Distinguish between *attributes* and *methods* in this class.

b Explain what it meant by the term *encapsulation*, how it is recorded in this UML diagram and how it is implemented in a Java class.

c For each method in the `Circle` class, determine

- the number of parameters;
- the type of any parameters;
- the return type;
- the equivalent method header in Java.

d Add an additional method into this UML diagram, `calculateDiameter`, which calculates and returns the diameter of the circle.

e Write the Java code for the `calculateDiameter` method.

2 The UML diagram below represents the design for a `Student` class.

Student
-studentNumber : String *-studentName : String* *-markForMaths : int* *-markForEnglish : int* *-markForScience : int* *-fee : double*
+Student(String, String) *+getNumber() : String* *+getName() : String* *+enterMarks(int, int, int)* *+getMathsMark() : int* *+getEnglishMark() : int* *+getScienceMark() : int* *+calculateAverageMark() : double* *+getFee() : double* *+setFee(double)*

You can see that students have a name, a number, some marks for subjects they are studying and the fee. Methods are then provided to process this data.

a What is indicated by the fact that certain attributes and methods have been underlined?

b Write the Java code for the parts of the class that have been underlined.

3 Consider the following class:

```
public class SomeClass
{
  private int x;

  public SomeClass( )
  {
    x = 10;
  }

  public SomeClass(int xIn)
  {
    x = xIn;
  }

  public void setX(int xIn)
  {
    x = xIn;
  }

  public int getX()
  {
    return x;
  }
}
```

a What would be the output from the following program?

```
public class ImplementinqClassesQ3a
{
  public static void main(String[] args)
  {
    SomeClass myObject = new SomeClass();
    System.out.println(myObject.getX());
  }
}
```

b What would be the output from the following program?

```
public class ImplementingClassesQ3b
{
  public static void main(String[] args)
```

```
    {
      SomeClass myObject = new SomeClass(5);
      System.out.println(myObject.getX());
    }
}
```

c Explain why the following program would not compile.

```
public class ImplementingClassesQ3c
{
  public static void main(String[] args)
  {
    SomeClass myObject = new SomeClass(5, 8);
    System.out.println(myObject.getX());
  }
}
```

d What would be the output from the following program?

```
public class ImplementingClassesQ3d
{
  public static void main(String[] args)
  {
    int y = 20;
    SomeClass myObject = new SomeClass(5);
    System.out.println(myObject.getX());
    test(y, myObject);
    System.out.println(y);
    System.out.println(myObject.getX());
  }
  static void test(int z, SomeClass classIn)
  {
    z = 50;
    classIn.setX(100);
  }
}
```

4 Identify some of the reasons why the object-oriented approach has become the norm for programming.

Programming exercises

1 a Implement the `Circle` class that was discussed in self-test question 1 above.

  b Add the `calculateDiameter` method into this class as discussed in self-test question 1d and 1e above.

  c Write a program to test out your class. This program should allow the user to enter a value for the radius of the circle, and then display the area, circumference and diameter of this circle on the screen by calling the appropriate methods of the `Circle` class.

  d Modify the tester program above so that the once the information has been displayed the user is able to reset the radius of the circle. The area, circumference and diameter of the circle should then be displayed again.

2 a Write the code for the `Student` class discussed in self-test question 2 above. You should note that in order to ensure that a **double** is returned from the `calculateAverageMark` method, you should specifically divide the total of the three marks by 3.0 and not simply by 3 (look back at chapter 2 to remind yourself why this is the case).

      Another thing to think about is what you choose for the initial values of the marks. If you choose to give each mark an initial value of zero, this could be ambiguous; a mark of zero could mean that the mark simply has not been entered – or it could mean the student actually scored zero in the subject! Can you think of a better initial value?
      You can assume that the fees for the student are set initially to 750.

  b Write a tester class to test out your `Student` class; it should create two or three students (or even better an array of students), and use the methods of the `Student` class to test whether they work according to the specification.

3 A system is being developed for use in a store that sells electrical appliances. A class called `StockItem` is required for this system. An object of the `StockItem` class will require the following attributes:

  ■ a stock number;
  ■ a name;
  ■ the price of the item;
  ■ the total number of these items currently in stock.

The first three of the above attributes will need to be set at the time a `StockItem` object is created – the total number of items in stock will be set to zero at this time. The stock number and name will not need to be changed after the item is created.
The following methods are also required:

  ■ a method that allows the price to be re-set during the object's lifetime;
  ■ a method that receives an integer and adds this to the total number of items of this type in stock;
  ■ a method that returns the total value of items of this type in stock; this is calculated by multiplying the price of the item by the number of items in stock;
  ■ methods to read the values of all four attributes.

The design of the `StockItem` class is shown in the following UML diagram:

StockItem
-stockNumber : String -name : String -price : double -totalStock : int
+StockItem(String, String, double) +setPrice(double) +increaseTotalStock(int) +getStockNumber() : String +getName() : String +getTotalStock() : int +getPrice() : double +calculateTotalPrice() : double

a Write the code for the `StockItem` class.

b Consider the following program, which uses the `StockItem` class, and in which some of the code has been replaced by comments:

```
import java.util.*;
public class TestProg
{
  public static void main(String[] args)
  {
    Scanner keyboard = new Scanner(System.in);
    Scanner keyboardString = new Scanner(System.in);
    String tempNumber;
    String tempName;
    double tempPrice;

    System.out.print("Enter the stock number: ");
    tempNumber = keyboardString.nextLine();
    System.out.print("Enter the name of the item: ");
    tempName = keyboardString.nextLine();
    System.out.print("Enter the price of the item: ");
    tempPrice = keyboard.nextDouble();

    // Create a new item of stock using the values that were entered by the user

    // Increase the total number of items in stock by 5

    // Display the stock number

    // Display the total price of all items in stock
  }
}
```

Replace the comments with appropriate code.

c **i** A further attribute, `salesTax`, is required. The value of this attribute should always be the same for each object of the class. Write the declaration for this attribute.

   ii Provide a class method, `setSalesTax`, for this class – it should receive a **double** and set the value of the sales tax to this value.

   iii Write a line of code that sets the sales tax for all objects of the class to 10 without referring to any particular object.

4 The class shown below keeps track of a pressure sensor in a laboratory.

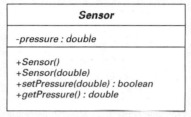

> **Sensor**
>
> -pressure : double
>
> +Sensor()
> +Sensor(double)
> +setPressure(double) : boolean
> +getPressure() : double

When a `Sensor` object is created using the first constructor, the initial pressure is set to zero. When it is created using the second constructor it is set to the value of the parameter.

The pressure should not be set to a value less than zero. Therefore, if the input parameter to the `setPressure` method is a negative number, the pressure should not be changed and a value of false should be returned. If the pressure is set successfully, a value of true should be returned.

a Write the code for the `Sensor` class.

b Develop a `SensorTester` program to test the `Sensor` class.

5 Consider a class that keeps track of the temperature within a nuclear reactor. The UML diagram is shown below:

> **Reactor**
>
> -temperature : int
> +MAX : int
> +MIN : int
>
> +Reactor()
> +getTemperature() : int
> +increaseTemperature(boolean)
> +decreaseTemperature(boolean)

When a `Reactor` object is created, the temperature is initially set to zero.

The `increaseTemp` method increases the temperature by 1, and the `decreaseTemp` method decreases the temperature by 1. However, the temperature must never be allowed to rise above a maximum value of 10 nor fall below a minumum value of –10. If an attempt is made to increase or decrease the temperature so it falls outside this range, then an alarm must be raised; the methods in this case should not increase or decrease the temperature but should return a value of **false**, indicating that the alarm should be raised. If the temperature is changed successfully, however, a value of **true** is returned.

a Write the code for the `Reactor` class.

b Develop a `ReactorTester` program to test the `Reactor` class.

6 Implement the changes to the bank application suggested at the very end of section 8.8. The source code for the `Bank` class and the `BankProgram` class is provided on the accompanying CD.

7 a In programming exercise 5 of the last chapter you were asked to develop a program to process a collection of rooms in an apartment. Now consider a collection class, `Apartment`, for this purpose. The `Apartment` class would store a collection of `Rectangle` objects, where each `Rectangle` object represents a particular room in the apartment. The UML diagram depicting the association between the `Apartment` class and the `Rectangle` class is shown below:

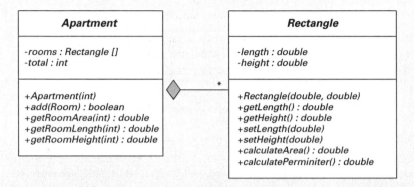

The attributes of the `Apartment` class consist of an array of `Rectangle` objects, representing the rooms in the apartment and an integer attribute, `total`, which keeps track of the number of rooms added into this array so far.

The methods of the `Apartment` class are described below:

+Apartment(int)

The constructor accepts an integer value representing the number of rooms in the apartment and sizes the `rooms` array accordingly.

+add(Room) : boolean

Adds the given room to the `rooms` array. Returns **true** if added successfully and **false** if the array is full.

+getRoomArea(int) : double

Returns the area of the given room number sent in as a parameter. If an invalid room number is sent in as a parameter this method should send back some dummy value (for example –999).

+getRoomLength(int) : double

Returns the length of the given room number sent in as a parameter. If an invalid room number is sent in as a parameter this method should send back some dummy value (for example –999).

+getRoomHeight(int) : double

Returns the height of the given room number sent in as a parameter. If an invalid room number is sent in as a parameter this method should send back some dummy value (for example –999).

Implement the Apartment class.

b Develop an `ApartmentTester` program to test the `Apartment` class.

8 Consider a scenario in which a university allows lecturers to borrow equipment. The equipment is available for use 5 days a week and for 7 periods during each day. When the equipment is booked for use, the details of the booking (room number and lecturer name) are recorded. When no booking is recorded, the equipment is available for use.

a Create a `Booking` class defined in the UML diagram below:

Booking
-room : String
-name : String
+Booking(String, String)
+getRoom() : String
+getName() : String

b Now a `TimeTable` class is defined to process these bookings. Its UML diagram is given below:

TimeTable
-times : Booking[][]
+TimeTable(int, int)
+makeBooking(int, int, Booking) : boolean
+cancelBooking(int, int) : boolean
+isFree(int, int) : boolean
+getBooking(int, int) : Booking
+numberOfDays() : int
+numberOfPeriods() : int

As you can see, the attribute of this class is a two-dimensional array of `Booking` objects. The methods of this class are defined below:

+TimeTable(int, int)
A constructor accepts the number of days per week and number of periods per day and sizes the timetable accordingly.
You should note that initially all elements in the array will of course have a **null** value – *a* **null** *value will represent an empty slot.*

+makeBooking(int, int, Booking): boolean
Accepts the booking details for a particular day and period and, as long as this slot is not previously booked and the day and period numbers are valid, updates the timetable accordingly. Returns **true** if the booking was recorded successfully and **false** if not.

+cancelBooking(int, int): boolean
Cancels the booking details for a particular day and period. Returns **false** if the given slot was not previously booked or the day and period number are invalid, and **true** if the slot was cancelled successfully.

+isFree(int, int): boolean

Accepts a day and period number and returns **true** if the day and period numbers are valid and the given slot is free, and **false** otherwise.

+getBooking(int, int): Booking

Accepts a day and period number and returns the booking for the given slot if the day and period number are valid and the slot has been booked or **null** otherwise.

+numberOfDays(): int

Returns the number of days associated with this timetable.

+numberOfPeriods(): int

Returns the number of periods associated with this timetable.

Implement this class in Java.

c Write a suitable tester for this class.

9 Add some additional methods such as nextByte and nextLong to the EasyScanner class.

CHAPTER
09

Inheritance

9.1 Introduction

One of the greatest benefits of the object-oriented approach to software development is that it offers the opportunity for us to *reuse* classes that have already been written – either by ourselves or by someone else. Let's look at a possible scenario. Say you wanted to develop a software system and you have, during your analysis, identified the need for a class called Employee. You might be aware that a colleague in your organization has already written an Employee class; rather than having to write your own class, it would be easier to approach your colleague and ask her to let you use her Employee class.

So far so good, but what if the Employee class that you are given doesn't quite do everything that you had hoped? Perhaps your employees are part-time employees, and you want your class to have an attribute like hourlyPay, or methods like calculateWeeklyPay and setHourlyPay, and these attributes and methods do not exist in the Employee class you have been given.

You may think it would be necessary to go into the old class and start messing about with the code. But there is no need, because object-oriented programming languages provide the ability to extend existing classes by adding attributes and methods to them. This is called **inheritance**.

9.2 Defining inheritance

Inheritance is the sharing of attributes and methods among classes. We take a class, and then define other classes based on the first one. The new classes *inherit* all the attributes and methods of the first one, but also have attributes and methods of their own. Let's try to understand this by thinking about the Employee class.

Say our Employee class has two attributes, number and name, a user-defined constructor, and some basic get- and set- methods for the attributes. We now define our PartTimeEmployee class; this class will *inherit* these attributes and methods, but can also have attributes and methods of its own. We will give it one additional attribute, hourlyPay, some methods to access this attribute and one additional method, calculateWeeklyPay.

This is illustrated in figure 9.1 which uses the UML notation for inheritance, namely a triangle.

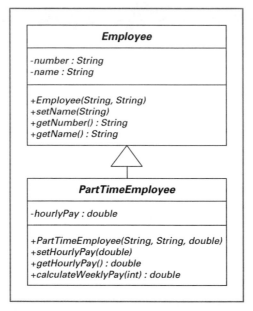

FIGURE 9.1 An inheritance relationship

You can see from this diagram that an inheritance relationship is a *hierarchical* relationship. The class at the top of the hierarchy – in this case the Employee class – is referred to as the **superclass** (or **base class**) and the PartTimeEmployee as the **subclass** (or **derived class**).

The inheritance relationship is also often referred to as an *is-a-kind-of* relationship; in this case a PartTimeEmployee *is a kind of* Employee.

9.3 Implementing inheritance in Java

The code for the Employee class is shown below:

THE *EMPLOYEE* CLASS

```java
public class Employee
{
  private String number;
  private String name;
  public Employee(String numberIn, String nameIn)
  {
    number = numberIn;
    name = nameIn;
  }
  public void setName(String nameIn)
  {
    name = nameIn;
  }
  public String getNumber()
  {
    return number;
  }
  public String getName()
  {
    return name;
  }
}
```

There is nothing new here, so let's get on with our `PartTimeEmployee` class. We will present the code first and analyse it afterwards.

THE *PARTTIMEEMPLOYEE* CLASS

```java
public class PartTimeEmployee extends Employee // this class is a subclass of Employee
{
  private double hourlyPay; // this attribute is unique to the subclass
  // the constructor
  public PartTimeEmployee(String numberIn, String nameIn, double hourlyPayIn)
  {
    super(numberIn, nameIn); // call the constructor of the superclass
    hourlyPay = hourlyPayIn;
  }
  // these methods are also unique to the subclass
  public double getHourlyPay()
```

```
{
  return hourlyPay;
}
public void setHourlyPay(double hourlyPayIn)
{
  hourlyPay = hourlyPayIn;
}
public double calculateWeeklyPay(int noOfHoursIn)
{
  return noOfHoursIn * hourlyPay;
}
}
```

The first line of interest is the class header itself:

```
public class PartTimeEmployee extends Employee
```

Here we see the use of the keyword **extends**. Using this word in this way means that the PartTimeEmployee class (the *subclass*) inherits all the attributes and methods of the Employee class (the *superclass*). So, although we haven't coded them, any object of the PartTimeEmployee class will have, for example, an attribute called name and a method called getNumber. A PartTimeEmployee is now a *kind of* Employee.

But can you see a problem here? The attributes have been declared as **private** in the superclass so although they are now part of our PartTimeEmployee class, none of the PartTimeEmployee class methods can directly access them – the subclass has only the same access rights as any other class!

There are a number of possible ways around this:

1   We could declare the original attributes as **public** – but this would take away the whole point of encapsulation.

2   We could use the special keyword **protected** instead of **private**. The effect of this is that anything declared as **protected** is accessible to the methods of any subclasses. There are, however, two issues to think about here. The first is that you have to anticipate in advance when you want your class to be able to be inherited. The second problem is that it weakens your efforts to encapsulate information within the class, since, in Java, **protected** attributes are also accessible to any other class in the same package (you will find out much more about the meaning of the word **package** in chapter 20).

The above remarks notwithstanding, this is a perfectly acceptable approach to use, particularly in situations where you are writing a class as part of a discrete application, and you will be aware in advance that certain classes will need to be subclassed. You will see an example of this in section 9.4.

Incidentally, in a UML diagram a **protected** attribute is indicated by a hash symbol, #.

3   The other solution, and the one we will use now, is to leave the attributes as **private**, but to plan carefully in advance which get- and set- methods we are going to provide.

After the class header we have the following declaration:

```
private double hourlyPay;
```

This declares an attribute, `hourlyPay`, which is unique to our subclass – but remember that the attributes of the superclass, `Employee`, will be inherited, so in fact any `PartTimeEmployee` object will have *three* attributes.

Next comes the constructor. We want to be able to assign values to the number and name at the time that the object is created, just as we do with an `Employee` object; so our constructor will need to receive parameters that will be assigned to the `number` and `name` attributes.

But wait a minute! How are we going to do this? The `number` and `name` attributes have been declared as **private** in the superclass – so they aren't accessible to objects of the subclass. Luckily there is a way around this problem. We can call the constructor of the superclass by using the keyword **super**. Look how this is done:

```
public PartTimeEmployee(String numberIn, String nameIn, double hourlyPayIn)
{
  super(numberIn, nameIn); // call the constructor of the superclass
  hourlyPay = hourlyPayIn;
}
```

After calling the constructor of the superclass, we need to perform one more task – namely to assign the third parameter, `hourlyPayIn`, to the `hourlyPay` attribute. Notice, however, that the line that calls **super** has to be the first one – if we had written our constructor like this it would not compile:

```
/* This version of the constructor would not compile - the call to super has to be
   the first instruction */

public PartTimeEmployee(String numberIn, String nameIn, double hourlyPayIn)
{
  hourlyPay = hourlyPayIn;
  super(numberIn, nameIn); // this call should have been the first instruction
}
```

The remaining methods of `PartTimeEmployee` are new methods specific to the subclass:

```
public double getHourlyPay()
{
  return hourlyPay;
}
```

```
public void setHourlyPay(double hourlyPayIn)
{
  hourlyPay = hourlyPayIn;
}
public double calculateWeeklyPay(int noOfHoursIn)
{
  return noOfHoursIn * hourlyPay;
}
```

The first two provide read and write access respectively to the hourlyPay attribute. The third one receives the number of hours worked and calculates the pay by multiplying this by the hourly rate. Program 9.1 demonstrates the use of the PartTimeEmployee class.

PROGRAM 9.1

```
import java.util.*;
public class PartTimeEmployeeTester
{
  public static void main(String[] args)
  {
    Scanner keyboard = new Scanner(System.in);
    Scanner keyboardString = new Scanner(System.in);
    String number, name;
    double pay;
    int hours;
    PartTimeEmployee emp;
    // get the details from the user
    System.out.print("Employee Number? ");
    number = keyboardString.nextLine();
    System.out.print("Employee's Name? ");
    name = keyboardString.nextLine();
    System.out.print("Hourly Pay? ");
    pay = keyboard.nextDouble();
    System.out.print("Hours worked this week? ");
    hours = keyboard.nextInt();
    // create a new part-time employee
    emp = new PartTimeEmployee(number, name, pay);
    // display part-time employee's details, including the weekly pay
    System.out.println();
```

```
    // the next two methods have been inherited from the Employee class
    System.out.println(emp.getName());

    System.out.println(emp.getNumber());

    System.out.println(emp.calculateWeeklyPay(hours));
  }
}
```

Here is a sample test run:

> *Employee Number?* **A103456**
>
> *Employee's Name?* **Mandy Lifeboats**
>
> *Hourly Pay?* **15.50**
>
> *Hours worked this week?* **20**
>
> *Mandy Lifeboats*
>
> *A103456*
>
> *310.0*

We can now move on to look at another inheritance example; let's choose the `Rectangle` class that we developed in the last chapter.

9.3.1 Extending the *Rectangle* class

We are going to define a new class called `ExtendedRectangle`, which extends the `Rectangle` class. First, let's remind ourselves of the `Rectangle` class itself.

THE *RECTANGLE* CLASS – a reminder

```
public class Rectangle
{
  // the attributes are declared first
  private double length;
  private double height;


  // then the methods


  // the constructor
  public Rectangle(double lengthIn, double heightIn)
  {
    length = lengthIn;
    height = heightIn;
  }
```

```
    // the next method allows us to read the length attribute
    public double getLength()
    {
      return length;
    }


    // the next method allows us to read the height attribute
    public double getHeight()
    {
      return height;
    }
    // the next method allows us to write to the length attribute
    public void setLength(double lengthIn)
    {
      length = lengthIn;
    }
    // the next method allows us to write to the height attribute
    public void setHeight(double heightIn)
    {
      height = heightIn;
    }
    // this method returns the area of the rectangle
    public double calculateArea()
    {
      return length * height;
    }


    // this method returns the perimeter of the rectangle
    public double calculatePerimeter()
    {
      return 2 * (length + height);
    }
}
```

The original `Rectangle` class had the capability of reporting on the perimeter and area of the rectangle. Our extended class will have the capability of sending back a string representation of itself composed of a number of symbols such as asterisks – for example:

```
*****
*****
*****
```

Now at first glance you might think that this isn't a string at all, because it consists of several lines. But if we think of the instruction to start a new line as just another character – which for convenience we could call <NEWLINE> – then our string could be written like this.

```
*****<NEWLINE>*****<NEWLINE>*****
```

In Java we are able to represent this <NEWLINE> character with a special character that looks like this:

```
'\n'
```

This is one of a number of special characters called **escape characters**, which are always introduced by a backslash (\). Another useful escape character is '\t' which inserts a tab.[1]

Our `ExtendedRectangle` class will need an additional attribute, which we will call `symbol`, to hold the character that is to be used to draw the rectangle. We will also provide a `setSymbol` method, and of course we will need a method that sends back the string representation. We will call this method `draw`. The new constructor will accept values for the length and height as before, but will also receive the character to be used for drawing the rectangle.

The design is shown in figure 9.2.

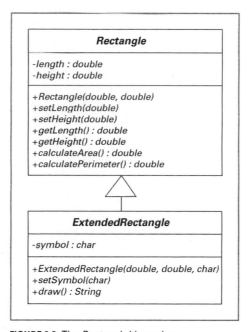

FIGURE 9.2 The *Rectangle* hierarchy

Now for the implementation. As well as those aspects of the code that relate to inheritance, there is an additional new technique used in this class – this is the technique known as **type casting**. Take a look at the complete code first – then we can discuss this new concept along with some other important features of the class.

---

[1] You would also have to place a backslash in front of a double quote (\ "), a single quote (\ ') or another backslash (\ \) if you wanted any of these to be output as part of a string. This is because the compiler would interpret these as having a special meaning such as terminating the string. You will see an example of this in section 10.5.

THE *EXTENDEDRECTANGLE* CLASS

```java
public class ExtendedRectangle extends Rectangle
{
  private char symbol;

  // the constructor
  public ExtendedRectangle(double lengthIn, double heightIn, char symbolIn)
  {
    super(lengthIn, heightIn);
    symbol = symbolIn;
  }
  public void setSymbol(char symbolIn)
  {
    symbol = symbolIn;
  }


  public String draw()
  {
    String s = new String(); // start off with an empty string
    int l, h;
    /* in the next two lines we type cast from double to integer so that we are able to count
       how many times we print the symbol */
    l = (int) getLength();
    h = (int) getHeight();
    for (int i = 1; i <= h; i++)
    {
      for (int j = 1; j <= l; j++)
      {
        s = s + symbol; // add the symbol to the string
      }
      s = s + '\n'; // add the <NEWLINE> character
    }
    return s; // return the string representation
  }
}
```

So let's take a closer look at all this. After the class header – which **extends** the Rectangle class – we declare the additional attribute, symbol, and then define our constructor:

```
public ExtendedRectangle(double lengthIn, double heightIn, char symbolIn)
{
   super(lengthIn, heightIn);
   symbol = symbolIn;
}
```

Once again we call the constructor of the superclass with the keyword **super**. After the constructor comes the setSymbol method – which allows the symbol to be changed during the rectangle's lifetime – and then we have the draw method, which introduces the new concept of **type casting**:

```
public String draw()
{
   String s = new String(); // start off with an empty string
   int l, h;
   l = (int) getLength();
   h = (int) getHeight();
   for (int i = 1; i <= h; i++)
   {
     for (int j = 1; j <= l; j++)
     {
       s = s + symbol; // add a symbol to end of the string
     }
     s = s + '\n'; // add a new line to the string
   }
   return s;
}
```

Inspect the code carefully – notice that we have declared two local variables of type **int**. In order to understand the purpose of these two variables, l and h, we need to explore this business of type casting, which means forcing an item to change from one type to another.

The draw method is going to create a string of one or more rows of stars or crosses or whatever symbol is chosen. Now the dimensions of the rectangle are defined as **double**s. Clearly our draw method needs to be dealing with whole numbers of rows and columns – so we must convert the length and height of the rectangle from **double**s to **int**s. There will obviously be some loss of precision here, but that won't matter in this particular case.

As you can see from the above code, type casting is achieved by placing the new type name in brackets before the item you wish to change. This is illustrated in figure 9.3.

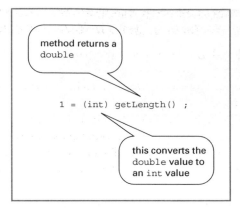

FIGURE 9.3 Type casting

Program 9.2 uses the `ExtendedRectangle` class. It creates a rectangle of length 10 and height 5, with an asterisk as the symbol; it then draws the rectangle, changes the symbol to a cross, and draws it again.

PROGRAM 9.2

```
public class ExtendedRectangleTester
{
  public static void main(String[] args)
  {
    ExtendedRectangle extRectangle = new ExtendedRectangle(10.2,5.3,'*');
    System.out.println(extRectangle.draw());
    extRectangle.setSymbol('+');
    System.out.println(extRectangle.draw());
  }
}
```

The output from program 9.2 is shown below:

```
* * * * * * * * * *
* * * * * * * * * *
* * * * * * * * * *
* * * * * * * * * *
* * * * * * * * * *

+ + + + + + + + + +
+ + + + + + + + + +
+ + + + + + + + + +
+ + + + + + + + + +
+ + + + + + + + + +
```

9.4 Method overriding

In chapter 5 you were introduced to the concept of polymorphism – the idea that we can have different methods with the same name, but whose behaviour is different. You saw in that chapter that one way of achieving polymorphism was by method *overloading*, which involves methods of the same class having the same name, but being distinguished by their parameter lists.

Now we are going to explore another way of achieving polymorphism, namely by **method overriding**. In order to do this we are going to extend the BankAccount class that we developed in the previous chapter. You will recall that the class we developed there did not provide any overdraft facility – the withdraw method was designed so that the withdrawal would take place only if the amount to be withdrawn did not exceed the balance.

Now let's consider a special account which is the same as the original account, but allows holders of the account to be given an overdraft limit and to withdraw funds up to this limit. We will call this account GoldAccount. Since a GoldAccount *is a kind of* BankAccount, we can use inheritance here to design the GoldAccount class. In addition to the attributes of a BankAccount, a GoldAccount will need to have an attribute to represent the overdraft limit, and should have get- and set- methods for this attribute. As far as the methods are concerned, we need to reconsider the withdraw method. This will differ from the original method, because, instead of checking that the amount to be withdrawn does not exceed the balance, it will now check that the amount does not exceed the total of the balance plus the overdraft limit. So what we are going to do is to rewrite – or *override* – the withdraw method in the subclass.

The design of the BankAccount class and the GoldAccount class appears in figure 9.4. You will notice that we have made a small change to the original BankAccount class. The balance attribute has a hash sign (#) in front of it instead of a minus sign. You will remember from our previous discussion that this means access to the attribute is **protected**, rather than **private**. The reason why we have decided to make this change is explained below.

You will also notice that the withdraw method appears in both classes – this, of course, is because we are going to override it in the subclass.

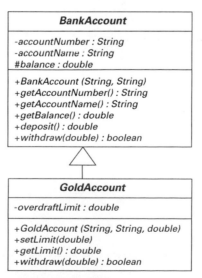

FIGURE 9.4 The UML diagram for the *BankAccount* hierarchy

You might already be thinking about how to code the `withdraw` method in the `GoldAccount` class. If you are doing this, you will probably have worked out that this method is going to need access to the `balance` attribute, which of course was declared as **private** in the `BankAccount` class, and (for good reason) was not provided with a `set-` method.

When we developed the `BankAccount` class in chapter 8, we developed it as a stand-alone class, and we didn't think about how it might be used in a larger application where it could be refined. Had we known about inheritance at that point we might have given the matter a little more thought, and realized that it would be useful if any subclasses of `BankAccount` that were developed in the future had access to the `balance` attribute. As we explained in section 9.3, we can achieve that by declaring that attribute as **protected** instead of **private**. That is what we have done here. The version of `BankAccount` that we are going to use in this chapter is therefore exactly the same as the previous one, with the single difference that the declaration of the `balance` attribute now looks like this, with the keyword **protected** replacing **private**:

```
protected double balance;
```

This new version of the `BankAccount` class is available on the CD, in the Chapter 9 folder.

Here is the code for the `GoldAccount` class:

THE *GOLDACCOUNT* CLASS

```java
public class GoldAccount extends BankAccount
{
  private double overdraftLimit;

  public GoldAccount(String numberIn, String nameIn, double limitIn)
  {
    super(numberIn, nameIn);
    overdraftLimit = limitIn;
  }

  public void setLimit(double limitIn)
  {
    overdraftLimit = limitIn;
  }

  public double getLimit()
    {
    return overdraftLimit;
  }

  public boolean withdraw(double amountIn)
```

```
    {
        if(amountIn > balance + overdraftLimit) /* the customer can withdraw up to the
                                                    overdraft limit */
        {
            return false; // no withdrawal was made
        }
        else
        {
            balance = balance - amountIn; // balance is protected so we have direct access to it
            return true; // money was withdrawn successfully
        }
    }
}
```

The thing that we are interested in here is the `withdraw` method. As we show below, the test in the `if` statement differs from the original method in the `BankAccount` class, in order to take account of the fact that customers with a gold account are allowed an overdraft:

withdraw **method in** BankAccount **class**

```
public boolean withdraw(double amountIn)
{
    if(amountIn > balance)
    {
        return false;
    }
    else
    {
        balance = balance - amountIn;
        return true;
    }
}
```

withdraw **method in** GoldAccount **class**

```
public boolean withdraw(double amountIn)
{
    if(amountIn > balance + overdraftLimit)
    {
        return false;
    }
    else
    {
        balance = balance - amountIn;
        return true;
    }
}
```

When we dealt with method *overloading* in chapter 5 we told you that the methods with the same name *within* a class are distinguished by their parameter lists. In the case of method *overriding*, the methods have the same parameter list but belong to different classes – the superclass and the subclass. In this case they are distinguished by the *object with which they are associated*. We illustrate this in program 9.3.

PROGRAM 9.3

```
public class OverridingDemo
{
    public static void main(String[] args)
    {
        boolean ok;
        //declare a BankAccount object
        BankAccount bankAcc = new BankAccount("123", "Ordinary Account Holder");
        //declare a GoldAccount object
```

```
    GoldAccount goldAcc = new GoldAccount("124", "Gold Account Holder", 500);


    bankAcc.deposit(1000);
    goldAcc.deposit(1000);


    ok = bankAcc.withdraw(1250); // the withdraw method of BankAccount is called
    if(ok)
    {
      System.out.print("Money withdrawn. ");
    }
    else
    {
      System.out.print("Insufficient funds. ");
    }
    System.out.println("Balance of " + bankAcc.getAccountName() + " is "
                                   + bankAcc.getBalance());

    System.out.println();


    ok = goldAcc.withdraw(1250);  // the withdraw method of GoldAccount is called
    if(ok)
    {
      System.out.print("Money withdrawn. ");
    }
    else
    {
      System.out.print("Insufficient funds. ");
    }
    System.out.println("Balance of " + goldAcc.getAccountName() + " is "
                                   + goldAcc.getBalance());

    System.out.println();
  }
}
```

In this program we create an object of the BankAccount class and an object of the GoldAccount class (with an overdraft limit of 500), and deposit an amount of 1000 in each:

```
BankAccount bankAcc = new BankAccount("123", "Ordinary Account Holder");
GoldAccount goldAcc = new GoldAccount("124", "Gold Account Holder", 500);
bankAcc.deposit(1000);
goldAcc.deposit(1000);
```

Next we attempt to withdraw the sum of 1250 from the BankAccount object and assign the return value to a **boolean** variable, ok:

```
ok = bankAcc.withdraw(1250);
```

The withdraw method that is called here will be that of BankAccount, because it is called via the BankAccount object, bankAcc.

Once this is done we display a message showing whether or not the withdrawal was successful, followed by the balance of that account:

```
if(ok)
{
  System.out.print("Money withdrawn. ");
}
  else
{
  System.out.print("Insufficient funds. ");
}
System.out.println("Balance of " + bankAcc.getAccountName() + " is "
                              + bankAcc.getBalance());
```

Now the withdraw method is called again, but in this case via the GoldAccount object, goldAcc:

```
ok = goldAcc.withdraw(1250);
```

This time it is the withdraw method of GoldAccount that will be called, because goldAcc is an object of this class. The appropriate message and the balance are again displayed.

The output from this program is shown below:

```
Insufficient funds. Balance of Ordinary Account Holder is 1000.0

Money withdrawn. Balance of Gold Account Holder is -250.0
```

As we would expect, the withdrawal from BankAccount does not take place – the balance is 1000, and since there is no overdraft facility a request to withdraw 1250 is denied.

In the case of the GoldAccount, however, a withdrawal of 1250 would result in a negative balance of 250, which is allowed, because it is within the overdraft limit of 500.

9.5 Abstract classes

Let's think again about our Employee class. Imagine that our business expands, and we now employ full-time employees as well as part-time employees. A full-time employee object, rather than having an hourly rate of pay, will have an annual salary. It might also need a method that calculates the monthly pay (by dividing the annual salary by 12).

Figure 9.5 shows the structure of an employee hierarchy with the two types of employee, the full-time and the part-time employee.

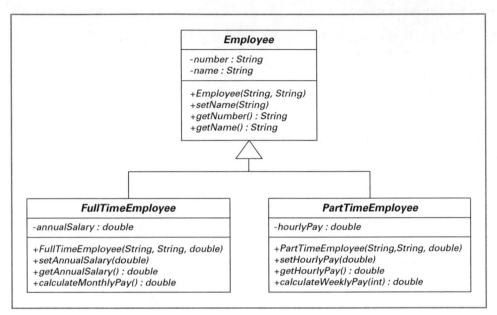

FIGURE 9.5 An inheritance relationship showing the superclass *Employee* and the subclasses *FullTimeEmployee* and *PartTimeEmployee*

Notice how the two subclasses contain the attributes and methods appropriate to the class. If you think about this a bit more, it will occur to you that *any* employee will always be either a full-time employee or a part-time employee. There is never going to be a situation in which an individual is just a plain old employee! So users of a program that included all these classes would never find themselves creating objects of the `Employee` class. In fact it would be a good idea to prevent people from doing this – and, as you might have guessed, there is a way to do so, which is to declare the class as **abstract**. Once a class has been declared in this way it means that you are not allowed to create objects of that class. In order to make our employee class abstract all we have to do is to place the keyword **abstract** in the header:

```
public abstract class Employee
```

The `Employee` class simply acts a basis on which to build other classes. Now, if you tried to create an object of the `Employee` class you would get a compiler error.

We have already seen the code for `Employee` and `PartTimeEmployee`; Here is the code for the `FullTimeEmployee` class:

THE *FULLTIMEEMPLOYEE* CLASS

```java
public class FullTimeEmployee extends Employee
{
  private double annualSalary;

  public FullTimeEmployee(String numberIn, String nameIn, double salaryIn)
  {
    super(numberIn,nameIn);
    annualSalary = salaryIn;
  }

  public void setAnnualSalary(double salaryIn)
  {
    annualSalary = salaryIn;
  }

  public double getAnnualSalary()
  {
    return annualSalary;
  }

  public double calculateMonthlyPay()
  {
    return annualSalary/12;
  }
}
```

As we said before, an inheritance relationship is often referred to as an "*is-a-kind-of*" relationship. A full-time employee is a *kind of* employee, as is a part-time employee. Therefore an object that is of type `PartTimeEmployee` is also of type `Employee` – an object is the type of its class, and also of any of the superclasses in the hierarchy.

Let's see how this relationship works in a Java program. Imagine a method which is set up to receive an `Employee` object. If we call that method and send in a `FullTimeEmployee` object or a `PartTimeEmployee` object, either is absolutely fine – because both are *kinds of* `Employee`. We demonstrate this in program 9.4.

PROGRAM 9.4

```java
public class EmployeeTester
{
  public static void main(String[] args)
  {
    FullTimeEmployee fte = new FullTimeEmployee("A123", "Ms Full-Time", 25000);
```

```
    PartTimeEmployee pte = new PartTimeEmployee("B456", "Mr Part-Time",30);
    testMethod(fte); // call testMethod with a full-time employee object
    testMethod(pte); // call testMethod with a part-time employee object
  }


  static void testMethod(Employee employeeIn) /* the method expects to receive an Employee
                                                  object */
  {
    System.out.println(employeeIn.getName());
  }
}
```

In this program `testMethod` expects to receive an `Employee` object. It calls the `getName` method of `Employee` in order to display the employee's name.

In the `main` method, we create two objects, one `FullTimeEmployee` and one `PartTime Employee`:

```
FullTimeEmployee fte = new FullTimeEmployee("A123", "Ms Full-Time", 25000);
PartTimeEmployee pte = new PartTimeEmployee("B456", "Mr Part-Time",30);
```

We then call `testMethod` twice – first with `FullTimeEmployee` object and then with the `PartTimeEmployee` object:

```
testMethod(fte); // call testMethod with a full-time employee object
testMethod(pte); // call testMethod with a part-time employee object
```

The method accepts either object, and calls the `getName` method. The output is, as expected:

```
  Ms Full-Time
  Mr Part-Time
```

9.6 Abstract methods

In program 9.4 we conveniently gave our objects the names "Ms Full-Time" and "Mr Part-Time" so that we could easily identify them in our output. In fact, it wouldn't be a bad idea – particularly for testing purposes – if every `Employee` type actually had a method that returned a string telling us the kind of object we were dealing with. Adding such a method – we could call it `getStatus` – would be simple. For the `FullTimeEmployee` the method would look like this:

```
public String getStatus()
{
  return "Full-Time";
}
```

For the `PartTimeEmployee`, `getStatus` would look like this:

```
public String getStatus()
{
  return "Part-Time";
}
```

It would be very useful if we could say, to anyone using any of the `Employee` types, that we *guarantee* that this class will have a `getStatus` method. That way, a developer could, for example, write a method that accepts an `Employee` object, and call that object's `getStatus` method, even without knowing anything else about the class.

As you have probably guessed, we *can* guarantee it! What we have to do is to write an **abstract** method in the superclass – in this case `Employee`. Declaring a method as **abstract** means that any subclass is *forced* to override it – otherwise there would be a compiler error. So in this case we just have to add the following line into the `Employee` class:

```
public abstract String getStatus();
```

You can see that to declare an **abstract** method, we use the Java keyword **abstract**, and we define the header, but no body – the actual implementation is left to the individual subclasses. Of course, **abstract** methods can only be declared in **abstract** classes – it wouldn't make much sense to try to create an object if one or more of its methods were undefined.

Now, having defined the **abstract** `getStatus` method in the `Employee` class, if we tried to compile the `FullTimeEmployee` or the `PartTimeEmployee` class (or any other class that extends `Employee`) without including a `getStatus` method we would be unsuccessful.

Once we have added the different `getStatus` methods into the `Employee` classes, we could re-write program 9.4 using the `getStatus` method in `testMethod`. We have done this in program 9.5:

PROGRAM 9.5

```
public class EmployeeTester2
{
  public static void main(String[] args)
  {
    FullTimeEmployee fte = new FullTimeEmployee("A123", "Ms Full-Time", 25000);
    PartTimeEmployee pte = new PartTimeEmployee("B456", "Mr Part-Time",30);
```

```
      testMethod(fte); // call testMethod with a full-time employee object
      testMethod(pte); // call testMethod with a part-time employee object
  }

  static void testMethod(Employee employeeIn) /* the method expects to receive an
                                                 Employee object */
  {
    System.out.println(employeeIn.getStatus());
  }
}
```

In program 9.5 it was clear at the time the program was compiled which version of getStatus was being referred to. The first time that the tester method is called a FullTimeEmployee object is sent in, so the getStatus method of FullTimeEmployee is called; the second time that the tester method is called, a PartTimeEmployee object is sent in, so the getStatus method of PartTimeEmployee is called. But now have a look at program 9.6, where, incidentally, we have made use of our EasyScanner class for input.

PROGRAM 9.6

```
public class EmployeeTester3
{

  public static void main(String[] args)
  {
    Employee emp; // a reference to an Employee

    char choice;
    String numberEntered, nameEntered;
    double salaryEntered, payEntered;

    System.out.print("Choose (F)ull-Time or (P)art-Time Employee: ");
    choice = EasyScanner.nextChar();

    System.out.print("Enter employee number: ");
    numberEntered = EasyScanner.nextString();

    System.out.print("Enter employee name: ");
    nameEntered = EasyScanner.nextString();

    if(choice == 'F' || choice == 'f')
```

```
   {
      System.out.print("Enter annual salary: ");
      salaryEntered = EasyScanner.nextDouble();

      // create a FullTimeEmployee object
      emp = new FullTimeEmployee (numberEntered, nameEntered, salaryEntered);
   }
   else
   {
      System.out.print("Enter hourly pay: ");
      payEntered = EasyScanner.nextDouble();

      // create a PartTimeEmployee object
      emp = new PartTimeEmployee (numberEntered, nameEntered, payEntered);
   }

   testMethod(emp); // call tester with the object created
 }

 static void testMethod(Employee employeeIn)
 {
    System.out.println(employeeIn.getStatus());
 }
}
```

In this program, we call `testMethod` only once, and allow the user of the program to decide whether a `FullTimeEmployee` object is sent in as a parameter, or a `PartTimeEmployee` object. You can see that at the beginning of the program we have declared a reference to an `Employee`:

```
Employee emp;
```

Although `Employee` is an **abstract** class, it is perfectly possible to declare a reference to this class – what we would not be allowed to do, of course, is to create an `Employee` *object*. However, as you will see in a moment, we can point this reference to an object of any subclass of `Employee`, since such objects, like `FullTimeEmployee` and `PartTimeEmployee`, are kinds of `Employee`.

You can see that we request the employee number and name from the user, and then ask if the employee is full-time or part-time. In the former case we get the annual salary and then create a `FullTimeEmployee` object which we assign to the `Employee` reference, `emp`.

```
if(choice == 'F' || choice == 'f')
{
   System.out.print("Enter annual salary: ");
```

```
    salaryEntered = input.nextDouble();

    // create a FullTimeEmployee object
    emp = new FullTimeEmployee (numberEntered, nameEntered, salaryEntered);
}
```

In the latter case we request the hourly pay and then assign emp to a new PartTimeEmployee object:

```
else
{
    System.out.print("Enter hourly pay: ");
    payEntered = input.nextDouble();

    // create a PartTimeEmployee object
    emp = new PartTimeEmployee (numberEntered, nameEntered, payEntered);
}
```

Finally we call the testMethod with emp:

```
testMethod(emp);
```

The getStatus method of the appropriate Employee object will then be called.

Here are two sample runs from this program:

Choose (F)ull-Time or (P)art-Time Employee: **F**

Enter employee number: **123**

Enter employee name: **Robertson**

Enter annual salary: **23000**

Full-Time

Choose (F)ull-Time or (P)art-Time Employee: **P**

Enter employee number: **876**

Enter employee name: **Adebayo**

Enter hourly pay: **25**

Part-Time

As you can see, we do not know *until the program is run* whether the getStatus method is going to be called with a FullTimeEmployee object or a PartTimeEmployee object – and yet when the get-Status method is called, the correct version is executed.

The technique which makes it possible for this decision to be made at run-time is quite a complex one, and differs slightly from one programming language to another.

9.7 The `final` modifier

You have already seen the use of the keyword **final** in chapter 2, where it was used to modify a variable and turn it into a constant. It can also be used to modify a class and a method. In the case of a class it is placed before the class declaration, like this:

```
public final class SomeClass
{

  // code goes here

}
```

This means that the class cannot be subclassed. In the case of a method it is used like this:

```
public final void someMethod()
{

  // code goes here

}
```

This means that the method cannot be overridden.

9.8 The *Object* class

One of the very useful things about inheritance is the *is-a-kind-of* relationship that we mentioned earlier. For example, when the ExtendedRectangle class extended the Rectangle class it became a kind of Rectangle – so, we can use ExtendedRectangle objects with any code written for Rectangle objects. When the PartTimeEmployee class extended the Employee class it became a kind of Employee. We have seen in section 9.5 that, in Java, if a method of some class expects to receive as a parameter an object of another class (say, for example, Vehicle), then it is quite happy to receive instead an object of a *subclass* of Vehicle – this is because that object will be *a kind of* Vehicle.

In Java, every single class that is created is in fact derived from what we might call a special "super superclass". This super superclass is called Object. So every object in Java is in fact *a kind of* Object. Any code written to accept objects of type Object can be used with objects of any type.

This allows us to create very generic methods – methods that can receive any kind of object. It also allows us to create generic arrays – arrays of Objects. In chapter 11 you will see an example of how we do precisely that.

To illustrate what we are saying, cast your mind back to the previous chapter, where we developed a collection class to hold BankAccount objects. This class had the following attribute:

```
private BankAccount[] list; // holds BankAccount objects
```

If we wanted to develop a generic class, we could replace this with:

```
private Object[] list; // holds objects of any type
```

Our add method would now look like this:

```
public boolean add(Object objectIn)
{
  if (!isFull())
  {
    list[total] = objectIn;
    total++;
    return true;
  }
  else
  {
    return false;
  }
}
```

This seems like a great idea, and it certainly can be very useful in some circumstances. However, there is a downside to generic classes too. Methods like search and depositMoney were methods which were relevant only to BankAccount objects, so we couldn't include those in a generic collection class – this sort of functionality would either have to be dealt with by the program using this class, or perhaps (as you will see in the case study in chapter 11) by creating a subclass that handles the specific functions we require.

There is another very important point about generic classes that we should mention. Consider a method like getItem that returned a BankAccount. In our new class it would look like this:

```
public Object getItem(int positionIn)
{
  if(positionIn < 1 || positionIn > total)
  {
    return null; // indicate invalid position
  }
  else
  {
    return list[positionIn - 1]; // subtract 1 to obtain the index
  }
}
```

This time the method returns an Object. A program that was using this method to retrieve BankAccount objects would need to be type cast in order to convert this Object to a BankAccount. For example, if an instance of our collection class called objectList had been declared, we might have this line:

```
BankAccount myAccount = (BankAccount) objectList.getItem(3);
```

In a similar way to that described in figure 9.3, we type cast from Object to BankAccount by placing the type name, BankAccount, in brackets before the item to be converted.

9.9 Wrapper classes and autoboxing

You might be wondering what you would do if you wanted to use an array of Objects to store a simple type such as an **int** or a **char** – or to pass such a type to a method that expects an Object. Java provides a very simple means of doing this.

To understand how it works you need to know about **wrapper** classes. For every primitive type, Java provides a corresponding class – the name of the class is similar to the basic type, but begins with a capital letter – for example Integer, Character, Float, Double. They are called *wrappers* because they "wrap" a *class* around the basic *type*. So an object of the Integer class, for example, holds an integer value. In future chapters you will find that these classes also contain some other very useful methods.

Imagine we had created an array of objects as follows:

```
Object[] anArray = new Object[20];
```

One way of storing an integer value such as 37 in this array would be as follows:

```
anArray[0] = new Integer(37);
```

The constructor of the Integer class accepts a primitive value and creates the corresponding Integer object – here we have created an Integer object from the primitive value 37, and this is now stored in the array.

Java, however, allows us to make use of a technique known as **autoboxing**. This involves the automatic conversion of a primitive type such as an **int** to an object of the appropriate wrapper class. This allows us to do the following:

```
anArray[0] = 37;
```

One way to retrieve this value from this array and assign it to an **int** would be:

```
Integer intObject = (Integer) anArray[0];
int x = intObject.getValue();
```

Notice we need to type cast from Object back to Integer; the Integer class provides a get Value method to retrieve the primitive value from the object.

However, Java also allows us to make use of a technique called **unboxing** that converts from the wrapper class back to the primitive type – so the above could be written as:

```
int x = (Integer) anArray[0];
```

Self-test questions

1 Below is a UML diagram for an inheritance relationship between two classes – `Vehicle` and `SecondHandVehicle`.

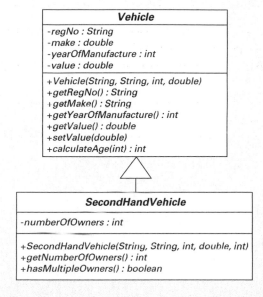

a By referring to the diagram, explain the meaning of the term *inheritance*.

b What do you think might be the function of each of the constructors?

c What do you think might be the reason for the fact that in the `Vehicle` class there is a set-method for the `value` attribute, but not for the other three?

d Write the header for the `SecondHandVehicle` class.

2 **a** Consider the following classes and arrange them into an inheritance hierarchy using UML notation:

b Write the top line of the class declaration for each of these classes when implementing them in Java.

c Explain what effect the **abstract** modifier has on a class and identify which, if any, of the classes above could be considered as abstract classes.

3 Consider once again an application to record the reading of a pressure sensor as discussed in programming exercise 4 of the previous chapter. Now assume a `SafeSensor` class is developed

that ensures that the pressure is never set above some maximum value. A `SafeSensor` *is a kind of* `Sensor`. The UML design is given below:

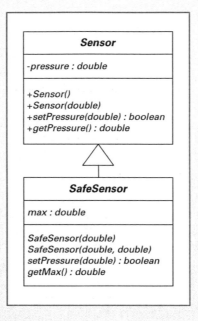

The `SafeSensor` class has two constructors. The first sets the maximum safe value to the given parameter and the actual value of the sensor reading to 10. The second constructor accepts two parameters; the first is used to set the maximum safe value and the second is used to set the initial value for the reading of the sensor.

The `setPressure` method is redefined so that only safe values (values no greater than the safe maximum value and no less than zero) are set.

a In the example above, distinguish between *method overriding* and *method overloading*.

b Below is one attempt at the Java code for the first `SafeSensor` constructor. Identify why it will not compile.

```
// THIS WILL NOT COMPILE!!
public SafeSensor(double maxIn)
{
  max = maxIn;
  pressure = 10;
}
```

c Here is another attempt at the Java code for the first `SafeSensor` constructor. Identify why it will not compile.

```
// THIS WILL NOT COMPILE!!
public SafeSensor(double maxIn)
{
  max = maxIn;
  super();
}
```

    d Write the correct code for the first `SafeSensor` constructor.

4 By referring to the `BankAccount` class of section 9.4, distinguish between **private**, **public** and **protected** access.

5 How are all classes in Java related to the `Object` class?

6 **a** Declare an array, `myList`, that can be used to hold up to 25 objects of *any* type.

    b Add a `BankAccount` object, with account number "001" and account name "A Kans", into the first position of this array.

    c Explain the term *type cast* and use this technique to deposit £200 into this first bank account.

7 Consider the following definition of a class called `Robot`:

```
public abstract class Robot
{
  private String id;
  private int securityLevel;
  private int warningLevel = 0;

  public Robot(String IdIn, int levelIn)
  {
    id = IdIn;
    securityLevel = levelIn;
  }

  public String getId()
  {
    return id;
  }

  public int getSecurityLevel()
  {
    return securityLevel;
  }

  public abstract void calculateWarningLevel();
}
```

i The following line of code is used in a program that has access to the Robot class:

```
Robot aRobot = new Robot("R2D2", 1000);
```

Explain why this line of code would cause a compiler error.

ii Consider the following class:

```
public class CleaningRobot extends Robot
{
  public String typeOfCleaningFluid;

  public CleaningRobot(String IdIn, int levelIn, String fluidIn)
  {
    super(IdIn, levelIn);
    typeOfCleaningFluid = fluidIn;
  }

  public String getTypeOfCleaningFluid()
  {
    return typeOfCleaningFluid;
  }
}
```

Explain why any attempt to compile this class would result in a compiler error.

8 What is the effect of the **final** modifier, when applied to both classes and methods?

9 Look back at program 9.4. What do you think would happen if you replaced this line of testMethod:

```
System.out.println(employeeIn.getName());
```

with the following line?

```
System.out.println(employeeIn.getAnnualSalary());
```

Give a reason for your answer.

Programming exercises

1 a Copy from the accompanying CD the `ExtendedRectangle` class, then implement program 9.2, the `ExtendedRectangleTester`. You will, of course, need to ensure that the `Rectangle` class itself is accessible to the compiler.

b Modify the `ExtendedRectangleTester` program so that the user is able to choose the symbol used to display the rectangle.

2 a Implement the `SafeSensor` class of self-test question 3. You will need to ensure that the `Sensor` class itself is accessible to the compiler.

b Write a tester class to test the methods of the `SafeSensor` class.

3 a Implement the `Vehicle` and the `SecondHandVehicle` classes of self-test question 1.
You should note that:

■ the `calculaeAge` method of `Vehicle` accepts an integer representing the current year, and returns the age of the vehicle as calculated by subtracting the year of manufacture from the current year;

■ the `hasMultipleOwners` method of `SecondHandVehicle` should return **true** if the `numberOfOwners` attribute has a value greater than 1, or **false** otherwise.

b Write a tester class that tests all the methods of the `SecondHandVehicle` class.

4 a Write a collection class that will hold a number of vehicle objects (as defined above), and will provide methods to add and delete vehicles, and to return a vehicle at a particular position in the list.

b Write a menu-driven program that uses the collection class to hold `Vehicles`. The menu should offer the following options:

> *1. Add a vehicle*
> *2. Display a list of vehicle details*
> *3. Delete a vehicle*
> *4. Quit*

5 a Modify the collection class developed in the previous programming exercise so that the class can hold, add and delete objects of *any* type.

b Modify the menu driven program you developed earlier to use this new generic collection to process a collection of vehicles.

c Now modify the menu driven program so that the generic collection class is used to process a collection of `Sensor` objects rather than `Vehicle` objects.

CHAPTER

Graphics

10

10.1 Introduction

At last it is time to learn about graphics programming. In this chapter you will start to move away from that rather uninteresting text screen you have been using and build attractive windows programs for input and output.

In order to do this you are going to be using the core Java graphics package known as **Swing**. This package provides the graphics tools and components that you need to produce the sort of windows programs that we have all become used to.

10.2 The Swing package

In the earlier versions of Java, graphical programming was achieved exclusively by making use of a package known as the **Abstract Window Toolkit (AWT)**. The AWT provides graphics classes that are based on an inheritance structure – at the top of this hierarchy is a basic `Component` class. This class contains a number of useful methods that are inherited by various subclasses such as `Button` or `Checkbox`, which are now an everyday feature of a graphics environment.

Nowadays, graphics in Java is achieved via the Swing package. The Swing classes build on the AWT classes to provide enhanced functionality and appearance. Figure 10.1 shows a few typical Swing components.

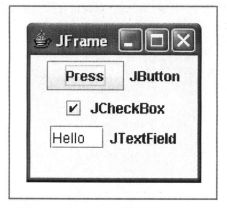

FIGURE 10.1 Some typical Swing components

Whereas AWT components have names such as `Frame`, `Button`, `Label` etc, you will see that the names of Swing components tend to start with the letter *J* – `JFrame`, `JButton`, and so on.

There is, in fact, a very different approach in terms of the way these two packages are implemented. When we use the AWT classes, any component that we create is associated with the corresponding component in the native operating system; so, for example, when we use methods of an AWT `Button` object, this communicates with a corresponding object – usually referred to as a **peer** – provided by, say, the Windows or Mac operating system. Consequently your button will look like a Windows or a Mac button. Components that rely on the native operating system are described as **heavyweight** components as they make extensive use of the system's resources.

In the case of Swing, however, most of the components are written in Java and all the code is provided as part of the Swing package. Components that are written in Java are called **lightweight** components.

The Swing package, along with the AWT, is part of the Java Foundation Classes (JFC).

10.3 The *SmileyFace* class

Our first graphics application is going to create a smiley face, as shown in figure 10.2.

FIGURE 10.2 The Smiley Face application

We have designed our `SmileyFace` class so that as soon as a new `SmileyFace` object is created, the graphic appears, as shown in figure 10.2. Thus, once the `SmileyFace` class is compiled, you can run it with a simple program that does nothing more than create a `SmileyFace` object, as shown in program 10.1 below.

PROGRAM 10.1

```
public class RunSmileyFace
{
  public static void main(String[] args)
  {
    new SmileyFace(); // call SmileyFace constructor
  }
}
```

Now we can get on with looking at the `SmileyFace` class itself. It is presented below. As you can see, there is quite a lot to it, so take a look at the code, and we will then go through it in detail.

THE *SMILEYFACE* CLASS

```
import java.awt.*;
import javax.swing.*;

public class SmileyFace extends JFrame
{

  public SmileyFace()
  {
    setTitle("Smiley Face");
    setDefaultCloseOperation(JFrame.EXIT_ON_CLOSE);
    setSize(250,220);
    setLocation(300,300);
    getContentPane().setBackground(Color.yellow);
    setVisible(true);
  }

  public void paint(Graphics g)
  {
    super.paint(g); // call the paint method of the superclass, JFrame
    g.setColor(Color.red);
    g.drawOval(85,75,75,75); // the face
    g.setColor(Color.blue);
    g.drawOval(100,95,10,10); // the right eye
```

```
    g.drawOval(135,95,10,10); // the left eye
    g.drawArc(102,115,40,25,0,-180); // the mouth
    g.drawString("Smiley Face", 90,175);
  }
}
```

There are a number of new concepts here. First, let's take a look at the **import** clauses:

```
import java.awt.*;
import javax.swing.*;
```

The first of these imports the standard Java Abstract Window Toolkit that we spoke about earlier. Although we are going to be using Swing, we still need many of the AWT classes for drawing and painting. The next clause imports the Swing package – the Swing classes come in a library called Javax (Java eXtension).

Now look at the class header:

```
public class SmileyFace extends JFrame
```

A JFrame is a Swing component that forms the visible window in which the graphic is displayed. By extending the JFrame class, we are making our SmileyFace class *a kind of* JFrame.

Now let's look at the constructor:

```
public SmileyFace()
{
  setTitle("Smiley Face");
  setDefaultCloseOperation(JFrame.EXIT_ON_CLOSE);
  setSize(250,220);
  setLocation(300,300);
  getContentPane().setBackground(Color.yellow);
  setVisible(true);
}
```

Since our class is a kind of JFrame we can use all of the JFrame methods to define its properties.

The order in which we set the properties is not especially important. In our case, the first thing we have done is to set the title of the frame by using the setTitle method of JFrame. As you can see, this method accepts a String – this String will form the title of the frame, as can be seen in figure 10.2.

The next line makes use of the JFrame method setDefaultCloseOperation. This method determines the behaviour of the frame when the user clicks on the *close* icon (the cross-hairs that you can see in the top right-hand corner in figure 10.2). This method accepts an integer – in order that you don't have to remember which integer does what, there are a number of pre-defined constants in the `JFrame` class, as follows:

- `JFrame.DISPOSE_ON_CLOSE`: The frame is destroyed.
- `JFrame.DO_NOTHING_ON_CLOSE`: Nothing happens.
- `JFrame.HIDE_ON_CLOSE`: The frame is hidden.
- `JFrame.EXIT_ON_CLOSE`: The program terminates.

As you can see, we have chosen to make the entire application end when the cross-hairs are clicked. Incidentally, this is a good point at which to let you know about the following command, which you might wish to use somewhere in a program should you want to terminate an application other than by the user clicking the exit icon on a frame:

```
System.exit(0);
```

Once we have set the default close operation, we set the size, location and colour of the `JFrame`. The `setSize` method takes two parameters, the width and the height respectively of the frame, measured in pixels – pixels are the little coloured dots that make up the image. We have chosen a frame measuring 250 by 220 pixels. The `setLocation` method determines the position of the top left-hand corner of the frame with respect to the top left-hand corner of the screen – the first parameter determines (in pixels) the distance across, the second the distance down.[1]

We set the background colour to yellow with the `setBackground` method. You can see, however, that we do not call the `setBackground` method of the frame itself; rather, we call the method of the frame's *content pane*. A `JFrame` is made up of a number of different `Containers`. The `Container` class is a class quite high up in the AWT/Swing hierarchy from which many other components are derived. One of the `Containers` that makes up a `JFrame` is known as the *content pane*, and it is this bit for which we set the background colour. You can see that we access it by calling the `getContentPane` method.

In the second semester you will find out how you can create your own colours – but until then, it is very convenient to use the pre-defined colours in the `Color` class that forms part of the AWT package. These are:

```
Color.black
Color.blue
Color.cyan
Color.darkGray
Color.gray
Color.green
Color.lightGray
Color.magenta
Color.orange
Color.pink
Color.red
Color.white
Color.yellow
```

---

[1] If we didn't set the location, the graphic would appear at position (0,0) – that is, at the top left-hand corner of the screen.

Finally, the frame does not automatically become visible when it is created – we have to make it visible by calling the setVisible method with the parameter **true**.

Now we come to the paint method:

```
public void paint(Graphics g)
{
  super.paint(g); // call the paint method of the superclass, Jframe
  g.setColor(Color.red);
  g.drawOval(85,75,75,75); // the face
  g.setColor(Color.blue);
  g.drawOval(100,95,10,10), // the right eye
  g.drawOval(135,95,10,10); // the left eye
  g.drawArc(102,115,40,25,0,-180); // the mouth
  g.drawString("Smiley Face", 90,175);
}
```

This special method is a method of the basic graphics class called Component, of which JFrame is an extension. Now it may have already occurred to you that we don't actually call this method anywhere. That is because we don't need to – when the component becomes visible, the paint method is automatically called. When this happens, an object of a core Java class called Graphics (which comes with the AWT package) is automatically sent into this method. A Graphics object has lots of useful methods. Before we look at those, take a note of the first line:

```
super.paint(g); // call the paint method of the superclass, Jframe
```

Using **super** in this way calls the relevant method of the superclass – in this case JFrame. Whenever we override paint, as we have done here, we should always call this method first. The paint method of a Swing component calls a number of necessary routines. Forgetting to call the paint method of the superclass leads to the painting process behaving erratically, which can be a source of much irritation.

The first method of the Graphics class that we use is setColor; this sets the foreground colour – in this case to red:

```
g.setColor(Color.red);
```

Then we use the drawOval method of the Graphics class to draw our circles. The first of these draws the big circle for the face itself:

```
g.drawOval(85,75,75,75);
```

The drawOval method takes four integer parameters. Referring to these as x, y, l, h, the oval that gets drawn fits into an imaginary rectangle that starts at position (x,y), and is l pixels long and h pixels high. This is illustrated in figure 10.3.

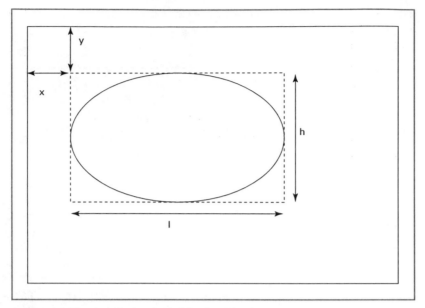

FIGURE 10.3 The *drawOval* method of the *Graphics* class

Notice that since we want a circle, we have made the values of l and h equal.

After we have drawn the big circle, we set the colour to blue and draw the right eye and left eye respectively:

```
g.setColor(Color.blue);
g.drawOval(100,95,10,10);
g.drawOval(135,95,10,10);
```

The next line draws the mouth:

```
g.drawArc(102,115,40,25,0,-180);
```

This requires some explanation. As you can see, this method requires six parameters, all integers. We shall call them x, y, l, h, α, θ. The first four define an imaginary rectangle as above. The arc is drawn so that its centre is the centre of this rectangle, as shown in figure 10.4.

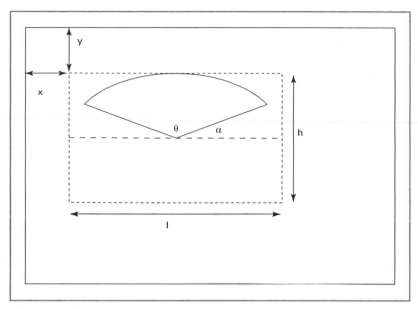

FIGURE 10.4 The *drawArc* method of the *Graphics* class

The next two parameters, α and θ, represent angles. The first, α, is the start angle – measured from an imaginary horizontal line pointing to the "quarter-past-three" position (representing zero degrees). The next, θ, is the finish angle. If θ is positive then the arc is drawn by rotating from the start position in an anti-clockwise direction; if it is negative we rotate in a clockwise direction. If this is not clear, you should try some experiments; play about with the SmileyFace class and see what happens.

The final line draws the string "Smiley Face" in the graphics window at the coordinates (90,175).

```
g.drawString("Smiley Face",90,175);
```

In addition to drawOval and drawArc, there are many other useful methods of the Graphics class that you might like to experiment with. Two particularly useful ones are:

    void drawLine (int x1, int y1, int x2, int y2)

Draws a line from point (*x1*, *y1*) to point (*x2*, *y2*).

    void drawRect (int x, int y, int w, int h)

Draws a rectangle of width *w* and height *h* with the top left-hand corner at point (*x*, *y*).

10.4 Event-handling in Java: The *ChangingFace* class

Now we are going to try to change our SmileyFace class into a ChangingFace class that can change its mood so it can be sad as well as happy. We are going to add a couple of buttons, as shown in figure 10.5.

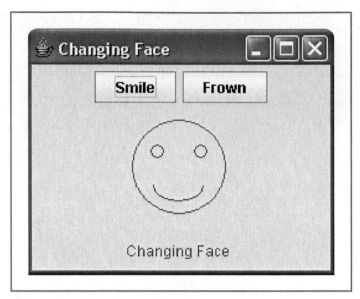

FIGURE 10.5 The *ChangingFace* class (still smiling)

You can see that we have now changed our title and caption from "Smiley Face" to "Changing Face" – because when we have finished we will be able to click on the *Frown* button and get the face to look like the one you see in figure 10.6.

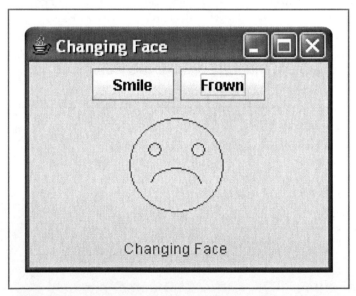

FIGURE 10.6 The *ChangingFace* class (frowning)

The code for our class is shown below. There are quite a lot of new concepts and techniques there, so we will discuss it in detail once you have had a look at it. You will notice immediately, however, an additional **import** statement (import java.awt.event.*), the unfamiliar words implements ActionListener in the header, and a method called actionPerformed.

THE *CHANGINGFACE* CLASS

```java
import javax.swing.*;
import java.awt.*;
import java.awt.event.*;

public class ChangingFace extends JFrame implements ActionListener
{
  private boolean isHappy = true; // will determine the mood of the face
  private JButton happyButton = new JButton("Smile");
  private JButton sadButton = new JButton("Frown");

  public ChangingFace()
  {
    // set the title
    setTitle("Changing Face");

    // choose a Flow Layout policy
    setLayout(new FlowLayout());

    // add the buttons to the frame
    add(happyButton); add(sadButton);

    // set the background to yellow
    getContentPane().setBackground(Color.yellow);

    // enable the buttons to listen for a mouse-click
    happyButton.addActionListener(this);
    sadButton.addActionListener(this);

    // configure the frame
    setDefaultCloseOperation(JFrame.EXIT_ON_CLOSE);
    setSize(250, 200);
    setLocation(300,300);
    setVisible(true);
  }

  public void paint(Graphics g)
  {
    // call the paint method of the superclass, Jframe
    super.paint(g);
    // paint the face
    g.setColor(Color.red);
```

```
    g.drawOval(85,75,75,75);

    g.setColor(Color.blue);

    g.drawOval(100,95,10,10);

    g.drawOval(135,95,10,10);

    g.drawString("Changing Face", 80,185);

    if(isHappy == true)

    {

      // draw a smiling mouth

      g.drawArc(102,115,40,25,0,-180);

    }

    else

    {

      // draw a frowning mouth

      g.drawArc(102,115,40,25,0,180);

    }

  }

  // this is where we code the event-handling routine

  public void actionPerformed(ActionEvent e)

  {

    if(e.getSource() == happyButton)

    {

      isHappy = true;

      repaint();

    }

    if(e.getSource() == sadButton)

    {

      isHappy = false;

      repaint();

    }

  }

}
```

We will start by looking at the instructions that are concerned with adding the buttons. These are in fact objects of the Swing component JButton. They are declared as attributes of the class, and initialized at the same time:

```
private JButton happyButton = new JButton("Smile");
private JButton sadButton = new JButton("Frown");
```

The JButton class has a constructor that allows us to create the buttons with the required caption by sending in this caption as a parameter.

Now consider the constructor of our ChangingFace class.

```
public ChangingFace()
{
  setTitle("Changing Face");
  setLayout(new FlowLayout());
  add(happyButton);
  add(sadButton);
  getContentPane().setBackground(Color.yellow);
  happyButton.addActionListener(this);
  sadButton.addActionListener(this);
  setDefaultCloseOperation(JFrame.EXIT_ON_CLOSE);
  setSize(250, 200);
  setLocation(300,300);
  setVisible(true);
}
```

The first thing we want to do, after setting the title, is to add the buttons to the frame. Now, a container, like our ChangingFace (which extends JFrame), always has a **layout** policy attached to it – this policy determines the way in which components are added to it. The default policy for a JFrame is called BorderLayout. We will explain how a border layout works later – what we want now is a policy called FlowLayout, which means that the components are just placed in the order in which they were added. When one row fills up then the next row starts to be filled. As you can see, we have changed the layout policy with this instruction:

```
setLayout(new FlowLayout());
```

Now we can add the buttons. To do this we use the add method, which is a method of the AWT class Container (from which JFrame is derived) and is therefore available to all the subclasses of Container.

Remember, of course, that the first two lines are short for:

```
this.add(happyButton);
this.add(sadButton);
```

After we add the buttons, we set the background to yellow.

As you can see, there are two more lines after this, which precede the final instructions that configure the frame. These are:

```
happyButton.addActionListener(this);
sadButton.addActionListener(this);
```

We won't discuss these just yet, but will talk about them further on.

The next thing we need to think about is writing the code that brings about the desired result when the buttons are pressed. This is called **event-handling**.

First, notice that we have an additional **import** statement:

```
import java.awt.event.*;
```

The *event* package contains all the classes (such as `ActionListener` below) that we need for handling events.

Now, let's take a closer look at the class header:

```
public class ChangingFace extends JFrame implements ActionListener
```

We have appended the words **implements** `ActionListener` to our class header. The `ActionListener` class is a special class called an **interface**. You will find out a lot more about interfaces in the second semester, but for now you just need to know that these classes contain *only abstract methods*. You will remember from chapter 9 that a class is forced to code any abstract method that it inherits. In this case `ActionListener` contains a method called `actionPerformed` to handle our events. Implementing an interface is very like extending a class, so any class that implements `ActionListener` *must* have an `actionPerformed` method. We will see how this is coded in a moment.

Before we do that, take a look at this new attribute we have included:

```
private boolean isHappy = true;
```

You can probably guess how we are going to use this – it will be set to **true** when the *Smile* button is pressed and **false** when the *Frown* button is pressed; the face will then be repainted with the appropriate expression. We have initialized it to **true**, so that the face will start off happy.

Now let's look at the two lines of the constructor that we mentioned before but didn't discuss:

```
happyButton.addActionListener(this);
sadButton.addActionListener(this);
```

These two lines are important. As we have said, when we use the keyword **implements** with an interface class like `ActionListener` we achieve an effect very similar to that achieved by inheritance – our class actually becomes *a kind of* `ActionListener`, just as if it were a subclass of some superclass, created with the keyword **extends**. The `JButton` class has a method called `addActionListener` that receives an object of the `ActionListener` class as a parameter – and since our class is now a kind of `ActionListener` we can send it to the `addActionListener` method of a `JButton`. The `ActionListener` that we send in is the class where the code for handling the event is to be found. In our case it is *this* class – hence the use of the keyword **this**. By adding an `ActionListener` to an object such as a button, we are making that object "listen" for a mouse-click. The program will then respond to this event – the mouse-click – by taking some action.

The action that it takes is determined by coding a special routine – this routine is called an **event-handler**. Before we come to that, however, we need to look at the `paint` method.

```
 public void paint(Graphics g)
{

  // call the paint method of the superclass, Jframe
  super.paint(g);

  // paint the face
  g.setColor(Color.red);
  g.drawOval(85,45,75,75);
  g.setColor(Color.blue);
  g.drawOval(100,65,10,10);
  g.drawOval(135,65,10,10);
  g.drawString("Changing Face", 80,155);
  if(isHappy == true)
  {
    // draw a smiling mouth
    g.drawArc(102,85,40,25,0,-180);
  }
  else
  {
    // draw a frowning mouth
    g.drawArc(102,85,40,25,0,180);
  }
}
```

As before, we begin by calling the paint method of the superclass, JFrame.

After drawing the face and the eyes as before we have two possibilities for the mouth – if isHappy is **true**, a smiling mouth is drawn. If not a frowning mouth is drawn. You should remember from the previous section how the drawArc method of a Graphics object works. If you look back at that section you will see that by changing the very last parameter from a negative value to a positive value the arc will be drawn anticlockwise instead of clockwise – this will make the mouth frown instead of smile. So if the isHappy attribute is set to **true** the mouth will smile – if not it will frown!

You will notice, by the way, that we have moved everything down on the screen in order to accommodate the buttons.

Now at last we come to the event-handler itself:

```
public void actionPerformed(ActionEvent e)
{
  if(e.getSource() == happyButton)
  {
    isHappy = true;
    repaint();
  }
```

```
  if(e.getSource() == sadButton)
  {
    isHappy = false;
    repaint();
  }
}
```

We determine what happens when the mouse-button is clicked by coding the actionPerformed method that is required by the ActionListener interface. When the mouse is clicked, this method is automatically sent an object of the class ActionEvent. This class has a method called getSource that returns the name of the object that was clicked on. We use this method in the condition of the **if** statement to find out which button was clicked. You can see that if it was the happyButton that was pressed, isHappy is set to **true** and then a special method – repaint – is called. We never call the paint method directly, because certain routines need to be carried out before paint is executed. Calling repaint performs these routines, and then calls the paint method so that the screen is repainted. The sadButton works in a similar way to the happyButton, but sets isHappy to **false**. Take one more look at the paint method to remind yourself how this works.

Program 10.2 runs the ChangingFace class.

PROGRAM 10.2

```
public class RunChangingFace
{
  public static void main(String[] args)
  {
    new ChangingFace();
  }
}
```

10.5 An interactive graphics class

The next class – which we have called PushMe – that we are going to develop is the first class that allows the user to input information via a graphics screen. The program isn't all that sophisticated, but it introduces the basic elements that you need to build interactive graphics classes.

This program allows the user to enter some text and then, by clicking on a button, to see the text that was entered displayed in the graphics window. You can see what it looks like in figure 10.7.

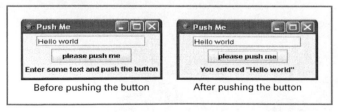

FIGURE 10.7 The *PushMe* class

As usual, we will show you the code first and discuss it afterwards:

THE *PUSHME* CLASS

```java
import javax.swing.*;
import java.awt.event.*;
import java.awt.*;


public class PushMe extends JFrame implements ActionListener
{
  private JTextField myTextField = new JTextField(15);
  private JButton myButton = new JButton("please push me");
  private JLabel myLabel = new JLabel("Enter some text and  push the button", JLabel.CENTER);

  // the constructor
  public PushMe()
  {
    setTitle("Push Me");
    setLayout(new FlowLayout());
    setDefaultCloseOperation(JFrame.EXIT_ON_CLOSE);
    setSize(220,120);
    setLocation(400, 300);
    add(myTextField);
    add(myButton);
    add(myLabel);
    myButton.addActionListener(this);
    setVisible(true);
  }


  // the event-handler
  public void actionPerformed(ActionEvent e)
  {
    String myText;
    myText = myTextField.getText();
    myLabel.setText("You entered " + "\"" + myText + "\"");
  }
}
```

As you can see, there are three components involved here, and we have declared them all as attributes of the class and initialized them at the same time:

```
private JTextField myTextField = new JTextField(15);
private JButton myButton = new JButton("please push me");
private JLabel myLabel    = new JLabel("Enter some text and push the button", JLabel.CENTER);
```

The first of the above three components is a `JTextField` – we have used the fact that it has a constructor which accepts an integer value (in this case 15) that allows you to specify the length of the text field to be displayed (in terms of columns).

Next we declare the `JButton`, which, as before, we have initialized with the required caption ("please push me").

Finally we have declared and instantiated a `JLabel`. The constructor that we are utilizing here takes two parameters: the text to be displayed and an integer value which determines the alignment of the text – 0 for left, 1 for centre and 2 for right; as you can see, we can use pre-defined constants for this, namely `JLabel.LEFT`, `JLabel.CENTER` and `JLabel.RIGHT`.

All of these components also have empty constructors (and others) that you can use if you wish.[2] You can change the properties later using the various methods that exist; for example, the `setText` method of the `JButton` class, the `setColumns` method of the `JTextField` class or the `setText` method of the `JLabel` class.

Next comes the constructor where we set some of the properties of the frame, add the buttons to the frame, and add the `ActionListener` to the button.

```
public PushMe()
{
  // set properties
  setTitle("Push Me");
  setLayout(new FlowLayout());
  setDefaultCloseOperation(JFrame.EXIT_ON_CLOSE);
  setSize(220,120);
  setLocation(400, 300);

  // add components
  add(myTextField);
  add(myButton);
  add(myLabel);

  // add actionListener to the button
  myButton.addActionListener(this);

  setVisible(true);

}
```

---

[2] You can find a detailed description of all the methods of the Java Foundation classes by looking at the API specifications on the official website of Sun Microsystems, www.java.sun.com.

Finally we have the event-handling routine:

```
public void actionPerformed(ActionEvent e)
{
  String myText;
  myText = myTextField.getText();
  myLabel.setText("You entered " + "\"" + myText + "\"");
}
```

Notice how we are using the getText method of the JTextField class to read the current "value" of the text in myTextField, and then using the setText method of the JLabel class to "transfer" it to myLabel. You should also notice that since there is only one component that is able to listen, it is not necessary to determine the source of the mouse-click. The final point to notice is the way in which we have managed to place quotes around the output text (as you can see in the second part of figure 10.7). As we referred to in chapter 9, we have had to place a backslash before each double quote that we want to insert into the string. If we didn't do that the compiler would simply assume that the double quote was there in order to end the string. You would have to do the same thing if you wanted to include a single quote, or the backslash itself.

Once again, a simple program such as program 10.3 will enable us to run the PushMe class.

PROGRAM 10.3

```
public class RunPushMe
{
  public static void main(String[] args)
  {
    new PushMe();
  }
}
```

10.6 A graphical user interface (GUI) for the *Rectangle* class

Up till now, when we wanted to write programs that utilize our classes, we have written text-based programs. Now that we know how to write graphics programs we can, if we wish, write graphical user interfaces for our classes. Let's do this for the Rectangle class we developed in chapter 8. The sort of interface we are talking about is shown in figure 10.8.

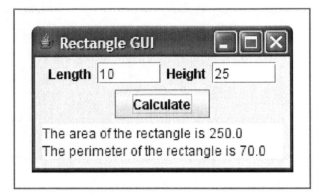

FIGURE 10.8 A GUI for the *Rectangle* class

Here is the code for the GUI:

THE GRAPHICAL USER INTERFACE FOR THE *RECTANGLE* CLASS

```java
import java.awt.*;
import java.awt.event.*;
import javax.swing.*;


public class RectangleGUI extends JFrame implements ActionListener
{
  // declare a new rectangle with a length and height of zero
  private Rectangle myRectangle = new Rectangle(0,0);


  // now declare the graphics components
  private JLabel lengthLabel = new JLabel("Length");
  private JTextField lengthField = new JTextField(5);
  private JLabel heightLabel = new JLabel("Height");
  private JTextField heightField = new JTextField(5);
  private JButton calcButton = new JButton("Calculate");
  private JTextArea displayArea = new JTextArea(2,20);


  public RectangleGUI()
  {
    setTitle("Rectangle GUI");
    setDefaultCloseOperation(JFrame.EXIT_ON_CLOSE);
    setLayout(new FlowLayout());
    setSize(240, 135);
    setLocation(300,300);


    // add the graphics components
    add(lengthLabel);
```

```java
        add(lengthField);
        add(heightLabel);
        add(heightField);
        add(calcButton);
        add(displayArea);

        // now add the ActionListener to the calcButton
        calcButton.addActionListener(this);

        setVisible(true);
    }


    // finally write the code for handling a mouse-click on the calcButton
    public void actionPerformed(ActionEvent e)
    {
      String lengthEntered = lengthField.getText();
      String heightEntered = heightField.getText();
      // make sure the fields aren't blank
      if(lengthEntered.length() == 0 || heightEntered.length() == 0)
      {
        displayArea.setText("Length and height must be entered");
      }
      else
      {
        // we have to convert the input strings to doubles (see below)
        myRectangle.setLength(Double.parseDouble(lengthEntered));
        myRectangle.setHeight(Double.parseDouble(heightEntered));

        // display area and perimeter of rectangle
        displayArea.setText("The area of the rectangle is "
        + myRectangle.calculateArea()
        + "\n"
        + "The perimeter of the rectangle is "
        + myRectangle.calculatePerimeter());
      }
    }
}
```

You can see that the first attribute that we declare is a `Rectangle` object, `myRectangle`, which we initialize as a new `Rectangle` with a length and height of zero (since the user hasn't entered anything yet):

```
private Rectangle myRectangle = new Rectangle(0,0);
```

After this we declare the graphics components; the only one of these that you have not yet come across is the `JTextArea`, which is the large text area that you see in figure 10.8, where the area and perimeter of the rectangle are displayed. As you can see, it is a useful component for entering and displaying text. We declared it like this:

```
private JTextArea displayArea = new JTextArea(2,20);
```

You can see that it has a constructor that allows you to fix the size by entering values for the number of rows and columns (in that order, by the way!).

After declaring and initializing the components, we have coded the constructor, which is straightforward – it simply adds these components to the frame, and then adds the `ActionListener` to the `calcButton`.

Next we have the event-handling routine for the `calcButton`; this is worth taking a look at:

```java
public void actionPerformed(ActionEvent e)
{
  String lengthEntered = lengthField.getText();
  String heightEntered = heightField.getText();
  // make sure the fields aren't blank
  if(lengthEntered.length() == 0 || heightEntered.length() == 0)
  {
    displayArea.setText("Length and height must be entered");
  }
  else
  {
    // convert the input strings to doubles (see below)
    myRectangle.setLength(Double.parseDouble(lengthEntered));
    myRectangle.setHeight(Double.parseDouble(heightEntered));
    displayArea.setText("The area of the rectangle is "
    + myRectangle.calculateArea()
    + "\n"
    + "The perimeter of the rectangle is "
    + myRectangle.calculatePerimeter());
  }
}
```

We have declared two local variables, `lengthEntered` and `heightEntered`, to hold the values entered by the user; these values are read (as `Strings`) using the `getText` method of `TextField`. Then we check that these are not of length zero (that is, that something has been entered). If one of the fields is empty we display an error message.

```
if(lengthEntered.length() == 0 || heightEntered.length() == 0)
{
  displayArea.setText("Length and height must be entered");
}
```

If there is no error, we use the setLength and setHeight methods of Rectangle to set the length and the height of myRectangle to the values entered. These methods of course expect to receive **doubles** – however, lengthEntered and heightEntered are Strings. We must therefore perform a conversion. To do this we use the parseDouble method of the Double class – one of the wrapper classes you learnt about in chapter 9:

```
myRectangle.setLength(Double.parseDouble(lengthEntered));
myRectangle.setHeight(Double.parseDouble(heightEntered));
```

Had we wanted to convert them to **ints**, we would have used the parseInt method of the Integer class.

Incidentally, if you want to do this the other way round and convert a **double** or an **int** to a String you can do so simply by concatenating it onto an empty String, as shown in the examples below:

```
String s = "" + 3;
```

or:

```
String s = "" + 3.12;
```

or even:

```
double d = 10.3;
int i = 20;
String s = "" + i + d;
```

Returning to the actionPerformed method, we now use the calculateArea and calculatePerimeter methods of Rectangle to display the area and perimeter of the rectangle in the text area. We have used the setText method of JTextArea to do this; we could also have used the append method – the difference is that this does not clear what was previously written in the area, whereas the setText method does.

You can write a little program for testing this class, as in the previous examples.

10.7 A metric converter

We thought that our next example would be a pretty useful one. Most of the world uses the metric system; however, if you are in the United Kingdom as we are, then you will still be only halfway there – sometimes using kilograms and kilometres, sometimes pounds and miles. Of course if you are in the USA (and you are not a scientist or an engineer) you will still be using the old imperial values for everything. Some might say it's time that the UK and the USA caught up with the rest of the world! But until that happens this little program, which converts back and forth from metric to imperial, is going to be very handy.

We will be building a `MetricConverter` class. Figure 10.9 shows what we are going to achieve.

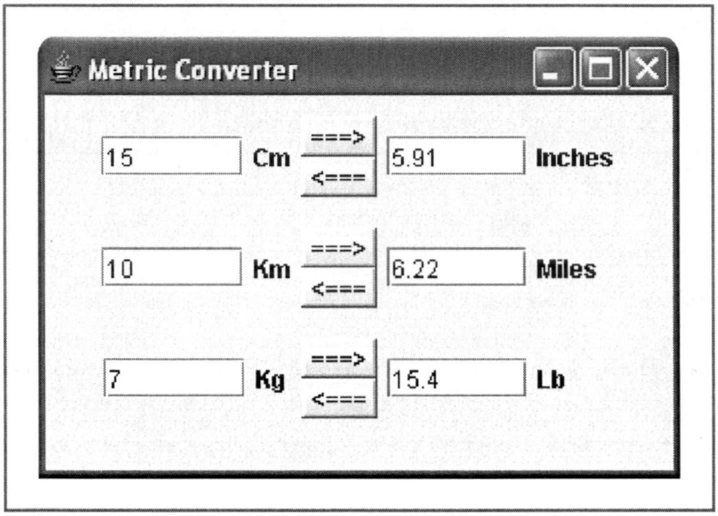

FIGURE 10.9 The metric converter

You might notice that the buttons in figure 10.9 have a slightly different look to them. This is because we have added a border, which is quite an easy thing to do with Swing components. To do this you need to import the appropriate package with the following statement:

```
import javax.swing.border.*;
```

There are many sorts of borders that can be added, and we will go into this in detail in the second semester – you will also see some other examples in the case study in the next two chapters. For now, however, we will just tell you how to add the above border (which is known as a *raised bevelled* border); you add such a border to a component – say, `myButton` – as follows:

```
myButton.setBorder(new BevelBorder(BevelBorder.RAISED));
```

You might want to try the effect of replacing `BevelBorder.RAISED` with `BevelBorder.LOWERED`.

In the `MetricConverter` class we have made extensive use of a Swing component called `JPanel`. A `JPanel` is a component that we don't actually see, but to which we can add other components; the `JPanel` can then be added to another container such as a `JFrame`. A `JPanel`, like most Swing components, is a lightweight component. A JFrame is in fact a heavyweight component.[3] One thing we should point out to you is that if you are going to paint a lightweight component then you use the paintComponent method, not the paint method (and call the paintComponent method of the superclass, just as we did with the paint method).

The MetricConverter class is now presented; it looks quite long, but most of it is just more of what you already know. There are, however, three concepts, **number formatting**, **layout policies** and **compound containers** that we need to discuss in some depth, and we do this straight after showing you the code.

THE *METRICCONVERTER* CLASS

```java
import java.awt.*;
import javax.swing.*;
import java.awt.event.*;
import java.text.*; // required for the DecimalFormat class
import javax.swing.border.*;


public class MetricConverter extends JFrame implements ActionListener
{
  // we declare the various components as attributes.

  // first the components for converting back and forth from inches to centimetres

  private JTextField cmText = new JTextField(6);
  private JLabel cmLabel = new JLabel("Cm");
  private JButton cmToInchButton = new JButton(" ===> ");
  private JButton inchToCmButton = new JButton(" <=== ");
  private JPanel inchCmButtons = new JPanel(); // compound container
  private JTextField inchText = new JTextField(6);
  private JLabel inchLabel = new JLabel("Inches");
  private JPanel inchCmPanel = new JPanel(); // compound container

  // next the components for converting back and forth from miles to kilometres

  private JTextField kmText = new JTextField(6);
  private JLabel kmLabel = new JLabel("Km");
  private JButton kmToMileButton = new JButton(" ===> ");
  private JButton mileToKmButton = new JButton(" <=== ");
  private JPanel mileKmButtons = new JPanel(); // compound container
  private JTextField mileText = new JTextField(6);
  private JLabel mileLabel = new JLabel("Miles  "); // extra spaces make all labels the same length
  private JPanel mileKmPanel = new JPanel(); // compound container
```

[3] The other heavyweight components are JWindow, JDialog and JApplet.

```
// finally the components for converting back and forth from pounds to kilograms

private JTextField kgText = new JTextField(6);
private JLabel kgLabel = new JLabel("Kg "); // extra spaces make all labels the same length
private JButton kgToPoundButton = new JButton(" ===> ");
private JButton poundToKgButton = new JButton(" <=== ");
private JPanel poundKgButtons = new JPanel(); // compound container
private JTextField poundText = new JTextField(6);
private JLabel poundLabel = new JLabel("Lb     "); // extra spaces make all labels the same length
private JPanel poundKgPanel = new JPanel();    // compound container

// the constructor adds the components to the object at the time it is created

public MetricConverter()
{
  inchCmButtons.setLayout(new BorderLayout()); // see discussion
  inchCmButtons.add("North", cmToInchButton);
  inchCmButtons.add("South", inchToCmButton);
  inchCmPanel.add(cmText);
  inchCmPanel.add(cmLabel);
  inchCmPanel.add(inchCmButtons);
  inchCmPanel.add(inchText);
  inchCmPanel.add(inchLabel);

  mileKmButtons.setLayout(new BorderLayout()); // see discussion
  mileKmButtons.add("North", kmToMileButton);
  mileKmButtons.add("South", mileToKmButton);
  mileKmPanel.add(kmText);
  mileKmPanel.add(kmLabel);
  mileKmPanel.add(mileKmButtons);
  mileKmPanel.add(mileText);
  mileKmPanel.add(mileLabel);
  poundKgButtons.setLayout(new BorderLayout()); // see discussion
  poundKgButtons.add("North", kgToPoundButton);
  poundKgButtons.add("South", poundToKgButton);
  poundKgPanel.add(kgText);
  poundKgPanel.add(kgLabel);
  poundKgPanel.add(poundKgButtons);
  poundKgPanel.add(poundText);
  poundKgPanel.add(poundLabel);

  add(inchCmPanel);
  add(mileKmPanel);
  add(poundKgPanel);
```

```
    // give raised borders to the buttons
    cmToInchButton.setBorder(new BevelBorder(BevelBorder.RAISED));
    cmToInchButton.setBorder(new BevelBorder(BevelBorder.RAISED));
    inchToCmButton.setBorder(new BevelBorder(BevelBorder.RAISED));
    kmToMileButton.setBorder(new BevelBorder(BevelBorder.RAISED));
    mileToKmButton.setBorder(new BevelBorder(BevelBorder.RAISED));
    kgToPoundButton.setBorder(new BevelBorder(BevelBorder.RAISED));
    poundToKgButton.setBorder(new BevelBorder(BevelBorder.RAISED));

    cmToInchButton.addActionListener(this);
    inchToCmButton.addActionListener(this);
    kmToMileButton.addActionListener(this);
    mileToKmButton.addActionListener(this);
    kgToPoundButton.addActionListener(this);
    poundToKgButton.addActionListener(this);

    setTitle("Metric Converter");
    setLayout(new FlowLayout());
    setDefaultCloseOperation(JFrame.EXIT_ON_CLOSE);
    setSize(320, 220);
    setLocation(300, 300);
    setVisible(true);
}

// now we code the event-handlers

public void actionPerformed(ActionEvent e)
{
  double d;
  String s;
  // format the output
  DecimalFormat df = new DecimalFormat("0.0#"); // see discussion that follows
  if (e.getSource() == cmToInchButton) // convert cm to inches
  {
    s = new String(cmText.getText());
    d = Double.parseDouble(s); // convert String to double
    d = d / 2.54; // convert to inches
    s = df.format(d); // format number for output
    inchText.setText(s);
  }
  if (e.getSource() == inchToCmButton) // convert inches to cm
  {
    s = new String(inchText.getText());
```

```
      d = Double.parseDouble(s); // convert String to double
      d = d * 2.54; // convert to cm
      s = df.format(d); // format number for output
      cmText.setText(s);
   }
   if (e.getSource() == kmToMileButton) // convert km to miles
   {
     s = new String(kmText.getText());
     d = Double.parseDouble(s); // convert String to double
     d = d / 1.609; // convert to miles
     s = df.format(d); // format number for output
     mileText.setText(s);
   }
   if (e.getSource() == mileToKmButton) // convert miles to km
   {
     s = new String(mileText.getText());
     d = Double.parseDouble(s); // convert String to double
     d = d * 1.609; // convert to km
     s = df.format(d); // format number for output
     kmText.setText(s);
   }
   if (e.getSource() == kgToPoundButton) // convert kg to pounds
   {
     s = new String(kgText.getText());
     d = Double.parseDouble(s); // convert String to double
     d = d * 2.2; // convert to pounds
     s = df.format(d); // format number for output
     poundText.setText(s);
   }


   if (e.getSource() == poundToKgButton) // convert pounds to kg
   {
     s = new String(poundText.getText());
     d = Double.parseDouble(s); // convert String to double
     d = d / 2.2; // convert to kg
     s = df.format(d); // format number for output
     kgText.setText(s);
   }
  }
}
```

10.8 Number formatting

In our `MetricConverter` application we have arranged for the numerical output to appear with no more than two numbers after the decimal point. In order to do this we have made use of the `DecimalFormat` class that resides in the `java.text` package. We have therefore included the following import statement:

```
import java.text.*;
```

Once you have access to this class you can create `DecimalFormat` objects in your program. These objects can then be used to format decimal numbers for you. The `DecimalFormat` constructor has one parameter, the format string. This string instructs the object on how you wish to format a given decimal number. Some of the important elements of such a string are given in table 10.1.

Character	Meaning
.	insert a decimal point
,	insert a comma
0	display a single digit
#	display a single digit or empty if no digit present

TABLE 10.1 Special DecimalFormat characters

In the Metric converter we created the following `DecimalFormat` object:

```
DecimalFormat df = new DecimalFormat("0.0#");
```

Here the decimal format object, `df`, is being informed on how to format any decimal numbers that may be given to it, as shown in figure 10.10.

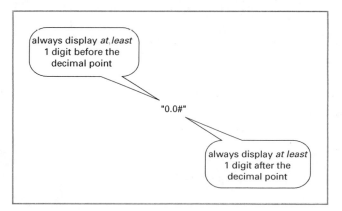

FIGURE 10.10 A format string used with the *DecimalFormat* class

Having created a `DecimalFormat` object, we could then create `String`, `s`, from a `double`, `d`, as follows:

```
String s = df.format(d);
```

Program 10.4 shows some examples:

PROGRAM 10.4

```
import java.text.*;

public class NumberFormatExample
{
  public static void main(String[] args)
  {
    double number = 4376.7863;

    DecimalFormat df1 = new DecimalFormat("###,##0.0#");
    DecimalFormat df2 = new DecimalFormat("###000.00");
    DecimalFormat df3 = new DecimalFormat("00.0");
    DecimalFormat df4 = new DecimalFormat("000000.00000");
    DecimalFormat df5 = new DecimalFormat("000,000.00####");

    System.out.println(df1.format(number));
    System.out.println(df2.format(number));

    System.out.println(df3.format(number));
    System.out.println(df4.format(number));
    System.out.println(df5.format(number));
  }
}
```

The output from program 10.4 is as follows:

```
4,376.79
4376.79
4376.8
004376.78630
004,376.7863
```

In the next chapter you will see how a similar technique can be used to output numbers as a particular currency.

10.9 Layout policies

We have already briefly described one layout policy, FlowLayout. In addition to this policy the AWT package provides other policies via a number of other classes called **layout managers**. We can create an object of one of these classes and attach it to a container, and thereafter that container will lay out the components it contains according to the policy of that layout manager. As we said earlier, the strategy of the only layout manager we have seen so far, FlowLayout, is simply to arrange the components in the order that they were added, starting a new row when necessary. If the window is resized the items move about accordingly, as shown in figure 10.11.

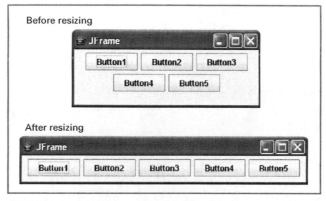

FIGURE 10.11 The effect of resizing when using the *FlowLayout* policy

Another commonly used layout manager is BorderLayout. This is the default policy for JFrame. Here the window is divided into five regions called North, South, East, West and Center as shown in figure 10.12.

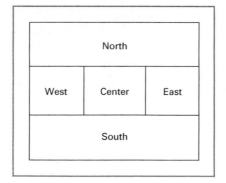

FIGURE 10.12 The *BorderLayout* Policy

If we use a border layout the components don't get moved around when the window is resized, as you can see from figure 10.13.

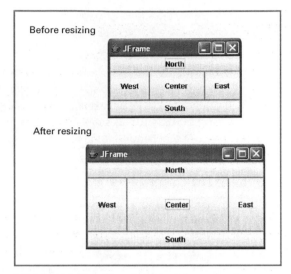

FIGURE 10.13 The effect of resizing when using the *BorderLayout* policy

The `MetricConverter` class uses a combination of `BorderLayout` and `FlowLayout` for its components, as explained below.

Some components (for example `JPanel`) have `FlowLayout` as their default layout policy and some (for example `JFrame`) have `BorderLayout`. If you wanted to change the policy of such a component – say `myPanel` – to `BorderLayout` you would do so as follows:

```
myPanel.setLayout(new BorderLayout());
```

The following line would then place a component called `myButton` in the `North` region:

```
myPanel.add("North", myButton);
```

There are a number of other layout managers that can be used, such as `GridLayout` and `CardLayout`, which we will introduce to you in the second semester.

10.10 Compound containers

A **compound container** is, as its name suggests, a container that contains other containers. Each container can use a different layout manager. One of the most useful components that we can use when we build graphics programs is a `JPanel`. As we have explained, this is a component that we don't actually see, but which can be used to hold other components.

In figure 10.14 we have adapted the graphic you saw in figure 10.13. Instead of adding a `JButton` in the East sector we have now added a `JPanel`. We have then added five `JButtons` to this `JPanel`, one in each sector.

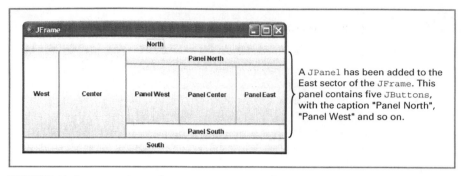

A `JPanel` has been added to the East sector of the `JFrame`. This panel contains five `JButtons`, with the caption "Panel North", "Panel West" and so on.

FIGURE 10.14 A compound container

We have used `JPanels` in the `MetricConverter` class. Figure 10.14 shows how each component is named and how we make use of compound containers by constructing the `MetricConverter` with three `JPanels` named `inchCmPanel`, `mileKmPanel` and `poundKgPanel`. The various components are added to these panels, which are then added to the `MetricConverter` itself. In each case one of these components is a `JPanel`, which contains the two buttons used to make the conversions (the ones with the arrows on them); these panels (`inchCmButtons`, `mileKmButtons` and `poundKgButtons`) have a `BorderLayout` policy so that the buttons remain one on top of the other however the window is sized.

Look carefully at figure 10.15 and then look back at the code to see how we build up the components that make up the class.

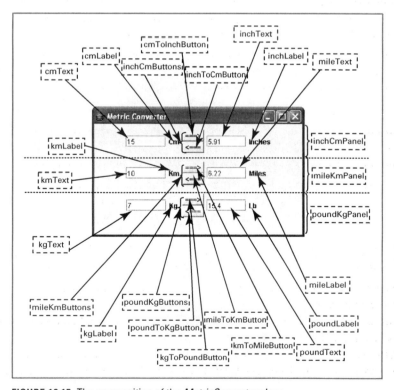

FIGURE 10.15 The composition of the *MetricConverter* class

10.11 GUIs for collections of objects

When we developed the GUI for our `Rectangle` class in section 10.6, we connected the GUI to a single instance of a `Rectangle` by declaring a `Rectangle` object as an attribute of the GUI class.

Many real-world examples will of course require you to manipulate more than one object – for example students, employees etc. One way to handle this would be to declare an array of objects as an attribute of the GUI class – you might want to try this out. The disadvantage of this approach, however, is that you would have to include in the event-handlers all the code for moving through the array (for example, to search it or to display items).

Another approach is to use a collection class and to declare an object of this class as an attribute of the GUI class. This is the approach that we have taken in the next two chapters, in which we develop a case study that deals with a student hostel.

Self-test questions

1 Distinguish between *lightweight* and *heavyweight* components.

2 **a** What is the role of *layout managers*?

   b Distinguish between the `FlowLayout` manager and the `BorderLayout` manager.

3 Which layout managers have been used in the following two graphics?

a 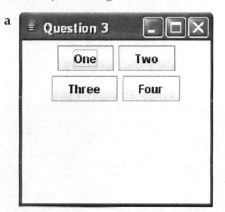   **b**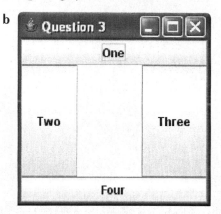

4 What is the default layout policy for:

   a a `JFrame`;

   b a `JPanel`?

5 A class called `Question5` has been written so that when an instance of this class is created, the following graphic appears:

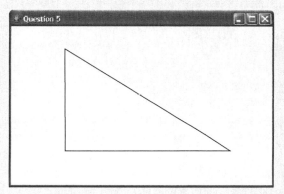

   a Write the necessary **import** statements for this class.

b Replace the comments in the constructor below with the appropriate code:

```
public Question5()
{
    // set the title to "Question 5"
    // disable the "close" icon
    // set the size of the frame to 500 x 400 pixels
    // set the location of the frame to (300,300)
    // set the background colour to yellow
    // make the frame visible
}
```

c Write the three lines of code that you would need to place in the paint method of the class in order to produce the triangle at the co-ordinates shown below:

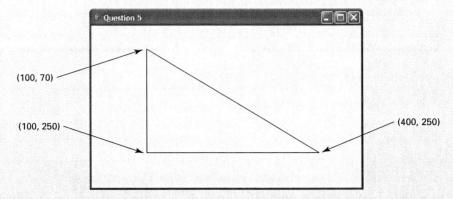

d Write the instruction that would be placed in a main method of a program in order to display the graphic.

6 Consider a class called Question6 which produces the following graphic in which two buttons can be used to change the background colour:

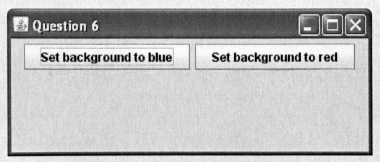

a Write the necessary **import** statements for this class.

    b Write the correct header for the class.

    c What is the name of the Swing component that you will need for the buttons?

    d Write the instruction that will make one of the buttons (say `button1`) listen for a mouse-click.

    e What is the name of the method that must be written to determine the action taken when the mouse is clicked on one of the buttons?

Programming exercises

1 Consider some changes or additions you could make to the `PushMe` class. For example, pushing the button could display your text in upper case – or it could say how many letters it contains. Maybe you could add some extra buttons.

2 Write the code that will produce the image shown in figure 10.13.

3 Implement the classes from tutorial questions 5 and 6.

4 Below is a variation on the `ChangingFace` class, which now has a neck and three possible moods!

Rewrite the original code to produce this new design.

*Hint: You will no longer be able to use a **boolean** variable like isHappy, because you need more than two possible values. Can you think of how to deal with this?*

In our version the top left-hand corner of the neck is at point (121,120); it is 3 pixels wide and 30 pixels long. The "thinking" mouth starts at point (102,100) and is 40 pixels long.

5 Add some additional features to the `MetricConverter` – for example Celsius to Fahrenheit or litres to pints.

6 Look back at the final version of the `Reactor` class that you wrote in programming exercise 5 of chapter 8. Now you can create a graphical user interface for it, instead of a text menu. A suggested interface is shown below, with an explanation of the different components used.

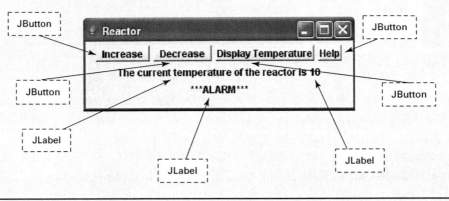

CHAPTER 11

Case study – part 1

❖ OBJECTIVES

By the end of this chapter you should be able to:

- ❖ describe each stage of the software development process;
- ❖ **design** a complete application using UML;
- ❖ **implement** a detailed UML design in Java;

- ❖ **document** your code using **Javadoc** comments;
- ❖ **test** a program using the strategies of **unit testing** and **integration testing**;
- ❖ document your test results professionally using a **test log**.

11.1 Introduction

The process of developing software requires us to carry out several tasks. They can be summarized as follows:

- **analysis and specification**: determining *what* the system is required to do (analysis) and writing it down in a clear and unambiguous manner (specification);
- **design**: making decisions about *how* the system is to be built in order to meet the specification;
- **implementation**: turning the design into an actual program;
- **testing**: ensuring that the system has been implemented correctly to meet the original specification;
- **installation**: delivering and setting up the completed system;
- **operation and maintenance**: running the final system and reviewing it over time – in light of changing requirements.

Rather than completely finishing one task before beginning the next, object-oriented languages like Java encourage systems to be developed a little bit at a time. So for example, we can build one class and test it (maybe in the presence of the client) before moving on to the next, rather than waiting for the whole system to be developed before testing and involving the client.

307

In the next two chapters we will demonstrate this process by developing a case study that will enable you to get an idea of how a commercial system can be developed from scratch; we start with an informal description of the requirements, and then specify and design the system using UML notation and pseudocode. From there we go on to implement our system in Java. Java applications, such as this, typically consist of many classes working together. When testing for errors we will start with a process of **unit testing** (testing individual classes) followed by **integration testing** (testing classes that together make up an application).

The system that we are going to develop will keep records of the residents of a student hostel. In order not to cloud your understanding, we have rather over-simplified things, keeping details of individuals to a minimum, and keeping the functionality fairly basic; you will have the opportunity to improve on what we have done in the practical exercises at the end of the next chapter.

11.2 The requirements specification

The local university requires a program to manage one of its student hostels, which contains a number of rooms, each of which can be occupied by a single tenant who pays rent on a monthly basis. The program must keep a list of tenants and their monthly payments. The information held for each tenant will consist of a name, a room number and a list of all the payments a tenant has made (month and amount) for one year. The program must allow the user to add and delete tenants, to display a list of all tenants, to record a payment for a particular tenant, and to display the payment history of a tenant.

11.3 The design

The two core classes required in this application are `Tenant` (to store the details of a tenant) and `Payment` (to store the details of a payment). We have made a number of design decisions about how the system will be implemented, and these are listed below:

- instances of the `Tenant` class and instances of the `Payment` class will each be held in a separate collection class, `PaymentList` and `TenantList` respectively;

- the collection classes `PaymentList` and `TenantList` are functionally very similar, so the common features of both classes will be captured in a generic `ObjectList` class. The `PaymentList` and `TenantList` classes can then inherit from this `ObjectList` class;

- the `Hostel` class, which will hold the `TenantList`, will also act as the graphical interface for the system.

The design of the system is shown in figure 11.1. In this design there are two arrows from one class to another. In UML these represent **associations**. An association is a link from objects of one class to objects of another class. For example, a *customer* might have one or more *accounts*; a *student* might have one or more *tutors*. The simplest form of association is a one-to-one relationship whereby a single instance of one class is associated with a single instance of another class – for example a *purchase transaction* and an *invoice*. You have already come across inheritance and aggregation – these are special examples of association.

In our example, the associations represented by the arrows are one-to-one associations – a `Tenant` requires a single instance of a `PaymentList` and a `Hostel` requires a single instance of a `TenantList`.

The `Hostel` class itself has not yet been designed and this will be left until the next chapter where we consider the overall system design and testing; for this reason it has been drawn with a dotted line.

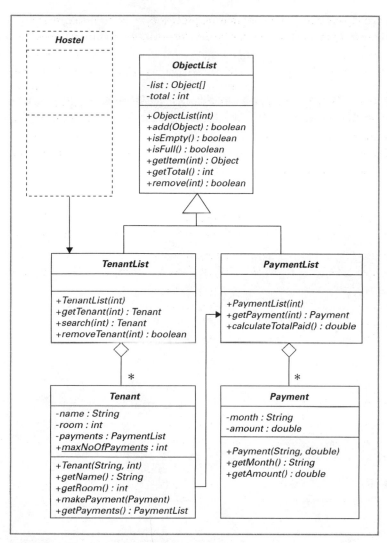

FIGURE 11.1 The design of the student hostel system

In order to implement this application we should start with those classes that do not depend on any other, so that they can be unit tested in isolation. For example, we should not start by implementing the `Tenant` class as it requires the `PaymentList` class to be implemented first. You can see from the associations in figure 11.1 that the only classes that do not require any other class for their implementation are the `Payment` class and the `ObjectList` class. Let's start with the `Payment` class.

11.4 Implementing the *Payment* class

The code for the Payment class is shown below:

THE *PAYMENT* CLASS

```java
// This class is used to store details of a single payment in a hostel

public class Payment
{
  private String month;
  private double amount;

  public Payment(String monthIn, double amountIn)
  {
    month = monthIn;
    amount= amountIn;
  }

  public String getMonth()
  {
    return month;
  }

  public double getAmount()
  {
    return amount;
  }
}
```

As you can see, this class is fairly simple and does not require any explanation.

Before incorporating this class into a larger program you would want to run it in order to test if it was working reliably. All applications require a class with a main method before they can be run. Eventually, when this class is incorporated into a larger program a suitable class with a main method will exist, but you'll want to test this class before an entire suite of classes have been developed. As we said before, testing an individual class in this way is often referred to as *unit testing*.

In order to unit test this class we will need to implement a separate class especially for this purpose. This new class will contain the main method and it will act as a **driver** for the original class. A driver is a special program designed to do nothing except exercise a particular class. If you look back at all our previous examples, this is exactly how we tested individual classes. Initially you should generate an object from the given class. Once an object has been generated we can then test that object by calling its methods. When testing your class by generating objects and calling methods, you will want to display results on the screen, such as the data stored within your object. We could access this data by calling the appropriate methods:

```
public class PaymentTester
{
  public static void main(String[ ] args)
  {
    Payment p1 = new Payment ("January", 175);
    // code to interrogate object data
    System.out.println("Month: " + p1.getMonth());
    System.out.println("Amount: " + p1.getAmount());
  }
}
```

This will display the expected output:

Month: January

Amount: 175.0

While having multiple output statements like this might be necessary in the final application, it is a rather cumbersome way of retrieving information from an object during the testing phase – when you will not be so concerned with the format of the output. What if your object had dozens of attributes? You would then need to call dozens of methods to read these attributes. It would be much more convenient to display the entire object on the screen with a single output statement such as this:

```
System.out.println (p1); // display entire object on the screen?
```

When an object is displayed in this way in a println (or print) instruction, what actually happens is that a special method of the object, called a toString method, is called. So this instruction could be considered a short-hand for the following instruction:

```
System.out.println (p1.toString());
```

This method should return a String representation of the object in question. However, we didn't write such a method when implementing the Payment class. The toString method is inherited from the Object class. Remember, from chapter 9, that all classes in Java inherit from the Object class. So the Payment class will also inherit any methods contained in the Object class – including this toString method. This means that, when we write an instruction such as this:

```
System.out.println (p1); // display Payment object on screen
```

we are actually calling the toString method of the Object class. Unfortunately, this method will not display the Payment object as we would wish. Here is an example of the output produced by this method:

Payment@19821f

What is this information that is being displayed? Well, the basic implementation of the toString method in the Object class just produces information on the *memory address* of the object in question.

In order for us to produce meaningful output here, we will need to *override* the toString method by providing our own implementation of this method in the Payment class. Here is one possible implementation:

```
public class Payment
{
  // original Payment attributes and methods here

  // override toString method of Object class
  public String toString()
  {
    return month+", "+amount;
  }
}
```

When implementing the toString method, you can choose how you wish the given object to be displayed. Here we have decided to display the attributes separated by a comma. Program 11.1 returns to the PaymentTester driver and makes use of this method:

PROGRAM 11.1

```
// a very simple driver program that makes use of the toString method

public class PaymentTester
{
  public static void main(String[ ] args)
  {
    Payment p1 = new Payment ("January", 175); // create object to test

    System.out.println(p1); // this will call the toString method in our Payment class
  }
}
```

Running this program will produce the following result:

January, 175.0

From this example, you can see how useful the `toString` method is. Many classes that are provided with the Java language, such as the `String` class, contain a `toString` method. It is worthwhile adding `toString` methods in the classes that you develop also, to allow them to be tested easily in this way.

Now let's move on to the more interesting parts of this system. This system requires us to develop two kinds of list, a `PaymentList` and a `TenantList`. Rather than develop the same code twice we are going to develop a generic `ObjectList` class and then use inheritance to add the specific attributes and methods that we need for a `PaymentList` and a `TenantList`.

11.5 The *ObjectList* class

The methods of the `ObjectList` class are very similar to a collection class that we showed you in chapter 8 – the `Bank` class. The main difference between the two classes is that in the `Bank` class the contained type was `BankAccount`, whereas in the `ObjectList` class the contained type is the generic type `Object`. As we said in chapter 9, this allows the list to store objects of any type.[1] Here is the code. This class has been commented using the `Javadoc` style of comments we briefly discussed in chapter 1. Take a look at it and then we will discuss it in more detail:

THE *OBJECTLIST* CLASS

```
/** This is a generic container class to store a list of objects
 *   @author Charatan and Kans
 *   @version 2nd September 2008
 */
public class ObjectList
{
  private Object[] list ;
  private int total ;


  /** Constructor intitializes an empty list
   *   @param sizeIn Used to set the maximum size of the list
   */
  public ObjectList(int sizeIn)
  {
    list = new Object[sizeIn];
    total = 0;
  }


  /** Adds an object to the end of the list
   *   @param objectIn The object to add
   *   @return Returns true if the object was added successfully and false otherwise
   */
```

---

[1] Later, in chapter 15, we will see that Java provides classes such as `ArrayList` that do a similar job to this `ObjectList` class.

```java
public boolean add(Object objectIn)
{
  if(!isFull())
  {
    list [total] = objectIn;
    total++;
    return true;
  }
  else
  {
    return false;
  }
}


/** Reports on whether or not the list is empty
 *  @return Returns true if the list is empty and false otherwise
 */
public boolean isEmpty()
{
  if(total==0)
  {
    return true;
  }
  else
  {
    return false;
  }
}


/** Reports on whether or not the list is full
 *  @return Returns true if the list is full and false otherwise
 */

public boolean isFull()
{
  if(total== list.length)
  {
    return true;
  }
  else
```

```
    {
      return false;
    }
  }


  /** Reads an object from a specified position in the list
   *  @param positionIn The position of the object in the list
   *  @return Returns the object at the specified position in the list
   *  or null if no object is at that position
   */
  public Object getItem(int positionIn)
  {
    if (positionIn <1 || positionIn > total)
    {
      return null;
    }
    else
    {
      return list [positionIn -1];
    }
  }


  /** Reads the number of objects stored in the list */
  public int getTotal()
  {
    return total;
  }


  /** Removes an object from the specified position in the list
   *  @param numberIn The position of the object to be removed
   *  @return Returns true if the item is removed successfully and false otherwise
   */
  public boolean remove(int numberIn)
  {
    if(numberIn >= 1 && numberIn <= total)
    {
      for(int i = numberIn-1; i <= total-2; i++)
      {
        list [i] = list [i+1];
      }
```

```
      total--;
      return true;
    }
    else
    {
      return false;
    }
  }


  /** Returns a string representation of the list */
  public String toString()
  {
    String items = ""; // initialize empty string
    for(int i =0; i < total; i++)
    {
      items = items + list[i].toString() + " "; // call toString of contained items
    }
    return "[ " + items +"]"; // surround list in square brackets
  }
}
```

You can see that we have included a `toString` method in this class, to assist in the testing process. In order to generate a `String` to represent this list, we have called the `toString` method of the contained items, joined these `Strings` together and surrounded them in a pair of square brackets:

```
public String toString()
{
  String items = ""; // initialize empty string
  for(int i =0; i < total; i++)
  {
    items = items + list[i].toString() + " "; // call toString of contained items
  }
  return "[ " + items +"]"; // surround list in square brackets
}
```

As this is class is considerably more complex class compared with the `Payment` class, we have documented this class with `Javadoc` comments which are explained below.

11.5.1 Javadoc

Sun's Java Development Kit contains a tool, `Javadoc`, which allows you to generate documentation for classes in the form of HTML files. In order to use this tool you must comment your classes in the `Javadoc` style. As we mentioned in chapter 1, `Javadoc` comments must begin with /** and end with */. `Javadoc` comments can also contain 'tags'. Tags are special formatting markers that allow you to record information such as the author of a piece of code. Table 11.1 gives some commonly used tags in `Javadoc` comments.

Tag	Information
@author	the name(s) of the code author(s)
@version	a version number for the code (often a date is used here)
@param	the name of a parameter and its description
@return	a description of the return value of a method

TABLE 11.1 Some *Javadoc* tags

The @author and @version tags are used in the `Javadoc` comment for the class as a whole. You can see examples of these tags at the top of the `ObjectList` class:

```
/** This is a generic container class to store a list of objects
 *   @author Charatan and Kans
 *   @version 2nd September 2008
 */
public class ObjectList
{
   // attributes and methods go here
}
```

You can see that, when `Javadoc` comments run over several lines, it is common (though not necessary) to begin each line with a leading asterix.

The @param and @return tags are used in the `Javadoc` comments preceding each method. For example, here are the `Javadoc` comments for the add method:

```
/** Adds an object to the end of the list
 *   @param objectIn The object to add
 *   @return Returns true if the object was added successfully and false otherwise
 */
public boolean add(Object objectIn)
{
  if(!isFull())
  {
    list [total] = objectIn;
    total++;
```

```
   return true;
  }
  else
  {
    return false;
  }
}
```

You can see that the `param` tag has been used to provide a comment on the parameter (`objectIn`) and the `return` tag has been used to comment the role of the **boolean** value returned by this method. The `Javadoc` HTML documentation files can then be generated either from the command line using the **javadoc** command:

javadoc ObjectList.java

or invoked directly by your IDE. Figure 11.2 gives part of the documentation generated for the `ObjectList` class.

Class ObjectList

```
java.lang.object
  └objectlist
```

```
public class objectlist
extents java.lang.object
```

This is a generic container class to store a list of objects

Version:
   2nd September 2008
Author:
   Charatan and Kans

Constructor Summary
`objectList(int sizeIn)`   Constructor intitialises an empty list

Method Summary	
boolean	`add(java.lang.object objectIn)` Adds on object to the end of the list
java.lang.object	`getItem(int positionIn)` Reads an object from a specified position in the list

FIGURE 11.2 Javadoc documentation generated for the *ObjectList* class

Comments, such as the `Javadoc` comments we added into the `ObjectList` class, provide one technique for documenting the code that you write. Documenting your code is important as it assists in the maintenance of that code, should it need to be modified in the future. Well documented code is also easier to fix if errors arise during development. As well as commenting your code, you should ensure that the code is well laid out so that it becomes easier to read and follow.

11.5.2 Code layout

Consistent and clear indentation is important to improve the readability of your programs. Look at the example programs that we have presented to you and notice the care we have taken with our indentation. We are following two simple rules all the time:

- keep braces lined up under the structure to which they belong;
- indent, by one level, all code that belongs within those braces.

For example, look at the add method of the ObjectList class:

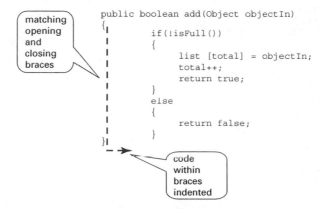

Notice how these rules are applied again with the braces of the inner **if...else** statements:

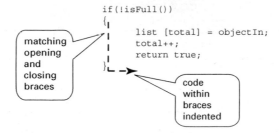

11.5.3 Testing the *ObjectList* class

To test the ObjectList class we need a driver that not only creates an ObjectList object, but also creates objects to add to this list. We will test the ObjectList class by adding a collection of simple String objects into this list.

We have quite a few methods to test in our ObjectList class, so we need to spend some time considering how we will go about testing these methods. For example, it would make sense to limit the size of our

ObjectList so that we can quickly fill up our list to check the isFull method. Here is one possible test strategy:

1 limit the size of the ObjectList to a relatively small number (say 4);

2 check to see if the isEmpty method returns **true**;

3 add four String items to this list (say "RED", "BLUE", "GREEN", and "YELLOW");

4 display the list to check the items have been added successfully;

5 check to see if the isFull method returns **true**;

6 remove one item (say item number 2);

7 display the list to ensure that the given item has been removed.

Once a strategy is chosen, the test results should be logged in a **test log**. A test log is a document that records the testing that took place during system development. Each row of the test log associates an *input* with an *expected output*. If the output is not as expected, reasons for this error have to be identified and recorded in the log.

Figure 11.3 illustrates a suitable test log to document the testing strategy we developed above.

TEST LOG			
Purpose: To test the ObjectList class			
Run Number:	**Date:**		
Action	**Expected Output**	**Pass/ Fail**	**Reason for failure**
	Prompt for size of list		
Enter 4	Display menu of options		
Select IS EMPTY option	Message "list is empty" Display menu of options		
Select ADD option	Prompt for String to add		
Enter "RED"	Display menu of options		
Select ADD option	Prompt for String to add		
Enter "BLUE"	Display menu of options		
Select ADD option	Prompt for String to add		
Enter "GREEN"	Display menu of options		
Select ADD option	Prompt for String to add		
Enter "YELLOW"	Display menu of options		
Select DISPLAY option	Message [RED BLUE GREEN YELLOW] Display menu of options		
Select IS FULL option	Message "list is full" Display menu of options		
Select REMOVE option	Prompt for position to remove		
Enter 2	Message "item removed" Display menu of options		
Select DISPLAY option	Message [RED GREEN YELLOW] Display menu of options		
Select EXIT	Program terminates		

FIGURE 11.3 Test log for the *ObjectList* class

Test logs such as this should be devised *before* the driver itself (and may even be developed before the class we are testing has been developed). The test log can then be used to prompt the development of the driver. As you can see by looking at the test log above, we assume that the driver is a menu driven program. Program 11.2 is one possible driver we could develop in order to process the actions given in this test log:

PROGRAM 11.2

```java
public class ObjectListTester
{
  public static void main(String[] args)
  {
    char choice;
    int size;
    ObjectList list; // declare ObjectList object to test

    // get size of list
    System.out.print("Size of list? ");
    size = EasyScanner.nextInt();
    list = new ObjectList(size); // create object to test
    // menu
    do
    {
      // display options
      System.out.println();
      System.out.println("[1] ADD");
      System.out.println("[2] REMOVE");
      System.out.println("[3] IS EMPTY");
      System.out.println("[4] IS FULL");
      System.out.println("[5] DISPLAY");
      System.out.println("[6] Quit");
      System.out.println();
      System.out.print("Enter a choice [1-6]: ");
      // get choice
      choice = EasyScanner.nextChar();
      System.out.println();
      // process choice
      switch(choice)
      {
        case '1': option1(list); break;
        case '2': option2(list); break;
        case '3': option3(list); break;
        case '4': option4(list); break;
```

```
        case '5': option5(list); break;
        case '6': System.out.println("TESTING COMPLETE"); break;
        default: System.out.print("1-6 only");
      }
  } while (choice != '6');
}


// ADD
static void option1(ObjectList listIn)
{
  System.out.print("Enter String: ");
  String str = EasyScanner.nextString();
  listIn.add(str);
}


// REMOVE
static void option2(ObjectList listIn)
{
  System.out.print("Enter position to remove: ");
  int pos = EasyScanner.nextInt();
  listIn.remove(pos);
}


// IS EMPTY
static void option3(ObjectList listIn)
{
  if (listIn.isEmpty())
  {
    System.out.println("list is empty");
  }
  else
  {
    System.out.println("list is NOT empty");
  }
}


// IS FULL
static void option4(ObjectList listIn)
{
  if (listIn.isFull())
  {
    System.out.println("list is full");
  }
```

```
    else
    {
      System.out.println("list is NOT full");
    }
  }


  // DISPLAY
  static void option5(ObjectList listIn)
  {
    System.out.println(listIn); // calls toString method of ObjectList
  }
}
```

We are now in a position to run the driver and check the actions documented in the test log:

Size of list? **4**

[1] ADD
[2] REMOVE
[3] IS EMPTY
[4] IS FULL
[5] DISPLAY
[6] Quit

Enter a choice [1-6]: **3**

list is empty

[1] ADD
[2] REMOVE
[3] IS EMPTY
[4] IS FULL
[5] DISPLAY
[6] Quit

Enter a choice [1-6]: **1**

Enter String: RED

[1] ADD
[2] REMOVE
[3] IS EMPTY
[4] IS FULL
[5] DISPLAY
[6] Quit

```
Enter a choice [1-6]: 1

Enter String: BLUE

[1] ADD
[2] REMOVE
[3] IS EMPTY
[4] IS FULL
[5] DISPLAY
[6] Quit

Enter a choice [1-6]: 1

Enter String: GREEN

[1] ADD
[2] REMOVE
[3] IS EMPTY
[4] IS FULL
[5] DISPLAY
[6] Quit

Enter a choice [1-6]: 1

Enter String: YELLOW

[1] ADD
[2] REMOVE
[3] IS EMPTY
[4] IS FULL
[5] DISPLAY
[6] Quit

Enter a choice [1-6]: 5

[ RED BLUE GREEN YELLOW ]

[1] ADD
[2] REMOVE
[3] IS EMPTY
[4] IS FULL
[5] DISPLAY
[6] Quit

Enter a choice [1-6]: 4

list is full
```

```
[1]  ADD
[2]  REMOVE
[3]  IS EMPTY
[4]  IS FULL
[5]  DISPLAY
[6]  Quit

Enter a choice [1-6]: 2

Enter position to remove: 2

[1]  ADD
[2]  REMOVE
[3]  IS EMPTY
[4]  IS FULL
[5]  DISPLAY
[6]  Quit

Enter a choice [1-6]: 5

[ RED GREEN YELLOW ]

[1]  ADD
[2]  REMOVE
[3]  IS EMPTY
[4]  IS FULL
[5]  DISPLAY
[6]  Quit

Enter a choice [1-6]: 6

TESTING COMPLETE
```

If unexpected results are produced during testing, you should stop and identify the cause of the error in the class that you are testing. Both the cause of the error and how the error was fixed should be documented in the test log. The driver can then be run again with a fresh test log and this process should continue until *all* results are delivered as predicted. In this case, however, the results were as expected, so we can now move on to developing the rest of our system.

11.6 The *PaymentList* class

The ObjectList class allows objects of any class to be stored in the list. The algorithms we used in the methods are the same as the Bank class that we discussed in chapter 8 so we will not discuss them further here. We need to specialize this class (using inheritance) so that it can be used to store Payment and Tenant objects exclusively. First let us look at the PaymentList class to store Payment objects. If you look back at the UML design in figure 11.1 you can see that after inheriting details from the ObjectList class, there is not a lot of extra work to be done to code the `PaymentList` class. We present the complete code for this class below, after which we discuss it.

THE *PAYMENTLIST* CLASS

```java
/** Collection class to hold a list of Payment objects
 *    @author Charatan and Kans
 *    @version 4th September 2008
 */
public class PaymentList extends ObjectList // inherit from ObjectList
{
  /** Constructor initializes the empty list and sets the maximium list size
   */
  public PaymentList(int sizeIn)
  { // call ObjectList constructor
     super(sizeIn);
  }
  /** Reads the payment at the given position in the list
   *  @param positionIn The position of the payment in the list
   *  @return Returns the payment at the given position in the list
   *  or null if no payment at that posiiton
   */
  public Payment getPayment(int positionIn)
  { // check for valid position
     if (positionIn <1 || positionIn > getTotal())
     {
       // no object found at given position
       return null;
     }
     else
     {
       // call inherited method and type cast
       return (Payment) getItem(positionIn);
     }
  }


  /** Returns the total value of payments recorded */
  public double calculateTotalPaid()
  {
     double totalPaid = 0; // initialize totalPaid
     // loop through all payments
     for (int i = 1; i <= getTotal();i++)
     { // add current payment to running total
```

```
        totalPaid = totalPaid + getPayment(i).getAmount();
    }
    return totalPaid;
    }
}
```

As you can see, this class requires no additional attributes and, apart from the new constructor, only two additional methods – `getPayment` and `calculateTotalPaid`. Let's have a look at each of these methods in turn.

The `getPayment` method is simply a wrapper for the `getItem` method from the inherited `ObjectList` class. The first thing we do is to check that the method has received a valid position as a parameter. If an invalid position is found the **null** value is returned:

```
if (positionIn <1 || positionIn > getTotal())
{
  // no object found at given position
  return null;
}
else
{
  // code to retrieve object at the valid position goes here
}
```

If you remember from chapter 9, we said that generic container classes can be used to store items of *any* type, but when returning such items from the container they must be type cast back to the appropriate type. The `get-Payment` method carries out this task of type casting the returned item back to an object of type `Payment`.

```
return (Payment) getItem(positionIn);
```

The advantage of this is that responsibility for type casting is taken away from the calling method, and given to `getPayment` itself. An example of the use of this method can be seen in the `calculateTotalPaid` method.

The `calculateTotalPaid` method uses a standard algorithm for computing sums from a list of items. We met such an algorithm in section 6.7.2. This algorithm can be expressed in pseudocode as follows:

```
SET totalPaid TO 0
LOOP FROM first item in list TO last item in list
BEGIN
  SET totalPaid TO totalPaid + amount of current payment
END
RETURN totalPaid
```

As with the `remove` method that we discussed in chapter 8, this algorithm can be implemented in Java with the use of a **for** loop. Notice how the position of the last item in the list is determined by the `getTotal` method; remember that we do not have access to the `total` attribute, since this was declared as **private** in the superclass.

```
double totalPaid = 0;
for (int i=1; i<= getTotal();i++)
{
  totalPaid = totalPaid + getPayment(i).getAmount();
}
return totalPaid;
```

The body of the loop takes the amount associated with the current payment and adds it to the running total. As you can see, the `getPayment` method is used to return the current payment and the `getAmount` method is used to find out the amount associated with that payment.

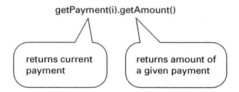

As we have said before, It is always important to test classes in order to ensure that they are functioning correctly before moving on to the rest of the development. Whereas the testing of the `Payment` class was an example of *unit testing*, testing this `PaymentList` class is an example of *integration testing* as it requires the `PaymentList` class working in conjunction with the `Payment` class and the `ObjectList` class. We leave the testing of this and the remaining classes to you as end of chapter programming exercises.

Before we look at the `TenantList` class we need to implement the `Tenant` class.

11.7 Implementing the *Tenant* class

As you can see from the UML diagram of figure 11.1, the `Tenant` class contains four attributes:

- `name`;
- `room`;
- `payments`;
- `maxNoOfPayments`.

The first two of these represent the name and the room of the tenant, respectively. The third attribute, `payments`, is to be implemented as a `PaymentList` object and the last attribute, `maxNoOfPayments`, is to be implemented as a **static** class attribute. The `maxNoOfPayments` attribute will also be implemented as a *constant* as we are assuming that tenants make a *fixed* number of payments in a year (twelve – one for each month). Since class constants can not be modified, it makes sense to allow them to be declared as **public**. Below is the code for the `Tenant` class.

THE *TENANT* CLASS

```java
/** Class used to record the details of a tenant
 *   @author Charatan and Kans
 *   @version 6th September 2008
 */
public class Tenant
{
  private String name;
  private int room;
  private PaymentList payments;
  public static final int maxNoOfPayments = 12;

  /** Constructor initializes the name and room number of the tenant
   *  and sets the payments made to the empty list
   */
  public Tenant(String nameIn, int roomIn)
  {
    name = nameIn;
    room = roomIn;
    payments = new PaymentList(maxNoOfPayments);
  }

  /** Reads the name of the tenant */
  public String getName()
  {
    return name;
  }

  /** Reads the room number of the tenant */
  public int getRoom()
  {
    return room;
  }

  /** Records a payment for the tenant */
  public void makePayment(Payment paymentIn)
  {
    payments.add(paymentIn); // call PaymentList method
  }
```

```
/** Reads the payments made by the tenant */
public PaymentList getPayments()
{
  return payments;
}
}
```

As there is nothing very new in this class, we don't really need to discuss it any further other than to point out that the payments attribute, being of type PaymentList, can respond to any of the PaymentList methods we discussed in section 11.6. The makePayment method illustrates this by calling the add method of PaymentList:

```
public void makePayment(Payment paymentIn)
{
  payments.add(paymentIn); // add method of PaymentList called
}
```

11.8 Implementing the *TenantList* class

The TenantList class, like the PaymentList class of section 11.6, inherits from the generic ObjectList class. As you can see from figure 11.1, the TenantList class requires no new attributes and, apart from the constructor, has only three new methods:

- getTenant;
- search;
- removeTenant.

The getTenant method behaves in much the same way as the getPayment method of the PaymentList class. That is, it acts as a wrapper for the getItem method of the generic ObjectList class and type casts the returned item back to an object of the correct type, which in this case is an object of type Tenant.

```
public Tenant getTenant(int positionIn)
{
  // call inherited method and type cast
  return (Tenant)getItem(positionIn);
}
```

The search method is unique to the TenantList class. Here is a reminder of its UML interface:

+search(int) : Tenant

The integer parameter represents the room number of the tenant that this method is searching for. The tenant returned is the tenant living in that particular room; if no tenant is found in that room then **null** is eturned.

We have already met an algorithm for searching an array in section 6.7.4 of this book. That algorithm dealt with searching an *entire* array and this was adapted in section 8.8.1 where we searched a *partially filled* array. This search method we are going to develop here is an example of searching a partially filled array so the code is similar to that in the Bank example of section 8.8.1. In the previous algorithms we returned a dummy value of –999 to indicate an unsuccessful search. In this case, however, we must return a value of **null** as we are returning an object, not an integer:

```
public Tenant search(int roomIn)
{
  for(int i=1;i<=getTotal();i++)
  {
    // find tenant with given room number
    if(getTenant(i).getRoom() == roomIn)
    {
      return getTenant(i);
    }
  }
  return null; // no tenant found with given room number
}
```

Notice that to check the room number of a particular tenant we call the getTenant method to identify the tenant, and then the getRoom method to identify this tenant's room number:

```
if(getTenant(i).getRoom() == roomIn)
{
  return getTenant(i);
}
```

Finally, let's look at the removeTenant method. The UML interface for this method is as follows:

+removeTenant(int) : boolean

Here the integer parameter represents the room number of the tenant that is to be removed from the list and the **boolean** return value indicates whether or not such a tenant has been removed successfully. From this interface we get the following method header:

```
public boolean removeTenant (int roomIn)
{
  // code for methods goes here
}
```

Most of the work of this method is going to be carried out by the `remove` method of the `ObjectList` class. The job of the `removeTenant` method is to determine which tenant to delete before calling the `remove` method. It is very similar to the `remove` method we looked at in the `Bank` example of section 8.8.1. In that case we looked for the bank account with the given account number whereas in this case we are looking for a tenant in a given room:

```
for(int i=1; i<=getTotal(); i++)
{
  // remove tenant with given room number
  if(getTenant(i).getRoom() == roomIn)
  {
    remove(i); // call remove method of ObjectList
    return true; // indicate success
  }
}
return false; // indicate failure
```

The complete code for the `TenantList` class is now presented below.

THE *TENANTLIST* CLASS

```
/** Collection class to hold a list of tenants
 *  @author Charatan and Kans
 *  @version 6th September 2008
 */
public class TenantList extends ObjectList
{
  /** Constructor initializes the empty list and sets the maximium
   *  list size
   */
  public TenantList(int sizeIn)
  {
    super(sizeIn); // call ObjectList constructor
  }
  /** Reads the tenant at the given position in the list
   *  @param positionIn The position of the tenant in the list
   *  @return Returns the tenant at the given position in the list
   *  or null if no tenant at that posiiton
   */
```

```
public Tenant getTenant(int positionIn)
{
  if (positionIn<1 || positionIn>getTotal()) // check for valid position
  {
    return null; // no object found at given position
  }
  else
  {
    // call inherited method and type cast
    return (Tenant) getItem(positionIn);
  }
}


/** Searches for the tenant in the given room number
 *  @param roomIn The room number to search for
 *  @return Returns the tenant in the given room or null if no tenant in the given room
 */
public Tenant search(int roomIn)
{
  for(int i = 1;i <= getTotal();i++)
  { // find tenant with given room number
    if(getTenant(i).getRoom() == roomIn)
    {
      return getTenant(i);
    }
  }
  return null; // no tenant found with given room number
}
/** Removes the tenant in the given room number
 *   @param roomIn The room number of the tenant to remove
 *   @return Returns true if the tenant is removed successfully or false otherwise
 */
public boolean removeTenant(int roomIn)
{
  for(int i = 1;i <= getTotal();i++)
  {
    // remove tenant with given room number
    if(getTenant(i).getRoom() == roomIn)
```

```
        {
            remove(i);
            return true;
        }
    }
    return false; // no tenant found with given room number
    }
}
```

All that remains for us to do to complete our case study in the next chapter is to design, implement and test the `Hostel` class, which will not only keep track of the tenants but will also act as the graphical user interface for the system.

Self-test questions

1 Describe the class associations given in the UML design of figure 11.1.

2 Produce suitable `Javadoc` comments for the `Payment` class.

3 The test log of section 11.5.3 did not include checks for the `getItem` and `getTotal` methods of the `ObjectList` class. It also did not include a check when attempting to add to a full list and removing from an empty list would fail. Modify the test log to include these checks.

4 Develop `toString` methods for the `Payment` and `Tenant` classes.

5 Develop a test log for testing the `TenantList` class.

Programming exercises

You will need to copy the entire suite of classes that make up the student hostel system from the accompanying CD.

1 Modify and then run the driver given in program 11.2 in light of the changes made to the test log in self-test question 3 above.

2 Amend the `Payment` and `Tenant` classes by including the `toString` methods you developed in self-test question 4 above.

3 Develop a suitable driver to test the `TenantList` class.

4 Use the test log you developed in self-test question 5 and the driver you developed in exercise 3 above to test the `TenantList` class.

CHAPTER

12

Case study – part 2

❖ OBJECTIVES

By the end of this chapter you should be able to:

- ❖ design an attractive graphical user interface;
- ❖ use pseudocode to design event handling routines;

- ❖ implement the design in Java using a variety of Swing based components.

12.1 Introduction

In the previous chapter we designed and developed the core classes required to implement the functionality of our *Student Hostel System*. We now go on develop a graphical user interface for this application.

12.2 Keeping permanent records

In practice, an application such as the *Student Hostel System* would not be much use if we had no way of keeping permanent records – in other words, of saving a file to disk. However, reading and writing files is something that you will not learn until your second semester. So, in the meantime, in order to make it possible to keep a permanent record of your data, we have created a special class for you to use; we have called this class `TenantFileHandler`. This class (along with the rest of the files from this case study) can be found on the accompanying CD.

The `TenantFileHandler` class has two **static** methods: the first, `saveRecords`, needs to be sent two parameters, an integer value indicating the number of rooms in the hostel, and a `TenantList`, which is a reference to the list to be saved; the second, `readRecords`, requires only a reference to a `TenantList` so that it knows where to store the information that is read from the file.

The `readRecords` method will be called when the application is first loaded (so this method call will therefore be coded into the constructor), and the `saveRecords` method will be called when we finish the application (and will therefore be coded into the event-handler of a "Save and Quit" button). We will also provide the option of exiting without saving, just in case, for any reason, the user should want to abandon any changes.

12.3 Design of the GUI

There will be two aspects to the design of the graphical interface. Firstly we need to design the visual side of things; then we need to design the algorithms for our event-handling routines so that the buttons do the jobs we want them to, like adding or displaying tenants.

Let's start with the visual design. We need to choose which graphics components we are going to use and how to lay them out. One way to do this is to make a preliminary sketch such as the one shown in figure 12.1. We have named our components so that it is obvious what kind of component we are talking about; for example, `nameField` is a `JTextField`, `addButton` is a `JButton` and `displayArea1` is a `JTextArea`.

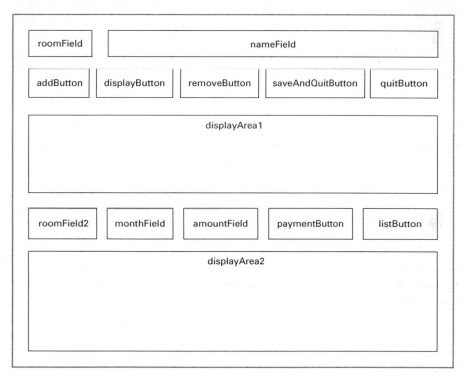

FIGURE 12.1 Preliminary design of the *Hostel* class

We are going to use a simple `FlowLayout` policy, so to get our components where we want them we will have to play about with the size of the components and the size of the frame. You can see from the design that we have not included any labels to mark the purpose of the text fields. For example the `roomField` has no associated label to indicate that a room number is to be entered into this field. Instead we will give such components a *titled border* indicating their purpose. As the name suggests, this is a facility in Swing to give a component a particular style of border that includes a title. We will examine this and other types of border in detail in chapter 17, but will introduce its use here in this case study. To help you see what we are aiming at, we have, with figure 12.2, "cheated" and let you look ahead at the end result. This shows the effect of running our Hostel interface in a 550 × 450 frame.

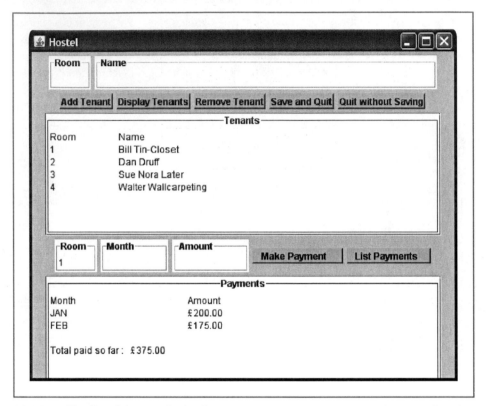

FIGURE 12.2 The *Hostel* class running in a frame

You can see that including titles (such as "Room" and "Name") in the border of a component such as a JTextField removes the need for labels. As you will see when we show you the complete code for the Hostel class, we will use the setBorder method of a component to set such borders.

Now that we know the components we need, it is an easy matter to complete the UML class diagram. Each of the components must be declared as an attribute of the class – and, in addition, there are two more attributes that we will need. First, we will need to hold information about the number of rooms available in the hostel, so we must declare an attribute of type **int** for this purpose; we have called our attribute noOfRooms. Second, we must, of course, declare an attribute of type TenantList (which we have called list) to keep track of the tenants in residence.

We are going to need only two methods: a constructor to add the components and read the data from the file, and an actionPerformed method for the event-handling routines.

The class design is shown in figure 12.3.

Hostel
-noOfRooms : int *-list : TenantList* *-roomField : JTextField* *-nameField : JTextField* *-addButton : JButton* *-displayButton : JButton* *-removeButton : JButton* *-saveAndQuitButton : JButton* *-quitButton : JButton* *-displayArea1 : JTextArea* *-roomField2 : JTextField* *-monthField : JTextField* *-amountField : JTextField* *-paymentButton : JButton* *-listButton : JButton* *-displayArea2 : JTextArea*
+Hostel(int) *+actionPerformed(ActionEvent)*

FIGURE 12.3 The UML design of the *Hostel* Class

12.4 Designing the event-handlers

As you can see, there are seven buttons that need to be coded so that they respond in the correct way when pressed. Our code for the `actionPerformed` method will therefore take the following form:

```
public void actionPerformed(ActionEvent e)
{
  if(e.getSource() == addButton)
  {
    // code for add button goes here
  }
  if(e.getSource() == displayButton)
  {
  // code for display button goes here
  }
  if(e.getSource() == removeButton)
  {
    // code for remove button goes here
  }
  if(e.getSource() == paymentButton)
  {
    // code for payment button goes here
  }
```

```
if(e.getSource() == listButton)
{
  // code for list button goes here
}
if(e.getSource() == saveAndQuitButton)
{
  // code for saveAndQuit button goes here
}
if(e.getSource() == quitButton)
{
  // code for quit button goes here
}
}
```

We have summarized below the task that each button must perform, and then gone on to design our algorithms using pseudocode:

The addButton

The purpose of this button is to add a new `Tenant` to the list. The values entered in `roomField` and `nameField` must be validated; first of all, they must not be blank; second, the room number must not be greater than the number of rooms available (or less than 1!); finally, the room must not be occupied. If all this is okay, then the new tenant is added (we will make use of the `add` method of `TenantList` to do this) and a message should be displayed in `displayArea1`. We can express this in pseudocode as follows:

```
read roomField
read nameField
IF roomField blank OR nameField blank
  display blank field error in displayArea1
ELSE IF roomField value < 1 OR roomField value > noOfRooms
  display invalid room number error in displayArea1
ELSE IF tenant found in room
  display room occupied error in displayArea1
ELSE
BEGIN
  add tenant
  blank roomField
  blank nameField
  display message to confirm success in displayArea1
END
```

The displayButton

Pressing this button will display the full list of tenants (room number and name) in `displayArea1`.

If all the rooms are vacant a suitable message should be displayed; otherwise the list of tenants' rooms and names should appear under appropriate headings, as can be seen in figure 12.3. This can be expressed in pseudocode as follows:

```
IF list is empty
  display rooms empty error in displayArea1
ELSE
BEGIN
  display header in displayArea1
  LOOP FROM first item TO last item in list
  BEGIN
    append tenant room and name to displayArea1
  END
END
```

The removeButton

Clicking on this button will remove the tenant whose room number has been entered in `roomField`.

As with the `addButton`, the room number entered must be validated; if the number is a valid one then the tenant is removed from the list (we will make use of the `remove` method of `TenantList` to do this) and a confirmation message is displayed. The pseudocode for this event-handler is given as follows:

```
read roomField
IF roomField blank
  display blank field error in displayArea1
ELSE IF roomField value < 1 OR roomField value > noOfRooms
  display invalid room number error in displayArea1
ELSE IF no tenant found in room
  display room empty error in displayArea1
ELSE
BEGIN
  remove tenant from list
  display message to confirm success in displayArea1
END
```

The paymentButton

This button records payments made by an individual tenant whose room number is entered in `roomField2`. The values entered in `roomField2`, `monthField` and `amountField` must be validated to ensure that none of the fields is blank, that the room number is a valid one and, if so, that it is currently occupied.

If everything is ok then a new payment record is added to that tenant's list of payments (we will make use of the `makePayment` method of `PaymentList` to do this) and a confirmation message is displayed in `displayArea2`. This design is expressed in pseudocode as follows:

```
read roomField2
read monthField
read amountField
IF roomField2 blank OR monthField blank OR amountField blank
  display fields empty error in displayArea2
```

```
ELSE IF roomField2 value < 1 OR roomField2 value > noOfRooms
  display invalid room number error in displayArea2
ELSE IF no tenant found in room
  display room empty error in displayArea2
ELSE
BEGIN
  create payment from amountField value and monthField value
  add payment into list
  display message to confirm success in displayArea2
END
```

The *listButton*

Pressing this button causes a list of payments (month and amount) made by the tenant whose room number is entered in `roomField2` to be displayed in `displayArea2`.

After validating the values entered, each record in the tenant's payment list is displayed. Finally, the total amount paid by that tenant is displayed (we will make use of the `calculateTotalPaid` method of `PaymentList` to do this). The pseudocode is given as follows:

```
read roomField2
IF roomField2 blank
display room field empty error in displayArea2
ELSE IF roomField2 value < 1 OR roomField2 value > noOfRooms
  display invalid room number error in displayArea2
ELSE IF no tenant found in room
  display room empty error in displayArea2
ELSE
BEGIN
  find tenant in given room
  get payments of tenant
  IF payments = 0
     display no payments error in displayArea2
  ELSE
  BEGIN
     display header in displayArea2
     LOOP FROM first payment TO last payment
     BEGIN
       append amount and month to displayArea2
     END
     display total paid in displayArea2
     blank monthField
     blank amountField
  END
END
```

The *saveAndQuitButton*

Pressing this button causes all the records to be saved to a file (here we make use of the `saveRecords` method of the `TenantFileHandler` class that we talked about in section 12.2); it then closes the frame, terminating the program.

It contains only two lines of code and we have therefore not written pseudocode for it.

The *quitButton*

Pressing this button terminates the program without saving the changes.

12.5 Implementing the *Hostel* class

The complete code for the `Hostel` class now appears below. When you see the code, you should notice that we have utilized the `NumberFormat` class (which is to be found in the `java.text` package) to print the amounts in the local currency. Also note the use of the `parseInt` method of the `Integer` class to convert the room values, entered as text, into integer values and the use of the `setBorder` method to set the border of a component (as discussed in section 12.3). We have also enhanced our text areas by making use of a new component called a *scroll pane*.

Study the code and the comments carefully and compare it with the pseudocode to make sure you understand it and we will explain the new concepts to you after that.

THE *HOSTEL* CLASS

```
import java.awt.*;
import java.awt.event.*;
import java.text.*;
import javax.swing.*;
import javax.swing.border.*;
/**GUI for the Hostel application
 *@author Charatan and Kans
 *@version 7th September 2008
 */
public class Hostel extends JFrame implements ActionListener
{
  // the attributes
  private  int noOfRooms;
  private  TenantList list;
  private  JButton addButton = new JButton("Add Tenant");
  private  JButton displayButton = new JButton("Display Tenants");
  private  JButton removeButton = new JButton("Remove Tenant");
  private  JTextField roomField = new JTextField(4);
  private  JTextField nameField = new JTextField(39);
  private  JButton saveAndQuitButton = new JButton("Save and Quit");
  private  JButton quitButton = new JButton("Quit without Saving");
```

```
private   JTextArea displayArea1 = new JTextArea(8,45);

private   JTextArea displayArea2 = new JTextArea(8,45);

private   JTextField roomField2 = new JTextField(4);

private   JTextField monthField = new JTextField(7);

private   JTextField amountField = new JTextField(8);

private JButton paymentButton = new JButton("   Make Payment      ");

private   JButton listButton = new JButton("   List Payments      ");


//the constructor
public Hostel (int numberIn)
{
  // initialse the number of rooms and the TenantList
  noOfRooms = numberIn;
  list = new TenantList(noOfRooms);


  // set layout policy to FlowLayout
  setLayout(new FlowLayout());
  // allow program to end when cross-hairs are clicked
 setDefaultCloseOperation(JFrame.EXIT_ON_CLOSE);
  // set appearance of JFrame
  setTitle("Hostel");
  setSize(550, 450);
  setLocation(400,100);
  getContentPane().setBackground(Color.cyan);
  // create a border style to be used for the JButtons
  BevelBorder raisedBevel = new BevelBorder(BevelBorder.RAISED);
  // add components
  add(roomField);
  /* The setBorder method is used to give a a component a titledborder.
     This version of the method accepts an appropriate TitleBoarder object */
  roomField.setBorder(new TitledBorder("Room"));
  // repeat this process for the nameField
  add(nameField);
  nameField. setBorder(new TitledBorder("Name"));
  //  JButtons are added, their background colours and borders set
  add(addButton);
  addButton.setBackground(Color.green);
  addButton.setBorder(raisedBevel);
  add(displayButton);
  displayButton.setBorder(raisedBevel);
  displayButton.setBackground(Color.green);
  add(removeButton);
```

```java
removeButton.setBackground(Color.green);
removeButton.setBorder(raisedBevel);
add(saveAndQuitButton);
saveAndQuitButton.setBackground(Color.green);
saveAndQuitButton.setBorder(raisedBevel);
add(quitButton);
quitButton.setBackground(Color.green);
quitButton.setBorder(raisedBevel);
/* By default the title of a component will be left justified.
   To choose another justification (in this case to centre the title) another version
   of the constructor is required.
   This takes a border style (we chose black line),
   the title (we chose "Tenants"),
   the justification (we chose Centre)
   and the title position (we chose Top) */


displayArea1.setBorder (new TitledBorder(new LineBorder(Color.black),
    "Tenants",TitledBorder.CENTER,TitledBorder.TOP));


// A JScrollPane created for displayArea1 (see discussion below)
JScrollPane p1 = new JScrollPane(displayArea1);
add(p1);


// the remaining components are added in a similar way
add(roomField2);
roomField2.setBorder(new TitledBorder("Room"));
add(monthField);
monthField.setBorder(new TitledBorder("Month"));
add(amountField);
amountField.setBorder(new TitledBorder("Amount"));
add(paymentButton);
paymentButton.setBackground(Color.green);
paymentButton.setBorder(raisedBevel);
add(listButton);
listButton.setBorder(raisedBevel);
listButton.setBackground(Color.green);
displayArea2.setBorder (new TitledBorder(new LineBorder(Color.black),
"Payments",TitledBorder.CENTER,TitledBorder.TOP));
// see discussion below about ScrollPanes
JScrollPane p2 = new JScrollPane(displayArea2);
add(p2);
// listeners given to buttons
addButton.addActionListener(this);
```

```
      displayButton.addActionListener(this);
      paymentButton.addActionListener(this);
      listButton.addActionListener(this);
      removeButton.addActionListener(this);
      listButton.addActionListener(this);
      saveAndQuitButton.addActionListener(this);
      quitButton.addActionListener(this);
      // read records from file into the list
      TenantFileHandler.readRecords(list);
      // make GUI visible
      setVisible(true);
   }


   // the event handlers
   public void actionPerformed(ActionEvent e)
   {
     if(e.getSource() == addButton)
     {
       String roomEntered = roomField.getText();
       String nameEntered = nameField.getText();
       // check for errors
       if(roomEntered.length() == 0 || nameEntered.length()== 0)
       {
         displayArea1.setText ("Room number and name must be entered");
       }
       else if(Integer.parseInt(roomEntered)< 1 || Integer.parseInt(roomEntered)>noOfRooms)
       {
         displayArea1.setText ("There are only " + noOfRooms + " rooms");
       }
       else if(list.search(Integer.parseInt(roomEntered)) != null)
       {
         displayArea1.setText("Room number " + Integer.parseInt(roomEntered) + " is occupied");
       }
       else  // ok to add a Tenant
       {
         Tenant t = new Tenant(nameEntered,Integer.parseInt(roomEntered));
         list.add(t);
         roomField.setText("");
         nameField.setText("");
         displayArea1.setText("New tenant in room " + roomEntered + " successfully added");
       }
     }
```

```
if(e.getSource() == displayButton)
{
  int i;
  if(list.isEmpty()) // no rooms to display
  {
    displayArea1.setText("All rooms are empty");
  }
  else // display rooms
  {
    displayArea1.setText("Room" +  "\t" +  "Name" +"\n");
    for(i = 1; i <=  list.getTotal(); i++ )
    {
      displayArea1.append(list.getTenant(i).getRoom()
      + "\t"
      + list.getTenant(i).getName() + "\n");
    }
  }
}


if(e.getSource()== removeButton)
{
  String roomEntered = roomField.getText();
  // check for errors
  if(roomEntered.length()== 0)
  {
    displayArea1.setText("Room number must be entered");
  }
  else if(Integer.parseInt(roomEntered) < 1 || Integer.parseInt(roomEntered)>noOfRooms)
  {
    displayArea1.setText("Invalid room number");
  }
  else if(list.search(Integer.parseInt(roomEntered))== null)
  {
    displayArea1.setText("Room number " +  roomEntered +  " is empty");
  }
  else // ok to remove Tenant
  {
    list.removeTenant(Integer.parseInt(roomEntered));
    displayArea1.setText("Tenant removed from room " +  Integer.parseInt(roomEntered));
  }
}

if(e.getSource() == paymentButton)
```

```
   {
      String roomEntered = roomField2.getText();
      String monthEntered = monthField.getText();
      String amountEntered = amountField.getText();
      // check for errors
      if(roomEntered.length()== 0 || monthEntered.length()== 0 || amountEntered.length()== 0)
      {
        displayArea2.setText("Room number, month and amount must all be entered");
      }
      else if(Integer.parseInt(roomEntered) < 1 || Integer.parseInt(roomEntered)>noOfRooms)
      {
        displayArea2.setText("Invalid room number");
      }
      else if(list.search(Integer.parseInt(roomEntered)) == null)
      {
        displayArea2.setText("Room number " +  roomEntered +  " is empty");
      }
      else // ok to process payment
      {
        Payment p = new Payment(monthEntered,Double.valueOf(amountEntered).doubleValue());
        list.search(Integer.parseInt(roomEntered)).makePayment(p);
        displayArea2.setText("Payment recorded");
      }
   }
if(e.getSource() == listButton)
   {
      int i;
      String roomEntered = roomField2.getText();
      // check for errors
      if(roomEntered.length()== 0)
      {
        displayArea2.setText("Room number must be entered");
      }
      else if(Integer.parseInt(roomEntered) < 1 || Integer.parseInt(roomEntered) > noOfRooms)
      {
        displayArea2.setText("Invalid room number");
      }
      else if(list.search(Integer.parseInt(roomEntered)) == null)
      {
        displayArea2.setText("Room number " + Integer.parseInt(roomEntered) + " is empty");
      }
```

```
  else // ok to list payments
  {
    Tenant t = list.search(Integer.parseInt(roomEntered));
    PaymentList p  = t.getPayments();
    if(t.getPayments().getTotal() == 0)
    {
      displayArea2.setText("No payments made for this tenant");
    }
    else
    {
      /* The NumberFormat class is similar to the DecimalFormat class that we used previously.
         The getCurrencyInstance method of this class reads the system values to
         find out which country we are in, then uses the correct currency symbol */
      NumberFormat nf = NumberFormat.getCurrencyInstance();
      String s;
      displayArea2.setText("Month" +  "\t\t" +  "Amount" +  "\n");
      for(i =  1; i <=  p.getTotal(); i++  )
      {
        s =  nf.format(p.getPayment(i).getAmount());
        displayArea2.append("" +
        p.getPayment(i).getMonth() +  "\t\t" + s + "\n");
      }
      displayArea2.append("\n" + "Total paid so far :   " + nf.format(p.calculateTotalPaid()));
      monthField.setText("");
      amountField.setText("");
    }
  }
}


if(e.getSource()== saveAndQuitButton)
{
  TenantFileHandler.saveRecords(noOfRooms,list);
  System.exit(0);
}
if(e.getSource()== quitButton)
{
  System.exit(0);
}
}
}
```

Before we complete our examination of the Hostel application we just draw your attention to a few new features. First, as discussed in section 12.3, we have given titled borders to some of our components by calling a component's setBorder method. For example, to give the roomField component a titled border we used the following:

```
roomField.setBorder(new TitledBorder("Room"));
```

You can see that the parameter to this method is a TitledBorder object, and the constructor for this object receives the title to be set (in this case "Room"). The default position of the title is the top left-hand corner of the component. For different positions, other forms of the TitledBorder constructor can be used (look at the code for an example of a centre-justified title). The TitledBorder class resides in a package. To make use of this class we need to include the following **import** statement at the top of the program:

```
import javax.swing.border.*;
```

We will look at border styles in more detail in chapter 17.

As well as titled borders we have also made use of **Scroll Panes** in this GUI. A scroll pane allows *scroll bars* to be added to visual components such as text areas. This is useful if the component sometimes needs to display more information than is possible in its visible area. In the case of our Hostel GUI, we have two text areas: displayArea1 and displayArea2. The former is used to display the details of all tenants while the latter is used to display the details of all payments. When the number of tenants or payments becomes large, a standard text area of a fixed size may not be sufficient to display all this information. So we have added scroll bars to these text areas by attaching scroll panes to them. We do this by simply calling the JScrollPane constructor as follows:

```
// creates a scroll pane from displayArea1
JScrollPane p1 = new JScrollPane(displayArea1);
```

It is then the scroll pane (p1) that is added to the frame, not the text area (displayArea1):

```
// add scroll pane to frame not the original text area
add(p1);
```

We will come across scroll panes again in the second semester.

Finally, one last new feature we made use of is the NumberFormat class. This class is similar to DecimalFormat that you met in chapter 10, except that it is designed specifically to convert decimal numbers and convert them into local currency formats. The getCurrencyInstance picks up the correct location by interrogating the system and it then returns an appropriate format object:

```
// generate a NumberFormat object
NumberFormat nf = NumberFormat.getCurrencyInstance();
```

This object's `format` method can then be used to take decimal numbers and format them as local currency values. So the following expression:

```
nf.format(p.calculateTotalPaid())
```

would take a decimal number and, as we are in the United Kingdom, would format the number to two decimal places with a pound sterling symbol (£).

The code needed to run the `Hostel` class now appears below as program 12.1. This program creates a hostel with five rooms; in the end of chapter exercises you will be given the opportunity to adapt this program so that the number of rooms can be entered by the user.

PROGRAM 12.1

```
public class RunHostel
{
  public static void main(String[] args)
  {
    // assume only 5 rooms available
    new Hostel(5);
  }
}
```

Before concluding this case study we shall consider how to test the application to ensure that it conforms to the original specification.

12.6 Testing the system

If you look back at the `Hostel` class you can see that much of the event-handling code is related to the validation of data entered from the graphical interface. Much of the testing for such a system will, therefore, be geared around ensuring that such validation is effective.

Amongst the types of validation we need to test is the display of suitable error messages when input text fields are left blank, or when inappropriate data has been entered into these text fields. Of course, as well as input validation, we also need to test the basic functionality of the system.

Figure 12.4 is one possible test log that may be developed for the purpose of testing the `Hostel` class.

TEST LOG			
Purpose: To test the Hostel class			
Run Number:	Date:		
Action	Expected Output	Pass/ Fail	Reason for failure
Display tenants	"Empty list" message		
Add tenant: Patel, Room Number blank	"Blank field" message		
Add tenant: blank, Room Number 1	"Blank field" message		
Add tenant: Patel, Room Number 1	Confirmation message		
Add tenant: Jones, Room Number 6	Error message: There are only 5 rooms		
Add tenant: Jones, Room Number 1	Error Message: Room 1 is occupied		
Add tenant: Jones, Room Number 2	Confirmation Message		
Display tenants	ROOM NAME		
	1 Patel		
	2 Jones		
List payments, Room Number 1	"Empty list" message		
Make payment: Room blank, Month			
January, Amount 100	"Blank field" message		
Make Payment: Room 1, Month			
blank, Amount 100	"Blank field" message		
Make payment: Room 1, Month			
January, Amount blank	"Blank field" message		
Make payment: Room 1, Month			
January, Amount 100	Confirmation message		
Make payment: Room 1, Month			
February, Amount 200	Confirmation message		
List payments: Room Number blank	"Blank field" message		
List payments, Room Number 1	MONTH AMOUNT		
	January £100		
	February £200		
	Total paid so far £300		
List payments: Room Number 2	"Empty list" message		
List payments: Room Number 5	"Room Empty" message		
Remove tenant: Room Number blank	"Blank field" message		
Remove tenant: Room Number 1	Confirmation Message		
Display tenants	2 Jones		
List payments: Room Number 1	"Room Empty" message		

FIGURE 12.4 A test log to ensure the reliability of the *Hostel* class

We include a few sample screen shots produced from running program 12.1 against this test log in figures 12.5–12.8. We will leave the complete task of running program 12.1 against the test log as a programming exercise at the end of this chapter.

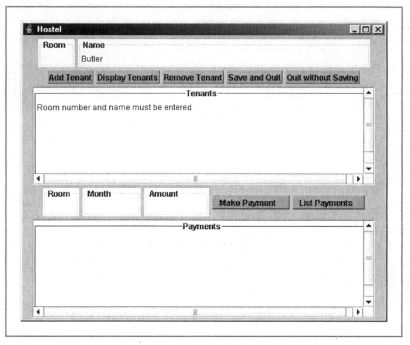

FIGURE 12.5 Error messages are produced in *displayArea1*. In this case an attempt is made to add a tenant without filling in the *roomField*

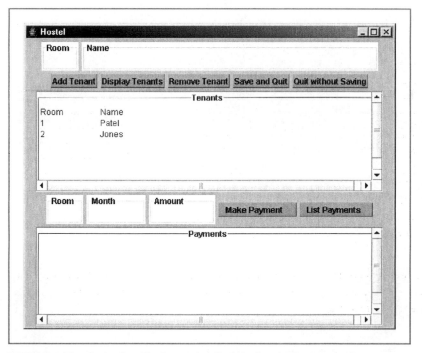

FIGURE 12.6 The *displayArea1* is also used to display a list of tenants entered

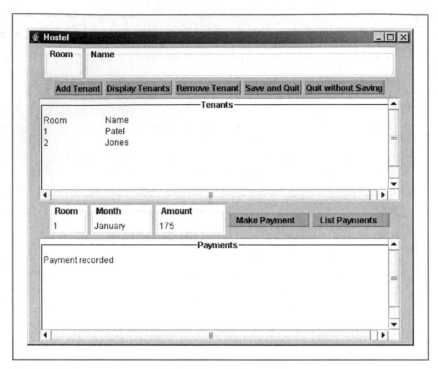

FIGURE 12.7 A payment is recorded for the tenant in room 1

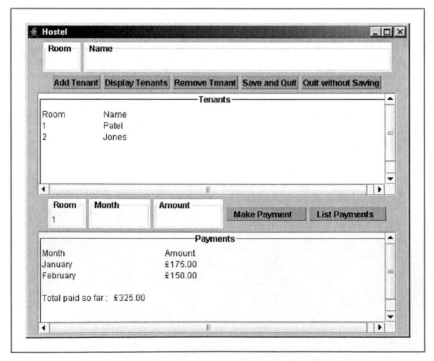

FIGURE 12.8 Details of the payments for room 1 are displayed in *displayArea2* when the *listButton* is pressed

12.7 What next?

Congratulations – you have now completed your first semester of programming; we hope you have enjoyed it. Many of you will be going on to at least one more semester of software development and programming – so what lies ahead?

Well, you have probably realized that there are still a few gaps in your knowledge and that some of the stuff that you have learnt can be developed further to give you the power to write multi-functional programs. Think, for example, about the case study we developed in this chapter; you will need to learn how to write the code that stores the information permanently on a disk; also, the user interface could be made to look a bit more attractive; and it would be helpful if our collection classes didn't make us decide in advance how many records we were allowed to have, so something a bit better than simple arrays would be useful.

And there is lots more; the standard Java packages provide classes for many different purposes; there is more to learn about interfaces; about dealing with errors and exceptions; about network programming; about programming for mobile devices; and about how to write programs that can perform a number of tasks at the same time.

Does all this sound exciting? We think so – and we hope that you enjoy your next semester as much as we have enjoyed helping you through this one.

Self-test questions

1 Explain how *titled borders* and *scroll panes* were used in the GUI for this application.

2 Use pseudocode to design the event handling routine for a `search` button. Clicking on the button should display the name of the tenant in the room entered in the `roomField` text box. The name is to be displayed in `displayArea1`. If no tenant is present in the given room, an error message should be displayed in `displayArea1`.

3 Modify the screen design in figure 12.1 to include the `search` button discussed in the question above.

4 How else might you improve the application developed in this case study?

Programming exercises

You will need to copy the entire suite of classes that make up the student hostel system from the accompanying CD.

1 Run program 12.1 against the test log given in figure 12.3.

2 Rewrite program 12.1 so that instead of fixing the number of rooms to 5, the user is asked how many rooms the hostel is to have.

3 Modify the `Hostel` class by adding the `search` button you considered in self-test questions 2 and 3 above.

4 Make any additions to the `Hostel` class that you considered in self-test question 4 above. For example, you might want to include additional validation to ensure that negative money values are never accepted for payments.

Semester Two

Interfaces and adapters

13

13.1 Introduction

Welcome back to the second semester of our programming course. We spent the first semester laying the foundations you would need to develop programs in Java. During that time you came a long way. You learnt about the idea of variables, control structures, methods and arrays, and then went on to develop your own classes and extend these classes using inheritance. Finally you developed applications consisting of many classes working closely together and interacting with users via attractive graphical interfaces. Along the way you also learnt about the UML notation and testing strategies. At the beginning of that semester you probably didn't expect to come as far as you have. Well, the second semester might look equally challenging but, with some help from us along the way, you can look forward to new and more advanced challenges.

In the first semester, until we developed our case study, the applications we created were fairly simple, consisting for the most part of only one or two classes. In reality, applications that are developed for commercial and industrial use comprise a large number of classes, and are developed not by one person, but by a team. Members of the team will develop different modules, which can later be integrated to form a single application. When groups of programmers work together in this way, they often have to agree upon how they will develop their own individual classes in order for them to be successfully integrated later. In this chapter we will see how these agreements can be formalized in Java programs by making use of a special kind of class called an **interface**. To demonstrate this we will begin by considering once again the testing process that we discussed in chapter 11.

13.2 An example

It is a very common occurrence that the attributes of a class should be allowed to take only a particular set of values. Think, for example, of the BankAccount class that we developed in the last semester. It is likely that the account number should be restricted to numbers that contain, say, precisely eight digits. Similarly, a Customer class might require that the customer number comprises a letter followed by four digits. In some cases there are constraints that exist not because we choose to impose them, but because they occur "naturally" – in the Rectangle class, for example, it would make no sense if an object of this class were to have a length or height of zero or less.

In such cases, every effort must be made when developing the class to prevent invalid values being assigned to the attributes. Constructors and other methods should be designed so that they flag up errors if such an attempt is made – and one of the advantages of object-oriented programming languages is precisely that they allow us to restrict access to the attributes in this way.

The above remarks notwithstanding, it is the case that in industrial-sized projects, classes will be very complex and will contain a great many methods. It is therefore possible that a developer will overlook a constraint at some point, and allow objects to be created that break the rules. It might therefore be useful if, for testing purposes, every object could contain a method, which we might call check, that could be used to check the integrity of the object.

In a particular project, people could be writing test routines independently of the people developing the modules, and these routines will be calling the check method. We need, therefore, to be able to *guarantee* that every object contains such a check method.

You learnt in chapter 9 that the way to guarantee that a class has a particular method is for that class to inherit from a class containing an **abstract** method – when a class contains an **abstract** method, then any subclass of that class is *forced* to override that method – if it does not do so, a compiler error occurs.

In our example, we need to ensure that our classes all have a check method that tests an object's integrity, so one way to do this would be to write a class as follows:

THE *CHECKABLE* CLASS

```
public abstract class Checkable
{
  public abstract boolean check();
}
```

Now all our classes could extend Checkable, and would compile successfully only if they each had their own check method.

While this would work, it does present us with a bit of a problem. What would happen, for example, if our Rectangle class were going to be part of a graphical application and needed to extend another class such as JFrame? This would be problematic, because, in Java, a class is not allowed to inherit from more than one superclass. Inheriting from more than one class is known as **multiple inheritance** and is illustrated in figure 13.1.

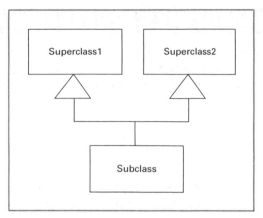

FIGURE 13.1 Multiple inheritance – not allowed
in Java

One reason that multiple inheritance is disallowed is that it can easily lead to ambiguity, and hence to programming errors. Imagine for example that the two superclasses shown in figure 13.1 both contained a method of the same name – which version of the method would be inherited by the subclass?

Luckily, there is a way around this, because Java allows a kind of *lightweight inheritance*, made possible by a construct to which you were introduced in chapter 10 – the **interface**.

13.3 Interfaces

As you learnt in chapter 10, an interface is a class in which *all* the methods are **abstract**. As you will recall, when we want a class to inherit the methods of an interface we use the word **implements**, rather than **extends**. Just as with inheritance, once a class implements an interface it has the same type as that interface, as well as being of the type of its own class. So, for example, if a class implements `ActionListener`, then any object of that class is a *kind of* `ActionListener` – in other words, it is of type `ActionListener`, as well as being of the type of its own class.

So far, `ActionListener` is the only interface you have come across. The Java Foundation Classes, particularly those associated with graphical applications, contain a great many more. Later in this chapter you will come across two of these – `MouseListener` and `MouseMotionListener`. Of course, it is perfectly possible for us to write our own interfaces, as we will do in a moment when we turn our `Checkable` class into an interface.

Figure 13.2 shows the UML notation for the implementation of interfaces – you can see that interfaces are marked with the <<interface>> tag, and that a circle is used to indicate a class implementing an interface.

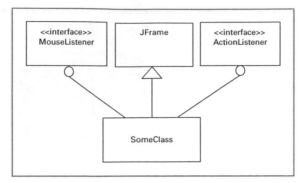

FIGURE 13.2 A class can inherit from only one superclass,
but can implement many interfaces

As can be seen in figure 13.2, while it is possible to *inherit* from only one class, it is perfectly possible to implement any number of interfaces. In this case SomeClass **extends** JFrame and **implements** MouseListener and ActionListener – because the methods are not actually coded in the interface, the problems with multiple inheritance that we described earlier do not arise.

A class is *obliged* to override all the methods of the interfaces that it implements. By implementing an interface we are *guaranteeing* that the subclass will have certain methods. In the case of the ActionListener interface, you are aware that this contains a single method, actionPerformed – so in figure 13.2, SomeClass is guaranteed to have an actionPerformed method. It is also guaranteed to have all the methods declared in MouseListener, an interface that you will meet in the next section.

So, in cases where we need a class such as Checkable in which all the methods are **abstract** we don't create a class – instead we create an interface.

Let's turn our Checkable class into an interface! The code looks like this:

THE *CHECKABLE* INTERFACE

```
public interface Checkable
{
  public boolean check();
}
```

Notice the word **interface** instead of **class** – and notice also that we don't have to declare our method as **abstract**, because by definition all methods of an **interface** are **abstract**.

Let's make the Rectangle class from chapter 8 checkable by implementing this interface – all we need to do is change the header, and code the check method. The class will now look like this:

THE *RECTANGLE* CLASS IMPLEMENTING THE *CHECKABLE* INTERFACE

```
public class Rectangle implements Checkable
{
  private double length;
  private double height;
```

```
public Rectangle(double lengthIn, double heightIn)
{
  length = lengthIn;
  height = heightIn;
}

public double getLength()
{
  return length;
}

public double getHeight()
{
  return height;
}

public void setLength(double lengthIn)
{
  length = lengthIn;
}

public void setHeight(double heightIn)
{
  height = heightIn;
}

public double calculateArea()
{
  return length * height;
}

public double calculatePerimeter()
{
  return 2 * (length + height);
}

public boolean check() /* we must implement this method as it is declared in the
                          Checkable interface */
{
  return length > 0 && height > 0;
}
}
```

You can see that the class now implements our `Checkable` interface:

```
public class Rectangle implements Checkable
```

The `check` method, which the class is forced to override, returns a value of **true** if the attributes are both greater than zero, and **false** otherwise:

```
public boolean check() // the check method of Checkable must be overridden
{
  return length > 0 && height > 0;
}
```

Other classes can implement the `Checkable` interface in a similar way. For example, a partial implementation of the `Customer` class that we talked about in section 13.2 might look like this:

THE *CUSTOMER* CLASS IMPLEMENTING THE *CHECKABLE* INTERFACE

```
public class Customer implements Checkable
{
  private String number;

  // other attributes

  public Customer(String numberIn)
  {
    number = numberIn;
  }
  public String getNumber()
  {
    return number;
  }

  public boolean check()
  {
    if(number.length() != 5)
    {
      return false;
    }
    else if(!Character.isLetter(number.charAt(0)))
    {
      return false;
    }
    else
```

```
   {
     for(int i = 1; i <= 4; i++)
     {
       if(!Character.isDigit(number.charAt(i)))
       {
         return false;
       }
     }
   }
   return true;
 }


 // other methods
}
```

You can see here how, in the check method, we check firstly that the string contains exactly five characters, and then check if the first character is a letter by making use of the isLetter method of the Character class. Finally we check that each of the remaining characters is a digit by using the isDigit method of the Character class.

In program 13.1 below we create four objects – two Rectangle objects and two Customer objects. In each case the first object breaks the rules that we have set for these two classes, whereas the second does not – the first Rectangle object is given a height of zero, while the first Customer object has a customer number containing only three characters.

PROGRAM 13.1

```
public class Checker
{
 public static void main(String[] args)
 {
   // create two rectangles
   Rectangle rectangle1 = new Rectangle(0, 8); // invalid: first attribute is zero
   Rectangle rectangle2 = new Rectangle(10, 8); // valid

   // create two customers
   Customer customer1 = new Customer("A37"); // invalid: number must be 1 letter and 4 digits
   Customer customer2 = new Customer("S1234"); // valid

   // send objects to the check method
   checkObject(rectangle1);
   checkObject(rectangle2);
   checkObject(customer1);
```

```
    checkObject(customer2);
  }

  static void checkObject(Checkable objectIn) // note that the type of the parameter is Checkable
  {
    if(objectIn.check()) // call the check method
    {
      System.out.println("Valid object");
    }
    else
    {
      System.out.println("Invalid object");
    }
  }
}
```

As you can see, we send the four objects in turn into a method called checkObject, which calls the object's check method.

The checkObject method accepts a parameter of type Checkable – and of course both the Rectangle objects and the Customer objects are of type Checkable because they implement the Checkable interface.

As expected, the output from the program is as follows:

```
Invalid object
Valid object
Invalid object
Valid object
```

Implementing an interface is rather like making a contract with the user of a class – it *guarantees* that the class will have a particular method or methods. In the above case, a developer will know that any object that implements Checkable will have a check method. This enables the developer to write methods such as checkObject that expect to receive an object of type Checkable, in the certain knowledge that the object – whether it is a Rectangle, Customer or any other class that implements this interface – will have a method called check.

13.4 Some more interfaces

We are now going to develop a program that makes use of two more interfaces that are provided with the AWT. It is a program with which you can amuse your friends. Figure 13.3 shows how it looks when it runs. We have called it – rather unimaginatively – the RedCircle game; a red circle always moves away from the cursor so you can never click on it, despite being told to do so! And if in desperation you start to click the mouse, the words "Keep Trying" flash onto the screen!

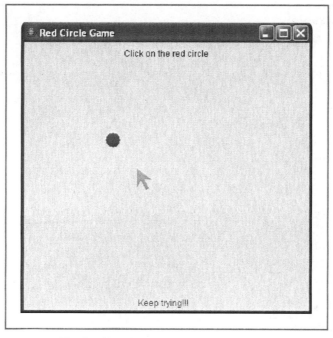

FIGURE 13.3 The *RedCircle* Application

As well as being a bit of fun it also introduces something new, namely the way to program a response to different mouse events like moving and dragging as well as just clicking. This will involve using two new interface classes instead of the single `ActionListener` interface that we have used before.

Here is the code for the class:

THE *REDCIRCLE* CLASS

```java
import java.awt.*;
import javax.swing.*;
import java.awt.event.*;


public class RedCircle extends JFrame implements MouseMotionListener, MouseListener
{
    private int xPos;
    private int yPos;
    private int width;
    private int height;
    private boolean mouseDown;

  // the constructor
  public RedCircle(int widthIn, int heightIn)
  {
    setTitle("Red Circle Game");
```

```
      addMouseMotionListener(this);

      addMouseListener(this);

      width = widthIn;

      height = heightIn;

      getContentPane().setBackground(Color.yellow);

      xPos = width/2 -20;

      yPos = height/2 - 20;

      setSize(width, height);

      setDefaultCloseOperation(JFrame.EXIT_ON_CLOSE);

      setLocation(300,300);

      setVisible(true);

   }


   // the paint method
   public void paint(Graphics g)
   {
     super.paint(g);
     g.drawString("Click on the red circle", width/2 - 60, 50);
     g.setColor(Color.red);
     g.fillOval(xPos,yPos,20,20);

     if(mouseDown)
     {
       g.drawString("Keep trying!!!", width/2 - 40, height - 10);
     }
   }


   /* The next two methods define what happens when the mouse is moved or dragged. They are
      part of the MouseMotionListener interface. The red circle always stays 50 pixels above
      and 50 pixels to the left of the cursor */

   public void mouseMoved(MouseEvent e)
   {
     xPos = e.getX() - 50;
     yPos = e.getY() - 50;
     repaint();
   }
   public void mouseDragged(MouseEvent e)
   {
     xPos = e.getX() - 50;
     yPos = e.getY() - 50;
     repaint();
```

```
    }

    /* The next two methods define what happens when the mouse button is pressed or released.
       They are part of the MouseListener interface */

    public void mousePressed(MouseEvent e)
    {
      mouseDown = true;
      repaint();
    }
    public void mouseReleased(MouseEvent e)
    {
      mouseDown = false;
      repaint();

    }

    /* The MouseListener interface also insists that we implement the next three methods.
       We are not actually going to use them here, so we have just left them blank */

    public void mouseClicked(MouseEvent e)
    {
    }

    public void mouseEntered(MouseEvent e)
    {
    }

    public void mouseExited(MouseEvent e)
    {
    }
}
```

The class itself is an extension of JFrame. You can see that here we are implementing *two* interfaces, MouseListener and MouseMotionListener; notice that the syntax is to separate them by a comma. As we have said previously, while we are not allowed to *extend* more than one class, it is perfectly possible to *implement* as many interfaces as we wish.

```
public class RedCircle extends JFrame implements MouseMotionListener, MouseListener
```

Both of these interfaces will, of course, have abstract methods which we then have to implement. The first one, MouseMotionListener, has two such methods which are described in table 13.1.

`mouseMoved`	Specifies the behaviour that occurs when the mouse is moved when no button is depressed.
`mouseDragged`	Specifies the behaviour that occurs when the mouse is moved with the left-hand button depressed.

TABLE 13.1 The methods of *MouseMotionListener*

The second interface, `MouseListener`, has five methods which are described in table 13.2.

`mousePressed`	Specifies the behaviour that occurs when the left-hand button is pressed.
`mouseReleased`	Specifies the behaviour that occurs when the left-hand button is released.
`mouseClicked`	Specifies the behaviour that occurs when the left-hand button is clicked on a component.
`mouseEntered`	Specifies the behaviour that occurs when the cursor enters a component.
`mouseExited`	Specifies the behaviour that occurs when the cursor leaves a component.

TABLE 13.2 The methods of *MouseListener*

The last three of the methods in table 13.2 are not used in this application so we have just left them blank – however, we have, of course, had to override them because they appear in the interface.

The declaration of the attributes is shown below; the first two integer attributes xPos and yPos will be used to keep track of the position of the red circle. The next two attributes, `width` and `height`, will be used to hold the width and the height of the frame that the program runs in. We have allowed this to be determined at run-time, by allowing the constructor to accept these values from the program that creates the RedCircle object. The other attribute, mouseDown, is a **boolean** variable and will be set to **true** while the left-hand button of the mouse is depressed, and **false** once it is released. The default value for a **boolean** attribute is **false**, which is in fact what we require to start off with:

```
private int xPos;
private int yPos;
private int width;
private int height;
private boolean mouseDown;
```

Next we have the constructor:

```
public RedCircle(int widthIn, int heightIn)
{
  setTitle("Red Circle Game");
  addMouseMotionListener(this);
```

```
    addMouseListener(this);
    width = widthIn;
    height = heightIn;
    getContentPane().setBackground(Color.yellow);
    xPos = width/2 -20;
    yPos = height/2 - 20;
    setSize(width, height);
    setDefaultCloseOperation(JFrame.EXIT_ON_CLOSE);
    setLocation(300,300);
    setVisible(true);
}
```

The first thing the constructor does, after setting the title, is to add the two listeners to the frame itself; remember that writing the method names without attaching them to an object is actually attaching them to **this** object, and is short for:

```
this.addMouseMotionListener(this);
this.addMouseListener(this);
```

The next thing it does is to assign the values received to width and height respectively and set the background colour.

The next thing we do is to get the circle to appear in the centre of the window when the frame first becomes visible. So we halve the width and height of the frame to find the central point of the window; to get the centre of the circle dead in the middle we subtract 20 (the radius of the circle) from the width and the height – remind yourself of the drawOval method in chapter 10 to understand why we have done this. The values calculated in this way are assigned to xPos and yPos.

As soon as the frame becomes visible, the paint method is called, and this is the one that we have coded next:

```
public void paint(Graphics g)
{
  super.paint(g);
  g.drawString("Click on the red circle", width/2 - 60, 50);
  g.setColor(Color.red);
  g.fillOval(xPos,yPos,20,20);
  if(mouseDown)
  {
    g.drawString("Keep trying!!!", width/2 - 40, height - 10);
  }
}
```

You will see soon that the paint method is called every time the mouse is moved. The first thing that is done (after calling the paint method of the superclass) is to draw the initial string that tells the user to click on the circle. Then we set the colour to red, and then draw the circle, this time using fillOval instead of drawOval to get a solid circle. The circle is drawn at position (xPos, yPos). Remember, this method gets called every time the program encounters a repaint command, and as we shall see in a moment this happens every time the mouse moves; and each time the screen gets repainted, xPos and yPos will have changed.

After the circle is drawn, the status of the mouse-button is tested by checking the value of mouseDown; as we said earlier, this attribute is going to be set to **true** if the left mouse-button is down, and **false** if not. If it is **true** the words "Keep Trying!!!" are drawn on the screen. We have tried to organize things so that this is drawn centred near the bottom of the window; you can see that we have used the dimensions of the frame to do this – we have set the x-coordinate to be half the frame width minus 40. The value of 40 is what we have estimated to be half the number of pixels taken up by the phrase "Keep Trying!!!". There are actually more accurate ways of doing this using font metrics, but we want to keep things simple at the moment, so we just had a go to see what it looked like, then tried again till we got it right! Similarly we have set the y-coordinate to be 10 pixels higher than the bottom of the window, and, as you will see when you run the program, this looks pretty good.

Now we come to the event-handling routines. This time, as we have mentioned, we are not using the ActionListener interface but are using two new interfaces, MouseMotionListener and MouseListener. The first method we implement, mouseMoved, is one of the two abstract methods of MouseMotionListener:

```java
public void mouseMoved(MouseEvent e)
{
  xPos = e.getX() - 50;
  yPos = e.getY() - 50;
  repaint();
}
```

This method is continually invoked while the mouse is moving; each time it is invoked xPos and yPos are assigned new values. The value assigned to each of them is always the value of the current coordinate of the cursor minus 50. After every assignment the window is repainted; thus, as the cursor moves, the circle moves too – always staying just north-west of it. Notice that the method is automatically sent an object of the MouseEvent class and that we use the getX and getY methods of this class to obtain the current coordinates of the cursor.

The other method of the MouseMotionListener interface, mouseDragged, determines what happens when the mouse is moved with the button held down (dragged). We have coded it in exactly the same way, so that dragging the mouse has the same effect as above.

The next two methods are declared in the MouseListener interface and determine what happens when the mouse-button is pressed and released. You can see that we have defined them so that when the button is pressed, the mouseDown attribute is set to **true** and the window is repainted; when the button is released it is set to **false**, and the window is repainted once again.

```
public void mousePressed(MouseEvent e)
{
  mouseDown = true;
  repaint();
}

public void mouseReleased(MouseEvent e)
{
  mouseDown = false;
  repaint();
}
```

As we have said, the MouseListener interface also insists that we implement the mouseClicked, mouseEntered and mouseExited methods. We are not actually going to use these here, so as you can see from the code we have just left them blank – for example:

```
public void mouseEntered(MouseEvent e)
{
}
```

Program 13.2 runs the class in a 400 × 400 frame.

PROGRAM 13.2

```
public class RunRedCircle
{
  public static void main(String[] args)
  {
    new RedCircle(400, 400);
  }
}
```

13.5 Adapters and inner classes

As you can see from the above example, using an interface means that we have to code *all* the interface methods, even those we are not interested in – for example in the RedCircle class we have had to code the methods mouseClicked, mouseEntered and mouseExited of the MouseListener interface, which are not relevant to our particular application.

There is a way around this, which is to use an **adapter**. An adapter is a special class that acts as an intermediary between our class and the interface, making it unnecessary to code all the methods, because the class can be extended in the normal way using inheritance. An adapter is created by writing a class that implements all the methods of the interface, leaving them blank if they are of type **void**, otherwise returning a dummy value. They can then be overridden by any subclass.

In the case of the Checkable interface from section 13.3, an adapter for this class would look like this:

THE *CHECKABLEADAPTER* CLASS

```
public class CheckableAdapter implements Checkable
{
  public boolean check()
  {
    return false;
  }
}
```

Our Rectangle class would than have the following header:

```
public class Rectangle extends CheckableAdapter
```

In this case this wouldn't have benefited us very much, because there are no additional methods that have to be coded and left blank. However, with an interface such as MouseListener this could be useful. An adapter is provided for every interface that comes with the standard Java packages. For example, the adapter equivalent for MouseListener is called MouseAdapter. Although we don't have access to the source code for this class, we could guess that it looks like this:

```
public class MouseAdapter implements MouseListener
{
  public void mousePressed(MouseEvent e)
  {
  }

  public void mouseReleased(MouseEvent e)
  {
  }

  public void mouseClicked(MouseEvent e)
  {
  }
```

```java
  public void mouseEntered(MouseEvent e)
  {
  }

  public void mouseExited(MouseEvent e)
  {
  }
}
```

Now, you might be wondering why we do not use adapters all the time. The reason is that very often the class that we want to extend is already extending another class. As we have mentioned before, in Java a class is allowed to inherit from one superclass only – multiple inheritance is not allowed. In the case of the RedCircle class, this class already extends JFrame; it cannot therefore also extend MouseAdapter.

There is a way, however, that we could use this adapter in the RedCircle class. Consider the following line in the constructor, which adds the MouseListener to the JFrame:

```java
addMouseListener(this);
```

As you know, the parameter indicates the class where the program can find the instructions for processing the event (in this case a MouseEvent). In the RedCircle class this code will be found in the class itself, hence the use of the keyword **this**. Another option would be to write a class, called, for example, RedCircleAdapter, for this express purpose; this class would extend MouseAdapter and would code the mousePressed and mouseReleased methods. The above line would then have to be changed to:

```java
addMouseListener(new RedCircleAdapter());
```

Of course, it might occur to you that the RedCircleAdapter class is not something that is ever going to be used for any other program, and it seems rather odd to write a separate class for such a narrow purpose. In cases like this, we can write what we call an **inner class** – which, as its name suggests, is a class written within another class. The way we have done this with the RedCircle class is shown below.

THE *REDCIRCLEWITHADAPTER* CLASS

```java
import java.awt.*;
import javax.swing.*;
import java.awt.event.*;
public class RedCircleWithAdapter extends JFrame implements MouseMotionListener
{
  private int xPos;
  private int yPos;
  private int width;
```

```java
private int height;
private boolean mouseDown;

// inner class
class RedCircleAdapter extends MouseAdapter
{
  public void mousePressed(MouseEvent e)
  {
    mouseDown = true;
    repaint();
  }
  public void mouseReleased(MouseEvent e)
  {
    mouseDown = false;
    repaint();
  }
}
// the constructor
public RedCircleWithAdapter(int widthIn, int heightIn)
{
  setTitle("Red Circle Game");
  addMouseMotionListener(this);
  addMouseListener(new RedCircleAdapter()); // create an object of the inner class
  width = widthIn;
  height = heightIn;
  getContentPane().setBackground(Color.yellow);
  xPos = widthIn/2 -20;
  yPos = heightIn/2 - 20;
  setSize(width, height);
  setDefaultCloseOperation(JFrame.EXIT_ON_CLOSE);
  setLocation(300,300);
  setVisible(true);
}
// the paint method
public void paint(Graphics g)
{
  super.paint(g);
  g.drawString("Click on the red circle", width/2 - 60, 50);
  g.setColor(Color.red);
  g.fillOval(xPos,yPos,20,20);
  if(mouseDown)
```

```
    {
      g.drawString("Keep trying!!!", width/2 - 40, height - 10);
    }
  }


  public void mouseMoved(MouseEvent e)
  {
   xPos = e.getX() - 50;
   yPos = e.getY() - 50;
   repaint();
  }


  public void mouseDragged(MouseEvent e)
    {
      xPos = e.getX() - 50;
      yPos = e.getY() - 50;
      repaint();
    }
}
```

The inner class, `RedCircleAdapter`, has been emboldened for clarity. Notice how it is possible to refer to attributes of the outer class (in this case `mouseDown`) in the inner class.

13.6 Polymorphism and polymorphic types

In this chapter we have seen how an object can have a number of different types. As well as being the type of its own class, it is also the type of any superclasses in the class hierarchy, and the type of any interfaces that it implements. You will recall that we have used the term *polymorphism* to refer to the phenomenon whereby methods and operators can have the same name, but exhibit different behaviour. A language like Java that allows objects to be of more than one type is said to support **polymorphic types.**

In general, polymorphism is an important feature of object-oriented languages, and it is worth our while spending a little more time summarizing the different ways in which polymorphism can be achieved.

13.6.1 Operator overloading

We have seen several examples of operators that are overloaded, and that can therefore behave differently depending upon the type of data they are manipulating. The + operator, for example, can be used for the concatenation of strings as well as for addition. The division operator, /, can be used for integer division as well as for division of real numbers. The particular function performed is determined by the operands. It should be noted that Java, as opposed to some other languages, does not allow the user to overload operators.

13.6.2 Method overloading

We are now very familiar with this type of polymorphism, whereby several methods in a class have the same name and are distinguished by their parameter lists. This is particularly useful for defining a number of different constructors, and you will find many examples in the Java Foundation Classes where a number of constructors are provided for a particular class. Just one of many examples is the `String` class where, among others, a constructor is provided with no parameters to create an empty string, and a constructor is provided that accepts a string value in order to initialize the new `String` object.

13.6.3 Method overriding

As we have seen, method overriding is a way of achieving polymorphism by redefining a method of a class within a subclass. Here methods are distinguished not by their parameter lists but by the object with which they are associated. As we have described in this and previous chapters, this is made even more powerful by having the ability to define abstract methods and therefore guaranteeing the existence of these methods further down the hierarchy.

13.6.4 Type polymorphism

Type polymorphism refers to the technique by which values of different types can be handled in a uniform way. Examples of this are the `System.out.print` and the `System.out.println` methods, which are set up to accept objects of many different types – **int**, **char**, **double**, `String` and so on. This is achieved, of course, by defining many different (overloaded) methods. In this way it is possible for a single method to appear to accept an object of any type. This is known as **parametric polymorphism.**

Another way to create a method that accepts more than one type was demonstrated in program 9.4, where a method was set up to accept an object of type `Employee`. We saw there how it was possible to call this method and send in objects of any subclass of `Employee` such as `FullTimeEmployee` or `PartTimeEmployee`. Because objects of a subclass are of the same type as the superclass, a method can effectively receive parameters of more than one type. As we saw, the behaviour of methods of these classes might be different, and hence this can be regarded as a kind of polymorphism – this is known as **subtype polymorphism**.

Self-test questions

1 Consider the design below of a `Game` class that makes reference to the `Checkable` interface discussed in this chapter:

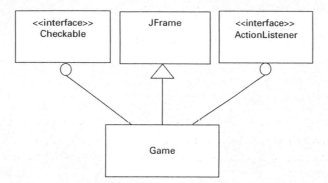

   a Write the top line of the `Game` class;

   b What methods need to be implemented in the `Game` class for this class to compile successfully?

2 Consider the following interface, called `SomeInterface`:

```
public interface SomeInterface
{
  public double SomeMethod(double x);
}
```

Now the following class is developed as shown below:

```
public class Question1 implements SomeInterface
{
  private double y;

  public double SomeMethod(int x)
  {
    return 2.5 * x;
  }
}
```

Explain why this class will not compile, and explain how it should be amended in order to rectify the problem.

3 Adapt the `BankAccount` class that we originally developed in chapter 8 so that it implements the `Checkable` interface of section 13.3. A valid `BankAccount` number will be defined as having eight digits, and the `check` method will therefore be overridden to reflect this.

4 a Explain the difference between an *interface* and an *adapter* in Java.

b Consider the following interface:

```java
public interface MyInterface
{
  public void method1();
  public int method2();
}
```

Write an adapter, `MyAdapter`, that could be used as an alternative to this interface.

5 Explain the purpose of *inner classes* and describe how they are used.

6 Consider the following two classes:

```java
public class HighClass
{
  private int num;
  private String str;

  public HighClass()
  {
    num = 10;
    str = "Hello ";
  }

  public HighClass(int numIn, String strIn)
  {
    num = numIn;
    str = strIn;
  }

  public void display(int mult)
  {
    System.out.println(100 + mult * num);
  }

  public void display(String strIn)
  {
    System.out.println(str + strIn);
  }
}
```

```
public class LowClass extends HighClass
{
  private char ch;

  public LowClass()
  {
    super();
    ch = 'Q';
  }

  public void display(String strIn)
  {
    System.out.println(strIn + ch);
  }
}
```

Give examples from these classes of:

a operator overloading;

b method overloading;

c method overriding;

d type polymorphism.

Programming exercises

1 Implement the `RedCircle` application from section 13.4.

2 Adapt program 13.1 so that it tests out the new version of `BankAccount` that you developed in self-test question 3.

3 Design and implement a program that allows the user to draw a rectangle by dragging the mouse. You should look at the `RedCircle` class to get some ideas for this – you will need to think about how you determine the start position of the rectangle, and how you will calculate its width and height.

4 Consider the following class:

```java
import java.awt.*;
import java.awt.event.*;
import javax.swing.*;

public class SomeGraphicsClass extends JFrame implements MouseListener
{
  private JButton aButton = new JButton("Press here");
  public SomeGraphicsClass()
  {
    setTitle("Question 4");
    setLayout(new FlowLayout());
    setDefaultCloseOperation(EXIT_ON_CLOSE);
    add(aButton);
    aButton.addMouseListener(this);
    setSize(300, 200);
  }

  public void mousePressed(MouseEvent e)
  {
  }

  public void mouseReleased(MouseEvent e)
  {
  }

  public void mouseEntered(MouseEvent e)
  {
  }

  public void mouseExited(MouseEvent e)
  {
  }

  public void mouseClicked(MouseEvent e)
  {
  }
}
```

Write the code for a class called `ExtendedGraphicsClass` that is a subclass of `Some GraphicsClass`. The class will have one additional attribute, a `JLabel`, initially displaying the text "The mouse button has not been pressed yet". The constructor must be overridden to enable this attribute to be added to the `JFrame` along with the `JButton`. It must also contain an instruction to make the frame visible.

The class will also override the methods `mousePressed` and `mouseReleased` so that, as shown below, the label will display the text "The mouse button has been pressed" when the mouse button is pressed, and "The mouse button has been released" when the mouse button is released.

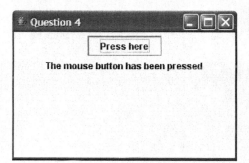   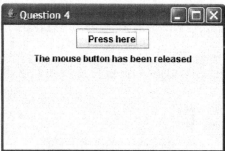

5 Experiment with the other methods of the `MouseListener` interface (`mouseEntered` and `mouseExited`) that you have not yet used.

For example, the simple little application shown below adds a button to a frame using a flow layout. The button is yellow, but turns red when the cursor moves over it. In this example we simply sized the button by adding some blank text, and then called its `setFocusPainted` method with a parameter of `false` in order to remove the highlighting around the text. The colour of the button is changed by calling its `setBackground` method.

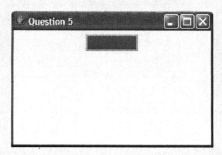

CHAPTER

14

Exceptions

❖ OBJECTIVES

By the end of this chapter you should be able to:

- ❖ explain the term **exception**;
- ❖ distinguish between **checked** and **unchecked** exception classes in Java;
- ❖ claim an exception using a **throws** clause;
- ❖ throw an exception using a **throw** command;
- ❖ catch an exception in a **try...catch** block;
- ❖ place cleanup code in a **finally** block;
- ❖ define and use your own exception classes.

14.1 Introduction

One way in which to write a program is to assume that everything proceeds smoothly and as expected – users input values at the correct time and of the correct format, files are never corrupt, array indices are always valid and so on. Of course, this view of the world is very rarely accurate. In reality, unexpected situations arise that could compromise the correct functioning of your program.

Programs should be written that continue to function even if unexpected situations should arise. So far we have tried to achieve this by carefully constructed **if** statements that send back error flags, in the form of **boolean** values, when appropriate. However, in some circumstances, these forms of protection against undesirable situations prove inadequate. In such cases the *exception handling* facility of Java must be used.

14.2 Pre-defined exception classes in Java

An **exception** is an event that occurs during the life of a program which could cause that program to behave unreliably. You can see that the events we described in the introduction fall into this category. For example, accessing an array with an invalid index could cause that program to terminate.

Each type of event that could lead to an exception is associated with a pre-defined *exception class* in Java. When a given event occurs, the Java run-time environment determines which exception has occurred and an object of the given exception class is generated. This process is known as **throwing** an exception.

These exception classes have been named to reflect the nature of the exception. For example, when an array is accessed with an illegal index an object of the `ArrayIndexOutOfBoundsException` class is thrown.

All exception classes inherit from the base class `Throwable`, which is found in the `java.lang` package. These subclasses of `Throwable` are found in various packages and are then further categorized depending upon the type of exception. For example, the exception associated with a given file not being found (`FileNotFoundException`) and the exception associated with an end of file having been reached (`EOFException`) are both types of input/output exceptions (`IOException`), which reside in the `java.io` package. Figure 14.1 illustrates part of this hierarchy.

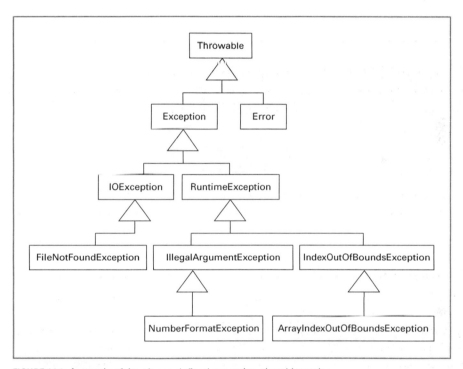

FIGURE 14.1 A sample of Java's pre-defined exception class hierarchy

As you can see from figure 14.1, there are two immediate subclasses of `Throwable`: `Exception` and `Error`. The `Error` class describes internal system errors that are very unlikely ever to occur (so-called "hard" errors). For example, one subclass of `Error` is `VirtualMachineError` where some error in the JVM has been detected. There is little that can be done in the way of recovery from such errors other than to end the program as gracefully as possible. All other exceptions are subclasses of the `Exception` class and it is these exceptions that programmers deal with in their programs. The `Exception` class is further subdivided. The two most important subdivisions are shown in figure 14.1, `IOException` and `RuntimeException`.

The `RuntimeException` class deals with errors that arise from the logic of a program. For example, a program that converts a string into a number, when the string contains non-numeric characters (`NumberFormatException`), or accesses an array using an illegal index (`ArrayIndexOutOfBounds-Exception`).

The IOException class deals with external errors that could affect the program during input and output. Such errors could include, for example, the keyboard locking, or an external file being corrupted.

Since nearly every Java instruction could result in a RuntimeException error, the Java compiler does not flag such instructions as potentially error-prone. Consequently, these types of errors are known as **unchecked** exceptions.[1] It is left to the programmer to ensure that code is written in such a way as to avoid such exceptions; for example, checking an array index before looking up a value in an array with that index. Should such an exception arise, it will be due to a program error and will not become apparent until run-time.

The Java compiler *does*, however, flag up those instructions that may generate all other types of exception (such as IOException errors) since the programmer has no means of avoiding such errors arising. For example, an instruction to read from a file may cause an exception because the file is corrupt. No amount of program code can prevent this file from being corrupt. The compiler will not only flag such an instruction as potentially error-prone, it will also specify the exact exception that could be thrown. Consequently, these kinds of errors are known as **checked exceptions**. Programmers have to include code to inform the compiler of how they will deal with checked exceptions generated by a particular instruction, before the compiler will allow the program to compile successfully.

14.3 Handling exceptions

Consider a simple program that allows the user to enter an aptitude test mark at the keyboard; the program then informs the user if he or she has passed the test and been allowed on a given course. We could use the nextInt method (from either our EasyScanner class or the original Scanner class) to allow the user to enter this mark. However, in order to show you how exceptions can be dealt with in your programs, we will not take this approach – instead we will devise our own class, TestException, that will contain a class method called getInteger. Before we do that, here is the outline of the main application:

```
public class AptitudeTest
{
  public static void main (String[] args)
  {
    int score;
    System.out.print ("Enter aptitude test score: ");
    score = TestException.getInteger(); // calling class method
    // test score here
  }
}
```

---

[1] Exceptions derived from Error are also unchecked.

Now let's look at an outline for the `TestException` class.

```
public class TestException
{
  // this method is declared 'static' as it is a class method
  public static int getInteger()
  {
    // code for method goes here
  }
}
```

The `getInteger` method must allow the user to enter an integer at the keyboard and then return that integer. There are many ways we could try to read an integer from the keyboard. As we have said, rather than make use of the `nextInt` method in the `Scanner` class, the approach we will take here will be to use a rather low-level method called `read` in the `System.in` object. So far we have used the `System.out` object to display information on the screen, but we have not explored the `System.in` object. This object is an object of the `InputStream` class that you will find out more about in chapter 18.

You will remember from chapter 2 that each character on the keyboard is represented by a Unicode number. For countries in which the standard western alphabet is used, the lower case letters 'a' through to 'z' are represented by the Unicode values 97 through to 122 inclusive. Special characters also have Unicode values. For example, the carriage return character has a Unicode value 13. The `InputStream` class provides a `read` method that is a bit like the `next` method of the `Scanner` class, except that it treats the `String` as a series of Unicode numbers. Each number is considered to be of type **byte**, so that the `String` itself is an array of bytes. Figure 14.2 illustrates the effect of the `read` method when someone enters the word "hello" at the keyboard.

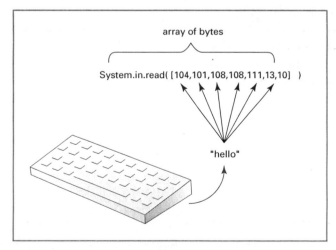

FIGURE 14.2 The 'read' method stores characters entered at the keyboard as an array of bytes

Notice that the array of bytes is not returned as a value. Instead they are placed into the parameter. Also note that the new-line character is given a Unicode value of 10.

The getInteger method will first have to take this array of bytes and convert it into a string. Luckily a version of the String constructor returns a String object from an array of bytes. We then remove any trailing spaces at the end of the String; this can be done with the String method trim as follows:

```
byte [] buffer = new byte[512]; // declare a large byte array
System.in.read(buffer); // characters entered stored in array
String s = new String (buffer); // make string from byte array
s = s.trim(); // trim string
```

Now, finally, we have to convert this string into an integer. We can use the parseInt method of the Integer class to allow us to do this:

```
int num = Integer.parseInt(s); // converts string to an 'int'
```

Our TestException class now looks like this:

```
// this is a first attempt, it will not compile!
public class TestException
{
  public static int getInteger()
  {
    byte [] buffer = new byte[512];
    System.in.read(buffer);
    String s = new String (buffer);
    s = s.trim();
    int num = Integer.parseInt(s);
    return num; // send back the integer value
  }
}
```

Unfortunately, as things stand, this class will *not* compile. The cause of the error is in the getInteger method, in particular the way we used the read method of System.in. Whenever this method is used, the Java compiler *insists* that we be very careful. To understand this better, take a look at the header for this read method, taken from the Java language specification, in particular the part we have emboldened:

```
public int read (byte[] b) throws IOException
```

Up until now, you have not seen a method header of this form. The words **throws** IOException are the new bits in this method header. In Java this is known as a method **claiming an exception**.

14.3.1 Claiming an exception

The term **claiming an exception** refers to a given method having been marked to indicate that it will pass on an exception object that it might generate. So the term **throws** IOException means that the method *could* cause an input/output exception in your program. The type of error that could take place while data is being read includes the loss of a network connection or a file being corrupted, for example.

Remember, when an exception occurs, an exception object is created. This is an unwanted object that could cause your program to fail or behave unpredictably, and so should be dealt with and not ignored. Rather than dealing with this exception object *within* the read method, the Java people decided it would be better if callers of this method dealt with the exception object in whatever way they felt was suitable. In effect, they *passed the error* on to the caller of the method (see figure 14.3).

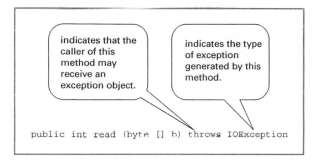

FIGURE 14.3 The 'throws' clause can be added to a method header to indicate that the method may generate an exception

As the type of exception generated (IOException) is not a subclass of RuntimeException, it is an example of a *checked exception*. In other words, the compiler *insists* that if the read method is used, the programmer deals with this exception in some way, and does not just ignore it as we did originally. That is why we had a compiler error initially. There are always two ways to deal with an exception:

1 deal with the exception within the method;

2 pass on the exception out of the method.

The developers of the read method decided to pass on the exception, so now our getInteger method has to decide what to do with this exception. In a while we will show you how to deal with an exception within a method, but for now we will just make our getInteger method pass on the exception too. We do this by simply adding a **throws** clause to our method:

```
import java.io.*; // for IOException class
public class TestException
{
  // adding this throws clause will allow this method to compile
  public static int getInteger() throws IOException
  {
    // as before
  }
}
```

Notice that, as the `IOException` class is in the io package, we now need the following **import** statement at the top of this class:

```
import java.io.*; // for IOException class
```

Now that the `getInteger` method has claimed the `IOException`, it *will* compile as we have not just *ignored* the exception, we have made a *conscious decision* to pass the exception on to any method that calls this `getInteger` method. Now, let's look at the `AptitudeTest` class again.

```java
// something wrong here!
public class AptitudeTest
{
  public static void main (String[] args)
  {
    int score;
    System.out.print("Enter aptitude test score: ");
    score = TestException.getInteger(); // calling class method
    // test score here
  }
}
```

Can you see what the problem with this program is? Well, this program will not compile now as the `main` method makes a call to our `getInteger` method, and this method may now throw an `IOException`! The `main` method now has to deal with this exception and not just ignore it. For the time being, to keep the compiler happy, we will just let the `main` method throw this exception as well. Here is the code:

PROGRAM 14.1

```java
import java.io.*; // for IOException
public class AptitudeTest
{
  // this main method will throw out any IOExceptions
  public static void main (String[] args) throws IOException
  {
    int score;
    System.out.print("Enter aptitude test score: ");
    // the 'getInteger' method may throw an IOException
    score = TestException.getInteger();
    if (score >= 50)
    {
      System.out.println("You have a place on the course!");
    }
```

```
    else
    {
      System.out.println("Sorry, you failed your test");
    }
  }
}
```

Dealing with the exception in the way we have is not a very good idea. We have effectively continually passed on the exception object until it gets thrown out of our program to the operating system. This may cause the program to terminate when such an exception occurs. Before we deal with this problem, let us show you a test run. Take a look at it as something very interesting happens.

```
Enter aptitude test score: 12w
java.lang.NumberFormatException: 12w
  at java.lang.Integer.parseInt(Integer.java:418)
  at java.lang.Integer.parseInt(Integer.java:458)
  at TestException.getInteger(TestException.java:10)
  at AptitudeTest.main(AptitudeTest.java:11)
```

As you can see, when asked to enter an integer, the user inadvertently added a character into the number (12**w**). This has led to an exception being generated and thrown out of our program. Again, looking at the output generated, you can see that when an exception is generated in this way the Java system gives you quite a lot of information. This information includes the name of the method that threw the exception, the class that the method belongs to, the line numbers in the source files where the error arose, and the type of exception that was thrown. Such information is referred to as the **stack trace** of the exception.

Look at the name of the exception that is thrown. It's not the one we were worried about, IOException, but NumberFormatException. This exception is raised when trying to convert a string into a number when the string contains non-numeric characters, as we were trying to do in this case within our getInteger method:

```
public static int getInteger() throws IOException
{
  // some code here
  int num = Integer.parseInt(s); /* will cause a NumberFormatException if string s
                                   contains non-numeric characters */
}
```

Why didn't the compiler warn us about this when we first used the parseInt method in our implementation of getInteger? Well, the reason is that the exception that could arise (NumberFormatException) is a subclass of RuntimeException and so is unchecked!

Notice that run-time exceptions do not need to be claimed in method headers in order for them to be thrown. For example, although the following is valid in Java, it is not *necessary* to claim the NumberFormatException in the header.

```
/* multiple exceptions can be claimed in the method header as follows by separating
   exception names with commas. However, run-time exceptions do not need to be claimed
   in this way */
public static int getInteger() throws IOException, NumberFormatException
{
  // some code here
}
```

The way we have dealt with exceptions so far has not been very effective. As you can see from the test run of program 14.1, continually throwing exceptions up to the calling method does not really solve the problem. It may keep the compiler happy, but eventually it means exception objects will escape from your programs and cause them to terminate. Instead, it is better at some point to handle an exception object rather than throw it. In Java this is known as **catching an exception.**

14.3.2 Catching an exception

One route for an exception object is *out* of the current method and *up to* the calling method. That's the approach we used in the previous section. Another way out for an exception object, however, is into a **catch** block. Once an exception object is trapped in a **catch** block, and that block ends, the exception object is effectively terminated. In order to trap the exception object in a **catch** block you must surround the code that could generate the exception in a **try** block. The syntax for using a **try** and **catch** block is as follows:

```
try
{
  // code that could generate an exception
}
catch (Exception e) // type of exception must be specified as a parameter
{
  // action to be taken when an exception occurs
}
// other instructions could be placed here
```

There are a few things to note before we show you this **try...catch** idea in action. First, any number of lines could be within the **try** block, and more than one of them could cause an exception. If none of them causes an exception the **catch** block is missed and the lines following the **catch** block are executed. If any one of them causes an exception the program will leave the **try** block and look for a **catch** block that deals with that exception.

Once such a **catch** clause is found, the statements within it will be executed and the program will then *continue* with any statements that follow the **catch** clause – it will *not* return to the code in the **try** clause. Look carefully at the syntax for the **catch** block:

```
catch (Exception e)
{
  // action to be taken when an exception occurs
}
```

This looks very similar to a method header. You can see that the **catch** block header has one parameter: an object, which we called e, of type Exception. Since *all* exceptions are subclasses of the Exception class, this will catch *any* exception that should arise. However, it is better to replace this exception class with the *specific* class that you are catching so that you can be certain *which* exception you have caught. As there may be more than one exception generated within a method, there may be more than one **catch** block below a **try** block – each dealing with a different exception. When an exception is thrown in a **try** block, the **catch** blocks are inspected in order – the first matching **catch** block is the one that will handle the exception.

Within the **catch** block, programmers can, if they choose, interrogate the exception object using some Exception methods, some of which are listed in table 14.1.

Method	Description
printStackTrace	prints (onto the console) a stack trace of the exception
toString	returns a detailed error message
getMessage	returns a summary error message

TABLE 14.1 Some methods of the *Exception* class

With this information in mind we can deal with the exceptions in the previous section in a different way. All we have to decide is where to catch the exception object. For now, we will leave the getInteger method as it is, and catch offending exception objects in the main method of program 14.2.

PROGRAM 14.2

```
import java.io.*;
public class AptitudeTest2
{
  public static void main (String[] args)
  {
    try
    {
      int score;
      System.out.print("Enter aptitude test score: ");
      // getInteger may throw IOException or NumberFomatException
      score = TestException.getInteger();
      if (score >= 50)
      {
        System.out.println("You have a place on the course!");
      }
```

```
      else
      {
        System.out.println("Sorry, you failed your test");
      }
    }
    // if something does goes wrong!
    catch (NumberFormatException e)
    {
      System.out.println("You entered an invalid number!");
    }
    catch (IOException e)
    {
      System.out.println(e); // calls toString method
    }
    // even if no exception thrown/caught, this line will be executed
    System.out.println("Goodbye");
  }
}
```

Notice that by catching an offending exception object there is no need to pass that object out of the method by raising that exception in the method header. Since we catch the IOException here, the throws IOException clause can be removed from the header of main. In program 14.2 we have chosen to print out an error message if an IOException is raised (by implicitly calling the toString method), whereas we have chosen to print our own message if a NumberFormatException is raised. Now look at a sample test run of program 14.2:

Enter aptitude test score: **12w**

You entered an invalid number!

Goodbye

As you can see, the user once again entered an invalid integer, but this time the program did not terminate. Instead the exception was handled with a clear message to the user, after which the program continued to operate normally.

14.4 The 'finally' clause

From the previous sections you can see that three courses of action may now take place in a try block:

1 the instructions within the **try** block are all executed successfully;

2 an exception occurs within the **try** block; the **try** block is exited and a matching **catch** block is found for this exception;

3 an exception occurs within the **try** block; the **try** block is exited but no matching **catch** block is found for this exception; so the exception is thrown from the method.

It may be the case that, no matter which of these courses of action takes place, you wish to execute some additional instructions before the method terminates. Often such a scenario arises when you wish to carry out some cleanup code, such as closing a file or a network connection that you have opened in the **try** block. The **finally** clause allows us to do this. The syntax for the **finally** clause is as follows:

```
try
{
  // code that could generate an exception
}
catch (Exception e) /* if one or more 'catch' clauses are specified, they must be given
                    before the 'finally' clause */
{
  // action to be taken when an exception occurs
}
finally
{
  // cleanup code goes here
}
// other instructions could be placed here
```

Notice that when **catch** clauses are specified, the **finally** clause must come directly *after* such clauses. If no such **catch** clauses are specified, the **finally** clause must follow directly after the **try** clause. Now, when the code in the **try** block is executed the following three courses of action can take place:

1 the instructions within the **try** block are all executed successfully; if there are any **catch** blocks specified they are skipped and the code in the **finally** block is executed;

2 an exception occurs within the **try** block; the **try** block is exited and a matching **catch** block is found for this exception, after which the code in the **finally** block is executed;

3 an exception occurs within the **try** block; the **try** block is exited but no matching **catch** block is found for this exception; so the code in the **finally** block is executed – after which the exception is thrown from the given method.

Program 14.3 is a simple demonstration of how the **finally** clause works under these three scenarios:

PROGRAM 14.3

```
public class TestTryCatchFinally
{
  public static void main(String[] args)
  {
    try
    {
      System.out.println("START TRY\n");
      String[] colours = {"RED","BLUE","GREEN"}; // initialize array
```

```
        System.out.print("Which colour? (1,2,3): ");
        String pos = EasyScanner.nextString(); // requires EasyScanner class
        // next line could throw NumberFormatException
        int i = Integer.parseInt(pos);
        // next line could throw ArrayIndexOutOfBoundsException
        System.out.println(colours[i-1]);
        System.out.println("\nEND TRY\n");
      }
    // include a catch only for ArrayIndexOutOfBoundsException
    catch(ArrayIndexOutOfBoundsException e)
    {
      System.out.println("\nENTER CATCH\n");
      System.out.println(e);
    }
    // this code will always be executed
    finally
    {
      System.out.println("\nENTER FINALLY\n");
      System.out.println("Goodbye\n");
    }
  }
}
```

This code should be fairly self-explanatory. Just notice that we have provided a **catch** block for the ArrayIndexOutOfBoundsException but we have not provided a **catch** block for the NumberFormatException, so such an exception would be thrown from main should it arise. Also, notice that we displayed messages to indicate when we are in each of the **try**, **catch** and **finally** blocks.

Here is one test run:

START TRY

Which colour? (1,2,3): **2**

BLUE

END TRY

ENTER FINALLY

Goodbye

Here the user enters a valid colour number, so the **try** block completes successfully. The **catch** block is skipped and the **finally** block is executed.

Here is another test run:

START TRY

Which colour? (1,2,3): **4**

```
ENTER CATCH

java.lang.ArrayIndexOutOfBoundsException: 3

ENTER FINALLY

Goodbye
```

Here the user enters an invalid colour number, but the **try** block does not complete as an `ArrayIndexOutOfBoundsException` is thrown. A matching **catch** block is found for this exception and executed. Upon completion of this **catch** block the program continues with the code in the **finally** block.

Here is the last test run:

```
START TRY

Which colour? (1,2,3): 2c

ENTER FINALLY

Goodbye

Exception in thread "main" java.lang.NumberFormatException:

For input string: "2c"

at java.lang.NumberFormatException.forInputString

                        (NumberFormatException.java:48)

at java.lang.Integer.parseInt(Integer.java:456)

at java.lang.Integer.parseInt(Integer.java:497)

at TestTryCatchFinally.main(TestTryCatchFinally.java:11)
```

In this case, the user entered an invalid number causing a `NumberFormatException` – so the **try** block did not complete successfully. However, there is no **catch** block provided for this exception. Without a **finally** clause this would have led to program termination *immediately* as the exception escapes from main. We have a **finally** clause, however, so this is executed *before* the program terminates with the offending exception.

These three test runs match the three scenarios we identified for **try...catch...finally** blocks earlier. You will notice from the three test runs above that, if the instructions inside the **finally** clause were written as normal below the **catch** clause (without putting them into a **finally** block), the first two test runs would have produced exactly the same result. This is because code following a **catch** block is always executed if no exception is thrown, or if an exception is thrown and a matching **catch** clause is found and executed. Only in scenario three, when an exception is thrown and no matching **catch** is found (perhaps because no **catch** clauses were specified), does the **finally** clause really make a difference to program flow.

You may well come across the third scenario when developing your programs, so the **finally** clause should be used here for cleanup code. Using the **finally** clause in scenarios one and two is optional.

14.5 Exceptions in GUI applications

In the previous section we showed you how the parseInt method could potentially result in a NumberFormatException being thrown. If this were not handled at some point, the exception object would escape out of your program and cause the program to terminate. However, this isn't the first time that you have used the parseInt method. You often had to use it when implementing GUI applications. In such applications all user input is initially considered a string, and in order to retrieve integer values from these strings you used the parseInt method (and to retrieve decimal values you used parseDouble). At the time, you never considered handling these exceptions, and your applications never seemed to terminate as a result of invalid data entry. For example, do you remember the Hostel case study of chapters 11 and 12? Figure 14.4 illustrates a sample screen shot when a user enters an invalid room number.

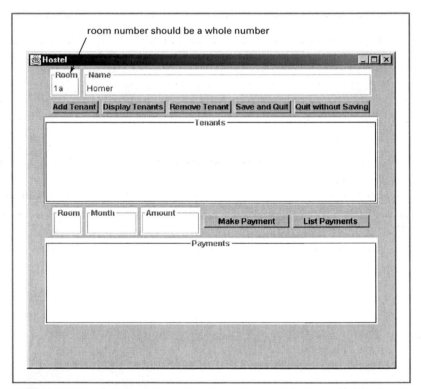

FIGURE 14.4 A sample screen shot from the 'Hostel' case study illustrating an invalid room number having been entered

When such an event occurred within a GUI application, the application seemed to continue operating regardless. After our discussion on exceptions this might seem surprising, as the text entered is being processed by a parseInt method. To remind you, here is a fragment from the event-handler:

```
if(e.getSource() == addButton)
{
  // some code here
  String roomEntered = roomField.getText(); // read text entered
  // the parseInt method could cause an exception!
  if(Integer.parseInt(roomEntered)< 1 || Integer.parseInt(roomEntered)>noOfRooms)
  {
    displayArea1.setText("There are only " + noOfRooms + " rooms");
  }
  // some code here
}
```

In fact, when an invalid number is entered as illustrated in figure 14.4, a `NumberFormatException` occurs but

- you will not see details of the exception in your graphics screen since they will always be displayed on your black console window (which may be hidden during the running of your application);
- exceptions do not terminate GUI applications; however, they may make them behave unpredictably.

So, if you uncover your black console screen you will see a list of exceptions that have been thrown during the running of your GUI applications – you may be surprised to see how many are actually thrown when you thought your program was operating correctly.

Often, graphical programs will continue to operate normally in the face of exceptions. To ensure this is the case you should still add exception handling code into your GUI applications. For example, we could amend the event-handler above as follows:

```
if(e.getSource() == addButton)
{
  try
  {
    // previous add button code goes here
  }
  // if any lines throw NumberFormatException this handler is activated
  catch (NumberFormatException nfe)
  {
    // display error message
    displayArea1.setText("Invalid room number");
  }
}
```

Notice we had to pick a different name for our exception object. We chose nfe (for NumberFormat-Exception) rather than just e as before, as we already have an object called e in this event-handler. Now if we run the application again, with the same input as depicted in figure 14.4 we get the response given in figure 14.5.

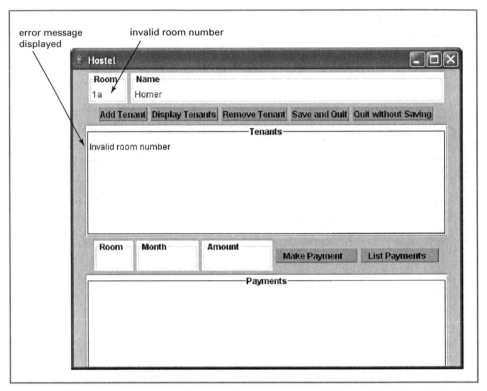

FIGURE 14.5 Exceptions can still be dealt with in GUI applications

14.6 Using exceptions in your own classes

So far we have mainly been dealing with how to handle exceptions that are thrown by pre-defined Java methods, such as read and parseInt. Up until now, the methods you have been writing yourself have not had to deal with exceptions unless they themselves used a Java method that throws an exception.

We have managed to avoid the need for exceptions by using **if** statements to monitor abnormal situations, and to send back **boolean** error values when appropriate, to warn users of our methods that something went wrong. In this way, exceptions never arose. As an example, think back to the Bank class of chapter 8. Some important parts of this class are presented again below.

THE *BANK* CLASS – a reminder

```
public class Bank
{
  // attributes
  private BankAccount[] list;
  private int total;
  // the constructor
  public Bank(int sizeIn)
  {
    // size array with parameter
    list = new BankAccount[sizeIn];
    total = 0;
  }

  // add an item to the array
  public boolean add(BankAccount accountIn)
  {
    if (!isFull()) // check if list is full
    {
      list[total] = accountIn;
      total++;
      return true; // indicate success
    }
    else
    {
      return false; // indicate failure
    }
  }

  // return an account at a particular place in the list
  public BankAccount getItem(int positionIn)
  {
    if(positionIn < 1 || positionIn > total)
    {
      return null; // indicate invalid index
    }
    else
    {
      return list[positionIn - 1];
    }
  }

  // return an account with the given account number
```

```java
public BankAccount getItem(String accountNumberIn)
{
  int index;
  index = search(accountNumberIn);
  if(index == -999) // check for error
  {
    return null; // indicate failure
  }
  else
  {
    return list[index]; // everything ok
  }
}


// deposit money in a specified account
public boolean depositMoney(String accountNumberIn, double amountIn)
{
  int index = search(accountNumberIn);
  if(index == -999) // check for error
  {
    return false; // indicate failure
  }
  else
  {
    list[index].deposit(amountIn);
    return true; // indicate success
  }
}


// withdraw money from a specified account
public boolean withdrawMoney(String accountNumberIn, double amountIn)
{
  int index = search(accountNumberIn);
  if(index == -999) // check for error
  {
    return false; // indicate failure
  }
  else
  {
    list[index].withdraw(amountIn);
    return true; // indicate success
  }
}
```

```
    // remove an account
    public boolean remove(String numberIn)
    {
      int index = search(numberIn);
      if(index == -999) // check for error
      {
        return false; // indicate failure
      }
      else
      {
        for(int i = index; i<= total-2; i++)
        {
          list[i] = list[i+1];
        }
        total--;
        return true; // indicate successful
      }
    }


    // search for an account
    private int search(String accountNumberIn)
    {
      for(int i = 0; i < total; i++)
      {
        BankAccount tempAccount = list[i];
        String tempNumber = tempAccount.getAccountNumber();
        if(tempNumber.equals(accountNumberIn))
        {
          return i;
        }
      }
      return -999; // when item is not found
    }


    // other methods go here
}
```

As you can see, the methods given above may not necessarily always be able to carry out their intended tasks successfully. For example, the add method would not be able to add a bank account to the list if the list were full. Similarly, the depositMoney method could not deposit money into a given bank account if that bank account number did not exist in the list. In each case, failure was indicated by returning some error value back to the caller. The add and depositMoney methods both return a **boolean** value of **false** to indicate failure. The getItem methods, on the other hand, both return a **null** value to indicate failure whereas the **private** search method returns a value of −999.

Within the methods themselves, **if...else** statements are used to prevent errors such as accessing an array with an invalid array index. Look again, for example, at the depositMoney method.

```
public boolean depositMoney(String accountNumberIn, double amountIn)
{
  int index = search(accountNumberIn);
  if(index == -999) // check for error
  {
    return false; // indicate failure
  }
  else
  {
    list[index].deposit(amountIn);
    return true; // indicate success
  }
}
```

The **if...else** statement checks that a valid array index has been returned by the search method, thus preventing an ArrayIndexOutOfBoundsException from being thrown. Sometimes the technique of avoidance and reporting of errors in **return** values does not work. In such cases exception-handling techniques can be used. As an example of this, consider the Bank constructor once again:

```
public Bank(int sizeIn)
{
  list = new BankAccount[sizeIn];
  total = 0;
}
```

What could potentially go wrong with a call to this constructor?

Well, the array is sized depending upon the value sent in as a parameter. That value can be any integer. A negative value would not be a valid array size, however, and this would cause an exception in your program. The name of the exception that is thrown can always be tested by writing a small **try...catch** block in a main method. Program 14.4 is one such simple tester program which uses an array of integers:

PROGRAM 14.4

```
/* the purpose of this class is just to test which exception is thrown when a negative
   array size is entered */

public class TrapException
{
  public static void main(String[] args)
```

```
  {
    try
    {
      // here write the code you are testing
      System.out.println("Enter size");
      int size = EasyScanner.nextInt(); // requires EasyScanner class
      int[] list = new int[size];
    }
    catch (Exception e) // this will catch any exception that is thrown
    {
      System.out.println(e); // will display the name of the exception
    }
  }
}
```

Notice that since all exceptions are of type `Exception`, the **catch** clause above will catch any exception that occurs. When testing your applications it might be a good idea to place the instructions inside `main` in such a **try...catch** block. Here is a sample test run:

Enter size

-5

java.lang.NegativeArraySizeException:

As you can see, this results in a `NegativeArraySizeException`. Returning to the `Bank` constructor, we could check if the parameter was negative within the constructor, but then how do we report back that an error has occurred? Usually we would make use of the return value, but constructors have no return value! The only way to report back errors from constructors is to make use of exceptions.

14.7 Throwing exceptions

In a way, the `Bank` constructor is already making use of exceptions to indicate that an error has occurred. It returns a `NegativeArraySizeException` to report the error. The issue that we have to deal with is – how do we inform users of this class that such an exception may be thrown?

One way of indicating that a method may throw an exception is to add the exception to the method header in a **throws** clause. As a first attempt we could amend the `Bank` constructor as follows:

```
// try this?
public Bank(int sizeIn) throws NegativeArraySizeException
{
  list = new BankAccount[sizeIn];
  total = 0;
}
```

However, it is not usually considered good programming practice for methods to claim unchecked exceptions in this way as it places no requirements on users of this method to acknowledge the exception. Another problem with claiming this particular exception is that the underlying implementation (an array) is revealed in the name of the exception. If in future a decision was made to replace the array representation with another representation, this exception name will not be valid.

Both of these problems could be solved by throwing a general exception (of type `Exception`), rather than a specific exception (like `NegativeArraySizeIndex` for example). A general exception will be checked by the compiler, forcing the caller to deal with this exception and not ignore it, and the exception name does not reveal the underlying representation. Here's how the header for the constructor would be amended if this were the chosen strategy:

```
public Bank(int sizeIn) throws Exception
{
  // some code here
}
```

Unfortunately, this approach does require some modifications to the actual body of the method. While the Java system will automatically detect and throw a specific exception object (of type `NegativeArrayIndexException`, for example), there is no event that will lead to a general exception object (of type `Exception`) being thrown. In order to throw a general exception object you must:

- detect the situation when such an exception should be thrown;
- write an instruction explicitly to throw the exception using the `throw` command;
- use the new command to generate an object of type `Exception`.

In the case of the constructor, the exception object will be thrown when the array size is less than zero. Here is the amended constructor:

```
public Bank (int sizeIn) throws Exception
{
  if (sizeIn < 0) // throw exception object under this condition
  {
     throw new Exception ("cannot set a negative size");
  }
  else
  {
    list = new BankAccount[sizeIn];
    total = 0;
  }
}
```

Notice that when you explicitly throw an exception object you may also pass along a message as a parameter, as we did in this case:

```
throw new Exception ("cannot set a negative size");
```

This message can be retrieved by the receiver of this exception object by calling its getMessage method. As an example of this, let us amend the Bank tester class from chapter 8 (BankProgram) to check for this exception:

```
public class BankProgram
{
  public static void main(String[] args)
  {
    try
    {
      // some code here
      System.out.print("Maximum number of accounts? ");
      size = EasyScanner.nextInt(); // requires EasyScanner class
      // call Bank constructor
      Bank myBank = new Bank(size); // may throw checked Exception
      // rest of code here
    }
    catch (Exception e)
    {
      System.out.println(e.getMessage());
    }
  }
  // other static methods here as before
}
```

Notice how throwing a checked exception object, from the Bank constructor, forced us in the BankProgram tester class to deal with the error – it could not be ignored. Here is a sample test run of the amended BankProgram class:

```
Maximum number of accounts? -5

cannot set a negative size
```

Notice also how the error message no longer reveals the underlying array representation. This approach of throwing general exceptions, while adequate, also has its drawbacks:

- the name of the exception does not explain the source of the problem; the getMessage method must be used to determine that;
- the **catch** clause we used to deal with the resulting exception object will catch *any* exception that is thrown, as all exceptions are derived from the exception class, but we may wish to handle other exceptions in a different way to the constructor exception.

If these issues affect your application, you will have to create your own exception classes rather than throwing general exceptions.

14.8 Creating your own exception classes

You can create your own exception class by inheriting from any pre-defined exception class. Generally speaking, if you wish your exception class to be unchecked then it should inherit from RuntimeException (or one of its subclasses), whereas if you wish your exception to be checked you can inherit from the general Exception class.

In the case of the Bank class we have decided to make the exception thrown by the constructor checked, so we will define our exception class by inheriting from the general Exception class. Remember, the problem that arose was the possibility of a negative size, so we will call this exception class NegativeSizeException. Look at the code first and then we will discuss it.

THE NEGATIVESIZEEXCEPTION CLASS

```
public class NegativeSizeException extends Exception
{
  public NegativeSizeException () // constructor without parameter
  {
    super("cannot set a negative size");
  }

  public NegativeSizeException (String message) // constructor with parameter
  {
    super (message);
  }
}
```

As well as inheriting from some exception class, user-defined exception classes should have two constructors defined within them. One should take no parameter and simply call the constructor of the superclass with a message of your choosing:

```
public NegativeSizeException ()
{
  super("cannot set a negative size"); // calls Exception constructor
}
```

The other constructor should allow a user-defined message to be supplied with the exception object:

```
public NegativeSizeException (String message)
{
  super (message); // message supplied as parameter
}
```

The Bank constructor can now be implemented as follows:

```java
public Bank (int sizeIn) throws NegativeSizeException
{
  if (sizeIn < 0) // throw exception object under this condition
  {
    throw new NegativeSizeException();
  }
  else
  {
    list = new BankAccount[sizeIn];
    total = 0;
  }
}
```

Now here is an outline of the amended tester:

```java
public class BankProgram
{
  public static void main(String[] args)
  {
    try
    {
      // some code here
      System.out.print("Maximum number of accounts? ");
      size = EasyScanner.nextInt();// requires EasyScanner class
      // Bank constructor may throw NegativeSizeException
      Bank myBank = new Bank(size);
      // rest of code here
    }
    catch (NegativeSizeException e) // to deal with Bank error
    {
      System.out.println(e.getMessage());
      System.out.println("due to error in Bank constructor");
    }
    catch (Exception e) // to catch all other errors
    {
      System.out.println("Some unforseen error");
      e.printStackTrace(); // print stack trace to determine cause
    }
  }
  // other static methods here as before
}
```

Notice how we added a general **catch** clause to catch any exceptions that we might not yet have considered. We have printed the stack trace in this error-handler to determine the exact cause of this unexpected error:

```
catch (Exception e)
{
  System.out.println("Some unforeseen error");
  e.printStackTrace();
}
```

During testing this is always a good strategy. However, you need to ensure that the general **catch** clause is the *last* **catch** clause you specify. For example, something like the following will not compile:

```
// this will not compile!
try
{
  // some code here
}
catch (Exception e) // catches all exceptions
{
  // some code here
}
catch (NegativeSizeException e) // will never be reached now!
{
  // some code here
}
```

The above will not compile as the first general **catch** clause (**catch** Exception) will catch *all* exception types (including NegativeSizeException). So any **catch** clauses below (such as catch NegativeSizeException) will never be reached. To write unreachable code in Java causes a compiler error.

14.9 Re-throwing exceptions

Ordinarily, when an exception is caught in a **catch** block, that exception has been dealt with. It is, however, possible to throw an exception from *within* a **catch** block. For example, let us consider the Bank constructor again. Here, an **if** statement was used to determine when to throw an exception object:

```
public Bank (int sizeIn) throws NegativeSizeException
{
  if (sizeIn < 0) // throw exception object under this condition
  {
    throw new NegativeSizeException();
  }
  else
  {
    list = new BankAccount[sizeIn];
    total = 0;
  }
}
```

We could, instead, have allowed the original NegativeArraySizeException to be thrown and then throw our own NegativeSizeException in a **catch** block as follows:

```
public Bank (int sizeIn) throws NegativeSizeException
{
  try // check for exceptions
  {
    list = new BankAccount[sizeIn];
    total = 0;
  }
  catch (NegativeArraySizeException e) // allow this to be caught
  {
    throw new NegativeSizeException ();// now throw our own exception
  }
}
```

This technique might be useful if the condition required for the **if** statement were difficult to formulate, or where there were several points in a method where an exception could be thrown. In the latter case, all these possible points of error could be included in a single **try** block.

14.10 Documenting exceptions

We finish off this chapter by looking at how to document methods that may throw exceptions, using the Javadoc style of comments discussed in chapter 11. The @throws tag should be used to document the name of any exceptions that may be thrown by a method. Here, for example, is the Bank constructor, documented with Javadoc comments:

```
/** Creates an empty collection of bank accounts
 * and fixes the maximum size of this collection
 *
 * @param sizeIn                 The maximum size of the collection
 *                               of bank accounts
 * @throws NegativeSizeException If the collection is sized
 *                               with a negative value
 */


public Bank (int sizeIn) throws NegativeSizeException
{
  // as before
}
```

Generally speaking, when documenting methods in this way, it is good practice to document *all* exceptions that a method may throw (be they checked or unchecked). Multiple `@throws` tags can be used to list multiple exceptions.

Self-test questions

1 What is an *exception*?

2 Distinguish between *checked* and *unchecked* exceptions and then identify which of the following exceptions are checked, and which are unchecked:

- `FileNotFoundException`;
- `NegativeArraySizeException`;
- `NumberFormatException`;
- `IOException`;
- `Exception`;
- `ArrayIndexOutOfBoundsException`;
- `RuntimeException`.

3 Explain the following terms:

a *claiming* an exception;

b *throwing* an exception;

c *catching* an exception.

4 What is the purpose of a **finally** clause?

5 Look at the program below and then answer the questions that follow:

```
public class ExceptionsQ5
{
  public static void main(String[] args)
  {
    int[] someArray = {12,9,3,11};
    int position = getPosition();
    display (someArray, position);
    System.out.println("End of program" );
  }


  static int getPosition()
  {
    System.out.println("Enter array position to display");
    String positionEntered = EasyScanner.nextString(); // requires EasyScanner class
    return Integer.parseInt(positionEntered);
  }
  static void display (int[] arrayIn, int posIn)
  {
    System.out.println("Item at this position is: " +arrayIn[posIn]);
  }
}
```

> **a** Will this result in any compiler errors?
>
> **b** Which methods could throw exceptions?
>
> **c** Identify the names of the exceptions that could be thrown and the circumstances under which they could be thrown.
>
> **6** When would it be appropriate to define your own exception class?

Programming exercises

1 Implement the program given in question 5 above. Now:

    a Rewrite `main` so that it catches any exceptions it may now throw by displaying a message on the screen indicating the exception thrown.

    b At the moment, the "End of program" message may not always be executed. Add an appropriate **finally** clause so that this message is always executed at the end of the program.

    c Add an additional **catch** clause in `main` to catch any unaccounted-for exceptions (within this **catch** clause, print out the stack trace of the exception).

    d Create your own exception class `InvalidPositionException` (make this a checked exception).

    e Rewrite the display method so that it throws the `InvalidPositionException` from a **catch** block.

    f Rewrite `main` to take account of this amended display method.

    g Document these exceptions using appropriate `Javadoc` comments.

2 The `Scanner` class has methods `nextInt` and `nextDouble` for reading an **int** and a **double** value from the keyboard, respectively. Both of these methods throw an exception if an appropriate numerical value is not entered.

    a Write a tester program to find out the name of this exception.

    b Develop a new version of the `EasyScanner` class, say `EasyScannerPlus`, so that instead of throwing exceptions the methods `nextInt` and `nextDouble` repeatedly display an error message and allow for data re-entry.

    c Write a tester program to test out the methods of your `EasyScannerPlus` class.

3 Look back at the timetable application that you developed in programming exercise 8 of chapter 8. Here is a reminder of the original design for the `TimeTable` class:

TimeTable
-times : Booking[][]
+TimeTable(int, int) ◆ *+makeBooking(int, int, Booking) : boolean* *+cancelBooking(int, int) : boolean* *+isFree(int, int) : boolean* *+getBooking(int, int) : Booking* *+numberOfDays() : int* *+numberOfPeriods() : int*

As you can see, several methods return **boolean** values. Some of these **boolean** values were sent to indicate errors. Now modify this class to make use of exceptions as follows:

a Develop a `TimeTableException` class (you can choose if you wish to make this a checked or an unchecked exception).

b Modify the `TimeTable` class so that the constructor, and the methods `makeBooking`, `cancelBooking` and `getBooking`, all throw a `TimeTableException` if an error occurs (this would mean that the methods `makeBooking` and `cancelBooking` no longer need to return **boolean** values).

c Modify the tester that you developed for the timetable application to take account of these exceptions.

4 Look back at the *Hostel* case study of chapters 11 and 12 and make use of exceptions where appropriate. Amend the `Javadoc` documentation for this application to include information on any exceptions you may have included.

CHAPTER 15

The Java Collections Framework

❖ OBJECTIVES

By the end of this chapter you should be able to:

❖ use the `ArrayList` class to store a **list** of objects;

❖ use the `HashSet` class to store a **set** of objects;

❖ use the `HashMap` class to store objects in a **map**;

❖ fix the type of elements within a collection using the **generics** mechanism;

❖ use an `Iterator` object to scan through a collection;

❖ create objects of your own classes, and use them in conjunction with Java's collection classes.

15.1 Introduction

An array is a very useful type in Java but it has its restrictions:

■ once an array is created it must be sized, and this size is fixed;

■ it contains no useful pre-defined methods.

Think back to the `Bank` class of chapter 8. We used an array to implement this class. In doing so we had to put an upper limit to the size of this collection of accounts. Sometimes, however, an upper limit is not known. Just creating a very big array is very wasteful of memory – and what happens if even this very big array proves to be too small? Another problem is that to carry out any interesting processing (like searching the array) required us to write complex algorithms.

One solution to the first problem would be to create a reasonably sized array and, when the array is full, copy this array into a slightly bigger array and use this new array and continue doing this every time the array gets full. A solution to the second problem would be to do as we did with the `ObjectList` class in chapter 11 – that is, wrap the array in a generic collection class and provide useful array methods (like searching) in this collection class.

Luckily we do not need to go to such lengths; the people from Sun have already done this for us. They have developed a group of generic collection classes that grow as more elements are added to them, and these classes provide lots of useful methods. This group of collection classes are referred to as the **Java Collections Framework**. These classes are all found in the `java.util` package so to access them we require the following **import** statement:

```
import java.util.*;
```

The collection classes themselves are organized around several collection interfaces that define different types of collections that we might be interested in using. Three important interfaces from this group are:

- `List`;
- `Set`;
- `Map`.

We will now examine these interfaces and some of the classes provided in the Java Collections Framework (JCF) which implement these interfaces.

15.2 The *List* interface and the *ArrayList* class

The `List` interface specifies the methods required to process an *ordered list* of objects. Such a list may contain duplicates. Examples of a list of objects include jobs waiting for a printer, emergency calls waiting for an ambulance and the names of players that have won the Wimbledon tennis tournament over the last 10 years. In each case ordering is important, and repetition may also be required. We often think of such a collection as a *sequence* of objects.

There are three implementations provided for the `List` interface in the JCF. They are `ArrayList`, `LinkedList` and `Vector`. Here we will look at the `ArrayList` class.

The `ArrayList` class is very similar to the `ObjectList` class that we developed in chapter 11. Like the `ObjectList` class, classes from the JCF (such as `ArrayList`) are *generic* collection classes. This means they can be used to store objects of *any* type.[1]

Let's use an `ArrayList` to store a queue of jobs waiting for a printer, and let us represent these jobs by a series of Job ID `String`s. The `ArrayList` constructor creates an empty list. Take a look at it and then we will discuss it, as it introduces a new concept:

```
// creates an ArrayList object - 'printQ'
ArrayList<String> printQ = new ArrayList<String>();
```

Creating an object by calling a constructor is nothing new, but what is that stuff in angled brackets after the class name `ArrayList`? Well, the stuff in angled brackets is a new feature introduced in Java 5.0 that allows us to *fix* the type of objects stored in a particular collection object. This feature is called **generics**.

---

[1] As we discussed before in chapter 9, generic collections cannot store primitive types like **int** and **double**. If primitive types are required then objects of the appropriate wrapper class (`Integer`, `Double` and so on) must be used. However, as discussed in chapter 9, *autoboxing* and *unboxing* (introduced in Java 5.0) automate the process of moving from a primitive type to its associated wrapper.

15.2.1 Generics

The **generics** mechanism allows us to send one or more types to a class (or interface) as a parameter. For this reason, such types are sometimes referred to as *parameterized types*. All the collection classes within the JCF have been modified, since Java 5.0, to allow us to make use of the generics mechanism to fix the type of elements within a collection.

In the case of the `printQ` object, we want each element within this collection to be of type `String`. To make use of generics to fix a collection's type, *angled brackets* are used to specify this type during object creation as follows. Here is the object creation again:

```
// this will make 'printQ' a list that holds String objects only
ArrayList<String> printQ = new ArrayList<String>();
```

You can see that it is easy to use the idea of generics to fix the type of the items within the collection. We just append the collection type with the type of the elements to be held in angled brackets.

Prior to Java 5.0 and the introduction of generics, we would have created the `printQ` object in the usual way:

```
// this is the old way of creating a 'printQ' object
ArrayList printQ = new ArrayList ();
```

This would have created a generic collection object, much like the creation of an `ObjectList` object from chapter 11. The objects stored in such a collection would all be of the generic `Object` type. While this allows such collection classes to be generic, there are several drawbacks with this old approach:

- As we saw in chapters 9 and 11, each time we retrieve items from such a collection, we must always remember to type cast back from `Object` to the actual type of the element.
- The compiler does not insist that the elements stored in the collection are of a consistent type. So, for example, the first item in the collection may be an object of type `String` and the second an object of some other class like `Rectangle`.
- Because the type of objects in the collection cannot be guaranteed to be anything other than the generic type `Object`, type casting to a specific type upon retrieval may not succeed. For example, we may assume the collection contains `String` objects, and type cast back to a `String` when we retrieve an item. But there is no guarantee that the object is *actually* a `String`. If it is not a `String` this will throw an unchecked `ClassCastException` at run-time.

Fixing the type of elements within a collection using the generics mechanism has the following benefits:

- it allows the compiler to check that items added into the collection are always of the correct type;
- it removes the need for type casting when we retrieve items from the collection;
- it avoids the possibility of `ClassCastExceptions`.

Of course, the generics mechanism can be used to fix *any* object type for the elements within a collection. For example, say we wished create a list of JButtons, we could do so as follows:

```
// this will make 'someButtons' a list of JButtons
ArrayList<JButton> someButtons = new ArrayList <JButton> ();
```

If, on the other hand, we wished to create a list of integers, we could do so like this:

```
// this will make 'someNumbers' a list of Integers
ArrayList <Integer> someNumbers = new ArrayList <Integer> ();
```

Notice that the Integer class must be used here, not the primitive **int** type. When using the collection classes within the JCF, we will always use the generics mechanism to fix the type of elements within the collection.

You should be aware that the type of any object created using this generics mechanism is now the class name *plus* the stuff in angled brackets. So, for example, if we were to write a method that received a list of strings, we would specify it as follows:

```
// this method receives an ArrayList<String> object
public void someMethod (ArrayList<String> printQIn)
{
  // some code here
}
```

15.2.2 Using the interface type instead of the implementation type

In order to create the object printQ, we have used the ArrayList class to implement the List interface. What if, at some point, we decide to change to the LinkedList implementation? Or some other implementation that might be available in the future? If we did this, then all references to the type of this object (such as in the method header of the previous section) would have to be modified to give the new class name.

There is an alternative approach. It is actually considered better programming practice to declare collection objects to be the type of the interface (List in this case) rather than the type of the class that implements this collection. So this would be a better way to create our printQ object:

```
// the type is given as 'List' not 'ArrayList'
List<String> printQ = new ArrayList<String>();
```

Notice that the interface type still needs to be marked as being a list of `String` objects using the generics mechanism. A method that receives a `printQ` object would now be declared as follows:

```
// this method receives a List<String> object
public void someMethod (List<String> printQIn)
{
  // some code here
}
```

The advantage of this approach is that we can change our choice of implementation in the future (maybe by using `LinkedList` or some other class that might be available that implements the `List` interface), without having to change the type of the object (which will always remain as `List`). This is the approach that we will take.

Now, let us look at some `List` methods.

15.2.3 *List* methods

The `List` interface defines two `add` methods for inserting into a list, one that inserts the item at the end of the list and one that inserts the item at a specified position in the list. Like arrays, `ArrayList` positions begin at zero. We wish to use the `add` method that adds items to the end of the list as we are modelling a queue here. This `add` method requires one parameter, the object to be added into the list:

```
printQ.add("myLetter.doc");
printQ.add("myFoto.jpg");
printQ.add("results.xls");
printQ.add("chapter.doc");
```

Notice that, since we have marked this list as containing `String` objects only, an attempt to add an object of any other type will result in a compiler error:

```
// will not compile as 'printQ' can hold Strings only!
printQ.add(new Rectangle(10, 20));
```

All the Java collection types have a `toString` method defined, so we can display the entire list to the screen:

```
System.out.println(printQ); // implicitly calling the toString method
```

When the list is displayed, the values in the list are separated by commas and enclosed in square brackets. So this `println` instruction would display the following list:

```
[myLetter.doc, myFoto.jpg, results.xls, chapter.doc]
```

As you can see, the items in the list are kept in the order in which they were inserted using the `add` method above.

As we said earlier, the `add` method is overloaded to allow an item to be inserted into the list at a particular position. When the item is inserted into that position, the item previously at that particular position and all items behind it shuffle along by one place (that is, they have their indices incremented by one). This `add` method requires two parameters, the position into which the object should be inserted, and the object itself. For example, let's insert a high priority job at the front of the queue:

```
printQ.add(0, "importantMemo.doc"); // inserts into front of the queue
```

Notice that the index is provided first, then the object. The index must be a valid index within the current list or it may be the index of the back of the queue. An invalid index throws an unchecked `IndexOutOf-BoundsException`.

Displaying this list confirms that the given job ("`importantMemo.doc`") has been added to the front of the queue, and all other items shuffled by one place:

[importantMemo.doc, myLetter.doc, myFoto.jpg, results.xls, chapter.doc]

If we wish to overwrite an item in the list, rather than insert a new item into the list, we can use the `set` method. The `set` method requires two parameters, the index of the item being overwritten and the new object to be inserted at that position. Let us change the name of the last job from "`chapter.doc`" to "`newChapter.doc`". This is the fifth item in the list so its index is 4:

```
printQ.set(4, "newChapter.doc");
```

If the index used in the `set` method is invalid, an `IndexOutOfBoundsException` is thrown once again. Displaying the new list now gives us the following:

[importantMemo.doc, myLetter.doc, myFoto.jpg, results.xls, newChapter.doc]

Lists provide a `size` method to return the number of items in the list, so we could have renamed the last job in the queue in the following way also:

```
printQ.set(printQ.size()-1, "newChapter.doc"); // last position is size-1
```

The `indexOf` method returns the index of the first occurrence of a given object within the list. It returns 1 if the object is not in the list. For example, the following checks the index position of the job "`myFoto.jpg`" in the list:

```
int index = printQ.indexOf("myFoto.jpg"); // check index of job
if (index != -1) // check object is in list
{
   System.out.println("myFoto.jpg is at index position: " +  index);
}
else // when job is not in list
{
   System.out.println("myFoto.jpg not in list");
}
```

This would display the following from our list:

myFoto.jpg is at index position: 2

Items can be removed either by specifying an index or an object. When an item is removed, items behind this item shuffle to the left (i.e. they have their indices decremented by one). As an example, let us remove the "myFoto.jpg" job. If we used its index, the following is required:

```
printQ.remove(2);
```

Once again, an `IndexOutOfBoundsException` would be thrown if this was not a valid index. This method returns the object that has been removed, which could be checked if necessary. Displaying the list would confirm the item has indeed been removed:

[importantMemo.doc, myLetter.doc, results.xls, newChapter.doc]

Alternatively, we could have removed the item by referring to it directly rather than by its index:[2]

```
printQ.remove("myFoto.jpg");
```

This method returns a **boolean** value to confirm that the item was in the list initially, which again could be checked if necessary.

Do you remember, from chapter 8, the complicated procedure for removing an item from an array? With a `List` we just use the `remove` method.

Behind the scenes you can guess how this `remove` method works. It looks in the list for the given `String` object ("myFoto.jpg"). It uses the `equals` method of the `String` class to identify a match. Once it finds such a match it shuffles items along in much the same way as our `remove` method from chapter 8.

Of course, as we have already said, these collection classes can be used to store objects of *any* type – not just `Strings`. For methods like `remove` to work properly, the contained object must have a properly defined `equals` method. We will return to this later in the chapter, when we look at how to use objects of our own classes in conjunction with the classes in the JCF.

The `get` method allows a particular item to be retrieved from the list via its index position. The following displays the job at the head of the queue:

```
// the first item is at position 0
System.out.println("First job is " + printQ.get(0));
```

This would display the following:

First job is importantMemo.doc

---

[2] If there were more than one occurrence of the object, the first occurrence would be deleted.

The `contains` method can be used to check whether or not a particular item is present in the list:

```
if (printQ.contains("poem.doc")) // check if value is in list
{
  System.out.println("poem.doc is in the list");
}
else
{
  System.out.println("poem.doc is not in the list");
}
```

Finally, the `isEmpty` method reports on whether or not the list contains any items:

```
if (printQ.isEmpty()) // returns true when list is empty
{
  System.out.println("Print queue is empty");
}
else
{
  System.out.println("Print queue is not empty");
}
```

15.3 Using the enhanced classes

In chapter 6 we showed you how the enhanced **for** loop can be used to iterate through an entire array. The use of this loop is not restricted to arrays, it can also be used with the List (and Set) implementations provided in the JCF. For example, here an enhanced **for** loop is used to iterate through the printQ list to find and display those jobs that end with a ".doc" extension:

```
for (String item: printQ) // iterate through all items in the printQ'list
{
  if(item.endsWith(".doc")) // check extension of the job ID
  {
    System.out.println(item); // display this item
  }
}
```

Notice that the type of each item in the printQ list is String. Within the loop we use the String method endsWith to check if the given job ID ends with the String ".doc". Assuming we had the following printQ:

[importantMemo.doc, myLetter.doc, results.xls, newChapter.doc]

424 Java in Two Semesters

the enhanced **for** loop above would produce the following output:

importantMemo.doc

myLetter.doc

newChapter.doc

If we do not wish to iterate through the *entire* list, or if we wish to *modify* the items within a list as we iterate through them, then (as we have said before) the enhanced **for** loop should not be used.

For example, if we wished to display the items in the printQ that are behind the head of the queue, the enhanced **for** loop is not appropriate as we are not processing the *entire* printQ. Instead the following standard **for** loop could be used:

```
// remember second item in list is at index 1!
for (int pos = 1; pos < printQ.size(); pos++)
{
    System.out.println(printQ.get(pos)); // retrieve item in printQ
}
```

Notice how the size method is used to determine the last index in the loop header. Within the loop, the get method is used to look up an item at the given index.

Again, if we assume we have the following printQ:

[importantMemo.doc, myLetter.doc, results.xls, newChapter.doc]

the **for** loop above would produce the following output:

myLetter.doc

results.xls

newChapter.doc

15.4 The *Set* interface and the *HashSet* class

The Set interface defines the methods required to process a collection of objects in which there is no repetition, and ordering is unimportant. Let's consider the following collections and consider if they are suitable for a set:

- a queue of people waiting to see a doctor;
- a list of number one records for each of the 52 weeks of a particular year;
- car registration numbers allocated parking permits.

The queue of people waiting to see a doctor cannot be considered to be a set as ordering is important here. Order may also be important when recording the list of number one records in a year. It would also be necessary to allow for repetition – as a record may be number one for more than one week. So a set is not a good choice for this collection. The collection of car registration numbers can be considered a set, however, as there will be no duplicates and ordering is unimportant.

Java provides three implementations of this `Set` interface: `HashSet`, `TreeSet` and `LinkedHashSet`. Here we will look at the `HashSet` class. The constructor creates an empty set. We will use the set to store a collection of vehicle registration numbers (as `Strings`):

```
// creates an empty set of String objects
Set<String> regNums = new HashSet<String>();
```

Again, notice that we have used the generics mechanism to indicate that this is a set of `String` objects, and we have given the type of this object as the interface `Set<String>`. Now let us look at some `Set` methods.

15.4.1 *Set* methods

Once a set is created the methods specified in the `Set` interface can be used. The `add` method allows us to insert objects into the set, so let us add a few registration numbers:

```
regNums.add("V53PLS");
regNums.add("X85ADZ");
regNums.add("L22SBG");
regNums.add("W79TRV");
```

We can display the entire set as follows:

```
System.out.println(regNums); // implicitly calling the toString method
```

The set is displayed in the same format as a list, in square brackets and separated by commas:

```
[W79TRV, X85ADZ, V53PLS, L22SBG]
```

Notice that, unlike lists, the order in which the items are displayed is not determined by the order in which the items were added. Instead, the set is displayed in the order in which the items are stored internally (and over which we have no control). This will not be a problem as ordering is unimportant in a set:

As with a list, the `size` method returns the number of items in the set:

```
System.out.println("Number of items in set: " + regNums.size() );
```

This would `print` the following onto the screen:

```
Number of items in set: 4
```

If we try to add an item that is already in the set, the set remains unchanged. Let us assume the four items above have been added into the set and we now try and add a registration number that is already in the set:

```
regNums.add("X85ADZ"); // this number is already in the set
System.out.println(regNums);
```

When this set is displayed, "X85ADZ" appears only once:

```
[W79TRV, X85ADZ, V53PLS, L22SBG]
```

The add method returns a **boolean** value to indicate whether or not the given item was successfully added. This value can be checked if required.

The remove method deletes an item from the set if it is present. Again, assuming that the four items given above are in the set, we can delete one item as follows:

```
boolean ok = regNums.add("X85ADZ"); // store boolean return value
if (!ok) //check if add method returned a value of false
{
  System.out.println("item already in the set!");
}
regNums.remove("X85ADZ");
```

If we now display the set, the given registration will have been removed:

```
[W79TRV, V53PLS, L22SBG]
```

As with the add method, the remove method returns a **boolean** value of **false** if the given item to remove was not actually in the set.

The Set interface also includes contains and isEmpty methods that work in exactly the same way as their List counterparts.

15.4.2 Iterating through the elements of a set

The enhanced **for** loop can be used to iterate through all the elements of a set. Let us look at an example.

In the UK the first letter of the registration number was at one time used to determine the time period when the vehicle came to market. A registration beginning with 'S', for example, denoted a vehicle that came to market between August 1998 and February 1999, while a registration beginning with 'T' denoted a vehicle that came to market between March 1999 and August 1999. The following enhanced **for** loop will allow us to iterate through the collection of registration numbers and display all registrations after 'T'.

```
for (String item: regNums) // iterate through all items in 'regNums'
{
  if (item.charAt(0) > 'T') // check first letter of registration
  {
    System.out.println(item); // display this registration
  }
}
```

Again, notice that the type of every element within our regNums set is String. Within the loop we use the String method charAt to check the first letter of registration. Assuming we have the following set of registration numbers:

```
[W79TRV, V53PLS, L22SBG]
```

the enhanced **for** loop above would produce the following result:

    W79TRV

    V53PLS

Let us consider a slightly different scenario now. Instead of simply displaying registration numbers after 'T', we now wish to modify the original `regNums` set so that registrations prior or equal to 'T' are removed. We could try using an enhanced **for** loop again:

```
// this will compile but is not safe!
for (String item: regNums) // iterate through all items in 'regNums'
{
  if (item.charAt(0) <= 'T') // check first letter of registration
  {
    regNums.remove(item); // remove this registration
  }
}
```

Here we are once again iterating over the elements of the `regNums` set. But this time, within the loop, we are attempting to *remove* the given element from the set. As we said in chapter 6, enhanced **for** loops should *not* be used to modify or remove elements from the original collection. To do so would not give a compiler error but it may cause your program to behave unpredictably. If we cannot use an enhanced **for** loop here, how else can we iterate over the elements in a set? Unlike an array, values in the set cannot be retrieved by an index value. Instead, to access the items in a set, the `iterator` method can be used to obtain an **iterator** object.

15.4.3 *Iterator* objects

An `Iterator` object allows the items in a collection to be retrieved by providing three methods defined in the `Iterator` interface (see table 15.1).

Method	Description	Inputs	Outputs
hasNext	Returns **true** if there are more elements in the collection to retrieve and **false** otherwise.	None	An item of type **boolean**.
next	Retrieves one element from the collection.	None	An item of the given element type.
remove	Removes from the collection	None	None the element that is currently retrieved.

TABLE 15.1 Methods of the *Iterator* interface

To obtain an `Iterator` object from the `regNums` set, the `iterator` method could be called as follows:

```
// the 'iterator' method retrieves an Iterator object from a set
Iterator<String> elements = regNums.iterator();
```

Here we have called the iterator method and stored the item returned by this method in a variable we have called `elements`. The generics mechanism has been used here to indicate that the `Iterator` object will be used to iterate over `String` objects only.[3]

```
Iterator<String> elements = regNums.iterator();
```

Once an `Iterator` object has been created, a **while** loop can be used to iterate through the collection, with the `hasNext` method the test of the loop. The body of the loop can then retrieve items with the `next` method and, if required, delete items with the `remove` method. Let us see how this would work with the `regNums` set.

```
/* an Iterator object can be used with a 'while' loop if we wish to iterate over a set and
    modify its contents */

// first create an Iterator object as discussed before
Iterator<String> elements = regNums.iterator();
// repeatedly retrieve items as long as there are items to be retrieved
while (elements.hasNext())
{
  String item = elements.next(); // retrieve next element from set
  if (item.charAt(0) <= 'T') // check first letter of registration
  {
    elements.remove(); // call Iterator method to remove registration
  }
}
```

Within the loop we call the `next` method of our `Iterator` object to retrieve the `next` item within the collection. Since we have specified the `Iterator` object to retrieve `String` objects, we know that this method will return a `String`. We have stored this `String` object in a variable we have called `item`:

```
// the String returned from the Iterator object is stored in a variable
String item = elements.next();
```

It is always a good idea to store the object returned by the `next` method in a variable, as the `next` method should be called only *once* within the loop. Storing the result in a variable allows us to refer to this object as many times as we like. In this case we refer to the object only once, in the test of the **if** statement:

```
if (item.charAt(0)<= 'T') // check the first character in this String
```

---

[3] If the type had been given simply as `Iterator`, instead of `Iterator<String>`, the elements in the collection would be treated by the iterator object to be of the generic `Object` type, rather than the specific `String` type.

If the registration number needs to be removed from the set, we may do so now safely – by calling the remove method of our `Iterator` object:

```
elements.remove(); // call Iterator method to remove current item
```

15.5 The *Map* interface and the *HashMap* class

The `Map` interface defines the methods required to process a collection consisting of *pairs* of objects. Rather than looking up an item via an index value, the first object of the pair is used. The first object in the pair is considered a **key**, and the second its associated **value**. Ordering is unimportant in maps, and keys are unique.

It is often useful to think of a map as a *look-up* table, with the key object the item used to look up (access) an associated value in the table. For example, the password of users of a network can be looked up by entering their username. Table 15.2 gives an example of such a look-up table.

Username	Password
lauraHaliwell	monkey
sarahThorsteinson	jasmine
bobbyMann	elephant
lucyLane	monkey
bernardAnderson	velvet

TABLE 15.2 A look-up table for users of a network

We can look up the password of a user by looking up their user name in table 15.2. The password of *lauraHaliwell*, for example, is *monkey*, whereas the password of *bobbyMann* is *elephant*. Notice that it is important we make usernames the key of the look-up table and *not* passwords. This is because usernames are unique – no two users can have the same username. However, passwords are not unique. Two or more users may have the same password. Indeed, in table 15.2, two users (*lauraHaliwell* and *lucyLane*) do have the same password (*monkey*).

Let us implement this kind of look-up table using a `Map`. As with the previous interfaces, there are three implementations provided for the `Map` interface: `HashMap`, `TreeMap` and `LinkedHashMap`. Here we will look at the `HashMap` class. The constructor creates the empty map:

```
Map<String, String> users = new HashMap<String, String>();
```

As before, the type of the collection is given as the interface: `Map`. Notice that to use the generics mechanism to fix the types used in a `Map` object, we must provide *two* types in the angled brackets. The first type will be the type of the key and the second the type of its associated value. In this case, *both* are `String` objects, but in general each may be of any object type.

To add a user's name and password to this map we use the `put` method as follows. The `put` method requires two parameters, the key object and the value object:

```
users.put("lauraHaliwell", "popcorn");
```

Note that the `put` method treats the first parameter as a key item and the second parameter as its associated value. Really, we should be a bit more careful before we add user IDs and passwords into this map – only user IDs that are not already taken should be added. If we did not check this, we would end up overwriting a previous user's password. The `containsKey` method allows us to check this. This method accepts an object and returns **true** if the object is a key in the map and **false** otherwise:

```
if (users.containsKey("lauraHaliwell")) // check if ID taken
{
  System.out.println("user ID already taken");
}
else // ok to use this ID
{
  users.put("lauraHaliwell", "popcorn");
}
```

Notice we do not need to check that the password is unique as multiple users can have the same password. If we did require unique passwords, the `containsValue` method could be used in the same way we used the `containsKey` method above.

Later a user might wish to change his or her password. The `put` method overrides the value associated with a key if that key is already present in the map. The following changes the password associated with "`lauraHaliwell`" to "`popcorn`":

```
users.put("lauraHaliwell", "popcorn");
```

The `put` method returns the value that was overwritten, or **null** if there was no value before, and this can be checked if necessary.

Later, a user might be asked to enter his or her ID and password before being able to access company resources. The `get` method can be used to check whether or not the correct password has been entered. The `get` method accepts an object and searches for that object among the keys of the map. If it is found, the associated value object is returned. If it is not found, the **null** value is returned:

```
System.out.print("enter user ID ");
String idIn = EasyScanner.nextString(); // requires EasyScanner class
System.out.print("enter password ");
String passwordIn = EasyScanner.nextString(); // requires EasyScanner class
// retrieve the actual password for this user
String password = users.get(idIn);
// password will be 'null' if the user name was invalid
```

```
if (password != null)
{
  if ( passwordIn.equals(password))// check password is correct
  {
    // allow access to company resources here
  }
  else // invalid password
  {
    System.out.println ("INVALID PASSWORD!");
  }
}
else // no such user
{
  System.out.println ("INVALID USERNAME!");
}
```

As you can see, once the user has entered what they believe to be their username and password, the actual password for the given user is retrieved using the `get` method.

We know the password retrieved will be of type `String` as we created our `Map` by specifying that both the keys and values of the `Map` object would be `Strings`. We can then check whether this password equals the password entered by calling the `equals` method of the `String` class:

```
if ( passwordIn.equals(password))
```

We have to be careful when we use the `equals` method to compare two objects in the way that we have done here. In this case, we are comparing the password entered by the user with the password obtained by the `get` method. However, the `get` method might have returned a **null** value instead of a password (if the key entered was invalid). The `equals` method of the `String` class does not return **false** when comparing a `String` with a **null** value; instead, it throws a `NullPointerException`. So, to avoid this exception, we must check that the value returned by the `get` method is not **null** *before* we use the `equals` method:

```
// check password returned is not 'null' before calling 'equals' method
if (password!= null)
{
  if ( passwordIn.equals(password))// now it is safe to call 'equals'
  {
    // allow access to company resources
  }
  else
  {
    System.out.println ("INVALID PASSWORD!")
  }
}
```

Note that the **null** value is always checked with primitive comparison operators (== for equality and != for inequality).

Like all the other Java collection classes, the HashMap class provides a toString method so that the items in the map can be displayed:

```
System.out.print(users); // implicitly calls 'toString' method
```

Key and value pairs are displayed in braces. Let us assume we have added two more users: "bobbyMann" and "sarahThorsteinson", with passwords "elephant" and "jasmine" respectively. Displaying the map would produce the following output:

{lauraHaliwell=popcorn, sarahThorsteinson=jasmine, bobbyMann=elephant}

As with a set, the order in which the items are displayed is not determined by the order in which they were added but upon how they have been stored internally.

In order to scan the items in the map, the keySet method can be used to return the set of keys.

```
// the keySet method returns the keys of the map as a set object
Set<String> theKeys = users.keySet();
```

Again, notice that we know this set of keys returned by the keySet method will be a set of String objects, so we mark the type of this set accordingly.

The set of keys can then be processed in the ways discussed in section 15.2: using either an enhanced **for** loop or by making use of the iterator method of sets.

For example, we might wish to display the contents of the map in our own way, rather than the format given to us by the toString method. An enhanced **for** loop can be used to iterate through the keys of the map; within the loop we can look up the associated password using the get method:

```
for(String item: theKeys)// iterate through the set of keys
{
  String password = users.get(item); // retrieve password value
  System.out.println(item + "\t" + password); // format output
}
```

This would display the map in the following table format:

lauraHaliwell	*popcorn*
sarahThorsteinson	*jasmine*
bobbyMann	*elephant*

As with the other collections, a map provides a remove method. In the case of map, a key value is given to the method. If the key is present in the map both the key and value pair are removed:

```
// this removes the given key and its associated value
users.remove("lauraHaliwell");
```

Displaying the map now shows the user's ID and password have been removed:

{sarahThorsteinson=jasmine, bobbyMann=elephant}

The remove method returns the value of the object that has been removed, or **null** if the key was not present. This value can be checked if necessary to confirm that the given key was in the map.

Finally, the map collection provides size and isEmpty methods that behave in exactly the same way as the size and isEmpty methods for sets and lists.

15.6 Using your own classes with Java's collection classes

In the examples above, we stuck to the pre-defined String type for the type of objects used in the collection classes of Java. However, objects of any class can be used inside these collections – including objects of your own classes. Care needs to be taken, however, when using your own classes. As an example, let us consider an application to store a collection of books that a person may own. Figure 15.1 gives the UML design for a Book class.

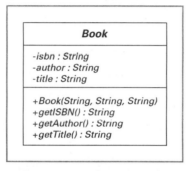

FIGURE 15.1 Initial design of the *Book* class

This class consists of an ISBN number, an author and a title. An ISBN number is a unique International Standard Book Number that is allocated to each new book title. Before we deal with a *collection* of books, here is the initial implementation of the Book class.

The *Book* class

```
public class Book
{
  private String isbn;
  private String title;
  private String author;

  public Book(String isbnIn, String titleIn, String authorIn)
  {
    isbn = isbnIn;
    title = titleIn;
```

```
    author = authorIn;
  }

  public String getISBN()
  {
    return isbn;
  }

  public String getTitle()
  {
    return title;
  }

  public String getAuthor()
  {
    return author;
  }
}
```

There is nothing new here so let's move on to see how objects of this class can be stored in the Java collection classes. To begin with, let's create a list to contain Book objects:

```
// create empty list to contain Book objects
List<Book> books = new ArrayList<Book>();
```

You can see that to indicate this list will hold Book objects, the Book type is given in angled brackets. Now let's add some book objects and display the list:

```
// create two Book objects
Book b1 = new Book("0123234521", "G Costanza", "Where's the luck?");
Book b2 = new Book("0823477542", "J Marr", "Half Empty");
// add Book objects to list
books.add(b1);
books.add(b2);
System.out.println(books); // implicitly call toString method of List
```

As things stand, this will display the following list on the screen:

```
[Book@6800d6e5, Book@681cd6e5]
```

This isn't exactly what we require! When Java collections are displayed on the screen by calling their toString method, each object in the collection is displayed by calling its own toString method. As we explained in chapter 11, this will call the default toString method inherited from the Object class, and all this does is display information on the memory address of the object.

If you wish to use objects of your own classes as objects in Java's `toString` method of the collection class, a meaningful `toString` method should be defined in your class.

Here is one possible `toString` method we could provide for our `Book` class:

```
public String toString()
{
  return "(" + isbn +", "+ author + ", " + title +")\n";
}
```

We create a single `String` by joining the ISBN, author and title `Strings`. To improve the look of this `String` we have separated the attributes by commas and have enclosed it in round brackets, plus we have added a new-line character at the end. Now if we print out the list we get the following:

```
[(0123234521, G Costanza, Where's the luck?) ,
(0823477542, J Marr, Half Empty)]
```

While you might wish to improve this `String` representation of a book further (maybe by adding more formatting), this is acceptable for testing purposes.

15.6.1 Defining an *equals* method

Another issue arises if we wish to use methods such as `contains` and `remove`. Methods such as these call the `equals` method of the contained object to determine whether or not a given object is in the collection. The `Book` class does not define its own `equals` method so again the inherited `equals` method of the `Object` class is called. This method is inadequate as it simply compares the memory address of two objects rather than the attributes of two objects. For example, the following would display **false** on the screen when we would want it to display **true**:

```
// check a book that is in the list
boolean check = books.contains(new Book("0823477542", "J Marr", "Half Empty"));
// display result
System.out.println(check);
```

To use objects of your own classes effectively, a meaningful `equals` method should be defined. One possible interpretation of two books being equal is simply that their ISBNs are equal, so the following `equals` method could be added to the `Book` class:

```
public boolean equals (Object objIn) // equals method must have this header
{
  Book bookIn = (Book) objIn; // type cast to a Book
  // check isbn
  return isbn.equals(bookIn.isbn);
}
```

Notice that the `equals` method must accept an item of type `Object`. The body of the method then needs to type cast this item back to the required type (`Book` in this case).

If you are using lists, these are the only two additional methods you need to provide in your class. Also, if you are using objects of your own classes only as *values* of a map, then again these are the only two additional methods you need to provide. If, however, you are using objects of your classes as keys of a map or as the items of a set, then you need to include an additional method in your classes: hashCode.

15.6.2 Defining a *hashCode* method

To understand how to define your own hashCode method you need to understand how the HashSet and HashMap implementations work. Both of these Java classes have been implemented using an array. Unlike the ArrayList class, however, (which has also been implemented using an array), the position of the items in the HashSet and HashMap arrays is not determined by the order in which they were added. Instead, the position into which items are added into these arrays is determined by their hashCode method.

The hashCode method returns an integer value from an object. This integer value determines where in the array the given object is stored. Objects that are equal (as determined by the equals method) should produce identical hashCode numbers and, ideally, objects that are not equal should return different hashCode numbers.

The reason for using hashCode numbers is that they considerably reduce the time it takes to search a given array for a given item. If items were stored consecutively, then a search of the array would require *every* item in the array being checked using the equals method, until a match was found. This would become very inefficient when the collection becomes very large. So, instead, the HashSet and HashMap classes make use of the hashCode method, so that when a search is required for an item, say x, that hashCode number is computed and this value is used to look up other items in the array. Then, only objects with the same hashCode number are compared to x using their equals method.

If you are using objects of your own classes, and you have not provided a hashCode method, the inherited hashCode method from the Object class is called. This does not behave in the way we would wish. It generates the hashCode number from the memory address of the object, so two "equal" objects could have different hashCode values. Program 15.1 demonstrates this.

PROGRAM 15.1

```
public class TestHashCode
{
  public static void main (String[] args)
  {
    // create two "equal" books
    Book book1 = new Book("0823477542", "J Marr", "Half Empty");
    Book book2 = new Book("0823477542", "J Marr", "Half Empty");
    // check their hashCode numbers
    System.out.println(book1.hashCode());
    System.out.println(book2.hashCode());
  }
}
```

This would produce the following hashCode numbers for the two "equal" books:

1745955844

1748315140

As you can see, the hashCode numbers do not match – even though the objects are "equal". This means that if we were searching for the given book in a HashSet or in the keys of a HashMap, the book would not be found, as only objects with identical hashCode values are checked. Also, we cannot ensure that objects in the HashSet or the keys of the HashMap will be unique, as two (or more) identical books (with different hashCode values) would both be stored in the underlying array at different array positions.

We need to define our own hashCode method for the Book class so that objects of this class can be used effectively with the HashSet and HashMap classes.

Luckily, all of Java's pre-defined classes (such as String) have a meaningful hashCode method defined. These hashCode methods return equal hashCode numbers for "equal" objects.

So one way of defining the hashCode number for an object of your class would be to add together the hashCode numbers generated by all the attributes to determine object equality. For Book equality we checked the ISBN only. This ISBN is a String, so all we need to do is to return the hashCode number of this String:

```
// this is a suitable hashCode method for our Book class
public int hashCode()
{
  // derive hash code by returning hash code of ISBN string
  return isbn.hashCode();
}
```

If you have more than one attribute that plays a role in determining object equality, then add each such hashCode number (assuming the attribute is not of primitive type) to determine your hashCode number.

If primitive attributes also play a part in object equality, they too can simply be added into your hash-Code formula by generating an integer value from each primitive attribute. Here is a simple set of guidelines for generating an integer value from the primitive types (although much more sophisticated algorithms exist than these!):

- **byte, short, int, long**: leave as they are;
- **float, double**: type cast to an integer;
- **char:** use its Unicode value;
- **boolean**: use an **if…else** statement to allocate 1 if the attribute is **true** and 0 if it is **false**.

15.7 Developing a collection class for *Book* objects

In the previous section we amended the Book class by supplying it with a toString method, an equals method and a hashCode method. If you look at the documentation of any class in the Java API you will see that it also possess these three methods. When developing classes professionally you should always include these methods. That way, objects of these classes can be used with any collection type.

Now we have a suitable Book class, we can store objects of this class in one of the Java collection classes. Which collection shall we use? There is no ordering required on the collection of books so we do not really need a list here. We could store these books in a set, but since each book has a unique ISBN it makes more sense to use a map and have ISBNs as the keys to the map, with Book objects themselves as the values of the map.

We will use this collection to help us develop our own class, `Library`, which keeps track of the books that a person may own. Figure 15.2 gives its UML design.

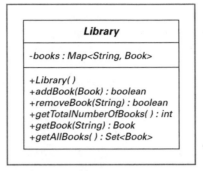

FIGURE 15.2 UML design for the *Library* class

Notice that the keys of the map are specified to be `String` objects (to represent ISBNs), and the values of the map are specified as `Book` objects.

Here is the implementation of the `Library` class. Take a look at it and then we will discuss it.

The *Library* class

```java
import java.util.*;
public class Library
{
  Map <String, Book> books; // declare map collection
  // create empty map
  public Library()
  {
    books = new HashMap<String, Book>();
  }


  // add the given book into the collection
  public boolean addBook(Book bookIn)
  {
    String keyIn = bookIn.getISBN(); // isbn will be key of map
    if (books.containsKey(keyIn)) // check if isbn already in use
    {
      return false; // indicate error
    }
    else // ok to add this book
    {
      books.put(keyIn, bookIn); // add key and book pair into map
      return true;
```

```java
    }
  }


  // remove the book with the given isbn
  public boolean removeBook(String isbnIn)
  {
    if (books.remove(isbnIn) != null) // check if item was removed
    {
      return true;
    }
    else // when item is not removed
    {
      return false;
    }
  }


  // return the number of books in the collection
  public int getTotalNumberOfBooks()
  {
    return books.size();
  }


  // return the book with the given isbn or null if no such book
  public Book getBook (String isbnIn)
  {
    return books.get(isbnIn);
  }


  // return the set of books in the collection
  public Set<Book> getAllBooks ()
  {
    Set<Book> bookSet = new HashSet<Book>(); // to store the set of books
    Set<String> theKeys = books.keySet(); // get the set of keys
    // iterate through the keys and put each value in the bookSet
    for (String isbn : theKeys)
    {
      Book theBook = books.get(isbn);
      bookSet.add(theBook);
    }
    return bookSet; // return the set of books
  }
}
```

Most of this class should be self-explanatory. Just consider how complicated some of these methods would have been if we had used an array instead of a map!

We just draw your attention to the `getAllBooks` method. The UML diagram indicates that this method should return a *set* of books. An alternative approach could have been to return the map itself, but it would be more useful for this method to return a set of objects, as a set is easier to scan than a map. It is fine to use a set as there is no repetition of books.

```
public Set<Book> getAllBooks ()
{
  // code to create this set goes here
}
```

There is no map method that returns the set of *values* in the map, so a suitable set needs to be created in this method:

```
Set<Book> bookSet = new HashSet<Book>();
```

This set is empty initially and we must fill it with book objects. In order to access these values we use the `keySet` method, which returns the set of keys. Remember the keys are `String` objects:

```
Set<String> theKeys = books.keySet();
```

An enhanced **for** loop can now be used to iterate over these ISBNs:

```
for (String isbn : theKeys)
{
  Book theBook = books.get(isbn);
  bookSet.add(theBook);
}
```

You can see that the ISBN number is used to retrieve the associated `Book` object by calling the `get` method of maps. The given book is then added to the set of books.

Finally, after this loop is complete and the set of books has been created, we can return this set from the method:

```
return bookSet;
```

That completes our discussion of the `Library` class. We leave the task of creating a tester for this class to the end of chapter exercises.

Self-test questions

1 Distinguish between the following types of collection in the Java Collections Framework:

   ■ `List`;
   ■ `Set`;
   ■ `Map`.

2 Identify, with reasons, the most appropriate Java collection type to implement the following collections:

   a an ordered collection of patient names waiting for a doctor;

   b an unordered collection of patient names registered to a doctor;

   c an unordered collection of `Employee` objects.

3 Consider the following instruction:

```
Map <String, Student> javaStudents = new HashMap<String, Student>();
```

   a Why is the type of this object given as `Map` and not `HashMap`?

   b What is the purpose of the stuff in angled brackets?

   c Assuming the object `javaStudents` has been created as above, why would the following line cause a compiler error?

```
javaStudents.put("U0012345", "Jeet");
```

4 Consider again the `StockItem` class from programming exercise 3 of chapter 8. Here is the UML diagram:

StockItem
-stockNumber : String
-name : String
-price : double
-totalStock : int
+StockItem(String, String, double)
+setPrice(double)
+increaseTotalStock(int)
+getStockNumber() : String
+getName() : String
+getTotalStock() : int
+getPrice() : double
+calculateTotalPrice() : double

   a Define an appropriate `toString` method for this class.

   b Define an appropriate `equals` method for this class.

   c Define an appropriate `hashCode` method for this class.

5 In section 15.4 a set called `regNums` was created to store a collection of car registration numbers. Write a fragment of code, which makes use of the `iterator` method, to remove all registration numbers ending in 'S'.

6 In chapter 8 we introduced a `BankAccount` class and a collection class to hold bank accounts called `Bank`. The `Bank` class was implemented using an array.

    a Which of Java's collection classes could be used to a implement the `Bank` class?

    b What modifications would be need to be made to the `BankAccount` class before objects of this class could be used in the collection type identified in part (a) of this question?

Programming exercises

1 Copy, from the accompanying CD, the `Book` and `Library` classes and then implement a tester for the `Library` class.

2 In this chapter we looked at an example of a printer queue. A *queue* is a collection where the first item added into the queue is the first item removed from the queue. Consequently, a queue is often referred to as a *first in first out* (FIFO) collection.

A *stack*, on the other hand, is a *last in first out* (LIFO) collection – much like a stack of plates, where the last plate added to the stack is the first plate removed from the stack. The method to add an item onto a stack is often called *push*. The method to remove an item from a stack is often called *pop*.

Below, we give the UML design for a `NameStack` class, which stores a stack of names.

NameStack
-stack : List<String>
+NameStack( ) +push(String) +pop( ) : String +size( ) : int +isEmpty( ) : boolean +toString( ) : String

A description of each `NameStack` method is given below:

`NameStack()`
Initializes the stack of names to be empty.

`push(String)`
Adds the given name onto the top of the stack.

`pop() : String`
Removes and returns the name at the top of the stack. Throws a `NameStackException` (which will also need to be implemented) if an attempt is made to pop an item from an empty stack.

▶ `size() : int`
Returns the number of names in the stack.

`isEmpty() : boolean`
Returns **true** if the stack is empty and **false** otherwise.

`toString() : String`
Returns a `String` representation of the stack of names.

a Implement the `NameStack` class. You will also need to implement a `NameStackException` class.

b Test the `NameStack` class with a suitable tester.

3   Consider an application that keeps track of the registration numbers of all cars that have a permit to use a company car park. It also keeps track of the registration numbers of the cars actually in the car park at any one time. While there is no limit to the number of cars that can have permits to park in the car park, the capacity of the car park is limited. Below we give the UML design for the `CarRegister` class:

CarRegister
-permit : Set<String> -parked : Set<String> -capacity : int
+CarRegister(int) +givePermit(String) : boolean +recordParking(String) : boolean +recordExit(String) : boolean +isParked(String) : boolean +isFull() : boolean +numberParked() : int +getPermit() : Set<String> +getParked() : Set<String> +getCapacity() : int

A description of each `CarRegister` method is given below:

`CarRegister(int)`
Initializes the `permit` and `parked` sets to be empty and sets the capacity of the car park with the given parameter. Throws a `CarRegisterException` (which will also need to be implemented) if the given parameter is negative.

`givePermit(String) : boolean`
Records the registration of a car given a permit to park. Returns **false** if the car has already been given a permit and **true** otherwise.

`recordParking(String) : boolean`
Records the registration of a car entering the car park. Returns **false** if the car park is full, or the car has no permit to enter the car park, and **true** otherwise.

`recordExit(String) : boolean`
Records the registration of a car leaving the car park. Returns **false** if the car was not initially registered as being parked and **true** otherwise.

▶ `isParked(String) : boolean`
Returns **true** if the car with the given registration is recorded as being parked in the car park and **false** otherwise.

`isFull() : boolean`
Returns **true** if the car park is full and **false** otherwise.

`numberParked() : int`
Returns the number of cars currently in the car park.

`getPermit() : Set<String>`
Returns the set of car registrations allocated permits.

`getParked() : Set<String>`
Returns the set of registration numbers of cars in the car park.

`getCapacity() : int`
Returns the maximum capacity of the car park.

a Implement the `CarRegister` class. You will also need to implement a `CarRegister-Exception` class.

b Test the `CarRegister` class with a suitable tester.

4 a Make the changes to the `BankAccount` class that you identified in part (b) of self-test question 6 above.

b Rewrite the `Bank` class to make use of the collection type identified in part (a) of self-test question 6 above, rather than an array.

c Produce a tester for this `Bank` class based on the original tester from chapter 8.

CHAPTER 16

Advanced graphics programming

❖ OBJECTIVES

By the end of this chapter you should be able to:

❖ use a number of difference layout managers;

❖ create **pull-down** and **pop-up** menus;

❖ create **dialogue windows, radio buttons** and **combo boxes**;

❖ use the JFileChooser class to access the computer's file system;

❖ use a **slider** to alter a value.

16.1   Introduction

In chapter 10 you learnt how to make use of some of the basic components of the Swing package. In this chapter you are going to learn how to utilize many more of these components, so that you can add features like menus, dialogues and radio buttons to your graphical interfaces.

There is a wealth of classes available in the Swing package, and we will introduce you to some of these classes to show you what is available, and to familiarize you with some of their methods by way of some simple examples. For a full description of the classes available, we strongly recommend that you visit the excellent Sun website (www.java.sun.com) and look at the API (Application Programming Interface) specifications, where all the Java classes and their methods are comprehensively described.

16.2   More layout policies

In chapter 10 we introduced you to the two most common layout managers, FlowLayout and BorderLayout; Swing containers normally have one of these as their default policy. However, there are a number of other, more complex, layout policies available, which we are going to introduce you to in this section.

16.2.1 The `GridLayout` policy

A grid layout policy divides the container into a number of rows and columns. Components are then placed into each cell in the order that they are added, starting at the top left-hand corner, and filling the top row, then when that row, is full moving onto the next row.

Figure 16.1 shows a program in which a `JFrame` has been divided into three rows and four columns, with a `JButton` placed into each cell.

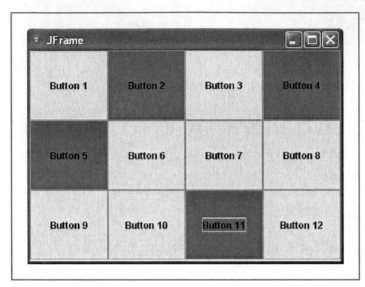

FIGURE 16.1 Buttons have been placed into all the cells of a `JFrame` with a `GridLayout` policy

The program has been designed so that all the buttons start off yellow, but each can be changed to red by clicking on the particular button. Clicking again will change it back to yellow.

Below is the class that we wrote to produce the `JFrame`. Take a look at it, then we will discuss it.

THE *GRIDLAYOUTEXAMPLE* CLASS

```java
import javax.swing.*;
import java.awt.*;
import java.awt.event.*;


public class GridLayoutExample extends JFrame implements ActionListener
{

  private JButton[] buttonArray = new JButton[12]; // declare an array of 12 JButtons


  public GridLayoutExample()
  {
    setLayout(new GridLayout(3, 4)); // set the layout policy to a GridLayout of 3 rows and 4 columns
```

```java
    setDefaultCloseOperation(JFrame.EXIT_ON_CLOSE);
    setTitle("JFrame");
    setSize(400, 300);
    setLocation(400, 300);

    for(int i = 0; i < buttonArray.length; i++)
    {
      buttonArray[i] = new JButton("Button" + (i+1)); // add a JButton into the array
      add(buttonArray[i]); // add the new JButton to the JFrame
      buttonArray[i].setBackground(Color.yellow); // set the colour of the JButton to yellow
      buttonArray[i].addActionListener(this); // add an actionListener to the button
    }
    setVisible(true);
  }


  public void actionPerformed(ActionEvent e)
  {
    for(int i = 0; i < buttonArray.length; i++)
    {
      if(e.getSource() == buttonArray[i]) /* check each button to see if it was
                                             the one pressed */
      {
        if(buttonArray[i].getBackground() == Color.yellow) // if the button is currently yellow
        {
          buttonArray[i].setBackground(Color.red); // set the colour of the button to red
        }
        else // if the button is not yellow
        {
          buttonArray[i].setBackground(Color.yellow); // set the colour to yellow
        }

        return; // there is no need to search the remaining buttons
      }
    }
  }

}
```

As you can see, the class has an attribute which is an array of 12 buttons:

```
private JButton[] buttonArray = new JButton[12];
```

It is perfectly possible to declare an array of graphical objects just as we can declare any other array, and this is a technique that you will find very useful in certain applications.

In the constructor we set the layout to a `GridLayout`:

```
setLayout(new GridLayout(3, 4));
```

The constructor accepts two integers representing the number of rows and columns respectively, so the above instruction produces the grid of three rows and four columns that you see in figure 16.1. Another constructor exists that accepts four integers, the last two representing, respectively, the horizontal and vertical gaps between columns.

After some lines that configure the window we use a **for** loop to add the buttons, set their initial colour to yellow with the `setBackround` method which is inherited by the `JButton` class, and add an `action-Listener` to each one:

```
for(int i = 0; i < buttonArray.length; i++)
{
  buttonArray[i] = new JButton("Button" + (i+1)); // add a JButton into the array
  add(buttonArray[i]); // add the new JButton to the JFrame
  buttonArray[i].setBackground(Color.yellow); // set the colour of the JButton to yellow
  buttonArray[i].addActionListener(this); // add an actionListioner to the button
}
```

We go round the loop 12 times, and on each iteration we add a new button, using the loop counter to give the buttons captions from *Button1* to *Button12*. Once the button is created it is added to the `JFrame`. As we have said, the `GridLayout` policy starts by placing the button in the top left cell, then continues along the row. When that row is filled the next row is started.

There is nothing very new in the `actionPerformed` method:

```
public void actionPerformed(ActionEvent e)
{
  for(int i = 0; i < buttonArray.length; i++)
  {
    if(e.getSource() == buttonArray[i]) // check each button to see if it was the one pressed
    {
      if(buttonArray[i].getBackground() == Color.yellow) // if the button is currently yellow
```

```
   {
     buttonArray[i].setBackground(Color.red); // set the colour of the button to red
   }
   else // if the button is not yellow
   {
     buttonArray[i].setBackground(Color.yellow); // set the colour to yellow
   }
   return; // there is no need to search the remaining buttons
  }
 }
}
```

It uses a **for** loop to check each button to see if it was clicked, then changes its colour. A **return** statement is used to terminate the method once the source of the click has been determined, and the necessary action taken – there is no need to continue to the end of the loop.

To display the graphic all you need to do is to write a program such as program 16.1 that creates an object of the class:

PROGRAM 16.1

```
public class RunGridLayoutExample
{
  public static void main(String[] args)
  {
    new GridLayoutExample();
  }
}
```

16.2.2 The `CardLayout` policy

Another very useful layout manager is CardLayout. The components in a container that implements a CardLayout policy are arranged like cards in a pack. The CardLayout class provides five methods that allow you to display each "card" in turn – these are first, next, previous, last and random. There is also a show method, which allows you to display a particular card by reference to a unique string assigned when the cards are added to a container (normally a JPanel). This layout policy is particularly useful when you want to break up a screen into different sections, so that the sections can be shown one at a time. The example that follows (figure 16.2) provides a possible start-up screen for a game – the screen is divided into three "cards" that allow players to choose their level, then the character they want to be, and finally the imaginary location for the game scenario. Buttons on either side allow the user to go back to a previous screen or to continue.

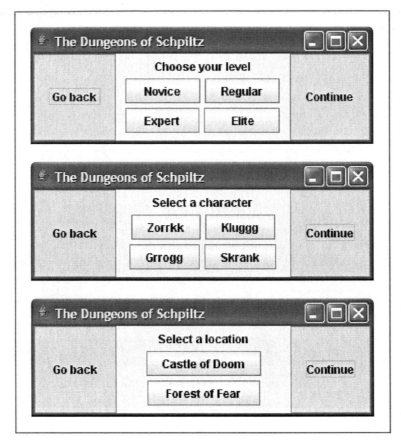

FIGURE 16.2 An example of the *CardLayout* manager, showing three different screens

The code for this class is shown below (only the "Go back" and "Continue" buttons have been made functional):

THE *CARDLAYOUTEXAMPLE* CLASS

```java
import javax.swing.*;
import java.awt.*;
import java.awt.event.*;


public class CardLayoutExample extends JFrame implements ActionListener
{
  // create a CardLayout object
  private CardLayout cardLayout = new CardLayout();


  // create a panel to hold the cards
  private JPanel centrePanel = new JPanel();
```

```java
// create the buttons for selecting the next and previous cards
private JButton nextButton = new JButton("Continue");
private JButton previousButton = new JButton(" Go back ");

// create the cards
private JPanel firstCard = new JPanel();
private JPanel secondCard = new JPanel();
private JPanel thirdCard = new JPanel();

// the constructor
public CardLayoutExample()
{
  // add labels and buttons to the cards
  firstCard.add(new JLabel("Choose your level"));
  firstCard.add(new JButton(" Novice "));
  firstCard.add(new JButton("Regular"));
  firstCard.add(new JButton(" Expert "));
  firstCard.add(new JButton("    Elite    "));
  secondCard.add(new JLabel("Select a character"));
  secondCard.add(new JButton("Zorrkk"));
  secondCard.add(new JButton("Kluggg"));
  secondCard.add(new JButton("Grrogg"));
  secondCard.add(new JButton("Skrank"));
  thirdCard.add(new JLabel("Select a location"));
  thirdCard.add(new JButton("Castle of Doom"));
  thirdCard.add(new JButton(" Forest of Fear "));

  previousButton.setBackground(Color.yellow);
  nextButton.setBackground(Color.yellow);

  // add the buttons and the centre panel to the frame
  add("West", previousButton);
  add("Center", centrePanel);
  add("East", nextButton);

  // set the layout of the centre panel to a CardLayout
  centrePanel.setLayout(cardLayout);

  // add the cards to the centre panel
  centrePanel.add(firstCard, "level");
  centrePanel.add(secondCard, "character");
  centrePanel.add(thirdCard, "location");
```

```
    // add Actionlisteners to the buttons
    nextButton.addActionListener(this);
    previousButton.addActionListener(this);

    // configure the frame
    setTitle("The Dungeons of Schpiltz");
    setSize(360,125);
    setLocation(300,300);
    setVisible(true);
  }


  // the event handler
  public void actionPerformed(ActionEvent e)
  {
    if(e.getSource() == nextButton)
    {
      cardLayout.next(centrePanel); // show the next card
    }
    else if(e.getSource() == previousButton)
    {
      cardLayout.previous(centrePanel); // show the previous card
    }
  }
}
```

The only things that we need to draw to your attention to are those to do with the `CardLayout` class. You can see that we have created a `CardLayout` object as an attribute:

```
private CardLayout cardLayout = new CardLayout();
```

We have also created a panel called `centrePanel` that is the component to which this layout is going to be attached:

```
private JPanel centrePanel = new JPanel();
```

The three different screens that you see in figure 16.2 – in other words, the "cards" – are created as `JPanels`:

```
private JPanel firstCard = new JPanel();
private JPanel secondCard = new JPanel();
private JPanel thirdCard = new JPanel();
```

In the constructor, the various buttons and labels are added to these cards – for example, for the first card we have:

```
firstCard.add(new JLabel("Choose your level"));
firstCard.add(new JButton(" Novice "));
firstCard.add(new JButton("Regular"));
firstCard.add(new JButton(" Expert "));
firstCard.add(new JButton("    Elite   "));
```

After that, the background colour of the two main buttons is set, and then the centrePanel is added to the main panel along with the buttons for going back and continuing:

```
add("West", previousButton);
add("Center", centrePanel);
add("East", nextButton);
```

When all that is done we set the layout of the centre panel using the cardLayout object that we defined previously:

```
centrePanel.setLayout(cardLayout);
```

Next we add the cards to the centre panel, and assign each one a unique string as described earlier:

```
centrePanel.add(firstCard,"level");
centrePanel.add(secondCard,"character");
centrePanel.add(thirdCard,"location");
```

Finally we add our ActionListeners to the two control buttons and configure the frame.

The actionPerformed method then makes use of the next and previous methods of CardLayout:

```
public void actionPerformed(ActionEvent e)
{
  if(e.getSource() == nextButton)
  {
    cardLayout.next(centrePanel);
  }
  else if(e.getSource() == previousButton)
  {
    cardLayout.previous(centrePanel);
  }
}
```

You can see that these two methods require that the component to which the cards are attached be sent in as a parameter. If we had wanted to use the show method here it would have taken the following form:

```
cardLayout.show(centrePanel, "location");
```

That would display the third card.

16.2.3 The "No Layout" policy

We should start this section with a word of warning – many people advise against using a "no layout" policy, so you should do so with care. Having no layout means that you have to position your objects on the screen by using absolute references, specified in pixels along and down from the top left corner. The main reason that some people don't like this technique is that once you have positioned your items, then it is hard to add further items without having to move everything around to accommodate the new components. Another reason is that there is no means of adjusting them when the window is resized. This is illustrated in figure 16.3.

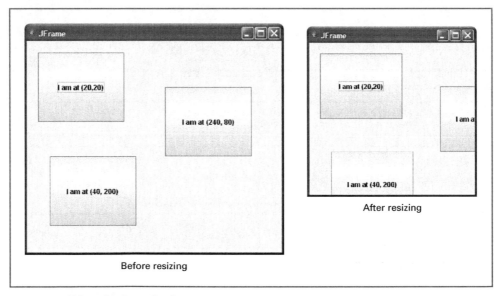

FIGURE 16.3 Using a "no layout" policy

In order to use no layout, you simply write the instruction:

```
setLayout(null);
```

Then, for each component that you add, you use the setBounds method of the component (inherited from the Component class), which has the following form:

```
setBounds(int x, int y, int width, int height)
```

Here x and y are the coordinates, in pixels, along and down from (0,0) at the top left corner – width and height determine the size of the component.

You can see how this is done in the class below, which we wrote to achieve the graphic that you see in figure 16.3. As you can see, we created three buttons, with captions to illustrate their coordinates, added them to the JFrame, and used the setBounds method to place them at various positions in the window.

THE *NOLAYOUTEXAMPLE* CLASS

```
import javax.swing.*;

public class NoLayoutExample extends JFrame
{

  private JButton button1 = new JButton("I am at (20,20)");
  private JButton button2 = new JButton("I am at (40, 200)");
  private JButton button3 = new JButton("I am at (240, 80)");

  public NoLayoutExample()
  {
    setLayout(null); // set to no layout
    setDefaultCloseOperation(JFrame.EXIT_ON_CLOSE);
    setTitle("JFrame");
    setSize(450,400);
    setLocation(400, 300);

    add(button1);
    add(button2);
    add(button3);

    // place buttons in frame
    button1.setBounds(20, 20, 150, 120);
    button2.setBounds(40, 200, 150, 120);
    button3.setBounds(240, 80, 150, 120);

    setVisible(true);
  }
}
```

The layout managers that you have come across so far should be enough for much of the programming that you will be doing. However, those of you who will be required to produce really professional interfaces may want to have even more control over the way things look. For this purpose the GridBagLayout manager is an ideal layout manager. However, this is a complex layout manager, and we are not going to go into its use here – those of you who wish to know about this manager should consult a Java reference text.

16.3 Making choices

One of the most common ways for an application to interact with the user is to provide a number of choices – just as we did with the text-based menus that we introduced you to in the first semester. With graphical applications, there are a number of ways of doing this, and in this section we present you with some of the ways that this can be done – we will show you how to create pull-down menus, pop-up menus, dialogue windows, radio buttons and combo boxes.

16.3.1 Pull-down menus

A pull-down menu is a very common way to offer choices to the user of a program. Such a menu is shown in figure 16.4. This is a very simple example; the program displays a flag consisting of three horizontal stripes. The colour of each stripe can be changed by means of the pull-down menus on the top bar.

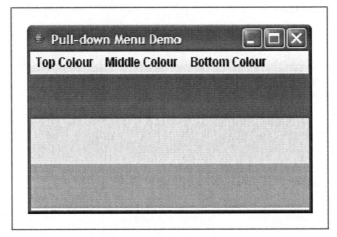

FIGURE 16.4 A *JFrame* with three pull-down menus

As an example, figure 16.5 shows the choices offered by the first menu.

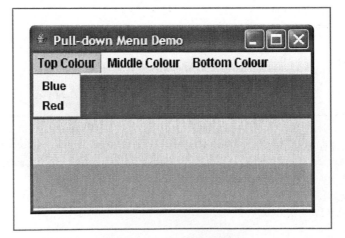

FIGURE 16.5 The options on the "Top Colour" menu

The code for the Flag class is presented below:

THE *FLAG* CLASS

```java
import java.awt.*;
import java.awt.event.*;
import javax.swing.*;


public class Flag extends JFrame implements ActionListener
{

  // declare and create three panels, one for each stripe
  private JPanel topPanel = new JPanel();
  private JPanel middlePanel = new JPanel();
  private JPanel bottomPanel = new JPanel();


  // declare and create the top menu bar
  private JMenuBar bar = new JMenuBar();


  // declare and create the three menus
  private JMenu topStripeMenu = new JMenu("Top Colour");
  private JMenu middleStripeMenu = new JMenu("Middle Colour");
  private JMenu bottomStripeMenu = new JMenu("Bottom Colour");


  // declare and create each menu item
  private JMenuItem blueStripe = new JMenuItem("Blue");
  private JMenuItem redStripe = new JMenuItem("Red");
  private JMenuItem whiteStripe = new JMenuItem("White");
  private JMenuItem yellowStripe = new JMenuItem("Yellow");
  private JMenuItem greenStripe = new JMenuItem("Green");
  private JMenuItem blackStripe = new JMenuItem("Black");


  // the constructor
  public Flag()
  {
    setTitle("Pull-down Menu Demo"); // set the title of the frame

    // set each stripe to an initial colour
    topPanel.setBackground(Color.red);
    middlePanel.setBackground(Color.yellow);
    bottomPanel.setBackground(Color.green);
```

```java
    // add menu items to the top stripe menu
    topStripeMenu.add(blueStripe);
    topStripeMenu.add(redStripe);

    // add menu items to the middle stripe menu
    middleStripeMenu.add(whiteStripe);
    middleStripeMenu.add(yellowStripe);

    // add menu items to the bottom stripe menu
    bottomStripeMenu.add(greenStripe);
    bottomStripeMenu.add(blackStripe);

    // add the menus to the menu bar
    bar.add(topStripeMenu);
    bar.add(middleStripeMenu);
    bar.add(bottomStripeMenu);

    // add the menu bar to the frame
    setJMenuBar(bar);

    // add listeners to each menu item
    blueStripe.addActionListener(this);
    redStripe.addActionListener(this);
    whiteStripe.addActionListener(this);
    yellowStripe.addActionListener(this);
    greenStripe.addActionListener(this);
    blackStripe.addActionListener(this);

    // select a GridLayout
    setLayout(new GridLayout(3,1));

    // add the panels to the frame
    add(topPanel);
    add(middlePanel);
    add(bottomPanel);

    // choose settings for the frame and make it visible
    setDefaultCloseOperation(JFrame.EXIT_ON_CLOSE);
    setSize(300,200);
    setVisible(true);
}
```

```java
  // the event handler
  public void actionPerformed(ActionEvent e)
  {
    if (e.getSource() == blueStripe)
    {
      topPanel.setBackground(Color.blue); // set top stripe to blue
    }
    if (e.getSource() == redStripe)
    {
      topPanel.setBackground(Color.red); // set top stripe to red
    }
    if (e.getSource() == whiteStripe)
    {
      middlePanel.setBackground(Color.white); // set middle stripe to white
    }
    if (e.getSource() == yellowStripe)
    {
      middlePanel.setBackground(Color.yellow); // set middle stripe to yellow
    }
    if (e.getSource() == greenStripe)
    {
      bottomPanel.setBackground(Color.green); // set bottom stripe to green
    }
    if (e.getSource() == blackStripe)
    {
      bottomPanel.setBackground(Color.black); // set bottom stripe to black
    }
  }
}
```

If you take a look at the attributes you will see that there are three aspects to creating a menu – there is the menu bar at the top and then the different menus – and each of these has its own list of menu items:

```java
// the top menu bar
private JMenuBar bar = new JMenuBar();

// the three menus
private JMenu topStripeMenu = new JMenu("Top Colour");
private JMenu middleStripeMenu = new JMenu("Middle Colour");
private JMenu bottomStripeMenu = new JMenu("Bottom Colour");
```

```
// the menu items
private JMenuItem blueStripe = new JMenuItem("Blue");
private JMenuItem redStripe = new JMenuItem("Red");
private JMenuItem whiteStripe = new JMenuItem("White");
private JMenuItem yellowStripe = new JMenuItem("Yellow");
private JMenuItem greenStripe = new JMenuItem("Green");
private JMenuItem blackStripe = new JMenuItem("Black");
```

Figure 16.6 clarifies how each of these items is used to create the menu.

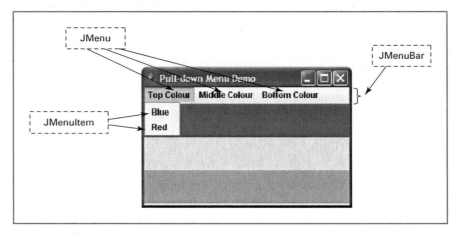

FIGURE 16.6 The components that make up a menu

Now we can look at the constructor. We start by assigning an initial colour to each stripe:

```
topPanel.setBackground(Color.red);
middlePanel.setBackground(Color.yellow);
bottomPanel.setBackground(Color.green);
```

After that, we add the individual menu items to the menus:

```
// add menu items to the top stripe menu
topStripeMenu.add(blueStripe);
topStripeMenu.add(redStripe);

// add menu items to the middle stripe menu
middleStripeMenu.add(whiteStripe);
middleStripeMenu.add(yellowStripe);

// add menu items to the bottom stripe menu
bottomStripeMenu.add(greenStripe);
bottomStripeMenu.add(blackStripe);
```

Next these menus are added to the menu bar:

```
bar.add(topStripeMenu);
bar.add(middleStripeMenu);
bar.add(bottomStripeMenu);
```

We now use the `setJMenuBar` method of `JFrame` to add the menu bar to the frame:

```
setJMenuBar(bar);
```

All the rest of the constructor is straightforward and does not require further explanation. Notice how we have used a `GridLayout` to get the stripes where we want them.

The `actionPerformed` method is also straightforward – we set the colour of a particular stripe according to the menu item that was selected. For example, the following sets the middle stripe to yellow:

```
if (e.getSource() == yellowStripe)
{
  middlePanel.setBackground(Color.yellow);
}
```

The flag can now be created with program 16.2:

PROGRAM 16.2

```
public class RunFlag
{
  public static void main(String[] args)
  {
    new Flag();
  }
}
```

16.3.2 Pop-up menus

An alternative to a pull-down menu is a pop-up menu. A pop-up menu is normally not available all the time, but pops up only when it is necessary, and then disappears. To demonstrate this we have created an application in which the menu is used simply to change the background colour of a frame, and is invoked by pressing a button. This is demonstrated in figure 16.7.

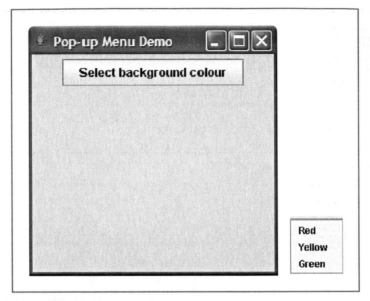

FIGURE 16.7 A pop-up menu

Here is the code for the PopupDemo class:

THE POPUPDEMO CLASS

```
import java.awt.*;
import java.awt.event.*;
import javax.swing.*;


public class PopupDemo extends JFrame implements ActionListener
{
  // declare and create the button
  private JButton button = new JButton("Select background colour");


  // declare and create the pop-up menu
  private JPopupMenu popup = new JPopupMenu();


  // declare and create the menu items
  private JMenuItem red = new JMenuItem("Red");
  private JMenuItem yellow = new JMenuItem("Yellow");
  private JMenuItem green = new JMenuItem("Green");


  // the constructor
  public PopupDemo()
  {
    setTitle("Pop-up Menu Demo"); // set the title of the frame
```

```java
    // add the menu items to the menu
    popup.add(red);
    popup.add(yellow);
    popup.add(green);

    // set the location of the pop-up menu
    popup.setLocation(260,180);

    // add ActionListeners to the menu items and to the button
    red.addActionListener(this);
    yellow.addActionListener(this);
    green.addActionListener(this);
    button.addActionListener(this);

    // choose a flow layout, then add the button to the frame
    setLayout(new FlowLayout());
    add(button);

    // remove the highlighting around the button text
    button.setFocusPainted(false);

    // choose settings for the frame and make it visible
    setDefaultCloseOperation(JFrame.EXIT_ON_CLOSE);
    setSize(250,250);
    setVisible(true);

  }


  // the event-handler
  public void actionPerformed(ActionEvent e)
  {
    if (e.getSource() == button)
    {
      popup.setVisible(true); // show the pop-up menu
    }
    if (e.getSource() == red)
    {
      getContentPane().setBackground(Color.red); // set background to red
      popup.setVisible(false);   // hide the pop-up menu
    }
    if (e.getSource() == yellow)
```

```
    {
      getContentPane().setBackground(Color.yellow); // set background to yellow
      popup.setVisible(false); // hide the pop-up menu
    }
    if (e.getSource() == green)
    {
      getContentPane().setBackground(Color.green); // set background to green
      popup.setVisible(false); // hide the pop-up menu
    }
  }
}
```

There is nothing here that is especially new; you have come across all the concepts before, so all we really have to draw your attention to is the line of code that declares and creates a new pop-up menu:

```
private JPopupMenu popup = new JPopupMenu();
```

The menu items are added to this menu in the constructor:

```
popup.add(red);
popup.add(yellow);
popup.add(green);
```

Notice how, in the `actionPerformed` method, the menu is made visible when the button is pressed, and then is hidden once the background colour has been selected.

Although this is unconnected to the concept of menus, we should also draw your attention to the use of the `setFocusPainted` method, which we have used here for the first time – calling this method with a parameter of **false** removes the highlighting around the text of the button when it is in focus:

```
button.setFocusPainted(false);
```

16.3.3 The *JDialog class* and the *JRadioButton* class

An alternative to a pop-up menu is a dialogue window. The Swing class that we use to produce such a window is the `JDialog` class. As with a pop-up menu, its purpose is to provide a means of communication between the user and the program. It is useful for those occasions when we do not want a part of a frame or window permanently devoted to this communication because it is only needed at particular times.

A `JDialog` object allows us to add any components we wish to it, so that we can provide the interface of our choice. In our example we are going to use radio buttons to change the background colour of a frame, just as we did with the pop-up menu. We could, had we wished, have used buttons instead. For other applications we could have added other components such as text boxes – a good example of this would be a dialogue that asked the user to enter his or her password; once this is done the dialogue window can be disposed.

The application is shown in figure 16.8.

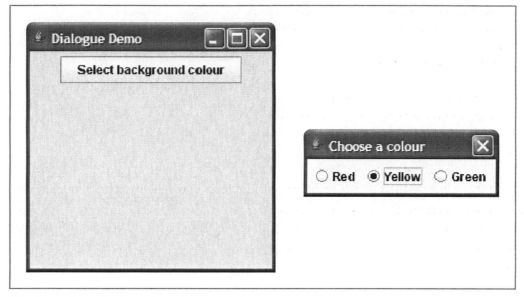

FIGURE 16.8 An application with a dialogue window

The code for this class, DialogDemo is shown below.

THE *DIALOGDEMO* CLASS

```java
import java.awt.*;
import java.awt.event.*;
import javax.swing.*;


public class DialogDemo extends JFrame implements ActionListener
{
  // declare and create the button
  private JButton button = new JButton("Select background colour");


  // declare and create the dialogue window
  private JDialog dialog = new JDialog();


  // declare and create a group for the radio buttons
  private ButtonGroup group = new ButtonGroup();


  // declare and create the radio buttons
  private JRadioButton red = new JRadioButton("Red");
  private JRadioButton yellow = new JRadioButton("Yellow");
  private JRadioButton green = new JRadioButton("Green");
```

```java
// the constructor
public DialogDemo()
{
  setTitle("Dialogue Demo"); // set the title of the frame

  // add the radio buttons to the group
  group.add(red);
  group.add(yellow);
  group.add(green);

  // set the layout policy of the dialogue window to flow layout
  dialog.setLayout(new FlowLayout());

  // set title of dialogue
  dialog.setTitle("Choose a colour");

  // add the radio buttons to the dialogue window
  dialog.add(red);
  dialog.add(yellow);
  dialog.add(green);

  // get the dialogue window to size itself
  dialog.pack();

  // set the location of the dialogue window
  dialog.setLocation(550,400);

  // add ActionListeners to the button and to the radio buttons
  button.addActionListener(this);
  red.addActionListener(this);
  yellow.addActionListener(this);
  green.addActionListener(this);

  // set the policy of the frame to flow layout
  setLayout(new FlowLayout());

  // add the button to the frame
  add(button);

  // remove the highlighting around the button text
  button.setFocusPainted(false);
```

```
    // configure the frame
    setDefaultCloseOperation(JFrame.EXIT_ON_CLOSE);
    setSize(250,250);
    setLocation(250,250);
    setVisible(true);
  }


  // the event handler
  public void actionPerformed(ActionEvent e)
  {
    if (e.getSource() == button)
    {
      dialog.setVisible(true); // make the dialogue window visible
    }


    // select correct action for each radio button
    if (e.getSource() == red)
    {
      getContentPane().setBackground(Color.red); // set background to red
    }
    if (e.getSource() == yellow)
    {
      getContentPane().setBackground(Color.yellow); // set background to yellow
    }
    if (e.getSource() == green)
    {
      getContentPane().setBackground(Color.green); // set background to green
    }
  }
}
```

By now you are familiar with much of this code. We will draw your attention to the specific instructions relating to the dialogue window and to the radio buttons. In fact, the `JDialog` class is very similar to `JFrame`, both being derived from the AWT `Window` class. As you can see, we have created the `JDialog` object with the following constructor:

```
private JDialog dialog = new JDialog();
```

As with a `JFrame`, the `JDialog` has a default `BorderLayout` policy, which, for simplicity, we have changed to a `FlowLayout`. The components are added to the dialogue box as follows.

```
dialog.add(red);
dialog.add(yellow);
dialog.add(green);
```

Notice also how we have used the container method `pack`, which, when there is a `FlowLayout` policy, makes the container adjust its size in order to lay the components out in the most compact manner:

```
dialog.pack();
```

With regard to the radio buttons, it is possible for the buttons to act independently, or, alternatively, as a group. In this case we require them to behave as a group, because we want only one button to be able to be selected at any given time. You can see that in order to do this, we have created a `ButtonGroup` object:

```
private ButtonGroup group = new ButtonGroup();
```

We add each button to the group as follows, so that they act together:

```
group.add(red);
group.add(yellow);
group.add(green);
```

16.3.4 Modal and non-modal dialogues

An object of the `JDialog` class can be **modal** or **non-modal**; in the above example, the `Dialog` constructor that we used – the empty constructor – creates a non-modal dialogue. This means that any listening components on the originating frame are still enabled and we can therefore interact with the frame even while the dialogue is visible. In our simple example, the only other listening component is the "close" icon; with the non-modal dialogue, we can still close the frame while the dialogue is visible.

A modal dialogue, on the other hand, works in such a way as to "freeze" any interaction with the parent frame until the dialogue is disposed of. To create a modal dialogue you can use a different constructor, which takes two parameters. The first is a reference to the originating frame. The second is a **boolean** parameter; if this parameter is **true** a modal dialogue will be created, if **false** a non-modal dialogue will be created.

Thus, in our example we could have created a modal dialogue with the following line:

```
private JDialog dialog = new JDialog(this, true);
```

This would make it impossible to close the frame while the dialogue window is visible.

You should also note that there is a constructor of `JDialog` which takes just one parameter, a reference to the originating frame. This constructor is useful in the case where the code for the frame resides in a different class to that of the dialogue; you will see an example of this in the case study in chapter 21.

16.3.5 The *JComboBox* class

The component known as a *combo box* – provided in Swing by the `JComboBox` class – should be familiar to everyone, as it is the most common means of providing a choice from a list of options. We have created once again a very simple class (`ComboBoxDemo`) to demonstrate this – here a combo box simply provides the choice of background colour for the frame. This is shown in figure 16.9.

FIGURE 16.9 The *ComboBoxDemo* class

The choices are revealed when the down arrow is clicked, as can be seen in figure 16.10.

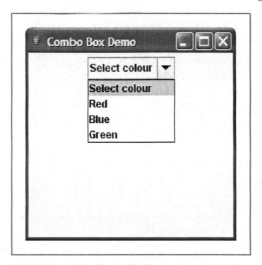

FIGURE 16.10 The *ComboBoxDemo* class – showing the options

Here is the code for our ComboBoxDemo class.

THE *COMBOBOXDEMO* CLASS

```java
import java.awt.*;
import java.awt.event.*;
import javax.swing.*;

public class ComboBoxDemo extends JFrame implements ActionListener
{
  // declare and create an array of strings
  private String[] colours = {"Select colour","Red", "Blue", "Green"};

  // declare and create a combo box
  private JComboBox box = new JComboBox(colours);

  // the constructor
  public ComboBoxDemo()
  {
    setTitle("Combo Box Demo"); // set the title of the frame

    // choose a flow layout, then add the combo box to the frame
    setLayout(new FlowLayout());
    add(box);

    // add an ActionListener to the combo box
    box.addActionListener(this);

    // configure the frame
    setDefaultCloseOperation(JFrame.EXIT_ON_CLOSE);
    setSize(250,250);
    setVisible(true);
  }

  public void actionPerformed(ActionEvent e)
  {
    // determine which item is selected
    String item = (String) box.getSelectedItem();
    if (item.equals("Red"))
    {
      getContentPane().setBackground(Color.red); // set background to red
    }
```

```
    if (item.equals("Blue"))
    {
      getContentPane().setBackground(Color.blue); // set background to blue
    }
    if (item.equals("Green"))
    {
      getContentPane().setBackground(Color.green); // set background to green
    }
    // set selected item to the first option so that "select colour" is displayed
    box.setSelectedIndex(0);
  }
}
```

Once again we will draw your attention to only a few points. First, notice that the JComboBox is created with a constructor that accepts an array of objects – normally Strings – that defines the choices. In the above class we defined the array of strings, colours, and then used this as the parameter:

```
private String[] colours = {"Select colour","Red", "Blue", "Green"};
private JComboBox box = new JComboBox(colours);
```

As is very common when using the combo box, the first option, "Select colour", is not actually an option but is there simply to direct the user.

An ActionListener is added to the combo box in the constructor:

```
box.addActionListener(this);
```

Note how, in the actionPerformed method, we use the getSelectedItem method of JComboBox to determine which item was selected. This method returns the selected item, an Object, which in this case must be type cast back to a String.

```
String item = (String) box.getSelectedItem();
```

Finally, note the last line of the actionPerformed method:

```
box.setSelectedIndex(0);
```

The setSelectedIndex method of JComboBox sets the selected item to the one indicated. In this case we require the selected item to be "Select colour", so that after the selection is made the user sees this displayed again. This is the first item in the list – index 0 of the array.

16.4 The *JFileChooser* class

A JFileChooser object interacts with your computer's operating system in order to enable you to search directories and select files. To illustrate the use of this class we will develop a class called FileHandler that will produce a frame containing a menu bar consisting of a couple of menu options. As well as the menu bar, it provides a text area, as shown in figure 16.11.

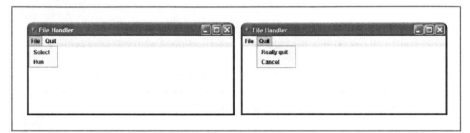

FIGURE 16.11 The *FileHandler* class

Choosing the *Select* option from the *File* menu will cause a dialogue window to appear as shown in figure 16.12.

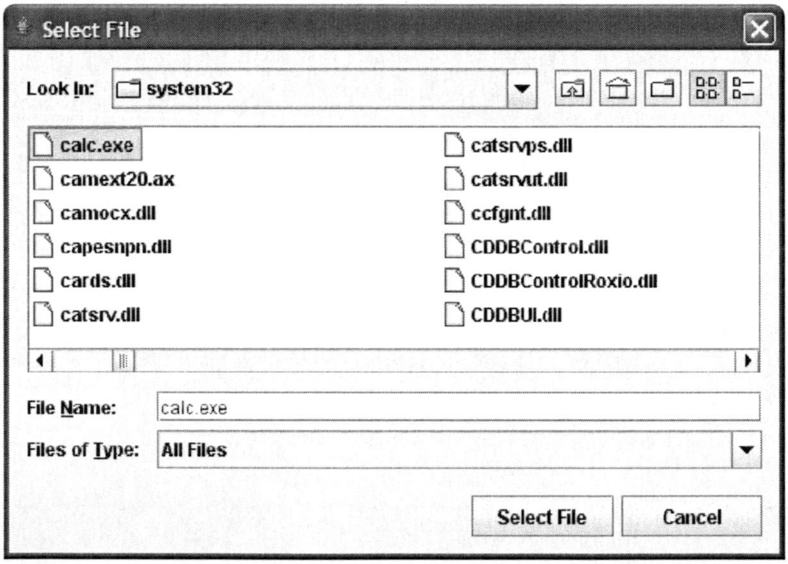

FIGURE 16.12 The file dialogue presented when the *Select* option is chosen

You can see that in figure 16.12 we have chosen the file called *calc.exe*, which is the calculator program that comes with the Windows operating system. Once we select this file a message appears in our text area, telling us the name of the file chosen. This is illustrated in figure 16.13.

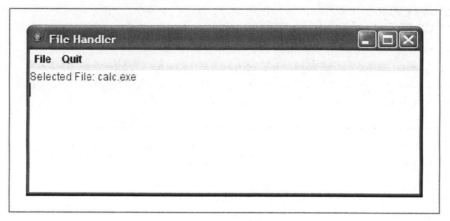

FIGURE 16.13 The name of the file we select appears in the text area

If the file we have chosen is an executable file, then selecting the *Run* option of the *File* menu will run the program, in this case the Windows calculator. When we get to chapter 18, we will learn more about handling files, and will be able to add an option to our menu which will allow us to look inside a file.

Once again, there is not a huge amount of new material here – there is the code for creating the JFileChooser object, and there is the running of the executable itself. We will discuss these after you have inspected the code for the FileHandler class.

THE *FILEHANDLER* CLASS

```java
import java.awt.event.*;
import java.io.*; // for the File class
import javax.swing.*;


public class FileHandler extends JFrame implements ActionListener
{
  // the attributes

  // declare a TextArea
  private JTextArea viewArea = new JTextArea(10,55);

  // declare the menu components
  private JMenuBar bar = new JMenuBar();
  private JMenu fileMenu = new JMenu("File");
  private JMenu quitMenu = new JMenu("Quit");
  private JMenuItem selectChoice = new JMenuItem("Select");
  private JMenuItem runChoice = new JMenuItem("Run");
  private JMenuItem reallyQuitChoice = new JMenuItem("Really quit");
  private JMenuItem cancelChoice = new JMenuItem("Cancel");
```

```java
// declare an attribute to hold the chosen file
private File chosenFile;

// the constructor
public FileHandler()
{
  setTitle("File Handler"); // set title of the frame

  add(viewArea); // add the text area

  // add the menus to the menu bar
  bar.add(fileMenu);
  bar.add(quitMenu);

  // add the menu items to the menus
  fileMenu.add(selectChoice);
  fileMenu.add(runChoice);
  quitMenu.add(reallyQuitChoice);
  quitMenu.add(cancelChoice);

  // add the menu bar to the frame
  setJMenuBar(bar);

  // add the ActionListeners
  selectChoice.addActionListener(this);
  runChoice.addActionListener(this);
  reallyQuitChoice.addActionListener(this);
  cancelChoice.addActionListener(this);

  // configure the frame
  setDefaultCloseOperation(JFrame.DO_NOTHING_ON_CLOSE);
  setSize(450,200);
  setVisible(true);
}

// the event handler
public void actionPerformed(ActionEvent e)
{
  if(e.getSource() == selectChoice)
  {
    // create a new JFileChooser object
    JFileChooser chooser = new JFileChooser();
```

```
        // show the dialogue
        chooser.showDialog(this, "Select File");


        // determine which file has been selected
        chosenFile = chooser.getSelectedFile();


        // display the name of the chosen file
        viewArea.append("Selected File: " + chosenFile.getName() + '\n');
    }


    if(e.getSource() == runChoice)
    {
      // create a RunTime object
      Runtime rt = Runtime.getRuntime();
      try
      {
        // run the file
        rt.exec(chosenFile.getPath());
      }

      // if the file name is null
      catch(NullPointerException npe)
      {
        viewArea.append("No file selected\n");
      }

      // if the file cannot be executed
      catch(IOException ioe)
      {
        viewArea.append("Not an executable file\n");
      }
    }
    if(e.getSource() == reallyQuitChoice)
    {
      System.exit(0);
    }


    if(e.getSource() == cancelChoice)
    {
      viewArea.append("Quit option cancelled\n");
    }
  }
}
```

First of all, you will notice that we have declared the following attribute:

```
private File chosenFile;
```

An object of the File class (which resides in the java.io package) will hold a representation of a file. Once we have selected a file, its details will be held in this attribute.

Now, let's take a look at the actionPerformed method. First there is the option associated with choosing the menu item that lets us select a file:

```
if(e.getSource() == selectChoice)
{
  // create a new JFileChooser object
  JFileChooser chooser = new JFileChooser();

  // show the dialogue
  chooser.showDialog(this, "Select File");

  // determine which file has been selected
  chosenFile = chooser.getSelectedFile();

  // display the name of the chosen file
  viewArea.append("Selected File: " + chosenFile.getName() + '\n');
}
```

After creating the JFileChooser object, we call its showDialog method to make the dialogue window visible. This requires two parameters. The first is a reference to the originating component (in our case **this** frame); the second is the text required on the *accept* button, in this case "Select File", as you saw in figure 16.12. Once the user has selected the file, the getSelectedFile method is called to return the file selected; this is then assigned to the chosenFile attribute. After this, we use the getName method of the File class to display the name of the file in the text area. If we had wanted the full path name to be displayed we could have used getPath instead of getName.

Here is the code for the runChoice option, which loads and runs the selected file.

```
if(e.getSource() == runChoice)
{
  Runtime rt = Runtime.getRuntime(); // create a RunTime object
  try
  {
    rt.exec(chosenFile.getPath()); // run the file
  }
```

```
   // if the file name is null
   catch(NullPointerException npe)
   {
     viewArea.append("No file selected\n");
   }


   // if the file cannot be executed
   catch(IOException ioe)
   {
     viewArea.append("Not an executable file\n");
   }
 }
```

As you can see, we are making use of a standard Java class called Runtime. We create an object of this class and then assign it the return value of the getRuntime method, which is a **static** method of the Runtime class. The object returned by this method contains information about the Java application that is currently running. Being armed with information about the current application, the Runtime object is able to execute a command – specific to the particular operating system – as a separate process in the computer's memory. It does this with its exec method, which executes the command that is sent in as a parameter. You can see from the above that we are sending in the full path name of the selected file (by using the getPath method of File). If the file is an executable file then it will be loaded and run.

You can see that two exceptions have been handled. The first is a NullPointerException, which would be thrown if the file name sent into the exec method were **null** – that is, if no file had been selected. The second is IOException. This would occur if the file was not executable.

All that is now required is a program such as program 16.3 to create an instance of the FileHandler class.

PROGRAM 16.3

```
public class RunFileHandler
{
  public static void main(String[] args)
  {
    new FileHandler();
  }
}
```

If you would prefer to navigate the file system with the more familiar dialogue window provided by the operating system, then you can make use of a class called FileDialog that is provided in the AWT package. Question 6 of the practical exercises will take you through the steps necessary to achieve this.

16.5 The *JSlider* class

A JSlider allows us to control the value of a variable by moving a sliding bar – a *slider* – which is used to vary a value of an integer within a particular range.

The JSlider class has a method called getValue which returns an integer representing the distance that the bar has been moved. An example should make it clear how this works; in figure 16.14 we have placed a slider at the top of a frame, and added a label to show the current value returned by getValue. When you run the program you will see that the default value of the range is 0 to 100.

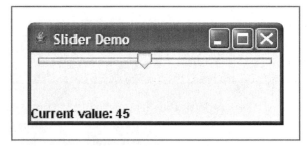

FIGURE 16.14 Using the *JSlider* class

Here is the code for this SliderDemo class:

THE *SLIDERDEMO* CLASS

```
import javax.swing.*;
import javax.swing.event.*;


public class SliderDemo extends JFrame implements ChangeListener
{
  // declare and initialize a horizontal slider
  private JSlider bar = new JSlider(JSlider.HORIZONTAL);

  // declare and initialize a label
  private JLabel valueLabel = new JLabel();

  // the constructor
  public SliderDemo ()
  {
    setTitle("Slider Demo"); // set the title of the frame

    // set the slider to its minimum value
    bar.setValue(0);
```

```java
      // add the slider to the top of the frame
      add("North", bar);
      // set the initial text for the label
      valueLabel.setText("Current value: 0");

      // add the label to the frame
      add("South", valueLabel);

      // add the listener to the slider
      bar.addChangeListener(this);

      // configure the frame
      setDefaultCloseOperation(JFrame.EXIT_ON_CLOSE);
      setSize(250,100);
      setLocation(300,300);
      setVisible(true);
   }

   // the event-handler
   public void stateChanged(ChangeEvent e)
   {
     // report on the current position of the bar
     valueLabel.setText("Current value: " + bar.getValue());
   }
}
```

Much of the code is self-explanatory. There are a few things to point out here, however. First, notice that we have maintained the BorderLayout policy for the frame and added the slider to the North sector. Second, you should observe that the constructor allows us to decide upon the orientation of the slider with a pre-defined integer parameter that can be either JSlider.HORIZONTAL or JSlider.VERTICAL. Third, you should note that the interface that we need to implement in this case is ChangeListener (provided in the javax.swing.event package). The method that handles the event is stateChanged, which receives a ChangeEvent object; notice how we report on the movement of the bar by using the getValue method:

```java
 public void stateChanged(ChangeEvent e)
 {
   valueLabel.setText("Current value: " + bar.getValue());
 }
```

Program 16.4 runs the SliderDemo class. If you run the program, you will see that the minimum and maximum values of the slider default to 0 and 100. If you require alternative limits there is an appropriate constructor provided – this takes two integer parameters, representing the minimum and maximum respectively.

PROGRAM 16.4

```java
public class RunSliderDemo
{
  public static void main(String[] args)
  {
     new SliderDemo();
  }
}
```

Self-test questions

1   The graphic below was created by declaring a class that **extends JFrame**:

a   Identify the layout manager that is attached to the frame, and write the line of code that would attach this layout manager.

b   Assuming that the centre square is a **JPanel** called **myPanel**, write the code that would attach the correct layout manager to this panel.

2   a   In the application shown below, identify the various ways that users are given for making choices.

b   What alternatives could have been used for selecting the age range?

3   The diagram below shows the options available in the "File" menu of the application shown in question 2.

Referring to this diagram, explain how a `JMenuBar`, a `JMenu` and a `JMenuItem` are used to construct a pull-down menu.

4 What is the difference between a *modal* and a *non-modal* dialogue?

5 In what circumstances might a *pop-up* menu be preferable to a *pull-down* menu?

6 What advantage does a `JDialog` have over a `JPopupMenu`?

7 Explain how a number of *radio butt*ons can be made to work together.

8 Distinguish between the `getName` and the `getPath` methods of the `File` class.

9 The diagram below shows some of the choices available under the "Select a country" option of the application shown in question 2.

Referring to the above diagram, explain how to determine which item has been selected from a `JComboBox`.

10 Write a fragment of code that will invoke the Windows Notepad program (`notepad.exe`), assuming that this is located in the directory `C:\Windows`.

11 What is the default range of a `JSlider`?

Programming exercises

1 Create the graphic that is shown in question 1 of the self-test questions.

2 A variation of the graphic shown in figure 16.1 appears below.

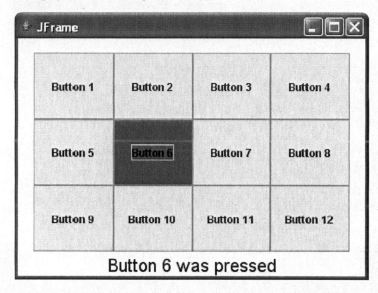

The graphic was created by adding a JPanel with a GridLayout to the central sector of a JFrame with a BorderLayout. JLabels with initially blank text were added to the other sectors.

Adapt the GridLayoutExample class from section 16.2 to produce the above graphic.

3 Adapt the hostel case study of chapters 11 and 12 so that it uses a JComboBox to enter the month.

4 Adapt the DialogDemo class of section 16.3.3 so that it uses a modal dialogue instead of a non-modal dialogue.

5 Create a graphical user interface for the Library class that we developed in chapter 15.

6 In section 16.4 you were told that there exists an alternative class to JFileChooser, namely FileDialog, which is a part of the AWT package. Using this class will furnish you with the

particular file dialogue provided by the operating system. For example, with Windows you would see something like this:

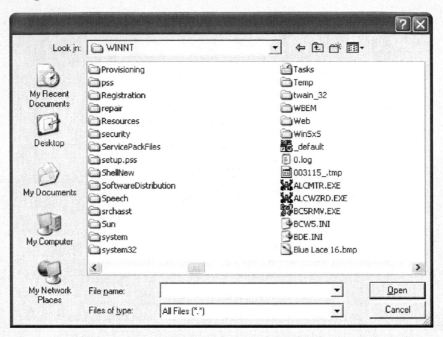

Adapt the `FileHandler` class from section 16.4, or write your own class so that it makes use of the `FileDialog` class. In order to do this you will need to import the AWT package:

```
import java.awt.*;
```

The methods of `FileDialog` are rather different from those of `JFileChooser`. The constructor takes a reference to the parent frame, so in most cases you would need a line that looks something like:

```
FileDialog chooser = new FileDialog(this);
```

To invoke the dialogue you will need to use the `setVisible` method:

```
chooser.setVisible(true);
```

To determine the file that has been selected, and its directory, you can use the following methods, which in this case – rather conveniently – return `Strings`:

```
file = chooser.getFile();
dir = chooser.getDirectory();
```

7 Adapt the SliderDemo from section 16.5 so that instead of printing an integer value, it draws an expanding square as the slider is moved. This is demonstrated in the following diagram:

8 Look back at programming exercise 3 from chapter 13, where you wrote a program that allowed the user to draw a rectangle by dragging the mouse. Adapt this program so that the user has the choice of drawing other shapes such as ovals and straight lines.

9 At the end of chapter 8 you were asked to develop a timetable application. You later enhanced this application by making use of exceptions at the end of chapter 14. Now, develop a GUI for this application, with the timetable displayed as a grid of `JTextAreas`. For example:

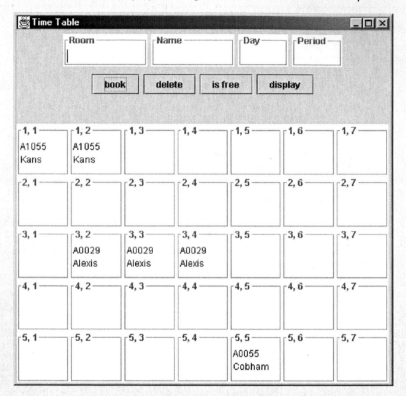

You should use the grid layout policy to achieve this timetable layout. Also make use of borders around the `JTextAreas` as discussed in chapter 12.

Enhancing the user interface

❖ OBJECTIVES

By the end of this chapter you should be able to:

❖ use a variety of Swing components;

❖ add **borders** and **icons** to components;

❖ create **message boxes** and **input boxes**;

❖ create your own colours and fonts;

❖ use some features of the `Graphics2D` class;

❖ explain some of the principles behind the creation of good user interfaces.

17.1 Introduction

The means by which a user communicates with a program is referred to as the **user interface** or **human–computer interface**. You have already discovered that using the Swing package enables you to produce very professional and attractive user interfaces. In this chapter we are going to introduce you to some more features of Swing so that you can enhance your user interfaces even further. We will also show you how you can improve your interfaces by creating your own colours and fonts. Finally, we provide some guidelines for good interface design.

17.2 The *Border* interface

As you saw in chapter 10, a very useful feature of Swing is the ability to add a variety of attractive borders to any component. All the basic components such as the `JButton` and the `JLabel` are derived from `JComponent`, and inherit its `setBorder` method, which can be used to add the border of your choice.

In the `javax.swing.border` package is a `Border` interface. In this package there are eight standard border classes that implement this interface. These are:

- `BevelBorder;`
- `SoftBevelBorder;`
- `LineBorder;`

- EtchedBorder;
- TitledBorder;
- MatteBorder;
- CompoundBorder;
- EmptyBorder.

Figure 17.1 shows examples of these borders.

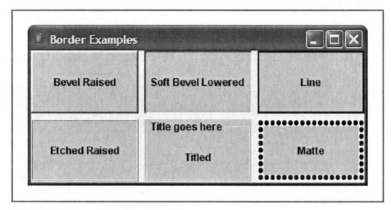

FIGURE 17.1 Examples of border styles

Each of these border classes has one or more constructors. The following fragment of code, with explanatory comments, shows the constructors that were invoked to produce the borders shown above:

```
// BevelBorder
/* the constructor takes an integer parameter, the value of which can be BevelBorder.RAISED
   or BevelBorder.LOWERED. There are other constructors that allow for the selection of
   highlight and shadow colours */
BevelBorder bevel = new BevelBorder(BevelBorder.RAISED);


// SoftBevelBorder - similar to BevelBorder
SoftBevelBorder soft = new SoftBevelBorder(SoftBevelBorder.LOWERED);


// LineBorder
/* the first parameter to the constructor defines the colour of the line; the second defines
   the thickness of the line. There is also a constructor that accepts one parameter for the
   colour only, the thickness defaulting to 1 */
LineBorder line = new LineBorder(Color.black, 2);


// EtchedBorder - similar to BevelBorder
EtchedBorder etched = new EtchedBorder(EtchedBorder.RAISED);
```

```
// TitledBorder
/* the String parameter determines the title. A number of other constructors exist to
    allow for positioning of the title */
TitledBorder titled = new TitledBorder("Title goes here");


// MatteBorder
/* the parameter determines the icon used to form the border - see next section. There are
    other constructors that allow adjustment of the insets, and a simple coloured line
    border */
MatteBorder matte = new MatteBorder(new ImageIcon("Circle.gif"));
```

Once created, a border can then be added to a component called, for example, `myLabel` with the following line of code:

```
myLabel.setBorder(bevel);
```

If you want to create more complex border combinations, you can use the `CompoundBorder` class in conjunction with the `EmptyBorder` class (which allows the insertion of empty space around components).

17.3 Combining text and graphics with the *Icon* interface

In the Swing package there is a very useful interface – the `Icon` interface. Any class that implements this interface can be passed into the `setIcon` method that is defined for many of the basic Swing components such as `JButton` or `JLabel`.

To demonstrate how this works we are going to define a simple class called `SquareIcon`, which will produce an icon consisting of a red square, the size of which can be passed into the constructor. Here is the code for the class:

THE *SQUAREICON* CLASS

```
import javax.swing.*;
import java.awt.*;


public class SquareIcon implements Icon // implement the Icon interface
{
  private int size;

  public SquareIcon(int sizeIn)
  {
    size = sizeIn;
  }
```

```
// all the following methods are required by the Icon interface
public void paintIcon(Component c, Graphics g, int x, int y)
{
    g.setColor(Color.red);
    g.fillRect(x, y, size, size);
}


public int getIconWidth()
{
  return size;
}


public int getIconHeight()
{
  return size;
}
}
```

There is a need for only one attribute, which will hold the width (and height) of the square. The constructor sets the value of this to whatever is sent in. The paintIcon method, which we are required to implement, is called automatically when the icon is created, and is automatically sent four attributes:

```
public void paintIcon(Component c, Graphics g, int x, int y)
{
  g.setColor(Color.red);
  g.fillRect(x, y, size, size);
}
```

Methods of the first parameter can be used to find out information (such as the foreground or background colour) of the component on which the icon is painted. The second parameter is the graphics context, and the final two are the coordinates at which the icon should be painted. These will have been calculated to take into account any borders that exist on the component.

The getWidth and getHeight methods have to be implemented at the insistence of the Icon interface.

The IconDemo class shown below creates a SquareIcon and adds this, together with some text, to a JButton.

THE *ICONDEMO* CLASS

```java
import javax.swing.*;
import java.awt.*;
import java.awt.event.*;

// adds an icon and text to a component
public class IconDemo extends JFrame implements ActionListener
{
  private JButton button = new JButton();
  private SquareIcon icon = new SquareIcon(30);

  public IconDemo()
  {
    button.setMargin(new Insets(0,0,0,0));
    button.setIcon(icon);        // adds the icon to the button
    button.setText("  Quit  "); // adds the text to the button
    add(button);
    button.addActionListener(this);

    // configure the frame
    setDefaultCloseOperation(JFrame.EXIT_ON_CLOSE);
    setSize(180,100);
    setVisible(true);
  }
  public void actionPerformed(ActionEvent e)
  {
    System.exit(0);
  }
}
```

You can see that we have used, respectively, the setIcon and setText methods of JButton (inherited from JComponent) to add our icon and then some text to the button.[1] Prior to this we called the setMargin method to set all the insets to zero; this has the effect of making the icon and text fill the whole button.

---

[1] There is also a version of the JButton constructor that accepts the desired icon as a parameter.

As usual, the application can be run with a program such as program 17.1.

PROGRAM 17.1

```
public class RunIconDemo
{
  public static void main(String[] args)
  {
    new IconDemo();
  }
}
```

The result of running this program is shown in figure 17.2.

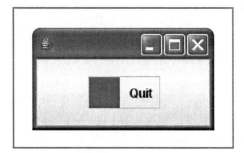

FIGURE 17.2 A button with an icon and text

17.4 The *ImageIcon* class

A very useful class that is defined in the Swing package, and which implements the Icon interface, is the ImageIcon class. This class allows you to create an icon from a file in .gif or .jpg format. We took a file called "Quit.gif", which consists of a red circle on a white background, and then, in our IconDemo class, replaced this line:

```
private SquareIcon icon = new SquareIcon(30);
```

with this one:

```
private ImageIcon icon = new ImageIcon("Quit.gif");
```

The result is shown in figure 17.3.

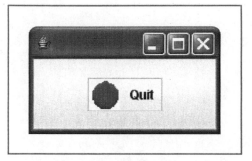

FIGURE 17.3 A button with an icon and text: in this case, the icon was created from a file.

If you want to add an image from a file to a `JFrame`, then you can use the `ImageIcon` class to add the image to a `JLabel`, which can then be added to the frame. This is illustrated in the `ImageHolder` class below:

The *ImageHolder* class

```
import javax.swing.*;

public class ImageHolder extends JFrame
{
  public ImageHolder()
  {
    ImageIcon image = new ImageIcon("Cover.jpg"); // create the image
    JLabel label = new JLabel(image); // add the image to a label
    add(label); // add the label to the frame
    setSize(360,530);
    setVisible(true);
  }
}
```

The result of running a program that creates an object of the `ImageHolder` class is shown in figure 17.4.

FIGURE 17.4 Displaying an image from a file

In this case we arranged for the frame to be big enough initially to hold the image; however, if you reduce the size of the frame you will see that eventually you only get to see part of the image. What would be useful here is for some scrollbars to be available so that we could move the image about within the frame. To do this we can use the `JScrollPane` class as shown below:

THE *IMAGEHOLDERWITHSCROLLPANE* CLASS

```java
import javax.swing.*;

public class ImageHolderWithScrollPane extends JFrame
{
  public ImageHolderWithScrollPane()
  {
    ImageIcon image = new ImageIcon("Cover.jpg"); // create the image
```

```
    JLabel label = new JLabel(image); // add the image to a label
    JScrollPane pane = new JScrollPane(label); // add the label to a scrollpane
    add(pane); // add the scrollpane to the frame
    setSize(250,340);
    setVisible(true);
  }
}
```

You will now find that when the size of the frame is reduced, scrollbars appear as shown in figure 17.5.

FIGURE 17.5 Displaying an image using the *JScrollPane* class

17.5 Creating message boxes and input boxes

In the Swing package there is a very useful class called JOptionPane. By making use of this class we can provide dialogue boxes of four possible types. These are described in table 17.1; examples of each can be seen in the application that we will describe shortly.

Option	Displays a list of buttons to enable the user to choose an option; see figure 17.6.
Input	Allows the user to enter data via a text field or list. Also provides an "OK" and a "Cancel" button; see figure 17.7.
Message	Displays a message and an "OK" button; see figures 17.8 and 17.9.
Confirm	Asks the user a question and provides "Yes" and "No" buttons for the answer; see figure 17.10.

TABLE 17.1 The *JOptionPane* dialogue types

To illustrate the use of these dialogues, we are going to create a "Magic Words" application, which could be used as the basis of a children's game. When the program first starts, the user is presented with an **option** dialogue as shown in figure 17.6.

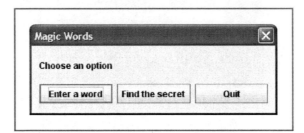

FIGURE 17.6 An option dialogue

The idea of the program (which you could easily adapt to make it a lot more interesting) is to allow the user to enter a word, and then be told whether or not the word entered was a "magic" word. The user can continue to enter words and try to work out the "secret" of what makes a particular word magical – the answer, in fact, is that magic words start and end with the same letter. As you can see here, the user can choose to find out the secret at any time.

If the user chooses to enter a word, the **input** dialogue shown in figure 17.7 appears.

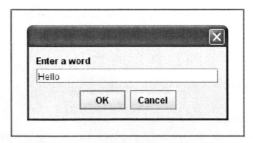

FIGURE 17.7 An input dialogue

Once the "OK" button is pressed a **message** dialogue appears, informing the user whether or not the word entered was a magic word (figure 17.8).

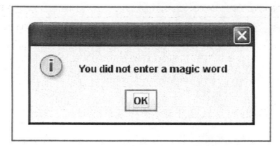

FIGURE 17.8 A message dialogue (information)

There are different types of message dialogue – the one shown in figure 17.8 is an information message dialogue. If no text had been entered, a different sort of dialogue – showing an error message – would appear as shown in figure 17.9.

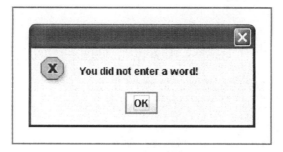

FIGURE 17.9 A message dialogue (error)

If the user chooses the "Find the secret" button from the option dialogue then a **confirm** dialogue appears as shown in figure 17.10.

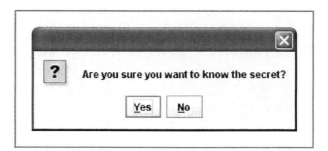

FIGURE 17.10 A confirm dialogue

Choosing the "Yes" button causes another information message box to appear, revealing the secret.

As you can see, we have designed this program to be a little bit like the old menu-driven programs that you started writing before you knew much about graphics. The `JOptionPane` class has allowed us to create a similar style of program but using graphical message boxes and input boxes instead of a text screen.

The code for this program is shown in program 17.2.

PROGRAM 17.2

```java
import javax.swing.*;

public class MagicWords
{
  public static void main(String[] args)
  {
    int result;
    do
    {

      // declare an array of strings to represent the choices
      String[] choice = {"Enter a word", "Find the secret", "Quit"};
      // create an option dialogue; the showOptionDialog method returns an integer
      result = JOptionPane.showOptionDialog
                          (null,
                           "Choose an option",
                           "Magic Words",
                           JOptionPane.DEFAULT_OPTION,
                           JOptionPane.PLAIN_MESSAGE,
                           null,
                           choice,
                           "Enter a word");

      switch(result)
      {
        case 0 : // the first button, "Enter a word", was pushed
                 enterWord();
                 break;
        case 1 : // the second button, "Find the secret", was pushed
                   findSecret();
      }
    }while(result != 2); // continue until the "Quit" button is pushed
    System.exit(0);
  }
  // helper methods

  static void enterWord()
  {
    char first, last;
    String word, message;
    // create an input dialogue; the showInputDialog method returns a string
```

```
    word = JOptionPane.showInputDialog
                            (null, "Enter a word",
                            null,
                            JOptionPane.PLAIN_MESSAGE);
  if(word != null) // the cross-hairs were not clicked on
  {
    if(word.length() != 0)
    {
      word = word.toUpperCase();
      first = word.charAt(0);
      last = word.charAt(word.length() - 1);
      if(first == last)
      {
        message = "You entered a magic word";
      }
      else
      {
        message = "You did not enter a magic word";
      }
      // create a message dialogue, giving information
      JOptionPane.showMessageDialog
                            (null, message,
                            null,
                            JOptionPane.INFORMATION_MESSAGE);
    }
    else
    {
      // create a message dialogue, showing an error
      message = "You did not enter a word!";
      JOptionPane.showMessageDialog
                            (null, message,
                            null,
                            JOptionPane.ERROR_MESSAGE);
    }
  }
}

static void findSecret()
{
  // create a confirm dialogue; the showConfirmDialog method returns an integer
    int answer;
```

```
        answer = JOptionPane.showConfirmDialog
                      (null,
                      "Are you sure you want to know the secret?",
                      null,
                      JOptionPane.YES_NO_OPTION,
                      JOptionPane.QUESTION_MESSAGE);
   if(answer == JOptionPane.YES_OPTION)
   {
     /* the message dialog defaults to an information message if the following
        constructor is used */
        JOptionPane.showMessageDialog
          (null,
          "A magic word starts and ends with the same letter");
   }
  }
}
```

As you can see, we have used the approach that we took in early chapters whereby a **do...while** loop controls the menu and a **switch** statement is used to process the user's choice. Our program is really more for demonstration purposes than anything else, and more commonly the JOptionPane class will be used as part of a more complex graphical application.

Let's take a look at some of the features of JOptionPane that we have used in the above program.

We have used four **static** methods of JOptionPane to create our dialogues; each of these methods has more than one version, but we will concentrate on the one we have used here – the others simply take a different combination of parameters.

We have begun by declaring an array of Strings, choice, to represent our three options:

```
String[] choice = {"Enter a word", "Find the secret", "Quit"};
```

The first thing that we have done within our **do...while** loop is to create an option dialogue (as shown in figure 17.6), for which purpose we use the showOptionDialog method:

```
result = JOptionPane.showOptionDialog
                          (null,
                          "Choose an option",
                          "Magic Words",
                          JOptionPane.DEFAULT_OPTION,
                          JOptionPane.PLAIN_MESSAGE,
                          null,
                          choice,
                          "Enter a word");
```

You can see that the version of this method that we have used takes eight parameters. The first of these is the parent component (that is, the component such as a `JFrame` or `JPanel` from which the dialogue was generated). In our program the dialogue was not generated from any other component, so this parameter is **null**.

The second parameter is a `String` – this determines the question or instruction that will appear in the dialogue – in our case "Choose an option".

The third parameter, also a `String`, determines the title.

The fourth parameter is an integer that will determine which buttons will appear on the dialogue box. Pre-defined constants exist for this purpose. The one we have used here is `JOptionPane.DEFAULT_OPTION`, which provides different defaults for the different types of dialogues. In the case of an option dialogue, the default is to provide no buttons other than those that determine our choices. However, as you will see below, for other types of dialogues we can choose other options such as `JOptionPane.OK_OPTION`, `JOptionPane.YES_NO_OPTION`, or finally, `JOptionPane.YES_NO_CANCEL_OPTION`.

The fifth parameter determines the icon that is displayed on the box. The possible options are shown in table 17.2.

`JOptionPane.PLAIN_MESSAGE`	No icon is displayed
`JOptionPane.INFORMATION_MESSAGE`	An information icon is displayed (see figure 17.8)
`JOptionPane.ERROR_MESSAGE`	An error icon is displayed (see figure 17.9)
`JOptionPane.QUESTION_MESSAGE`	A question icon is displayed (see figure 17.10)
`JOptionPane.WARNING_MESSAGE`	A warning icon is displayed

TABLE 17.2 Message types available in the *JOptionPane* class

The sixth parameter can be an `Icon` of your choice – **null** in our case.

The seventh parameter is the array of `Strings` that represents our list of options.

The final parameter determines the option that is initially highlighted.

The `showOptionDialog` method returns an integer, which we have assigned to `result`. The value of this integer represents the option selected – 0 for the first, 1 for the second and so on. In our case, pushing the "Quit" button will cause a value of 2 to be returned, and this is used to terminate the **do...while** loop. A return value of 0 causes the `enterMarks` method to be called. Let's take a closer look at this.

After declaring some variables, we create an input dialogue (figure 17.7) by calling the `showInput-Dialogue` method of `JOptionPane`:

```
word = JOptionPane.showInputDialog
              (null, "Enter a word", null, JOptionPane.PLAIN_MESSAGE);
```

The version of this method that we have used here returns the string that was entered, and takes four parameters representing, respectively, the parent component, the message, the title and the message type.

The next bit of this method tests for a **null** return value (caused by closing the dialogue with the crosshairs) and then, if all is well, goes on to determine whether or not a magic word was entered. It then assigns either the string "You entered a magic word" or the string "You did not enter a magic word" to a `String` variable, `message`. If no word was entered it assigns the string "You did not enter a word" to `message`.

If a word was entered, the `showMessageDialogue` method of `JOptionPane` is called:

```
JOptionPane.showMessageDialog(null, message, null, JOptionPane.INFORMATION_MESSAGE);
```

This method has the same parameter list as above; you can see that we have used `message` as the second parameter, and have chosen an information message as the message type. You can see the result in figure 17.8.

If no word was entered we again create a message box, but this time it is an error message (figure 17.9).

If the user had selected the "Find the secret" from the original option dialogue, this would have caused the helper method `findSecret` to be called. This method calls the `showConfirmDialog` method of `JOptionPane`:

```
answer = JOptionPane.showConfirmDialog (null,
                        "Are you sure you want to know the secret?",
                        null,
                        JOptionPane.YES_NO_OPTION,
                        JOptionPane.QUESTION_MESSAGE);
```

The first three parameters here are the same as above, as is the final one. The one before the last represents the option type required.

The method returns an integer that is assigned to a variable called `answer`. The possible return values are shown in table 17.3.

`JOptionPane.YES_OPTION`	The "Yes" button was pressed
`JOptionPane.NO_OPTION`	The "No" button was pressed
`JOptionPane.CANCEL_OPTION`	The "Cancel" button was pressed
`JOptionPane.OK_OPTION`	The "OK" button was pressed
`JOptionPane.CLOSED_OPTION`	The dialogue was closed by clicking on the cross-hairs

TABLE 17.3 Possible return values from the *showConfirmDialog* method

You can see from the code that if the "Yes" button were pressed, then an information message box is created, explaining the secret of a magic word.

17.6 Creating new colours

Those of you who have studied some elementary physics will know that there are three primary colours, red, green and blue;[2] all other colours can be obtained by mixing these in different proportions.

---

[2] Don't confuse this with the mixing of coloured paints, where the rules are different. In the case of mixing coloured lights (as on a computer monitor) we are dealing with reflection of light – in the case of paints we are dealing with absorption, so the primary colours, and the rules for mixing, are different. For paints the primary colours are red, blue and yellow.

Mixing red, green and blue in equal intensity produces white light; the colour we know as black is in fact the absence of all three. Mixing equal amounts of red and green (and no blue) produces yellow light; red and blue produce a mauvish colour called magenta; and mixing blue and green produces cyan, a sort of turquoise.

Residing in the AWT package is a class called `Color`. We have already been using the pre-defined attributes of this class such as `red`, `green`, `blue`, `lightGray` and so on. However, it is perfectly possible to create our own colours. A new colour is created by mixing any of the primary colours, which can be added in different degrees of intensity. This intensity for each colour can range from a minimum of zero to a maximum of 255. So there are 256 possible intensities for each primary colour, and the total number of different colours available to us is therefore 256 × 256 × 256, or 16,777,216. To create our new colour we simply use the constructor of the `Color` class, which accepts three integer parameters, representing the intensity of red, green and blue respectively.

The `ColourTester` class tests out a few new colours that we have created as well as demonstrating the principles we mentioned earlier about mixing the primary colours.

THE *COLOURTESTER* CLASS

```java
import java.awt.*;
import javax.swing.*;

public class ColourTester extends JFrame
{
  public ColourTester()
  {
    // configure the frame
    setDefaultCloseOperation(JFrame.EXIT_ON_CLOSE);
    setSize(150,160);
    setVisible(true);
  }

  public void paint(Graphics g)
  {
    super.paint(g); // call the paint method of the superclass

    // create six new colours of our own
    Color magenta = new Color(255,0,255);
    Color cyan = new Color(0,255,255);
    Color black = new Color(0,0,0);
    Color purple = new Color(210,100,210);
    Color orange = new Color(250,150,0);
    Color brown =  new Color(200,150,150);

    // draw a string in each of the new colours
    g.setColor(magenta);
```

```
    g.drawString("This is magenta", 10,40);
    g.setColor(cyan);
    g.drawString("This is cyan", 10,60);
    g.setColor(black);
    g.drawString("This is black", 10,80);
    g.setColor(purple);
    g.drawString("This is purple", 10,100);
    g.setColor(orange);
    g.drawString("This is orange", 10,120);
    g.setColor(brown);
    g.drawString("This is brown", 10,140);
  }
}
```

Figure 17.11 shows the result (in monochrome here, of course) of running a program that creates an object of this class.

FIGURE 17.11 Creating new colours

17.7 Creating new fonts

Creating our own fonts is a similar process to that of creating colours, this time making use of the Font class which again resides in the AWT package. The Font constructor takes three attributes – two strings representing a font name and a style respectively, and an integer representing the font size.

To achieve platform independence, Java provides a number of "logical" font names. These are "Serif", "SansSerif", "Monospaced", "Dialog" and "DialogInput". Using one of these as the font name means that the

JVM will select a system font that matches the particular style specified. It is also possible to use the names of system fonts such as "Arial" or "Times New Roman", but this does assume that these fonts are present on the particular machine. The possible styles are Font.PLAIN, Font.BOLD and Font.ITALIC; the last two of these can be combined by using the plus sign. The FontTester class below shows examples of the different options.

THE *FONTTESTER* CLASS

```java
import java.awt.*;
import javax.swing.*;

public class FontTester extends JFrame
{

  public FontTester()
  {
    setDefaultCloseOperation(JFrame.EXIT_ON_CLOSE);
    setSize(260,260);
    setVisible(true);
  }

  public void paint(Graphics g)
  {
    super.paint(g); // call the paint method of the superclass

    // create seven new fonts of our own
    Font font1 = new Font("SansSerif",Font.PLAIN,16);
    Font font2 = new Font("Serif",Font.PLAIN,20);
    Font font3 = new Font("Monospaced",Font.PLAIN,30);
    Font font4 = new Font("Dialog",Font.BOLD,20);
    Font font5 = new Font("DialogInput",Font.BOLD,20);
    Font font6 = new Font("Serif",Font.ITALIC,30);
    Font font7 = new Font("Serif",Font.ITALIC + Font.BOLD,16);

    // draw a string in each of the new fonts
    g.setFont(font1);
    g.drawString("This is font1", 10,47);
    g.setFont(font2);
    g.drawString("This is font2", 10,75);
    g.setFont(font3);
    g.drawString("This is font3", 10,105);
    g.setFont(font4);
    g.drawString("This is font4", 10,135);
```

```
    g.setFont(font5);
    g.drawString("This is font5", 10,165);
    g.setFont(font6);
    g.drawString("This is font6", 10,200);
    g.setFont(font7);
    g.drawString("This is font7", 10,230);
  }
}
```

Figure 17.12 shows the result of creating an object of this class.

FIGURE 17.12 Creating new fonts

17.8 The `Graphics2D` class

This `Graphics2D` class is an extension of the `Graphics` class. It is used to create sophisticated graphics applications and provides the developer with a way to have more control over such things as geometry and coordinate transformations, and to produce advanced complex colour effects and text layouts.

The aim of this section is simply to draw your attention to the existence of this class; the complexities are such that any detailed discussion should be part of a text that is dedicated to producing sophisticated graphical applications such as computer games.

All we will do here is to provide a little application to show you some of the possibilities available. For this purpose, we have created a class called `Graphics2DExamples` – the result of creating an instance of this class is shown in figure 17.13.

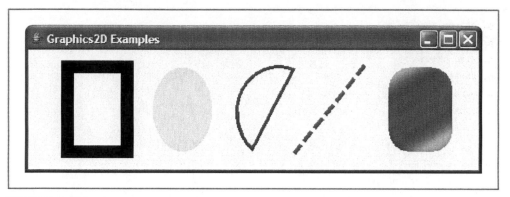

FIGURE 17.13 Using the Graphics2D class

Here is the code for Graphics2DExamples. As usual, you should take a look at it and then read the explanation that follows:

THE *GRAPHICS2DEXAMPLES* CLASS

```java
import java.awt.*;
import javax.swing.*;
import java.awt.geom.*;

public class Graphics2DExamples extends JFrame
{
  public Graphics2DExamples()
  {
    // configure the frame
    super("Graphics2D Examples");
    setSize(540, 175);
    setLocation(300, 400);
    setDefaultCloseOperation(JFrame.EXIT_ON_CLOSE);
    setVisible(true);
  }

  public void paint(Graphics g)
  {
    super.paint(g); // call the paint method of JFrame
    Graphics2D g2g = (Graphics2D) g; // type cast the Graphics object to a Graphics2D object

    // create a rectangle
    Rectangle2D.Double rectangle = new Rectangle2D.Double(50, 50, 70, 100);

    // create an ellipse
    Ellipse2D.Double ellipse = new Ellipse2D.Double(150, 50, 70, 100);
```

```
    // create an arc
    Arc2D.Double arc = new Arc2D.Double(250, 50, 100, 110, 70, 160, Arc2D.CHORD);


    // create a line
    Line2D.Double line = new Line2D.Double(400, 50, 320, 150);


    // create a rounded rectangle
    RoundRectangle2D.Double roundRect = new RoundRectangle2D.Double(430, 50, 75, 100, 50, 50);


    // set the width of the brush stroke to 15 pixels
    g2g.setStroke(new BasicStroke(15));


    // draw the rectangle
    g2g.draw(rectangle);


    // set the colour of the brush to yellow then draw the ellipse, filled
    g2g.setPaint(Color.yellow);
    g2g.fill(ellipse);


    // set the colour of the brush to blue and the width to 4 pixels, then draw the arc
    g2g.setPaint(Color.blue);
    g2g.setStroke(new BasicStroke(4));
    g2g.draw(arc);


    // declare a single element array to define the width of the dashes
    float dashes[] = { 10 };


    // define the style of a dashed line
    g2g.setStroke(new BasicStroke(5, BasicStroke.CAP_SQUARE, BasicStroke.JOIN_ROUND, 10, dashes, 0));


    // set the colour of the brush to red then draw the line
    g2g.setPaint(Color.red);
    g2g.draw(line);


    // define a gradient so that the shape is painted in gradually changing colours
    g2g.setPaint(new GradientPaint(10, 40, Color.red, 45, 100, Color.green, true));


    // draw the rounded rectangle, filled
    g2g.fill(roundRect);
  }
}
```

As you are aware, the `paint` method is called as soon as the object becomes visible. If you take a look at that method, you will see that after calling the `paint` method of the superclass (as usual) the `Graphics` object is type cast to a `Graphics2D` object, thus giving it all the capabilities of that class, while retaining those of the `Graphics` class:

```
Graphics2D g2g = (Graphics2D) g;
```

The next thing we do is to define a number of shapes using classes from the `java.awt.geom` package. The first of these is a rectangle:

```
Rectangle2D.Double rectangle = new Rectangle2D.Double(50, 50, 70, 100);
```

The syntax here is unfamiliar. The classes of `java.awt.geom`, such as `Rectangle2D`, can be specified in either **double** or **float** dimensions – so there is an alternative class that could be used called `Rectangle2D.Float`. In fact `Double` and `Float` are **static** *nested* classes – you can see that the syntax is to separate them from the main class with the dot operator. Classes such as `Rectangle2D` implement the `Shape` interface defined in the `java.awt` package.

The constructor of `Rectangle2D` requires four parameters of type **double**, representing pixels. The first two specify the position of the top left hand corner of the rectangle (as usual, measured along and down from the top left-hand corner of the component). The next two specify, respectively, the width and height of the rectangle.

Next we create an ellipse:

```
Ellipse2D.Double ellipse = new Ellipse2D.Double(150, 50, 70, 100);
```

As you can see, we use the `Ellipse2D.Double` class. the parameters are similar to those of the constructor of the `Rectangle2D.Double` class, but in this case represent the coordinates of the top left-hand corner of the framing rectangle, and its width and height.

The next shape we produce is an arc:

```
Arc2D.Double arc = new Arc2D.Double(250, 50, 100, 110, 70, 160, Arc2D.CHORD);
```

Here we make use of the `Arc2D.Double` class. The constructor that we have used takes seven parameters. As before, the first two determine the coordinates of the top-left hand corner of the framing rectangle (of the ellipse of which the arc is a part); the second two determine the width and height.

The next two parameters are the angles at which we start and stop drawing the arc, anti-clockwise from the quarter-past-three position which represents zero degrees.

The final parameter is the style of the arc. Here we have used `Arc2D.CHORD` – figure 17.14 shows the effect we would have got had we used the other alternatives, `Arc2D.OPEN` and `Arc2D.PIE`.

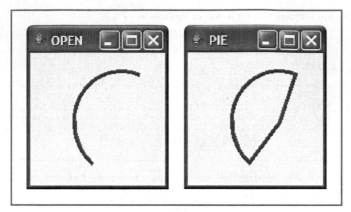

FIGURE 17.14 An OPEN style arc and a PIE style arc

Next we define a line:

```
Line2D.Double line = new Line2D.Double(400, 50, 320, 150);
```

The constructor of `Line2D.Double` is very straightforward – the first two parameters represent the start coordinates of the line, the second two represent the end coordinates.

Finally we create a rounded rectangle:

```
RoundRectangle2D.Double roundRect
                        = new RoundRectangle2D.Double(430, 50, 75, 100, 50, 50);
```

The first four parameters of the constructor of `RoundRectangle2D.Double` are the same as `Rectangle2D.Double`. The last two represent the width and height of the round corners.

Having specified our shapes, we now need to **render** them. Rendering is the process of drawing an image from a model, such as the ones we have specified above. The `Graphics2D` class provides two principal rendering methods, `draw` and `fill`. The former draws the shape with a brushstroke in a style that we can specify as in the examples that follow. The latter draws a solid shape. They both require a `Shape` object as a parameter, and, as we have said, the classes of `Java.awt.geom` all implement the `Shape` interface.

First we will draw the rectangle that we defined earlier. Before doing so we specify the style of the brushstroke:

```
g2g.setStroke(new BasicStroke(15));
```

You can see that we use the `setStroke` method of `Graphics2D` class. This method requires a `Stroke` object as parameter. `Stroke` is an interface defined in `java.awt`, and it is implemented by the class `BasicStroke`. `BasicStroke` has a number of constructors – the one we use here accepts a single **float** value which defines the thickness of the brushstroke.[3] Here we have set the brushstroke to be 15 pixels wide.

---

[3] If you wish to use a decimal value such as 15.5, you must specify that this is a **float** by using the notation 15.5f. If you do not do this, the compiler will take this to be a **double**, and you will get a compiler error.

Now we can draw the rectangle, which you see in figure 17.13:

```
g2g.draw(rectangle);
```

As we have not specified a colour it will be drawn in black, which is the default.

Now we want to draw the ellipse. First we set the colour of the brush to yellow:

```
g2g.setPaint(Color.yellow);
```

As you see, we use the `setPaint` method of `Graphics2D` for this purpose. This method expects to receive a `Paint` object; the `Color` class implements the `Paint` interface, so we can send a `Color` object in as a parameter.

Now we draw the ellipse – we want a solid object this time so we use the `fill` method:

```
g2g.fill(ellipse);
```

Now we draw the arc – we set the colour to blue and the width of the brushstroke to 4:

```
g2g.setPaint(Color.blue);
g2g.setStroke(new BasicStroke(4));
g2g.draw(arc);
```

Next we draw the line – we are going to draw a dashed line which requires us to use a more complex constructor of `BasicStroke`. One of the parameters required by this constructor is an array of **floats**. This determines the length of each dash. If we just want all the dashes to be the same length, as we do here (10 pixels), then all we need to do is to create a one-element array:

```
float dashes[] = { 10 };
```

Now we set the stoke style:

```
g2g.setStroke(new BasicStroke(5, BasicStroke.CAP_SQUARE,  BasicStroke.JOIN_ROUND, 10, dashes, 0));
```

The first parameter sets the width of the line. The second determines the style of the end of the dashes – here we have chosen CAP_SQUARE. You can experiment with the others – CAP_ROUND and CAP_BUTT – yourselves. The next two parameters determine how the corner will look if lines are joined, so they don't affect us here. Again you can experiment with the styles (JOIN_ROUND, JOIN_BEVEL, JOIN_MITER) yourselves. The second of these two determines the limit to which a line can be trimmed when it is joined; as we have said, that will not affect our demonstration here, but once again you could try some experiments if you wish. The next parameter is the **float** array that we defined earlier – dashes. The final parameter indicates the start index of the dashes array (this is only relevant if you have defined different lengths for each dash – in our case we simply start at the first – and only – index, 0).

We are now able to set the colour and draw the line:

```
g2g.setPaint(Color.red);
g2g.draw(line);
```

Finally we want to draw our rounded rectangle. We want to do this using gradually changing colours, and to achieve this effect we call the `setPaint` method with an object of a class called `GradientPaint`:

```
g2g.setPaint(new GradientPaint(10, 40, Color.red, 45, 100, Color.green, true));
```

You can see that the constructor of `GradientPaint` requires seven parameters. The first two of these specify the point where the gradient effect will start. The third parameter is the starting colour, and the fourth and fifth specify the point where the gradient effect ends. The sixth is the ending colour. The final, **boolean**, parameter specifies whether you want the gradient effect to simply go from the first colour to the last (acyclic – **false**) or to start and end with the same colour (cyclic – **true**). We chose the latter. Once again you can conduct your own experiments using different values.

Having specified the gradient we can draw the filled shape:

```
g2g.fill(roundRect);
```

As we have said, all that we have done in this section is whet your appetite. If you are going on to produce applications such as computer games you will want to consult a specialist text to explore the true power of the `Graphics2D` class.

17.9 Guidelines for creating good user interfaces

Nowadays users expect to access their programs via attractive graphical interfaces, using mice, pull-down or pop-up menus, icons and so on. A great deal has been written about the human–computer interface, and there has been much research on the subject. Here we summarize a few of these ideas in order to furnish you with some simple guidelines to help you when you are creating user interfaces for your applications:

- The first rule is to keep it simple. Resist the temptation to show off your programming skills by making your interface too flashy or overly complex. The usual result of this is to put the user off the program.
- Don't use too many colours on one screen; the psychological effect of this can be to make the user feel bombarded by too much at one time.
- Try not to mix too many fonts. Although the idea of having a number of different fonts might sound tempting at first, the effect of this is recognized as having a negative effect on the eye.
- Think carefully about how the user might navigate through the program – don't bury menu options or different screens in large numbers of layers. Always provide a simple route back to the main program menu or screen – and apart from that, provide just one way back and one way forward.

- Think carefully about who is going to be using the program. Will it be an expert user or a novice user? What sort of language are you using, and is it appropriate for the type of user in question? For example, a dialogue window that says "Sorry, but the file you have requested does not exist" is likely to be far more helpful to the average user than "File I/O error".

- Think carefully about the needs of users with disabilities. For example, people with visual impairments require such things as strongly contrasting colours for background and foreground; also such users are likely to benefit greatly from sound prompts. However, a program that actually *relied* on sound prompts would be useless to a deaf person. There is now UK and EU legislation that needs to be adhered to when creating computer programs that might be used for people with special needs – any professional developer needs to be familiar with the laws in this area.

Self-test questions

1   Identify the types of dialogue that appear in the figures below:

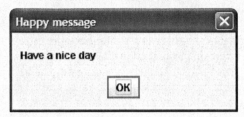

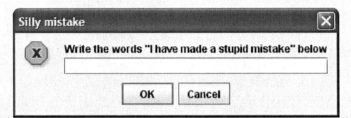

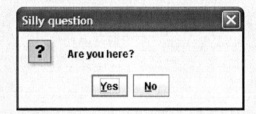

2   Write fragments of code to create each of the JOptionPanes shown in question 1.

3   Explain the principle behind the creation of colours on a monitor.

4   What issues would you take into account in regard to interface design when considering the needs of users with disabilities?

5   Take a look at the interface below that somebody has designed; referring to the guidelines given in section 17.9 for creating good interfaces, identify the features that you consider to be poor design:

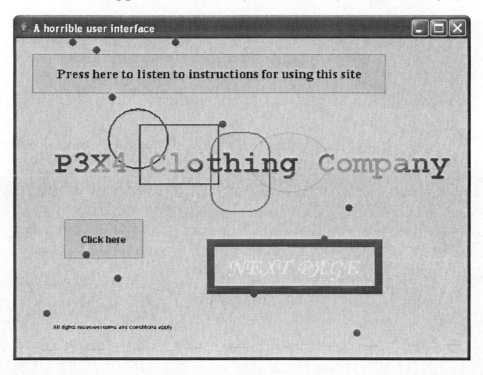

Programming exercises

1   Write a short program to create the dialogues from question 1 of the self-test questions.

2   Look back at section 17.2 in which examples of the different border styles were presented. Experiment with other style combinations by using the various constructors and methods that you learnt about in that section.

3   Making good use of the JOptionPane class (section 17.5), design and implement a program that would help primary school children to test their arithmetic.

4   Adapt the library application you developed in programming exercise 5 of the last chapter by adding a password facility. You can use the JPasswordField class, which extends JTextField. To hide the input you should use the setEchoChar method, which takes as a parameter the character that echoes on the screen when each key is pressed (traditionally a star).

Working with files

18

18.1 Introduction

When we developed our case study in chapters 11 and 12 it became apparent that in reality an application such as that one wouldn't be much use unless we had some way of storing our data permanently – even when the program has been terminated and the computer has been switched off. You will remember that in those chapters, because you had not yet learnt how to do this, we provided a special class called `TenantFileHandler` that enabled you to keep permanent records on disk.

Now it is time to learn how to do this yourself. As you are no doubt already aware, a named block of externally stored data is called a **file**.

When we are taking an object-oriented approach, as we have been doing, we tend not to separate the data from the behaviour; however, when it comes to storing information in files then of course it is only the data that we are interested in storing. When referring to data alone it is customary to use the terms **record** and **field**. A record refers to a single data instance – for example a person, a stock-item, a student and so on; a **field** refers to what in the object-oriented world we would normally call an attribute – a name, a stock number, an exam mark etc.

In this chapter we will learn how to create files, and write information to them, and to read the information back when we need it. We start by looking at this process in the overall context of input and output,

or I/O as it is often called; you will then go on to learn a number of different techniques for keeping permanent copies of your data.

18.2 Input and output

Any computer system must provide a means of allowing information to come in from the outside world
(**input**) and, once it has been processed, to be sent out again (**output**). The whole question of input and
output, particularly where files are concerned, can sometimes seem rather complex, especially from the
point of view of the programmer.

As with all aspects of a computer system, the processes of input and output are handled by the computer
hardware working in conjunction with the system software – that is, the operating system (Windows XP,
Windows Vista or Unix, for example). The particular application program that is running at the time normally deals with input and output by communicating with the operating system, and getting it to perform
these tasks in conjunction with the hardware.

All this involves some very real complexity and involves a lot of low-level details that a programmer is not
usually concerned with; for example, the way in which the system writes to external media such as disks, or
the way it reconciles the differences between the speed of the processor with the speed of the disk-drive.

18.3 Input and output devices

The most common way of getting data input from the outside world is via the keyboard; and the most
common way of displaying output data is on the screen. Therefore, most systems are normally set up so
that the *standard* input and output devices are the keyboard and the screen respectively. However, there are
many other devices that are concerned with input and output: magnetic and optical disks for permanent
storage of data; flash memory; network interface cards and modems for communicating with other computers; and printers for producing hard copies.

We should bear in mind that the process, in one sense, is always the same, no matter what the input or
output device. All the data that is processed by the computer's central processing unit in response to program
instructions is stored in the computer's main memory or RAM (Random Access Memory). Input is the transfer
of data from some external device to main memory whereas output is the transfer of data from main memory
to an external device. In order for input or output to take place, it is necessary for a channel of communication to be established between the device and the computer's memory. Such a channel is referred to as a
stream. The operating system will have established a **standard input stream** and a **standard output stream**,
which will normally be the keyboard and screen respectively. In addition to this, there is usually a **standard
error stream** where error messages can be displayed; this is normally also set to the screen. All of these
default settings for the standard streams can be changed either via the operating system or from within the
program itself.

In previous chapters you have seen that the `System` class has two attributes called `in` and `out`. In addition to this, it has an additional attribute called `err`; these objects are already set up to provide access to the
standard input, output and error streams. The attribute `in` is an object of a class called `InputStream`. This
class provides some low-level methods to deal with basic input – they are low-level because they deal with
sequences of bytes, rather than characters. A higher-level class, `InputStreamReader` can be wrapped

around this class to deal with character input; `InputStreamReader` objects can subsequently be wrapped by another class, `BufferedReader`, which handles input in the form of strings.

This rather complex way of reading from the keyboard is how things were done before Java 5.0 provided the `Scanner` class. Program 18.1 illustrates how you would get keyboard input in this manner.

PROGRAM 18.1

```java
import java.io.*;
public class KeyboardInput
{
  public static void main(String[] args)
  {
    InputStreamReader input = new InputStreamReader (System.in);
    BufferedReader reader = new BufferedReader(input);

    try
    {
      System.out.print("Enter a string: ");
      String test = reader.readLine();
      System.out.println("You entered: " + test);
    }

    catch(IOException e)
    {
      e.printStackTrace();
    }
  }
}
```

You can see that the `readLine` method of `BufferedReader` is used to get a string of characters from the keyboard; as you would expect, the method reads characters from the keyboard until the user presses the return key. It throws an `IOException` if an error (such as a keyboard lock) occurs during the process, and this has to be handled.

In this chapter, instead of dealing with input and output to the standard streams, we are going to be dealing with the input and output of data to external disk drives in the form of files – but, as you will see, the principles are the same.

18.4 File-handling

The output process, which consists of transferring data from memory to a file, is usually referred to as **writing**; the input process, which consists of transferring data from a file to memory, is referred to as **reading**. Both of these involve some low-level detail to do with the way in which data is stored physically on the disk. As programmers we do not want to have to worry more than is necessary about this process – which, of course, will differ from one machine to the next and from one operating system to the next. Fortunately, Java makes it quite easy for us to deal with these processes. As we shall see, Java provides low-level classes which create **file streams** – input or output streams that handle communication between main memory and a named file on a disk. It also provides higher-level classes which we can "wrap around" the low-level objects, enabling us to use methods that relate more closely to our logical way of thinking about data. In this way we are shielded from having to know too much detail about the way our particular system stores and retrieves data to or from a file.

As we shall see, this whole process enables us to read and write data in terms of units that we understand – for example, in the form of strings, lines of text, or basic types such integers or characters; Java even allows us to store and retrieve whole objects.

18.4.1 Encoding

Java supports three different ways of encoding data – that is, representing data on a disk. These are **text**, **binary** and **object**.

Text encoding means that the data on the disk is stored as characters in the form used by the external system – most commonly ASCII. Java, as we know, uses the Unicode character set, so some conversion takes place in the process, but fortunately the programmer does not have to worry about that. As an example, consider saving the number 107 to a text file – it will be saved as the character '1' in ASCII code (or whatever is used by the system) followed by the character '0', followed by the character '7'. A text file is therefore readable by a text editor (such as Windows Notepad).

Binary encoding, on the other hand, means that the data is stored in the same format as the internal representation of the data used by the program to store data in memory. So the number 107 would be saved as the binary number 1101011. A binary file could not be read properly by a text editor, as we shall see in section 18.6.

Finally, there is object-encoding which is a powerful mechanism provided by Java whereby a whole object can be input or output with a single command.

You are probably asking yourself which is the best method to use when you start to write applications that read and write to files. Well, if your files are going to be read and written by the same application, then it really makes very little difference how they are encoded. Just use the method that seems the easiest for the type of data you are storing. However, do bear in mind that if you wanted your files to be read by a text editor then you must, of course, use the text encoding method.

18.4.2 Access

The final thing that you need to consider before we show you how to write files in Java is the way in which files are accessed. There are two ways in which this can take place – **serial** access and **random** access. In the first (and more common) method, each item of data is read (or written) in turn. The operating system provides what is known as a **file pointer**, which is really just a location in memory that keeps track of where we have got to in the process of reading or writing to a file.

Another way to access data in a file is to go directly to the record you want – this is known as random access, and is a bit like going straight to the clip you want on a DVD; whereas serial access is like using a video tape, where you have to work your way through the entire tape to get to the bit you want. Java provides a class (`RandomAccessFile`) that we can use for random access. We will start, however, with serial access.

18.5 Reading and writing to text files

In this and the following section we are going to use as an example a very simple class called Car; the code for this class is given below, and the source code is provided on the accompanying CD:

THE *CAR* CLASS

```java
public class Car
{
  private String registration;
  private String make;
  private double price;

  public Car(String registrationIn, String makeIn, double priceIn)
  {
    registration = registrationIn;
    make = makeIn;
    price = priceIn;
  }

  public String getRegistration()
  {
    return registration;
  }

  public String getMake()
  {
    return make;
  }

  public double getPrice()
  {
    return price;
  }
}
```

Program 18.2 below is a very simple menu-driven program that manipulates a list of cars, held in memory as a List; it provides the facility to add new cars to the list, to remove cars from the list and to display the details of all the cars in the list. As it is a demonstration program only, we have not bothered with such things as input validation, or checking if the list is empty before we try to remove an item.

The difference between this and other similar programs that we have discussed before is that the list is kept as a permanent record – as we mentioned before, we did a similar thing in our case study in chapter 12, but there the process was hidden from you.

The program is designed so that reading and writing to the file takes place as follows: when the quit option is selected, the list is written as a permanent text file called Cars.txt; each time the program is run, this file is read into memory.

The program is presented below; notice that we have provided two helper methods, writeList and readList, for the purpose of accessing the file; as we shall explain, the writeList method also deals with creating the file for the first time. Notice also that, for convenience, we are making use of the EasyScanner class that we developed in chapter 8.

PROGRAM 18.2

```
import java.util.*; // required for List and ArrayList
import java.io.*; // required for handling the IOExceptions

public class TextFileTester
{
  public static void main(String[] args)
  {
    char choice;
    // create an empty list to hold Cars
    List<Car> carList = new ArrayList<Car>();
    // read the list from file when the program starts
    readList(carList);
    // menu options
    do
    {
      System.out.println("\nText File Tester");
      System.out.println("1. Add a car");
      System.out.println("2. Remove a car");
      System.out.println("3. List all cars");
      System.out.println("4. Quit\n");
      choice = EasyScanner.nextChar();
      System.out.println(); switch(choice)
      {
        case '1' : addCar(carList);
                   break;
        case '2' : removeCar(carList);
                   break;
        case '3' : listAll(carList);
                   break;
        case '4' : writeList(carList); // write to the file
                   break;
```

```
      default : System.out.print
                ("\nPlease choose a number from 1 - 4 only\n ");
    }
  }while(choice != '4');
}


// method for adding a new car to the list
static void addCar(List<Car> carListIn)
{
  String tempReg;
  String tempMake;
  double tempPrice;

  System.out.print("Please enter the registration number: ");
  tempReg = EasyScanner.nextString();
  System.out.print("Please enter the make: ");
  tempMake = EasyScanner.nextString();
  System.out.print("Please enter the price: ");
  tempPrice = EasyScanner.nextDouble();
  carListIn.add(new Car(tempReg, tempMake, tempPrice));
}


/* method for removing a car from the list - in a real application this would need to
   include some validation */
static void removeCar(List<Car> carListIn)
{
  int pos;
  System.out.print("Enter the position of the car to be removed: ");
  pos = EasyScanner.nextInt();
  carListIn.remove(pos - 1);
}


// method for listing details of all cars in the list
static void listAll(List<Car> carListIn)
{
  for(Car item : carListIn)
  {
    System.out.println(item.getRegistration()
                    + " "
                    + item.getMake()
                    + " "
                    + item.getPrice());
  }
}
```

```java
// method for writing the file
static void writeList(List<Car> carListIn)
{
  try
  {
    /* create a FileWriter object, carFile, that handles the low-level details of writing
       the list to a file which we have called "Cars.txt" */
    FileWriter carFile = new FileWriter("Cars.txt");
    /* now create a PrintWriter object to wrap around carFile; this allows us to user
       high-level functions such as println */
    PrintWriter carWriter = new PrintWriter(carFile);
    // write each element of the list to the file
    for(Car item : carListIn)
    {
      carWriter.println(item.getRegistration());
      carWriter.println(item.getMake());
      // println can accept a double, then write it as a text string
      carWriter.println(item.getPrice());
    }
    // close the file so that it is no longer accessible to the program
    carWriter.close();
  }

  // handle the exception thrown by the FileWriter methods
  catch(IOException e)
  {
    System.out.println("There was a problem writing the file");
  }
}


// method for reading the file
static void readList(List<Car> carListIn)
{
  String tempReg;
  String tempMake;
  String tempStringPrice;
  double tempDoublePrice;
  try
  {
    /* create a FileReader object, carFile, that handles the lowlevel details of reading the
       list from the "Cars.txt" file */
    FileReader carFile = new FileReader("Cars.txt");
```

```
      /* now create a BufferedReader object to wrap around carFile; this allows us to
         user high-level functions such as readLine */
      BufferedReader carStream = new BufferedReader(carFile);
      // read the first line of the file
      tempReg = carStream.readLine();
      /* read the rest of the first record, then all the rest of the records until the end of
         the file is reached */
      while(tempReg != null) // a null string indicates end of file
      {
        tempMake = carStream.readLine();
        tempStringPrice = carStream.readLine();
        // as this is a text file we have to convert the price to double
        tempDoublePrice = Double.parseDouble(tempStringPrice);
        carListIn.add(new Car(tempReg, tempMake, tempDoublePrice));
        tempReg = carStream.readLine();
      }
      // close the file so that it is no longer accessible to the program
      carStream.close();
    }

    // handle the exception that is thrown by the FileReader constructor if the file is not found
    catch(FileNotFoundException e)
    {
      System.out.println("\nNo file was read");
    }

    // handle the exception thrown by the FileReader methods
    catch(IOException e)
    {
      System.out.println("\nThere was a problem reading the file");
    }
  }
}
```

It is only the writeList and readList methods that we need to analyse here – none of the other methods involves anything new. Let's start with writeList. The first thing to notice is that, after declaring a Car object, we enclose everything in a **try** block. This is because all the methods (including the constructor) of the FileWriter class that we are going to use throw IOExceptions in situations in which the file cannot be written (for example if the disk is full).

The first thing we need to do (within the **try** block) is to open a file in which to keep our records. To do this we use the class called `FileWriter`; this is one of the classes we talked about earlier that provide the low-level communication between the program and the file. By opening a file we establish a *stream* through which we can output data to the file. We create a `FileWriter` object, `carFile`, giving it the name of the file to which we want to write the data:

```
FileWriter carFile = new FileWriter("Cars.txt");
```

In this case we have called the file `Cars.txt`.[1] Creating the new `FileWriter` object causes the file to be opened in output mode – meaning that it is ready to receive data; if no file of this name exists then one will be created. Opening the file in this way (in output mode) means that any data that we write to the file will wipe out what was previously there. That is what we need for this particular application, because we are simply going to write the entire list when the program terminates. Sometimes, however, it is necessary to open a file in **append** mode; in this mode any data written to the file would be written after the existing data. To do this we would simply have used another constructor, which takes an additional (**boolean**) parameter indicating whether or not we require append mode:

```
FileWriter carFile = new FileWriter("Cars.txt", true);
```

The next thing we do is create an object, `carWriter`, of the `PrintWriter` class, sending it the `carFile` object as a parameter.

```
PrintWriter carWriter = new PrintWriter(carFile);
```

This object can now communicate with our file via the `carFile` object; `PrintWriter` objects have higher-level methods than `FileWriter` objects (for example `print` and `println`) that enable us to write whole strings like we do when we output to the screen.

Now we are ready to write each `Car` in the list to our file – we can use a **for** loop for this:

```
for(Car item : carListIn)
{
  carWriter.println(item.getRegistration());
  carWriter.println(item.getMake());
  carWriter.println(item.getPrice());
}
```

On each iteration we use the `println` method of our `PrintWriter` object, `carWriter`, to write the registration number, the make and the price of the car to the file; `println` converts the price to a `String` before writing it. Notice also that the `println` method inserts a newline character at the end of the string

---

[1] As we have not supplied an absolute pathname, the file will be saved in the current directory.

that it prints; if we did not want the newline character to be inserted, we would use the `print` method instead.

Now that we have finished with the file it is most important that we *close* it. Closing the file achieves two things. First, it ensures that a special character, the end-of-file marker,[2] is written at the end of the file. This enables us to detect when the end of the file has been reached when we are reading it – more about this when we explore the `readList` method. Second, closing the file means that it is no longer accessible by the program, and is therefore not susceptible to being written to in error. We close the file by calling the `close` method of `PrintWriter`:

```
carWriter.close();
```

Finally we have to handle any `IOExceptions` that may be thrown by the `FileWriter` methods:

```
catch(IOException e)
{
  System.out.println("There was a problem writing the file");
}
```

In a moment we will explore the code for reading the file. But bear in mind that if we were to run our program and add a few records, and then quit the program, we would have saved the data to a text-file called `Cars.txt`, so we should be able to read this file with a text editor. When we did this, we created three cars, and then looked inside the file using Windows Notepad. Figure 18.1 shows the result.

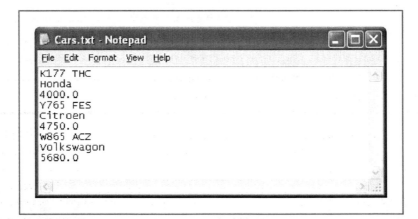

FIGURE 18.1 Viewing a text file with Windows Notepad

As we have written each field using the `println` statement, each one, as you can see, starts on a new line. If our aim were to view the file with a text editor as we have just done, then this might not be the most suitable format – we might, for example, have wanted to have one record per line; we could also have printed

---

[2] Most systems use ASCII character 26 as the end-of-file marker.

some headings if we had wished. However, it is actually our intention to make our program read the entire file into our list when the program starts – and as we shall now see, one field per line makes reading the text file nice and easy. So let's take a look at our readList method.

First, we need to declare some variables to hold the value of each field as we progressively read through the file. Remembering that this is a text file we declare three Strings:

```
String tempReg;
String tempMake;
String tempStringPrice;
```

But the last of these will have to be converted to a **double** before we store it in the list so we also need a variable to hold this value once it is converted:

```
double tempDoublePrice;
```

Now, as before, we put everything into a **try** block, as we are going to have to deal with the exceptions that may be thrown by the various methods we will be using.

The first thing we need to do is to open the file that we wish to read; we create an object – carFile – of the class FileReader which deals with the low-level details involved in the process of reading a file. The name of the file, Cars.txt, that we wish to read is sent in as a parameter to the constructor; this file is then opened in read mode.

```
FileReader carFile = new FileReader("Cars.txt");
```

Now, in order that we can use some higher-level read methods, we wrap up our carFile object in an object of a class called BufferedReader. We have called this new object carStream.

```
BufferedReader carStream = new BufferedReader(carFile);
```

Now we are going to read each field of each record in turn, so we will need some sort of loop. The only problem is to know when to stop – this is because the number of records in the file can be different each time we run the program. There are different ways in which to approach this problem. One very good way (although not the one we have used here), if the same program is responsible for both reading and writing the file, is simply to write the total number of records as the first item when the file is written. Then, when reading the file, this item is the first thing to be read – and once this number is known a **for** loop can be used to read the records.

However, it may well be the case that the file was written by another program (such as a text editor). In this case it is necessary to check for the end-of-file marker that we spoke about earlier. In order to help you understand this process we are using this method here, even though we could have used the first (and perhaps simpler) method.

This is what we have to do: we have to read the first field of each record, then check whether that field began with the end-of-file marker. If it did, we must stop reading the file, but if it didn't we have to carry on and read the remaining fields of that record. Then we start the process again for the next record.

Some pseudocode should make the process clear; we have made this pseudocode specific to our particular example:

```
BEGIN
    READ the registration number field of the first record
    LOOP While the field just read does not contain the end-of-file marker
    BEGIN
        READ the make field of the next record
        READ the price field of the next record
        CONVERT the price to a double
        CREATE a new car with details just read and add it to the list
        READ the registration number field of the next record
    END
END
```

The code for this is shown below:

```
tempReg = carStream.readLine();
while(tempReg != null) // a null string indicates end of file
{
  tempMake = carStream.readLine();
  tempStringPrice = carStream.readLine();
  tempDoublePrice = Double.parseDouble(tempStringPrice);
  carListIn.add (new Car(tempReg, tempMake, tempDoublePrice));
  tempReg = carStream.readLine();
}
```

Notice that we are using the `readLine` method of `BufferedReader` to read each record. This method reads a line of text from the file; a line is considered anything that is terminated by the newline character. The method returns that line as a `String` (which does not include the newline character). However, if the line read consists of the end-of-file marker, then `readLine` returns a **null**, making it very easy for us to check if the end of the file has been reached. In section 18.7 you will be able to contrast this method of `BufferedReader` with the `read` method, which reads a single character only.

Once we have finished with the file, we mustn't forget to close it!

```
carStream.close();
```

Finally, we must handle any exceptions that may be thrown by the methods of `FileReader`; first, the constructor throws a `FileNotFound` exception if the file is not found:

```
catch(FileNotFoundException e)
{
  System.out.println("\nNo file was read");
}
```

All the other methods may throw `IOExceptions`:

```
catch(IOException e)
{
  System.out.println("\nThere was a problem reading the file");
}
```

18.6 Reading and writing to binary files

In many ways, it makes little difference whether we store our data in text format or binary format; but it is, of course, important to know the sort of file that we are dealing with when we are reading it. For example, in the previous section you saw that we needed to convert a `String` to a **double** when it came to handling the price of a car. However, it is important for you to be familiar with the ways of handling both types of file, so now we will show you how to read and write data to a binary file using exactly the same example as before.

The only difference in our program will be the `writeList` and `readList` methods. First, let's look at the code for the new `writeList` method:

```
static void writeList(List<Car> carListIn)
{
  try
  {
    FileOutputStream carFile = new FileOutputStream("Cars.bin");
    DataOutputStream carWriter = new DataOutputStream(carFile);
    for(Car item : carListIn)
    {
      carWriter.writeUTF(item.getRegistration());
      carWriter.writeUTF(item.getMake());
      carWriter.writeDouble(item.getPrice());
    }
    carWriter.close();
  }
  catch(IOException e)
  {
    System.out.println("There was a problem writing the file");
  }
}
```

You can see that the process is similar to the one we used to write a text file, but here the two classes that we are using are `FileOutputStream` and `DataOutputStream` which deal with the low-level and high-level processes respectively. The `DataOutputStream` class provides methods such as `writeDouble`, `writeInt` and `writeChar` for writing all the basic scalar types, as well a method called `writeUTF` for writing strings. UTF stands for *Unicode Transformation Format*, and the method is so called because it converts the Unicode characters (which are used in Java) to the more commonly used ASCII format when it writes the string to a file.

Before moving on to the `readList` method it is worth reminding ourselves that a file written in this way – that is, a binary file – cannot be read by a text editor. And to prove the point, figure 18.2 shows the result of trying to read such a file in Windows Notepad.

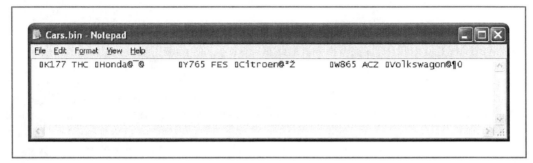

FIGURE 18.2 Trying to read a binary file with a text editor

So now we can look at the `readList` method:

```java
static void readList(List<Car> carListIn)
{
  String tempReg;
  String tempMake;
  double tempPrice;
  boolean endOfFile = false;
  try
  {
    FileInputStream carFile = new FileInputStream("Cars.bin");
    DataInputStream carStream = new DataInputStream(carFile);
    while(endOfFile == false)
    {
      try
      {
        tempReg = carStream.readUTF();
        tempMake = carStream.readUTF();
        tempPrice = carStream.readDouble();
        carListIn.add(new Car(tempReg, tempMake, tempPrice));
      }
      catch(EOFException e)
```

```
      {
        endOfFile = true;
      }
    }
    carStream.close();
  }
  catch(FileNotFoundException e)
  {
    System.out.println("\nThere are currently no records");
  }


  catch(IOException e)
  {
    System.out.println("There was a problem reading the file");
  }
}
```

You can see that the two classes we use for reading binary files are `FileInputStream` for low-level access and `DataInputStream` for the higher-level functions; they have equivalent methods to the those we saw previously when writing to files.

The most important thing to observe in this method is the way we test whether we have reached the end of the file. In the case of a binary file we can do this by making use of the fact that the `DataInputStream` methods throw `EOFExceptions` when an end of file marker has been detected during a read operation. So all we have to do is declare a **boolean** variable, `endOfFile`, which we initially set to **false**, and we use this as the termination condition in the **while** loop. Then we enclose our read operations in a **try** block, and, when an exception is thrown, `fileNotFound` is set to **true** within the **catch** block, causing the **while** loop to terminate.

18.7 Reading a text file character by character

As you will have realized by now, there are many ways in which we can deal with handling files, and the methods we choose will depend largely on what it is we want to achieve.

In this section we will show you how to read a text file character by character – this is a useful technique if we do not know anything about the structure of the file. The way we have done this is to add a new option to the `FileHandler` class that we developed in section 16.4. We have added a *Display contents* option to the File menu. To demonstrate this we created a file called `Poem.txt` with a text editor, and when we selected it and displayed its contents we got the result shown in figure 18.3.

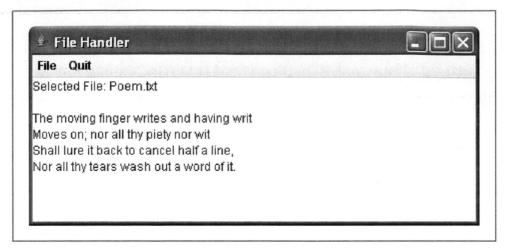

FIGURE 18.3 Using the *Display contents* option of the *FileHandler* class

The technique that we used to do this was to read each character of the file, display it in the viewing area, then move on to the next character. We have designed the program to stop either when the end of the file has been reached or when a stipulated maximum number of characters has been read. We put this last condition in as a safeguard in case the user should try to display a very large file by mistake.

Here is the code for the event-handler for the new menu option, which we called `displayContents-Choice`:

```
if(e.getSource() == displayContentsChoice)
{
  try
  {
    final int MAX = 1000;
    FileReader testFile = new FileReader(chosenFile.getName());
    BufferedReader textStream = new BufferedReader(testFile);
    int ch; // to hold the integer (Unicode) value of the character
    char c; // to hold the character when type cast from integer
    int counter = 0; // to count the number of characters read so far
    ch = textStream.read(); // read the first character from the file
    c = (char) ch; // type cast from integer to character
    viewArea.append("\n");
    /* continue through the file until either the end of the file is reached (in which
       case -1 is returned) or the  maximum number of characters stipulated have been read */
    while( ch != -1 && counter <= MAX)
    {
      counter++; // increment the counter
      viewArea.append("" + c); // display the character
```

```
      ch = textStream.read(); // read the next character
      c = (char) ch;
    }
    textStream.close();
    viewArea.append("\n");
  }


  catch(IOException ioe)
  {
    if(chosenFile == null) // no file selected
    {
      viewArea.append("No file selected\n");
    }
    else
    {
      viewArea.append("There was a problem reading the file\n");
    }
  }
}
```

The main thing to notice here is that we are using the `read` method of `BufferedReader`; this method reads a single character from the file and returns an integer, the Unicode value of the character read. If the character read was the end-of-file marker then it returns −1, making it an easy matter for us to check whether the end of the file has been reached. In the above example, as explained earlier, we stop reading the file if we have reached the end or if more than the maximum number of characters allowed has been read; here we have set that maximum to 1000. You can see that in the above method, after each read operation, we type cast the integer to a character, which we then display in the view area.

18.8 Object serialization

If you are going to be dealing with files that will be accessed only within a Java program, then one of the easiest ways to do this is to make use of two classes called `ObjectInputStream` and `ObjectOutputStream`. These classes have methods called, respectively, `readObject` and `write-Object` that enable us to read and write whole objects from and to files. The process of converting an object into a stream of data suitable for storage on a disk is called **serialization**.

Any class whose objects are to be read and written using the above methods must implement the interface `Serializable`. This is a type of interface that we have not actually come across before – it is known as a **marker** and in fact contains no methods. Its purpose is simply to make an "announcement" to anyone using the class; namely that objects of this class can be read and written as whole objects. In designing a class we can, then, choose not to make our class `Serializable` – we might want to do this for security reasons (for example, to stop whole objects being transportable over the Internet) or to avoid errors in a distributed environment where the code for the class was not present on every machine.

In the case of our `Car` class, we therefore need to declare it in the following way before we can use it in a program that handles whole objects:

```
public class Car implements Serializable
```

Note that the `Serializable` interface resides within the `java.io` package, so this package needs to be imported for us to access it.

Now we can rewrite the `writeList` and `readList` methods of program 18.2 so that we manipulate whole objects. First the `writeList` method:

```
static void writeList(List<Car> carListIn)
{
  try
  {
    FileOutputStream carFile = new FileOutputStream("Cars.obf");
    ObjectOutputStream carStream = new ObjectOutputStream(carFile);

    for(Car item : carListIn)
    {
      carStream.writeObject(item);
    }
    carStream.close();
  }
  catch(IOException e)
  {
    System.out.println("There was a problem writing the file");
  }
}
```

You can see how easy this is – you just need one line to save a whole object to a file by using the `write-Object` method of `ObjectOutputStream`.

Now the `readList` method:

```
static void readList(List<Car> carListIn)
{
  boolean endOfFile = false;
  Car tempCar;
  try
  {
    // create a FileInputStream object, carFile
    FileInputStream carFile = new FileInputStream("Cars.obf");
    // create an ObjectInputStream object to wrap around carFile
```

```
    ObjectInputStream carStream = new ObjectInputStream(carFile);
    // read the first (whole) object with the readObject method
    tempCar = (Car) carStream.readObject();
    while(endOfFile != true)
    {
      try
      {
        carListIn.add(tempCar);
        // read the next (whole) object
        tempCar = (Car) carStream.readObject();
      }
      /* use the fact that readObject throws an EOFException to check whether the end of the
         file has been reached */
      catch(EOFException e)
      {
        endOfFile = true;
      }
    }
    carStream.close();
  }

catch(FileNotFoundException e)
{
  System.out.println("\nNo file was read");
}

catch(ClassNotFoundException e) // thrown by readObject
{
  System.out.println ("\nTrying to read an object of an unknown class");
}

catch(StreamCorruptedException e) // thrown by the constructor
{
  System.out.println("\nUnreadable file format");
}

catch(IOException e)
{
  System.out.println("There was a problem reading the file");
}
}
```

Again you can see how easy this is – a whole object is read with the readObject method.

We should draw your attention to a few of the exception handling routines we have used here – first, notice that we have once again made use of the fact that readObject throws an EOFException to check for the end of the file. Second, notice that readObject also throws a ClassNotFoundException, which indicates that the object just read does not correspond to any class known to the program. Finally, the constructor throws a StreamCorruptedException, which indicates that the input stream given to it was not produced by an ObjectOutputStream object – underlining the fact that reading and writing whole objects are complementary techniques that are specific to Java programs.

One final thing to note – if an attribute of a Serializable class is itself an object of another class, then that class too must be Serializable in order for us to be able to read and write whole objects as we have just done. You will probably have noticed that in the case of the Car class, one of its attributes is a String – fortunately the String class does indeed implement the Serializable interface, which is why we had no problem using it in this way in our example.

Before moving on, it is worth noting that all the Java collection classes such as HashMap and ArrayList are themselves Serializable.

18.9 Random access files

All the programs that we have looked at so far in this chapter have made use of serial access. For small applications this will probably be all you need – however, if you were to be writing applications that handled very large data files it would be desirable to use random access methods. Fortunately Java provides us with this facility.

The class that we need is called RandomAccessFile. This enables us to open a file for random access. Random access files can be opened in either read–write mode or in read-only mode; the constructor therefore takes, in addition to the name of the file, an additional String parameter which can be either "rw" or "r", indicating the mode in which the file is to be opened.

In addition to methods similar to those of the DataOutputStream class (such as writeUTF, readDouble and so on), RandomAccessFile has a method called seek. This takes one attribute, of type long, which indicates how many bytes to move the file-pointer before starting a read or write operation.

So now we have the question of how far to move the pointer – we need to be able to calculate the size of each record. If we are dealing only with primitive types, this is an easy matter. These types all take up a fixed amount of storage space, as shown in table 18.1.

byte	**1 byte**
short	2 bytes
char	2 bytes
int	4 bytes
long	8 bytes
float	4 bytes
double	8 bytes
boolean	1 bit[3]

TABLE 18.1 Size of the primitive types

The difficulty comes when a record contains `Strings`, as is commonly the case. The size of a `String` object varies according to how many characters it contains. What we have to do is to restrict the length of each string to a given amount; let's take the `Car` class as an example. The data elements of any `Car` object consist of two `Strings` and a **double**. We will make the decision that the two `String` attributes – registration number and make – will be restricted to 10 characters only. Now, any `String` variable will always take up one byte for each character, plus two extra bytes (at the beginning) to hold an integer representing the length of the `String`. So now we can calculate the maximum amount of storage space we need for a car as follows:

```
registration (String)      12 bytes

make (String)              12 bytes

price (double)              8 bytes

TOTAL                      32 bytes
```

This still leaves us with one problem – what if the length of one of the `String` attributes entered is actually less than 10? The best way to deal with this is to pad the string out with spaces so that it always contains *exactly* 10 characters. This means that the size of every `Car` object will always be exactly 32 bytes – you will see how we have done this when you study program 18.3. This program uses a rather different approach to the one we have used so far in this chapter. Two options (as well as a *Quit* option) are provided. The first, the option to add a car, simply adds the car to the end of the file. The second, to display the details of a car, asks the user for the position of the car in the file then reads this record directly from the file. You can see that there is now no need for a `List` in which to store the cars.

Study the program carefully – then we will discuss it. Note that we have made use of our `EasyScanner` class here.

---

[3] Allow for 1 byte when calculating storage space.

PROGRAM 18.3

```java
import java.io.*;

public class RandomFileTester
{
  static final int CAR_SIZE = 32; // each record will be 32 bytes
  public static void main(String[] args)
  {
    char choice;
    do
    {
      System.out.println("\nRandom File Tester");
      System.out.println("1. Add a car");
      System.out.println("2. Display a car");
      System.out.println("3. Quit\n");
      choice = EasyScanner.nextChar(); // note the use of EasyScanner
      System.out.println();
      switch(choice)
      {
        case '1' : addCar();
                   break;
        case '2' : displayCar();
                   break;
        case '3' : break;
        default : System.out.print("\nChoose 1 - 3 only please\n ");
      }
    }while(choice != '3');
  }

  static void addCar()
  {
    String tempReg;
    String tempMake;
    double tempPrice;
    System.out.print("Please enter the registration number: ");
    tempReg = EasyScanner.nextString();
    //limit the registration number to 10 characters
    if(tempReg.length() > 10)
    {
      System.out.print("Ten characters only - please re-enter: ");
      tempReg = EasyScanner.nextString();
    }
```

```java
   // pad the string with spaces to make it exactly 10 characters long
   for(int i = tempReg.length() + 1 ; i <= 10 ; i++)
   {
       tempReg = tempReg.concat(" ");
   }


   // get the make of the car from the user
   System.out.print("Please enter the make: ");
   tempMake = EasyScanner.nextString();

   // limit the make number to 10 characters
   if(tempMake.length() > 10)
   {
     System.out.print("Ten characters only - please re-enter: ");
     tempMake = EasyScanner.nextString();
   }
   // pad the string with spaces to make it exactly 10 characters long
   for(int i = tempMake.length() + 1; i <= 10; i++)
   {
     tempMake = tempMake.concat(" ");
   }


   // get the price of the car from the user
   System.out.print("Please enter the price: ");
   tempPrice = EasyScanner.nextDouble();


   // write the record to the file
   writeRecord(new Car(tempReg, tempMake, tempPrice));
}


static void displayCar()
{
  int pos;
  // get the position of the item to be read from the user
  System.out.print("Enter the car's position in the list: ");
  pos = EasyScanner.nextInt(); // read the record requested from file
  Car tempCar = readRecord(pos);
  if(tempCar != null)
  {
    System.out.println(tempCar.getRegistration().trim()
      + " "
```

```
            + tempCar.getMake().trim()

            + " "

            + tempCar.getPrice());
    }
    else
    {
      System.out.println("Invalid postion") ;
    }
  }
  static void writeRecord(Car tempCar)
  {
    try
    {
      // open a RandomAccessFile in read-write mode
      RandomAccessFile carFile = new RandomAccessFile("Cars.rand", "rw");
      // move the pointer to the end of the file
      carFile.seek(carFile.length());
      // write the three fields of the record to the file
      carFile.writeUTF(tempCar.getRegistration());
      carFile.writeUTF(tempCar.getMake());
      carFile.writeDouble(tempCar.getPrice());
      // close the file
      carFile.close();
    }
    catch(IOException e)
    {
      System.out.println("There was a problem writing the file");
    }
  }


  static Car readRecord(int pos)
  {
    String tempReg;
    String tempMake;
    double tempPrice;
    Car tempCar = null; // a null value will be returned if there was a problem reading the record
    try
    {
      // open a RandomAccessFile in read-only mode
      RandomAccessFile carFile = new RandomAccessFile("Cars.rand","r");
```

```
      // move the pointer to the start of the required record
      carFile.seek((pos-1) * CAR_SIZE);
      // read the three fields of the record from the file
      tempReg = carFile.readUTF();
      tempMake = carFile.readUTF();
      tempPrice = carFile.readDouble();
      // close the file
      carFile.close();
      // use the data just read to create a new Car object
      tempCar = new Car(tempReg, tempMake, tempPrice);
   }
   catch(FileNotFoundException e)
   {
     System.out.println("\nNo file was read");
   }

   catch(IOException e)
   {
     System.out.println("There was a problem reading the file");
   }
   // return the record that was read
   return tempCar;
  }
}
```

You can see that in the addCar method we have called writeRecord with a Car object as a parameter. Let's take a closer look at the writeRecord method. First the line to open the file in read–write mode:

```
RandomAccessFile carFile = new RandomAccessFile ("Cars.rand", "rw");
```

Now the instruction to move the file pointer:

```
carFile.seek(carFile.length());
```

You can see how we use the seek method to move the pointer a specific number of bytes; here the correct number of bytes is the size of the file (as we want to write the new record at the end of the file), so we use the length method of RandomAccessFile to determine this number.

Now we can move on to look at the readRecord method. You can see that this is called from within the displayCar method, with an integer parameter, representing the position of the required record in the file.

The file is opened in read-only mode:

```
RandomAccessFile carFile = new RandomAccessFile ("Cars.rand","r");
```

Then the seek method of RandomAccessFile is invoked as follows:

```
carFile.seek((pos-1) * CAR_SIZE);
```

You can see that the number of bytes through which to move the pointer has been calculated by multiplying the size of the record by one less than the position. This is because in order to read the first record we don't move the pointer at all; in order to read the second record we must move it 1 × 32 bytes; for the third record 2 × 32 bytes; and so on.

The final thing to note about program 18.3 is that in the displayCar method we have used the trim method of String to get rid of the extra spaces that we used to pad out the first two fields of the record.

Here is a test run from the program (starting off with an empty file):

```
Random File Tester
1. Add a car
2. View a car
3. Quit

1

Please enter the registration number: R54 HJK
Please enter the make: Vauxhall
Please enter the price: 7000

Random File Tester
1. Add a car
2. View a car
3. Quit

1

Please enter the registration number: T87 EFU
Please enter the make: Nissan
Please enter the price: 9000

Random File Tester
1. Add a car
2. View a car
3. Quit

2

Enter the car's position in the list: 2
T87 EFU Nissan 9000.0
```

Self-test questions

1 Explain the principles of *input* and *output* and identify different input and output devices.

2 What is meant by the term *input/output* stream?

3 Distinguish between *text, binary* and *object encoding* of data.

4 Program 18.2 is to be adapted so that the user is simply asked to enter a number of cars, which, when that process is finished, saves those cars to a text file. The program then terminates. The file does not have to be read from within the program, but should be able to be read by a text editor such as Windows Notepad. The format should be as follows:

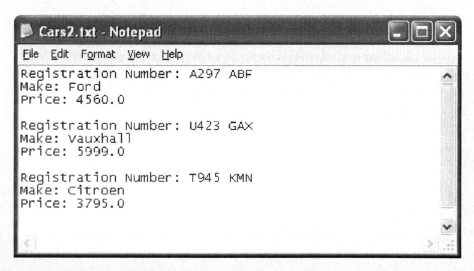

```
Cars2.txt - Notepad
File  Edit  Format  View  Help
Registration Number: A297 ABF
Make: Ford
Price: 4560.0

Registration Number: U423 GAX
Make: Vauxhall
Price: 5999.0

Registration Number: T945 KMN
Make: Citroen
Price: 3795.0
```

Adapt the `writeList` method accordingly.
Hint: remember that a blank line is obtained by calling println with no parameters.

5 What is the difference between *serial access* files and *random access* files?

6 Explain the purpose of the `Serializable` interface.

7 Calculate the number of bytes required to store an object of a class, the attributes of which are declared as follows:

```
private int x;
private char c;
private String s;
```

You can assume that the `String` attribute will always consist of exactly 20 characters.

Programming exercises

You will need to have access to the Car *class, the source code for which is available on the CD – or you can simply copy it from this chapter. The source code for programs 18.2 and 18.3 is also on the CD.*

1 Run program 18.2 then adapt it so that it handles binary files, as described in section 18.6.

2 Adapt program 18.2 so that it behaves in the way described in question 4 above.

3 Add the *Display Contents* option to the `FileHandler` class from chapter 16, as described in section 18.7.

4 Adapt program 18.2 so that it uses object encoding, as explained in section 18.8 (don't forget that the `Car` class must implement the `Serializable` interface).

5 Adapt the `Library` application of chapter 15 so that it keeps permanent records.

6 In chapter 12 the case study made use of a file called `TenantFileHandler` that we wrote for you. This is available on the CD. Study this class carefully, so that you are sure you understand it, then modify it so that it uses:

   a text encoding;

   b object encoding.

Multi-threaded programs

19.1 Introduction

In this chapter you are going to learn how to make a program effectively perform more than one task at the same time – this is known as **multi-tasking**, and Java provides mechanisms for achieving this within a single program.

19.2 Concurrent processes

If you have been using computers for only a few years, then you will probably think nothing of the fact that your computer can appear to be doing two or more things at the same time. For example, a large file could be downloading from the web, while you are listening to music and typing a letter into your word processor. However, those of us who were using desktop computers in the 1980s don't take this for granted! We can remember the days of having to wait for our document to be printed before we could get on with anything else – the idea of even having two applications like a spreadsheet and a database loaded at the same time on a personal computer would have been pretty exciting!

In recent years "dual core" computers have become available on a fairly wide scale – such computers have more than one processor, so it does not seem quite so extraordinary that they can perform more than one task at a time. However, multi-tasking has been possible for many years on machines with a single processor – and at first sight this does seem rather extraordinary. The way this is achieved is by some form of **time-slicing**; in other words, the processor does a little bit of one task, then a little bit of the next and so on – and it does this so quickly that it appears that it is all happening at the same time.

A running program is usually referred to as a **process**; two or more processes that run at the same time are called **concurrent** processes. Normally, when processes run concurrently each has its own area in memory where its program code and data are kept, and each process's memory space is protected from any other process. All this is dealt with by the operating system; modern operating systems such as Windows and Unix have a process management component whose job it is to handle all this.

19.3 Threads

We have just introduced the idea of a number of programs – or processes – operating concurrently. There are, however, times when we want a *single* program to perform two or more tasks at the same time. Whereas two concurrent programs are known as processes, each separate task performed by a single program is known as a **thread**. A thread is often referred to as a **lightweight process**, because it takes less of the system's resources to manage threads than it does to manage processes. The reason for this is that threads do not have completely separate areas of memory; they can share code and data areas. Managing threads, which also works on a time-slicing principle, is the job of the JVM working in conjunction with the operating system.

In all the programs we have developed so far, we have always waited for one task to complete before another one starts. So now let's develop a program where this is not the case.

What we are going to try to achieve with this program is a simple counter as shown in figure 19.1.

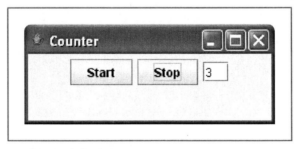

FIGURE 19.1 A simple counter

The intention is that when we press the "Start" button the numbers 1 to 10 will keep flashing by in the window; pressing the "Stop" button should stop this process and clicking on the crosshairs should terminate the application. Intuitively you might think that the way to do this would be to have a loop that keeps flashing the numbers, and which is controlled by some **boolean** variable, so that the loop continues while the variable is set to **true**, and stops when it is set to **false**.

This is what we have tried in our first attempt, which we have called CounterVersionOne. We should warn you, though, that it doesn't do the job, and could make your system hang up.

THE *COUNTERVERSIONONE* CLASS

```java
/* this class doesn't do what we intend! in fact, it could make your system hang up, so we
   don't recommend you try it!*/

import java.awt.*;
import java.awt.event.*;
import javax.swing.*;

public class CounterVersionOne extends JFrame implements ActionListener
{
  private JButton startButton = new JButton("Start");
  private JButton stopButton = new JButton("Stop");
  private JTextField counterWindow = new JTextField(2);
  private boolean go; // it is intended that this variable should control the loop

  public CounterVersionOne()
  {
    setTitle("Counter");
    add(startButton);
    add(stopButton);
    add(counterWindow);
    startButton.addActionListener(this);
    stopButton.addActionListener(this);

    setDefaultCloseOperation(JFrame.EXIT_ON_CLOSE);
    setLayout(new FlowLayout());
    setSize(250,100);
    setLocation(300,300);
    setVisible(true);
  }

  private void startCounterRunning()
  {
    // continuously display the numbers 1 to 10
    int count = 1;
    while(go)
    {
      counterWindow.setText("" + count);
      count++;
      if(count > 10) // reset the counter if it has gone over 10
      {
        count=1;
```

```
      }
    }
}

  public void actionPerformed(ActionEvent e)
  {
    if(e.getSource() == startButton)
    {
      go = true;
      startCounterRunning();
    }
    else if(e.getSource() == stopButton) /* this doesn't actually work, because the
                                           startCounterRunning method is still executing! */
    {
      go = false;
    }
  }
}
```

It is quite easy to see how this program is intended to work. Pressing the "Start" button sets a **boolean** attribute, go, to **true** and then calls the startCounterRunning, method, which looks like this:

```
private void startCounterRunning()
{
  int count = 1;
  while(go)
  {
    counterWindow.setText("" + count);
    count++;
    if(count > 10)
    {
      count=1;
    }
  }
}
```

You can see that this method involves a **while** loop that is controlled by the value of the go attribute; while it is **true** the loop continuously displays the numbers 1 to 10 in the text window.

Pressing the "Stop" button sets the value of go to **false**, with the intention that the loop will terminate. However, if you create an object of this class, as in program 19.1, you will find that pressing the "Stop" button has no effect, and pressing the crosshairs won't terminate the application! In fact it is likely that your whole system will hang up.

PROGRAM 19.1

```java
public class RunCounterVersionOne
{
  public static void main(String[] args)
  {
    new CounterVersionOne();
  }
}
```

Can you see what's wrong here? The answer is that there is only one *thread of control*. The program, as always, starts with the first line of the `main` method and carries on to the end of this method; in this case this involves simply creating a `CounterVersionOne` object. If the mouse is clicked on the "Start" button then, as we have seen, the loop is started. But because there is only a single thread, this is all that can happen. The whole program is now tied up in this loop; it doesn't matter how often you click on the "Stop" button, the program will never get the chance to process this event, because it is busy executing the loop.

What we need is to set up a separate thread that can busy itself with the loop, while another thread carries on with the rest of the program. Luckily Java provides us with a `Thread` class that allows us to do exactly that.

19.4 The *Thread* class

The `Thread` class provides a number of different methods that allow us to create and handle threads in our Java programs. The `Thread` class implements an interface called `Runnable`; this provides a method called `run`, which must be implemented. The code for this method determines the action that takes place when the thread is started.

One of the simplest ways to create a thread is to extend the `Thread` class. Let's do this with our previous example, and create a class called `CounterThread`; this is shown below.

THE *COUNTERTHREAD* CLASS

```java
import javax.swing.*;

public class CounterThread extends Thread
{
  private JTextField counterWindow; // this is the window where the numbers are displayed
  private boolean go = true; // this variable controls the loop

  // the text window where the numbers are displayed is sent in as a parameter to the constructor
  public CounterThread(JTextField windowIn)
  {
    counterWindow = windowIn;
  }
```

```
  public void run()
  {
    int count = 1;
    while(go)
    {
      counterWindow.setText("" + count);

      // Some additional code is going to go here later to improve our program

      count++;
      if(count > 10) // reset the counter if it has gone over 10
      {
        count=1;
      }
    }
  }


  // this method will stop the numbers being displayed
  public void finish()
  {
    go = false;
  }
}
```

You can see that the business of displaying the numbers in the text window is now the responsibility of this class, and the instructions are placed within the run method. This method needs to know where to display the output, so the JTextField object has been passed into the constructor and assigned to an attribute of the class, making it accessible to the run method. You will see shortly that, in fact, we do not actually call this run method directly.

We have also provided a finish method that sets go back to **false**, and therefore terminates the thread.

Now we can write our new class, which we have called CounterVersionTwo:

THE *COUNTERVERSIONTWO* CLASS

```
import java.awt.*;
import java.awt.event.*;
import javax.swing.*;


public class CounterVersionTwo extends JFrame implements ActionListener
```

```
{
  private JButton startButton = new JButton("Start");
  private JButton stopButton = new JButton("Stop");
  private JTextField counterWindow = new JTextField(2);
  private CounterThread thread;

  public CounterVersionTwo()
  {
    setTitle("Counter");
    add(startButton);
    add(stopButton);
    add(counterWindow);

    startButton.addActionListener(this);
    stopButton.addActionListener(this);

    setDefaultCloseOperation(JFrame.EXIT_ON_CLOSE);
    setLayout(new FlowLayout());
    setSize(250,100);
    setLocation(300,300);
    setVisible(true);
  }

  public void actionPerformed(ActionEvent e)
  {
    if(e.getSource() == startButton)
    {
      //create a new thread
      thread = new CounterThread(counterWindow);
      // start the thread
      thread.start();
    }
    else if(e.getSource() == stopButton)
    {
      // stop the thread
      thread.finish();
    }
  }
}
```

You can see that pressing the "Start" button creates a new thread and starts it running by calling the object's start method, which automatically calls the run method; as we mentioned above, the run method should not be called directly, but should always be called by invoking `start`. Pressing the "Stop" button calls the thread's `finish` method.

If you create an object of this class you will see that it now does what we wanted. Pressing "Start" will, as before, cause the numbers to rush by in the display window. You might notice, however, that the way they are displayed is a little erratic; pressing "Stop" does indeed stop the thread – but you might notice that the program does not always respond immediately, but instead continues to display the numbers for a little while before actually stopping. The reason for this slightly erratic behaviour is explained in the section that follows, which also shows how we can improve matters.

19.5 Thread execution and scheduling

As we explained earlier, concurrency, with a single processor, is achieved by some form of time-slicing. Each process or thread is given a little bit of time – referred to as a **quantum** – on the CPU, then the next process or thread takes its turn and so on.

Now, as you can imagine, there are some very complex issues to consider here. For example, what happens if a process that currently has the CPU cannot continue because it is waiting for some input, or perhaps is waiting for an external device like a printer to become available? When new processes come into existence, when do they get their turn? Should all processes get an equal amount of time on the CPU or should there be some way of prioritizing?

The answers to these questions are not within the domain of this book. However, it is important to understand that the responsibility for organizing all this lies with the operating system; in the case of multi-threaded Java programs this takes place in conjunction with the JVM. Different systems use different **scheduling algorithms** for deciding the order in which concurrent threads or processes are allowed CPU time. This is hidden from the user, and from the programmer. In the case of an application such as our counter program, all we can be sure about is the fact that one thread has to complete a quantum on the CPU before another thread gets its turn – we cannot, however, predict the amount of time that will be allocated to each thread; hence the slightly unpredictable behaviour that we have seen.

Fortunately, however, we are not totally at the mercy of the operating system and the JVM. The `Thread` class provides some very useful methods, one of which is a method called `sleep`. This method forces a thread to give up the CPU for a specified amount of time, even if it hasn't completed its quantum. The time interval, in milliseconds, is passed in as a parameter. During this time, other threads can be given the CPU. The `sleep` method could throw an `InterruptedException` and must be enclosed in a **try…catch** block.

So in our `CounterThread` example above, we could rewrite our `run` method as shown below – the additional code is emboldened:

```
public void run()
{
  int count = 1;
  while(go)
  {
    counterWindow.setText("" + count);
    try
```

```
   {
     sleep(1); //force the thread to sleep for 1 msec
   }
   catch(InterruptedException e)
   {
   }
   count++;
   if(count > 10)
   {
     count = 1;
   }
 }
}
```

You can see that now, on every iteration of the loop, we force the thread to sleep for 1 millisecond; this gives any other thread the chance to get a turn on the CPU. So when we run this program in a frame, the "Stop" button responds straight away. This is because, after each number is displayed, the thread rests for a millisecond and the main thread has a chance to get the CPU, so events like mouse-clicks can be processed. The other advantage of using the `sleep` method here is that the cycle can now be timed; you can try altering the sleep time to, say, 500 milliseconds or 1 second, and watch the numbers being displayed accordingly. You might want to adapt this program so that the interval is passed in as a parameter.

In many programs that involve more than one thread you will find it necessary to force a thread to stop after one or more iterations to allow other events to be processed (rather than relying on the unpredictable scheduling of the operating system). If you do not want the thread to wait a specific period of time before resuming, then you can use the `yield` method rather than `sleep`; `yield` does not require any parameters.

19.6 An alternative implementation

Very often it is not possible to extend the `Thread` class, because the class we are writing needs to extend another class such as a `JPanel` or `JFrame`. The `Thread` class provides an alternative constructor that takes as a parameter a `Runnable` object where it expects to find the code for the `run` method.

So, the alternative approach involves creating a class that implements the `Runnable` interface, and then declaring a separate `Thread` object, either within this class or as a separate class. Study the following version of our `CounterThread`:

THE *ALTERNATIVECOUNTER* CLASS

```
import javax.swing.*;

public class AlternativeCounter implements Runnable // implement the Runnable interface
{
  private JTextField counterWindow;
  private boolean go = true;
```

```
// a thread object is now created as an attribute of the class
private Thread cThread = new Thread(this);

public AlternativeCounter(JTextField windowIn)
{
  counterWindow = windowIn;
}

public void run()
{
  int count = 1;
  while(go)
  {
    counterWindow.setText("" + count);
    count++;
    try
    {
      // the sleep method of the thread object is called
      cThread.sleep(1);
    }
    catch(InterruptedException e)
    {
    }
    if(count > 10)
    {
      count = 1;
    }
  }
}

public void begin() // a separate method is now required to start the thread
{
  cThread.start();
}

public void finish()
{
  go = false;
}
}
```

As can be seen from the comments, there are three changes that have been made.

First, a new `Thread` object is created as an attribute. As we explained before, the object where the `run` method is to be found is passed as a parameter; in the above example, it is **this** object itself that we must pass in.

Second, in the `run` method, we previously called the `sleep` method of **this** object. We can no longer do this, of course, because the `AlternativeCounter` class does not extend the `Thread` class. Instead, we call the `sleep` method of the thread object, `cThread`.

Finally, we have had to create a new method, `begin`, which calls the `start` method of `cThread`. Again, we have had to do this because our `AlternativeCounter` class is not an extension of `Thread`, and therefore does not have a `start` method of its own.

In order to make use of this new class we have had to rewrite `CounterVersionTwo`; we have named the new version of this class `CounterVersionThree`:

THE *COUNTERVERSIONTHREE* CLASS

```java
import java.awt.*;
import java.awt.event.*;
import javax.swing.*;


public class CounterVersionThree extends JFrame implements ActionListener
{
  private JButton startButton = new JButton("Start");
  private JButton stopButton = new JButton("Stop");
  private JTextField counterWindow = new JTextField(2);

  /* we are now using the AlternativeCounter class instead of the CounterThread class that we
     used in version two */
  private AlternativeCounter aCounter;

  public CounterVersionThree()
  {
    setTitle("Counter");
    add(startButton);
    add(stopButton);
    add(counterWindow);

    startButton.addActionListener(this);
    stopButton.addActionListener(this);

    setLayout(new FlowLayout());
    setDefaultCloseOperation(JFrame.EXIT_ON_CLOSE);
    setSize(250,100);
```

```
    setLocation(300,300);
    setVisible(true);
  }


  public void actionPerformed(ActionEvent e)
  {
    if(e.getSource() == startButton)
    {
      aCounter = new AlternativeCounter(counterWindow);
      /* this time we have to use the object's begin method; it does not have a start method
         as it is not an extension of Thread */
      aCounter.begin();
    }
    else if(e.getSource() == stopButton)
    {
      aCounter.finish();
    }
  }
}
```

You can see that the only real difference in this version is that we now have to call the begin method of the AlternativeCounter object, instead of the start method as we were able to do in version two.

19.7 Synchronizing threads

In section 19.5 we explained that under normal circumstances the behaviour of two or more threads executing concurrently is not coordinated, and we are not able to predict which threads will be allocated CPU time at any given moment. Uncoordinated behaviour like this is referred to as is **asynchronous** behaviour.

It is, however, often the case that we require two or more concurrently executing threads or processes to be coordinated – and if they were not, we could find we had some serious problems. There are many examples of this. One of the most common is that of a **producer–consumer** relationship, whereby one process is continually producing information that is required by another process. A very simple example of this is a program that copies a file from one place to another. One process is responsible for reading the data, another for writing the data. Since the two processes are likely to be operating at different speeds, this would normally be implemented by providing a *buffer*, that is, a space in memory where the data that has been read is queued while it waits for the write process to access it and then remove it from the queue.

It should be fairly obvious that it could be pretty disastrous if the read process and the write process tried to access the buffer at the same time – both the data and the indices could easily be corrupted. In a situation like this we would need to treat the parts of the program that access the buffer as **critical sections** – that is, sections that can be accessed only by one process at a time.

Implementing critical sections is known as **mutual exclusion**, and fortunately Java provides a mechanism for the implementation of mutual exclusion in multi-threaded programs. In this book we are not going to go into any detail about how this is implemented, because the whole subject of concurrent programming is a vast one, and is best left to texts that deal with that topic. What we intend to do here is simply to explain the mechanisms that are available in Java for coordinating the behaviour of threads.

Java provides for the creation of a **monitor**, that is, a class whose methods can be accessed by only one thread at a time. This entails the use of the modifier `synchronized` in the method header. For instance, a `Buffer` class in the above example might have a `read` method declared as:

```
public synchronized Object read()
{
   .....
}
```

Because it is `synchronized`, as soon as some object invokes this method a **lock** is placed on it; this means that no other object can access it until it has finished executing. This can, however, cause a problem known as **busy waiting**. This means that the method that is being executed by a particular thread has to go round in a loop until some condition is met, and as a consequence the CPU time is used just to keep the thread going round and round in this loop until it times out – not very efficient! As an example of this, consider the `read` and `write` methods that we talked about in the example above. The `read` method would not be able to place any data in the buffer if the buffer were full – it would have to loop until some data was removed by the `write` method; conversely, the `write` method would not be able to obtain any data if the buffer were empty – it would have to wait for the `read` method to place some data there.

Java provides methods to help us avoid busy waiting situations. The `Object` class has a method called `wait`, which suspends the execution of a thread (taking it away from the CPU) until it receives a message from another thread telling it to wake up. The object methods `notify` and `notifyAll` are used for the purpose of waking up other threads. Sensible use of these methods allows programmers to avoid busy waiting situations.

19.8 Thread states

A very useful way to summarize what you have learnt about threads is by means of a **state transition diagram**. Such a diagram shows the various states that an object can be in, and the allowed means of getting from one state to another – the **transitions**. The state transition diagram for a thread is shown in figure 19.2.

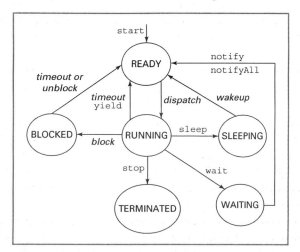

FIGURE 19.2 The state transition diagram for a thread

As we have said, much of the thread's life-cycle is under the control of the operating system and the JVM; however, as you have seen, some transitions are also under the control of the programmer. In figure 19.2 the transitions that are controlled by the operating system and the JVM are italicized; those that the programmer can control are in plain font.

As you have seen, a thread is brought into existence by invoking its `start` method. At this point it goes into the **ready** state. This means it is waiting to be allocated time on the CPU; this decision is the responsibility of the operating system and JVM. Once it is **dispatched** (that is given CPU time), it is said to be in the **running** state. Once a thread is running, a number of things can happen to it:

- It can simply time out and go back to the **ready** state; you have seen that it is possible for the programmer to force this to happen by ensuring that its `yield` method is invoked.

- The programmer can also arrange for the `sleep` method to be called, causing the thread to go into the **sleeping** state for a given period of time. When this time period has elapsed the thread wakes up and goes back to the ready state.

- The programmer can use the `wait` method to force the thread to go into the **waiting** state until a certain condition is met. Once the condition is met, the thread will be informed of this fact by a `notify` or `notifyAll` method, and will return to the ready state.

- A thread can become **blocked**; this is normally because it is waiting for some input, or waiting for an output device to become available. The thread will return to the ready state when either the normal timeout period has elapsed or the input/output operation is completed.

- When the `run` method finishes the thread is terminated. It is actually possible to use the `stop` method of `Thread` for this purpose, but it can be very dangerous to stop a thread in the middle of its execution; it could, for example, be in the middle of writing to a file. It is far better to use a control variable instead, so that the thread terminates naturally.

19.9 Animations

One of the more practical ways of utilizing threads is to produce animations. Clearly, an application that uses animated graphics is going to consist of some sort of continuous loop that displays a serious of different images.

Let's start off by animating our familiar `SmileyFace` program. The following class, when instantiated, produces a face that changes its expression from smile to frown once a second:

THE *ANIMATEDFACE* CLASS

```java
import java.awt.*;
import javax.swing.*;


public class AnimatedFace extends JFrame implements Runnable
{
  private boolean isHappy;


  // a separate thread is required to run the animation
  private Thread thread1;
```

```
public AnimatedFace()
{
  isHappy = true;

  setDefaultCloseOperation(JFrame.EXIT_ON_CLOSE);
  setSize(250,250);
  setLocation(300,300);
  getContentPane().setBackground(Color.yellow);
  setVisible(true);

  // create a new thread
  thread1 = new Thread(this);
  // start the thread
  thread1.start();
}


public void run()
{
  while(true)   // a continuous loop
  {
    // on each iteration of the loop the mood is changed.....
    if(isHappy == true)
    {
      isHappy = false;
    }
    else
    {
      isHappy = true;
    }
    // ..... and the face is repainted
    repaint();
    try
    {
      thread1.sleep(1000);
    }
    catch(InterruptedException e)
    {
    }
  }
}
```

```
public void paint(Graphics g)
{
   super.paint(g);
   g.setColor(Color.red);
   g.drawOval(85,75,75,75);  // the face
   g.setColor(Color.blue);
   g.drawOval(100,95,10,10); // the right eye
   g.drawOval(135,95,10,10); // the left eye
   g.drawString("Animated Face", 82,175);
   if(isHappy == true)
   {
      // draw a smiling mouth
      g.drawArc(102,115,40,25,0,-180);
   }
   else
   {
      // draw a frowning mouth
      g.drawArc(102,115,40,25,0,180);
   }
}
```

As you can see, this time we have done everything in one class, the constructor of which creates and starts the thread. The run method consists of a loop that goes on forever until the thread is destroyed. On each iteration of the loop the mood is changed, the face is repainted, and the thread is forced to sleep for one second.

Program 19.2 runs the AnimatedFace as usual.

PROGRAM 19.2

```
public class RunAnimatedFace
{
   public static void main(String[] args)
   {
      new AnimatedFace();
   }
}
```

19.9.1 Animation using a series of images

The traditional way of producing animations in film has been to display a continuous series of images, which, to the eye, gives the impression of movement. In this section we are going to use that technique here to create an animated application.

Our animation is going to depict an old-style vinyl record going round on a turn-table; it is not, perhaps, the most imaginative animation ever, but we have no doubt that you will be able to be far more artistic and produce some spectacular animations of your own! There are eight images involved here, as shown in figure 19.3.

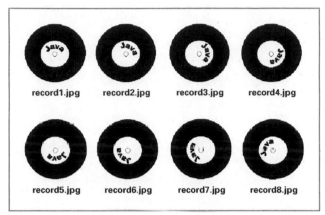

FIGURE 19.3 The images used with the *Record* class

The code for the class is presented below.

THE *RECORD* CLASS

```java
import java.awt.*;
import javax.swing.*;

public class Record extends JFrame implements Runnable
{
  // declare some constants
  public static final String fileName = "record";
  public static final int numberOfImages = 8;
  public static final int SLEEP_TIME = 100;

  private JLabel label = new JLabel();
  private ImageIcon image;
  private Thread animationThread;

  public Record()
  {
    // create a new thread
    animationThread = new Thread(this);

    // add the label to the frame and centre the image
    add("Center",label);
    label.setHorizontalAlignment(JLabel.CENTER);
```

```java
    // configure the frame
    setTitle("Revolving Record");
    setDefaultCloseOperation(JFrame.EXIT_ON_CLOSE);
    getContentPane().setBackground(Color.white);
    setSize(300,300);
    setVisible(true);

    // start the thread
    animationThread.start();
}


public void run()
{
  int currentImage = 0;
  String strImage;
  while(true)
  {
    strImage = fileName + (currentImage+1) + ".jpg";
    image = new ImageIcon(strImage);

    label.setIcon(image);

    try
    {
      animationThread.sleep(SLEEP_TIME);
    }
    catch(InterruptedException e)
    {
    }
    currentImage++;
    if(currentImage == numberOfImages)
    {
      currentImage = 0;
    }
  }
}
}
```

As you can see, we have declared a number of attributes, so we will start by looking at these:

```
public static final String fileName = "record";
public static final int numberOfImages = 8;
public static final int SLEEP_TIME = 100;

private JLabel label = new JLabel();
private ImageIcon image;
private Thread animationThread;
```

The first three of these are constants that we will use later on. Once we have declared them, we declare a JLabel, which will later be added to the frame. This JLabel will hold a series of images in turn, and so for this purpose we declare an ImageIcon. Finally we declare a Thread.

Now let's look at the constructor:

```
animationThread = new Thread(this);
add("Center",label);
label.setHorizontalAlignment(JLabel.CENTER);
setTitle("Revolving Record");
setDefaultCloseOperation(JFrame.EXIT_ON_CLOSE);
getContentPane().setBackground(Color.white);
setSize(300,300);
setVisible(true);
animationThread.start();
```

Most of this is really self-explanatory. We create a new thread, we add the label to the centre of the frame, and set its alignment to JLabel.CENTER; we then configure the frame and finally we start the thread.

Now the run method:

```
public void run()
{
  int currentImage = 0;
  String strImage;
  while(true)
  {
    strImage = fileName + (currentImage + 1) + ".jpg";
    image = new ImageIcon(strImage);
    label.setIcon(image);
    try
    {
      animationThread.sleep(SLEEP_TIME);
```

```
    }
    catch(InterruptedException e)
    {
    }
    currentImage++;
    if(currentImage == numberOfImages)
    {
      currentImage = 0;
    }
  }
}
```

The body of this method consists of an infinite loop. On each iteration we use an integer variable, `currentImage`, to construct the name of the image – "record1.jpg", "record2.jpg" and so on – and then set the label's icon to this image. After each new image is displayed, the thread is made to sleep for a given period. The value of `currentImage` is then incremented, and set back to zero once all eight images have been displayed.

19.10 The *Timer* class

Now that you understand the concept of multi-threaded programs, we can introduce you to the `Timer` class. This class conveniently provides a facility for scheduling threads. The way a `Timer` object works is to generate `ActionEvents` at fixed intervals. We therefore have to associate a `Timer` object with an `ActionListener` object. Whenever it generates an `ActionEvent`, the instructions in the `actionPerformed` method associated with the `Timer`'s `ActionListener` are executed. We will illustrate this by adapting our `Record` class – it will behave exactly as before, but now we will use a `Timer`. The code for our new class, `RecordVersion2`, is shown below:

THE *RECORDVERSION2* CLASS

```
import java.awt.*;
import java.awt.event.*;
import javax.swing.*;


public class RecordVersion2 extends JFrame implements ActionListener
{
  public static final String fileName = "record";
  public static final int numberOfImages = 8;
  public static final int SLEEP_TIME = 100;
```

```
private ImageIcon image;
private JLabel label = new JLabel();
private int currentImage = 0;

// declare a Timer
private Timer animationTimer;

public RecordVersion2()
{
  // create a new Timer object
  animationTimer = new Timer(SLEEP_TIME, this);

  // add the label to the frame and centre the image

  add(label);
  label.setHorizontalAlignment(JLabel.CENTER);
  label.setIcon(new ImageIcon ("record1.jpg"));

  // configure the frame
  setTitle("Revolving Record");
  setDefaultCloseOperation(JFrame.EXIT_ON_CLOSE);
  getContentPane().setBackground(Color.white);
  setSize(300,300);
  setVisible(true);

  // start the Timer
  animationTimer.start();
}

// the instructions for the Timer
public void actionPerformed(ActionEvent e)
{
  String strImage = fileName + (currentImage+1) + ".jpg";
  image = new ImageIcon(strImage);
  label.setIcon(image);
  currentImage++;
  if(currentImage == numberOfImages)
  {
    currentImage = 0;
  }
}
}
```

You can see that we have declared an object of the `Timer` class, `animationTimer`, as an attribute, and have instantiated it in the constructor:

```
animationTimer = new Timer(SLEEP_TIME, this);
```

The constructor of the `Timer` requires two parameters – an integer representing the interval during which it must wait before performing the action again, and a reference to an `ActionListener` where it will expect to find an `actionPerformed` method containing the instructions it is to perform each time the given interval elapses. Our `RecordVersion2` class is an `ActionListener` because it implements the `ActionListener` interface. The final instruction in the constructor starts the `Timer`:

```
animationTimer.start();
```

As you can see from the code, the instructions that were previously part of the thread's `run` method in our original version are now placed in the `actionPerformed` method – there is no need to make them part of a loop, because this is taken care of by the `Timer` itself.

Before finishing with timers, we will do one more thing – we will adapt our class by adding a "Stop" and "Start" button to it. Figure 19.4 shows how it is going to look.

FIGURE 19.4 The new version of the *Record* class

In this case the `actionPerformed` method is going to have to deal with the buttons – that is, it will ensure that the timer is started when the "Start" button is pressed and stopped when the "Stop" button is pressed. Therefore the `actionPerformed` method associated with the timer cannot be declared as part of this class;

we need to write a separate class for this purpose. The easiest way to do this is to write an inner class, because that will enable us to access the attributes. You can see how we do that below – we have called the inner class `TimerListener` – notice how we create a new object of this class when we create the `Timer` object in the constructor.

THE *RECORDVERSION3* CLASS

```java
import java.awt.*;
import java.awt.event.*;
import javax.swing.*;

public class RecordVersion3 extends JFrame implements ActionListener
{

  public static final String fileName = "record";
  public static final int numberOfImages = 8;
  public static final int SLEEP_TIME = 10;

  private ImageIcon image;
  private JLabel label = new JLabel();
  private JButton startButton = new JButton("Start");
  private JButton stopButton = new JButton("Stop");
  private int currentImage = 0;
  private Timer animationTimer;

  // define an inner class to hold the timer instructions
  class TimerListener implements ActionListener
  {
    public void actionPerformed(ActionEvent e)
    {
      String strImage = fileName + (currentImage + 1) + ".jpg";
      image = new ImageIcon(strImage);
      label.setIcon(image);
      currentImage++;
      if(currentImage == numberOfImages)
      {
        currentImage = 0;
      }
    }
  }
```

```java
public RecordVersion3()
{
  // create a new Timer object
  animationTimer = new Timer(SLEEP_TIME, new TimerListener());


  setDefaultCloseOperation(JFrame.EXIT_ON_CLOSE);
  setLayout(new FlowLayout());
  // add the buttons and label to the frame and centre the image
  add(startButton);
  add(stopButton);
  add(label);
  label.setHorizontalAlignment(JLabel.CENTER);
  label.setIcon(new ImageIcon ("record1.jpg"));


  startButton.addActionListener(this);
  stopButton.addActionListener(this);


  // configure the frame
  setTitle("Revolving Record");
  getContentPane().setBackground(Color.white);
  setSize(300,300);
  setVisible(true);
}


public void actionPerformed(ActionEvent e)
{
  if(e.getSource() == startButton)
  {
    animationTimer.start(); // start the timer
  }
  else
  {
    animationTimer.stop(); // stop the timer
  }
}
}
```

Self-test questions

1 Explain how concurrency is achieved by means of *time-slicing*.

2 Distinguish between *threads* and *processes*.

3 What is the difference between *asynchronous* and *synchronized* thread execution?

4 What is meant by the terms *critical section* and *mutual exclusion*? How are Java programs made to implement these concepts?

5 Explain how *busy waiting* can be avoided in Java programs.

6 The class below has had its `run` method replaced by a comment.

```
public class Threads6 extends JFrame implements Runnable
{
  private JLabel label = new JLabel("Hello");
  private Thread thread1;

  public Threads6()
  {

    label.setHorizontalAlignment(JLabel.CENTER);
    add(label);
    thread1 = new Thread(this);
    setTitle("Question 6");
    setDefaultCloseOperation(JFrame.EXIT_ON_CLOSE);
    setSize(200,100);
    setVisible(true);

    thread1.start();
  }


  public void run()
  {
    // code goes here
  }
}
```

a Replace the comment with code so that when an object of the class is created it will produce a frame containing a label whose caption changes once every second from "Hello" to "Goodbye". This is shown below:

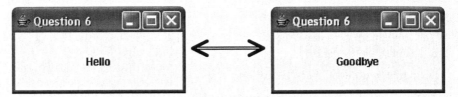

b Adapt the code so that the interval between changes can be determined at the time the object is created.

Programming exercises

1 Design some experiments that will help you to observe the behaviour of threads. A suggestion is to provide a `Thread` class with an id number that can be allocated at the time an object is created; the `run` method could simply print out this id a given number of times. A program could then be written to create and run a number of threads concurrently so that the output can be studied. You could vary the number of times the threads loop before terminating and see if there is any observable difference.

2 Implement the programs from this chapter. The images that you need for the `Record` class are on the CD. Try to design some animations of your own.

3 Modify the `CounterVersionTwo` class (with the `sleep` method implemented) so that:

a the sleep interval is passed in as a parameter from the main program;

b two separate counters run concurrently as shown below; each counter could be made to operate with a different sleep interval.

CHAPTER

Packages

20

20.1 Introduction

rom as early as the second chapter of this book you have been using the idea of a *package*, in order to access classes residing in external folders. In this chapter we will take a more in-depth look at Java's package concept and see how you can deploy your own applications by making use of this package concept.

20.2 Understanding packages

A **package**, in Java, is a *named collection* of *related classes*. You have already been using packages to access pre-written classes. For example, to draw geometric shapes you made use of the Graphics class which resides in the awt package. To format text you used classes in the text package. To produce attractive GUIs you used classes such as JButton and JLabel from the swing package. Giving meaningful names to a set of related classes in this way makes it easy for programmers to locate these classes when required. Packages can themselves contain other packages. For example, as well as containing related visual component classes, the awt package also contains the event package, since this group of classes is still logically related to Java's Abstract Window Toolkit.

The package name actually corresponds to the *name of the directory* (or folder as some operating systems call it) in which all the given classes reside. All pre-defined Java packages themselves reside in a global

Java directory, named simply `java`. This directory is not itself a package but a store for other packages. Figure 20.1 illustrates this hierarchy of packages.

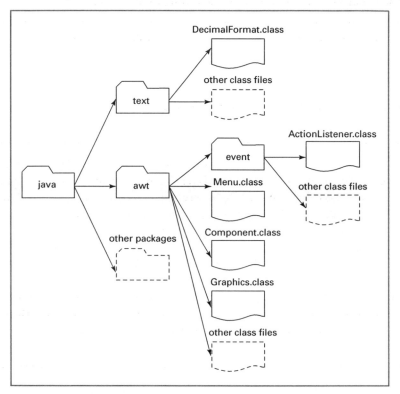

FIGURE 20.1 A sample of the Java package hierarchy

As you can see from figure 20.1, packages contain class files (that is, the compiled Java byte code), not source files (the original Java instructions). This means the location of the original Java source files is unimportant here. They may be in the same directory as the class files, in another directory or, as in the case of the pre-defined Java packages, they may even no longer be available.

20.3 Accessing classes in packages

Suppose you are writing the code for a new class. You will recall how you can give it access to a class contained within a package. Just referencing the class won't work. For example, let's assume a class you are writing needs a `DecimalFormat` object. The following will not compile:

```
public class SomeClass
{
  private DecimalFormat someFormatObject; // a problem here
}
```

This won't compile because the compiler won't be able to find a class called `DecimalFormat`. One way to tell the compiler where this class file resides is, as you already know, to add an **import** statement above the class. This class is in the `text` package so the following would be appropriate:

```
import java.text.*; // allows compiler to find the DecimalFormat.class file


public class SomeClass
{
  private DecimalFormat someFormatObject; // now this will compile
}
```

The asterisk allows you to have access to *all* class files in the given package. Can you see how the **import** statement matches the directory structure we illustrated in figure 20.1? Effectively the compiler is being told to look for classes in the `text` directory (package), which in turn is in the java directory (whose location is already known to the Java run-time system). The location of a file is often referred to as the **path** to that file. In the Windows operating systems this path would be expressed as follows:

```
java\text\
```

In other operating systems forward slashes may be used instead of backward slashes. The Java **import** statement simply expresses this path but uses dots instead of backward or forward slashes. Note that there can only ever be one '.*' in an **import** statement and the '.*' must follow a package name. However, you can have as many **import** statements as you require. Here are some examples of valid and invalid **import** statements:

```
import java.*.*; // illegal as contains more than one '.*'
import java.*; // illegal as 'java' is not a package
import java.text.*; // fine, allows access to classes in text package
import java.awt.event.*; // fine, allows access to classes in event package
```

If you want, you could list a *specific* class file instead of accessing all the files in a package as follows:

```
// this will allow the compiler to find the DecimalFormat class only
import java.text.DecimalFormat;
```

However, as there is no overhead in allowing access to all files in a package, we will use the asterisk notation in this book.

It is actually possible to access classes from within packages *without* the need for an **import** statement. To do this, references to any such classes must be appended onto the package name itself. Returning to the

DecimalFormat example, we could have removed the **import** statement and referred to the package directly in the class as follows:

```
public class SomeClass
{
  /* appending the class name onto the package name avoids the need to import the
     given package */

  private java.text.DecimalFormat someFormatObject;
}
```

The package plus class name is in fact the proper name for this class. An **import** statement just provides us with a convenient shorthand so that we do not always have to include the package name with the class name. As you can imagine, having to append the class name onto the package name every time we use a class from a package would be very cumbersome, so the **import** statement is preferable. There are times, however, when the long name is necessary.

The long class name can be useful when the class name on its own clashes with the name of another class. For example, let us assume we have developed our own class called Graphics – perhaps as part of a game application. Giving this name to the class is not a great idea as there already is a Graphics class in the awt package, but it is possible to choose this name if we wish. Now, let us assume that the constructor for this class takes two integer coordinates. We might require both our Graphics class in a program and the Graphics class in the awt package:

```
import java.awt.*; // for the awt Graphics class
import javax.swing.*; // for swing components

// something wrong in this class!
public class Game extends JPanel // this class can do some drawing
{
  // some code here

  // call constructor of our Graphics class
  Graphics moveCar = new Graphics (20, 40);
  // more code here

  public void paint (Graphics g) // this is the awt Graphics class
  {
    // call methods of awt Graphics class here
  }
}
```

As you can see, we are referencing two `Graphics` classes here: our own `Graphics` class:

```
Graphics moveCar = new Graphics (20, 40);
```

and the awt `Graphics` class in the `paint` method:

```
public void paint (Graphics g)
{
  // call methods of awt Graphics class here
}
```

Not surprisingly, this will result in a compiler error! When the compiler tries to find a class it initially looks in the *current folder* before it looks in any package folders. Assuming our own `Graphics` class is in the same folder as this `Game` class, it will decide that this is the `Graphics` class we are interested in. So, when we come to call the methods of the awt `Graphics` class (such as `drawOval`) the compiler will complain, as our `Graphics` class has no such methods in it!

To resolve this name clash, we can use the extended package name to differentiate between the two classes.

```
public void paint (java.awt.Graphics g)
{
  // call methods of awt Graphics class here
}
```

Now we no longer have a name clash with our class and the compiler can process references to both classes.

20.4 Developing your own packages

You might be surprised to know that all the classes that you have developed so far already reside in a *single* package. This may seem strange as you didn't instruct the compiler to add your classes to any package. In fact, what actually happens is that if you don't specifically ask your classes to be put in a package, then they all get added to some large unnamed package.

In order to locate and deploy your class files easily, and avoid any name clashes in the future, it might be a good idea to use named packages to organize your classes.

As an example, let's go back to our *Hostel* application from chapters 11 and 12 and create a unique package in which to put our class files – we will call this package `hostelApp`.[1] To instruct the compiler that

---

[1] We will stick to the standard Java convention of beginning package names with a lower-case letter.

you wish to add the classes that make up this application into a package called `hostelApp`, simply add the following **package** command at the top of each of the original source files:

```
package hostelApp;
```

This line instructs the compiler that the class file created from this source file must be put in a package called `hostelApp`. Here, for example, is the `Payment` class with this **package** line added:

```
package hostelApp; // add this line to the top of the source file


public class Payment
{
  // as before
}
```

When you compile this class you will find that a directory called `hostelApp` will have been created and the resulting `Payment.class` file will be placed into this directory.[2]

All the classes that make up this *Hostel* application (such as `Tenant`, `Hostel` and so on) will need to be amended in a similar way:

1 add the following line to the top of each source file

    `package hostelApp;`

2 ensure that the compiled class files are placed in the `hostelApp` directory.

Now the last step. We need to import this package into programs like any other package. If you had developed the `hostelApp` package in this way, and written program 12.1 (the driver for the hostel application) as normal (outside of a package), the program would no longer compile:

PROGRAM 12.1 – will not compile now!

```
public class RunHostel
{
  public static void main(String[] args)
  {
    new Hostel(5); // something wrong here!
  }
}
```

---

[2] If you are developing a class from scratch that you wish to add into a package, your Java IDE can be used so that the package line is inserted into your code for you and the required directory structure created. If you are using your Java IDE to *revisit* classes previously written outside of a package (as in this example), you may need to ensure that the resulting directory structure is reflected in the project you are working on. Refer to your IDE's documentation for details about how to do this.

The instruction that makes reference to the `Hostel` class will cause an error because that class no longer resides in the same directory as every other class file, but instead resides in its own package directory – `hostelApp`. The obvious answer is to import that package into this file. Program 20.1 amends program 12.1 accordingly:

PROGRAM 20.1

```
import hostelApp.*; // import classes from our package


public class RunHostel
{
  public static void main(String[] args)
  {
    new Hostel(5); // now this line will compile
  }
}
```

20.5 Package scope

Up until now we have declared all our classes to be **public**. This has meant they have been visible to all other classes. When we come to adding our classes into our own packages, this becomes particularly important. This is because *classes can be made visible outside of their package only if they are declared as* **public**. Unless they are declared as **public**, classes by default have what is known as **package** scope. This means that they are visible *only to other classes within the same package*.

Not all classes in the package need be declared as **public**. Some classes may be part of the implementation only and the developer may not wish them to be made available to the client. These classes can have **package** scope instead of **public** scope. In this way, packages provide an extra layer of security for your classes.

In the case of our *Hostel* application, we might choose to make only the `Hostel` class **public**, and keep all the other files required in this application hidden within the package by giving them package scope. To give a class package scope, just remove the **public** modifier from in front of the class declaration. For example, returning to the `Payment` class, we can give this package scope as follows:

```
package hostelApp; // this class is added into the package


class Payment // this class has package scope
{
  // as before
}
```

Now, when the `hostelApp` package is imported into another class, this other class has access only to the `Hostel` class; not to classes like `Payment` which are hidden in the package with package scope. This is demonstrated in the code fragment below:

```
import hostelApp.*; // this imports only the public classes in the package
public class SomeOtherClass
{
  Payment p = new Payment(); // will not compile as Payment is hidden in the hostelApp package
}
```

If you begin to develop your own packages and have trouble importing them, it could be that you have to modify the **classpath** variable.

The classpath is a special **environment variable**. Environment variables provide your operating system with information such as the location of important files in your system. The special environment variable related to the location of Java packages is the classpath variable.

20.6 Setting the *classpath* environment variable

The details of how the classpath environment variable is set will differ from one operating system to another. In Windows, for example, you place an instruction such as the one below in the `autoexec.bat` file using an application like Microsoft WordPad.

> **SET CLASSPATH = C:\ jCreator\myProjects**

If you are working in a `UNIX` environment you would use the `setenv` command. Check with your tutor the exact method to use. Note that the classpath is not the location of *classes* in packages, but the location of *packages* themselves. It would be wrong to set the classpath as follows:

> **SET CLASSPATH = C:\jCreator\myProjects\hostelApp**

This is because the `hostelApp` directory does not contain a package – it *is* a package. It is possible to set more than one location in your classpath, if necessary, by separating these locations by a semi-colon. For example:

> **SET CLASSPATH = C:\java\lib; C:\jCreator\myProjects**

Here the classpath has been set to look in the `lib` directory for packages, as well as the `myProjects` directory.

20.7 Running applications from the command line

Way back in chapter 1, we discussed the process of compiling and running Java programs. If you remember, we said that if you are working within a Java IDE you will have simple icons to click in order to carry out these procedures. If, however, you are working from a command line, like a DOS prompt for example, you would use the **javac** command (followed by the name of the source file) to compile a source file and **java** (followed by the name of a class) to run an application.

When you run a class that resides in a package you must amend this slightly. As an example let's once again consider the *Hostel* application. When you run an application you must run the class that contains the main method. Program 20.1 provided such a class for running the *Hostel* application. We called this class RunHostel. This class file was *not* part of a package, so it can be run simply from the command line as follows:

> **java RunHostel**

Notice that the .class extension is not added to the name of the class. When you type the **java** command you are in fact running the java.exe program, which is an implementation of the Java Virtual Machine. This command will run the given class assuming the classpath has been set appropriately. If the classpath had not been previously set we could specify it as part of this command by making use of the −cp switch as follows:

> **java -cp C:\jCreator\myProjects RunHostel**

Note that the parameter cp, indicating the classpath, is prefixed with a minus sign. Now let's assume that we provided a similar class, with a main method, as part of the hostelApp package. This class will be identical to RunHostel, but we will send in a different number of rooms to the Hostel constructor. It is called RunHostelFromPackage. The code is presented in program 20.2 below.

PROGRAM 20.2

```
package hostelApp; // add this class to our package

public class RunHostelFromPackage
{
  public static void main(String[] args)
  {
    new Hostel(10);
  }
}
```

Notice that, to add this class to the hostelApp package, we had to include the package hostelApp line to the top of the class. Now, to run this class from the command line we could try the following:

> **java RunHostelFromPackage**

Unfortunately this won't work as the system won't be able to find a class of the given name. In order to run a class that is contained within a package you must append the class name onto the name of the package. So, in this case you can run this class by using the following command:

java hostelApp.RunHostelFromPackage

Note that even if this class had the same name as the original program, RunHostel, the package name would have allowed the correct class file to have been found and executed.

Before we move on, let's just stop and have a look at the parameter that we always give to main methods:

```
public static void main(String[] args)
```

As you know, this means that main is given an array of String objects as a parameter. How are these String objects passed on to main? Up until now we have not discussed them at all. Well, values for these strings can be passed to main when you run the given class from the command line. Often, as in our previous program, there is no need to pass any such strings and this array of strings is effectively empty. Sometimes, however, it is useful to send in such parameters. They are sent to main from the command line by listing the strings, one after the other after the name of the class as follows:

java ClassName firstString secondString otherStrings

As you can see, the strings are separated by spaces. Any number of strings can be sent in this way. For example, if a program were called ProcessNames, two names could be sent to it as follows:

java ProcessNames Aaron Quentin

Notice that, were the strings to contain spaces, they must be enclosed in quotes:

java ProcessNames "Aaron Kans" "Quentin Charatan"

These strings will be placed into main's array parameter (args), with the first string being at args[0], the second at args[1] and so on. The number of strings sent to main is variable. The main method can always determine the number of strings sent by checking the length of the array (args.length). Program 20.3 is a simple implementation of the ProcessNames class.

PROGRAM 20.3

```
public class ProcessNames
{
  public static void main(String[] args)
  {
    if (args.length != 0)// check some arguments have been sent
    {
      // loop through all elements in the 'args' array
```

```
    for (int i = 0; i<args.length; i++)

    {

      // access individual strings in array

      System.out.println("hello " + args[i]);

    }

  }

}

}
```

We can run this program from the command line as follows:

java ProcessNames "Batman and Robin" Superman

Notice "Batman and Robin" needed to be surrounded by quotes as it has spaces in it, whereas Superman does not. Running this program would produce the obvious result:

hello Batman and Robin

hello Superman

20.8 Deploying your packages

A very common way of making your packages available to clients is to convert them to JAR files. A JAR file (short for Java Archive) has the extension .jar and is simply a compressed file. Most IDEs provide a means of creating JAR files; however, very often the file created is simply a flat file containing the relevant .class files. If this is all you want then that is fine. However, in most cases you want your client to be able to import the package into an application, and in order to do this the JAR file must have a *structure*. Let's take as an example the hostelApp package from section 20.4. If we want to include in our JAR file the RunHostel.class file (which contained the main method to run the application) as well as the hostelApp package, and we wish to call our JAR file hostel.jar, then the structure of the JAR file would have to be as shown in figure 20.2.

FIGURE 20.2 The correct structure of a JAR file

If, in a Windows environment, the `hostel.jar` file were placed in the directory `C:\jCreator\my Projects`, then the correct classpath statement would be:

> **SET CLASSPATH = C:\jCreator\myProjects\hostel.jar**

As you can see, the JAR file acts as the directory in which the package resides.

A JAR file such as the one above can by created by using the `jar.exe` application. This application is provided with the JDK and also with most standard IDEs. Assuming that we are in the directory containing the `hostelApp` package and the `RunHostel.class` file then the correct statement to create the above package is:

> **jar cvf hostel.jar RunHostel.class hostelApp**

As you can see, there are various switches that are used with the `jar` program. The ones used above have the following effect:

- **c:** create a new JAR file;
- **v:** provide full (verbose) output to report on progress;
- **f:** provide a name for the JAR file.

After these switches comes the name of the output file – `hostel.jar` in our case. Finally we must list the files we wish to be included. In the above example we require the `RunHostel.class` file, and the package directory, `hostelApp`.

20.8.1 Creating "executable" JAR files

If you are working in a graphics environment, and there is a JVM installed on your computer, then it is possible to create a JAR file that will run the program by double-clicking on its icon.

When we create our JAR file, a text file called a manifest file is automatically created. The default file normally has the filename `manifest.mf` and would look something like this:

```
Manifest-Version: 1.0
Created-By: 1.6.0_11 (Sun Microsystems Inc.)
```

However, if we want our JAR file to be executable, then we need to include in the manifest file information about which class in the package is the one with the `main` method. If this class is part of the package it would need to be included in the package directory (as with the `RunHostelFromPackage` example in section 20.7). Alternatively, it could be in the directory that contains the package, in which case the package would be specified in the **import** statement.

So, to include information about which class is the `main` class, we need to have a line added to the manifest file. We do this by creating a text file which we get the `jar.exe` program to merge with the default file. Assuming that our `main` class is called `RunHostel`, we would need to create a text file with the following line:

```
Main-Class: RunHostel
```

But be warned here – be sure to follow this line with a carriage return. If you do not do this, then this line will not be merged with the manifest file, causing much frustration!

Now, assuming that we are currently in a directory containing our text file (which we have named `myManifest.mf`), the file `RunHostel.class`, and the directory `hostelApp` (containing the files in the package), we could create the executable file with the following line:

```
jar cvfm RunHostel.jar myManifest.mf RunHostel.class hostelApp
```

The additional "m" switch after the "c", "v" and "f" switches stands for "merge", and indicates that we wish to merge the file stated with the default manifest file. You can see that after providing the name of our file we have listed what to include – the file `RunHostel.class` and the directory `hostelApp`. The resulting manifest file will now look like this:

```
Manifest-Version: 1.0
Created-By: 1.6.0_11 (Sun Microsystems Inc.)
Main-Class: RunHostel
```

Now double-clicking on the resulting JAR file's icon will run the application.

If you are using a Windows operating system there is another way you could provide an icon that will run your application, without creating a JAR file. You can create a shortcut to the file `javaw.exe`, the JVM specifically designed to run in a Windows graphical environment. You can then set the shortcut's properties so that the `main` class is added as a parameter. Figure 20.3 shows an example of this – it assumes that the required classes are in the directory `C:\Hostel`; note that we have included the classpath here as described in section 20.7.

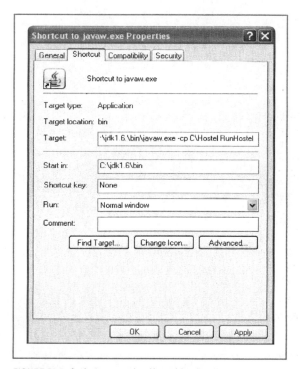

FIGURE 20.3 A shortcut to the *Hostel* Application

20.8.2 Splash screens

You will notice, from running Java applications (and indeed any application), that there can be a delay in making the request to run an application (for example by double-clicking on an icon as discussed in the previous section) and the application actually starting. This is because it takes a short while to load the necessary resources to run that application. With a Java program this includes the time it takes to load the JVM and any necessary packages.

Many applications display an opening screen while the actual program loads so that the user knows that the application is starting up. This screen is often referred to as a **splash screen**. A splash screen could just consist of a simple image, or it could also include information such as copyright statements and a progress bar.

A splash screen could be created as a simple opening frame in your Java application, but since one purpose of the splash screen is to load *before* your application loads, this is not an ideal way of implementing a splash screen.

Java 6 solves this problem by allowing a splash screen image to be included in your JAR file. The splash screen image can be any GIF, PNG, or JPG file and can include animation. You can use any drawing applications such as Microsoft Paint to create your image. Figure 20.4 gives the splash screen image we created for our Hostel application.

FIGURE 20.4 A splash screen image created for the *Hostel* application

We have saved this image as a JPG with the name hostelSplash.jpg.

To include this splash screen in our Hostel application we need to amend the manifest file as follows:

```
Main-Class: RunHostel
Splash-Image: hostelSplash.jpg
```

As you can see we add an additional line indicating the name of the file containing the splash screen image. Once again, remember to include a carriage return at the end of this manifest file.

When we create our JAR file, we need to include this splash screen image amongst the list of files to be compressed:

```
jar cvfm RunHostel.jar myManifest.mf RunHostel.class hostelSplash.jpg hostelApp
```

Now, when we run the executable JAR file the splash screen image will be displayed. The splash screen image will close automatically once the first screen of the application is loaded and displayed.

If you are running the application from the command line (and the splash image is in the same directory as your main class), then you can just include the splash image in the command line command by making use of the new -splash switch as follows:

```
java –splash: hostelSplash.jpg RunHostel
```

Self-test questions

1 What role do *packages* have in the development of classes?

2 Identify valid and invalid **import** statements amongst the following list:

```
import java.*;

import java.swing.*;

import java.awt.JButton;

import javax.swing.JButton;

import javax.swing.JButton.*;

import java.text.*.*;

import javax.swing.*;
```

3 What does it mean for a class to have *package scope*?

4 Consider the following outline of a class, used in a computer game, that makes reference to the JButton class:

```
public class GameController
{
   private JButton myButton;
   // more code here
}
```

At the moment the line referencing the JButton class will not compile. Identify three different techniques to allow this class with a JButton attribute to compile.

5 What is the purpose of the **classpath** environment variable?

6 You were asked to develop a timetable application in programming exercise 8 of chapter 8. Later, in programming exercise 3 of chapter 14 you were asked to enhance this application with exceptions. Finally you were asked to develop a GUI for this application in programming exercise 9 of chapter 16.

   a How would you place the classes that make up the timetable application into a package called timetableApp?

   b How would you modify the main class (that runs this application) if it was *not* to be included as part of the timetableApp package?

   c If the main class is called RunTimeTable, how would you run this application from the command line?

   d What is the purpose of a *JAR* file and a *manifest file* in Java?

   e What would you include in a manifest file for the timetable application?

> **f** Assuming a suitable manifest file for the timetable application has been written and called timetable `timeTableManifest.mf`, what command would you use to create the necessary executable JAR file?
>
> **g** What purpose does a *splash screen* serve and how would such a splash screen be created for the timetable application?

Programming exercises

1 Make the changes discussed in this chapter so that the *Hostel* application is now part of a package called `hostelApp`. Include a splash screen as discussed in section 20.8.2.

2 At the moment program 20.1 (`RunHostel`) fixes the number of rooms the hostel can handle:

```
import hostelApp.*;


public class RunHostel
{
  public static void main(String[] args)
  {
    new Hostel(5); // rooms fixed to 5
  }
}
```

a Amend this class so that the number could be sent in as a command line parameter. If no value has been sent in via the command line, the program should size the hostel with a default value of 5 rooms.

b Write the command to run this application from the command line to create a hostel with 25 rooms.

3 Make the changes to the timetable application, discussed in self-test question 6 above, so that the application can be run by clicking an executable JAR file. To include a splash screen as discussed in part (g) you will need to create a splash screen image using any suitable drawing application.

4 There are several Java packages that we have not yet explored. Browse your Java documentation to find out about what kind of classes these packages offer. For example, the `lang` package contains a class called `Math`, which has a **static** method called `random` designed to generate random numbers. There is also a random number class, `Random`, in the `util` package. Read your Java documentation to find out more about these random number generation techniques. Then write a program that generates five lottery numbers from 1 to 50 using:

a the **static** random method of the `Math` class in the `lang` package;

b the random number class, `Random`, in the `util` package.

CHAPTER 21

Advanced Case Study

21.1 Introduction

You have covered quite a few advanced topics now in this second semester. In this chapter we are going to take stock of what you have learnt by developing an application that draws upon all these topics. We will make use of Java's package notation for bundling together related classes; we will implement interfaces; we will catch and throw exceptions; we will make use of the collection classes in the `java.util` package; and we will store objects to file. We will also make use of many Swing components to develop an attractive graphical interface.

As with the case study we presented to you in the first semester, we will discuss the development of this application from the initial stage of requirements analysis, through to final implementation and testing stages. Along the way we will look at a few new concepts.

21.2 System overview

The application that we will develop will keep track of planes using a particular airport. So as not to over-complicate things, we will make a few assumptions:

■ there will be no concept of *gates* for arrival and departure – passengers will be met at a runway on arrival and be sent to a runway on departure;

588

- planes entering airport airspace and requesting to land are either called in to land on a free runway, or are told to join a queue of circling planes until a runway becomes available;
- once a plane departs from the airport it is removed from the system.

21.3 Requirements analysis and specification

Many techniques are used to determine system requirements. Amongst others, these include interviewing the client, sending out questionnaires to the client, reviewing any documentation if a current system already exists and observing people carrying out their work. A common way to document these requirements in UML is to develop a **use case model**. A use case model consists of **use case diagrams** and **behaviour specifications**.

A *use case diagram* is a simple way of recording the *roles* of different users within a system and the services that they require the system to deliver. The users (people or other systems) of a system are referred to as **actors** in use case diagrams and are drawn as simple stick characters. The roles these actors play in the system are used to annotate the stick character. The services they require are the so-called *use cases*. For example, in an ATM application an actor may be a customer and one of the use cases (services) required would be to withdraw cash. A very simple use case diagram for our application is given in figure 21.1.

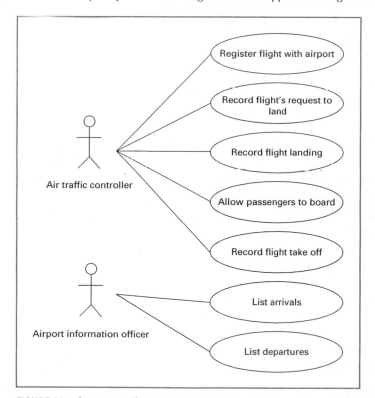

FIGURE 21.1 A use case diagram for the airport application

Figure 21.1 depicts the actors in this application (air traffic controllers and information officers) and the services these actors require (registering a flight, listing arrivals and so on). Once a list of use cases has been identified, *behaviour specifications* are used to record their required functionality. A simple way of recording behaviour specifications is to give a simple textual description for each use case. Table 21.1 contains behaviour specifications for each use case given in figure 21.1. Note that the descriptions are always given from the users' point of view.

Register flight with airport	An air traffic controller registers an incoming flight with the airport by submitting its unique flight number and its city of origin. If the flight number is already registered by the airport, the software will signal an error to the air traffic controller.
Record flight's request to land	An air traffic controller records an incoming flight entering airport airspace, and requesting to land, by submitting its flight number. As long as the plane has previously registered with the airport, the air traffic controller is given an unoccupied runway number on which the plane will have permission to land. If all runways are occupied, however, this permission is denied and the air traffic controller is informed to instruct the plane to circle the airport. If the plane has not previously registered with the airport, the software will signal an error to the air traffic controller.
Record flight landing	An air traffic controller records a flight landing on a runway at the airport by submitting its flight number and the runway number. If the plane was not given permission to land on that runway, the software will signal an error to the air traffic controller.
Allow Passengers to board	An air traffic controller allows passengers to board a plane currently occupying a runway by submitting its flight number and its destination city. If the given plane has not yet recorded landing at the airport, the software will signal an error to the air traffic controller.
Record flight take off	An air traffic controller records a flight taking off from the airport by submitting its flight number. If there are planes circling the airport, the first plane to have joined the circling queue is then given permission to land on that runway. If the given plane was not at the airport, the software will signal an error to the air traffic controller.
List arrivals	The airport information officer is given a list of planes whose status is either due-to-land, waiting-to-land, or landed.
List departures	The airport information officer is given a list of planes whose status is currently waiting-to-depart (taking on passengers).

TABLE 21.1 Behaviour specifications for the airport application

As the system develops, the use case descriptions may be modified as detailed requirements become uncovered. These descriptions will also be useful when testing the final application, as we will see later.

21.4 Design

The detailed design for this application is now presented in figure 21.2. It introduces some new UML notation. Have a look at it and then we will discuss it.

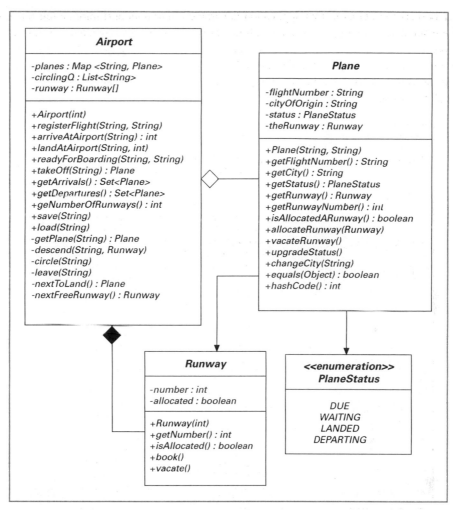

FIGURE 21.2 Detailed design for the airport application

As you can see from figure 21.2, an `Airport` class has been introduced to represent the functionality of the system as a whole. You can see that the **public** methods of the `Airport` class correspond closely to the use cases identified during requirements analysis and specification. The **private** methods of the `Airport` class are there simply to help implement the functionality of the class.

The requirements made clear that there would be *many* planes to process in this system. Since the airport exists regardless of the number of planes at the airport, the relationship between the `Airport` and `Plane` class is one of containment, as indicated with a hollow diamond. It made sense to consider the collection classes in the `java.util` package at this point. As we record planes in the system, and process these planes, we will always be using a plane's flight number as a way of identifying an individual plane. A `Map` is the obvious collection to choose here, with flight numbers the *keys* of the `Map` and the planes associated with these flight numbers as *values* of the `Map`.

The one drawback with a `Map`, however, is that it is not ordered on input. When considering which plane in a circling queue of planes to land, ordering is important, as the first to join the queue should be the first to land. So we have also introduced a `List` to hold the flight numbers of circling planes. Notice that the contained `Plane` type requires `equals` and `hashCode` methods to work effectively with these collection classes.

The airport will also consist of a number of runways. In fact the airport cannot exist without this collection of runways. The airport is said to be *composed of* a number of runways as opposed to *containing* a number of planes. Notice that the UML notation for **composition** is the same as that for containment, except that the diamond is filled rather than hollow. We use an array to hold this collection of `Runway` objects.

Turning to the contained classes, the `Runway` class provides methods to allow for the runway number to be retrieved, and for a runway to be booked and vacated. The `Plane` class also has access to a `Runway` object, to allow a plane to be able to book and vacate runways. You can see that as well as each plane being associated with a runway, the plane also has a flight number, a city and a status associated with it. The arrows from the `Plane` class to the `PlaneStatus` and `Runway` classes indicate the direction of the association. In this case a `Plane` object can send messages to a `Runway` and `PlaneStatus` object, but not vice versa.

The status of a plane is described in the `PlaneStatus` diagram. This diagram is the UML notation for an *enumerated type*.

21.4.1 Enumerated types in UML

A type that consists of a few possible values, each with a meaningful name, is referred to as an **enumerated type**. The status of a plane is one example of an enumerated type. This status changes depending upon the plane's progress to and from the airport:

- when a plane registers with the airport, it is *due* to land;
- when a plane arrives in the airport's airspace, it is *waiting* to land (this plane may be told to come in and land, or it may have to circle the airport until a runway becomes available);
- when a plane touches down at the airport, it has *landed*;
- when a plane starts boarding new passengers, it is *departing* the airport.

You can see from the design of the system that such a type is captured in UML by marking this type with `<<enumeration>>` as shown in figure 21.3.

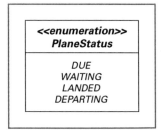

FIGURE 21.3 The UML design of the enumerated *PlaneStatus* type

We need to mark this UML diagram with `<<enumeration>>` so that it is not confused with a normal UML class diagram. With a normal UML class diagram, attributes and methods are listed in the lower portion. With an enumerated type diagram, the possible values of this type are given in the lower portion of the diagram, with each value being given a meaningful name. An attribute that is allocated a `PlaneStatus` type, such as `status` in the `Plane` class, can have any one of these values.

This completes our design analysis, so now let's turn our attention to the Java implementation.

21.5 Implementation

Since we are developing an application involving several classes, it makes sense to bundle these classes together into a single package. We will call this package `airportSys`. This means that all our classes will begin with the following **package** statement:

```
package airportSys;
```

This will allow our entire suite of classes to be imported into another application with the following **import** statement:

```
import airportSys.*;
```

It is a good idea to hide implementation-level exceptions (such as `ArrayIndexOutOfBoundsException`) from users of the application and, instead, always throw some general application exception. In order to be able to do this, we define our own general `AirportException` class.

THE *AIRPORTEXCEPTION* CLASS

```
package airportSys; // add to package

/**
 * Application Specific Exception
 *
 * @author Charatan and Kans
 * @version 1st November 2008
 */
public class AirportException extends Exception
{
  /**
   * Default Constructor
   */
  public AirportException ()
  {
    super("Error: Airport System Violation");
  }
```

```
/**
 * Constructor that accepts an error message
 */
public AirportException (String msg)
{
    super(msg);
}
}
```

Notice that, as with all the classes we shall develop here, we have added `Javadoc` comments into the class definition. Now let's consider the remaining classes. First of all, we will look at the implementation of the enumerated `PlaneStatus` type.

21.5.1 Implementing enumerated types in Java

A simple enumerated type mechanism was included in Java 5.0. In order to define an enumerated type such as `PlaneStatus`, the **enum** keyword has been introduced. The `PlaneStatus` type can now be implemented simply as follows:

```
// this is the new way of defining enumerated types in Java
public enum PlaneStatus
{
    DUE, WAITING, LANDED, DEPARTING
}
```

You can see how easy it is to define an enumerated type. When defining such a type, do not use the **class** keyword, use the **enum** keyword instead. The different values for this type are then given within the braces, separated by commas.

These values create class constants with the given names. The type of each class constant is `PlaneStatus` and variables can now be declared of this type. For example, here we declare a variable of the `PlaneStatus` type and assign it one of these class constant values:

```
PlaneStatus status; // declare PlaneStatus variable
status = PlaneStatus.DEPARTING; // assign variable a class constant
```

The variable `status` can take no other values, apart from those defined in the enumerated `PlaneStatus` type. Each enumerated type you define will also have an appropriate `toString` method generated for it, so values can be displayed on the screen:

```
System.out.println("Value = " + status);
```

Assuming we created this variable as above, this would display the following:

```
Value = DEPARTING
```

As well as a `toString` method, a few other methods are generated for you as well, and the **switch** statement can be used in conjunction with enumerated type variables. We will see examples of these features when we look at the code for the other classes in this application.

Of course, we must remember to add this `PlaneStatus` type into our `airportSys` package:

THE PLANESTATUS TYPE

```java
package airportSys; // add to package


/**
 * Enumerated plane status type.
 *
 * @author Charatan and Kans
 * @version 1st November 2008
 */
public enum PlaneStatus
{
   DUE, WAITING, LANDED, DEPARTING
}
```

21.5.2 The *Runway* class

Here is the code for the Runway class, take a look at it and then we will discuss it.

THE *RUNWAY* CLASS

```java
package airportSys; // add class to package
import java.io.*; // for Serializable interface


/**
 * This class is used to store details of a single runway.
 *
 * @author Charatan and Kans
 * @version 2nd November 2008
 */
public class Runway implements Serializable
{
  // attributes
  private int number;
  private boolean allocated;
```

```java
/**
 * Constructor sets the runway number
 * @param       numberIn            Used to set the runway number
 * @throws      AirportException    When the runway number is less than 1
 */
public Runway (int numberIn) throws AirportException
{
  if (numberIn <1)
  {
    throw new AirportException ("invalid runway number "+numberIn);
  }

  number = numberIn;
  allocated = false; // runway vacant intially
}


/**
 * Returns the runway number
 */
public int getNumber()
{
  return number;
}
/**
 * Checks if the runway has been allocated
 * @return    Returns true if the runway has been allocated and false otherwise
 */
public boolean isAllocated()
{
  return allocated;
}
/**
 * Records the runway as being booked
 */
public void book()
{
  allocated = true;
}
/**
 * Records the runway as being vacant
 */
```

```
  public void vacate()
  {
    allocated = false;
  }
}
```

There is not much that needs to be said about this class. As we may wish to save and load objects from our system, we have to remember to indicate that this class is `Serializable`.

```
public class Runway implements Serializable
```

Notice that we have defined this as a **public** class so that it is accessible outside of the package. We did this as a runway is a generally useful concept in many applications; declaring this class **public** allows it to be reused outside of the `airportSys` package. In fact, we have declared most of our classes **public** for this reason.

21.5.3 The *Plane* class

Here is the code for the `Plane` class. Have a close look at it and then we will discuss it.

THE *PLANE* CLASS

```
package airportSys;
import java.io.*;


/**
 * This class stores the details of a single plane
 *
 * @author Charatan and Kans
 * @version 2nd November 2008
 */
public class Plane implements Serializable
{
  // attributes
  private String flightNumber;
  private String city;
  private PlaneStatus status;
  private Runway theRunway;

  /**
    * Constructor sets initial flight details of plane
```

```java
 * @param      flightIn        The plane's flight number
 * @param      cityOfOrigin    The plane's city of origin
 */
public Plane(String flightIn, String cityOfOrigin)
{
  flightNumber = flightIn;
  city = cityOfOrigin;
  status = PlaneStatus.DUE; // initial plane status set to DUE
  theRunway = null; // indicates no runway allocated
}


/**
 * Returns the plane's flight number
 */
public String getFlightNumber()
{
  return flightNumber;
}


/**
 * Returns the city asscoiated with the flight
 */
public String getCity()
{
  return city;
}


/**
 * Returns the current status of the plane
 */
public PlaneStatus getStatus()
{
  return status;
}


/**
 * Returns the runway allocated to this plane or null if no runway allocated
 */
public Runway getRunway()
{
  return theRunway;
}
```

```java
/**
 * Returns the runway number allocated to this plane
 * @throws AirportException if no runway allocated
 */
public int getRunwayNumber()throws AirportException
{
  if (theRunway == null)
  {
    throw new AirportException("flight "+flightNumber+" has not been allocated a runway");
  }
  return theRunway.getNumber();
}


/**
 * Checks if the plane is allocated a runway
 * @return   Returns true if the plane has been allocated a runway and false otherwise
 */
public boolean isAllocatedARunway()
{
  return theRunway != null;
}


/**
 * Allocates the given runway to the plane
 * @throws   AirportException if runway parameter is null or runway already allocated
 */
public void allocateRunway(Runway runwayIn)throws AirportException
{
  if (runwayIn == null) // check runway has been sent
  {
    throw new AirportException ("no runway to allocate");
  }
  if (runwayIn.isAllocated()) // check if runway already allocated
  {
    throw new AirportException ("runway already allocate");
  }
  theRunway = runwayIn;
  theRunway.book();
}
```

```java
/**
 * De-allocates the current runway
 * @throws      AirportException if no runway allocated
 */
public void vacateRunway() throws AirportException
{
  if (theRunway == null)
  {
    throw new AirportException ("no runway allocated");
  }
  theRunway.vacate();
}


/**
 * Upgrades the status of the plane.
 * @throws AirportException when trying to upgrade a DEPARTING status
 */
public void upgradeStatus() throws AirportException
{
  switch(status)
  {
    case DUE: status = PlaneStatus.WAITING; break;
    case WAITING: status = PlaneStatus.LANDED; break;
    case LANDED: status = PlaneStatus.DEPARTING; break;
    case DEPARTING: throw new AirportException ("Cannot upgrade DEPARTING status");
  }
}


/**
 * Changes the city associated with the plane
 */
public void changeCity (String destination)
{
  city = destination;
}


/**
 * Checks whether the plane is equal to the given object
 */
public boolean equals(Object objIn)
```

```
  {
    if (objIn!=null)
    {
      Plane p = (Plane)objIn;
      return p.flightNumber.equals(flightNumber);
    }
    else
    {
      return false;
    }
  }


  /**
   * Returns a hashcode value
   */
  public int hashCode()
  {
    return flightNumber.hashCode();
  }
}
```

Again, most of the points we raised with the Runway class are relevant to this Plane class. It needs to be Serializable and it is declared **public**.

Since Plane objects will be used in collection classes we have provided this class with an equals and a hashCode method. You can see that both of these methods make use of the plane's flight number.

In addition, you should look at the way in which we dealt with the status attribute. During class design we declared this attribute to be of the enumerated PlaneStatus type, so it has been implemented as follows:

```
private PlaneStatus status;
```

We can then assign this attribute values from the enumerated PlaneStatus type. For example, in the constructor, we initialize the status of a plane to DUE:

```
public Plane(String flightNumberIn, String cityOfOrigin)
{
  flightNumber = flightNumberIn;
  city = cityOfOrigin;
  status = PlaneStatus.DUE;
  theRunway = null;
}
```

The getStatus method returns the value of the status attribute, so the appropriate return type is PlaneStatus:

```
public PlaneStatus getStatus()
{
  return status;
}
```

The upgradeStatus method is interesting as it demonstrates how the **switch** statement can be used with enumerated type variables such as status:

```
public void upgradeStatus() throws AirportException
{
  switch(status) // this is an enumerated type variable
  {
    // 'case' statements can check the different enumerated values
    case DUE: status = PlaneStatus.WAITING; break;
    case WAITING: status = PlaneStatus.LANDED; break;
    case LANDED: status = PlaneStatus.DEPARTING; break;
    case DEPARTING: throw new AirportException ("Cannot upgrade DEPARTING status");
  }
}
```

Here we are upgrading the status of a plane as it makes its way to, and eventually from, the airport. Notice that the value of the status attribute is checked in the **case** statements, but this value is *not* appended onto the PlaneStatus class name. For example:

```
// just use a status name here
case DUE: status = PlaneStatus.WAITING; break;
```

However, in all other circumstances, such as assigning to the status attribute, the enumerated value *does* have to be appended onto the PlaneStatus class name:

```
// use class + status name here
case DUE: status = PlaneStatus.WAITING; break;
```

You can see that we should not be upgrading the status of a plane if its current status is DEPARTING, so an exception is thrown in this case:

```
case DEPARTING: throw new AirportException ("Cannot upgrade DEPARTING status");
```

Before we leave this class, also notice that by adding a runway attribute, `theRunway`, into the `Plane` class we can send messages to (access methods of) a Runway object, for example:

```
public void allocateRunway(Runway runwayIn)throws AirportException
{
  // some code here
  theRunway.book(); // 'book' is a 'Runway' method
}
```

21.5.4 The *Airport* class

The `Airport` class encapsulates the functionality of the system. It does not include the interface to the application. As we have done throughout this book, the interface of an application is kept separate from its functionality. That way, we can modify the way we choose to implement the functionality without needing to modify the interface, and vice versa. Examine it closely, being sure to read the comments, and then we will discuss it.

THE *AIRPORT* CLASS

```
package airportSys;
import java.util.*;
import java.io.*; // for IOException


/**
 * Class to provide the functionality of the airport system
 *
 * @author Charatan and Kans
 * @version 4th November 2008
 */
public class Airport
{
  // attributes
  private Map<String, Plane> planes; // registered planes

  private List<String> circlingQ; // flight numbers of circling planes
  private Runway []runway; // runways allocated to the airport

  /**
   * Constructor creates an empty collection of planes, and allocates runways to the airport
   * @param    numIn The number of runways
   * @throws    AirportException with a negative runway number
   */
```

```java
public Airport (int numIn) throws AirportException
{
  try
  {
    // intialize runways
    runway = new Runway [numIn];
    for (int i = 0; i<numIn; i++)
    {
      runway[i] = new Runway (i+1);
    }
    // no planes allocated to airport
    planes = new HashMap<String, Plane>();
    circlingQ = new ArrayList<String>();
  }
  catch (Exception e)
  {
    throw new AirportException("Invalid Runway Number");
  }
}


/**
 * Registers a plane with the airport
 * @param      flightIn The plane's flight number
 * @param      cityOfOrigin The plane's city of origin
 * @throws     AirportException if flight number already registered.
 */
public void registerFlight (String flightIn, String cityOfOrigin) throws AirportException
{
  if (planes.containsKey(flightIn))
  {
    throw new AirportException ("flight "+flightIn+" already registered");
  }
  Plane newPlane = new Plane (flightIn, cityOfOrigin);
  planes.put(flightIn, newPlane);
}


/**
 * Records a plane arriving at the airport
 * @param      flightIn The plane's flight number
 * @throws     AirportException if plane not previously registered
 *                or if plane already arrived at airport
 */
```

```java
public int arriveAtAirport (String flightIn) throws AirportException
{
  Runway vacantRunway = nextFreeRunway(); // get next free runway
  if (vacantRunway != null) // check if runway available
  {
    descend(flightIn, vacantRunway); // allow plane to descend on runway
    return vacantRunway.getNumber(); // return booked runway number
  }
  else // no runway available
  {
    circle(flightIn); // plane must join circling queue
    return 0; // indicates no runway available to land
  }
}


/**
 * Records a plane landing on a runway
 * @param       flightIn The plane's flight number
 * @param       runwayNumberIn The runway number the plane is landing on
 * @throws      AirportException if plane not previously registered
 *              or if the runway is not allocated to this plane
 *              or if plane has not yet signalled its arrival at the airport
 *              or if plane is already recorded as
 *              having landed.
 */
public void landAtAirport (String flightIn, int runwayNumberIn) throws AirportException
{
  Plane thisPlane = getPlane(flightIn); // throws exception if invalid
  if (thisPlane.getRunwayNumber() != runwayNumberIn)
  {
    throw new AirportException ("flight "+flightIn+" should not be on this runway");
  }
  if (thisPlane.getStatus() == PlaneStatus.DUE)
  {
    throw new AirportException ("flight "+flightIn+" not signalled its arrival");
  }
  if (thisPlane.getStatus().compareTo(PlaneStatus.WAITING) >0)
  {
    throw new AirportException ("flight "+flightIn+" already landed");
  }
```

```java
    thisPlane.upgradeStatus(); // upgrade status from WAITING to LANDED
}


/**
 * Records a plane boarding for take off
 * @param      flightIn The plane's flight number
 * @param      destination The city of destination
 * @throws     AirportException if plane not previously registered
 *             or if plane not yet recorded as landed
 *             or if plane already recorded as ready for take off
 */
public void readyForBoarding(String flightIn, String destination) throws AirportException
{
  Plane thisPlane = getPlane(flightIn); // throws exception if invalid
  if (thisPlane.getStatus().compareTo(PlaneStatus.LANDED)<0)
  {
    throw new AirportException ("flight "+flightIn+" not landed");
  }
  if (thisPlane.getStatus() == PlaneStatus.DEPARTING)
  {
    throw new AirportException ("flight "+flightIn+" already registered to depart");
  }
  thisPlane.upgradeStatus(); // upgrade status from LANDED to DEPARTING
  thisPlane.changeCity(destination); // change city to destination city
}


/**
 * Records a plane taking off from the airport
 * @param      flightIn The plane's flight number
 * @throws     AirportException if plane not previously registered
 *             or if plane not yet recorded as landed
 *             or if the plane not previously recorded as ready for take off
 */
public Plane takeOff (String flightIn) throws AirportException
{
  leave(flightIn); // remove from plane register
  Plane nextFlight = nextToLand(); // return next circling plane to land
  if (nextFlight != null) // check circling flight exists
  {
    // allocate runway to circling plane
    Runway vacantRunway = nextFreeRunway();
    descend(nextFlight.getFlightNumber(), vacantRunway);
```

```
      return nextFlight;
    }
    else // no circling planes
    {
      return null;
    }
  }


  /**
   * Returns the set of planes due for arrival
   */
  public Set<Plane> getArrivals()
  {
    Set<Plane> planesOut = new HashSet<Plane>(); // create empty set
    Set<String> items = planes.keySet(); // get all flight numbers
    for(String thisFlight: items) // check status of all
    {
      Plane thisPlane = planes.get(thisFlight);
      if (thisPlane.getStatus() != PlaneStatus.DEPARTING)
      {
        planesOut.add(thisPlane); // add to set
      }
    }
    return planesOut;
  }


  /**
   * Returns the set of planes due for departure
   */
  public Set<Plane> getDepartures()
  {
    Set<Plane> planesOut = new HashSet<Plane>(); // create empty set
    Set<String> items = planes.keySet();
    for(String thisFlight: items)
    {
      Plane thisPlane = planes.get(thisFlight);
      if (thisPlane.getStatus() == PlaneStatus.DEPARTING)
      {
        planesOut.add(thisPlane); // add to set
      }
    }
```

```
   return planesOut;
 }


/**
 * Returns the number of runways
 */
public int getNumberOfRunways()
{
   return runway.length;
}


/**
 * Saves airport object to file
 * @param      fileIn The name of the file
 * @throws     IOException if problems with opening and saving to given file
 */
public void save(String fileIn)throws IOException
{
   FileOutputStream fileOut = new FileOutputStream(fileIn);
   ObjectOutputStream objOut = new ObjectOutputStream (fileOut);
   objOut.writeObject(planes);
   objOut.writeObject(circlingQ);
   objOut.writeObject(runway);
   objOut.close();
}


/**
 * Loads airport object from file
 * @param      fileName The name of the file
 * @throws     IOException if problems with opening and loading given file
 * @throws     ClassNotFoundException if objects in file not of right type
 */
public void load (String fileName) throws IOException, ClassNotFoundException
{
   FileInputStream fileInput = new FileInputStream(fileName);
   ObjectInputStream objInput = new ObjectInputStream (fileInput);

   planes = (Map<String, Plane>) objInput.readObject();
   circlingQ = (List<String>) objInput.readObject();
   runway = (Runway[])objInput.readObject();
   objInput.close();
}
```

```java
// helper methods

/**
 * Returns next free runway or null if no free runway
 */
private Runway nextFreeRunway()
{
  for (int i = 0; i < runway.length; i++)
  {
    if (!runway[i].isAllocated())
    {
      return runway[i];
    }
  }
  return null;
}


/**
 * Returns the registered plane with the given flight number
 * @throws     AirportException if flight number not yet registered.
 */
private Plane getPlane(String flightIn) throws AirportException
{
  if (!planes.containsKey(flightIn))
  {
  throw new AirportException ("flight "+flightIn+" has not yet registered");
  }
  return planes.get(flightIn);
}


/**
 * Records a plane descending on a runway
 * @param        flightIn The plane's flight number
 * @param        runwayIn The runway the plane will be landing on
 * @throws       AirportException if plane not previously registered
 *               or if plane already arrived at airport
 *               or if plane already allocated a runway
 */
private void descend (String flightIn, Runway runwayIn) throws AirportException
{
  Plane thisPlane = getPlane(flightIn); // throws exception if invalid
```

```java
    if (thisPlane.getStatus().compareTo(PlaneStatus.WAITING) > 0)
    {
      throw new AirportException ("flight "+flightIn+ " already at airport has status of "
                                  +thisPlane.getStatus());
    }
    if (thisPlane.isAllocatedARunway())
    {
      throw new AirportException ("flight "+flightIn+ " has already been allocated runway "
                                  +thisPlane.getRunwayNumber());
    }
    thisPlane.allocateRunway(runwayIn);
    if (thisPlane.getStatus() == PlaneStatus.DUE)
    {
      thisPlane.upgradeStatus();// upgrade status from DUE to WAITING
    }
}


/**
 * Records a plane joining the planes circling the airport
 * @param      flightIn The plane's flight number
 * @throws     AirportException if plane not previously registered or if plane already arrived
 */
private void circle (String flightIn) throws AirportException
{
  Plane thisPlane = getPlane(flightIn); // throws exception if invalid
  if (thisPlane.getStatus() != PlaneStatus.DUE)
  {
    throw new AirportException ("flight "+flightIn+" already at airport");
  }
  thisPlane.upgradeStatus(); // updrage status from DUE to WAITING
  circlingQ.add(flightIn);
}


/**
 * Records a plane taking off from the airport
 * @param      flightIn The plane's flight number
 * @throws     AirportException if plane not plane not previously registered
 *             or if plane not yet recorded as landed
 *             or if the plane not previously recorded as ready for take off
 */
private void leave (String flightIn) throws AirportException
```

```
{
  Plane thisPlane = getPlane(flightIn); // throws exception if invalid
  // throw exceptions if plane is not ready to leave airport
  if (thisPlane.getStatus().compareTo(PlaneStatus.LANDED)<0)
  {
    throw new AirportException ("flight "+flightIn+" not yet landed");
  }
  if (thisPlane.getStatus() == PlaneStatus.LANDED)
  {
    throw new AirportException ("flight "+flightIn+" must register to board");
  }
  // process plane leaving airport
  thisPlane.vacateRunway(); // runway now free
  planes.remove(flightIn); // remove plane from list
}


/**
 * Locates next circling plane to land
 * @return      Returns the next circling plane to land or null if no planes
 */
private Plane nextToLand()throws AirportException
{
  if (!circlingQ.isEmpty()) // check circling plane exists
  {
    String flight = circlingQ.get(0);
    circlingQ.remove(flight);
    return getPlane(flight); // could throw exception if not in list
  }
  else // no circling plane
  {
    return null;
  }
}
}
```

There is not a lot that is new here, but we draw your attention to a few implementation issues.

First, in the constructor you can see that we catch a general exception, in case something goes wrong when allocating the array, and throw our application-specific exception when this occurs:

```
public Airport (int numIn) throws AirportException
{
  try
  {
    // array exceptions may be thrown here
    runway = new Runway [numIn];
    for (int i = 0; i < numIn; i++)
    {
      runway[i] = new Runway (i+1);
    }
    // code to initialize other collections here
  }
  catch (Exception e)// catch array exceptions
  {
    // re-throw AirportException
    throw new AirportException("Invalid Runway Number");
  }
}
```

Most of the other **public** methods simply check for a list of exceptions, and then upgrade the plane's status as it makes its way to and eventually from the airport.

Here, for example, is the method that records a plane that has previously landed at the airport, being ready to board new passengers for a new destination:

```
/**
 * Records a plane ready for boarding new passengers
 * @param      flightIn The plane's flight number
 * @param      destination The city of destination
 * @throws     AirportException if plane not previously registered
 *             or if plane not yet recorded as landed
 *             or if plane already recorded as ready for boarding
 */
public void readyForBoarding(String flightIn, String destination)throws AirportException
{
  Plane thisPlane = getPlane(flightIn); // may throw AirportException
  // check for other exceptions
  if (thisPlane.getStatus().compareTo(PlaneStatus.LANDED)<0)
```

```
    {
      throw new AirportException ("flight "+flightIn+" not landed");
    }
    if (thisPlane.getStatus() == PlaneStatus.DEPARTING)
    {
      throw new AirportException ("flight "+flightIn+" already registered to depart");
    }
    thisPlane.upgradeStatus(); // upgrade status from LANDED to DEPARTING
    thisPlane.changeCity(destination); // change city to destination city
}
```

The first thing we need to do in this method is to check whether or not an `AirportException` needs to be thrown. The `Javadoc` comments make clear that there are three situations in which we need to throw such an exception.

First, an exception needs to be thrown if the given flight number has not been registered with the airport. At some point we also need to retrieve the `Plane` object from this flight number. Calling the helper method `getPlane` will do both of these things for us, as it throws an `AirportException` if the flight is not registered.

```
// retrieves plane or throws AirportException if flight is not registered
Plane thisPlane = getPlane(flightIn);
```

To check for the remaining exceptions we need to check that the plane currently has the appropriate status to start taking on passengers. The `getStatus` method of a plane returns the status of a plane for us. We know from the previous section that this method returns a value of the enumerated type `PlaneStatus`.

As well as having a `toString` method generated for you when you declare an enumerated type such as `PlaneStatus`, a `compareTo` method (to allow for comparison of two enumerated values) is also generated. This method works in exactly the same way as the `compareTo` method you met when looking at `String` methods. That is, it returns 0 when the two values are equal, a number less than 0 when the first value is less than the second value and a number greater than 0 when the first value is greater than the second value. One enumerated type value is considered *less than* another if it is listed before that value in the original type definition. So, in our example, DUE is *less than* WAITING, which is *less than* LANDED and so on. If a plane has a status that is less than LANDED it has not yet landed, so cannot be ready to board passengers – an `AirportException` is thrown:

```
// use 'compareTo' method to compare two status values
if (thisPlane.getStatus().compareTo(PlaneStatus.LANDED)<0)
{
  throw new AirportException ("flight "+flightIn+" not yet landed");
}
```

We also need to throw an `AirportException` if the plane already has a status of `BOARDING`. Although the `compareTo` method can be used to check for equality as well, with most classes it is common to use an `equals` method to do this. An `equals` method is generated for any enumerated type, such as `PlaneStatus`, that you define. However, because of the way enumerated types are implemented in Java, the simple equality operator (==) can also be used to check for equality:

```
// equality operator can be used to check if 2 enumerated values are equal
if (thisPlane.getStatus() == PlaneStatus.DEPARTING)
{
  throw new AirportException ("flight "+flightIn+" already registered to depart");
}
```

Having checked for exceptions, we can now indicate that this plane is ready for boarding by upgrading its status (from `LANDED` to `DEPARTING`), and by recording the flights new destination city:

```
// we have cleared all the exceptions so we can update flight details now
thisPlane.upgradeStatus(); // upgrades status from LANDED to DEPARTING
thisPlane.changeCity(destination); // changes city to destination city
```

The inequality operator (!=) can be used with enumerated types, to check for inequality of two enumerated type values. An example of this can be seen in the implementation of the `arrivals` method:

```
/**
 * Returns the set of planes due for arrival
 */
public Set<Plane> getArrivals()
{
  Set<Plane> planesOut = new HashSet<Plane>(); // create empty set
  Set<String> items = planes.keySet(); // get all flight numbers
  for(String thisFlight: items) // check status of all
  {
    Plane thisPlane = planes.get(thisFlight);
    if (thisPlane.getStatus() != PlaneStatus.DEPARTING)
    {
      planesOut.add(thisPlane); // add to set
    }
  }
    return planesOut;
}
```

Here we create an empty set of planes. We then add planes into this set if they do not have a status of
DEPARTING:

```
// use inequality operator to check if status does not equal some value
if (thisPlane.getStatus() != PlaneStatus.DEPARTING)
{
  planesOut.add(thisPlane);
}
```

Before we leave this section, let us take a look at the save and load methods that allow us to save and load
the attributes in our application. We have three attributes here, planes (the Map of registered planes),
circlingQ (the List of flight numbers of the planes circling the airport) and runway (the array of
runways).

Since we have declared our Plane and Runway classes to be Serializable, and because enumerated types such as PlaneStatus and collection classes such as Map and List are already Serializable,
it is a simple matter to write these objects to a file, and read them from a file.

```
/**
 * Saves attributes to file
 *
 * @param     fileIn The name of the file
 * @throws    IOException if problems with opening and saving to given file
 */
public void save(String fileIn)throws IOException
{
  FileOutputStream fileOut = new FileOutputStream(fileIn);
  ObjectOutputStream objOut = new ObjectOutputStream (fileOut);
  // write three attributes to file
  objOut.writeObject(planes);
  objOut.writeObject(circlingQ);
  objOut.writeObject(runway);
  // close file
  objOut.close();
}


/**
 * Loads attributes from file
 * @param     fileName The name of the file
 * @throws    IOException if problems with opening and loading given file
 * @throws    ClassNotFoundException if objects in file not of right type
 */
public void load (String fileName) throws IOException, ClassNotFoundException
```

```
{
  FileInputStream fileInput = new FileInputStream(fileName);
  ObjectInputStream objInput = new ObjectInputStream (fileInput);
  // read three attributes from file
  planes = (Map<String, Plane>) objInput.readObject();
  circlingQ = (List<String>) objInput.readObject();
  runway = (Runway[])objInput.readObject();
  // close file
  objInput.close();
}
```

Notice that when we load the attributes from file, we must indicate their type. The collection class types need to be marked using the generics mechanism:

```
// indicate the type of each collection using generics mechanism
planes = (Map<String, Plane>) objInput.readObject();
circlingQ = (List<String>) objInput.readObject();
```

There is nothing particularly new in the remaining methods. Take a look at the comments provided to follow their implementation.

21.6 Testing

In chapters 11 and 12 we looked at the concepts of unit testing and integration testing. We have left unit testing to you as a practical task, but we will spend a little time here considering integration testing. A useful technique to devise test cases during integration testing is to review the behaviour specifications of use cases, derived during requirements analysis.

Remember, a use case describes some useful service that the system performs. The behaviour specifications capture this service from the point of view of the user. When testing the system you take the place of the user, and you should ensure that the behaviour specification is observed.

Often, there are several routes through a single use case. For example, when registering a plane, either the plane could be successfully registered, or an error is indicated. Different routes through a single use case are known as different **scenarios**. During integration testing you should take the place of the user and make sure that you test *each* scenario for *each* use case. Not surprisingly, this is often known as **scenario testing**. As an example, reconsider the "*Record flight's request to land*" use case:

An air traffic controller records an incoming flight entering airport airspace, and requesting to land at the airport, by submitting its flight number. As long as the plane has previously registered with the airport, the air traffic controller is given an unoccupied runway number on which the plane will have permission to land. If all runways are occupied, however, this permission is denied and the air traffic controller is informed to instruct the plane to circle the airport. If the plane has not previously registered with the airport an error is signalled.

From this description three scenarios can be identified:

Scenario 1

An air traffic controller records an incoming plane entering airport airspace and requesting to land at the airport, by submitting its flight number, and is given an unoccupied runway number on which the plane will have permission to land.

Scenario 2

An air traffic controller records an incoming plane entering airport airspace and requesting to land at the airport, by submitting its flight number. The air traffic controller is informed to instruct the plane to circle the airport as all runways are occupied.

Scenario 3

An air traffic controller records an incoming plane entering airport airspace and requesting to land at the airport, by submitting its flight number. An error is signalled as the plane has not previously registered with the airport.

Similar scenarios can be extracted for each use case. During testing we should walk through each scenario, checking whether the outcomes are as expected.

21.7 Design of the GUI

Figure 21.4 illustrates the interface design we have chosen for the *Airport* application. The type of Swing components used have been labelled.

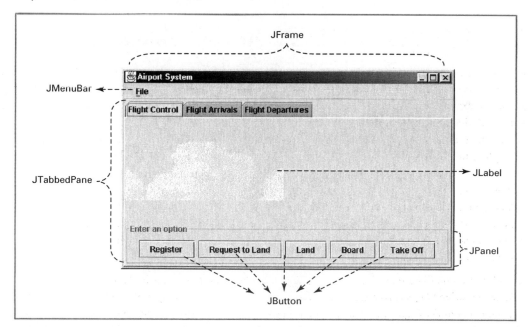

FIGURE 21.4 A Swing-based design for the airport GUI

Notice that we have used a label (JLabel) to hold a GIF image here:

```
JLabel jlblPicture = new JLabel(); // create JLabel component
jlblPicture.setIcon(new ImageIcon ("clouds.gif")); // add image
```

As you can see from figure 21.4, most of the Swing components we use (such as JFrame and JLabel) have already been introduced to you. However, the JTabbedPane is a Swing component that we have not yet looked at.

21.8 The *JTabbedPane* class

The JTabbedPane class provides a very useful Swing component for organizing the user interface. You can think of a JTabbedPane component as a collection of overlapping tabbed "cards", on which you place other user interface components.[1] A particular card is revealed by clicking on its **tab**. This allows certain parts of the interface to be kept hidden until required, thus reducing screen clutter.

A JTabbedPane component can consist of any number of tabbed cards. Each card is actually a *single* component of your choice. If you use a container component such as a JPanel, you can effectively associate many components with a single tab (see figure 21.5).

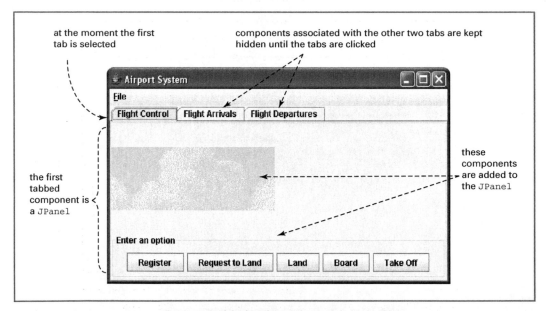

FIGURE 21.5 A JTabbedPane allows parts of the interface to be revealed selectively

---

[1] A similar effect can be achieved by using the CardLayout manager discussed in chapter 16, but the JTabbedPane involves considerably less coding effort and provides a more sophisticated interface.

The simplest way to construct a `JTabbedPane` component is to use the empty constructor as follows:

```
JTabbedPane tabs = new JTabbedPane();
```

We can now add tabbed components to the `JtabbedPane`.[2] When adding a tabbed component to a `JTabbedPane`, you call the `addTab` method. The method requires two parameters – the first is the title that will appear on the tab and the second the component to add. The "Flight Control" tab can be created as follows:

```
// create a JPanel component
JPanel controlPanel = new JPanel();

// other components can be added to this panel either now or later

// add this panel to the JTabbedPane component and give the tab a title
tabs.addTab("Flight Control", controlPanel);
```

The "Flight Arrivals" and "Flight Departures" tabs both consist of a text area for displaying plane details. Figure 21.6 shows the airport GUI after selecting the "Flight Arrivals" tab.

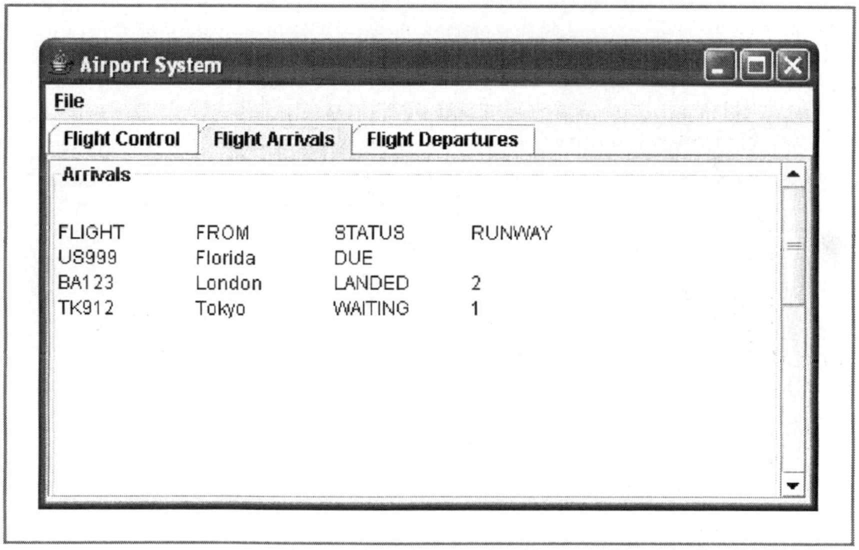

FIGURE 21.6 Both "Flight Arrivals" and "Flight Departures" consist of a text area

In this case, we do not need to associate a tab with a `JPanel`, as the tab will only reveal a single component: the text area. Our text areas require scroll panes, however. To add scroll bars to a `JTextArea`, the

---

[2] By default, the tabs you add will appear at the top of the `JTabbedPane` (as in figure 21.4). A version of the `JTabbedPane` constructor allows you to choose whether they appear at the top, the bottom, the left or the right.

`JTextArea` component has to be added to a `JScrollPane` component. The `JScrollPane` is then added to the `JTabbedPane` as follows:

```
// create text area
JTextArea jtaArrivals = new JTextArea(30,20);
// add text area to scroll pane
JScrollPane jspArrivals = new JScrollPane(jtaArrivals);
// add scroll pane to JTabbedPane component
tabs.addTab("Flight Arrivals", jspArrivals);
```

Notice that we have begun the name of Swing components with a summary of the type of component, so the name of the `JTextArea` component begins with 'jta' and so on.

21.9 The *AirportFrame* class

The GUI for the airport application is contained within a `JFrame`. The `JFrame` will need the `Airport` object to be one of its attributes so that it can be modified. The outline of this class is given below:

THE *AIRPORTFRAME* CLASS

```
package airportSys; // add to package
import java.awt.*; // for Layout managers and Color
import java.awt.event.*; // for ActionListener interface
import javax.swing.*; // for Swing components
import javax.swing.border.*; // for Swing borders
import java.io.*; // for File input, output
import java.util.*; // for Set class


/**
 * Class to provide GUI for Airport application
 *
 * @author Charatan and Kans
 * @version 5th November 2008
 */
public class AirportFrame extends JFrame implements ActionListener
{
  //attributes
  private Airport myAirport; // reference to Airport object
  // code to declare graphical components here
/**
 * Constructor initializes Airport object and arranges the GUI components
 * @param numIn The number of runways
 */
```

```
public AirportFrame(int numIn)
{
  try // check for Exceptions
  {
    myAirport = new Airport (numIn); // send number of runways
  }
  catch (AirportException ae)
  {
    ae.printStackTrace(); // display error to console
    JOptionPane.showMessageDialog (this,"AIRPORT SYSTEM VIOLATION",
                       "Error", JOptionPane.ERROR_MESSAGE);
    System.exit(1); // indicates exit with error
  }


  // rest of code left to complete
}


/**
 * Process button presses and update arrivals and departures information
 */
public void actionPerformed (ActionEvent e)
{
  // code to respond to button clicks and menu selections here
  listArrivals(); // update arrivals tab
  listDepartures(); // update departures tab
}
private void listArrivals()
{
  // code to display arrivals information in arrivals text area
}
private void listDepartures()
{
  // code to display departures information in departures text area
}
}
```

As you can see, the outline of this class follows a familiar pattern. Adding the detail should be a simple matter and we leave this to you as a practical task. Our implementation can also be copied from the accompanying CD. We will just draw your attention to one or two Swing features that we have decided to incorporate into our implementation that will be new to you.

First, we have added **tool tips** to our buttons. A tool tip is an informative description of the purpose of a GUI component. This informative description is revealed when the user places the cursor over the component. Figure 21.7 shows the tool tip that is revealed when the cursor is placed over the "Land" button.

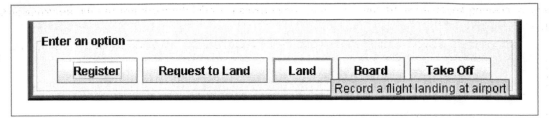

FIGURE 21.7 A tool tip is revealed when the mouse is placed over the "Land" button

Adding a tool tip to a Swing component is easy; just use the `setToolTipText` method:

```
// create Swing component
JButton jbtnLand = new JButton ("Land");
// add tool tip text
jbtnLand.setToolTipText("Record a flight landing at the airport");
```

We have also created **short cut** key access to our File menu. Ordinarily, a graphical component is selected by clicking on it with a mouse. Sometimes it is convenient to provide keyboard access to such items (this might be useful, for example, when the user does not have access to a working mouse). In the case of our GUI, the file menu can be selected with a mouse or by pressing the ALT and F keys simultaneously (ALT-F). It is clear that this is an alternative method of accessing the "File" menu by the fact that the 'F' of "File" is underlined (see figure 21.8).

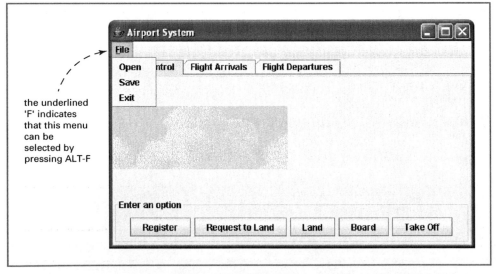

FIGURE 21.8 A keyboard shortcut provides a useful alternative for accessing graphical components

Again, creating keyboard short cuts for Swing components is straightforward; just use the `setMnemonic` method:

```
// create Swing component
JMenu fileMenu = new JMenu("File");
// add keyboard shortcut
fileMenu.setMnemonic('F');
```

21.10 Airport dialogue boxes

Whenever a button is selected in the "Flight Control" screen, a dialogue box is required to get and process user input. We have defined five dialogue classes for this purpose:

- `RegisterDialog`;
- `RequestToLandDialog`;
- `LandingDialog`;
- `BoardingDialog`;
- `TakeOffDialog`.

The button responses are coded in the `actionPerfomed` method of the `AirportFrame` class. Here, for example, is how we generate a `RegisterDialog` in response to the selection of the "Register" button:

```
public void actionPerformed (ActionEvent e)
{
  if (e.getSource()==jbtnRegister) // "Register" Button selected
  {
    // generate Register Dialogue Box
    new RegisterDialog(this,"Registration form", myAirport);
  }
  // more processing here
}
```

As you can see, our dialogue constructor takes three parameters:

```
new RegisterDialog(this,"Registration form", myAirport);
```

The first is the parent frame (`this`), the second is the title of the dialogue box ("Registration form") and the final parameter is a reference to our `Airport` object (`myAirport`). The last parameter is required as each dialogue box must update the airport object in some way or another.

You already know how to create dialogue classes from chapters 16 and 17. You may wish to model your dialogue boxes on ours (see figures 21.9–21.13).

FIGURE 21.9 This dialogue box is created when the "Register" button is selected

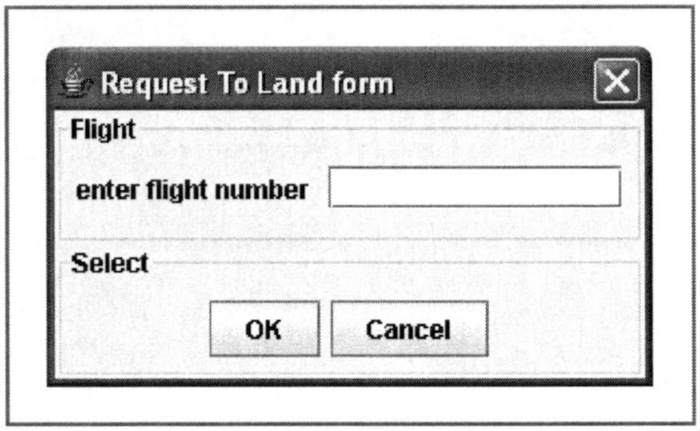

FIGURE 21.10 This dialogue box is created when the "Request to Land" button is selected

FIGURE 21.11 This dialogue box is created when the "Land" button is selected

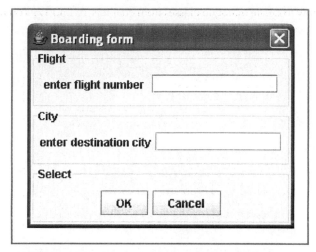

FIGURE 21.12 This dialogue box is created when the "Board" button is selected

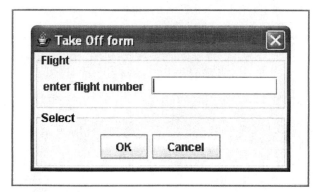

FIGURE 21.13 This dialogue box is created when the "Take Off" button is selected

21.10.1 Implementing the Airport dialogue boxes

The `Airport` dialogue boxes contain Swing components such as `JPanel`, `JLabel`, and `JTextField`, which you have met before. We leave their implementation to you. Before we do that, you may wish to consider using inheritance to reduce the coding task.

If you look back at the dialogue boxes in figures 21.9–21.13 you can see that, although no two are identical, they all share many common features. It makes sense to generalize these common features into a base class, `AirportDialog` say, and then use inheritance to develop the specialized dialogue classes (see figure 21.14).

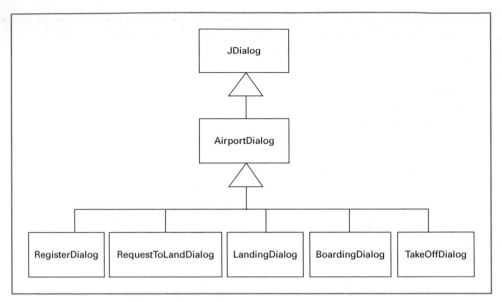

FIGURE 21.14 Common dialogue features are encapsulated in a base `AirportDialog` class

As an example of the visual components that are common to all the `Airport` dialogue boxes, look back at the "Request To Land" dialogue box and the "Take Off" dialogue boxes. These dialogue boxes contain only visual components that are common to all dialogue boxes (see figure 21.15).

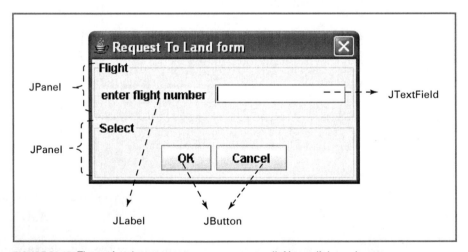

FIGURE 21.15 These visual components are common to all *Airport* dialogue boxes

Here is the code for the `AirportDialog` base class. Take a look at it and then we will discuss it.

THE *AIRPORTDIALOG* CLASS

```java
package airportSys;
import java.awt.*;
import java.awt.event.*;
import javax.swing.*;
import javax.swing.border.*;

/**
 * This is an abstract class for a general Airport dialog
 *
 * @author Charatan and Kans
 * @version 6th November 2008
 */
abstract class AirportDialog extends JDialog implements ActionListener
{
  // notice we have given some attributes 'protected' access
  protected JPanel flightPanel = new JPanel();
  protected JPanel buttonPanel = new JPanel();
  private JLabel jlbFlightNumber = new JLabel ("enter flight number ");
  protected JTextField jtfFlight = new JTextField(12);
  protected JButton jbtnOk = new JButton ("OK");
  private JButton jbtnCancel = new JButton ("Cancel");
  protected Airport associatedAirport; // airport object

  public AirportDialog(JFrame frameIn, String titleIn, Airport airportIn)
  {
    super(frameIn, true); // associate dialog with parent frame
    associatedAirport = airportIn; // make link to airport object
    // position dialog and set title
    setLocation(100,200);
    setTitle(titleIn);
    // add visual components
    flightPanel.add(jlbFlightNumber);
    flightPanel.add(jtfFlight);
    flightPanel.setBorder(new TitledBorder("Flight"));
    buttonPanel.add(jbtnOk);
    buttonPanel.add(jbtnCancel);

    buttonPanel.setBorder(new TitledBorder("Select"));
    // we will disuss the next two lines after this code
    jbtnOk.addActionListener(this);
    jbtnCancel.addActionListener(new CancelButtonListener());
  }
```

```
// this inner class implements the Actionlistener for the 'Cancel' button
private class CancelButtonListener implements ActionListener
{
  public void actionPerformed(ActionEvent event)
  {
    dispose(); // destroys the dialog box
  }
}
}
```

Most of this code should be straightforward to follow. There are just a few things we want to point out to you. First, notice that we declared some attributes as **protected** rather than **private**:

```
protected JPanel flightPanel = new JPanel();
protected JPanel buttonPanel = new JPanel();
private JLabel jlbFlightNumber = new JLabel ("enter flight number ");
protected JTextField jtfFlight = new JTextField(12);
protected JButton jbtnOk = new JButton ("OK");
private JButton jbtnCancel = new JButton ("Cancel");
protected Airport associatedAirport;
```

The use of the **protected** modifier, as opposed to **public** or **private**, was explained in chapter 9. An attribute that is declared as **protected** can be accessed by a method of a subclass, or by any class within the same package.

In chapter 9 we told you that declaring attributes as **protected** has two drawbacks. First, it is not always possible to anticipate in advance that a class will be subclassed; second, **protected** access weakens encapsulation, because access is given to all classes within the package, not just the subclasses. For these reasons we have mostly chosen not to use **protected**, but rather to plan carefully when deciding on which attributes are to have get- and set- methods. On this occasion, however, we have relaxed our rule and used **protected**, because neither of the above problems actually applies: we do know in this case that other classes will need to inherit from this class – and because this class is not declared as **public** within our package, we do not need to worry about weakening encapsulation. The advantage of doing this is, of course, that we are able to cut out a considerable amount of additional coding by accessing these attributes directly in subclasses. Notice that the Airport object is a **protected** attribute here as all dialogues will require access to this attribute.

One last thing we need to tell you about the AirportDialog class is the way we dealt with the event-handling code. There are two buttons in this class, the 'Cancel' button and the 'OK' button, which require event-handling code.

The behaviour of the 'OK' button will vary from dialogue box to dialogue box, so that will be left for each inherited class to define, in an actionPerformed method.[3] The behaviour of the 'Cancel' button will be

---

[3] In fact, each subclass *must* implement this method as this base class (AirportDialog) claims to implement the ActionPerformed interface.

the same for all dialogue boxes, however – to simply dispose of the dialogue. So it is appropriate to implement the behaviour for this button in this base class. However, we have a small problem here. If we define an `actionPerformed` method in the base class (for the 'Cancel' button) and an `actionPerformed` method in an inherited class (for the 'OK' button), the inherited class method will always override the base class method! For that reason we have defined an inner class (see section 13.5), `CancelButtonListener`, which contains its own `actionPerformed` method:

```
abstract class AirportDialog extends JDialog implements ActionListener
{
  // some code here

  // this Actionlistener will be implemented in the inherited classes
  jbtnOk.addActionListener(this);
  /* this action listener will be the same for all classes so it is implemented once here in
     the base class, in an inner class below */
  jbtnCancel.addActionListener(new CancelButtonListener());

  // inner class contains actionPerformed method for the 'Cancel' button
  private class CancelButtonListener implements ActionListener
  {
    public void actionPerformed(ActionEvent event)
    {
      dispose(); // destroys the dialog box
    }
  }
}
```

Finally, program 21.1 imports the `airportSys` package and runs the application with four runways:

PROGRAM 21.1

```
import airportSys.*; // import all the classes from this package

public class RunAirport
{
  public static void main (String[] args)
  {
    new AirportFrame(4); // generate GUI with 4 runways
  }
}
```

Self-test questions

1 In section 21.6 we developed scenarios for the use case *"Register flight arrival"*. Develop scenarios for all the other use cases in table 21.1.

2 What is the difference between *containment* and *composition* in UML?

3 Consider an enumerated type, Light. This type can have one of three values: RED, AMBER and GREEN. It will be used to display a message to students, indicating whether or not a lecturer is available to be seen.

    a Specify this type in UML.

    b Implement this type in Java.

    c Declare a Light variable, doorLight;

    d Write a **switch** statement that checks doorLight and displays "I am away" when doorLight is RED, "I am busy" when doorLight is AMBER and "I am free" when doorLight is GREEN.

4 Identify the benefits offered by the JTabbedPane component.

5 How can the tool tip *"This button stops the game"* be added to a JButton icalled jbStop?

6 How can a JMenu item called viewMenu be allocated a short cut key "V"?

Programming exercises

1 Copy, from the accompanying CD, the classes that make up the airport application. Make any further enhancements that you wish to this application. For example, you may wish to consider using JOptionPane dialogues to provide information and error messages such as those given below:

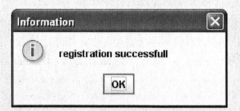
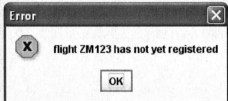

2 Develop tester programs for the Runway, Plane and Airport classes.

3 Create an executable JAR file to run the airport application and include a splash screen.

Java in a network environment

❖ OBJECTIVES

By the end of this chapter you should be able to:

❖ describe the **client–server** model;

❖ explain the difference between an application and an **applet**;

❖ explain the purpose of the `init`, `start`, `stop` and `destroy` methods;

❖ implement Java applets using the `JApplet` class;

❖ describe **Java Database Connectivity (JDBC)** technology;

❖ write a Java program that accesses a remote database and executes SQL queries on that database;

❖ explain the function of the Java `Socket` and `ServerSocket` classes;

❖ write a simple **client–server** application using **sockets**.

22.1 Introduction

In this chapter we are going to explore some of the ways in which Java can be used to write programs that communicate over a network. We will be restricting ourselves to programs that involve some sort of data transfer, as opposed to programs which are themselves distributed over a network and which need to call the methods of remote objects. There is in fact a Java mechanism for the latter situation – *Remote Method Invocation (RMI)*. We will not be dealing with RMI here, however, because there are many theoretical issues involved and the subject is better placed in a book that deals primarily with networking.

Network programs rely very much on the concept of a **client** and a **server**. A server program provides some sort of service for other programs – clients – normally located on a different machine. The service it provides could be one of many things – it could send some files to the client; it could send web pages to the client; it could read some data from the local machine and send that across, maybe having done some processing first; it could perform a complex calculation; it could print some material on a local printer. The possibilities are endless.

It should be noted that the distinction between a client and server can become blurred: a program acting as a client in one situation could also act as a server in another, and vice versa. It is also important to note that it is often the case that a machine, rather than a program, is referred to as a server. This usually happens when a machine is dedicated to running a particular server program – typically a file server – and does very little else. Strictly speaking, we should refer to the machine that a server runs on as the host.

Communication between a client and a server could be over a local area network, a wide area network, or over the Internet. Server programs that offer a service via the Internet have to obey a particular set of rules or protocols to ensure that the client and server are "speaking the same language". Common examples are File Transfer Protocol (FTP) for servers that send files, and Hypertext Transfer Protocol (HTTP) for services that send web pages to a client.

In this chapter we are going to explore three types of program:

- first, we will look at **applets** – programs that are downloaded from a remote site to run on the local machine under the control of a browser;

- second, we will show you how to communicate with a database server operating either locally or on a remote machine in order to store and retrieve data from the database;

- finally, we will look at the notion of **sockets** – special programs that allow data to pass between two programs running on different computers.

22.2 Applets

An applet is a Java program that can be downloaded from the World Wide Web and run in a browser such as Internet Explorer or Firefox. The fact that Java runs on a virtual machine and is therefore platform independent means that the type of operating system running on the client machine is unimportant.

As you know, applications, as opposed to applets, are made runnable by providing a class that contains a `main` method. The `main` method provides the overall means of controlling the program. However, an applet, as we have said, runs in a browser. Control of the applet thus becomes the responsibility of the browser and there is no need for a `main` method – if there were a `main` method in the class, it would simply be ignored when the applet ran.

You will have observed that in this book, apart from the earlier very simple text-based programs, we have organized things in such a way that the `main` method is never included in the functional class, but instead is placed in a separate "driver" class. In many of the graphical applications that we have developed, we have provided a class whose `main` method does nothing more than create an instance of a class that extends a `JFrame`.

22.2.1 Running an applet in a browser

In order to run an applet in a browser (or in one of the applet viewers provided with most Java IDEs), we need to include an instruction in a web page that tells the browser to load the applet and run it. Web pages are written in a special language known as Hypertext Markup Language (HTML), or one of its associated languages such as Extensible Markup Language (XML). HTML code is interpreted by browsers such as Firefox and Internet Explorer to produce the formatted text and graphics that we are used to seeing.

We are not going to go into any detail here about how to write HTML or XML; we will talk only about the commands you need in order to get your applets running. Commands in HTML are called tags and are enclosed in angle brackets. The tag that we are interested in here is the one that tells the browser to load and run a Java class. This uses the key word *applet*, as we shall see in a moment.

Cast your mind back to the `ChangingFace` class from chapter 10. We are going to make two changes, which are described below:

- the class will extend `JApplet` instead of `JFrame`;
- the constructor will be replaced with a special method called `init` (short for *initialize*), and the code that we originally had in the constructor will now be placed in this special `init` method.

The `ChangingFaceApplet` class is shown below:

THE *CHANGINGFACEAPPLET* CLASS

```java
import javax.swing.*;
import java.awt.*;
import java.awt.event.*;

public class ChangingFaceApplet extends JApplet implements ActionListener
{
  private boolean isHappy = true; // will determine the mood of the face
  private JButton happyButton = new JButton("Smile");
  private JButton sadButton = new JButton("Frown");

  public void init() // initialization routines are placed in this method
  {
    // use a flow layout
    setLayout(new FlowLayout());

    // add the buttons to the panel
    add(happyButton);
    add(sadButton);

    // set the background to yellow
    getContentPane().setBackground(Color.yellow);

    // make the buttons transparent
    happyButton. setOpaque(false);
    sadButton.setOpaque(false);

    // enable the buttons to listen for a mouse-click
    happyButton. addActionListener(this);
    sadButton.addActionListener(this);
  }

public void paint(Graphics g)
{
  // call the paint method of the superclass, JApplet
  super.paint(g);
```

```
    g.setColor(Color. red);
    g.drawOval(85,45,75,75);
    g.setColor(Color. blue);
    g.drawOval(100,65,10,10);
    g.drawOval(135,65,10,10);
    g.drawString("Changing Face", 80,155);
    if(isHappy == true)
    {

      // draw a smiling mouth
      g.drawArc(102,85,40,25,0,-180);
    }
    else
    {

      // draw a frowning mouth
      g.drawArc(102,85,40,25,0,180);
    }
}


// the event-handling routine
public void actionPerformed(ActionEvent e)
{
    if(e.getSource() == happyButton)
    {
      isHappy = true;
      repaint();
    }
    if(e.getSource() == sadButton)
    {
      isHappy = false;
      repaint();
    }
  }
}
```

We have provided below the bare minimum HTML code that will load and run this class in a browser; it doesn't add any headings, or attempt to produce a pretty webpage – those of you who know HTML or XML will be able to add those features if you wish:

```
<HTML>
  <APPLET CODE = "ChangingFaceApplet.class" WIDTH = "250"HEIGHT = "175" >
  </APPLET>
</HTML>
```

As some of you might know, HTML tags often have an opening and a closing version, the latter starting with a forward slash (/). The relevant text is contained within these tags. So in our example the HTML tags tell the browser that the text contained represents an HTML page. The text within the APPLET tags provides the information about the applet that needs to be loaded; this is done with special words (called *attributes* just to confuse us!) which are part of the tag. In this case we provide the name of the class (with the CODE attribute) and the dimensions of the applet window (with the attributes WIDTH and HEIGHT). Figure 22.1 shows the ChangingFace class running in a browser.

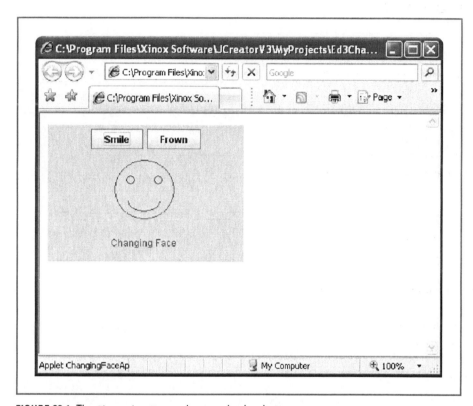

FIGURE 22.1 The ChangingFace class running in a browser

Of course, it is necessary to have the correct file (in this case ChangingFaceApplet.class) in the same directory as the HTML file; alternatively it is possible to make absolute references to directories in the HTML code, but you should look at books on HTML in order to find out more about this. Do notice, however, that it is the compiled byte code that you need (that is, the file with the .class extension), and not the Java source code.

22.2.2 Special applet methods

In addition to the init method there are three other special applet methods that you can code if you wish; start, stop and destroy. Together with the paint method these are automatically called in a special order which is explained in table 22.1 below.

Method	Invocation
init	Invoked the first time the applet is loaded (or reloaded) by a browser
start	Invoked after init when the applet is first loaded (or reloaded) and then invoked each time the applet is made visible again by returning to the page
paint	Invoked immediately after start
stop	Invoked when the applet is hidden (by pointing the browser at a different page)
destroy	Invoked after stop when the applet is abandoned (by closing the browser)

TABLE 22.1 The special applet methods (working with the paint method)

22.2.3 Guidelines for creating applets

As you have seen, when creating applets, as opposed to applications, there are a few differences that you need to be aware of. These are summarized below:

1 Ensure that your class extends the JApplet class.

2 Place any initialization routines, such as setting initial values, in an init or a start method rather than in a constructor.

3 Do not include a main method, as any code in the main method is ignored by the browser.

4 Make sure that any input and output goes through the Swing interface – the user will not normally see the text console when using a browser.

5 Do not include any buttons or other controls that attempt to terminate the program – applets terminate when the page is closed in the browser.

6 Always declare your class as public.

To help you to understand more about creating applets, you will be given the opportunity in the exercises at the end of the chapter to rewrite the RedCircle class from chapter 13 as an applet.

22.3 Accessing remote databases

It is not an uncommon occurrence that we need to develop an application that requires the use of data that is held on a database which is stored either locally or on a remote site. Java is able to access such a database by means of a technology called **Java Database Connectivity (JDBC)**; manufacturers of database management systems provide JDBC drivers by means of which Java programs can access their databases. A driver is a piece of software that enables communication between two programs, or between a software program and a piece of hardware, by translating the output of one program into a form understood by the other one.

To make life even easier for us, there is a package known as java.sql. This package provides the means by which our Java programs can contain commands written in standard SQL (Structured Query Language), which is the well-established means of writing database instructions. In this chapter we are not going to teach you SQL, but will assume you are familiar with some basic commands. The example we are going to use is for a MySQL database. MySQL, a shareware product, has proved to be very popular with developers over recent years, and its popularity continues to grow; more information can be obtained from www.mysql.org. The developers of MySQL provide a driver known as Connector/J (formerly known as mm.mysql), which can be downloaded. It needs to be unzipped and its contents stored to a folder to which the classpath has been set. The driver itself is called `Driver.class` and, once the package is unzipped, will reside in the hierarchy `org.gjt.mm.mysql` – so you can see that the classpath must be set to the folder that contains the `org` directory.

For our example we have set up a little database called *ElectricalStore* that contains a table called *products*. This table is described below (table 22.2); it is assumed that you are familiar with relational databases and the data types available.

Field	Data type	Length
SerialNumber	char	(7)
Make	char	(10)
Description	char	(20)
Price	decimal	(10, 2)

TABLE 22.2 The *Products* table

We have populated this database, and, in order to query it, we have developed a class called `ProductQuery`. This class, once an instance of it is created, executes just one SQL statement:

```
select * from products;
```

Those of you who are familiar with SQL will know that this query retrieves all the fields from all the records in the *products* table. The information obtained is then displayed in a text area as you can see from figure 22.2.

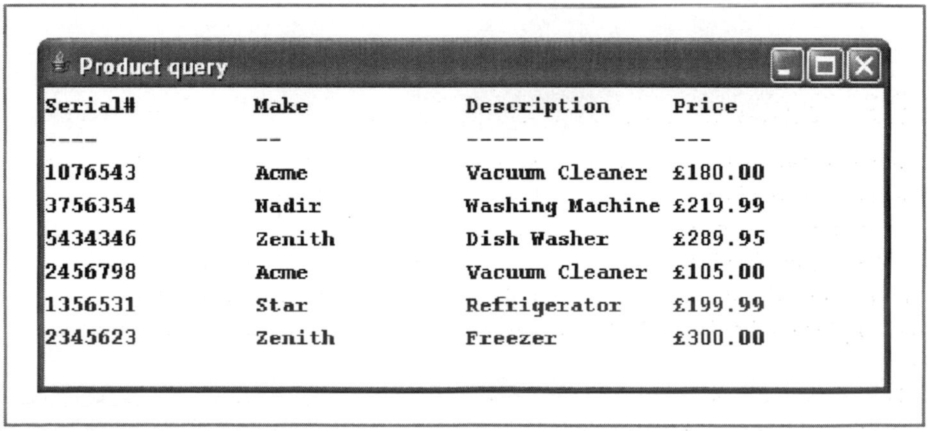

```
Product query                                    [_][□][✕]
Serial#          Make           Description      Price
----             --             ------           ---
1076543          Acme           Vacuum Cleaner   £180.00
3756354          Nadir          Washing Machine  £219.99
5434346          Zenith         Dish Washer      £289.95
2456798          Acme           Vacuum Cleaner   £105.00
1356531          Star           Refrigerator     £199.99
2345623          Zenith         Freezer          £300.00
```

FIGURE 22.2 Displaying the information from the *ElectricalStore* database

Take a look at the `ProductQuery` class below, and then we will go through it with you.

THE *PRODUCTQUERY* CLASS

```java
import java.sql.*;
import javax.swing.*;
import java.awt.*;

public class ProductQuery extends JFrame
{

  // the attributes
  public static final String DRIVER = "org.gjt.mm.mysql.Driver";
  public static final String URL = "jdbc:mysql://localhost/ElectricalStore";
  public static final String USERNAME = "U1098765";
  public static final String PASSWORD = "scott";

  private Connection con;
  private Statement st;
  private ResultSet result;
  private JTextArea display = new JTextArea(25,25);

  // the constructor
  public ProductQuery()
  {

    // configure the frame and text area
    setTitle("Product query");
    add("Center",display);
    setSize(520,250);
    setVisible(true);
    display.setTabSize(16);
    display.setFont(new Font("DialogInput", Font.BOLD, 14));

    try
    {

      // load the MySQL jdbc driver
      Class.forName(DRIVER);

    }
    catch(ClassNotFoundException e)
    {
      display.setText("Driver not found");
    }
```

```
    try
    {

      // connect to the database
      con = DriverManager.getConnection(URL, USERNAME, PASSWORD);


      // create an SQL statement
      st = con.createStatement();


      // execute an SQL query
      result = st.executeQuery("select * from products");


      // create a heading
      display.setText("Serial#" + "\t" + "Make" + "\t" +
                          "Description" + "\t" + "Price" + "\n");
      display.append("——-" + "\t" + "—" + "\t" +
                          "———-" + "\t" + "—-" + "\n");


      // display results
      while(result.next()) // move to next record
      {

        // retrieve and display first field
        display.append(result.getString(1) + "\t");
        // retrieve and display second field
        display.append(result.getString(2) + "\t");
        // retrieve and display third field
        display.append(result.getString(3)+ "\t");
        // retrieve and display fourth field
        display.append("£" + result.getString(4)+ "\n");


      }
    }


    catch(SQLException e) // handle the SQLException
    {
      e.printStackTrace();
    }
  }
}
```

You can see that we have declared some String constants as attributes – these will be explained later, when they are used. After these, we have declared a Connection object, a Statement object and a ResultSet object, none of which you have previously encountered. These are part of the java.sql package, and we will explain them in a moment. The final attribute declaration is a JTextArea object, display, which will be used to display the results.

The first thing we do in the constructor, after configuring the frame and the text area, is to load the driver:

```
try
{
  Class.forName(DRIVER);
}
catch(ClassNotFoundException e)
{
  display.setText("Driver not found");
}
```

You can see we are using a method of a Java class called Class. Objects of the Class class are constructed by the Java Virtual Machine and they hold representations of all the running classes. The **static** method forName loads a class into memory, and returns a representation of that class. The class is located by a string representing its file name. In this case the string, DRIVER, was defined as an attribute:

```
public static final String DRIVER = "org.gjt.mm.mysql.Driver";
```

You can see we have given a full path reference to the MySQL driver. Notice that the forName method throws a checked exception, ClassNotFoundException, if the class is not found, so we have had to enclose it in a **try...catch** block.

Once the driver is loaded we establish a connection to the database as follows:

```
con = DriverManager.getConnection(URL, USERNAME, PASSWORD);
```

The class DriverManager is located in the java.sql package, along with Connection, Statement and ResultSet. The getConnection method of DriverManager establishes a connection with the database referred to by the parameter URL, which was defined in the attribute declarations as:

```
public static final String URL = "jdbc:mysql://localhost/ElectricalStore";
```

This is the correct format for the MySQL database called *ElectricalStore* residing on the local machine. Other databases will require a slightly different format, the details of which can be found in the documentation for that product. Note that *localhost* is the way in which operating systems refer to the local machine – it is in fact an alias for IP (Internet Protocol) address 127.0.0.1, the normal loopback IP. If the database were located on another machine on the network, then this would be replaced by its name or IP address.[1] As you can see, the getConnection method receives, in addition to the url (uniform resource locator), the user name and password; if this is not required, there is a version of getConnection that accepts the url only.

The method returns a Connection object, which we have assigned to the attribute con. A Connection object created in this way has a number of methods that allow communication with the database. One of these methods is called createStatement, and it is the next one we use:

```
st = con.createStatement();
```

As you saw, we declared a Statement object, st, as an attribute and this is now assigned the return value of the createStatement method. A Statement object is used for executing SQL statements and returning their results; in the next line we use its executeQuery method:

```
result = st.executeQuery("select * from products");
```

The data returned by executing the query is assigned to a ResultSet object, result. A ResultSet object holds a tabular representation of the data, and a pointer is maintained to allow us to navigate through the records. The next method moves the pointer to the next record, returning **false** if there are no more records. The individual fields are returned with methods such as getString, getDouble and getInt. You can see how we have used these methods in the ProductQuery class:

```
while(result.next())
{
  display.append(result.getString(1) + "\t");
  display.append(result.getString(2) + "\t");
  display.append(result.getString(3)+ "\t");
  display.append("£" + result.getString(4)+ "\n");
}
```

The version of getString that we have used here takes an integer representing the position of the field – in our example 1 is the *SerialNumber*, 2 is *Make* and so on. There is also a version of getString that accepts the name of the field. So, for example, we could have used, for the second field:

```
display.append(result.getString("Make") + "\t");
```

Since all we are doing is displaying the data, we have used getString for the last field, even though it holds numeric data – this saved us the trouble of doing any formatting on it. If we had wished to do any processing with this data, we could have used the getDouble method to retrieve it as a **double** rather than a String.

You should note that all the above methods may throw SQLExceptions, hence the use of the **try...catch** block.

---

[1] The system administrator will, of course, have had to set up the correct permissions for the database.

22.3.1 Connecting to Microsoft databases

The Microsoft Foundation has its own technology for database connectivity, known as Open Database Connectivity (ODBC). The latest Java versions include what is called a JDBC-to-ODBC bridge driver to enable a Java program to interact with a Microsoft database such as Access. In order to do this it is necessary to configure the database using the Windows ODBC Data Source Administrator tool; this is accessed via the control panel. This allows you to assign a name to a particular database; this name can then be used in the Java program. If for example we created an Access database similar to the one in the previous example, and we then assigned the name *ElectricalStore* to it using the ODBC tool, the correct format for the url string would be:

```
"jdbc:odbc:ElectricalStore"
```

We would have had to previously load the appropriate driver, which, as we said, is packaged with Java. Its full path name is:

```
"sun.jdbc.odbc.JdbcOdbcDriver"
```

22.4 Sockets

In chapter 18 you were introduced to the idea of a *stream* – a channel of communication between the computer's main memory and some external device such as a disk. In that chapter you were shown how Java provides high-level classes that hide from the programmer the low-level details of how data is stored on a disk or other device. Just as the external storage of data is a complicated business, so too is the transmission of data across a network.

A **socket** is a software mechanism that is able to hide from the programmer the detail of how data is actually transmitted, in a not dissimilar way to that in which the high-level file handling classes protect the programmer from the details of external storage. Sockets were originally developed for the Unix operating system and they enabled the programmer to treat a network connection as just another stream to which data can be written and from which it can be read. Sockets have since been developed for other operating systems such as Windows, and fortunately for Java.

In order to understand sockets it is also necessary to understand the concept of a port. A machine on a network is referred to by its IP (Internet Protocol) address. However, any particular server can perform a number of different functions, and therefore needs to be able to distinguish between different types of request, such as email requests, file transfer requests, requests for web pages and so on. This is accomplished by assigning each type of request a special number known as a *port*. Many port numbers are now internationally recognized, and so all computers will agree on their meaning. For example, a request on port 80 will always be expected to be an HTTP request; port 22 is reserved for Telnet[2] requests; port 21 is for FTP (File Transfer Protocol) requests. A client program can therefore assume that server programs will be using these ports for those particular services.

All sockets must be capable of doing the following:

- connect to a remote machine;
- send data;

---

[2] Telnet is a special protocol used for interactive remote command-line sessions.

■ receive data;

■ close a connection.

A socket which is to be used for a server must additionally be able to:

■ bind to a port (that is, to associate the server with a port number);

■ listen for incoming data;

■ accept connections from a remote server on the bound port.

The Java `Socket` class has methods that correspond to the first four of the above; the `ServerSocket` class provides methods for the last three.

22.5 A simple server application

The server we are going to build is going to offer a very simple service to a client; it will wait to receive two integers, and then it will send back the sum of those two integers. Clearly this would not in reality be a very useful server – a real-world server would be offering a far more complex service – perhaps performing some very complicated processing, or retrieving data from a database running on the same machine, or maybe printing on a printer local to the server. However, our simple addition server demonstrates the principles of a client–server protocol very nicely.

The application will display a frame containing a text area in which it reports on its behaviour – it will tell us when it is waiting for a connection, when a connection has been established with a client, when the numbers to be added have been received, and when the information has been sent back to the client.

The `AdditionServer` class is presented below – have a look at it and then we'll take you through it.

THE *ADDITIONSERVER* CLASS

```java
import java.net.*;
import java.io.*;
import javax.swing.*;


public class AdditionServer extends JFrame
{

  private JTextArea textWindow = new JTextArea();
  private int port;

  // the constructor
  public AdditionServer(int portIn)
  {

    port = portIn;
    setTitle("Addition Server");
```

```
   add("Center",textWindow);
   setDefaultCloseOperation(JFrame.EXIT_ON_CLOSE);
   setSize(400, 300);
   setVisible(true);
   startServer();
}

private void startServer()
{

   // declare a "general" socket and a server socket
   Socket connection;
   ServerSocket listenSocket;

   // declare low level and high level objects for input
   InputStream inStream;
   DataInputStream inDataStream;

   // declare low level and high level objects for output
   OutputStream outStream;
   DataOutputStream outDataStream;

   // declare other variables
   String client;
   int first, second, sum;
   boolean connected;

   while(true) // an infinite loop
   {
     try
     {

       // create a server socket
       listenSocket = new ServerSocket (port);
       textWindow.append("Listening on port " + port + "\n");

       // listen for a connection from the client
       connection = listenSocket.accept();
       connected = true;
       textWindow.append("Connection established" + "\n");

       // create an input stream from the client
       inStream = connection.getInputStream();
       inDataStream = new DataInputStream(inStream);
```

```
        // create an output stream to the client
        outStream = connection.getOutputStream ();
        outDataStream = new DataOutputStream(outStream);

        // wait for a string from the client
        client = inDataStream.readUTF();
        textWindow.append("Address of client: " + client + "\n");
        while(connected)
        {

            // read an integer from the client
            first = inDataStream.readInt();
            textWindow.append("First number received: " + first + "\n");

            // read an integer from the client
            second = inDataStream.readInt();
            textWindow.append("Second number received: " + second + "\n");

            sum = first + second;
            textWindow.append("Sum returned: " + sum + "\n");

            // send the sum to the client
            outDataStream.writeInt(sum);

        }
    }

    catch (IOException e)
    {
        connected = false;
    }
    }

    }
}
```

You can see that we have declared a text area as an attribute, as well as an integer to hold the port number that the server is to bind to. As you can see, this is accepted by the constructor and assigned to this attribute; thus the port is selected by the user of this class. The rest of the constructor is concerned with configuring the frame and then calling a **private** method startServer.

The startServer method begins by declaring a number of variables:

```
// declare a "general" socket and a server socket
Socket connection;
ServerSocket listenSocket;

// declare low level and high level objects for input
InputStream inStream;
DataInputStream inDataStream;

// declare low level and high level objects for output
OutputStream outStream;
DataOutputStream outDataStream;

// declare other variables
String client;
int first, second, sum;
boolean connected;
```

The first two variables are, respectively, a Server and a ServerSocket. As this is a server application it requires both the general functionality of the Socket class and the specialist functionality of the ServerSocket class.

Next we declare the objects that we will need to establish an input stream with the client. We have come across the classes InputStream and DataInputStream before, in chapter 18. The former allows communication at a low level in the form of bytes; the latter allows the high-level communication in the form of strings, integers, characters and so on with which we are familiar.

After this we declare objects of OutputStream and DataOutputStream that we will need to establish the output stream. Finally we make some other declarations that we will need later on.

Now we start an infinite loop. The idea is that the server will accept a connection request from a client, and when that client is finished making requests it will be ready to receive connections from other clients; this will continue until the server is terminated.

From now everything is placed in a **try** block, because the constructor of the ServerSocket class and its accept method may both throw IOExceptions.

The first instruction in the **try** block looks like this:

```
listenSocket = new ServerSocket(port);
```

We are creating a new ServerSocket object and binding it to a particular port. In order to get the server to listen for a client requesting a connection on that port, we call the accept method of the ServerSocket class; we also place a message on the screen to tell us that the server is listening for a request:

```
textWindow.append("Listening on port " + port + "\n");
connection = listenSocket.accept();
```

The accept method returns an object of the Socket class, which we assign to the connection variable that we declared earlier.

The server is now listening for requests from clients on that port. This information is displayed in the text window as shown in figure 22.3.

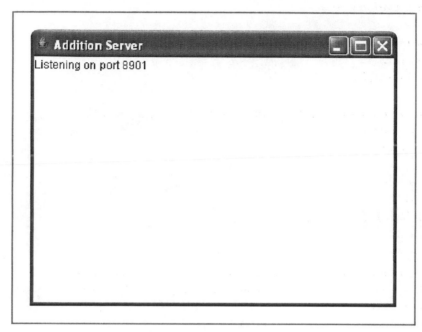

FIGURE 22.3 The server is listening for a request from a client

Once the connection is established we set the **boolean** variable, connected, to **true** and display a message:

```
connected = true;
textWindow.append("Connection established" + "\n");
```

The next thing we do is call the getInputStream method of the Socket object, connection. This returns an object of the InputStream class, thus providing a stream from client to server. We then wrap this low-level InputStream object with a high-level DataInputStream object, in the same way as we did when handling files in chapter 18:

```
inStream = connection.getInputStream();
inDataStream = new DataInputStream(inStream);
```

We then create an output stream in the same way:

```
outStream = connection.getOutputStream ();
outDataStream = new DataOutputStream(outStream);
```

As you will see shortly, we have designed our client to send its IP address to the server once it is connected. So our next instructions to the server are to wait to receive a string on the input stream, and then to display a message.

```
client = inDataStream.readUTF();
textWindow.append("Connection established with " + client + "\n" );
```

Figure 22.4 shows the text window after the connection has been made.

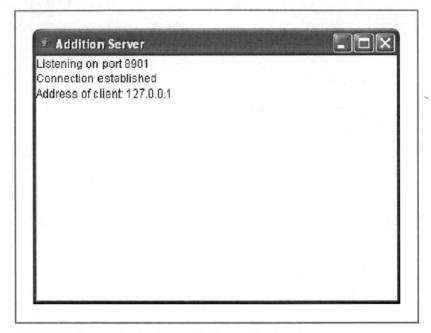

FIGURE 22.4 A connection has been established with a client

Once a connection has been established we want the server to perform the addition calculation for the client as many times as the client requires. Thus we provide a **while** loop that continues until the connection is lost:

```
while(connected)
{
  // read an integer from the client
  first = inDataStream.readInt();
  textWindow.append("First number received: " + first + "\n");
  // read an integer from the client
  second = inDataStream.readInt();
  textWindow.append("Second number received: " + second   + "\n");
  sum = first + second;
```

```
    textWindow.append("Sum returned: " + sum + "\n");
    // send the sum to the client
    outDataStream.writeInt (sum);
}
```

You can see that we read two integers from the input stream, displaying them each time. We then calculate and display the sum which we send back to the client on the output stream. Figure 22.5 shows an example of this.

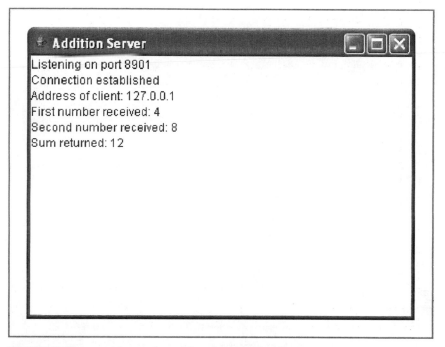

FIGURE 22.5 The server has performed the request for the client

The accept method of ServerSocket throws an IOException when the connection is lost. Therefore we have coded the **catch** block so that the connected variable that controls the inner **while** loop is set to **false**, so that when the client closes the connection the server will no longer expect to receive integers, but will return to the top of the outer **while** loop, and wait for another connection request:

```
catch (IOException e)
{
  connected = false;
}
```

We can run our server with program 22.1, which in this example will bind the server to port 8901:

PROGRAM 22.1

```
public class RunAdditionServer
{
  public static void main (String[] args)
  {
    new AdditionServer(8901);
  }
}
```

Now we can go on and build a client application that will communicate with the server.

22.6 A simple client application

Our AdditionClient is shown in figure 22.6.

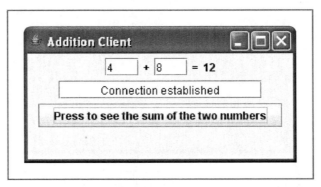

FIGURE 22.6 The addition client

You can see from the diagram how the client is going to work. The connection is established as soon as the application starts; then the user is free to enter numbers and press the button to send the numbers to the server and display the result. The middle text box is used to display messages regarding the connection.

Here is the code for the AdditionClient:

THE *ADDITIONCLIENT* CLASS

```
import java.net.*;
import java.io.*;
import javax.swing.*;
import java.awt.*;
```

```java
import java.awt.event.*;

public class AdditionClient extends JFrame implements ActionListener
{

  // declare the visual components
  private JTextField firstNumber = new JTextField(3);
  private JLabel plus = new JLabel("+");
  private JTextField secondNumber = new JTextField(3);
  private JLabel equals = new JLabel("=");
  private JLabel sum = new JLabel();
  private JTextField msg = new JTextField(20);
  private JButton addButton = new JButton("Press to see the sum of the two numbers");

  // declare low level and high level objects for input
  private InputStream inStream;
  private DataInputStream inDataStream;

  // declare low level and high level objects for output
  private OutputStream outStream;
  private DataOutputStream outDataStream;

  // declare a socket
  private Socket connection;

  // declare attributes to hold details of remote machine and port
  private String remoteMachine;
  private int port;

  // constructor
  public AdditionClient(String remoteMachineIn, int portIn)
  {

    remoteMachine = remoteMachineIn;
    port = portIn;
    // add the visual components
    add(firstNumber);
    add(plus);
    add(secondNumber);
    add(equals);
    add(sum);
    add(msg);
    add(addButton);
```

```
   // configure the frame
   setLayout(new FlowLayout());
   setTitle("Addition Client");
   msg.setHorizontalAlignment(JLabel.CENTER);
   addButton.addActionListener(this);
   setDefaultCloseOperation(JFrame.EXIT_ON_CLOSE);
   setSize(300, 150); setLocation(300,300);
   setVisible(true);

   // start the helper method that starts the client
   startClient();
}
private void startClient()
{

   try
   {

      // attempt to create a connection to the server
      connection = new Socket(remoteMachine, port);
      msg.setText("Connection established");

      // create an input stream from the server
      inStream = connection.getInputStream();
      inDataStream = new DataInputStream(inStream);

      // create an output stream to the server
      outStream = connection.getOutputStream();
      outDataStream = new DataOutputStream(outStream);

      // send the host IP to the server
      outDataStream.writeUTF(connection.getLocalAddress().getHostAddress());
   }
   catch (UnknownHostException e)
   {
     msg.setText("Unknown host");
   }
   catch (IOException except)
   {
     msg.setText("Network Exception");
   }


}
```

```
public void actionPerformed(ActionEvent e)
{

  try
  {

    // send the two integers to the server
    outDataStream.writeInt(Integer.parseInt(firstNumber.getText()));
    outDataStream.writeInt(Integer.parseInt(secondNumber.getText()));

    // read and display the result sent back from the server
    int result = inDataStream.readInt();
    sum.setText("" + result);

  }
  catch(IOException ie)
  {
     ie.printStackTrace();
  }
 }
}
```

We have declared a number of attributes, mostly concerned with the graphics components and with the input and output streams. We have also declared an object of the Socket class, and we have additionally declared a string, remoteMachine, and an integer, port. Both of these will be initialized via the constructor in order to allow the user of the class to specify the remote machine on which the server is running and the port on which it is listening.

Thus the constructor accepts a String and an **int**, which it assigns to remoteMachine and port respectively. The rest of the constructor is concerned with adding components to the frame and configuring it. Finally the constructor calls the **private** method startClient.

The startClient method itself begins with a **try** block. This is necessary because the constructor of the Socket class potentially throws two exceptions. It is called like this:

```
connection = new Socket(remoteMachine, port);
```

Creating a new Socket in this way broadcasts a message requesting a response from the remote machine specified (either by its network name or its IP address), listening on the port in question. If the connection is established, and no exception is therefore thrown, the constructor goes on to display the message "Connection established" in the message area, and then to initialize the input and output streams. It finishes with this instruction:

```
outDataStream.writeUTF(connection.getLocalAddress().getHostAddress());
```

You will recall that we programmed the server so that the first thing it did after the connection was established was to wait for a string from the client. Here you can see how the client sends its address to the server on the output stream. It calls the `getLocalAddress` method of the `Socket` class. This returns an object of the `InetAddress` class. The `InetAddress` class holds a representation of an IP address and enables us to obtain the host name, or the IP address (as a `String`), with the methods `getHostName` and `getHostAddress` respectively.

Now we have to catch the exceptions that can be thrown by the constructor. If the host we are trying to connect to is unknown, then an `UnknownHostException` is thrown:

```
catch (UnknownHostException e)
{
  msg.setText("Unknown host");
}
```

You can see that in this case an appropriate message is placed in the message area. If there is another network error (perhaps no server is running on the specified host), then an `IOException` is thrown:

```
catch (IOException except)
{
  msg.setText("Network Exception");
}
```

The `actionPerformed` method determines what happens when we press the button that gets the server to perform the addition for us:

```
public void actionPerformed(ActionEvent e)
{
  try
  {
    outDataStream.writeInt(Integer.parseInt(firstNumber.getText()));
    outDataStream.writeInt(Integer.parseInt(secondNumber.getText()));

    int result = inDataStream.readInt();
    sum.setText("" + result);
  }
  catch(IOException ie)
  {
    ie.printStackTrace();
  }
}
```

This is straightforward: we send the two numbers to the server and read the response. We enclose everything in a **try...catch** block so that the exceptions thrown by the readInt and writeInt methods are handled.

The socket example here is clearly rather elementary. Java provides a very wide range of possibilities for communication via sockets, for example secure sockets and sockets for multicasting. This is beyond the scope of this book, but it is hoped that we have given you a flavour of what is available so that those of you who want to develop your skills in this area are able to move forward. To help you do that we are going to provide one further, rather more complex, example.

22.7 A client–server chat application

The final application that we are going to develop is a chat application. Figure 22.7 shows the sort of thing we are talking about.

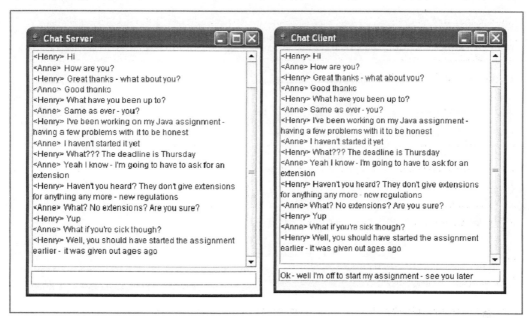

FIGURE 22.7 A client–server chat application

The first thing to point out is that the only difference between the client and the server is the fact that initially the server waits for the client to initiate a connection – once the connection is established the behaviour is the same.

Both the client and the server have to be able to listen for connections, and at the same time be capable of sending messages entered by the user. They will therefore need to be multi-threaded. The main thread will allow the user to enter messages which it will send to the remote program. The other thread will listen for messages from the remote application and display them in the text area.

When the thread is created it will need to receive a reference to the text area where the messages are to be displayed, and a reference to the socket connection. It will need to create an input stream which must be associated with this connection. Its run method must be written so that the thread continuously waits for messages on the input stream and then displays them in the text area. Both the client and the server classes will need to create an object of this thread and start the thread running.

We have designed our application so that rather than having a button that has to be pressed, the message is sent and echoed in the text area when the <Enter> key is pressed. As you will see in a moment, in order to achieve this the class must implement the `KeyListener` interface. This has methods `keyPressed`, `keyReleased` and `keyTyped`; they receive an object of the `KeyEvent` class, one of whose methods is `keyChar`, which returns the character that was pressed. This can be used to see if it was the <Enter> key (`'\n'`) that was pressed.

We'll begin by looking at the code for the server:

THE *CHATSERVER* CLASS

```java
import java.net.*;
import java.io.*;
import javax.swing.*;
import java.awt.event.*;
import java.awt.*;

public class ChatServer extends JFrame implements KeyListener
{
  // declare and initialize visual components
  private JTextArea textWindow = new JTextArea(20, 30);
  private JTextField inputWindow = new JTextField(30);
  private JScrollPane pane = new JScrollPane(textWindow);

  private OutputStream outStream; // for low level output
  private DataOutputStream outDataStream; // for high level output

  private ChatListener listener; /* a reference to the listening thread (discussed in
                                    detail later) */

  private int port; // to hold the port number chosen by the user
  private String name; // to hold the name chosen by the user

  // the constructor
  public ChatServer(int portIn, String nameIn)
  {
    port = portIn;
    name = nameIn;

    // configure the text window where the messages are displayed
    textWindow.setLineWrap(true);
```

```java
    textWindow.setWrapStyleWord(true);
    textWindow.setEditable(false);

    // add a KeyListener to the input window so that messages can be sent by pressing <Enter>
    inputWindow.addKeyListener(this);

    // configure the frame
    setTitle("Chat Server");
    setLayout(new FlowLayout());
    add(pane);
    add(inputWindow);
    setDefaultCloseOperation(JFrame.EXIT_ON_CLOSE);
    setSize(350, 400);
    setVisible(true);

    // start the server
    startServer();
}

private void startServer()
{
    // declare a "general" socket and a server socket
    Socket connection;
    ServerSocket listenSocket;

    try
    {
        // create a server socket
        listenSocket = new ServerSocket (port);

        // listen for a connection from the client
        connection = listenSocket.accept();

        // create an output stream to the connection
        outStream = connection.getOutputStream ();
        outDataStream = new DataOutputStream(outStream );

        // create a thread to listen for massages
        listener = new ChatListener(textWindow, connection);
        listener.start(); // start the thread
    }
```

```java
      catch (IOException e)
      {
        textWindow.setText("An error has occurred");
      }
    }


    // handle a "key typed" event
    public void keyTyped(KeyEvent e)
    {
      String text;
      if(e.getKeyChar()=='\n') // if the <Enter> key was pressed
      {
        // echo the message typed in the input window (including the name) in the text area
        text = inputWindow.getText();
        textWindow.append("<" + name + "> " + text + "\n");

        // clear the input window
        inputWindow.setText("");

        // send the message to the client
        try
        {
          outDataStream.writeUTF("<" + name + "> " + text + "\n");
        }
        catch(IOException ie)
        {
        }
      }
    }


    // implement the remaining methods of KeyListener
    public void keyReleased(KeyEvent e)
    {
    }

    public void keyPressed(KeyEvent e)
    {
    }
}
```

We start by declaring and initializing the visual components that we need:

```java
private JTextArea textWindow = new JTextArea(20, 30);
private JTextField inputWindow = new JTextField(30);
private JScrollPane pane = new JScrollPane(textWindow);
```

The JTextArea will be used for displaying the conversation, as can be seen in figure 22.7. The JTextField is used to enter the message – as can be seen this is placed below the JTextArea. The text area is placed in a JScrollPane so that the window scrolls once it becomes filled with text.

Next comes the declaration of the objects of OutputStream and DataOutputStream needed to establish the output stream:

```java
private OutputStream outStream; // for low level output
private DataOutputStream outDataStream; // for high level output
```

As we said earlier, we will need a separate thread that will listen to messages. For this purpose we will declare a separate class, ChatListener, which we will discuss in a while. The next declaration is a reference to an object of this class which will be instantiated when the server is started:

```java
private ChatListener listener;
```

Finally we declare an integer and a string which will hold, respectively, the port number and user name which will be chosen by the user:

```java
private int port;
private String name;
```

The constructor accepts two parameters:

```java
public ChatServer(int portIn, String nameIn)
```

These are assigned to the relevant attributes:

```java
port = portIn;
name = nameIn;
```

Next we change the properties of the text area where the conversation is viewed. We set it to wrap the text so that a new line is started when the right-hand side of the window is reached, preserving whole words; then we disable the editing function of the area so that text cannot be typed in.

```
textWindow.setLineWrap(true);
textWindow.setWrapStyleWord(true);
textWindow.setEditable(false);
```

Next we add a `KeyListener` to the text field where the messages are typed:

```
inputWindow.addKeyListener(this);
```

This will enable it to listen for a key press and respond appropriately when the <Enter> key is pressed. You will see how this is done in a moment when we explore the `keyTyped` method.

Finally we configure the frame and add the components, and then call the `startServer` method:

```
setTitle("Chat Server");
setLayout(new FlowLayout());
add(pane);
add(inputWindow);
setDefaultCloseOperation(JFrame.EXIT_ON_CLOSE);
setSize(350, 400);
setVisible(true);
startServer();
```

We can look at the `startServer` method now.

```
private void startServer()
{
  // declare a "general" socket and a server socket
  Socket connection;
  ServerSocket listenSocket;

  try
  {
    // create a server socket
    listenSocket = new ServerSocket(port);

    // listen for a connection from the client
    connection = listenSocket.accept();

    // create an output stream to the connection
    outStream = connection.getOutputStream ();
    outDataStream = new DataOutputStream(outStream );
```

```
    // create a thread to listen for messages
    listener = new ChatListener(textWindow, connection);

    listener.start(); // start the thread

  }
  catch (IOException e)
  {
    textWindow.setText("An error has occurred");
  }
}
```

There is nothing here that is particularly new – you have already seen how we create a server socket and listen for a connection; and you have seen how we associate a data stream with that connection. Notice, however, the last two lines of the **try** block. Here we create an instance of ChatListener (the thread that we need in order for the server to be able listen for remote messages), and send to it a reference to the text window and a reference to the connection. We then start the thread.

Let's look at the ChatListener class now:

THE *CHATLISTENER* CLASS

```
import javax.swing.*;
import java.io.*;
import java.net.*;
import java.awt.*;

public class ChatListener extends Thread
{
  private InputStream inputStream; // for low level input
  private DataInputStream dataInputStream; // for high level input
  private JTextArea window; // a reference to the text area where the message will be displayed
  private Socket connection; // a reference to the connection

  // constructor receives references to the text area and the connection
  public ChatListener(JTextArea windowIn, Socket connectionIn)
  {
    window = windowIn;
    connection = connectionIn;

    try
```

```
    {
      // create an input stream from the remote machine
      inputStream = connection.getInputStream();
      dataInputStream = new DataInputStream(inputStream);
    }
    catch(IOException e)
    {
    }
  }

  public void run()
  {
    String msg;
    while(true)
    {
      try
      {
        msg = dataInputStream.readUTF(); // read the incoming message
        window.append(msg); // display the message

        // ensure that the window scrolls correctly (see discussion below)
        window.setCaretPosition(window.getCaretPosition() + msg.length());
      }
      catch(IOException e)
      {
      }
    }
  }
}
```

As you can see, the attribute declarations include references to the objects that will be needed for the input stream, as well as a reference to a `JTextField` and a `Socket`. The constructor receives a `JTextField` object and a `Socket` object, and these are assigned to the relevant attributes. A `ChatListener` object will therefore have access to the text window and the connection associated with the parent object. The constructor then goes on to establish the input stream:

```
public ChatListener(JTextArea windowIn, Socket connectionIn)
{
  window = windowIn;
  connection = connectionIn;
```

```
try
{
  // create an input stream from the remote machine
  inputStream = connection.getInputStream();
  dataInputStream = new. DataInputStream(inputStream);
}
catch(IOException e)
{

}
}
```

Now the run method:

```
public void run()
{
  String msg;
  while(true)
  {
    try
    {
      msg = dataInputStream.readUTF(); // read the incoming message
      window.append(msg); // display the message

      // ensure that the window scrolls correctly (see discussion below)
      window.setCaretPosition(window.getCaretPosition() + msg. length());
    }
    catch(IOException e)
    {

    }
  }
}
```

You can see that once the thread is started, an infinite loop is implemented so that it continuously reads messages from the data stream, and then displays the message in the text area associated with the server or client program that created the thread.

The final instruction in the **try** block is there only in order to accommodate a slightly quirky feature of the JScrollPane class which means that the window doesn't scroll properly when the remote message is received. We have dealt with this by moving the caret (the cursor where text can be entered when the JTextArea is editable) to the end of the text – this forces the bar down to the bottom of the window.

Now we can look at the client application:

```java
import java.net.*;
import java.io.*;
import javax.swing.*;
import java.awt.event.*;
import java.awt.*;

public class ChatClient extends JFrame implements KeyListener
{
  // declare and initialize visual components
  private JTextArea textWindow = new JTextArea(20,30);
  private JTextField inputWindow = new JTextField(30);
  private JScrollPane pane = new JScrollPane(textWindow);

  private OutputStream outStream; // for low level output
  private DataOutputStream outDataStream; // for high level output

  private ChatListener listener;

  private int port; // to hold the port number of the server
  private String remoteMachine; // to hold the name chosen by the user

  private String name;

  // the constructor
  public ChatClient(String remoteMachineIn, int portIn, String nameIn)
  {
    port = portIn;
    name = nameIn;
    remoteMachine = remoteMachineIn;

    // configure the text window where the messages are displayed
    textWindow.setLineWrap(true);
    textWindow.setWrapStyleWord(true);
    textWindow.setEditable(false);

    // add a KeyListener to the input window so that messages can be sent by pressing <Enter>
    inputWindow.addKeyListener(this);
```

```java
    // configure the frame
    setTitle("Chat Client");
    setLayout(new FlowLayout());
    add(pane);
    add(inputWindow);
    setDefaultCloseOperation(JFrame.EXIT_ON_CLOSE);
    setSize(350, 400);
    setVisible(true);

    // start the client
    startClient();
}

private void startClient()
{
  // declare a "general" socket
  Socket connection;

  try
  {
    // create a connection to the server
    connection = new Socket (remoteMachine, port);

    // create output stream to the connection
    outStream = connection.getOutputStream();
    outDataStream = new DataOutputStream (outStream);

    // create a thread to listen for messages
    listener = new ChatListener(textWindow, connection);
    listener.start(); // start the thread
  }

  catch(UnknownHostException e)
  {
    textWindow.setText("Unknown host");
  }

  catch (IOException e)
  {
    textWindow.setText("An error has occured");
  }
}
```

```
    // handle a "key typed" event
    public void keyTyped(KeyEvent e)
    {
      String text;
      if(e.getKeyChar()=='\n')
      {
        // echo the message typed in the input window (including the name) in the text area
        text = inputWindow.getText();
        textWindow.append("<" + name + "> " + text + "\n");

        // clear the input window
        inputWindow.setText("");

        // send the message to the server
        try
        {
          outDataStream.writeUTF("<" + name + "> " + text + "\n");
        }
        catch(IOException ie)
        {
        }

      }
    }


    // implement the remaining methods of KeyListener
    public void keyReleased(KeyEvent e)
    {
    }

    public void keyPressed(KeyEvent e)
    {
    }
}
```

As you can see, there is not a great deal of difference between the client and the server. The only significant differences are:

■ The client needs to know the address of the host that is running the server, so there is an additional attribute, a string, to hold this address. The constructor accepts an additional parameter to receive this value, which it assigns to the attribute.

■ In the startClient method there is no need for a ServerSocket; instead the socket is created by establishing the connection with the remote machine:

```
connection = new Socket(remoteMachine, port);
```

In order to use the application it is necessary to start the server with a program such as program 22.2:

PROGRAM 22.2

```java
import javax.swing.*;


public class RunChatServer
{


  public static void main(String[] args)
  {
    String port, name;
    port = JOptionPane.showInputDialog
            (null, "Enter the port number", null, JOptionPane.PLAIN_MESSAGE);
    name = JOptionPane.showInputDialog
            (null, "Choose a user name", null, JOptionPane. PLAIN_MESSAGE);

    new ChatServer(Integer.valueOf(port), name);


  }
}
```

This particular program allows the user to enter the port number followed by the chosen user name via a JoptionPane, as shown in figure 22.8.

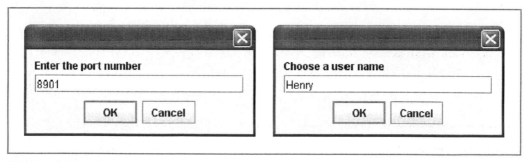

FIGURE 22.8 Starting the chat server

Program 22.3 shows a similar program for starting the client, which additionally prompts the user for the address of the host machine that is running the server. The user of the server must of course inform the client of the address of the host and the port number.

PROGRAM 22.3

```java
import javax.swing.*;

public class RunChatClient
{

  public static void main(String[] args)
  {
    String host;
    String port;
    String name;

    host = JOptionPane.showInputDialog
          (null, "Enter the address of the host machine", null, JOptionPane.PLAIN_MESSAGE);
    port = JOptionPane.showInputDialog
          (null, "Enter the port number that the host listens on", null, JOptionPane.PLAIN_MESSAGE);
    name = JOptionPane.showInputDialog
          (null, "Choose a user name", null, JOptionPane.PLAIN_MESSAGE);

    new ChatClient  (host, Integer.valueOf(port), name);
  }
}
```

Self-test questions

1 Explain the principles of *client–server* architecture.

2 What is the difference between an *applet* and an *application* in Java?

3 Explain the purpose of the following methods of the JApplet class, and describe the order in which they, and the paint method, are called:

- init;
- start;
- stop;
- destroy.

4 The figure below shows the RedCircle application from chapter 13 converted to an applet and running in a browser.

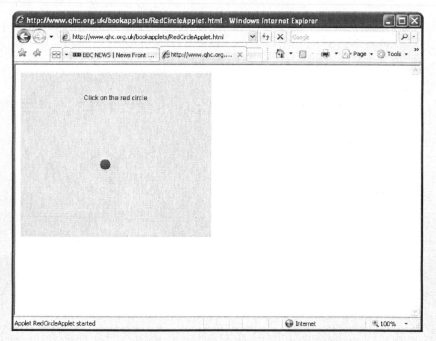

A partial implementation is shown below, highlighting the changes made to the original class:

THE *REDCIRCLEAPPLET* CLASS

```
import java.awt.*;
import javax.swing.*;
import java.awt.event.*;
// class extends JApplet instead of JFrame
```

```java
public class RedCircleApplet extends JApplet implements MouseMotionListener, MouseListener
{
  private final int width = 350; // initialized here
  private final int height = 300; // initialized here


  // other attributes as before


  public void init()
  {
    // add the MouseListener and the MouseMotionListener to the applet
    // set the background colour
  }


  public void start()
  {
    // centre the red circle
  }


  public void paint(Graphics g)
  {
    // as before
  }


  public void mouseMoved(MouseEvent e)
  {
    // as before
  }
  public void mouseDragged(MouseEvent e)
  {
    // as before
  }


  public void mousePressed(MouseEvent e)
  {
    // as before
  }
  public void mouseReleased(MouseEvent e)
```

```
    {
      // as before
    }


    public void mouseClicked(MouseEvent e)
    {
      // as before
    }


    public void mouseEntered(MouseEvent e)
    {
      // as before
    }


    public void mouseExited(MouseEvent e)
    {
      // as before
    }
}
```

   a Explain the division of tasks between the `init` method and the `start` method.

   b Complete the code for the class.

   c Write the HTML instructions for running this applet in a browser.

5 Explain the technology known as Java Database Connectivity (JDBC).

6 Explain the function and purpose of the Java `Socket` and `ServerSocket` classes.

Programming exercises

1 Implement the applets that we developed in this chapter. You should find that your IDE provides an applet viewer in which to test and run the applets. However, you may then wish to run these in a browser and eventually to upload them to a remote website. Make sure that the `.class` file is in the same directory as the HTML file that loads the applet.

2 Implement the `RedCircleApplet` class from question 4 above, and try running it in a browser.

3 Look back at the `MetricConverter` class from chapter 10 and convert this to an applet.

4 If you have a database program such as MySQL, then implement the `ProductQuery` class – either by adapting it for your own database, or by creating the *ElectricalStore* database.

5 If you have a Microsoft database system such as Access, then try to adapt the `ProductQuery` class to interact with this database. You should read section 22.3.1 carefully and make sure you configure your database using the Windows ODBC Data Source Administrator tool.

6 Write a server application that tells jokes to the client, and lets the client respond. A good example would be a classic "Knock Knock" joke. The client would receive the message "Knock Knock" from the server, and would be expected to reply "Who's there?" and so on. You could adapt the program so that a different joke is told each time a client connects (that is, if you actually know that many "Knock Knock" jokes!).

CHAPTER

Mobile Java

23

❖ OBJECTIVES

By the end of this chapter you should be able to:

❖ explain the need for the **Java Micro Edition (ME)**;

❖ describe the two configurations supported by Java ME;

❖ explain the terms **MIDP** and **MIDlet**, and describe the life cycle of a MIDlet;

❖ create a mobile application using a **TextBox**;

❖ create a mobile application using a **Canvas**;

❖ add command buttons to a mobile application;

❖ explain the term **sprite**, and write a simple sprite;

❖ program the arrow keys and number keys to move a sprite on the screen;

❖ use the **Timer** class to produce an animation for a mobile device;

❖ provide the user of a mobile program with a list of choices.

23.1 Introduction

Throughout this book we have worked with the standard Java platform for programming applications that run on a computer with a JVM installed. However, the Java technology also provides an alternative platform that allows us to write programs for small, portable devices such as mobile phones, PDAs, web telephones and set-top boxes.

The standard Java platform is not suitable for small devices such as these, because they have limited resources such as memory and screen resolution. Programs for these devices must be specially tailored in order that they can run on either a **Kilobyte Virtual Machine (KVM)**, which is the run-time environment for small mobile devices like mobile phones, or a **Compact Virtual Machine (CVM)**, which is the run-time environment for larger mobile devices such as set-top boxes.

Consequently, programs designed for these devices must be specifically tailored for this purpose. The Java technology provides an alternative platform for developing and running applications suitable for small devices; this platform is known as the **Java Micro Edition** (Java ME).

23.2 Java Micro Edition

Java Micro Edition, which is still often referred to by its old name Java 2 Platform Micro Edition (or J2ME), is a complete software development kit (SDK) specially designed so that Java can run on devices such as mobile phones, PDAs and set-top boxes. It consists of:

- a set of programming APIs that have been designed specifically to develop programs that run on a KVM/CVM;
- an integrated development environment for developing programs for small devices;
- a mobile phone emulator for running applications prior to transferring them to the device;
- a tool that produces `.jar` files so that applications can be transferred and installed on a mobile device.

Figure 23.1 shows the integrated development environment that is provided with the micro edition.

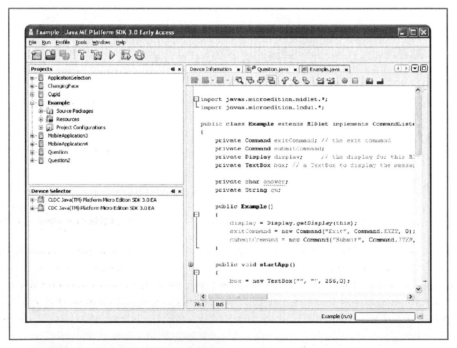

FIGURE 23.1 The IDE provided as part of the Java Micro Edition

In figure 23.2, you can see the program running in the emulator.

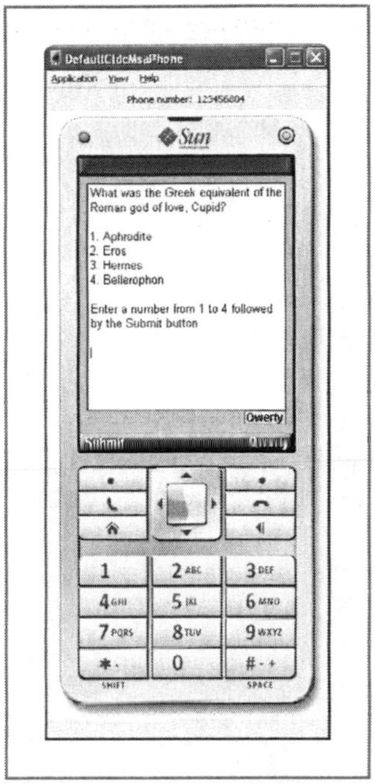

FIGURE 23.2 A program running in the emulator

The Micro Edition software development kit can be downloaded from Sun Microsystems at:

```
java.sun.com/javame
```

This site is hugely informative, and contains all the latest information about Java ME; it also provides a complete description of the Java ME APIs.

23.3 Java ME configurations and profiles

The micro edition currently defines two **configurations**. A configuration is a specification that defines the characteristics of a device in terms of its software requirements, and includes such things as the type and amount of available memory, the type and speed of the processor and the network connections available to the device. A particular configuration will define a strict subset of Java class libraries that are the minimum required for a particular virtual machine. Java Micro Edition currently supports two configurations:

- **Connected Limited Device Configuration (CLDC)**
  CLDC defines software requirements for small devices such as mobile phones and PDAs. CLDC is associated with mobile devices that allow users to download small applications known as **MIDlets**. CLDC applications normally run on a KVM.

- **Connected Device Configuration (CDC)**
  CDC is concerned with larger devices such as smart phones, web telephones and set-top boxes. CDC applications normally run on a CVM.

In this chapter we will concern ourselves with CLDC only.

A particular configuration can be extended by defining one or more sets of classes known as a **profile**. For writing downloadable applications for network-connectable mobile devices there exists the **Mobile Information Device Profile (MIDP)**. MIDP, combined with CLDC, is the Java run-time environment for today's most popular devices, such as mobile phones and PDAs.

23.4 Developing MIDP applications

MIDP applications are called **MIDlet**s. A MIDlet is written by extending the `MIDlet` class. Just as an applet needs no `main` method because control is the concern of the browser, a MIDlet needs no `main` method because program control is the responsibility of the run-time environment running on the mobile device.

The `MIDlet` class contains a number of methods, three of which are declared as **abstract**. In order to understand their purpose it is necessary to understand that a `MIDlet` can be in one of three possible states, *Paused*, *Active* or *Destroyed*.

When a MIDlet is loaded it goes into the *Paused* state. Various initialization routines are then performed, after which the MIDlet goes into the *Active* state and the `startApp` method is called. This method is called every time the MIDlet moves from the *Paused* to the *Active* state, so any initialization routines can be divided between this method and the constructor depending on whether they should be called only when the MIDlet is created or every time it becomes active again. The difference is quite subtle, and often does not make a lot of difference, although it is normal to initialize display objects in the constructor.

Once a MIDlet is active it can be returned to the *Paused* state, either by the device itself, or as a result of the MIDlet calling the `notifyPaused` method. When it goes into the *Paused* state, the `pauseApp` method is called, and should there be any routines required at this point they should be placed in this method. Once in the *Paused* state, it can be resumed by the device, or as a result of the `resumeRequest` method being called.

A MIDlet can terminate as a result of the user ending the MIDlet or the program calling the `notify-Destroyed` method. If this action is performed by the host platform then the `destroyApp` method is called with a parameter of **true**, causing the MIDlet to terminate and release all resources, stop any active timers and terminate any background threads. In this case it is not necessary for the MIDlet to call the `notify-Destroyed` method. If it is terminated from within the program, then it is normal to call the `destroyApp` method with an argument of **false** so that it doesn't immediately terminate, but continues until any necessary data is saved. The `notifyDestroy` method is then called. You will see later that this is normal way to code an *Exit* button.

23.5 Your first mobile program

Let's stick with tradition and make our first program a "Hello world" program.

Before we show you the code, we should point out one thing – this first version does not provide an *Exit* button, so don't load this onto your phone because the only way to exit the program would be to turn your phone off.

Take a look at the code below and then we will take you through it:

THE *HELLOWORLD* MIDLET

```
import javax.microedition.midlet.*;
import javax.microedition.lcdui.*;

public class HelloWorld extends MIDlet
{
  private Display display;     // the display for this MIDlet
  private TextBox box;         // a text box to display the message

  public HelloWorld()
  {
    display = Display.getDisplay(this); // get an instance of the display object
  }

  public void startApp()
  {
    box = new TextBox("First Micro Program", "Hello world", 256, 0); // create the text box
    display.setCurrent(box); // set the current display to the text box
  }

  public void pauseApp()
  {
  }

  public void destroyApp(boolean unconditional)
  {
  }
}
```

You can see that we have imported two packages:

```
import javax.microedition.midlet.*;
import javax.microedition.lcdui.*;
```

The first of these contains the `MIDlet` class, while the second contains the various classes needed to display our output on the screen of a device such as a mobile phone. We are therefore going to need to import these packages for all our programs.

The class header shows that we are extending the `MIDlet` class:

```
public class HelloWorld extends MIDlet
```

After the header we declare two attributes that are used later in the program. The first is used in the constructor:

```
private Display display;

public HelloWorld()
{
  display = Display.getDisplay(this);
}
```

As you can see, we are making use of the `Display` class which is part of the `lcdui` package. The `Display` class defines objects that are capable of being placed on the display. It is used to manage the display and input of the device. One `Display` object is automatically associated with every MIDlet.

One of the methods of `Display` is `getDisplay`, which we use in the constructor as shown above. This gets an instance of the `Display` object associated with the MIDlet and we can then use the methods of this object to manage our display, as you will see in a moment.

Following the constructor there are the three methods that are declared as **abstract** in the MIDlet class, and therefore must be implemented. The only one that we have implemented here is the `startApp` method, which, you will recall, is called each time the application moves from the *Paused* state to the *Active* state:

```
public void startApp()
{
  box = new TextBox("First Micro Program", "Hello world", 256, 0);
  display.setCurrent(box);
}
```

The first line instantiates a `TextBox` object that was declared as an attribute. The `TextBox` class, which resides in the `lcdui` package, is very similar to the `JTextArea` that we have encountered before in the standard edition of Java. The constructor takes four parameters – two strings and two integers. The first two represent the heading and the initial text respectively. The third represents the maximum size in characters. The fourth is an integer value corresponding to a number of available constraints that can be placed on the type of entry (for example numeric only). A value of zero means that there will be no constraints on the input.

The next line calls the `setCurrent` method of the `Display` object that we obtained when the constructor was called. It requires an object of type `Displayable` to be sent in. `Displayable` is a top-level class in the `lcdui` package from which classes such as `TextBox` are derived. As its name suggests, this method determines which object will be visible on the display – in this case the `TextBox` that we created above.

Figure 23.3 shows the program running in the emulator. You can see that pressing the keys on the keypad will enter more text; depending on how we choose the input type with the *Qwerty* key (explained below), the keys can be used in the same way that they are used to write text messages.

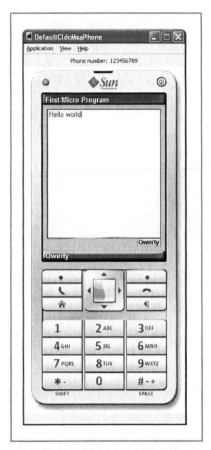

FIGURE 23.3 The *Hello world* program running in an emulator

You can also see that the right-hand "soft" key is labelled *Qwerty*. At the moment, pressing this doesn't do anything because we haven't programmed our application to listen for commands. However, you will see that when we add commands to our application, the system assigns functions to the two soft keys. When the display is set to a `TextBox`, one key is automatically given the function of letting us choose the type of input we require, the default being *Qwerty* (that is, all the symbols available on a *Qwerty* keyboard). For you to see the other options, we need to program the application so that it listens for key presses – and at the same time we should also provide the user with the ability to exit the program properly by assigning this function to the other soft key. This is shown in figure 23.4.

FIGURE 23.4 The *Hello world* program
with an exit button

Take a look at the program code before we take you through it:

THE *HELLOWORLDWITHEXITCOMMAND* MIDLET

```
import javax.microedition.midlet.*;
import javax.microedition.lcdui.*;

public class HelloWorldWithExitCommand extends MIDlet implements CommandListener
{
  private Command exitCommand; // the exit command
  private Display display;    // the display for this MIDlet
  private TextBox box; // a text box to display the message
```

```
    public HelloWorldWithExitCommand()
    {
      display = Display.getDisplay(this); // get an instance of the display object
      exitCommand = new Command("Exit", Command.EXIT, 0); // create the exit command
    }

    public void startApp()
    {
      box = new TextBox("Hello world with exit command", "Hello world", 256,0); /* create the
                                                              text box */
      box.addCommand(exitCommand); // add the exit command to the text box
      box.setCommandListener(this); // enable the text box to listen for commands

      display.setCurrent(box); // set the current display to the text box
    }

    public void pauseApp()
    {
    }

    public void destroyApp(boolean unconditional)
    {
    }


    public void commandAction(Command c, Displayable d)
    {
      if (c == exitCommand) // destroy the MIDlet
      {
        destroyApp(false);
        notifyDestroyed();
      }
    }
}
```

The first thing to draw your attention to is the class header:

```
public class HelloWorldWithExitCommand extends MIDlet implements CommandListener
```

You can see that we are implementing the CommandListener interface. This is the interface required in order that the application can listen for events. It contains the method CommandAction which is used to handle the events. We will discuss the implementation of this method in a moment. Before we do that, you should note that we have declared the following attribute:

```
private Command exitCommand;
```

and we have instantiated this attribute in the constructor:

```
exitCommand = new Command("Exit", Command.EXIT, 0);
```

The Command class makes it possible for us to assign instructions to either keys or menu items, depending on the device. As MIDlets are intended to be portable, the final decision about how the commands are assigned is left to the run-time environment. On a mobile phone there are normally two soft keys to which commands can be assigned; if there are more than two commands, then the system will assign a menu to one of the keys, giving access to the further commands.

Although the final decision is left to the system, we are able to give it "hints" by means of the constructor of the Command class. As you can see from the above, the constructor takes three parameters. The first provides the label for the button or menu item. The next two are concerned with the hint that we give to the run-time environment to help it decide where to place the command. Thus, the second parameter is an integer that tells the system the kind of command that we are dealing with. There are pre-defined values for this in the Command class, and they are explained in table 23.1.

BACK	A command that returns the user to the previous screen
CANCEL	A command that abandons the operation before it has been started
EXIT	A command that requests that the MIDlet terminates the application in an orderly fashion
HELP	A command that requests help
ITEM	A command that is associated with a particular component of the user interface
OK	A command that gives a positive answer to a dialogue implemented on the screen
SCREEN	A command that relates to some aspect of the current screen that does not fit into any of the other categories
STOP	A command that stops an operation in progress

TABLE 23.1 The *Command type* parameters

The final parameter is an integer that tells the system the priority of this command relative to others (with 1 being the highest, 2 the next highest and so on). This will help the run-time environment to decide, in the case of a number of commands, whether to assign the command to a key or a menu, and how to order the items on the menu. An exit command is always assigned to a soft key, and we have therefore set this parameter to zero, thus not given it a priority since it is not necessary in this case.

As we have said above, in the case of a TextBox, another command is always assigned. Figure 23.5 shows the menu provided by this command.

FIGURE 23.5 The effect of pressing the *Qwerty* soft key

Turning our attention to the `startApp` method, you can see that we have added the following lines:

```
box.addCommand(exitCommand);
box.setCommandListener(this);
```

Here we are adding the command to the `TextBox`, and adding the `CommandListener` in a similar way to that in which we have added `Actionlisteners` to Swing components in the past.

Finally we can look at the event handler, `commandAction`, which is declared as **abstract** in the `CommandListener` interface:

```
public void commandAction(Command c, Displayable d)
{
  if (c == exitCommand)
  {
    destroyApp(false);
    notifyDestroyed();
  }
}
```

This method is called whenever a command is selected. It automatically receives two parameters representing the command selected and the current display. If the exit command was selected (in fact the only possibility here) then the application is terminated by calling `destroyApp` and `notifyDestroyed` as explained in section 23.4 above.

23.6 The `Canvas` class

In the examples in the previous section we used a `TextBox` to display information. However, the most common way of displaying information on a mobile device is to make use of the `Canvas` class, which can be used to display graphics on the screen. Like `TextBox`, it is derived from `Displayable`, and has access to the methods for adding commands.

Let's start by adapting the `SmileyFace` class from chapter 10 for a mobile device. You can see the result in figure 23.6.

FIGURE 23.6 The *SmileyFace* application

The `Canvas` class is an abstract class, and the way to utilize it is to create a class that extends `Canvas`. The entire code for the application appears below – you can see that our `Canvas` class, `SmileyFaceCanvas`, has been written as an inner class. This is a useful way to do things because it means we have access to the attributes of the main class if we need them.

THE *SMILEYFACE* MIDLET

```java
import javax.microedition.lcdui.*;
import javax.microedition.midlet.*;

public class SmileyFace extends MIDlet implements CommandListener
{
  private Display display; // the display for this MIDlet
  private Command exitCommand;  // exit command
  private Canvas canvas;   // the canvas

  public SmileyFace()
  {
    display = Display.getDisplay(this); // get an instance of the display object
    exitCommand = new Command("Exit", Command.EXIT, 0); // create the exit command
  }

  public void startApp()
  {
    canvas = new SmileyFaceCanvas(); // create the canvas
    canvas.addCommand(exitCommand); // add the exit command to the canvas
    canvas.setCommandListener(this); // enable the canvas to listen for commands
    display.setCurrent(canvas); // set the current display to the canvas
  }

  public void pauseApp()
  {
  }

  public void destroyApp(boolean unconditional)
  {
  }

  public void commandAction(Command c, Displayable d)
  {
    if (c == exitCommand) // destroy the MIDlet
    {
      destroyApp(false);
      notifyDestroyed();
    }
  }

  // define the canvas as an inner class
  class SmileyFaceCanvas extends Canvas
```

```
  {
    public void paint(Graphics g)
    {
      // get the width and height of the canvas
      int width = getWidth();
      int height = getHeight();

      // create an Image the same size as the Canvas.
      Image image = Image.createImage(width, height);

      // get a graphics object that will render to this image
      Graphics smileyFace = image.getGraphics();

      // define a font
      Font font = Font.getFont(Font.FACE_PROPORTIONAL, Font.STYLE_PLAIN, Font.SIZE_LARGE);

      smileyFace.setFont(font); // set the font
      smileyFace.setColor(255,255,0); // set the colour to yellow
      smileyFace.fillRect(0, 0, width, height); // fill the canvas with the chosen colour
      smileyFace.setColor(255, 0, 0); // set colour to red
      smileyFace.drawArc(width/2 - 40, height/2 - 40, 80, 80, 0, 360); // the face
      smileyFace.setColor(0, 0, 255); // set colour to blue
      smileyFace.drawArc(width/2 - 25, height/2 - 20, 10, 10, 0, 360); // the right eye
      smileyFace.drawArc(width/2 + 15, height/2 - 20, 10, 10, 0, 360); // the left eye
      smileyFace.drawArc(width/2 - 20, height/2, 40, 25, 0, -180); // the mouth

      // draw the caption
      smileyFace.drawString("Smiley Face", width/2, 200, Graphics.TOP | Graphics.HCENTER);

      // draw the image
      g.drawImage(image, 0, 0, Graphics.TOP | Graphics.LEFT);
    }
  }
}
```

We'll begin by examining the inner class, `SmileyFaceCanvas`, which you can see extends `Canvas`. We need to define a `paint` method for the canvas, and we have begun this method by using the `getWidth` and `getHeight` methods of `Canvas` to determine its width and height:

```
int width = getWidth();
int height = getHeight();
```

After this, we declare and create an object of the Image class, which resides in the lcdui package; this class is able to hold information about a graphics image that exists independently of the particular display device:

```
Image image = Image.createImage(width, height);
```

You can see that in order to do this we use the createImage method of Image to create an image of the desired width and height. In order to render our image we need to create a Graphics object and associate this with the image. We do this by using the getGraphics method of Image:

```
Graphics face = image.getGraphics();
```

Now we define a font, using the getFont method of the Font class which again comes as part of the lcdui package:

```
Font font = Font.getFont(Font.FACE_PROPORTIONAL, Font.STYLE_PLAIN, Font.SIZE_LARGE);
```

The method requires three parameters to define the face, style and size of the font. We have used the pre-defined constants of the Font class, which are summarized in table 23.2 below.

Face	Style	Size
FACE_MONOSPACE	STYLE_BOLD	STYLE_LARGE
FACE_PROPORTIONAL	STYLE_ITALIC	STYLE_MEDIUM
FACE_SYSTEM	STYLE_PLAIN	STYLE_SMALL
	STYLE_UNDERLINED	

TABLE 23.2 The pre-defined constants of the *Font* class

After this, we draw our face, using the same principles as we did originally in chapter 10. You should note, however that the methods that we are using are those associated with the Graphics object smileyFace that we associated with our image, not the Graphics object, g, that was received as a parameter; we use that object in a moment to actually draw the image.

Here are the lines which render the face:

```
smileyFace.setFont(font); // set the font
smileyFace.setColor(255,255,0); // set the colour to yellow
smileyFace.fillRect(0, 0, width, height); // fill the canvas with the chosen colour
smileyFace.setColor(255, 0, 0); // set colour to red
smileyFace.drawArc(width/2 - 40, height/2 - 40, 80, 80, 0, 360); // the face
smileyFace.setColor(0, 0, 255); // set colour to blue
```

```
smileyFace.drawArc(width/2 - 25, height/2 - 20, 10, 10, 0, 360); // the right eye
smileyFace.drawArc(width/2 + 15, height/2 - 20, 10, 10, 0, 360); // the left eye
smileyFace.drawArc(width/2 - 20, height/2, 40, 25, 0, -180); // the mouth
```

You can see that we begin by setting the font to our chosen design, and then choosing the colour for the background. The `setColor` method of the micro edition of the `Graphics` class takes three integer parameters representing red, green and blue; yellow is obtained by combining red and green as explained in chapter 17. We have used `fillRect` to apply the background colour.

The micro edition of the `Graphics` class does not have a `drawOval` method, so we have had to use `drawArc` for the circles by drawing an arc through 360 degrees. Notice how we have used the width and height dimensions to centre the face.

Finally we have drawn the caption:

```
smileyFace.drawString("Smiley Face", width/2, 200, Graphics.TOP | Graphics.HCENTER);
```

Here the `drawString` method takes four parameters. The first is the string itself; the next two are the coordinates of what is called the anchor point. The anchor point is determined by the last parameter and is the point on a piece of text or an image around which it is centred. We can define the anchor point by combining various pre-defined constants from the `Graphics` class with the bar symbol (|). They are described in table 23.3.

Constant	Description
HCENTER	Text and images are centred horizontally around the anchor point
VCENTER	Text and images are centred vertically around the anchor point
LEFT	The anchor point is positioned to the left of the text or image
RIGHT	The anchor point is positioned to the right of the text or image
TOP	The anchor point is positioned above the text or image
BOTTOM	The anchor point is positioned below the text or image
BASELINE	The anchor point is positioned at the baseline of the text

TABLE 23.3 Constants of the *Graphics* class for centring text and images

In our example the anchor point (the left coordinate of which is half the width of the visible screen) is centred horizontally and at the top of the text.

The final line of the `SmileyFace` class draws the image:

```
g.drawImage(image, 0, 0, Graphics.TOP | Graphics.LEFT);
```

You can see that in this case we have anchored the image by its top left corner, which is placed at coordinate (0, 0) so that it fills the whole screen.

Now we can turn our attention to the rest of the program, which you can see is not so very different from the previous program in which we used a `TextBox`.

Instead of a `TextBox` we have now declared a `Canvas`:

```
private Canvas canvas;
```

In the `startApp` method we now create the `Canvas` object (instead of a `TextBox` object), add the commands to it and set the current display to this object.

```
public void startApp()
{
  Canvas canvas = new SmileyFaceCanvas();
  canvas.addCommand(exitCommand);
  canvas.setCommandListener(this);
  display.setCurrent(canvas);
}
```

23.7 Adding more commands

In our examples so far the applications have just had one command, the *Exit* command, and this has been added by the run-time environment to one of the soft keys. To illustrate how another command can be added, we will turn our `SmileyFace` into a `ChangingFace`, just as we did in chapter 10. You can see the result in figure 23.7.

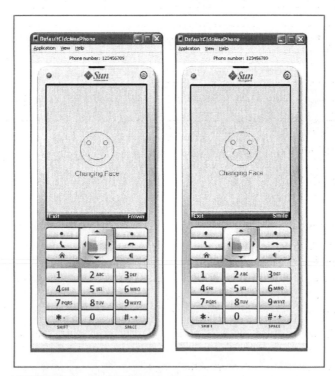

FIGURE 23.7 The *ChangingFace* application

The code for the application is shown below:

THE *CHANGINGFACE* MIDLET

```java
import javax.microedition.lcdui.*;
import javax.microedition.midlet.*;

public class ChangingFace extends MIDlet implements CommandListener
{
  private Display display; // the display for this MIDlet

  private Command exitCommand; // exit command
  private Command frownCommand; // frown command
  private Command smileCommand; // smile command
  private Canvas canvas; // the canvas
  private boolean isHappy = true; // boolean attribute to determine the mood of the face

  public ChangingFace()
  {
    display = Display.getDisplay(this); // get an instance of the display object
    exitCommand = new Command("Exit", Command.EXIT, 0); // create the exit command
    frownCommand = new Command("Frown", Command.SCREEN,1); // create the frown command
    smileCommand= new Command("Smile", Command.SCREEN,1); // create the smile command
  }

  public void startApp()
  {
    canvas = new ChangingFaceCanvas(); // create the canvas
    canvas.addCommand(exitCommand); // add the exit command to the canvas
    canvas.addCommand(frownCommand); /* add frown command to the canvas (but not the
                                  smile command yet) */
    canvas.setCommandListener(this); // enable the canvas to listen for commands
    display.setCurrent(canvas); // set the current display to the canvas
  }

  public void pauseApp()
  {
  }

  public void destroyApp(boolean unconditional)
  {
  }
```

```java
public void commandAction(Command c, Displayable d)
{
  if(c == exitCommand) // destroy the MIDlet
  {
    destroyApp(false);
    notifyDestroyed();
  }

  if(c == frownCommand)
  {
    d.removeCommand(frownCommand); // remove the frown comand
    d.addCommand(smileCommand), // add the smile comand
    isHappy = false; // set attribute to false so the face frowns when canvas is repainted
    canvas.repaint(); // repaint the canvas
  }

  if(c == smileCommand)
  {
    d.removeCommand(smileCommand); // remove the smile comand
    d.addCommand(frownCommand); // add the frown comand
    isHappy = true; // set attribute to true so the face smiles when canvas is repainted
    canvas.repaint(); // repaint the canvas
  }
}


// define an inner class
class ChangingFaceCanvas extends Canvas
{
  public void paint(Graphics g)
  {
    // get the width and height of the canvas
    int width = getWidth();
    int height = getHeight();

    // create an Image the same size as the Canvas.
    Image image = Image.createImage(width, height);

    // get a graphics object that will render to this image
    Graphics changingFace = image.getGraphics();

    // define a font
    Font font = Font.getFont(Font.FACE_PROPORTIONAL, Font.STYLE_PLAIN, Font.SIZE_LARGE);
```

```
        changingFace.setFont(font); // set the font
        changingFace.setColor(255,255,0); // set the colour to yellow
        changingFace.fillRect(0, 0, width, height); // fill the canvas with the chosen colour
        changingFace.setColor(255, 0, 0); // set colour to red
        changingFace.drawArc(width/2 - 40, height/2 - 40, 80, 80, 0, 360); // the face
        changingFace.setColor(0, 0, 255); // set colour to blue
        changingFace.drawArc(width/2 - 25, height/2 - 20, 10, 10, 0, 360); // the right eye
        changingFace.drawArc(width/2 + 15, height/2 - 20, 10, 10, 0, 360); // the left eye
        if(isHappy)
        {
          changingFace.drawArc(width/2- 20, height/2,40,25,0,-180); // smiling mouth
        }
        else
        {
          changingFace.drawArc(width/2- 20, height/2,40,25,0,180); // frowning mouth
        }

        // draw the caption
        changingFace.drawString("Changing Face", width/2, 200, Graphics.TOP | Graphics.HCENTER);

        // draw the image
        g.drawImage(image, 0, 0, Graphics.TOP | Graphics.LEFT);
      }
    }
  }
```

As we did in chapter 10, we have declared a **boolean** attribute, isHappy, to determine whether the face smiles or frowns. The ChangingFace canvas is defined as an inner class, so it will be able to see this attribute. Apart from the name, the new canvas will differ from the previous one only when it comes to drawing the mouth:

```
if(isHappy)
{
  changingFace.drawArc(width/2- 20 ,height/2,40,25,0,-180); // smiling mouth
}
else
{
  changingFace.drawArc(width/2- 20 ,height/2,40,25,0,180); // frowning mouth
}
```

The changes to the rest of the class are just to do with the new command. We have declared two new commands as attributes:

```
private Command frownCommand; // frown command
private Command smileCommand; // smile command
```

You might be wondering why we have declared two separate commands, rather than just one, since the key will be used as a toggle. The reason is that once a Command object has been created, the caption cannot be altered. So we could have had a single Command object with a caption such as *Change*, but it is nicer to have the caption saying "Frown" when the face is smiling, and vice versa.

Along with the *Exit* command, we instantiated both these new commands in the constructor:

```
frownCommand = new Command("Frown", Command.SCREEN,1);
smileCommand = new Command("Smile", Command.SCREEN,1);
```

However, in the `startApp` method we have added only the *Exit* command and the *Frown* command:

```
canvas.addCommand(exitCommand);
canvas.addCommand(frownCommand);
```

The reason for this is that we will start the face smiling, so the command we need at this time is the one that will change it to a frowning face. When it is frowning, the *Frown* command should be removed and the *Smile* command added. Look at the `CommandAction` method:

```
public void commandAction(Command c, Displayable d)
{
  if (c == exitCommand)
  {
    destroyApp(false);
    notifyDestroyed();
  }

  if (c == frownCommand)
  {
    d.removeCommand(frownCommand);
    d.addCommand(smileCommand);
    isHappy = false;
    canvas.repaint();
  }
```

```
    if (c == smileCommand)
    {
      d.removeCommand(smileCommand);
      d.addCommand(frownCommand);
      isHappy = true;
      canvas.repaint();
    }
}
```

You can see that if the *Frown* button was the one that was pressed, then we use the `removeCommand` method of `Displayable` to remove the *Frown* command and the `addCommand` method to add the *Smile* command. We then set the `isHappy` attribute to **false**. If it was the *Smile* button that was pressed, we do the opposite. In both cases we repaint the canvas.

23.8 Sprites

In the world of computer games and computer graphics the term **Sprite** refers to an image or animation that can be integrated into a larger application. In Java we can define a sprite by writing a MIDlet that has some basic methods that can be used for painting and movement, and then use this MIDlet in our applications.

An example `Sprite` class is defined below:[1]

THE *SPRITE* CLASS

```
import javax.microedition.lcdui.*;

public class Sprite
{
  public Image image; // declare an image
  public int x; // the x-coordinate
  public int y; // the y-coordinate


  public Sprite(Image imageIn) // the constructor
  {
    image = imageIn; // set the current image
  }
```

---

[1] When you read the instructions for using the Java ME software development kit, you will see that sometimes it is preferable to define additional classes in the same file as the `main` class. If you do this, then you should not declare the class as **public**, because a single file should contain only one **public** class. Also remember that you would not need the **import** statement if this had already been coded. See the instructions for using the micro edition SDK on the CD.

```
public void paint(Graphics g)
{
  // draw the image at position (x, y) using the centre of the image as the anchor point
  g.drawImage(image, x, y, Graphics.VCENTER | Graphics.HCENTER);
}


public Image getImage()  // get the current image
{
  return image;
}


public int getX() // get the current x-coordinate
{
  return x;
}


public void setX(int xIn) // set the x-coordinate
{
  x = xIn;
}


public int getY() // get the current y-coordinate
{
  return y;
}


public void setY(int yIn) // set the y-coordinate
{
  y = yIn;
}
}
```

You can see that the MIDlet has attributes that will contain information about the position of the sprite and the image it holds. The constructor accepts an object of the Image class and assigns it to the relevant attribute:

```
public Sprite(Image imageIn) // the constructor
{
  image = imageIn; // set the current image
}
```

You can also see that `set-` and `get-` methods are provided for the coordinates, and that the `paint` method draws the image at the current location:

```
public void paint(Graphics g)
{
  // draw the image at position (x, y) using the centre of the image as the anchor point
  g.drawImage(image, x, y, Graphics.VCENTER | Graphics.HCENTER);
}
```

We will now develop an application that makes use of this sprite. The program will allow a red ball to be moved around the screen by using the arrow keys. Although the application itself is not especially exciting, you should be able to see how the techniques used could easily be adapted to produce more complex applications such as games. Figure 23.8 shows the application.

FIGURE 23.8 The *RedBall* application

The code for the application (apart from the `Sprite` class) appears below. Take a look at it and then we will go through it with you.

THE *REDBALL* MIDLET

```java
import javax.microedition.lcdui.*;
import javax.microedition.midlet.*;

public class RedBall extends MIDlet implements CommandListener
{
  private Display display; // the display for this MIDlet
  private RedBallCanvas canvas; // the canvas
  private Command exitCommand; // exit command

  public RedBall()
  {
    display = Display.getDisplay(this); // get an instance of the display object
    exitCommand = new Command("Exit", Command.EXIT, 1); // create the exit command
  }

  public void startApp()
  {
    canvas = new RedBallCanvas(); // create the canvas
    canvas.addCommand(exitCommand); // add the exit command to the canvas
    canvas.setCommandListener(this); // enable the canvas to listen for commands
    display.setCurrent(canvas); // set the current display to the canvas
  }

  public void pauseApp()
  {
  }

  public void destroyApp(boolean unconditional)
  {
  }

  public void commandAction(Command c, Displayable d)
  {
    if (c == exitCommand) // destroy the MIDlet
    {
      destroyApp(false);
      notifyDestroyed();
    }
  }
}
```

```java
// define the canvas as an inner class
class RedBallCanvas extends Canvas
{
 private Sprite ball; // declare a Sprite object
 private int width; // to hold the width of the canvas
 private int height; // to hold the height of the canvas

 RedBallCanvas()
 {
     width = getWidth(); // get the width of the canvas
     height = getHeight(); // get the height of the canvas

     // load the image
     Image ballImage;
     try
     {
       ballImage = Image.createImage("/ball.png"); // create an image
       ball = new Sprite(ballImage); // create a new sprite with this image

       // set the initial position of the sprite to the centre of the screen
       ball.setX(width/2);
       ball.setY(height/2);
     }
     catch (Exception e)
     {
       System.err.println("Problem loading image " + e);
     }
 }

 public void paint(Graphics g)
 {
   g.setColor( 255, 255, 255 ); // set colour to white
   g.fillRect( 0, 0, width, height ); // paint a white background

   ball.paint(g); // paint the sprite
 }

 public void keyPressed(int keyCode)
 {
   int key = getGameAction(keyCode);
```

```java
    if(key == LEFT) // move the sprite left
    {
      int newX = ball.getX()-12;
      if (newX < 12)
      {
        newX = 12;
      }
      ball.setX(newX);
    }
    else if(key == RIGHT) // move the sprite right
    {
      int newX = ball.getX()+12;
      if (newX > width-12)
      {
        newX = width-12;
      }
      ball.setX(newX);
    }
    else if(key == UP) // move the sprite up
    {
      int newY = ball.getY()-12;
      if (newY < 12)
      {
        newY = 12;
      }
      ball.setY(newY);
    }
    else if(key == DOWN) // move the sprite down
    {
      int newY = ball.getY()+12;
      if (newY > height-36)
      {
        newY = height-36;
      }
      ball.setY(newY);
    }
    repaint(); // repaint the canvas
  }
 }
}
```

You can see that the interesting part of this program is in the canvas, which we have called `RedBallCanvas` and have once again defined as an inner class.

We have declared a `Sprite` object as an attribute, and then in the constructor, after obtaining the width and height of the canvas, we have loaded the image from a file called `ball.png`. Images need to be in Portable Network Graphics format (with a `.png` extension) and should be located in the compiler's default directory for resources, which is the `src` directory. We load the image like this:

```
Image ballImage;
try
{
  ballImage = Image.createImage("/ball.png");
  ball = new Sprite(ballImage);
  ball.setX(width/2);
  ball.setY(height/2);
}
catch (Exception e)
{
  System.err.println("Problem loading image " + e);
}
```

You can see that we make use of the `createImage` method of `Image` in order to create the image from a file. Placing a forward slash in front of the file name indicates that the file is in the default directory.

Having created the image, we create a new `Sprite` object, sending in the image as a parameter. You will remember that we provided our `Sprite` class with a `setX` and `setY` method, and we now call these with parameters of `width/2` and `height/2` respectively so that the image is placed in the centre of the canvas.

The `createImage` method throws a number of exceptions and we have therefore placed it in a **try...catch** block.

After the constructor comes the `paint` method:

```
public void paint(Graphics g)
{
  g.setColor( 255, 255, 255 ); // set colour to white
  g.fillRect( 0, 0, width, height ); // paint a white background

  ball.paint(g); // paint the sprite
}
```

As you can see, this paints a white background and then calls the paint method that we defined in our `Sprite` class.

Finally, we implement the `keyPressed` method of `Canvas`. This is one of a number of methods of the `Canvas` class that listens for events – in this case for a key press. It is automatically sent an integer object representing the key code of the key that was pressed. Our implementation looks like this:

```
public void keyPressed(int keyCode)
{
  int key = getGameAction(keyCode);

  if(key == LEFT) // move the sprite left
  {
    int newX = ball.getX()-12;
    if (newX < 12)
    {
      newX = 12;
    }
    ball.setX(newX);
  }
  else if(key == RIGHT) // move the sprite right
  {
    int newX = ball.getX()+12;
    if (newX > width-12)
    {
      newX = width-12;
    }
    ball.setX(newX);
  }
  else if(key == UP) // move the sprite up
  {
    int newY = ball.getY()-12;
    if (newY < 12)
    {
      newY = 12;
    }
    ball.setY(newY);
  }
  else if(key == DOWN) // move the sprite down
  {
    int newY = ball.getY()+12;
    if (newY > height-36)
    {
      newY = height-36;
    }
    ball.setY(newY);
  }
  repaint(); // repaint the canvas
}
```

The integer parameter that is sent to the `keyPressed` method corresponds to the code returned by the key that was pressed. For convenience, in the first line we have used the `getGameAction` method of `Canvas` to translate the key code into an integer that corresponds to one of the pre-defined constants `LEFT`, `RIGHT`, `UP` or `DOWN`. Had we not used the `getGameAction` method, we could have used the raw key code for the arrow keys as shown in table 23.4. This also shows the values returned for the number keys (which is their Unicode value), should we want to use these for any purpose.

Key	Key code returned
UP arrow	−1
DOWN arrow	−2
LEFT arrow	−3
RIGHT arrow	−4
Keypad number 0	48
Keypad number 1	49
Keypad number 2	50
Keypad number 3	51
Keypad number 4	52
Keypad number 5	53
Keypad number 6	54
Keypad number 7	55
Keypad number 8	56
Keypad number 9	57

TABLE 23.4 Key codes

After this, we take appropriate action according to which key was pressed. For example, if the `LEFT` key was pressed, the new x attribute of our `Sprite` is set 12 pixels to the left – this corresponds to the radius of the ball, and you can see that we have organized it so that if we try to move the ball past the left side of the screen (that is, when the centre is less than 12 pixels from the screen) then the x coordinate is reset to 12 so that the ball remains at the edge of the screen. Similar techniques are used for the other directions, although the bottom of the screen is estimated to be 36 pixels away instead of 12 to take account of the space taken up by the button caption. After the coordinate has been reset the screen is repainted.

As you can see, there is nothing new that we need to add to the rest of the program, which simply assigns the canvas to the screen and adds the exit button; all of the work has been done in the `Sprite` class and the `RedBallCanvas` class.

23.9 Using a timer

In chapter 19 we made use of the `Timer` class in the Swing package to allow a thread to schedule a task for future execution. Here we will use the `Timer` class in `java.util`. This class enables us to define a `TimerTask` object that can be scheduled for one-time execution, or for repeated execution at regular intervals.

In our next application we will adapt the `RedBall` program so that the ball bounces continuously, moving from the top to the bottom of the screen.[2]

The code appears below – it uses the `Sprite` class again, so make sure that this is available to the compiler by following the instructions on the CD.

THE *BOUNCINGREDBALL* MIDLET

```java
import javax.microedition.lcdui.*;
import javax.microedition.midlet.*;
import java.util.*; // for the Timer and TimerTask classes

public class BouncingRedBall extends MIDlet implements CommandListener
{
  private Display display; // the display for this MIDlet
  private BouncingRedBallCanvas canvas; // the canvas
  private Command exitCommand;  // exit command

  private final long interval = 50; // the time interval

  public BouncingRedBall()
  {
    display = Display.getDisplay(this); // get an instance of the display object
    exitCommand = new Command("Exit", Command.EXIT, 1); // create the exit command
  }

  public void startApp()
  {
    canvas = new BouncingRedBallCanvas(); // create the canvas
    canvas.addCommand(exitCommand); // add the exit command to the canvas
    canvas.setCommandListener(this); // enable the canvas to listen for commands
    display.setCurrent(canvas); // set the current display to the canvas

    Timer timer = new Timer(); // create a timer object

    // schedule the timer to perfom the task specified in the TimerTask (Bounce) defined below
    timer.scheduleAtFixedRate(new Bounce(), 0, interval);
  }

  public void pauseApp()
  {
  }
```

---

[2] That is to say, with a coefficient of restitution of 1, for the physicists among you!

```
public void destroyApp(boolean unconditional)
{
}

public void commandAction(Command c, Displayable d)
{
  if (c == exitCommand) // destroy the MIDlet
  {
    destroyApp(false);
    notifyDestroyed();
  }
}

// define a canvas as an inner class
class BouncingRedBallCanvas extends Canvas
{
  private Sprite ball;
  private int width;
  private int height;
  private boolean onTheWayUp = true;

  BouncingRedBallCanvas()
  {
    width = getWidth();
    height = getHeight();

    // load the image
    Image ballImage;
    try
    {
      ballImage = Image.createImage("/ball.png");
      ball = new Sprite(ballImage);
      ball.setX(width/2);
      ball.setY(height/2);
    }
    catch (Exception e)
    {
      System.err.println("Problem loading image " + e);
    }
  }

  public void paint(Graphics g)
  {
    g.setColor( 255, 255, 255 ); // set colour to white
```

```
      g.fillRect( 0, 0, width, height ); // paint a white background

      ball.paint(g); // paint the sprite
    }


    public void moveBall()
    {
      int newY, currentY;
      currentY = ball.getY();
      if (onTheWayUp)
      {
        newY = currentY - 12; // move the ball up by 12 pixels
        if(currentY < 12) // the ball has reached the top of the screen
        {
          onTheWayUp = false;
        }
      }
      else
      {
        newY = currentY + 12; // move the ball down by 12 pixels
        if(currentY > height - 36) // the ball has reached the bottom of the screen
        {
          onTheWayUp = true;
        }
      }
      ball.setY(newY);
      canvas.repaint(); // repaint the canvas
    }
  }


  // define a timer task as an inner class
  class Bounce extends TimerTask
  {
    public void run()
    {
      canvas.moveBall();  // call the moveBall method
    }
  }
}
```

As you can see, we have once again defined a canvas (BouncingRedBallCanvas) as an inner class. It differs from the previous class in two respects. Firstly, we have a new attribute, initialized to **true**:

```
private boolean onTheWayUp = true;
```

Secondly, we have removed the keyPressed method, but have added the following method:

```
public void moveBall()
{
  int newY, currentY;
  currentY = ball.getY();
  if (onTheWayUp)
  {
    newY = currentY - 12; // move the ball up by 12 pixels
    if(currentY < 12) // the ball has reached the top of the screen
    {
      onTheWayUp = false;
    }
  }
  else
  {
    newY = currentY + 12; // move the ball down by 12 pixels
    if(currentY > height - 36) // the ball has reached the bottom of the screen
    {
      onTheWayUp = true;
    }
  }
  ball.setY(newY);
  canvas.repaint(); // repaint the canvas
}
```

This method is fairly self-explanatory. If the ball is on its way up then its y-coordinate is reduced by 12 pixels. If it has reached the top then onTheWayUp is set to **false**, so that the next time the method is invoked it moves down by 12 pixels until it reaches the bottom, at which point onTheWayUp becomes **true** again. The canvas is repainted after each change.

We have defined an additional inner class, Bounce, which extends the TimerTask class available in java.util. The TimerTask class has a run method in which we can define a task for future scheduling:

```
class Bounce extends TimerTask
{
  public void run()
  {
    canvas.moveBall();  // call the moveBall method
  }
}
```

As you can see, all that the `run` method does is to call the `moveBall` method of our canvas.

In the `BouncingRedBall` MIDlet itself we have declared a constant that will be used as the timer interval; we have set it to 50, so that the action will repeat every 50 milliseconds.

In the `startApp` method we declare a `Timer` object and then use its `scheduleAtFixedRate` method, which, as its name suggests, allows a task to be scheduled to repeat at a specified interval:

```
Timer timer = new Timer();
timer.scheduleAtFixedRate(new Bounce(), 0, interval);
```

The `scheduleAtFixedRate` method requires three parameters representing, respectively, a timer task, a delay period and the interval at which the task repeats – 50 milliseconds in this case.

23.10 Selecting items from a list

The final application that we are going to show you is one that provides a list of items from which you can choose. We will keep it simple, and just provide a choice between running our simple *Hello World* program (with buttons) and the *Smiley Face* program. You will see that it demonstrates rather nicely how easy it is to change the screen simply by reloading the display.

Figure 23.9 shows the list; the items are selected by moving up or down with the arrow keys and then pressing the selection button, which, on the emulator, is the central button; different devices will of course differ in their design.

FIGURE 23.9 A list of items to be selected

The code appears below:

THE *APPLICATIONSELECTION* MIDLET

```
import javax.microedition.lcdui.*;
import javax.microedition.midlet.*;

public class ApplicationSelection extends MIDlet implements CommandListener
{
  private Display display; // the display for this MIDlet
  private Command exitCommand; // exit command
  private Command backCommand; // back command
  private TextBox box; // the text box
  private Canvas canvas; // the canvas
  private List itemList; // the list of choices
  private String[] items = {"Hello World", "Smiley Face"}; // the items on the list

  public ApplicationSelection()
  {
    display = Display.getDisplay(this); // get an instance of the display object
    exitCommand = new Command("Exit", Command.EXIT, 0); // create the exit command
    backCommand = new Command("Back", Command.EXIT, 1); // create the back command
  }

  public void startApp()
  {
    box = new TextBox("Hello world", "Hello world", 256,0); // create the text box

    // add the commands to the text box and enable it to listen for commands
    box.addCommand(backCommand);
    box.addCommand(exitCommand);
    box.setCommandListener(this);

    canvas = new SmileyFaceCanvas(); // create the canvas

    // add the commands to the canvas and enable it to listen for commands
    canvas.addCommand(backCommand);
    canvas.addCommand(exitCommand);
    canvas.setCommandListener(this);

    itemList = new List("Select Item", List.IMPLICIT); // create the list of items
    for (int i = 0; i < items.length; i++) // add the items to the list
```

```
      {
        itemList.append(items[i], null);
      }

      itemList.addCommand(exitCommand); // add the exit command to the list
      itemList.setCommandListener(this); // enable the list to listen for commands

      display.setCurrent(itemList); // set the current display to the list
    }

    public void pauseApp()
    {
    }

    public void destroyApp(boolean unconditional)
    {
    }

    public void commandAction(Command c, Displayable d)
    {
      if (c == exitCommand) // destroy the MIDlet
      {
        destroyApp(false);
        notifyDestroyed();
      }

      if(c == backCommand)
      {
        display.setCurrent(itemList); // return to the list of items
      }
      if (d == itemList)
      {
        int index = itemList.getSelectedIndex(); // determine which item was selected
        if(index == 0) // the first item was selected
        {
          display.setCurrent(box); // set the current display to the text box
        }
        if(index == 1) // the second item was selected
```

```
      {
      display.setCurrent(canvas); // set the current display to the canvas
      }
    }
  }


// define the SmileyFace canvas as an inner class
class SmileyFaceCanvas extends Canvas
{
  public void paint(Graphics g)
  {
    // get the width and height of the canvas
    int width = getWidth();
    int height = getHeight();


    // create an Image the same size as the canvas
    Image image = Image.createImage(width, height);


    // get a graphics object that will render to this image
    Graphics smileyFace = image.getGraphics();


    // define a font
    Font font = Font.getFont(Font.FACE_PROPORTIONAL, Font.STYLE_PLAIN, Font.SIZE_LARGE);


    smileyFace.setFont(font); // set the font
    smileyFace.setColor(255,255,0); // set the colour to yellow
    smileyFace.fillRect(0, 0, width, height); // fill the canvas with the chosen colour
    smileyFace.setColor(255, 0, 0); // set colour to red
    smileyFace.drawArc(width/2 - 40, height/2 - 40, 80, 80, 0, 360); // the face
    smileyFace.setColor(0, 0, 255); // set colour to blue
    smileyFace.drawArc(width/2 - 25, height/2 - 20, 10, 10, 0, 360); // the right eye
    smileyFace.drawArc(width/2 + 15, height/2 - 20, 10, 10, 0, 360); // the left eye
    smileyFace.drawArc(width/2 - 20, height/2, 40, 25, 0, -180); // the mouth
    smileyFace.drawString("Smiley Face", width/2, 200,
    Graphics.TOP | Graphics.HCENTER); // the caption
    g.drawImage(image, 0, 0, Graphics.TOP | Graphics.LEFT); // draw the image
  }
 }
}
```

You can see that in the list of attributes we have made the following declarations:

```
private List itemList;
private String[] items = {"Hello World", "Smiley Face"};
```

The `List` class provides us with a screen containing a number of choices – so we have declared an object, `itemList`, of this class. To facilitate the process of adding the choices we have provided an array of strings, `items`, containing the names of the items that are going to appear on the list.

Looking at the `startApp` method, you can see that we have declared our `TextBox`, then added two commands and then added the command listener to the box. Note that we have declared and instantiated (in the constructor) an additional button, `backCommand`, which we will use to return to the previous screen.

```
box = new TextBox("Hello world", "Hello world", 256,0);
box.addCommand(backCommand);
box.addCommand(exitCommand);
box.setCommandListener(this);
```

Next, we have done the same thing with the canvas (having declared the `SmileyFaceCanvas` class as an inner class as before):

```
canvas = new SmileyFaceCanvas();
canvas.addCommand(backCommand);
canvas.addCommand(exitCommand);
canvas.setCommandListener(this);
```

After that, we deal with the list:

```
itemList = new List("Select Item", List.IMPLICIT);
for (int i = 0; i < items.length; i++)
{
  itemList.append(items[i], null);
}

itemList.addCommand(exitCommand);
itemList.setCommandListener(this);
```

First we create the new list. The constructor of `List` requires two parameters. The first is the title and the second is the type of list required. The most common type is `IMPLICIT` whereby an item is selected and that selection is immediately applied. The other options, `EXCLUSIVE` and `MULTIPLE`, allow items to be tagged and then applied by some further action.

You can see that next we use the append method of List to add each item to the list. The first parameter of this method is a String, representing the name of the item; the second is an Image; this provides for the facility of adding an image to the title. If we do not require an image then this parameter is set to **null**.

Finally we add the exitCommand to the list, and then add the command listener.

Now we come to the CommandAction method:

```java
public void commandAction(Command c, Displayable d)
{
  if (c == exitCommand)
  {
    destroyApp(false);
    notifyDestroyed();
  }

  if(c == backCommand)
  {
    display.setCurrent(itemList);
  }

  if (d == itemList)
  {
    int index = itemList.getSelectedIndex();
    if(index == 0)
    {
      display.setCurrent(box);
    }
    if(index == 1)
    {
      display.setCurrent(canvas);
    }
  }
}
```

You can see that we use the getSelectedIndex method of List to determine which item was selected; they are numbered in order, starting at zero. Once the chosen item is determined, it is a simple matter to set the display to the TextBox or Canvas appropriately – this illustrates how easy it is to simply switch displays as we require.

You should also notice how we have coded the action associated with the backCommand so that choosing this will take us back to our list.

It is interesting to note that when the `TextBox` is selected there are actually three commands available – as well as the *Exit* command and the *Back* command there is also the *Qwerty* command that accompanies the `TextBox`. However, as we mentioned before, a regular mobile phone normally has only two soft keys. Figure 23.10 shows how this is dealt with by providing a menu. The second image shows the result of selecting the menu.

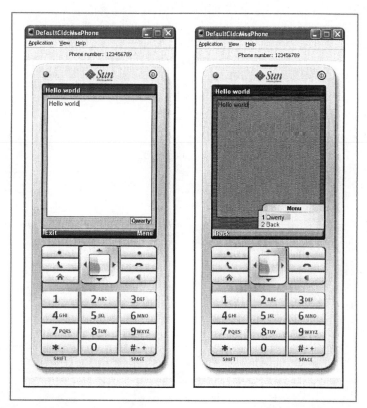

FIGURE 23.10 A screen with more than two commands available

Self-test questions

1 Explain why there needs to be a special edition of Java for small devices, and describe the two configurations supported by Java ME.

2 Explain the terms *MIDP* and *MIDlet*.

3 Describe the life cycle of a MIDlet, and explain the purpose of the three **abstract** MIDLet methods.

4 Take a look at the `Sprite` class that we developed in section 23.8. Adapt this class so that it provides for diagonal movement.

5 Study the `BouncingRedBall` class that we defined in section 23.9. In the `BouncingRedBall` class we defined a `moveBall` method. Adapt that method so that it:

  a moves the ball from left to right instead of up and down;

  b behaves in a more interesting way – for example, bounces up and down more realistically, so that the height of the upward bounce is a little less each time (this will take some thought!).

Programming exercises

1 Following the instructions on the CD, install the JAVA ME software development kit and implement the programs from this chapter.

2 Try to implement a program such as the one shown below, which allows an image to be moved to different positions on the screen by pressing one of the soft keys.

3 Making use of the `Timer` class, animate the `ChangingFace` application so that the face continuously changes expression.

4 Modify the `RedBall` application so that it makes use of the modified `Sprite` class that you developed in self-test question 4.

5 Implement the changes you made to the `BouncingRedBall` application in self-test question 5.

6 The image below shows a simple quiz program that makes use of a `TextBox`.

By exploring the methods of `TextBox`, try to develop a game such as this.

Some methods of `TextBox` that you might find especially useful are:

`String getString()`
Returns the contents of the text box.

`void setString(String text)`
Sets the contents of the text box, replacing any existing text.

`void insert(String text, int pos)`
Inserts a string at a particular position (where `pos` is number of characters from the beginning).

`int getCaretPosition()`
Returns the current input position.

Java in context

❖ OBJECTIVES

By the end of this chapter you should be able to:

❖ provide a brief history of the development of the Java language;

❖ identify the potential problems with **pointers, multiple inheritance** and **aliases**;

❖ develop **clone** methods to avoid the problem of aliases;

❖ identify **immutable objects**;

❖ explain the benefits of Java's **garbage collector**.

24.1 Introduction

Originally named *Oak*, Java was developed in 1991 by Sun Microsystems. At the time, the intention was to use it to program consumer devices such as video recorders, mobile phones and televisions. The expectation was that these devices would soon need to communicate with each other. As it turned out, however, this concept didn't take off until later. Instead, it was the growth of the Internet through the World Wide Web that was to be the real launch pad for the language.

The original motivation behind its development explains many of its characteristics. In particular, the **size** and **reliability** of the language became very important.

24.2 Language size

Generally, the processor power of a system controlling a consumer device is very small compared with that of a PC; so the language used to develop such systems should be fairly compact. Consequently, the Java language is relatively small and compact when compared with other traditional languages. At the time Java was being developed, C++ was a very popular programming language. For this reason the developers of Java decided to stick to conventional C++ syntax as much as possible. Consequently, Java syntax is very similar to C++ syntax.

Just because the Java language is relatively small, however, does not mean that it is not as powerful as some other languages. Instead, the Java developers were careful to remove certain language features that they felt led to common program errors. These include the ability for a programmer to create **pointers** and the ability for a programmer to develop **multiple inheritance** hierarchies.

24.2.1 Pointers

A pointer, in programming terms, is a variable containing an address in memory. Of course, Java programmers can do something very similar to this – they can create *references*. Figure 24.1 repeats an example we showed you in chapter 7.

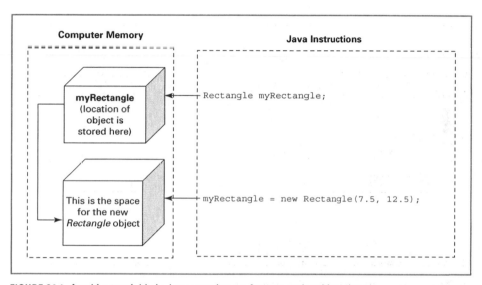

FIGURE 24.1 An object variable in Java contains a reference to the object data

In figure 24.1, the variable `myRectangle` contains a reference (address in memory) of a `Rectangle` object. The difference between a *reference* and a *pointer* is that the *programmer* does not have control over which address in memory is used – the *system* takes care of this. Of course, internally, the system creates a pointer and controls its location. In a language like C++ the programmer can directly manipulate this pointer (move it along and back in memory). This was seen as giving the programmer greater control. However, if this ability is abused, critical areas of memory can easily be corrupted. For this reason the Java language developers did not allow users to manipulate pointers directly.

24.2.2 Multiple inheritance

Inheritance is an important feature of object-oriented languages. Many object-oriented languages, such as C++ and Eiffel, allow an extended form of inheritance known as multiple inheritance. When programming in Java, a class can only ever inherit from at most one superclass. Multiple inheritance allows a class to inherit from more than one superclass (see figures 24.2 and 24.3).

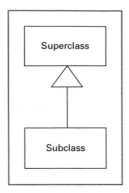

FIGURE 24.2 Single
inheritance

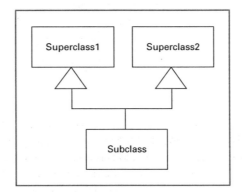

FIGURE 24.3 Multiple inheritance

The Java developers decided not to allow multiple inheritance for two reasons:

■ it is very rarely required;

■ it can lead to very complicated inheritance trees, which in turn lead to programming errors.

As an example of multiple inheritance, consider a football club with various employees. Figure 24.4 illustrates an inheritance structure that might be arrived at.

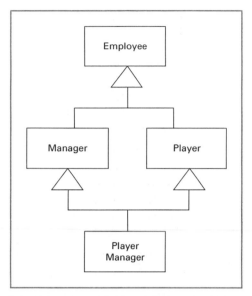

FIGURE 24.4 A combination of single and multiple inheritance

Here, a `PlayerManager` inherits from both `Player` and `Manager`, both of which in turn inherit from `Employee`! As you can see, this is starting to get a little messy. Things become even more complicated when we consider method overriding. If both `Player` and `Manager` have a method called `payBonus`, which method should be called for `PlayerManager` – or should it be overridden?

Although Java disallows multiple inheritance, it does offer a type of multiple inheritance – interfaces. As we have seen in previous chapters, a class can inherit from only one base class in Java but can implement many interfaces.

24.3 Language reliability

The Java language developers placed a lot of emphasis on ensuring that programs developed in Java would be reliable. One way in which they did this was to provide the extensive exception-handling techniques that we covered in chapter 14. Another way reliability was improved was to remove the ability for programmers to directly manipulate pointers, as we discussed earlier in this chapter. Errors arising from pointer manipulation in other languages are very common. A related problem, however, is still prevalent in Java but can be avoided to a large extent. This is the problem of **aliasing**.

24.3.1 Aliasing

Aliasing occurs when the *same* memory location is accessed by variables with *different* names. As an example, we could create an object, `r1`, of the `Rectangle` class as follows:

```
Rectangle r1 = new Rectangle (10, 20);
```

We could then declare a new variable, r2, which could reference the same object:

```
Rectangle r2 = r1;
```

Here r2 is simply a different name for r1 – in other words, an **alias**. The effect of creating an alias is illustrated in figure 24.5.

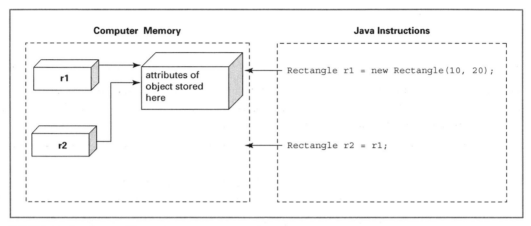

FIGURE 24.5 Copying an object reference creates an alias.

In practice, a programmer would normally create an alias only with good reason. For example, in chapter 8, when we deleted bank accounts from a list, we were able to make good use of aliasing by assigning an object reference to a different object with a statement like:

```
list[i] = list[i+1];
```

After this instruction, list[i] is pointing to the same object as list[i+1]. In this case that was the intention. However, a potential problem with a language that allows aliasing is that it could lead to errors arising inadvertently. Consider, for example, a Customer class that keeps track of just two bank accounts. Here is the outline of that class:

```
public class Customer
{
  // two private attributes to hold bank account details
  private BankAccount account1;
  private BankAccount account2;

  // more code here

  // two access methods
  public BankAccount getFirstAccount()
```

```
    {
      return account1;
    }


    public BankAccount getSecondAccount()
    {
      return account2;
    }
}
```

Consider the methods getFirstAccount and getSecondAccount. In each case we have sent back a reference to a **private** attribute, which is itself an object. We did this to allow users of this class to interrogate details about the two bank accounts, with statements such as:

```
BankAccount tempAccount = someCustomer.getFirstAccount();
System.out.println("balance of first account = "+tempAccount.getBalance());
```

Let us assume that this produced the following output:

```
balance of first account = 250.0
```

This is fine, but the tempAccount object that we have just created is now an alias for the **private** BankAccount object in the Customer class. It can be used to manipulate this **private** BankAccount object without going through any Customer methods. To demonstrate this, let us withdraw money from the alias:

```
tempAccount.withdraw(100); // withdraw 100 from alias
```

Now let us go back and examine the bank account in the Customer class:

```
double balance = someCustomer.getFirstAccount().getBalance();
System.out.println("balance of first account = " + balance);
```

In this case we have retrieved the first bank account and its balance in one instruction. We then display this balance, giving the following output:

```
balance of first account = 150.0
```

The balance of this internal account has been reduced by 100 without the Customer class having any control over this! From this example you can see how dangerous aliases can be.

There are a few examples in this book where we have returned references to **private** objects, but we have been careful not to take advantage of this by manipulating **private** attributes in this way. However, the important point is that they *could* be manipulated in that way. In order to make classes extra secure (for example, in the development of safety-critical systems), aliasing should be avoided.

The problem of aliases arises when a copy of an object's *data* is required but instead a copy of the object's *reference* is returned. These two types of copies are sometime referred to as *deep copy* (for a copy of an object's data) and *shallow copy* (for a copy of an object's reference). By sending back a shallow copy, the original object can be manipulated, whereas a deep copy would not cause any harm to the original object.

In order to provide such a deep copy, a class should define a method that returns an exact copy of the object data. Such a method exists in the `Object` class, but this should be overridden in any user-defined class. The method is called `clone`. We want to send back copies of `BankAccount` objects, so we need to include a `clone` method in the original `BankAccount` class.

24.3.2 Overriding the *clone* method

You have seen examples of overriding `Object` methods before. In chapter 15, for instance, we overrode the `toString` and `hashCode` methods in the `Object` class. There is one important difference, however, between the `clone` method and other `Object` methods such as `hashCode` and `toString`. The `clone` method is declared as **protected** in the `Object` class, whereas methods such as `hashCode` and `toString` are declared as **public**.

Methods which are **protected** can only be called from within the same package (`Object` is in the `java.lang` package), or *within* subclasses. Methods which are **protected** are *not* part of the external interface of a class.

So if we wish to provide a `clone` method for any class, we are *forced* to override the `clone` method from `Object`. When we override this method we must make it **public** and not **protected**. When over-riding methods you are able to give them wider access modifiers but not less – so a **protected** method can be overridden to be **public**, but not vice versa. The return type of the `clone` method is always `Object`:

```
// clone methods you write must have this interface
public Object clone() // must be a public method
{
  // code goes here
}
```

There were sound security reasons for the Java developers forcing you to override the `clone` method if you wish objects of your classes to be cloned, rather than allow objects of *all* classes to use the `clone` method in the `Object` class because you might be developing a class in which you did not want objects of that class to be cloned.

However, we *do* want to provide the original `BankAccount` class with a `clone` method. Such a method would allow the `Customer` class to send back clones of `BankAccount` objects, rather than aliases as it is currently doing. Here is the outline of the BankAccount class with one possible implementation of such a method:

```java
public class BankAccount
{
  // private attributes as before
  private String accountNumber;
  private String accountName;
  private double balance;
  // previous methods go here
  // now provide a clone method
  public Object clone()
  {
    // call contsructor to create a new object identical to this object
    BankAccount copyOfThisAccount = new BankAccount (accountNumber, accountName);
    /* after this the balance of the two bank accounts might not be the same,
       so copy the balance as well */
    copyOfThisAccount.balance = balance;
    // finally, send back this copy
    return copyOfThisAccount;
  }
}
```

Notice that in order to set the balance of the copied bank account, we have directly accessed the **private** balance attribute of the copy:

```java
copyOfThisAccount.balance = balance;
```

This is perfectly legal as we are in a BankAccount class, so all BankAccount objects created within this class can access their **private** attributes. Now, whenever we need to copy a BankAccount object we just call the clone method. For example:

```java
// create the original object
BankAccount ourAccount = new BankAccount ("98765432", "Charatan and Kans");
// now make a copy using the clone method, notice a type cast is required
BankAccount tempAccount = (BankAccount) ourAccount.clone();
// other instructions here
```

The clone method sends back an exact copy of the original account, not a copy of the reference (see figure 24.6).

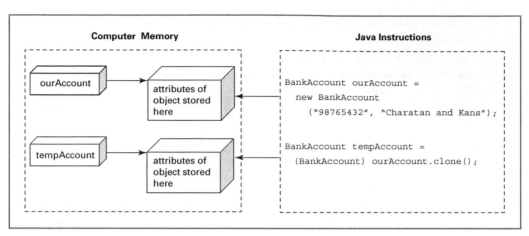

FIGURE 24.6 The *clone* method creates a copy of an object

Now, whatever we do to the copied object will leave the original object unaffected, and vice versa.

In a similar way, we can ensure that classes that contain BankAccount objects do not inadvertently send back references (and hence aliases) to these objects:

```
public class Customer
{
  // as before here

  // next two methods now send back clones, not aliases
  public BankAccount getFirstAccount()
  {
    return (BankAccount)account1.clone();
  }
  public BankAccount getSecondAccount()
  {
    return (BankAccount)account2.clone();
  }
}
```

Now, in our earlier example, the problem is removed because of the use of the clone method in the Customer class, as illustrated in the fragment below:

```
Customer someCustomer = new Customer();

// some code to update someCustomer here
```

```
/* now a temporary variable is created to read details of first account but this
   is not an alias it is a clone */
BankAccount tempAccount = someCustomer.getFirstaccount();
System.out.println("balance of first account = " + tempAccount.getBalance());
// assume the balance is displayed as 500
temp.withdraw(100); /* because temp is a clone the private BankAccount attribute
                       account1 is unaffected */
System.out.println("balance of first account = " + someCustomer.getFirstAccount().getBalance());
// the balance of the customer's first account will still be 500
```

24.3.3 Immutable objects

We said that methods that return references to objects actually create aliases and that this can be dangerous. However, these aliases are not *always* dangerous. Consider the following features of the original BankAccount class:

```
public class BankAccount
{
  private String accountNumber;

  // other attributes and methods here

  public String getAccountNumber()
  {
    return accountNumber;
  }
}
```

In this case the getAccountNumber method returns a reference to a **private** String object (account-Number). This is an alias for the **private** String attribute. However, this alias causes no harm as there are no String methods that allow a String object to be altered. So, this alias cannot be used to alter the **private** String object.

Objects which have no methods to alter their state are known as **immutable objects**. String objects are immutable objects. Objects of classes that you develop may also be immutable depending on the methods you have provided. If such objects are immutable, you do not have to worry about creating aliases of these objects and do not need to provide them with clone methods. For example, let's go back to the Library application (consisting of a collection of Book objects) that we developed in chapter 15. Rather than show you the code, figure 24.7 shows you the UML design for the Library and Book classes.

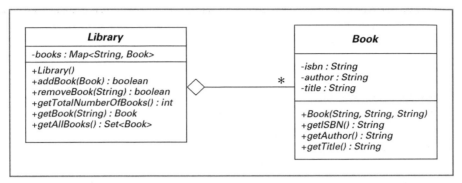

FIGURE 24.7 Design for the *Library* application

As you can see, the `Library` class contains a collection of `Book` objects. These `Book` objects are part of the **private** books attribute in the `Library` class. However, the `getBook` method returns a reference to one of these `Book` objects and so sends back an alias. This is not a problem, however, because if you look at the design of the `Book` class the only methods provided are `get` methods. In other words, there are no `Book` methods that can alter the attributes of the `Book` object once the `Book` object has been created. A `Book` object is an immutable object.

24.3.4 Using the *clone* method of the *Object* class

Although the `clone` method in the `Object` class is not made available as part of your class's external interface, it can be used *within* classes that you develop. In particular, you might wish to use it within a `clone` method that you write yourself, as it does carry out the task of copying an object for you – albeit with some restrictions.

The `clone` method from the `Object` class copies the *memory contents* allocated to the object attributes. This is sometimes referred to as a *bit-wise copy*. This means that it makes exact copies of attributes that are of primitive type, and it makes copies of references for attributes that are objects. Of course, a copy of a reference gives you an alias – but if the object in question is immutable, this is not a problem. This means that:

- if a class's attributes are all of primitive type, then make your `clone` method just call the clone method of `Object`;
- if a class's attributes include objects, and these objects are *all* immutable, then again make your `clone` method just call the `clone` method of `Object`;
- if a class's attributes include any objects which are *not* immutable, then you *cannot* rely upon the `clone` method of `Object` to make a sensible copy and so you must write your own instructions for providing a clone.

Bearing these points in mind, let us revisit the `clone` method for our `BankAccount` class.

```
public class BankAccount
{
  // attributes
  private String accountNumber;
  private String accountName;
  private double balance;

  public Object clone()
  {
    // code goes here
  }


    // other code here
}
```

To make a copy of a BankAccount object we need a new bank account with an identical account number, name and balance. The balance attribute is of type **double**, so a bit-wise copy would be fine here. The account name and number are both String objects; since String are immutable, a bit-wise copy is fine here also. This means the *entire* object can be safely copied using the clone method of Object. Here is a first attempt at using this method within our own clone method – it will not compile!

```
// this attempt to clone a BankAccount will not compile
public Object clone()
{
  // call 'clone' method of superclass Object
  return super.clone();
}
```

This will not compile at the moment because the clone method of Object checks whether developers of this class really want to allow cloning to go ahead.

To indicate that developers do want cloning to go ahead, they have to mark their class as implementing the Cloneable interface. This interface, much like Serializable, contains no methods. It is just used to mark a class with some extra information. So, in order to call the clone method of Object, we need to mark the BankAccount class as follows:

```
// marking this class Cloneable allows us to call clone method of Object
public class BankAccount implements Cloneable
{
  // code here can use 'super.clone()'
}
```

There is one last thing we need to do in order to use the clone method of the Object class. This method throws a checked CloneNotSupportedException if the calling class does not implement the Cloneable interface. Of course, we know our class does implement this interface, but as this is a checked exception, we still need to provide a **try...catch** around the call to super.clone() to keep the compiler happy. Here is the modified BankAccount class:

```
// mark that objects of this class can be cloned
public class BankAccount implements Cloneable
{
  // attributes as before
  private String accountNumber;
  private String accountName;
  private double balance;


  // this method allows BankAccount objects to be cloned
  public Object clone()
  {
    try
    {
      return super.clone(); // call 'clone' from Object
    }
    catch (CloneNotSupportedException e) // will never be thrown!
    {
      return null;
    }
  }
  // other code here
}
```

Whether or not you use super.clone() in your implementation of the clone method, it is always a good idea to mark your class Cloneable, so it is clear that objects from your class can be cloned.

24.3.5 Garbage collection

When an object is created using the **new** operator, a request is being made to grab an area of free computer memory to store the object's attributes. Because this memory is requested during the running of a program, not during compilation, the compiler cannot guarantee that enough memory exists to meet this request. Memory could become exhausted for two related reasons:

- continual requests to grab memory are made when no more free memory exists;
- memory that is no longer needed is not released back to the system.

These problems are common to all programming languages and the danger of memory exhaustion is a real one for large programs, or programs running in a small memory space. Java allows both of the reasons listed above to be dealt with effectively and thus ensures that programs do not crash unexpectedly.

First, exception-handling techniques can be used to monitor for memory exhaustion and code can be written to ensure the program terminates gracefully. More importantly, Java has a built-in **garbage collection** facility to release unused memory. This is a facility that regularly trawls through memory looking for locations used by the program, freeing any locations that are no longer in use.

For example consider program 24.1 below.

PROGRAM 24.1

```
import java.util.*;

public class Tester
{
  public static void main(String[] args)
  {
    char ans;
    Scanner keyboard = new Scanner (System.in);
    Rectangle object; // reference to object created here
    do
    {
      System.out.print("Enter length: ");
      double length = keyboard.nextDouble();
      System.out.print("Enter height: ");
      double height = keyboard.nextDouble();
      // new object created each time we go around the loop
      object = new Rectangle(length, height);
      System.out.println("area = "+ object.calculateArea());
      System.out.println("perimeter = "+ object.calculatePermeter());
      System.out.print("Do you want another go? ");
      ans = keyboard.next.charAt(0);
    } while (ans == 'y' || ans == 'Y');
  }
```

Here, a new object is created each time we go around the loop. The memory used for the previous object is no longer required. In a language like C++ the memory occupied by old objects would not be destroyed unless the programmer added instructions to do so. So if the programmer forgot to do this, and this happened on a large scale in your C++ program, the available memory space could easily be exhausted. The Java system, however, regularly checks for such unused objects in memory and destroys them.

Although automatic garbage collection does make extra demands on the system (slowing it down while it takes place), this extra demand is considered by many to be worthwhile by removing a heavy burden on programmers. Nowadays many programming languages, such as C# (pronounced "C Sharp"), also include a garbage collection facility.

24.4 The role of Java

While Java began life as a language aimed primarily at programming consumer devices, it has evolved into a sophisticated application programming language, competing with languages such as C++, Visual Basic and C#, to develop a wide range of applications. The security and reliability offered by the language has allowed the use of Java to be spread from desktop applications to network systems, web-based applications, set-top boxes, smart cards, computer games, mobile phones and many more. To see an example of the enormous range of applications powered by Java visit the Sun site at:

`http://www.java.com/en/java_in_action`

Table 24.1 gives the TIOBE programming community index of the ten most popular programming languages for February 2009.[1]

Position Feb 2009	Position Feb 2008	Programming language
1	1	Java
2	2	C
3	5	C++
4	3	Visual Basic
5	4	PHP
6	8	C#
7	7	Python
8	6	Pearl
9	9	Delphi
10	10	JavaScript

TABLE 24.1 TIOBE programming community index

You can see that Java is at the top of this table, as it was last year. In fact it has been top of this index for the last four years.

24.5 What next?

This chapter marks the end of our Java coverage for your second semester in programming. Although you have covered a lot of material, there is still more that you can explore. For example, there are some packages that we have not had space to discuss here. Table 24.2 lists a few you might wish to study further.

---

[1] The TIOBE index is a respected measure of the popularity of a programming language. For details of the table itself and of how it was compiled go to **http://www.tiobe.com/index.php/content/paperinfo/tpci/index.html**

Package name	Description
java.beans	Contains classes such as Beans, that relate to the development of reusable visual components within a rapid application development environment.
java.math	Contains classes such as BigInteger and BigDecimal that do not have upper and lower limits on their number ranges, and so allow for extremely rigorous calculations.
java.rmi	Contains classes such as RMISecurityManager for dealing with remote method calling within a distributed environment.
javax.xml.parsers	Contains classes such as DocumentBuilder that allow you to parse an XML document. To parse a document means to check that it is valid and then to take some action.

TABLE 24.2 Some additional Java packages

You might find out more about packages such as these in advanced modules on your course. In the meantime, don't forget you can get further information on the Java language at the Sun website, www.java.sun.com/docs.

Now that you have completed two semesters of programming we are pretty certain that you will have come to realize what an exciting and rewarding activity it can be. So whether you are going on to a career in software engineering, or some other field in computing – or even if you are just going to enjoy programming for its own sake, we wish you the very best of luck for the future.

Self-test questions

1   Distinguish between a *pointer* and a *reference*.

2   What does the term *multiple inheritance* mean and why does Java disallow it?

3   Consider the following class:

```
public class Critical
{
  private int value;
  public Critical (int valueIn)
  {
    value = valueIn;
  }.
  public void setValue(int valueIn)
  {
    value = valueIn;
  }
  public int getValue ()
  {
    return value;
  }
}
```

a Explain why `Critical` objects are not immutable.

b Write fragments of code to create `Critical` objects and demonstrate the problem of aliases.

c Develop a `clone` method in the `Critical` class (make use of the `clone` method of `Object` here).

d Write fragments of code to demonstrate the use of this `clone` method.

4   Look back at the classes from the two case studies of chapters 11, 12 and 21.

a Which methods in these classes return aliases?

b Which aliases could be dangerous?

c How can these aliases be avoided?

5   What are the advantages and disadvantages of a *garbage collection* facility in a programming language?

Programming exercises

1 Implement the `Critical` class of self-test question 3 and then write a tester program to demonstrate the problem of aliases.

2 Amend the `Critical` class by adding a `clone` method as discussed in self-test question 3(c) and then amend the tester program you developed in the previous programming exercise to demonstrate the use of this `clone` method.

3 Implement the changes you identified in self-test question 4, in order to remove the aliases that might have been present in the classes from the two case studies.

4 Review all the classes that you have developed so far and identify any problems with aliases. Provide appropriate `clone` methods to avoid these aliases.

Index

A

abstract classes 253–6
abstract methods 256–60
Abstract Window Toolkit (AWT),
  graphics 270–1
access, file-handling 519
actors, requirements analysis/
  specification 589–90
actual parameters,
  methods 102–3, 110
adapters 373–7
addButton, event-handling 340
AdditionClient class, network
  environment 650–5
AdditionServer class, network
  environment 643–50
advanced case study 588–630
  airport 588–630
  Airport class 603–16
  airport dialogue boxes 623–30
  AirportFrame class 620–3
  design 590–3
  GUI 617–18
  implementation 593–616
  JTabbedPane class 618–20
  Plane class 597–603
  requirements analysis/
    specification 589–90
  Runway class 595–7
  system overview 588–9
  testing 616–17
aggregation
  Bank class 208
  composition 208
  objects 208
airport, advanced case
  study 588–630
Airport class, advanced case
  study 603–16
airport dialogue boxes, advanced
  case study 623–30
AirportFrame class, advanced
  case study 620–3
algorithms, methods 105
aliasing 719–22
animations
  multi-threaded programs 558–64
  series of images 560–4

API *see* Application Programming
  Interface
append mode, files 525
applets 9–11, 632–6
  browsers 632–5
  guidelines for creating 636
  special applet methods 635–6
Application Programming
  Interface (API) 445, 671–5
application software 4
ApplicationSelection
  MIDlet 707–13
arithmetic operators 25–7
ArrayList class
  Java Collections
    Framework 417–23
  List interface 417–23
arrays 121–62
  array maximum 137–8
  array membership 139–40
  array search 140–1
  array summation 138–9
  creating 122–5
  elements, accessing 125–9
  enhanced 'for' loop 135–6
  final program 141–7
  index value 124–5
  'for' loop 135–6
  memory 123–5, 131–2
  methods 132–5
  methods, some useful
    array 136–47
  MonthlyTemperatures
    program 150–6
  multi-dimensional 147–50
  of objects 184–7
  one-dimensional 147
  passing arrays as
    parameters 129–32
  ragged 156–8
  returning an array from a
    method 132–5
  two-dimensional 147–50
assignment operator 23–5
assignments in Java 23–5
associations, design 308–9
asynchronous behaviour,
  multi-threaded programs 556

attributes
  class(es) 165, 205–6
  initializing attributes 205–6
autoboxing 263–4
AWT *see* Abstract Window Toolkit

B

Bank class 208–27
  exceptions 400–5
  testing 220–7
BankAccount class 181–4
  designing 198–201
  static keyword 201–5
base class (superclass) 238
behaviour specifications,
  requirements analysis/
  specification 589–90
binary encoding 519
binary files 529–31
  reading and writing to 529–31
blocked state, multi-threaded
  programs 558
Book class, Java Collections
  Framework 433–5
Book objects
  collection classes 437–40
  Java Collections
    Framework 437–40
Border interface 487–9
BorderLayout, graphics 299–300
BouncingRedBall MIDlet 702–7
braces 13
'break' statement 83–6
  removing 'break'
    statements 55–7
browsers, applets 632–5
busy waiting, multi-threaded
  programs 557

C

calling a method 95, 98–9
Canvas class 684–9
card layout policy 449–54
case study 307–56
  see also advanced case study
  airport 588–630

code layout 319
design 308–9, 337–9
Hostel class 343–51
integration testing 308
Javadoc 316–19
ObjectList class 313–25
Payment class 310–13
PaymentList class 325–8
records, keeping
     permanent 336–7
requirements specification 308
student hostel 307–56
Tenant class 328–30
TenantList class 330–4
test log 320–5
unit testing 308
catching an exception 392–4
CDC *see* Connected Device
  Configuration
ChangingFace class,
  event-handling 277–84
ChangingFace MIDlet 689–94
ChangingFaceApplet class
  633–5
chat application, network
  environment 655–68
ChatClient class 664–8
ChatListener class 661–3
ChatServer class 656–61
Checkable class 360
Checkable interface 362–6
checked exceptions 386
choices, graphics 456–71
claiming an exception 389–92
class(es) 12–13, 163–90
  see also packages
  abstract classes 253–6
  AdditionClient class 650–5
  AdditionServer class 643–50
  Airport class 603–16
  AirportFrame class 620–3
  ArrayList class 417–23
  attributes 165, 205–6
  Bank class 208–27, 400–5
  BankAccount class 181–4,
    198–201
  base class (superclass) 238
  Book class 433–5
  Canvas class 684–9
  ChangingFace class 277–84
  ChangingFaceApplet
    class 633–5
  ChatClient class 664–8
  ChatServer class 656–61
  Checkable class 360

collection classes 208–27
Console class 180–1
as data types 163–5
derived class (subclass) 238
dot operator 169
EasyScanner class 206–7
encapsulation 168, 192–3
FontTester class 505–6
Graphics2D class 505–6
Hostel class 343–51
IconDemo class 490–2
ImageHolder class 493–5
ImageIcon class 492–5
implementing 191–236
initializing attributes 205–6
inner classes 373–7
input and output 168
interactive graphics
  class 284–7
JComboBox class 469–71
JDialog class 464–9
JFileChooser class 472–7
JRadioButton class 464–8
JSlider class 478–80, 485
JTabbedPane class 618–20
Library class 438–40
methods 165
Metric Converter class 292–6
Object class 261–3, 726–8
ObjectList class 313–25
objects 165–6
passing objects as
  parameters 207–8
Payment class 310–13
PaymentList class 325–8
Plane class 597–603
PushMe class 284–7
Rectangle class 166–72,
  192–8, 243–8, 287–91
RedCircle class 367
Runway class 595–7
Scanner class 31–4, 179–80
SmileyFace class 271–7
SmileyFaceCanvas 684–9
Sprite class 694–702
SquareIcon class 489–90
static keyword 201–5
String class 173–5
subclass (derived class) 238
superclass (base class) 238
Tenant class 328–30
Thread class 549–52
Timer class 564–8
UML 191–4
wrapper classes 263–4

classpath environment variable,
  packages 578–9, 582
CLDC *see* Connected Limited
  Device Configuration
client application, network
  environment 650–5
client-server chat application,
  network environment 655–68
client-server model, network
  environment 631–2
clone method
  Object class 726–8
  overriding the 722–5
code layout, case study 319
collection classes 208–27
  Bank class 208–27
  Book objects 437–40
collections of objects, GUI 302
colours
  creating new 502–4
  user interface 502–4
ColourTester class 503–4
combo boxes, graphics 469–71,
  482–3
command line, running
  applications from 578–81
comments, program 14
Compact Virtual Machine
  (CVM) 673
comparison operator, 'if'
  statement 42–3
compiling programs 4–5
composition
  aggregation 208
  Bank class 208
  objects 208
  UML 592
compound containers,
  graphics 300–1
concatenation operator 16
concurrent processes,
  multi-threaded programs 545–6
confirm dialogue, user
  interface 497–502
Connected Device Configuration
  (CDC), Java Micro Edition 675–6
Connected Limited Device
  Configuration (CLDC), Java
  Micro Edition 675–6
console applications 8
Console class 180–1
constants, creating 25
constructor, objects 167
'continue' statement 86–7
creating constants 25

critical sections, multi-threaded programs 556
CVM *see* Compact Virtual Machine

D

data types 20–1
databases, accessing remote
  JDBC 636–42
  Microsoft databases 642
  ODBC 642
declaring methods 96–8
declaring variables 21–3
defining methods 96–8
derived class (subclass) 238
design
  advanced case study 590–3
  associations 308–9
  case study 308–9, 337–9
  event-handling 339–43
  GUI 337–9
dialogue windows, graphics 464–77
dispatched thread, multi-threaded programs 558
displayButton, event-handling 340–1
'do...while' loop 78–83
documentation, Javadoc 316–19
documenting exceptions 411–12
dot operator
  class(es) 169
  methods 169
double-branched selection, 'if...else' statement 46–7

E

EasyScanner class 206–7
embedded software 4
encapsulation
  class(es) 168, 192–3
  UML 192–3
encoding, file-handling 519
enhanced classes, Java Collections Framework 423–4
enhanced 'for' loop, arrays 135–6
enumerated types, UML 592–5
environment variables, *classpath* environment variable 578–9, 582
equals method, Java Collections Framework 435–6
escape characters 245

event-handling
  ChangingFace class 277–84
  design 339–43
  graphics 277–84
  pseudocode 340–3
exceptions 125, 384–415
  Bank class 400–5
  catching 392–4
  checked 386
  claiming an exception 389–92
  creating your own exception classes 408–10
  documenting 411–12
  'finally' clause 394–7
  GUI applications 398–400
  handling 386–94
  pre-defined exception classes in Java 384–6
  re-throwing 410–11
  throwing 384–6, 405–7
  unchecked 386
  using exceptions in your own classes 400–5
expressions, in Java 26–9
extends, keyword 240

F

fields, data 516
file-handling
  access 519
  encoding 519
file pointer 519
file streams, file-handling 519
files 516–44
  append mode 525
  binary files 529–31
  file-handling 518–19
  input and output 517–18
  object serialization 533–6
  random access files 536–42
  serialization 533–6
  text files 520–9
final
  keyword 25
  modifier 261
final program, arrays 141–7
'finally' clause, exceptions 394–7
first mobile program, Java Micro Edition 676–84
first program 11–16
FlowLayout, graphics 281, 299–300
fonts

creating new 504–6
user interface 504–6
FontTester class 505–6
'for' loop 65–75
  arrays 135–6
  body of the loop 70–4
  enhanced 135–6
  loop counter, revisiting 74–5
  loop counter, varying 68–70
formal parameters, methods 100–1, 103–15

G

garbage collection 728–30
generics, Java Collections Framework 418–19
graphical user interface (GUI) 8–9
  see also user interface
  advanced case study 617–18
  collections of objects 302
  design 337–9
  exceptions 398–400
  Rectangle class 287–91
  short cut keys 622–3
  tool tips 621–3
graphics 270–306
  advanced graphics programming 445–86
  animations 558–64
  AWT 270–1
  BorderLayout 299–300
  ChangingFace class 277–84
  choices 456–71
  combining text and graphics 489–92
  combo boxes 469–71, 482–3
  compound containers 300–1
  dialogue windows 464–77
  event-handling 277–84
  FlowLayout 281, 299–300
  interactive graphics class 284–7
  JComboBox class 469–71
  JDialog class 464–9
  JFileChooser class 472–7
  JRadioButton class 464–8
  JSlider class 478–80, 485
  layout managers 281, 299–300
  layout policies 299–300, 445–55
  Metric Converter class 292–6
  number formatting 297–8
  pop-up menus 461–4
  pull-down menus 456–61
  PushMe class 284–7

radio buttons 464–8
slider 478–80, 485
SmileyFace class 271–7
Swing package 270–1
Graphics2D class 505–6
grid layout policy 446–9
grouping 'case' statements,
'switch' statement 54–5
GUI *see* graphical user interface

H

hashCode method, Java
Collections Framework 436–7
HashMap class, Java Collections
Framework 429–33
HashSet class, Java Collections
Framework 424–9
header 13
HelloWorld MIDlet 676–84
Hostel class, case study 343–51
human-computer interface *see*
graphical user interface (GUI);
user interface

I

Icon interface 489–92
IconDemo class 490–2
IDEs *see* Integrated Development
Environments
'if' statement 40–6
comparison operator 42–3
multiple instructions
within 44–6
'if...else' statement 46–8
double-branched
selection 46–7
nested 'if...else' statement 50–2
single-branched selection 46
ImageHolder class 493–5
ImageIcon class 492–5
images *see* graphics
immutable objects 725–6
index value, arrays 124–5
inheritance 237–69
defining 238
implementing 238–48
object-oriented
programming 227
private access 239–48
public access 239–48
inner classes 373–7
input and output
class(es) 168

devices 517–18
files 517–18
methods 99–103, 168
standard error stream 517–18
standard input stream 517–18
standard output stream 517–18
streams 517–19
input boxes, user interface
495–502
input in Java 31–4
input validation, 'while'
loop 76–8
instantiation, objects 167
integer 20
Integrated Development
Environments (IDEs) 7–8
integration testing, case study 308
interactive graphics class 284–7
interfaces 359–73
see also graphical user interface
(GUI); user interface
List interface 417–23
iteration 63–94
'break' statement 83–6
'continue' statement 86–7
'do...while' loop 78–83
'for' loop 65–75
picking the right loop 83
'while' loop 76–8, 83
Iterator objects, Java Collections
Framework 427–9

J

JAR files, executable,
packages 582–5
Java applications 8–11
Java Collections
Framework 416–44
ArrayList class 417–23
Book class 433–5
Book objects 437–40
enhanced classes 423–4
equals method 435–6
generics 418–19
hashCode method 436–7
HashMap class 429–33
HashSet class 424–9
interface type 419–20
Iterator objects 427–9
Library class 438–40
List interface 417–23
List methods 420–3
Map interface 429–33
Set interface 424–9

Set methods 425–7
using your own classes
with 433–7
Java Database Connectivity
(JDBC) 636–42
Java Development Kit (JDK) 6–7
Java in context 716–33
Java Micro Edition 674–6
CDC 675–6
CLDC 675–6
configurations 675–6
first mobile program 676–84
MIDlets 675–6
MIDP 676
profiles 675–6
selecting items from a
list 707–13
sprites 694–702
TextBox 677–84
timers 702–7
Java Runtime Environment
(JRE) 5–6
Java Virtual Machine (JVM) 5–6
Javadoc
case study 316–19
documentation 316–19
JComboBox class 469–71
JDBC *see* Java Database
Connectivity
JDialog class 464–9
JDK *see* Java Development Kit
JFileChooser class 472–7
JRadioButton class 464–8
JRE *see* Java Runtime Environment
JSlider class 478–80, 485
JTabbedPane class, advanced
case study 618–20
JVM *see* Java Virtual Machine

K

keyword 13
extends 240
final 25
super 241, 247
Kilobyte Virtual Machine
(KVM) 673

L

language reliability 719–30
language size 716–17
layout managers, graphics 281,
299–300
layout policies

advanced graphics
        programming 445–55
graphics 299–300, 445–55
Library class, Java Collections
        Framework 438–40
lightweight process, threads 546
List interface
        ArrayList class 417–23
        Java Collections
                Framework 417–23
List methods, Java Collections
        Framework 420–3
listButton, event-handling 342
local variables, methods 107–9
lock, multi-threaded programs 557
logical operators 48–50
loop *see* iteration

M

machine code 4
Map interface, Java Collections
        Framework 429–33
marker interface, object
        serialization 533
memory
        arrays 123–5, 131–2
        methods 109
        passing arrays as
                parameters 131–2
        stack 109
menu driven programs,
        methods 114–17
message boxes, user
        interface 495–502
method overloading 109–13,
        249, 251
        polymorphism 110, 378
method overriding 249–53
        polymorphism 378
methods 13, 95–120
        abstract methods 256–60
        actual parameters 102–3, 110
        algorithms 105
        array methods, some
                useful 136–47
        arrays 132–5
        calling a method 95, 98–9
        class(es) 165
        declaring 96–8
        defining 96–8
        dot operator 169
        examples 103–7
        formal parameters 100–1,
                103–15

input and output 99–103, 168
local variables 107–9
memory 109
menu driven programs 114–17
method overloading 109–13,
        249, 251, 378
parameters 100–15
passing parameters 102
returning an array from a
        method 132–5
stack (memory) 109
String class 173–5
variable scope 107–9
Metric Converter class,
        graphics 292–6
Microsoft databases, ODBC 642
MIDlets
        ApplicationSelection
                MIDlet 707–13
        BouncingRedBall MIDlet 702–7
        ChangingFace MIDlet 689–94
        HelloWorld MIDlet 676–84
        Java Micro Edition 675–6
        RedBall MIDlet 696–702
        SmileyFace MIDlet 684–9
Mobile Information Device Profile
        (MIDP), Java Micro Edition 676
mobile Java 673–715
modal/non-modal dialogues 468–9
modulus 26–7
monitor, multi-threaded
        programs 557
MonthlyTemperatures program,
        arrays 150–6
multi-dimensional arrays 147–50
multi-tasking, multi-threaded
        programs 545
multi-threaded programs 545–70
        alternative
                implementation 553–6
        animations 558–64
        asynchronous behaviour 556
        blocked state 558
        busy waiting 557
        concurrent processes 545–6
        critical sections 556
        dispatched thread 558
        lock 557
        monitor 557
        multi-tasking 545
        mutual exclusion 556–7
        processes 546
        producer-consumer
                relationship 556
        ready state 558

running state 558
sleeping state 558
state transition diagram 557–8
synchronizing threads 556–7
Thread class 549–52
thread execution 552–3
thread scheduling 552–3
thread states 557–8
time-slicing 546
Timer class 564–8
transitions 557–8
waiting state 558
multiple inheritance 360–1,
717–19
mutual exclusion, multi-threaded
programs 556–7

N

nesting, nested 'if…else'
        statement 50–2
network environment 631–72
        accessing remote
                databases 636–42
        AdditionServer class 643–50
        applets 632–6
        chat application 655–68
        ChatListener class 661–3
        client application 650–5
        client-server chat
                application 655–68
        client-server model 631–2
        JDBC 636–42
        ODBC 642
        server application 643–50
        sockets 642–3
no layout policy 454–5
number formatting,
        graphics 297–8

O

Object class 261–3
        clone method 725–6
object encoding 519
object-oriented 163–6
object-oriented programming
        benefits 227
        inheritance 227
object serialization, files 533–6
ObjectList class, case study 313–25
objects
        aggregation 208
        arrays of objects 184–7
        class(es) 165–6

collections of objects 302
composition 208
constructor 167
creating 167
instantiation 167
passing objects as
    parameters 207–8
reference 166–7
ODBC *see* Open Database
Connectivity
one-dimensional arrays 147
Open Database Connectivity
(ODBC) 642
operator overloading,
polymorphism 377
option dialogue, user
interface 496–7
output and input *see* input and
output
output in Java 14–16, 30–1
overloaded 27
overloading, method *see* method
overloading

P

packages 31, 571–87
accessing classes 572–5
classpath environment
    variable 578–9, 582
deploying 581–5
developing 575–7
hierarchy 571–2
JAR files, executable 582–5
running applications from the
    command line 578–81
scope 577–8
splash screens 584–5
parameters
methods 100–15
passing arrays as
    parameters 129–32
passing objects as
    parameters 207–8
passing arrays as
parameters 129–32
memory 131–2
passing objects as parameters,
class(es) 207–8
passing parameters, methods 102
Payment class, case study 310–13
paymentButton,
event-handling 341–2
PaymentList class,
case study 325–8

Plane class, advanced
    case study 597–603
platform-independent 5
pointers 717
polymorphic types 377–8
polymorphism 377–8
method overloading 110, 378
pop-up menus, graphics 461–4
primitive types 20–1
print, output in Java 14–16
private access 193, 195–6
inheritance 239–48
processes
concurrent 546
multi-threaded programs 546
producer-consumer relationship,
multi-threaded programs 556
program code 4
program design 34
programming in Java 5–11
pseudocode 34
event-handling 340–3
'while' loop 77
public 13
public access 193, 196–7
inheritance 239–48
pull-down menus,
graphics 456–61
PushMe class 284–7

Q

quantum, thread execution 552
quitButton, event-handling 343

R

radio buttons, graphics 464–8
ragged arrays 156–8
random access, file-handling 519
random access files 536–42
re-throwing exceptions 410–11
reading
to binary files 529–31
file-handling 518–19
to text files 520–9
text files character by
    character 531–3
ready state, multi-threaded
programs 558
real number 20
records
data 516
keeping permanent
    (case study) 336–7

Rectangle class 166–72
designing 192–4
extending 243–8
GUI 287–91
implementing 194–8
private access 195–6
public access 196–7
RectangleTester program
    170–2
RedBall MIDlet 696–702
RedCircle class 367
reference, objects 166–7
reliability, language 719–30
removeButton,
event-handling 341
removing 'break' statements,
'switch' statement 55–7
requirements analysis/
specification
actors 589–90
advanced case study 589–90
behaviour
    specifications 589–90
use case diagrams 589–90
use case model 589–90
requirements specification,
case study 308
role of Java 730
running applications from the
    command line 578–81
running state, multi-threaded
programs 558
Runway class, advanced
    case study 595–7

S

saveAndQuitButton,
event-handling 343
scalar types 20–1
Scanner class 31–4, 179–80
keyboard input 179–80
scenario testing 616–17
scheduling, threads 552–3
scope
packages 577–8
variables 107–9
selection 38–62
double-branched 46–7
single-branched 46
sequence 38–9, 47
serial access, file-handling 519
serialization, files 533–6
server application, network
environment 643–50

Set interface, Java Collections Framework 424–9
Set methods, Java Collections Framework 425–7
short cut keys, GUI 622–3
single-branched selection, 'if...else' statement 46
size of language 716–17
sleeping state, multi-threaded programs 558
slider, graphics 478–80, 485
SmileyFace class 271–7
SmileyFace MIDlet 684–9
SmileyFaceCanvas 684–9
sockets, network environment 632, 642–3
software 3–4
source code 4
splash screens, packages 584–5
Sprite class 694–702
sprites, Java Micro Edition 694–702
SquareIcon class 489–90
stack (memory)
    methods 109
    variables 109
standard error stream 517–18
standard input stream 517–18
standard output stream 517–18
state transition diagram, multi-threaded programs 557–8
static keyword, class(es) 201–5
streams
    file streams 519
    input and output 517–19
String class, methods 173–5
strings 16, 172–8
    comparing 176–7
    entering strings containing spaces 177–8
    obtaining strings from the keyboard 172–3
    String class methods 173–5
student hostel, case study 307–56
subclass (derived class) 238
super, keyword 241, 247
superclass (base class) 238
Swing package, graphics 270–1
'switch' statement 52–7
    grouping 'case' statements 54–5
    removing 'break' statements 55–7
synchronizing threads, multi-threaded programs 556–7

syntax 5
system overview, advanced case study 588–9
system software 4

T

Tenant class, case study 328–30
TenantList class, case study 330–4
test log, case study 320–5
testing
    advanced case study 616–17
    integration testing 308
    scenario testing 616–17
    the system 351–4
    unit testing 308
text encoding 519
text files
    reading and writing to 520–9
    reading character by character 531–3
TextBox, Java Micro Edition 677–84
Thread class, multi-threaded programs 549–52
thread states, multi-threaded programs 557–8
threads *see* multi-threaded programs
throwing exceptions 384–6, 405–7
    re-throwing exceptions 410–11
time-slicing, multi-threaded programs 546
Timer class, multi-threaded programs 564–8
timers, Java Micro Edition 702–7
tool tips, GUI 621–3
transitions, multi-threaded programs 557–8
try...catch block 392–4, 404–5
two-dimensional arrays 147–50
    creating 148
    initializing 148–9
    processing 149–50
type casting 27, 245–8
type polymorphism 378

U

UML *see* Unified Modeling Language
unchecked exceptions 386
Unified Modeling Language (UML)

composition 592
designing classes 191–4
encapsulation 192–3
enumerated types 592–5
Rectangle class 192–4
unit testing, case study 308
use case diagrams, requirements analysis/specification 589–90
use case model, requirements analysis/specification 589–90
user interface 9–10, 487–515
    see also graphical user interface (GUI)
    Border interface 487–9
    colours 502–4
    ColourTester class 503–4
    combining text and graphics 489–92
    confirm dialogue 497–502
    enhancing 487–515
    fonts 504–6
    FontTester class 505–6
    Graphics2D class 505–6
    guidelines for good user interfaces 512–13
    Icon interface 489–92
    IconDemo class 490–2
    ImageIcon class 492–5
    input boxes 495–502
    message boxes 495–502
    option dialogue 496–7
    SquareIcon class 489–90

V

variable scope, methods 107–9
variables
    declaring 21–3
    local 107–9
    scope 107–9
    stack (memory) 109

W

waiting state, multi-threaded programs 558
'while' loop 76–8, 83
    input validation 76–8
    pseudocode 77
wrapper classes 263–4
writing
    to binary files 529–31
    file-handling 518–19
    to text files 520–9